Union Soldiers and the Northern Home Front

THE NORTH'S CIVIL WAR SERIES
Paul A. Cimbala, series editor

Union Soldiers and the Northern Home Front

WARTIME EXPERIENCES, POSTWAR ADJUSTMENTS

Edited by
PAUL A. CIMBALA
and
RANDALL M. MILLER

FORDHAM UNIVERSITY PRESS
New York
2002

The North's Civil War, No. 18
ISSN 1089–8719
Library of Congress Cataloging-in-Publication Data

Union soldiers and the northern home front : wartime experiences, postwar adjustments / edited by Paul A. Cimbala and Randall M. Miller.— 1st ed.
      p.   cm. — (The North's Civil War ; no. 18)
   Includes bibliographical references and index.
   ISBN 0-8232-2145-8 (hardcover) — ISBN 0-8232-2146-6 (pbk.)
   1. United States—History—Civil War, 1861–1865—Social aspects.
   2. United States—History—Civil War, 1861–1865—Influences.
   3. Soldiers—United States—Social conditions—19th century.
   4. Veterans—United States—Social conditions—19th century.
   5. Northeastern States—Social conditions—19th century.   6. Civil-military relations—Northeastern States—History—19th century.
   I. Cimbala, Paul A. (Paul Alan), 1951–   II. Miller, Randall M.
   III. Series.

E468.9 .U44   2002
973.7′41—dc21   2001040884

02   03   04   05   06   5   4   3   2   1
First Edition

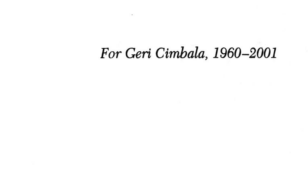

For Geri Cimbala, 1960–2001

CONTENTS

ACKNOWLEDGMENTS

WE WOULD LIKE to thank the librarians at Fordham University, the New York Public Library, Saint Joseph's University, the Civil War Library and Museum, Haverford College, the Historical Society of Pennsylvania, the Library Company of Philadelphia, and the University of Pennsylvania for their assistance in preparing this volume. Thanks also to the Saint Joseph's University Faculty Development Fund for supporting the preparation of this collection. We are especially grateful to Carol Digel, the historian of the Darley Society, for tracking down a copy of Felix O. C. Darley's *News From the Front*, which we've used for our cover illustration. Ms. Digel put us in touch with Ray Hester, who with his wife Judith founded the Darley Society and is its present executive director. Mr. and Mrs. Hester, owners of the Darley Manor Inn, Darley's former home in Claymont, Delaware, are also owners of the Darley print. They graciously provided a copy of the illustration for our use, hoping that its presence on our cover will prompt more people to seek out Darley's wonderful art and book illustrations.

The contributors to this volume made our editorial work that much easier by providing us with well-written, well-researched essays. We thank them for their cooperation and their patience.

Megan McClintock, one of our contributors, passed away before this book's publication. She was an extraordinary scholar who will be missed by the profession. The editors thank her father, Thomas C. McClintock, Professor Emeritus of History at Oregon State University, for providing additional information required for completing this volume.

Once again, Fordham University Press provided us with the encouragement and support required for completing this volume. Saverio Procario, Mary Beatrice Schulte, Anthony Chiffolo, Jacky Philpotts, and Loomis Mayer eased our burdens. Finally, the editors wish to thank Linda Patterson Miller and Elizabeth C. Vozzola for living with another one of these projects for much too long a time.

INTRODUCTION

Randall M. Miller

IN 1944, Ezra T. Hazeltine of South Bend, Washington, mailed a privately printed twelve-page booklet to "Aunt Polly's descendants." In doing so, he completed one of the last tasks of his late father, who had, with the aid of family materials and relatives, compiled "a summary of the Civil War experiences of his beloved grandmother," Mary Abbot "Polly" Hazeltine (1813–1892).

In 1862, Mrs. Hazeltine had left her husband and children in Busti, Chautauqua County, New York, for the Annapolis Junction hospital in Maryland. She went to find her son Clark, of the 49th New York Volunteer Infantry, who had taken ill during McClellan's retreat from the failed Peninsula Campaign. According to her daughter, Polly Hazeltine "had never traveled, and had met very few people outside her own circle." But news of her boy's condition sent her racing southward and seemingly into a new life. Having lost one son to the war the preceding spring, she did not want to give up another so far from home.

Mrs. Hazelton found Clark, but the doctor running the hospital resented her presence and interfered with her ministrations. Not to be intimidated, she went to Washington to complain of the hospital's conditions. An investigation led to the doctor's removal, and under a new administration at the hospital, Mrs. Hazeltine nursed her son back to health. She also attended numerous other stricken soldiers in the ward over a two-month stay. Known as "Mother" by the men, she became something of a saint among them for her care. While busy in hospital work, she confessed that "I don't worry about home." Nevertheless, she did write home regularly and also started a journal of her experiences, and she kept up a correspondence with the soldiers after she returned home. Years after the war, veterans in western New York recalled Mrs. Hazeltine's service with reverence. She had saved lives at Annapolis Junction, and she had shown what courage meant. Or so the story goes.[1]

The story of Mary Abbot Hazeltine, as related by her admiring family, hardly seems worthy of so long an introduction. But her story, as lived and remembered, says much about the way northerners experienced the Civil War. Though far away from the threatening presence of armies, refugees, or outlaws that afflicted many southern communities, the people of the rural and village North did not escape the war. They sent their men and boys off to fight, and they supplied them with all manner of clothes, blankets, foodstuffs, sweets, and so much more, including news from home. As soldiers "hardened" during the war and "lightened" their load by shedding all but the most necessary items to survive, the physical commerce between home front and camp slackened, but the news always mattered.

People at home did not forget their men. Rather than being isolated from the war, as some historians would have it, people on the home front wanted to participate in it. They wanted to get information about the war from their kinfolk and townsfolk fighting in it, to go to the military encampments whenever possible, and even to visit the battlefields. They were eager to do something to hasten victory on the field and bring the boys home. The need for such contact no doubt was felt more keenly in rural areas and small towns such as Busti, Chautauqua County, New York, where the departure of anyone altered social rhythms and affected someone everyone knew, at least indirectly. Regiments raised from such places were extensions of the community, closely watched and worried over. News from the front demanded a response—such as a mother rushing to her dying soldier son's side.

The admiration for Mrs. Hazeltine, in her day and after, was the consequence of her action. No one much commented on the proper sphere of women or duties to husband and children at home when the soldier son fell ill and his mother left to attend him. Mrs. Hazeltine's going to the hospital at Annapolis Junction simply extended the

---

[1] On the history of Mrs. Hazeltine's service, see "Mary Abbot Hazeltine 1813–1892," typescript of reminiscences, in Mary A. Hazeltine Memoirs and Letters, Warren County Historical Society, Warren, Pa. The collection also includes Mrs. Hazeltine's letters from her time at the hospital, a letter from a soldier at the hospital, and several family members' reminiscences relating stories from soldiers and about her. All quotations are from the family members' reminiscences.

home front. As some historians insist, the war might have been too horrible to report in truth and the soldiers too much changed by war to tell what soldiering really meant, but when mothers went off to hospitals, observing the swill carts take the pine coffins to the bone yard, as Mrs. Hazeltine did, or when wounded soldiers limped home, the distance between home front and soldier closed. Keeping diaries, letters, and memoirs, and telling and re-telling the stories of the men and women who joined in the great cause sealed the union of home front and soldier after the war.

For Mrs. Hazeltine and her descendants there were not "two wars." To be sure, civilians at home and soldiers away played different roles. Some soldiers were so shaken by war's horrors or taken up with the thrill of battle that they became forever estranged from the home front, and as the war entered its third winter, soldiers' letters reveal an impatience with those at home.[2] But in the end, most of those at home and those away at war did not go their separate ways. They would not have it so. Therein was the meaning of Mrs. Hazeltine's story for the soldiers she saved in her day and the memory of her saved by three generations of her descendants.

In the letters, diary, and memories of Mrs. Hazeltine's service and those of the soldiers with whom she had contact, the character of the war as experienced by civilians and soldiers comes into bolder relief. Most significant is the way such documents point to evolving relation-

---

[2] Examples of such feelings are legion. Typical is the correspondence of Joseph E. Kaucher of Reading, Pennsylvania. In 1863, he reassured his mother that he was not "lousy" with vermin and urged those at home to "hurry and get well" before he returned. A year later, Kaucher carped about bad sausage and stale news from home. He also demanded that his mother destroy his letter, as he burned hers after reading them because his affairs were his own and he did not want "every Tom, Dick, and Jerry sticking his nose into my business." Kaucher also confessed that he liked the service and "would not be lazing around Reading for any amount of money." Samuel E. Peters, of the 93rd New York State Battalion, in his letters home to his brother James, of Evans, New York, would have understood Kaucher's feelings. Peters compared the peace and tranquility of home and family to the miseries and violence of army life, but found home boring when he returned on furlough and longed to return to the glory of battle. Yet neither soldier completely cut his emotional ties with home. Kaucher kept the Bible his mother gave him and expected to return to a normal life when the war ended, as did Peters and so many other soldiers writing home. Joseph Kaucher to mother, April 3, 1863 and February 1, 1864, and Kaucher to "Dear Parents," April 8, 1864, Kaucher Papers, Berks County Historical Society, Reading, Pa.; and Samuel E. Peters to James Peters, October 28, 1862 through October 14, 1864, S. E. Peters Letters (photocopies), Balch Institute for Ethnic Studies, Philadelphia, Pa.

ships as the war moved from the early optimism of easy victories and a return home by Christmas to the grim business of a long, ever more demanding conflict. Soldiers coped with the new kind of war by assuming new identities for a time, but so, too, did those at home. The sheer busyness of maintaining the old ways demanded that those at home step up the pace of life and think beyond their local world. With men-folk at the front, those who remained behind managed and watched over the farm or trade for the absentees. They took up the tasks of writing to their soldiers, supplying them, and organizing relief for them, and, as best they could, attending to the physical, emotional, and spiritual needs of the widows, orphans, and others at home who suffered from the war.

Those at home might never have been able to understand the ambivalence, even emptiness and loneliness, returning veterans first felt as they tried to reenter the communities they had left, but they did embrace them. However, in those northern locales where the war had widened political, economic, and social cleavages, the reentry of soldiers into the "community" proved more problematical. For African Americans returning to small towns in the North, the reentry forced the town to grapple with a larger definition of "community" that might recognize and respect the full citizenship of all who had stood for the Union. Yet in their own trial by fire, civilians and communities had changed, too. The change was not so much as William Dean Howells's hero Silas Lapham observed upon returning home, that he had "got back to another world" wherein the "day of small things was past" and not likely "ever [to] come again in this country."[3] The change for much of northern society was not yet one of scale but of identity, and it included a newly found sense of common purpose and connection to "the nation." Perhaps in no other way was the long-term meaning of the northern home front more different than the southern.

The prevailing view among those few historians who have studied the northern home front is that the war did not transform the North because the Union did not have to change much to bring about victory. No "total war" gripped northern society, as it did southern, and the demands war made in conscription, inflation, limits on political

---

[3] William Dean Howells, *The Rise of Silas Lapham* (1885; reprint ed., New York: Oxford University Press, 1996), 17.

dissent, and even emancipation were unevenly, even erratically, spread. They required an adjustment more than a restructuring of northern society.[4] To be sure, particular groups, especially women reformers and African Americans, emerged from the war almost as "new Americans," fired by the experience of organizing for and winning not only the war but a broader claim to freedom in their own society. Intellectuals, people involved in organized relief, and many veterans also came to think of themselves in national terms and to appreciate the advantages of coordinated, national effort. Their postwar associations bespoke their new identities and interests. But most northerners fought to save the Union rather than recast it, even as the Union of 1861 became during the war a "nation, under God," dedicated to a "new birth of freedom" and the preservation of democratic government. In his Gettysburg Address, Abraham Lincoln had called on all northerners, but especially those not in uniform, to stand resolutely by and for the cause, not to build a new order, but rather to realize the promise of freedom first heralded by the founding generation in 1776. Later, in their memorials to the war, northerners celebrated continuity and fidelity rather than change. They were the true heirs of the Founding Fathers.

The essays in this book do not so much challenge the general view as test it. To understand the relationship between the Union soldier and the northern home front, it is necessary to consider and compare

---

[4] The literature on the northern home front and the Union soldier is comparatively sparse when set against that examining the southern experience. The two best overall treatments of the northern home front are Phillip Shaw Paludan, "A People's Contest": The Union and the Civil War, 1861–1865 (New York: Harper & Row, 1988); and J. Matthew Gallman, The North Fights the Civil War: The Home Front (Chicago: Ivan R. Dee, 1994). For an insightful review of the historiography of the northern home front, see Phillip Shaw Paludan, "What Did the Winners Win?" in James M. McPherson and William J. Cooper, Jr., eds., Writing the Civil War: The Quest to Understand (Columbia: University of South Carolina Press, 1998), 174–200. Paludan's observations about what has been done and needs to be done become more salient when read along with Reid Mitchell's instructive essay, "Not the General but the Soldier: The Study of Civil War Soldiers," in ibid., 81–95. An earlier collection that brought together case studies of several northern communities and raised the question why social historians had forgotten the Civil War and that attempted to point directions to help historians find their way is Maris Vinovskis, ed., Toward a Social History of the American Civil War (New York: Cambridge University Press, 1990). William Blair and William Pencak, eds., Making and Remaking Pennsylvania's Civil War (University Park: Penn State University Press, 2001), does for one state what Union Soldiers and the Northern Home Front tries to do over a broader reach.

the ways particular communities, groups, and organizations met the challenges of war during and after the struggle. This collection of original essays offers an initial foray, especially with regard to such varied experiences as recruitment, wartime correspondence, benevolence and organized relief, race relations, definitions of freedom and citizenship, claims to public memory and space, and efforts to write the history of the war. It does so by stretching across a wide geographic area, by largely pulling examples from the kinds of small-town and rural communities that formed the marrow of northern society, communities that provided most of the North's soldiers and much of its character. It also stands as an invitation to assay other northern home fronts to gauge the extent to which war changed society and the ways soldiers and civilians adjusted to the demands of war and of one another.

If no single conclusion emerges from these studies, a common perspective does. The essays in this book suggest that to see the relationship between Union soldier and northern society, one might think in terms of the stereoscopic view so popular in Civil War days. Only by looking simultaneously with both eyes through the common lens is it possible to see the whole picture. Just so for the soldier and the citizen.

Union Soldiers and the Northern Home Front

1
Filling the Ranks

1

"We Are All in This War": The 148th Pennsylvania and Home Front Dissension in Centre County during the Civil War

Carol Reardon

IN OCTOBER 1862, a small filler item in the *Central Press*, the weekly Republican newspaper of Bellefonte, Pennsylvania, reminded the citizens of Centre County that "we are all in this war—those who fight and those who stay at home that their brethren may fight; those who give their hearts to the enemy, and those whose heart-strings are lacerated by every ball that comes from a rebel rifle."[1] The notice attempted to appeal to that rural region's sense of unity recently shredded by several months of heated partisan debate about the changing political goals and military policies of the Lincoln administration. That summer, Centre Countians had begun to question sharply the continued efficacy of the conflict; no single community endeavor illustrated so well the contentiousness of those times than the challenge of raising a regiment of local men to answer their part of the July 1862 call for 300,000 more three-year volunteers. Destined always to reflect the strained times in which it was raised, the new 148th Pennsylvania Infantry and its fate in camp and in battle provided a point of intersection and debate for Centre County's Lincoln administration supporters and opponents.

Although historians such as James M. McPherson and Earl J. Hess have made a strong case for the relative importance of political values in convincing an individual soldier to enlist and then stay the course in the ranks, scholars are just beginning to consider seriously the

---

[1] *Bellefonte Central Press*, October 17, 1862.

importance of community values on the conduct of the Civil War. As Reid Mitchell observes, such values "were crucial to the way in which Americans made war from 1861 to 1865."[2] Political sentiment comprised a key component of those community values; it could help to unite a town or a county behind the war effort or work against federal policies. Significantly, as Thomas Kemp shows in his study of two New Hampshire towns, a community's political attitudes might well influence both the number of its sons who go to war and the men's willingness to do so: Republican Claremont sent a higher proportion of its sons than Democratic Newport.[3]

Centre County's experience, however, is not so easily explained. Over the course of the conflict, political sentiment in this rural central Pennsylvania county of small farm towns and mining and logging villages shifted dramatically from support for the war to moderate but substantial opposition to it. That reversal of public opinion first manifested itself in the late summer of 1862, precisely when Lincoln's call for more soldiers reached rural central Pennsylvania and the 148th Pennsylvania Infantry was raised.

In 1860, it would have seemed impossible for Centre County to show any sign of disloyalty to the Lincoln administration and its policies. The new president had won 3,021 votes, against 2,400 for all his opponents combined.[4] Centre County voters felt a genuine commitment to the preservation of the Constitution and the Union, and some freely expressed their willingness to take up arms to do so even before Lincoln was inaugurated. In January 1861, when South Carolina troops fired on *The Star of the West*, the relief ship sent to Fort Sumter, James A. Beaver of the Bellefonte Fencibles militia company wrote, "The nation must be preserved. . . . If we have a nationality, it must be continued, supported, upheld."[5] When war finally came,

---

[2] Reid Mitchell, "The Northern Soldier and His Community," in *Toward a Social History of the American Civil War: Exploratory Essays*, ed. by Maris A. Vinovskis (Cambridge, Eng.: Cambridge University Press, 1990), 79–80.

[3] See Thomas R. Kemp, "Community and War: The Civil War Experience of Two New Hampshire Towns," in Vinovskis, *Toward a Social History of the American Civil War*, 31–77.

[4] John Blair Linn, *History of Centre and Clinton Counties, Pennsylvania* (n. p.: Lewis H. Ewert, 1883), 102.

[5] Frank A. Burr, *Life and Achievements of James Addams Beaver: Early Life, Military Services and Public Career* (Philadelphia: Furguson Brothers & Co., 1882), 23.

hundreds of local men answered Lincoln's first call for ninety-day volunteers in the dark days after Fort Sumter. When they were mustered out three months later, many of these same men re-enlisted for three years of service, leaving home again in ranks filled with even more of their neighbors. By the end of 1861, Centre County had sent off to war nearly two thousand men from its total 1860 population of 27,000 residents.

But by the summer of 1862, the political climate in Centre County had changed. Few men who heard the call to join a new Centre County regiment in the second summer of the war signed on with the enthusiasm of the "Boys of '61." They considered their course of action with genuine deliberation. Some of those who cited political reasons to explain their reluctance to enlist were ardent Republicans, but they represented more moderate civic values than those embraced by the Radical element of their party, a segment that supported a more vigorous prosecution of the war that would both preserve the Union and end slavery.

This brand of political moderation had been apparent even in early 1861, when most Centre Countians, including Beaver and many other Republican activists, had expressed sincere hopes that the Union might be preserved without resort to force of arms. In those days before the outbreak of hostilities, they had embraced as a hero their local Republican Congressman James T. Hale, who had worked tirelessly with Senator John J. Crittenden's compromise committee to avoid war.[6] The firing on Fort Sumter had changed some minds, but it did not alter the desire of many who still sought a peaceful resolution that preserved the Constitution and the Union. Moreover, fighting to end slavery won few supporters in Centre County, even among its most ardent Republicans. That they likely would not send forth their sons willingly to fight a war for abolition seemed to be apparent as early as the summer of 1861, when few recruits from the Democratic strongholds of eastern Centre County's so-called German townships answered the call to arms. The sentiment extended into the population at large, and the slightest hint that the war might become a crusade to end slavery cast a pall over even non-political events; a once-popular religious revival meeting in August 1861

---

[6] Linn, *History of Centre and Clinton Counties*, 104.

ended early when local residents stayed away in droves "because some preachers are to[o] hard Republicans or Politicians."[7]

If Centre Countians felt so strongly about the nature and aims of this war in 1861, the call for more troops in the summer of 1862 arrived at a very bad time. The war had not gone well for the North in recent months. The thrill of early spring victories had given way to stalemate around Corinth in the west and the Army of the Potomac's withdrawal from the gates of Richmond in the east. On July 7, Lincoln called for 300,000 additional three-year volunteers to fill the bloodied ranks.

That call reached Centre County at a time when several related issues had already begun to fuel a major shift in its citizens' attitudes toward the war. Defeat in the Seven Days Battles and slow progress in Mississippi proved bothersome. Many Centre Countians wondered if the passage of the Second Confiscation Act in July 1862 instituted a dangerous federal policy that violated individual property rights, involved civilians too directly in the war, or, worst of all, signified that the war really had changed into a crusade for abolition. Their fears seemed to be validated with arrival of news that, in July 1862, Major General John Pope had begun to impose harsher restrictions on slave-owning Virginia civilians. Hints that Lincoln might issue an emancipation proclamation or formally approve the raising of regiments of black soldiers unnerved Centre Countians, too. And now, in late July, as Lee's army began to march north and few northerners seemed willing to answer Lincoln's call for troops, Centre Countians grew nervous about rumors that the administration might turn to conscription to fill the depleted ranks.

Stepping in at this moment to ignite these various latent dissatisfactions into full-blown political dissension in Centre County came P. Gray Meek, the new editor of the *Bellefonte Democratic Watchman*. An ardent opponent of the Lincoln administration, Meek purchased a half-interest in the weekly newspaper in July 1862. He previously had attacked Lincoln in the paper's pages during the 1860 campaign, but its owners had fired him when his radical rhetoric caused a decline in subscriptions and a drop in advertisers.[8] Now

---

[7] Entry for August 22, 1861, Wesley Bierly Diary, Civil War Miscellaneous Collection, Archives, United States Army Military History Institute, Carlisle, Pa. (hereinafter cited as USAMHI).

[8] Linn, *History of Centre and Clinton Counties*, 348.

with far more editorial control than he had earlier possessed, he launched a tirade of vicious attacks on the president and on all elements of his conduct of the war.

Most effectively, Meek played upon concerns about recent battlefield defeats. He printed "The Dead Soldier," a piece designed to call attention to the ultimate cost of war's folly. "Dead, dead, how mournfully fall the words upon the hearts of those, who but a few months ago, crowded about the departing soldier, to grasp tearful eye, while thoughts of the horrors and dangers that must henceforth surround his life intrude themselves," the writer had intoned. He asked readers to consider any single one of the many Pennsylvanian combat deaths at the Seven Days: "Sad and heart broken these friends wept his loss, in the mountains and centre of the Old Keystone, while he slept his last sleep, leagues from any one who ever called him friend."[9]

Local Republicans feared that recent battlefield defeats and Meek's anti-administration tirades might doom efforts to fill Centre County's quota under the July call for new recruits. They worried about political embarrassment if they failed to produce enough willing volunteers, thus exposing unwilling neighbors to possible conscription. But they also considered opportunities for accruing political benefits if they could meet, or even exceed the county's quota. Republicans decided to try to rally their fellow citizens to support the organization of a special Centre County regiment.

Congressman Hale and Bellefonte attorney Hugh McAllister, a local Republican party leader, spearheaded the enlistment drive. They issued their call for volunteers in upbeat and patriotic terms, downplaying the threat of conscription that might follow if the ranks went unfilled. To build still more momentum, they called for a public meeting at the county courthouse in Bellefonte on August 2, 1862.

The well-advertised meeting drew a large and enthusiastic crowd. Hale spoke at length, and a committee of local citizens presented a set of nine resolutions for the people's approval. The separate items reveal much about both the way in which Centre Countians viewed this war and how much they would do to support goals with which they agreed.

Initial resolutions addressed standard themes. The first called

---

[9] *Bellefonte Democratic Watchman*, July 18, 1862.

upon the citizens of Centre County to deplore the current rebellion as "unauthorized, uncalled for and desperately wicked." The second endorsed President Lincoln's leadership. The third mourned the soldier dead, both victims of bullets and of disease, and called for a public pledge to provide all possible aid to local soldiers disabled by wounds or exposure.

After these more general commitments, the resolutions took on the pressing issues of the day. The crowd endorsed a fourth resolution to fill Centre County's new quota for three-year volunteers. Recruits would receive tangible evidence of their community's appreciation for their services, as the crowd endorsed a fifth resolution to permit the Centre County commissioners to borrow $10,000 for five years to pay a $50 bounty to each resident who now enlisted.

The public meeting endorsed two additional resolutions about war aims that revealed much about community sentiment and clearly placed Centre County's most active Republicans among the party's moderates. Preserving the Union, stated the sixth resolution, could be the "only legitimate object of the war." All patriotic northerners easily could embrace this goal, Hale and McAllister argued, and thus they all should "surrender party prejudices and predilections upon the altar of his country" for the rest of the war. Any loyal Centre County man, regardless of political allegiance, should "devote his energies, his property, and if need be his life to the accomplishment of so important and so noble an object." Clearly uncomfortable with the Radical element of their party, the resolution's authors stated in a seventh resolution that they viewed slavery as being of "minor importance" at this critical time. Indeed, one must "distrust the judgment and doubt the patriotism of those who seek to give it preeminence by making the support they owe the government of the country to depend on the adoption" of any single specific policy regarding slavery.[10]

These first seven resolutions apparently comprised the intended agenda for the public meeting, but rapidly changing events required the local committee to tack on two final items. Weak initial response to Lincoln's call for 300,000 three-year troops generated rumors that the president would demand that state militias enroll 300,000 addi-

---

[10] *Bellefonte Central Press*, August 8, 1862; and *Bellefonte Democratic Watchman*, August 8, 1862.

tional nine-month volunteers. In cases of extreme national emergency, these state militiamen could be called into federal service. Much worse, in states unable to enlist their quotas of three-year volunteers, some nine-month men might be drafted for the longer term of service to make up the shortfall. Worried that the administration might take such an action—and Lincoln in fact did issue the call for additional state militia enlistments only two days after the Bellefonte meeting—Hale and McAllister presented an eighth resolution to extend the coverage of the County Relief Fund that supported families of three-year volunteers to include the dependents of any Centre County militiamen drafted into federal service. In so doing, they did not lose sight of their primary mission to raise a regiment of three-year volunteers. In their final resolution, they won the crowd's acceptance of a suggestion to give all long-term recruits both a $50 county bounty and a guarantee of family support from the County Relief Fund during their absence; nine-month men would get only the latter.[11]

With public approval apparently secured, recruiting for the Centre County regiment began in earnest. With the enthusiasm of the first rush to the colors long faded, each successful enlistment required great effort on the part of recruiting officers. Plenty of men seeking commissions in the new regiment had obtained authorization from the state to organize companies, but during the first three weeks of August, few of them found it easy to overcome the reluctance of many potential recruits while fighting off competing recruiters.

Who answered the call to arms to join the Centre County regiment in the late summer of 1862? Years later, one veteran shed the best possible light on the new recruits. They had not enlisted "for pecuniary gain," he wrote. "It was not because they were ignorant of the consequences of the step they were about to take. . . . It was pure patriotism that constrained them to stand by the Union in the fearful conflict; they felt it their duty to go and they went."[12]

In truth, when patriotism could be counted among motivating factors for enlistment, deliberation rather than enthusiasm shaped its expression. For example, neighbors considered Robert M. Forster, a

---

[11] *Bellefonte Central Press*, August 8, 1862; and *Bellefonte Democratic Watchman*, August 8, 1862.

[12] Adjt. J.W. Muffly, comp., *The Story of Our Regiment: A History of the 148th Pennsylvania Volunteers* (Des Moines, Iowa: Kenyon Printing, 1904), 994–95.

middle-aged man with a wife and three sons, a man who was an "intelligent [sic] progressive farmer," merchant, and postmaster of "Farmers High School [modern-day State College, Pennsylvania]," to be an unlikely candidate for enlistment. But Forster was a "man of strong convictions" who—despite many compelling reasons not to enlist—finally "entered the service because" of his political beliefs.[13]

More often, however, factors other than patriotism informed men's decisions to enlist. A significant number of draft-eligible men in Miles Township decided to enlist voluntarily now so they could serve together in family groups, rather than risk being drafted later as individuals. One father-son pair and at least thirteen sets of brothers signed up with the same recruiting officer with a guarantee of serving in the same company.[14]

At times it took more than an impassioned appeal to patriotism to sway the unconvinced. Martin Dolan attended a "log rolling"—a community "frolic" to fell and burn trees to clear new farmland—in the northern part of Centre County. With his "genial manner and impressive Irish brogue," he announced his plans to raise a company for the new regiment. He convinced few to sign up, however, until he suggested that potential recruits rendezvous at Milesburg—at his tavern.[15]

Others found their way into the ranks quite unexpectedly. D. H. Young left home one August morning uncertain whether to answer his country's call or to take care of aging parents. He referred the matter to Providence, he later recalled, by writing "Stay" and "Go" on two pieces of paper and asking a trusted friend to pick one. The slip read "Go," so he did.[16] At a recruiting rally at Martha's Furnace, a wealthy local man encouraged others to enlist and expressed regret that his business obligations kept him from going himself. Young Daniel Baumgardner rose and said to the crowd: "Gentlemen, I pity this poor man, who would offer his life for his country, if it were not for his possessions. . . . No, gentlemen, it is not for such men but for us who have nothing to leave but our families, no difference whether we are able to leave them anything to live on or not; our lives are not

---

[13] Ibid., 569.
[14] Ibid., 563–64.
[15] Ibid., 674.
[16] Ibid., 650.

worth much at any rate or we would be rich."[17] The wealthy man was shamed into enlisting along with Baumgardner.

Patriotism certainly did not motivate twenty-four-year-old John McIvison to enlist. Despite the regimental historian's later declaration that nobody joined the new regiment for money, the unemployed McIvison, a man without prospects, bowed to his mother's and sister's pressure to enlist, because they wanted to be able to draw benefits from the County Relief Fund.[18]

The need for new soldiers compelled recruiters to accept a significant number of boys under eighteen for service in the Centre County regiment. Underage boys could enroll legally with a parent's permission, but recruiting officers seldom demanded such evidence. Many young recruits left classrooms at Pine Grove Academy to follow Professor E. T. Thomas—a well-known public supporter of political moderation—when he reluctantly decided to go to war. Likewise, many more left the Boalsburg Academy to follow Professor James J. Patterson, whose public statements on the war made it clear that he, too, felt much the same way Thomas did.

Local opponents of the war effort watched the initial recruiting activities with great interest. Some unleashed a barrage of criticism on those who had called the public meeting to raise support for the Centre County regiment but then had failed to back their words with actions. Editor Meek suggested that Hale and McAllister especially should *enroll themselves as volunteers*, and thus set the example." That would demonstrate true patriotism and prove the earnestness of their words. "Other men have gone to war as good by nature as James T. Hale and H. N. McAllister. Why should not *they* go and spill some of *their* blood if need be for the country which they profess to love so well." As affluent men, both could certainly afford to go without concern for their families' welfare. If their country needed soldiers so badly, Meek wrote, "We can spare them, about as well as anybody else in town, and in view of the great crisis which is now

---

[17] Ibid., 724.

[18] Sallie McIvison to brother John McIvison, September 21, 1862, John McIvison Letters, Special Collections, Paterno Library, Penn State University, University Park (hereinafter cited as PSU). Sallie responded to John's initially positive view of soldier life with the comment, "I am glad your pleased with Solgier life; it will please you for you never liked to work to well." Subsequent letters are filled with references to McIvison's mother attempting to get financial support from the County Relief Fund.

upon us, we cannot conceive how, in the name of Heaven, a couple of such stout able-bodied men as they, can stay at home? Go, JAMES T. HALE and H. N. McALLISTER, go, for God's sake, go!"[19]

Meek's pointed personal criticisms targeted others, too. Recalling the Wide Awakes' boast in 1860 that they would raise thousands of troops if needed, Meek now wondered "why these chaps do not now go, when Old Abe so earnestly appeals to them to come. Not one has volunteered under the late call."[20] He seemed to delight in relating a contemporary riddle that asked for a definition of "plenty." The answer was: "Men who think everybody—but themselves—ought to respond with alacrity to the call for three thousand troops."[21]

Interestingly enough, recruiters purposefully decided to target Penn, Haines, Gregg, and Miles Townships, some of Centre County's most heavily German communities, with strong Democratic leanings and a poor record for answering earlier calls for soldiers. Attorney McAllister had blasted their "lethargy," and now he, along with Capt. William H. Blair, the county's new conscription officer, organized a public meeting at Millheim in Penn Township on August 18 to raise recruits for the Centre County regiment. Abandoning the positive inducements with which he began most of his recruiting speeches, McAllister now argued at length that it was in the county's best interest to fill its quota with volunteers. If the men of Penn Township did not go willingly now, the draft certainly would fall most heavily on the communities in the county. The effort yielded few recruits, however. As the meeting broke up, a local man asked for guidance from a prominent leader of the town, a gentleman who once had served as a county commissioner. In the presence of McAllister and Blair, the former official told the questioner that he would never have to join the army if he did not want to do so. If he was drafted, he simply could take refuge in the wilds of the nearby mountains.[22]

When new recruit Reverend L. C. Edmonds tried to entice enlistments from his own congregation, he heard one of his German parishoners mutter *"Mer sut den Schwartz Republikaner uf der strose um schiese,"* which the recorder of the incident translated as "Some one ought to shoot down this black Republican upon our street."

[19] *Bellefonte Democratic Watchman*, August 2, 1862.
[20] Ibid.
[21] Ibid., August 22, 1862.
[22] Muffly, *The Story of Our Regiment*, 33–34.

Several women whose friends had reluctantly answered Edmonds's call openly wished that the first bullet fired by the Confederates would kill the preacher.[23]

In public political meetings, in local Democratic papers, and other community events during August 1862, antiwar and anti-Lincoln proponents continued to raise questions about the conflict's conduct and its changing aims. With so many residents actively weighing their options, critics of the war seemed determined to make potential recruits seriously consider all the implications of their decision to enlist. "Ever go to a military ball?" began one short article. The grizzled old veteran in the story answered that he had not, but then added, "I once had a military ball come to me, and what do think, madam, it took my leg off."[24]

In a region where support for the war once had rested solidly on only a single foundation—that of preservation of the Union—some local Democrats attempted to dissuade enlistments by playing upon real fears that the conflict might become a struggle to end slavery or to extend the rights of citizenship to blacks. When Republican Senator James Lane announced the opening of recruiting stations for two regiments of black troops in faraway Kansas, a Centre Countian commented that "it is perfectly proper that a black regiment should go with a *black*guard."[25] When word arrived that Massachusetts and Rhode Island had begun to enroll black soldiers, editor Meek used the opportunity to wonder why those two states felt "compelled to call upon a servile and inferior race to fight their battles for them." He marveled at the irony that "Great(?) Massachusetts, with its hundreds of thousands of able bodied men, its boasted wealth, and its *boasted valor* cannot find within its limits brave men enough to fill its quota of 300,000 men without calling about its *negro* population! Oh, wonderful greatness!"[26]

Either Democratic sympathizers succeeded in raising doubts in sufficient numbers of Centre Countians' minds or the decision to enlist proved too difficult for even loyal men to make hastily. In any case, recruiting for the new Centre County regiment progressed so slowly that some residents grew impatient with what they perceived

---

[23] Ibid., 618.
[24] *Bellefonte Democratic Watchman*, August 8, 1862.
[25] Ibid., August 15, 1862.
[26] Ibid., August 22, 1862.

to be signs of growing disloyalty in their midst. A crowd physically assaulted editor Meek in Bellefonte, while onlookers urged on the attackers. A warrant for his arrest was issued for *"inducing men not to enlist in the army,"* a move described by a fellow Democratic newspaperman as "a malicious attempt to injure the character of the Junior [editor] in the eyes of the community." Meek's friend felt compelled to include a stern warning to those who would harm critics of government policy: "Remember, this is a free country; and so long as a man is guiltless of treason . . . he has a *right* to the free expression of his opinion."[27]

Administration supporters in Centre County no doubt felt deep dismay to discover that they could not hide its growing political dissension. In nearby Altoona in Blair County, a man who had read recent issues of Meek's Bellefonte newspaper damned it as "one of the most contemptible, Jeff Davis truckling sheets with which we have ever defiled our fingers." Noting Centre County's flagging enthusiasm for meeting the president's latest call for troops, he marveled that any community could be so unconcerned about the fate of the Union "unless perchance, there should be a locality inhabited by such truth perverters and treason abetters as these men who edit the *Watchman.*" He added, "If the people of Bellefonte of Centre County are at all imbued with the sentiments promulgated by the *Watchman* we do not wonder that they are unconcerned, and that they are willing to let the Union slide."[28]

Administration supporters had good reason to worry. After three weeks of hard effort, response to the call for recruits had slowed so much that McAllister and other local Republican leaders called for a second public meeting at the county courthouse. By August 22, the ardent patriotic spirit of the August 2 meeting had evaporated. The official announcement of the meeting now appealed to the people's fears: the gathering would be held to "raise money for bounty to volunteers to fill our quota of 600,000 men called for by the President of the United States and thus save the disagreeable necessity of a draft."[29]

At this second well-attended and attentive public meeting, McAl-

[27] Ibid., August 8, 1862.

[28] *Altoona Tribune*, reprinted as comic relief in the *Bellefonte Democratic Watchman*, August 8, 1862.

[29] *Bellefonte Central Press*, August 22, 1862.

lister and Blair shared the stage. Although the county's conscription officer, Blair urged voluntary enlistment so he could "acquiesce in the will of the people" and conscript none of them. He and McAllister then won the crowd's support for three resolutions. First, they again approved the payment of a $50 county bounty for each recruit already enrolled, and, as an added incentive for immediate enlistment, promised the same sum to any man who signed up before September 1. Second, they reasserted their views about the true goals of this war: restoration of the authority of the government "with or without slavery as will best promote the accomplishment of this great work." Third, they approved Lincoln's response to New York editor Horace Greeley's antislavery "Plea for Twenty Million," in which the president had administered a "severe and merited rebuke, alike to those who withhold their support from the National Administration because it does not devote all its energies to maintain or to abolish the institution of slavery."[30] McAllister made it so clear that he still considered the war primarily as a conflict to preserve the Union that even a local Democrat explained that the attorney "was not in favor of the abolition of slavery, further than it came as an incident."[31]

By mid-August, well before meeting enlistment goals, small groups of Centre County's newest recruits got the call to leave for Harrisburg for formal muster into federal service. The sorrow of leavetaking overwhelmed affected families. Nobody knew what lay ahead. Henry Clay Campbell recalled later that "fathers were wiping the tears from their eyes; mothers and sisters were weeping aloud. I think Pine Grove has never witnessed another scene like that, and after forty years I am persuaded that those left behind were the real sufferers during the war. We were soon on our way, cheering and singing, little realizing what was in future for us all."[32] But no bands played, the singing soon died down, and all in all, the Centre County soldiers and their families experienced a far more somber departure than had the "Boys of '61."

For those who stayed behind, personal sadness mingled with other painful emotions. Pride mixed with fear in one resident's mind as he

---

[30] Ibid., August 29, 1862; and *Bellefonte Democratic Watchman*, August 29, 1862.
[31] *Bellefonte Democratic Watchman*, August 29, 1862.
[32] Henry Clay Campbell Memoir, Civil War Miscellaneous Collection, USAMHI.

watched a group of new volunteers leave. He took pleasure in knowing that Centre County "will have somewhere in the neighborhood of 2500 soldiers in the field," but he knew as well that "hopes have been entertained that there would be no necessity for a draft in this county, but we think that is scarcely possible. We have a good many men yet to raise and the probability is that it will have to be done by a draft."[33]

Arrival at Camp Curtin brought the new recruits their first taste of army life. Private Lemuel Osman recalled his first meal in camp: "Such a dinner! Hard tack and pork as thick as a cheese." Best of all, the Centre County boys learned they had not really left "home" far behind at all. "I looked up and down the ranks for the company to see how the rosy-cheeked lads were taking it, and lo! to my surprise," Osman reported, "I saw in the ranks with the boys, a cracker and a piece of fat pork in his hand, Governor Curtin, who was having lots of fun with the boys, and who, by his presence and good humor, helped to hearten the situation."[34]

A native son of Bellefonte, Curtin knew many of the men in ranks personally and certainly he intended nothing more than to offer his good wishes to his neighbors. But this meeting became only the first of many, and, back home, the connection between Curtin and the new Centre County regiment helped forge an unrealistic image of that unit as a Republican organization in total support of all elements of the administration's war effort.

It is easy to see how such a perception developed. The political controversy that had swirled around the recruiting of the regiment continued to grow after the recruits left. In some towns, local Republicans were embarrassed to discover that the mere display of a blue uniform could trigger protests. When Reverend Edmonds, now a lieutenant serving with the "Centre County regiment," returned home briefly to tie up personal business, he announced his intention to preach one final sermon—and he planned to wear his uniform when he did so. He so greatly "roused the hostile sentiment of the community" that a committee of vestrymen warned him not to do it, and a close personal friend pleaded with him to change his mind. Reverend Edmonds refused to be intimidated and delivered his fare-

---

[33] *Bellefonte Democratic Watchman*, August 22, 1862.
[34] Muffly, *The Story of Our Regiment*, 599.

well sermon in uniform to "the compliments of loyal men and women" but also to "the curses of those whose sympathies were with the other side."[35]

Worse, local Republicans learned that despite their hard work they had not raised a full Centre County regiment after all. Only about seven hundred Centre County men—enough to fill about seven companies—had enlisted for three-year service. A full regiment required about a thousand men organized into ten companies. On September 8, 1862, when it officially entered federal service as the 148th Pennsylvania, the Centre County regiment had to fill its ranks with three additional companies raised in Jefferson, Indiana, and Clarion Counties.

Not inclined to take this defeat lightly, local Republicans worked hard to maintain the fiction that the 148th was, indeed, the "Centre County regiment." Even before formal muster, many of the captains of the unit's Centre County companies—with attorney McAllister's collaboration—requested from Governor Curtin the appointment of Bellefonte attorney James A. Beaver, currently serving as lieutenant colonel of the 45th Pennsylvania, to be promoted to colonel of the new regiment.[36] Beaver knew his peacetime law partner arranged the move, but he did not seem to view his promotion as part of a larger political statement on the part of Centre County's Republicans. Perhaps because he had been stationed in South Carolina, far from the recent dissension back in Pennsylvania, he wrote to his mother merely that he was gratified by the promotion that came as "evidence of the confidence and good-will of my fellow-citizens at home."[37]

On September 10, Colonel Beaver received orders to take the 148th Pennsylvania to war. The regiment left for the front just as Lee's army invaded Maryland, but the new regiment played no part in the bloody battle of Antietam on September 17. It went instead to Cockeysville, Maryland, to guard the Baltimore and Ohio railroad and settle down to the routine of garrison life.

A soldier signing himself "Monitor" described the 148th Pennsylvania's encampment and activities for readers of the *Central Press*.

---

[35] Ibid., 618–19.

[36] Hugh N. McAllister to James A. Beaver, August 28, 1862, box 15, James A. Beaver Papers, PSU.

[37] James A. Beaver to Mother, August 22, 1862, quoted in Burr, *Life and Achievements of James Addams Beaver*, 43.

He hoped to encourage friends and family at home to follow the fate of the 148th closely, for "Old Centre is well represented in this regiment." He regretted he had no exciting stories of battles and glories to report yet, but he knew that "when the coveted opportunity presents itself [the regiment] will show to the country that the mountains and valleys of Old Centre produce as brave men and true as ever 'Greece nurtured in her glory's time.' "[38] That time did not come soon, but even in mid-October, a correspondent signing himself as "Wendel" reminded readers to "expect to hear a good account of us—Centre county *has* been tried, as the long list of killed and wounded in the old 45th will testify."[39]

But fewer and fewer citizens at home seemed to accept the worth of such great sacrifice. Centre County supporters of Lincoln and Union noted that despite the departure of their neighbors in the 148th Pennsylvania for an uncertain future at the front, the voices of discontent had grown louder since the formal announcement of the Emancipation Proclamation in late September. They feared that Republican office holders might be defeated in the upcoming fall elections by this rising wave of local disillusionment. If Centre County reversed its course and fell into the Democratic camp, an editor for the *Central Press* wrote, "it would be a rebuke of the general Administration." Worse, any such move coming so soon after the recent departure of their friends and neighbors with the 148th Pennsylvania represented a betrayal of their citizen-soldiers, a "burning reproach of old *loyal Centre*, who has now upwards of 2000 soldiers in the field fighting for freedom."[40]

Nonetheless, clearly understanding his neighbors' shifting political sentiments, Congressman Hale—a leader of the drive to raise the Centre County regiment—decided to bolt the Republican party. He hoped that the strength of his character and his consistent moderate stance on slavery and the conduct of the war would secure his reelection as an independent candidate. He made a wise move. The fall elections of 1862 shocked Centre County Republicans. Democratic candidates swept local races. Worse, Hale soundly beat a "Regular Republican" challenger by a margin that clearly included the votes

---

[38] *Bellefonte Central Press*, September 26, 1862.
[39] Ibid., October 10, 1862.
[40] Ibid.

of many Democrats who so respected his independent stand that their own party had nominated no opponent.[41]

Center Countians of both major parties never forgot the change of political fortunes that followed the fall elections of 1862. For the rest of the war, they returned again and again to the fortunes of their friends and neighbors in the Centre County regiment born in the heat of 1862's contentious political atmosphere to express their support for the war effort or to decry its conduct. By the time the regiment joined the Army of the Potomac in Virginia, in the dark days after Fredericksburg, local Republicans who now viewed the soldiers of the 148th Pennsylvania as the most loyal standard bearers of the Lincoln administration would not have believed that its ranks included soldiers such as Private McIvison, who, of the recent terrible fight at Fredericksburg, wrote, "we lost about Seventeen thousand so no abolitionist there need tell you that we only lost a few hundred; I seen graves forty feet long."[42] Local Democrats, on the other hand, would have found it equally unsettling to learn that the 148th Pennsylvania included soldiers willing to praise the Stars and Stripes as "the glorious emblem of liberty, which all men irrespective of clime or birth," could live under and "partake of the liberties which it grants."[43]

Centre County's political partisanship and antiwar sentiment of the fall of 1862 grew worse in the late winter and early spring of 1863. It even began to infect the families and friends of soldiers in the 148th Pennsylvania. While Calvin Fisher served as regimental surgeon, his clergyman brother at home condemned "this awful war—and what concerns does it cause to hundreds and thousands of Families and what desolation and sorrow does it spread. May the Lord have mercy upon us."[44]

At the front, soldiers in the 148th Pennsylvania heard more and

---

[41] Linn, *History of Centre and Clinton Counties*, 136.

[42] John McIvison to Mother, Sister, and Brother, December 25, 1862, John McIvison Letters, PSU.

[43] "John McIvison" to Sister, January 22, 1863, ibid. An examination of the McIvison letter reveals that this soldier was only partially literate and often got other soldiers to write home for him. This quotation was written in the hand of one of McIvison's comrades. Its content is entirely inconsistent with political sentiments McIvison expressed in other letters.

[44] Reverend Peter Fisher to Alfred Fisher, November 30, 1862, Benjamin F. Fisher Papers, USAMHI.

more about increasing signs of disloyalty among their neighbors and friends at home. After a series of vicious antiwar attacks published in Bellefonte, attorney McAllister wrote Colonel Beaver that "the Democratic Watchman is the vilest sheet published in the State," and editor P. Gray Meek was "an avowed secessionist and at heart a traitor." In McAllister's mind, the increasing popularity of Meek's paper represented only the most obvious sign of a growing Copperhead organization in Centre County. He only hoped that because "the *Copperhead* loves to strike in the dark," the area's loyal men would soon "drag him forth and expose him to the world in the light of day."[45] James M. Thompson, another of the colonel's acquaintances, concurred that something needed to be done to root out home front disloyalty and suggested that the 148th Pennsylvania itself should play a leading role in it. "We have . . . a good many copperheads in the county that your Centre County Regiment should by all means send their respects to. Whilst you have led a thousand of our bravest young men to face the daring rebels, a . . . thousand more traitors than the rebels you are now confronting remain at home to thwart the government in all its endeavors to crush the rebellion."[46]

Thompson also suggested that Beaver encourage his men to send their "private opinions to the presses to be distributed for the copperheads to read." He especially targeted readers in "those german townships" where "a larger percentage of the people have imbibed those traitorous ideas and prejudices than the other townships."[47] There is no evidence that Beaver acted on this suggestion, but a Centre County man in Company C of the 49th Pennsylvania—a unit raised to great local enthusiasm in 1861, and whose members counted many friends in the ranks of the 148th Pennsylvania— offered up his scathing commentary. He and his brothers-in-arms in the 148th Pennsylvania and all of Centre County's commands, he noted, had observed "with sorrow and shame the too evident decline of that patriotic enthusiasm which prompted you, the people of our native county, to send us, your neighbors, sons and brothers to the defense of our nation's unity." He asked all loyal residents of Centre County to dismiss Democratic claims that the troops were demoral-

---

[45] Hugh N. McAllister to James A. Beaver, March 17, 1863, box 15, James A. Beaver Papers, PSU.

[46] James M. Thompson to James A. Beaver, March 18, 1863, box 15, ibid.

[47] Ibid.

ized or dispirited. "Permit us to remind you that we are *soldiers*; that we enlisted—with a full knowledge of all the meaning of that act—in the service of our Government," he wrote. He reminded them, too, that "we fight for no General—we follow any one who may be appointed to lead us. We care for no man's glory and no party a success; while there is war in the land we belong in the party in whose hands is placed under the Providence of God the destinies of our country, for it we fight."[48]

That spring, Centre County Republicans organized Union League Societies to rally those still loyal to the administration. James Thompson did not know "whether their influence will be sufficient to control the bainful bosh and ignorance of the new Democratic party [the Copperheads]."[49] But in Virginia, Private Isaac Sweetwood expressed no confidence in the success of the movement. "[Y]ou were talking about them haveing a meeting in bellefonte Union League," he wrote a friend at home, adding, "i Suppose tha think tha will give thar party that nam in order to get the majority[.] tha had better Start up the wideawakes a gane."[50]

Still, reports about Governor Curtin's visits to their camp continued to fuel notions back home that the 148th Pennsylvania represented loyal Centre County. Private Solomon Dale broke from his usual pattern of recording the weather and daily labors to record his pleasure with the governor's visit and speech in late March.[51] Curtin came again in late April to watch the regiment break camp for its first full season of active campaigning and its imminent baptism of fire at Chancellorsville on May 1–3.

The 148th Pennsylvania appears only briefly in most studies of that battle, but as part of Brigadier General Winfield S. Hancock's division of the II Corps, it performed well. Six companies served with distinction on a reinforced skirmish line that protected the Union left flank; the remaining four companies—all raised in Centre County— marched into a fruitless effort to stem the massed Confederate as-

---

[48] *Bellefonte Central Press*, March 20, 1863.

[49] James M. Thompson to James A. Beaver, March 18, 1863, box 15, James A. Beaver Papers, PSU.

[50] Isaac Sweetwood to "Friend," May 15, 1863, vol. 261, Fredericksburg National Military Park Library, Fredericksburg, Va. Sweetwood was killed in action at Spotsylvania on May 10, 1864.

[51] Entry for March 27, 1863, Solomon Dale Diary, Pennsylvania Military Museum Archives, Boalsburg, Pa.

sault on May 3 that forced the Union army to withdraw. Colonel Beaver fell badly wounded, and the four companies with him took very heavy losses. Governor Curtin revisited the regiment's camp shortly after the battle. He found that "many noble fellows known to him had fallen; many others were suffering from painful wounds; and withal there was no success to cheer and compensate." As Captain Robert H. Forster recalled, "Vain indeed were his efforts to cancel his sad emotions," adding that after the governor nearly broke down while trying to speak, "few that heard his touching and pathetic words will ever forget it."[52]

The Union defeat at Chancellorsville and the brutal handling of the 148th Pennsylvania gave home front observers another chance to weigh in on the war's purpose and progress. Supporters of the administration's effort urged all citizens to put aside their political differences while the county awaited the arrival of the casualty lists. Regardless of one's political stand, wrote the editor of the *Central Press*, in wartime, everyone pays a price, and although brave soldiers died on faraway battlefields, the cost to their critics who mocked their deaths could be much higher:

> History is merciless, but just . . . its verdicts are irreversible, its probe goes down, through the self-inflicted wounds, down to the bone, and elicits groans and tears from even the third generation. If in these times he be asked "Where does he stand?" history, neighborhood, tradition, will assign that man to his proper place—among the doubtful . . . For men will ask—"Who is this man?" and where did he stand in the dark days of peril, when the false fell away and the weak held their peace?"[53]

As bad news trickled back from Virginia into many Centre County homes, administration loyalists reechoed their praise of their soldiers in the 148th Pennsylvania as the true heroes of the republic. As Attorney McAllister wrote to Colonel Beaver, the regiment acquitted itself so well on the battlefield, he could not repress the pride he felt that "is identified with the government." He hoped a time would come when it would "treat any Copperheads in the land with execration, scorn and contempt."[54]

---

[52] Robert H. Forster, "Address to the Veterans Club of Howard on September 20, 1877," in Linn, *History of Centre and Clinton Counties*, 132.

[53] *Bellefonte Central Press*, May 15, 1863.

[54] Hugh N. McAllister to James A. Beaver, May 22, 1863, box 15, James A. Beaver Papers, PSU.

When the tally was complete, at least forty-eight local men were counted among the Union dead at Chancellorsville, some of the most horribly wounded perishing in agony when they could not be rescued from brush fires. The editors of the *Central Press* honored these men as martyrs. At the end of a long list of the regiment's casualties, the editor noted that "the 148 PV have acquitted themselves nobly, and their praise is universal in this army."[55] For their part, the soldiers already knew that this weekly would treat their sacrifice with respect. As Surgeon Fisher wrote his brother after listing personal friends who died or fell wounded, "If you can[,] get a copy of the Bellefonte Central Press of this week which will publish all" the names of the regiment's casualties.[56]

By comparison, the *Democratic Watchman* responded to the 148th Pennsylvania's crushing losses at Chancellorsville in quite different tones. The editor portrayed the casualties as neither fallen heroes nor as martyrs to a worthy cause. After a stark list of the names of the dead and wounded in badly bloodied Company H followed this commentary: "Our county has sustained a much heavier loss in this last battle than at any other during the war. We are just at the beginning if force alone is to settle the difficulties, and how much better would it be could we close the bloody history, without the loss of another man."[57] A week later, at the top of a list of the entire regiment's casualties, the editor urged citizens to try and recall the faces of "friends who but a short time since were enjoying the pleasures of home, that are now suffering in Hospitals, maimed; some of them for life," or to remember "the ghastly faces of the brave dead." In somber tones, the Democratic editor intoned, "A continuation of the war can only bring more lists of the kind. It can only make more suffering and sorrow, more graves and cripples, more destruction and death. . . . Can we force another State to love us? Answer honestly or more lists like the following will tell."[58]

The pattern of reporting the battles of the 148th Pennsylvania set after Chancellorsville continued throughout the war, as home front supporters and opponents of the war continued to debate the issues against the backdrop of their fellow citizens' fortunes on the battle-

---

[55] *Bellefonte Central Press*, May 22, 1863.
[56] Calvin Fisher to Brother, May 19, 1863, Benjamin Fisher Papers, USAMHI.
[57] *Bellefonte Democratic Watchman*, May 15, 1863.
[58] Ibid., May 22, 1863.

field. After Chancellorsville, when Lee headed north into Pennsylvania, the Democratic press of Centre County advised noncompliance with a draft to fill the ranks of the state's emergency militia, asserting that "if we are good Democrats" the invading Confederates would leave them alone. The editor of the *Central Press*, by contrast, used the recent sacrifices of the 148th Pennsylvania to condemn those who supported such a stand: "A great many of you have sons and brothers, friends and relatives at this very moment who are battling for the Government and lending a helping hand to suppress the rebellion, yet at the same time you cry for peace and do all in your power to paralyze the energies of the Government. Shame on you!"[59]

A few weeks later, on July 2, at Gettysburg, the 148th Pennsylvania marched into a veritable hail of Confederate bullets in the Wheatfield. Even though the battle ended with a Union victory, another thirty-one men from the regiment lay dead or mortally wounded.

As word of the great battle filtered back home, the *Central Press* mourned the community's newest heroes: "This once splendid body of men—the pride of Centre County—is fast dwindling down. Much was expected of it when they entered the service, and more could not be expected of them than they have accomplished." At Gettysburg, "too many of them enriched the soil of Gettysburg with their life's blood." The cost had been high, but "well may Centre County be proud of their noble sons, and while we shower praise and congratulations on those who have escaped the monster death, let us not forget that gallant band who offered up their lives as willing sacrifice for the honor and defence of this country."[60] Some lightly wounded soldiers from the regiment came home to recuperate, and the *Central Press* greeted them with praise: "Now, may they be able to point with pride to their wounds and say, 'I was a soldier of the 148th Pa. Vols. and received these wounds in fighting for my country.'"[61] The *Democratic Watchman* dutifully printed a list of the names of the regiment's dead and wounded, too, but for commentary, it also published a local resident's account of his recent trip to Gettysburg, replete with complaints about unburied bodies, dead horses, and a stench "described as almost intolerable." The editor added only, "Save us from any more such awful scenes."[62]

---

[59] *Bellefonte Central Press*, June 12, 1863.
[60] Ibid., July 17, 1863.
[61] Ibid., August 7, 1863.
[62] *Bellefonte Democratic Watchman*, July 17, 1863.

In the aftermath of Gettysburg and on the eve of the 1863 fall elections, efforts by Centre County Republicans to portray the 148th Pennsylvania as a haven of administration loyalists grew even more intense. To try and recapture control of county politics, local Republicans—and even some moderate Democrats who found the cant of Meek and his ilk intolerable—announced the formation of the "Loyal Union Party." In preparing a slate of candidates for the fall elections, attorney McAllister announced Captain Forster of the 148th as the new party's nominee for state legislator.[63] As a soldier and a one-time Democrat, Forster seemed to McAllister to be an ideal candidate. Although surprised by a nomination he had not sought and skeptical about his chances of winning, Forster reluctantly agreed to run: "I feel that I would sooner be defeated as a Union candidate, than elected on the platform upon which the so-called Democrats of Pennsylvania are at present standing," he wrote. He expressed dissatisfaction with the conduct of his own party back home, adding, "I have yet to learn that to be a Democrat a man must sympathise with treason and give 'aid and comfort' to this monster accursed rebellion, as a large majority of those who now control the Democratic organization do." He also made it clear that if he won, he would go to Harrisburg, but if he lost, he planned to remain with his men, now "within very easy shelling range of the enemy's position across the Rapidan."[64]

Despite his own Republican sympathies, Colonel Beaver did not approve of such home front interference with his command. He endorsed Forster's right to accept nomination for state office, noting that "much as I am opposed to soldiers mingling in politics, I cannot but remember that the citizen soldier is as much interested in the Government which he defends as others who pursue . . . peaceful avocations of life." But he expressed as well considerable dismay about the way in which folks at home—including his own law partner—attempted to manipulate his regiment to strengthen their political influence miles away from the front lines. Noting Forster's stated preference to remain in the field, Beaver made clear his desire that the captain's wish would "be sustained by those who have placed

---

[63] Hugh N. McAllister to James A. Beaver, September 10, 1863, box 15, James A. Beaver Papers, PSU.

[64] *Bellefonte Central Press*, October 2, 1863.

his name before the people without any knowledge or application of his."[65]

Beaver's rebuke apparently meant little to Centre County Republicans as the fall elections neared. Governor Curtin was running for reelection, and local Republican leaders considered ways in which soldiers' votes might help their native son. McAllister went so far as to demand Colonel Beaver's direct assistance: "You will much oblige by sending me immediately a list of the men in your regiment—voters in Centre County—who can render most aid." He even asked the colonel to list the men in "the order of their relative importance."[66] Not long after this, rumors that loyal Republican soldiers might obtain furloughs to go home to vote swept through the regiment. "I am living in hop[e]s of gitting home to vote this faul for Cirtain," wrote Pvt. William Williams in September, explaining that "I would like to see Cirtain a lecting a gain[.] I think we can't git a better man then he is." Suspecting that many of his fellow soldiers felt the same way, he added "[I]f we git home we show them [the Democrats] a trick or two."[67]

There is no evidence to suggest that Colonel Beaver actually did approve furlough applications based on political affiliation, although a number of soldiers from the regiment were home on leave during the election. Private Williams was not one of the fortunate ones, but even without his vote, Curtin won reelection handily. When he heard the news, Williams crowed, "I would like to here some of them copper heds talks since the el[ec]tion." He took equal pleasure in hearing about the good treatment enjoyed by those fortunate soldiers home on leave that fall: "I herd that some of the solders that went home to vote stood a good chance whith the girls[.] I am glad to here that the solders Stance whith the girls."[68] Curtin's win provided Centre County's Lincoln loyalists with their sole victory, however. As predicted, Captain Forster and the rest of the Union Party slate in the county went down to defeat.

The war's hardest days for the 148th Pennsylvania came in the

---

[65] Ibid.

[66] Hugh N. McAllister to James A. Beaver, September 12, 1863, box 15, James A. Beaver Papers, PSU.

[67] William Williams to Brother, September 26, 1863, copy in possession of author.

[68] William Williams to Brother, October 25, November 13, 1863, copies in possession of author.

spring of 1864. The regiment lost only one man killed in hard fighting on May 5 and 6 at the Wilderness, Grant's opening gambit during the Overland Campaign. At Spotsylvania, however, between May 10 and May 16, sixty-seven soldiers in the regiment were killed or fell mortally wounded, and other Centre County commands—especially its two companies in the 49th Pennsylvania—suffered heavily as well. As fragments of bad news reached the editoral offices of the *Central Press*, the editor warned: "We have reason to fear that it is the fate of many in Centre county to mourn the loss of a father, husband, son or brother." But he assured readers that no death had been meaningless, as each had "offered up his life upon the sacred altar of our common country in fighting the ignoble and traitorous hordes arrayed against the existence of the Union."[69] In early June, the bad news continued: sixteen more men from the 148th Pennsylvania fell at Cold Harbor.

Among the dead at Cold Harbor was the 148th's Lieutenant James B. Cook. The *Democratic Watchman* lamented the futility of Cook's death, noting that "only a few weeks ago the lieutenant was among us in the full vigor of robust health. Today he sleeps beneath the sod of the Old Dominion, a sacrifice to the dreadful Moloch of war." As the list of local dead lengthened, the *Democratic Watchman's* editor advised Grant that it would be no disgrace to admit defeat and stop the killing. Describing Robert E. Lee as "the accomplished master of the art of war," the editor considered the capture of Richmond to be "one of the impossibilities" of this costly war.[70]

The heavy losses among their comrades did not reforge the men of the 148th Pennsylvania into the embodiment of the image imposed upon it by Centre County's pro-administration advocates as its representatives in the field. The conservative political sentiments of the soldiers themselves changed little over the course of the war. Even after the losses they took in battle, the duty-bound or draft-inspired recruits of August 1862 never embraced their cause with the enthusiasm of the "Boys of '61." Still, although few Centre County Republicans expressed surprise in 1864 when local voters cast only 2,410 ballots for Lincoln and a solid 3,256 for Democrat George McClellan, the results from the front stunned them into silence. In the

---

[69] *Bellefonte Central Press*, May 20, 1864.
[70] *Bellefonte Democratic Watchman*, May 27, 1864.

"Centre County regiment," 199 soldiers cast ballots. Lincoln won 127 votes, but George McClellan won a sizeable seventy-two, not much of a vote of confidence in their commander-in-chief.[71] The Republican press at home remained quiet about these results, as if crushed by undeniable evidence that even their vaunted Centre County regiment had turned on them. Local Republicans easily could have celebrated the results of the vote in one company in the 49th Pennsylvania—Centre Countians who had volunteered in 1861 without bounties or the threat of a draft—who all voted for Lincoln.[72] But they now so completely linked support for the administration with the fate of the 148th Pennsylvania that they took little note of their successes.

Even if it failed to live up to the expectations of Republican leaders at home, the 148th Pennsylvania became one of the hardest fighting regiments in the Army of the Potomac. Between their first fight at Chancellorsville in May 1863 and final disbanding in June 1865, 1,339 men served in the regiment. Of those, 210 men were killed or mortally wounded in battle, a full 15.6 percent. At least 379 more fell wounded, some more than once. Four officers and 121 enlisted men died of disease. Confederates captured at least 138 soldiers from the 148th Pennsylvania; sixty-two of them died in southern prison camps. Company C's seven officers who fell dead from Confederate bullets set an army record for commissioned losses in a unit of that size. They paid in blood for a high place among the "Three Hundred Fighting Regiments" named by William F. Fox in his masterful tabulation of regimental records and statistics.[73]

In later years, the survivors of the Centre County regiment recalled little about the home front dissension or the way in which party-controlled presses used soldiers' blood to promote their own

[71] United States War Department, *The War of the Rebellion: A Compilation of the Official Records of the Union and Confederate Armies,* 70 vols. in 128 (Washington, D. C.: Government Printing Office, 1880–1901), series 1, vol. 42, pt 3, 561. Despite the usual interpretation that the soldier vote helped to guarantee his reelection, Lincoln actually lost to McClellan in a number of hard-fighting regiments, including the 5th New Hampshire (McClellan, 29; Lincoln, 26) and the 116th Pennsylvania of the Irish Brigade (McClellan, 58; Lincoln, 54).

[72] Entry for October 11, 1864, Christian Dale Diary, Pennsylvania Military Museum Archives.

[73] William F. Fox, *Regimental Losses in the American Civil War, 1861–1865* (Albany, N.Y.: Albany Publishing Co., 1889), 302.

causes. They erected monuments to salute their service to the nation, and they wrote an eloquent regimental history. Mostly they seemed perfectly satisfied to concur with the sentiments of unsuccessful political candidate and former captain Robert Forster, who, at the unveiling of their regimental monument in the Wheatfield at Gettysburg, expressed his deepest thanks to God that the war made the nation "safe for all time to come from another War of Rebellion."[74]

[74] Muffly, *The Story of Our Regiment*, 885.

2

"Volunteer While You May": Manpower Mobilization in Dubuque, Iowa

Russell L. Johnson

> Come, then, fellow citizens, come to the rescue. Come
> from your workshops, your stores, your farms and your
> labors. Come without distinction of party or nationality.
> Come without regard to position in society and without
> care for position in the army, save that of brave soldier in
> your country's cause. Come of your own free will . . . vol-
> unteer while you may.
>
> *Dubuque Daily Times*, July 16, 1862

HISTORIANS HAVE LONG DEBATED who enlisted in the Union Army
and why. The most extensive portion of this historiography focuses
on conscription legislation and the contemporary assertion that it was
"a rich man's war and a poor man's fight." One group of scholars
argues that the draft laws are best described as "class legislation," as
they allowed drafted men to buy their way out of the service for a
sum roughly equal to an average worker's annual income. Another
group of scholars disagrees, arguing that the law operated fairly because communities acted to help their residents purchase exemption;

* The author wishes to thank Shelton Stromquist, Malcolm Rohrbough, Linda
Kerber, Kenneth Cmiel, and Kathleen Diffley for their comments on an earlier version of this material, and Paul A. Cimbala and Randall M. Miller for contributing to
refining this essay. The research was conducted in part with funds provided by the
State Historical Society of Iowa, Inc. and the Louis A. Pelzer Dissertation Fellowship
of the University of Iowa Graduate College.

claims of a poor man's fight, therefore, lack "objective reality."[1] A second historiographic thread attempts to argue the poor man's fight question by tracing groups of soldiers into the 1860 census to identify more specifically the men who enlisted. The results have been mixed at best. The three most prominent such analyses find essentially the same patterns of enlistment from a total of four New England communities, but whereas one scholar asserts that this pattern demonstrates a poor man's fight, the other two claim the opposite.[2] A final historiographic thread tries to broaden the discussion beyond the narrow poor man's fight issue by using soldiers' letters and diaries to discern their motivations for enlisting and fighting. These analyses have interesting things to say about soldiers' motivations for fighting once in the army, but rather less value in explaining why some men enlisted whereas others did not.[3]

---

[1] For the "poor man's fight" interpretation, see, e.g., Fred A. Shannon, *Organization and Administration of the Union Army 1861–1865*, 2 vols. (Cleveland: Arthur H. Clark Co., 1928), quotation from 2: 308; Robert Sterling, "Civil War Draft Resistance in the Middle West" (Ph.D. dissertation, Northern Illinois University, 1974); and Peter Levine, "Draft Evasion in the North During the Civil War, 1863–1865," *Journal of American History* 67 (March 1981): 816–34. Disagreement comes from James M. McPherson, *Battle Cry of Freedom: The Civil War Era* (New York: Oxford University Press, 1988), esp. 600–9; Eugene C. Murdock, "Was It a 'Poor Man's Fight'?" *Civil War History* 10 (September 1964): 241–45; Murdock, *One Million Men: The Civil War Draft in the North* (Madison: State Historical Society of Wisconsin, 1971); Hugh Earnhart, "Commutation: Democratic or Undemocratic," *Civil War History* 12 (June 1966): 132–42; James W. Geary, "Civil War Conscription in the North: A Historiographical Review," *Civil War History* 32 (September 1986) 208–28; and Geary, *We Need Men: The Union Draft in the Civil War* (DeKalb: Northern Illinois University Press, 1991).

[2] See Maris A. Vinovskis, "Have Social Historians Lost the Civil War? Some Preliminary Demographic Speculations," *Journal of American History* 76 (June 1989): 34–58 (dealing with Newburyport, Mass.); W. J. Rorabaugh, "Who Fought for the North in the Civil War? Concord, Massachusetts, Enlistments," *Journal of American History* 73 (December 1986): 695–701; Thomas R. Kemp, "Community and War: The Civil War Experience of Two New Hampshire Towns," in *Towards a Social History of the American Civil War: Exploratory Essays*, ed. by Maris A. Vinovskis (Cambridge, Eng.: Cambridge University Press, 1990), 31–77. Rorabaugh argues for the poor man's fight interpretation.

[3] See, for example, Gerald Linderman, *Embattled Courage: The Experience of Combat in the American Civil War* (New York: The Free Press, 1987); James M. McPherson, *What They Fought For, 1861–1865* (Baton Rouge: Louisiana State University Press, 1994); McPherson, *For Cause and Comrades: Why Men Fought in the Civil War* (New York: Oxford University Press, 1997); Earl J. Hess, *The Union Soldier in Battle: Enduring the Ordeal of Combat* (Lawrence: University Press of Kan-

Much of this scholarship is limited in important ways. The focus on conscription, for example, oversimplifies the complicated process of manpower mobilization for the Union Army. Initial recruiting efforts relied on voluntarism, and only when that faltered did the North turn to conscription laws. Even so, conscription had its greatest impact as a threat to spur volunteering and encourage communities to make greater efforts to fill their quotas with volunteers. In fact, fewer than 10 percent of Union Army soldiers were conscripts; adding draft substitutes, the number rises to just 10.2 percent.[4] Accordingly, when historians focus on conscription, they miss the largest part of the story, the part that produced 90 percent of Union soldiers. They also miss a number of important questions. James M. McPherson, for example, argues that northern recruiting relied upon a "carrot-and-stick" system, with progressively larger bonuses for enlistment—called bounties—as the carrot and the draft as the stick. But how did the carrot and stick function together to produce the needed soldiers? More specifically, to whom did the carrot appeal, and who was the stick used to threaten? And who benefited most from the system that evolved? These questions are missing from McPherson and others' analyses.[5]

Further, neither these questions nor the answers can be found in existing analyses of who enlisted from particular communities and why. Part of the problem is confusion over the meaning of the word "poor" for mid-nineteenth-century Americans. How else can we explain discovery of similar patterns of enlistment leading to diametrically opposed conclusions in existing analyses of enlistments on the community level? Indeed, this result suggests that it is time for historians to put aside the "poor man's fight" notion and develop new ways to think about who served in the Union Army and the meaning

---

sas, 1997); Joseph Allan Frank and George A. Reaves, *"Seeing the Elephant": Raw Recruits at the Battle of Shiloh* (Westport, Conn.: Greenwood Press, 1989), 30–37; and Joseph Allan Frank, *With Ballot and Bayonet: The Political Socialization of American Civil War Soldiers* (Athens: University of Georgia Press, 1998).

[4] For percentages see Geary, *We Need Men*, 84–85. Even limiting consideration to the years when the federal draft law was in force, 1863–1865, conscripts and substitutes comprised only 13 percent of the total enlistments.

[5] McPherson, *Battle Cry*, 492–94 and 600–9; Geary, *We Need Men*, 65 also uses the carrot and stick metaphor. Though McPherson is cited in the text, the flaw of paying too much attention to the draft and not enough to the functioning of the overall system occurs in much of the historiography of the recruiting system, including among those who argue the system was class-biased.

of that service. However, the analysis of soldiers' motivations does not yet represent a viable alternative. The existing analyses rely on surveys of greater or lesser numbers of letters and diaries from soldiers across the country, but they divorce the men from their home communities and personal circumstances by considering only the men's existence as soldiers. Moreover, the general conclusion in analyses of motivation that soldiers enlisted from an ideological commitment tells us little. In their letters and diaries, nearly everyone in the North—volunteer or civilian, war supporter or war opponent— repeated the same "themes of liberty and republicanism" that are said to signal the soldiers' commitment. The question remains: Why did some with this commitment enlist whereas many others did not?[6]

Although the broad outline of the recruiting system was the same throughout the North, a community-level analysis allows a more detailed look at how the system functioned in order to answer some of these questions.[7] Dubuque, Iowa, the community chosen for this

---

[6] McPherson, *What They Fought For*, 6 and especially 27–46. By contrast, because the older interpretation (for example see Bell I. Wiley, *The Life of Billy Yank: The Common Soldier of the Union* [Indianapolis: Bobbs-Merrill Co., 1952]) held that the soldiers had *no* ideological beliefs, recovering their ideological commitment is an important corrective. For the pervasiveness of liberty and republicanism in nineteenth-century rhetoric see, for example, Steven J. Watts, *The Republic Reborn: War and the Making of Liberal America* (Baltimore: Johns Hopkins University Press, 1987), especially 63–107, which shows Americans interpreting the War of 1812 as a battle for "liberty and republicanism" as well as to purify society; Jean Baker, *Affairs of Party: The Political Culture of Northern Democrats in the Mid-Nineteenth Century* (Ithaca: Cornell University Press, 1983; reprint, New York: Fordham University Press, 1998), which argues that republicanism was the primary language of opposition to authority in the mid-nineteenth century; and Steven J. Ross, *Workers on the Edge: Work, Leisure, and Politics in Industrializing Cincinnati, 1788–1890* (New York: Columbia University Press, 1985), which describes a century-long contest between workers and capitalists for control of the language of republicanism. Also see Willard Waller, *On the Family, Education, and War: Selected Writings*, ed. by William J. Goode, Frank F. Furstenberg, and Larry R. Mitchell (Chicago: University of Chicago Press, 1970), 323–24, which argues that "the most obvious change in [social] mores" during wartime is "the reversion to the tribal morality which commands solidarity within the group and enmity to those outside." Such solidarity—reflected in the soldiers' ideological commitment—is, according to Waller, "a necessary precondition of war."

[7] Two analyses of recruiting on the local level might be noted here: Iver Bernstein, *The New York City Draft Riots: Their Significance in American Society and Politics in the Age of the Civil War* (New York: Oxford University Press, 1990); and Grace Palladino, *Another Civil War: Labor, Capital, and the State in the Anthracite Regions of Pennsylvania, 1840–1868* (Urbana: University of Illinois Press, 1990). Both

analysis, was a former mining town whose population of thirteen thousand made it the eightieth largest city in the country in 1860. With its location on the Mississippi River, in the late 1850s, Dubuque occupied a prominent place in upper-Midwest commercial networks. The Panic of 1857 and a second downturn after southern secession closed the Mississippi, however, prompted many local boosters to re-think their commitment to commerce as the basis for the city's future greatness. The local economy did not recover until 1863, after which Dubuque began the development that would see it emerge as a sig-nificant manufacturing center. The city was also Iowa's "Gibraltar of Democracy," steadfastly maintaining its allegiance to the Democratic party even as most of the rest of Iowa turned Republican. It contin-ued supporting Democrats throughout the war, and the outspoken-ness of its war critics earned it a reputation as "a Secession hole." However, the city met all of its enlistment quotas during the war with volunteers and never held a draft. Indeed, in September 1864, when the draft came closest to becoming operational, war opponents worked most actively to help the city avoid it. The recruiting system in Dubuque passed through a series of phases—voluntarism, coer-cion, controlled market, and free market. In each phase, local war supporters placed particular emphasis on pushing working and poor people into the army.[8]

Recruiting during the first year of the war relied on pure volunta-rism. Men who aspired to commissions as officers sought approval of the state governor and then opened recruiting offices and advertised for recruits. Once they had filled a company (80 to 100 officers and men), it would be assigned to a regiment (a group of ten companies), officially sworn or "mustered" into the army, and sent to a camp of rendezvous and training to await the completion of the regimental

---

Bernstein and Palladino, however, focus on conscription, not the broader pattern of recruiting.

[8] Quotations from Leland L. Sage, *William Boyd Allison: A Study in Practical Politics* (Iowa City: State Historical Society of Iowa, 1956), 22 ("Gibraltar"); and *Dubuque Daily Times*, January 21, 1862 (quoting the *Philadelphia Press* on Du-buque as a "Secession hole") (hereinafter cited as *Times*). Population and ranking from U.S. Department of Commerce, Bureau of the Census, *Eighth Census of the United States, 1860*, vol. 4: *Mortality and Miscellaneous Statistics* (Washington, D.C.: Government Printing Office, 1866), xviii–xix. For more on Dubuque's early history and development, see Russell Lee Johnson, "An Army for Industrialization: The Civil War and the Formation of Urban-Industrial Society in a Northern City" (Ph.D. dissertation, University of Iowa, 1996), chapters 1–3.

organization. After a longer or shorter stay in camp, depending on how quickly the regiment filled, the new soldiers would be sent to the field. These volunteer regiments carried state designations—the 1st Iowa Infantry, for example—and throughout the war the Union maintained a separation between this "volunteer army" and the Regular Army. The former represented by far the largest share of the Union's fighting force, although the latter also grew in size during the war.

Dubuque easily recruited two companies for the 1st Iowa Infantry, a regiment formed to serve for ninety days under President Lincoln's initial call for troops in April 1861. In fact, so many men offered to enlist that the city could have created four companies if they had been wanted. For subsequent troop calls, however, the local recruiting field became more and more crowded—there was no lack of aspiring officers—but volunteers grew increasingly scarce. In addition to state organizations, Regular Army recruiters saw Dubuque as a convenient base of operation for reaching potential recruits in a large geographic area and thus swelled the number of recruiting offices in the city. From August 1861 until the recruiting environment was changed in 1863, Dubuque never had fewer than five recruiting offices. With the recruiting field that badly fragmented, all struggled to fill their companies.[9]

Other difficulties arising in 1861 dampened the volunteer spirit. Guns, for example, were scarce. "If no arrangement has yet been made for arms for this State," Iowa's Governor Samuel Kirkwood wrote the War Department in April 1861, "do, for God's sake, send us some." A few months later Kirkwood added that "the delay in furnishing [arms and equipment] to other regiments discourages enlistments." Once received, the arms themselves further discouraged enlistments. The Dubuque *Herald*'s Franc Wilkie, traveling with the 1st Iowa Infantry, described the guns given to that regiment as "infinitely more dangerous to friend than enemy." And, as Kirkwood told the War Department, "our boys don't feel willing to carry [such guns] to the field to meet men armed with better weapons."[10]

---

[9] This broad overview of the recruiting field in Dubuque is based on a close examination of the local newspapers for the war years.

[10] For quotations in text, see United States War Department, *The War of the Rebellion: A Compilation of the Official Records of the Union and Confederate Armies*, 70 vols. in 128 (Washington, D.C.: Government Printing Office, 1880–1901), series

The situation with other material elements of military service was little, if any better. The 1st Iowa veterans made quite a spectacle in Dubuque when they returned home in August 1861, dressed in brand new uniforms given to them specifically for the occasion, but for most of the period of their service the men were dressed "in tatters to an extent . . . that would excite the profoundest contempt of the seediest beggar." Nor was the food given the 1st Iowa likely to boost enlistments. During one four-day march covering seventy-eight miles, for instance, members of the regiment were issued only one cup of corn meal mush per day as their rations. The soldiers supplemented this unhealthy diet with further corn foraged from surrounding fields. The other great staple of the soldiers' diet was pork. "Oh ye gods, how I do loathe the cursed pork," Franc Wilkie declared. "Its scrofulous, greasy, foul-looking slices cover every platter—it reposes in superlative nastiness in every barrel!" A member of a 1st Iowa company recruited in the city of Burlington, who claimed to have never eaten pork in his life before joining the army, considered the amount of pork fed the soldiers a measure of the country's lack of regard for them.[11]

The homecoming parade for the 1st Iowa veterans gave a short-term boost to recruiting in Dubuque, and many members of the 1st Iowa subsequently reenlisted. But the stories Wilkie and the veterans told of supply problems as well as drudgery in the army discouraged enlistments in the longer term. Military recruiters thus needed to counter these negative stories, and they began using more advertising to do so. The earliest advertisements for recruits had been simple

3, vol. 1, 163 and 489–99 (hereinafter cited as *Official Records*); and Franc B. Wilkie, *The Iowa First: Letters from the War* (Dubuque: *Dubuque Herald*, 1861), 24. See also Eugene F. Ware, *The Lyon Campaign in Missouri* (Topeka, Kans.: Crane & Company, 1907; reprint, Iowa City: The Press of the Camp Pope Bookshop, 1991), 79–80, 155–56, 196, and 346; *Official Records*, series 3, vol. 1, 162, 220, 221, 353, 407, 560–61, and 790; Cyril B. Upham, "Arms and Equipment for the Iowa Troops in the Civil War," *Iowa Journal of History and Politics* 16 (January 1918): 3–52 (especially 15–23); and Dan Elbert Clark, *Samuel Jordan Kirkwood* (Iowa City: State Historical Society of Iowa, 1917), 187–88.

[11] Josiah Conzett, "My Civil War: Before, During and After, 1861–1865," typescript of unpublished memoir written in 1909, Center for Dubuque Area History, Loras College, Dubuque, Iowa, 10–11; Wilkie, *Iowa First*, 69, 94–95; and entries for July 22–25, 1861, in Andrew Y. McDonald, *The Personal Civil War Diary of Andrew Young McDonald, April 23, 1861 to September 12, 1861* (Dubuque: A. Y. McDonald Manufacturing Co., 1956). Also Ware, *Lyon Campaign*, 211, 346.

and straightforward, such as a brief notice for "applicants" to fill a company for the 1st Iowa in April 1861. Advertisements later in 1861, however, stressed the advantages of service in a particular company and asserted that material conditions in the army were better than rumored. An advertisement for a sharpshooter company, for example, said members would do "NO GUARD DUTY" and receive "DRY WINTER QUARTERS." John Ruehl, trying to raise a company of Germans for the 16th Iowa Infantry, offered "Pay and Subsistence . . . from the day of Enlistment," with "CLOTHES [TO] BE FURNISHED AS SOON AS THE MEN ARE IN CAMP." In its effort to promote Ruehl's company, the Republican, pro-war Dubuque *Times* added that "Beer," along with "rations and clothing," would start "from the date of enlistment." As part of an abortive attempt in 1861 to raise an Irish regiment in Iowa, John H. O'Neill's advertisement explained that the regiment would "have the power to select its own Chaplin [*sic*]," guaranteeing that Catholic Irishmen would not have to endure a Protestant chaplain.[12]

Despite such creative appeals, only a few companies managed to complete their organizations in late 1861; of the preceding examples, only Ruehl's German company attracted enough volunteers to be mustered into service. Although many circumstances combined to slow the pace of volunteering, local war supporters laid the blame at the feet of Dennis A. Mahony, the erstwhile editor of the *Herald*. Whereas historians usually focus on the federal draft law of 1863 as the major cause of the complaint that the Civil War was a rich man's war and a poor man's fight, Mahony stressed the war's class elements from its beginning. It was an article of Mahony's faith that "to a great extent" the volunteers came from among "those who have the least interest in the result of the contest"—namely, the poor and working class. In an August 1861 editorial, for example, Mahony asked "whose turn is it next" to enlist? "The Democrats of the North, and especially those in the humbler walks of life, have done a reasonably fair share of service in the Army and of fighting; is it not time now that those who provoked the war and who clamor loudest for its continuance enter the lists for a while and do their share of service? Come on ye talking Patriots, and fill up the ranks." In September 1861, Mahony

---

[12] Examples in the text from *Dubuque Daily Herald*, November 15, 1861 (hereinafter cited as *Herald*); *Times*, January 9, 11, 1862; and *Herald*, September 17, 1861.

even advocated the establishment of a federal draft, suggesting it would be the only way to get those who did "not show as much zeal in fighting as in talking" into the army. Thus when lawyer and vocal war supporter William Mills argued that Mahony's class rhetoric helped "to prevent 'ignorant Irishmen' from enlisting," Mahony had a ready answer. Mills was not an "ignorant Irishman," so what was his excuse for not enlisting?[13]

War supporters in Dubuque responded to Mahony's class rhetoric by accusing him of "discouraging enlistments." Republicans and other war supporters in the city believed that Mahony controlled the working-class and Irish voters, who could never be accused of "reasoning or thinking for themselves." If the pages of the *Herald* contained little but criticism of the war effort and conditions in the military, therefore, those who read it would be less likely to volunteer. Mahony, according to the Dubuque *Times* in June 1861, tried "to keep the readers of his paper from fighting the battles of their country." But the deeper point, as Mills's "ignorant Irishmen" comment suggests, is that war supporters expected the poor and working class to provide a large proportion of the soldiers from the city. That the *Herald's* antiwar position interfered with that expectation would become crystal clear in August 1862.[14]

Recruiting for the Civil War entered a second phase in 1862. In April, the new secretary of war, Edwin Stanton, whether because of over-confidence about the war's speedy conclusion or because he hoped to gain control of the unwieldy system he inherited from his predecessor, closed down the recruiting service; the Union Army stopped accepting new recruits. In June, confidence dissipated or control established, Stanton rescinded his order and recruiting resumed the following month. It resumed under changed circumstances, however. On July 17, the Militia Act became law, adding an

---

[13] For 1861 Mahony class rhetoric, for example see, *Herald*, July 2, August 2, September 7, 18, and October 2, 1861; see also *Herald*, September 14, 19, 1861. Broader explanations for the 1861 recruiting downturn include lack of preparedness, the dashing of early expectations that the war would be short, and the numerous systemic and logistic difficulties that arose. See, for example, Sterling, "Civil War Draft Resistance," 36–42, 45; and Geary, *We Need Men*, 7.

[14] For ideas about Mahony's support from and control of workers and the Irish, see, for example, *Times*, April 4, June 26, September 11, 1861; and April 2, 3, June 11, September 12, October, 10, 11, 23, November 4, December 19, 1862; and June 5, 1863.

element of coercion. Now, if volunteering continued at its slow pace, state governors could draft men to serve for up to nine months. Iowa never held a Militia Act draft, but still state authorities considered the draft a great success in the state. "Our whole State appears to be volunteering," Governor Kirkwood informed the War Department in August. His chief military aide added "I like a draft." State authorities thus left little doubt that they considered the draft primarily valuable as a threat to stimulate volunteering rather than as a tool for putting men in uniform directly. Iowa proceeded to fill—indeed, to far exceed—its quotas of volunteers in the last months of 1862.[15]

In Dubuque, the *Times* asserted that it was "fallacious" to suppose that the "government has gone through all [the] expense and trouble of listing the militia [that is, those liable to a draft] merely for the purpose of getting up a big scare." Nevertheless, the paper did its best to promote "a big scare," admonishing the men of Dubuque to "volunteer while you may." Reporting rumors was one tactic. The paper regularly asserted that the draft would be held "any day" or "next week." Similarly, the paper periodically announced that the last chance to enlist had arrived; August 15, August 22, September 9, October 7, and December 31 were all said to be the last day to volunteer before the draft was held. Occasionally, in its efforts to maintain the scare, the *Times* even lent credence to absurdities. On September 18, for example, the paper repeated a "street rumor" that the governor had ordered an immediate draft of 16,000 men from Dubuque; the city's population in 1860—males and females, adults and children—was only 13,000.[16]

A second method for keeping the draft scare alive was to cite state authorities on the matter. In late September, the *Times* published a letter from Governor Kirkwood that said "a draft is imminent." On October 22, the paper published an order from the Iowa adjutant general's office that it interpreted as saying that regiments in the field

---

[15] Quotes from Clark, *Samuel Jordan Kirkwood*, 232; and *Official Records*, series 3, vol. 2, 339. For the over-confidence interpretation, see Shannon, *Organization*, 1: 266; for control interpretation, see McPherson, *Battle Cry*, 437; and, for a lengthier discussion of the historiography, Geary, *We Need Men*, 7–8. Seven states held militia drafts in 1862 (Geary, *We Need Men*, 47). Geary, the closest scholar of the Militia Act, concludes that its designer, Senator Henry Wilson (R-MA), intended it more as an emancipation measure than as a way to raise an army.

[16] See, for examples, *Times*, August 15, 22, September 9, 18, October 7, 25, November 12, 20, 26, December 5, 30, 1862; and January 7, 1863.

that had become depleted through attrition "must be filled immediately, or the draft will fill them"; in reality, the order said the draft *might* be used to fill the existing regiments. Dubuquers serving on Kirkwood's military staff were quoted as another source of "official" information. On one occasion, one of these men, "Colonel" Henry Wiltse, stated "authoritatively" that the draft would be held in Dubuque on November 28.[17]

The third, and most effective, way to remind people about the impending draft was through recruiting advertisements, which worked best because they ran day after day. When recruiting resumed in July 1862, the field in Dubuque remained as crowded as ever. Between July 11 and August 21, 1862, no fewer than fifteen new recruiting offices opened in the city, not counting organizations already in the field that sent officers to the city in an effort to replenish their depleted ranks. The character of the recruiting pitches again changed. Whereas in late 1861, recruiters had emphasized material conditions—uniforms, prompt pay, "dry quarters," leadership—in late 1862, a reminder of the draft accompanied nearly every recruiting pitch, either as part of the advertisement or in a news item directing attention to it. The advertisement for a company called the "Herron Rifles," for example, featured draft-related information in four lines of text and only near the bottom in small print added that the "best of arms and equipments [were] all ready" for the volunteers. Joseph Dorr, an officer in the 12th Iowa Infantry, returned to Dubuque seeking recruits. His advertisement in the *Times* stressed that "drafting will commence immediately" on September 1, so men would be wise to enlist in the 12th Infantry before then.[18]

By themselves, the constant draft reminders and assurances that the draft would take place were insufficient. Men still needed to be convinced that volunteering was a better option than gambling that their name would not come up in the draft. To be a drafted soldier, the *Times* asserted, was "a disgrace," and conscripts' "duties are usually more disagreeable, and they are not so well officered as others."

---

[17] *Times*, September 29, October 22, November 21, 1862. Governor's staff members received the rank of colonel though they never actually served in the army.

[18] For opening of new recruiting offices, see *Times*, July 11, 26, August 1, 5, 8, 10, 12, 13, 14, 21, 1862 (some days saw more than one recruiting office open); for Dorr, see *Times*, August 20, 1862. For other examples, see *Times*, August 12, 14, October 7, November 20, December 5, 1862.

The paper published a variety of misleading or false information to reinforce the point. The purpose of ads like Joseph Dorr's, for example, was to remind prospective soldiers that volunteers could choose their branch of service, the officers they would serve under, and their comrades; conscripts would be assigned wherever they were needed. Although the choice difference was essentially accurate, it was only guaranteed for men who joined an organization such as Dorr's, which was already in the field. A new company might be sent anywhere, as a group of prospective sharpshooters from Dubuque discovered. When the Iowa sharpshooter regiment failed to materialize, these volunteers found their company absorbed into the 6th Iowa Cavalry, and they found themselves pursuing Indians in the Dakota Territory, rather than rebels in the South. In 1864, Dubuque's DeWitt C. Cram, captain of the company, expressed the disappointment some members of the 6th Cavalry experienced. "I regret much that I am obliged to serve my turn in this service. . . . Of all things, I would like to get into the Southern Service." Even volunteers, in other words, did not always receive their choice of service, a possibility omitted from the recruiting pitches.[19]

More seriously, the *Times* distorted the pay and length of service of volunteers compared to conscripts. The paper told prospective soldiers that volunteer privates received $13 monthly pay, whereas drafted privates were paid just $11 per month. This was not true. Although there was a pay difference between volunteers and conscripts—because under the Militia Act the latter did not receive an enlistment bounty—volunteers and drafted men received the same monthly pay. On August 1, the paper presented a detailed analysis of army pay. A volunteer soldier received $102 in bounty and premium[20] plus $13 per month, which the *Times* computed as $21.58 per month for a one-year enlistment; this was more even than the "high wages for [civilian] labor" the paper had reported the previous day. Con-

---

[19] *Times*, July 26, October 7, 1862; January 20, 1863; V. J. Williams to Brig. Gen. S. R. Curtis, December 29, 1862, in Williams, 6th Iowa Cavalry, Compiled Service Records, Record Group 94, National Archives, Washington, D.C. (hereinafter cited by name, unit, RG 94); and DeWitt Cram to S. P. Adams of Dubuque, March 4, 1864, in Cram, 6th Iowa Cavalry, RG 94.

[20] The "premium" was a $2 per recruit payment to individuals presenting new recruits at a recruiting depot. It could be paid to an enlistment broker—someone who made a business of rounding up potential recruits and bringing them in—or to the volunteer soldier himself, if he came in on his own.

scripts supposedly earned only $11 per month, and in case anyone forgot, the paper repeated the point three weeks later. In reality, however, because a volunteer from Iowa at this point in the war had to commit himself for not one year but three, the compensation for volunteers was actually as low as $15.83 per month—just $2.83 more per month than conscripts actually earned. The *Times* scarcely mentioned that anyone drafted under the Militia Act would serve for only nine months, not three years. The one time it did mention this fact, the paper commented that a law extending nine-month enlistments indefinitely could be passed at any time after the men were in the service.[21]

In sum, the question became, "Will you take a generous bounty and an honorable enlistment, or endure the discredit of a forcible draft?" Even though this question affected all men of draft age, the *Times* directed it with particular emphasis toward the poor and working class. War supporters argued that these groups had the most to gain—or lose—in the war. Although Republicans said they were being forced by the secessionists to adopt an emancipation policy, the policy would be good, not bad for white workers. Among other things, abolition would elevate the status of all labor and firmly establish the superiority of white working men. Accordingly, poor and working-class whites should be eager to enlist; the war was being fought for their interests. War supporters further argued that the South, as well as its northern "Tory" allies like Dennis Mahony, sought to expand slavery into the northern states and western territories, ending in "the serfdom of the entire laboring classes." The North's war aim, in contrast, was to preserve the North and West as "homes for free white laborers" and as "an asylum for the oppressed white laborers." If workers were concerned about competition for jobs from freed slaves, the *Times* assured them that a northern victory coupled with an emancipation policy was the best way for Dubuque to "keep white"; no African Americans would move north if they could enjoy the "blessing of liberty" in the South.[22]

Taking the draft scare and this exposition of the North's war goals

---

[21] *Times*, July 19, 26, 31, August 1, 22, October 7, 1862. One example of the "high wages for labor" the *Times* cited was the $20 per month boatmen on the Erie Canal earned.

[22] For quotations, see *Times*, July 23, September 20, November 6, 13, 1862. See also, Geary, *We Need Men*, 37.

together reveals the extent to which the recruiting effort in 1862 was directed toward securing poor and working-class enlistments. While stressing the inevitability of the draft and the desirability of avoiding it, war supporters emphasized favorable material conditions— housing, food, clothing, and medical care—that might be better than workers in Dubuque could expect, given the continuing economic depression and with winter approaching. They further promoted the idea that pay in the army was better than even some of the best civilian pay for workers, but asserted that only volunteers could take advantage. Also, by volunteering, men could spare themselves some of the less desirable aspects of military service. And finally, war supporters argued that working-class whites would be helping themselves by preserving the Union and destroying slavery.

At the same time, however, the Militia Act specifically exempted some of those in whose interest the war was allegedly being fought. Much to the displeasure of some war supporters, non-naturalized immigrants and workers in a number of artisan and unskilled occupations could not be drafted. In response, at the same time it promoted the 1862 draft scare, the *Times* worked for the creation of an Iowa Irish regiment. In August, after two weeks of items pressing for such a regiment, two Dubuque Irishmen, George M. O'Brien and John H. O'Neill, came forward and offered to recruit one.[23] Everyone knew, though, that Dennis Mahony was the real leader of the local Irish community. In fact, Mahony had offered to raise an Irish regiment in 1861, but doubting his loyalty, Governor Kirkwood had commissioned someone else, who made little progress during the following year. In 1862, therefore, C. C. Flint, a former Republican newspaper editor in Dubuque, lobbied Kirkwood to change his mind. Mahony was poor and ambitious, Flint argued, and so would accept the commission, the 1861 snub notwithstanding. Commissioning Mahony would also be a good way to redirect his formidable talents away from war opposition. Another Dubuque resident, John T. Brazill, wrote to

---

[23] See *Times*, August 1, 3, 5, 9, 13, 19, 1862, for some of Irish Regiment campaign. See also, *Official Records*, series 3, vol. 2, 257, 294, 322, 331, 334, 346, 348, 358, 392, 395, 396, 398, 458–59, 512. Working-class exemptions in the Militia Act included telegraph operators and "constructors," locomotive engineers, steamboat engineers, stage drivers who carry the mail, pilots, mariners, and workmen in arsenals, gun factories, and gunpowder mills; ibid., series 3, vol. 2, 257, 294, 322, 334, 346, 348, 358, 398.

the governor on August 10: "Mahony is loyal. He has more influence than any other in the state over the Irish and no other would be so good."[24]

Four days after Brazill wrote, circumstances changed dramatically. In the early morning hours of August 14, U.S. Marshal Herbert Hoxie, a former state Republican party chairman, swept into Dubuque and arrested Mahony. Mahony was sent by boat to Burlington, Iowa, and two days later went by rail to Washington, where he was incarcerated in the Old Capitol Prison.[25] Although Hoxie asserted that he acted under authority of a recent War Department order directing the arrest of people "discouraging enlistments," reasons for the arrest remain murky. The *Herald*, for example, continued to publish, and according to local war supporters expressed "even more violent and reckless opposition to the government" under Mahony's replacement. Further, the Lincoln administration seems not to have known what to do with Mahony and others arrested at roughly the same time. No charges were ever filed against Mahony, and all efforts by his friends to find out the charges came to nought. In the end, after languishing for three months in prison, Mahony was released and sent back to Iowa, where he resumed his opposition to the war.[26]

---

[24] C. C. Flint to S. J. Kirkwood, August 4, 1862, Correspondence, Disloyal Sentiments, 1861–1866, folder 1, Records of the Iowa Adjutant General's Office, Record Group 101, Iowa Historical Society, Des Moines. Brazill letter quoted from Hubert H. Wubben, "The Dubuque *Herald* in the Fight for the Northwest" (M. A. thesis, University of Iowa, 1958), 103. For Mahony and the Irish regiment, see D. A. Mahony, *Prisoner of State* (New York: George W. Carleton, 1863), 392–94; also Randolph W. Lyon, *Dubuque: The Encyclopedia* (Dubuque: First National Bank of Dubuque, 1991), 71.

[25] Sources on Mahony's arrest include *Times*, August 15, 17, 1862; Mahony, *Prisoner of State*, esp. 117–46, 247–48, 399–410; John A. Marshall, *American Bastille: A History of the Illegal Arrests and Imprisonment of American Citizens in the Late Civil War* (Philadelphia: T. W. Hartley, 1869), 403–16.

[26] *Herald*, August 8, 1862; *Times*, November 14, 1862. For interpretation of the arrest, see Phillip Shaw Paludan, *"A People's Contest": The Union and Civil War, 1861–1865* (New York: Harper & Row, 1988), 239–40; and Allan Nevins, *Ordeal of the Union*, vol. 6: *The War for the Union: War Becomes Revolution* (New York: Charles Scribner's Sons, 1960), 316–17.

While in prison, Mahony received the Democratic nomination for Congress in the district, a fact that Mahony and some of his supporters thought explained the arrest. But electoral failure for Democrats in that district was largely predetermined by gerrymandering; the Republican majority in the state legislature offset Dubuque County's Democratic strength by placing it in an otherwise Republican district. Mahony carried only Dubuque County in the election and even there ran behind most

It seems most significant that the period of Mahony's incarceration corresponded with the draft scare and especially the renewed effort to raise an Irish regiment in Iowa. With Mahony disposed of and Irish recruiting under way, the *Times* celebrated. It "looks as though we are to have an Irish regiment sure." The paper promoted the Irish regiment on an almost daily basis, using several types of items, including the draft scare. Though the draft exempted immigrants, naturalized citizens and anyone who had ever voted could be drafted. Therefore, the only way for Catholics to be sure of serving with a Catholic chaplain was to volunteer and choose the Irish regiment.[27] The *Times* also reprinted the speeches of nationally prominent military men and civilians advocating Irish enlistments.[28] Favorable notice of Irishmen already in the army became common.[29] The final element of the campaign for an Irish regiment involved republican arguments: the Federal government protected Irish immigrants from the tyranny of the British monarchy, so the Irish owed the government protection from its despotic enemies, too. Mahony himself had used this argument the year before to respond to the first accusations that he was disloyal.[30]

Local war supporters had further cause for celebration in August 1862. Beginning in July, they had argued in favor of an additional

---

of the rest of the Democratic ticket. For this interpretation of the arrest, see Mahony, *Prisoner of State*, 169–70; Franc B. Wilkie, *Pen and Powder* (Boston: Ticknor and Company, 1888), 9; and Sage, *William Boyd Allison*, 49–50, 54. See also *Times*, October 22, 1862, for election results; and Paul S. Pierce, "Congressional Districting in Iowa," *Iowa Journal of History and Politics* 1 (July 1903): 341–43.

[27] There was a message for Protestant, non-Irish in this, too—be drafted, and you may wind up in the Irish Regiment. *Times*, August 13, September 9, December 10, 1862.

[28] For example, see *Times*, August 16, 26, September 14, 1862. In Dubuque itself, Mortimer Hayden—a prewar Democrat and commander of the 3rd Iowa Artillery Battery—gave a speech on August 2 and exhorted "the Irish to Come to the Rescue." See Solon M. Langworthy Diary, 251, Iowa Historical Society, Iowa City.

[29] For example, see *Times*, August 5, 16, September 4, 1862. This was a refinement of a broader *Times* policy of giving favorable notice to Democrats in the army. Compare *Times*, August 19, 1862, in which John H. O'Neill was praised, to *Times*, March 29, 30, 1861, in which O'Neill was denounced for antiwar views.

[30] For example, see *Times*, September 18, October 10, 12, 25, November 23, 1862; for Mahony's use of this argument, see *Herald*, September 17, 1861. See also the advertisement for the 1861 version of the Irish regiment in the same *Herald* edition. This "protection from tyranny" argument was sometimes stated more generically in reference to immigrants, because, of course, it could also apply to Germans; for example, see *Times*, October 9, 1862.

local bounty to spur volunteering. Henry Pettit, an assistant editor at the *Times*, summarized the point best, saying, "Let those who cannot go [into the army], offer inducements to those who will. Money inducements. Those are the best arguments now-a-days." War supporters initially thought wealthier private citizens should offer their own bounties; soon, however, they began pressing for local government to act. Near the end of July, an "Unconditional Union Democrat" wrote to the *Times* decrying the "criminal indifference" of the Democratic mayor and city council and urging that citizen meetings be held to "secure a liberal bounty to volunteers." Several meetings were indeed held, and some money for bounties was collected, but local bounties made little progress until August 19, 1862, when a special session of the County Board of Supervisors approved a $50 bounty for anyone enlisting before September 1. The *Times* asserted that this could never have happened without the arrest of Mahony five days earlier.[31]

Results from the bounty were encouraging. Poor and working-class men who had hesitated to enlist because they had seen the families of earlier volunteers suffer when local arrangements for their support broke down now came forward. Speaking for himself and others he knew, Ernst Renner, a lawyer and farmer from Peru Township in Dubuque County who enlisted as a lieutenant in the 21st Iowa Infantry, explained that the $50 county bounty added to the promise of a $25 advance on their federal bounty money, a $2 enlistment premium, and a month's pay in advance overcame many men's reluctance. "We gladly went," he noted, "trusting that our monthly pay would suffice to provide further for our families." In this they were due to be disappointed. The irregularity of army pay and the difficulties of sending it to Dubuque meant that their families still suffered. Renner himself was eventually dismissed from the army for drawing pay twice for the same pay period in order to send more money to his distressed and increasingly estranged family.[32]

[31] *Times*, July 13, 19, 23 (Pettit), 26 (Union Democrat), August 20, 1862; Franklin T. Oldt, *History of Dubuque County, Iowa* (Chicago: Goodspeed, 1911), 284; and, for reports of citizen meetings, *Times*, July 26, August 1, 3, 9, 12, 13, 14, 17, 1862.

[32] *Times*, September 13, 1862; and Ernst Renner, 21st Iowa Infantry, RG 94. For more on the failure of efforts to support soldiers' families, see Russell L. Johnson, " 'A Debt Justly Due': The Relief of Civil War Soldiers and Their Families in Dubuque," *The Annals of Iowa* 55 (summer 1996): 207–38.

Although the bounty produced results, recruiting for the Irish regiment proceeded poorly. Nothing local government, the *Times*, or O'Brien and O'Neill did spurred sufficient enlistments. Finally, after Mahony's release from prison in November 1862, the *Times* abandoned the Irish regiment idea, later adding that the project should never have been started. "How an Irish regiment could be . . . formed in a community where almost the only paper read by those who are wanted to fill its ranks is almost wholly devoted to opposing the Government and sustaining the rebellion, and the most influential men among them openly denounce the Government and oppose the war is something that ought to have been thought of months ago. It would have saved not a little public and private expense." The paper printed the official death notice of the Irish regiment in January 1863. An order from the Iowa adjutant general's office announced that the Irish regiment recruits would form the nucleus for the 7th Iowa Cavalry. George O'Brien would become lieutenant colonel of the 7th Cavalry; John O'Neill, recently elected city attorney on the Democratic ticket, would be left out. Although they had not been officially mustered into the service, the Irish regiment recruits were told they would be treated as deserters if they resisted enlistment in the 7th Cavalry with its Protestant chaplain.[33]

Further revealing the emphasis on poor and working-class enlistments, after the collapse of the Irish regiment, war supporters in Dubuque almost immediately came out in favor of arming black soldiers. Previously, the *Times* had considered that the "last step of degradation." Once it became clear that the city would raise no Irish regiment, however, the *Times* began adjusting its rhetoric to support African American enlistments. It started by publishing letters from soldiers in favor of taking this step. In December, for example, George M. Staples, a Dubuque doctor serving as physician in the 14th Iowa Infantry, wrote to say that he had seen numerous blacks grab guns in the heat of battle and join the fray, and "I have not yet heard that our men felt disgraced thereat." The *Times* itself waited until February 6, 1863, before openly endorsing the idea of black soldiers: "There is no reason why Negroes should be rejected when Indians are accepted, and no reason why both should not be enlisted

---

[33] *Times*, August 26, October 16, November 22, 1862; and January 10, 11, 13, 1863.

. . . under proper discipline and control." Less than a month later, federal law allowed the recruiting of African American regiments.[34]

The end of 1862 brought an end to the militia draft scare. On December 30, a page-one editorial in the *Times* said that the period allowed by Governor Kirkwood to fill quotas will expire "with tomorrow . . . and if the requisite authority shall be given to him by the War Department he will proceed to enforce the Draft." The paper then did some math to show that, even though the state had enlisted about 22,000 men since July, Iowa was still 7,000 men short on its quotas. Therefore, it argued, Democrats were wrong to assert that Iowa had filled its quotas and that Kirkwood merely planned to use the draft as a partisan weapon.[35] But Kirkwood convinced the War Department that 10,570 three-years men enlisted to meet the state's quota under the call for nine-months militia were four times as valuable as the same number of nine-months men; the extra beyond the nine-months quota was then applied to meet deficiencies under other troop calls. On January 7, 1863, the first item in the *Times'* City News column reported that Kirkwood said there would be no draft in Iowa.[36]

Changes to federal recruiting policy in 1863 reflected the success of the 1862 draft scare and the use of small local bounties in places such as Dubuque. In March 1863, the Enrollment Act became law, creating a national draft structure. This law maintained the element of coercion that had been introduced by the Militia Act, but further attempted to control the soldier market with a "commutation" provision. Commutation allowed a drafted man to avoid service by paying a $300 fee to the government and had the effect of limiting the price a draft substitute could receive to the same amount. Shortly thereafter, the federal government increased the amount of its enlistment

---

[34] *Times*, July 12, 30, December 18, 1862; and January 20, February 6, March 29, 1863.

[35] *Times*, December 30, 1862. The paper did not mention the draft on December 31. The idea that Republicans might use the draft for partisan purposes was not so far-fetched. On two occasions before the fall 1862 election, the *Times* published the list of people claiming exemption from the draft as immigrants. The paper reminded its readers to stay vigilant at the polls, because no one could both vote and claim exemption as a non-citizen. *Times*, September 9, October 10, 1862. Other cities in Iowa likewise published their lists; see *Times*, September 18, 1862. Geary, *We Need Men*, 44, cites evidence from other states of Republicans considering the use of the draft as a political weapon.

[36] *Times*, January 7, 1863.

bounty. The first to benefit from bounty changes were three-year soldiers who had enlisted in 1861. These men had received at most a $100 bounty when they enlisted; some had not received even that. From June 1863 to April 1864, any of these soldiers who re-enlisted were given a $400 bounty. In October 1863, the $100 bounty still in effect for new volunteers was raised to $300 for anyone enlisting for three years in an existing regiment. Then, in December 1863, the bounty for new, three-year volunteers in new regiments was also increased to $300. Federal bounties temporarily ended in April 1864, but in July 1864, the bounty for all white soldiers—veteran, new volunteer, or conscript—was set at $100 per year for up to three years. The Enrollment Act guaranteed conscripts the same bounty as volunteers.[37]

Although Dennis Mahony had advocated a federal draft as early as September 1861, he came out in opposition to the Enrollment Act. According to the title of a pamphlet he wrote, it was one of *The Four Acts of Despotism* of the Lincoln administration. He began his analysis with the argument that the Enrollment Act was unconstitutional because it by-passed state militia organizations; the federal government had no constitutional power to raise troops independent of the states, he asserted. But since in 1861 he himself had proclaimed the federal government's power "under the constitution to 'draft' men for the public service," he quickly passed over that argument and focused on the discriminatory nature of the commutation and substitution clauses. He had been attacking the class biases of the war effort from its beginning, so this argument allowed him greater consistency, as allowing individuals to purchase exemption for $300 was self-evidently class legislation. "Does the poor man owe more to the Government than the rich man that he should be compelled to give his life, while the rich man is required to give but a portion of his superabundant wealth?" he asked. "Is a rich man's life, in a government of equals, more valuable than a poor man's life?" It was in effect "military slavery" for the poor. If there had to be monetary

---

[37] Black soldiers received a $10 bounty after November 1863; before that they received no bounty. *Official Records*, series 3, vol. 5, 672 covers changes in bounty amounts. For discussion of Enrollment Act and evolution of bounty system, see Geary, *We Need Men*, 65–77, 103–15; McPherson, *Battle Cry*, 600–11; Sterling, "Civil War Draft Resistance," 150–61, 314–18; Shannon, *Organization*, 2: 11–46; and Murdock, *One Million Men*, 178–217.

exemptions, he argued, a better system would have been to base the exemption fee on the ability to pay.[38]

Local war supporters' most effective voice in 1863 was the then proprietor of the *Times*, G. T. Stewart, who welcomed the new draft law. In January 1863, after the failure of the Irish regiment, Stewart had called building the army by voluntary enlistments "an expedient" that had failed and needed to be replaced by "a system." Stewart undertook the defense of the Enrollment Act. He first effectively refuted Mahony's claim that the central government could not raise troops independent of the state militias. Citing the constitutional power of Congress to raise and support armies, Stewart noted that in the landmark *McCullough vs. Maryland* case, the Supreme Court had declared Congress' right to enact laws to carry out its delegated powers. Furthermore, he defended the class bias in the $300 exemption fee. "Men whose services at home are more valuable to themselves, or to others than the amount required, are thus retained there," he asserted, "while those go whose services in the army are more valuable to themselves and others there than at home." And if poor people were forced into the choice between paying $300 they did not have or joining the army, Stewart left no doubt who they should blame: "For every volunteer discouraged from entering the ranks by [Democratic] lies, we must now furnish a conscript." It was, in other words, workers' own fault for believing and supporting Mahony.[39]

The workers of Dubuque did not immediately face this choice, however, as Iowa continued to fill its quotas without conscripts. In Dubuque, efforts to promote volunteering during the Enrollment Act period followed earlier patterns. Threatening a draft to scare people into the army remained the most prominent tactic. Over the course of two weeks in July 1863, for example, while other parts of the country were experiencing the first draft under the Enrollment

---

[38] D. A. Mahony, *The Four Acts of Despotism: Comprising I, the Tax Bill with All Amendments; II, the Finance Bill; III, the Conscription Act; IV, the Indemnity Bill; with Introduction and Comments* (New York: Van Evrie, Horton 1863), 7, 19–24. See also *Herald*, September 19, 1861. Mahony's pamphlet consisted of about thirty pages of commentary followed by the complete texts of the laws in question. He also denounced the tax and finance laws as class legislation.

[39] *Times*, January 27, July 24, August 25, 1863. See also *Times*, March 26, May 9, July 23, 26, August 4, 5, 1863.

Act, the *Times* tried to whip up a draft scare. The paper asserted that "in some parts of the State the Draft is about to commence immediately" and "will scoop nearly every man fit for military duty in the State." In the fall of 1863, the paper repeated the tactic, with special reference to Dubuque's situation. "Although deficient under every call," it argued, "Dubuque County has escaped the draft by the large surplus of volunteers furnished from other portions of the State. . . . But from the impending draft there will be no such escape." The paper added for the first time that failure to report after being drafted was equivalent to desertion, and "the punishment of desertion *is death*." But no draft had yet been held in Iowa.[40]

Army recruiters also continued to feature the draft prominently in their advertisements. In May 1863, for instance, Joseph Dorr, promoted to colonel of the new 8th Iowa Cavalry, asserted his regiment would be "undoubtedly the last Volunteer Regiment [from Iowa] . . . as *active* preparations are going on all over the State for the enforcement of the conscription." Sergeant Frank Udell, back in town recruiting for the 6th Iowa Cavalry in March 1864, noted that his regiment was stationed in Dakota and expected to go to Idaho soon. He added that "frontier service is the healthiest and most pleasant in the army," but volunteering was the only way to be certain of assignment to a particular regiment.[41]

In the environment created by the Enrollment Act, war supporters further promoted enlistments with the old tactics of emphasizing differences between volunteers and drafted men, and arguing that the working class had the most to gain from enlisting. "True," the *Times'* assistant editor, 1st Iowa veteran George Ballou, allowed in July 1863, conscripts "will receive the same *pay and bounty*" as volunteers. "But will money compensate brave and loyal men for the sneers and jeers of their comrades or the cold words and looks of those they leave at home?" The drafted man's descendants "will have to bear the stigma" as well. Moreover, the drafted men will not get promotions, will not get "credit for the hardships and sufferings they may en-

---

[40] *Times*, July 11, 12, 15, 25, November 3, December 5, 17, 23, 31, 1863; and January 5, February 12, 1864. See also, *Times*, May 17, 26, July 16, August 15, 19, 25, September 10, October 15, 29, 1863; and March 4, 1864.

[41] *Times*, May 27, 1863 (Dorr), March 18, 1864 (Udell). For others, see *Times*, July 24, October 3, November 12, December 2, 1863.

dure," and "must go as *forced men* among veteran soldiers who *vol-unteered* to defend their country."[42]

Working people and the poor were still said to have the most to gain by service in the army. In April 1864, the *Times* cited some "Good Advice" from the *Catholic Telegraph* to "newly arrived emigrants." Immigrants should head West where opportunities were greater, but more importantly they should first join the army to sustain the government "which enables the poor to live decently and comfortably." And in August 1864, George Ballou did some strange arithmetic to assert that pay in the army was $442 per year for a three-year enlistment, "in addition to 'board and clothes.'" "This is better pay than most laboring men can get in any other business," Ballou argued. In fact, however, at the time an army private earned just $292 per year, which compared unfavorably to wages in Dubuque. In 1861, mechanics in Dubuque earned between $250 and $400 per year, and according to the 1860 manufacturing census, the average annual wages paid per employee in Dubuque County manufactories was $332.13.[43]

Given their emphasis on working-class and poor enlistments, war supporters naturally objected when Democrats laid plans, should the draft come, to raise the $300 draft commutation fee for those too poor to pay it. In July 1863, the Democratic State Central Committee made it party policy to support paying commutation for the poor, and in September, the Dubuque County Supervisors issued county bonds to create a commutation fund. The *Times* reacted by pointing out what it considered the inconsistency of denouncing the Enrollment Act and especially commutation as "unconstitutional" and "abominable" while making plans so that "its benefits may be enjoyed by the poor men of the State." The paper also cited a decision from the

---

[42] *Times*, July 12, 1863. See also November 13, December 5, 17, 23, 1863. On July 22, 1863, an anomalous note snuck into Ballou's "City News" columns, when he asserted that "there should be no encouragement given, in or out of the army, to the idea that the fact of being conscripted carries a stigma to the conscript." That comment was at odds with everything that preceded and followed it.

[43] *Times*, April 27, August 8, 1864. See also April 7, 1861; and U.S. Dept. of Commerce, *Bureau of the Census, 8th Census of the United States 1860*, vol. 3: *Manufacturing* (Washington, D. C.: Government Printing Office, 1865), 155. See also *Times*, December 31, 1863. Ballou gave no indication of the source of his $442 per year number. The $292 figure in the text comes from $100 in bounty per year plus $16 per month ($192 per year) pay; the $2 premium was also paid, which would add 66 cents per year for a three-year enlistment.

Maine Supreme Court that declared taxation for such a purpose unconstitutional. Soon, however, the *Times* went further, quoting an argument from the pro-war Burlington (Iowa) *Hawkeye* that offering to pay commutation for poor men amounted to "a wholesale effort to impede the operation of the enrollment act."[44] But raising money to "purchase the freedom (as the rich are provided to do for themselves, [*sic*]) of each poor white man who may be drafted in Iowa," as the Iowa Democratic party put it, only represented "a wholesale effort to impede" the draft if the purpose of the law was to force the poor and working class into the army. This suggests very strongly who war supporters wanted to reach with the Enrollment Act and stands in contrast to the assertions of historians that there was no intentional or unintentional class bias in the law.

Further evidence comes from the repeal of commutation for all except conscientious objectors in July 1864. Commutation, which had been intended to hold substitute prices to what Republicans in Congress considered a reasonable level—no one would pay more than $300 to a substitute when they could pay that sum directly to the government for exemption—had in fact produced more money than men.[45] Although Iowa Democrats never needed to carry out their plans for extending the benefits of commutation to poorer people, other states did; individuals also acted, forming draft insurance clubs that paid commutation for anyone paying a small fee (usually about $25). In passing the Enrollment Act, Congress had not anticipated these means of extending commutation's benefits to a broader segment of the public. Seeing their creation thus perverted, congressional Republicans sacrificed it.[46]

---

[44] *Times*, August 5, September 10, 20, 1863, but see also *Times*, August 1, 13, 1863. The Maine Court's opinion said, in part, "Were a town to raise money to be distributed to favored individuals, the tax assessed for such a purpose could not for a moment be upheld." At the same time, Republicans in Dubuque were criticizing Democrats for arguing that it would be illegal to tax everyone to provide funds specifically for the relief of soldiers' families.

[45] By way of illustration, in the first draft under the Enrollment Act (in July 1863), only 9,881 drafted men personally entered the service, whereas 26,002 furnished substitutes and 52,288 paid commutation; in the next draft (April 1864), the same numbers were 3,416, 8,911, and 32,678. For these numbers, see Sterling, "Civil War Draft Resistance," 401–4, 424.

[46] For discussion of commutation and its repeal, see Geary, *We Need Men*, 49–64, 103–50. Geary's interpretation, it should be noted again, disagrees with that pursued here. For instance, Geary argues there was no class bias in commutation, as the

The repeal of commutation established a freer marker for soldier-labor and most benefited those men who were willing to go into the army. Under the original terms of the Enrollment Act, neither prospective volunteers nor substitutes could sell their services to the highest bidder. Once the federal bounty was increased from $100 to $300, moreover, there was little incentive to being a substitute at all, because the substitute fee would be at most $300 and by becoming a substitute the soldier forfeited his $300 federal bounty. In this system the main beneficiaries were the people thereby enabled to stay out of the army.

After repeal, prospective volunteers and substitutes could shop around for the best price. In May 1863, before repeal, for example, Daniel Darrow advertised in the *Times* his willingness to go as a substitute for "any one . . . on payment of the $300 as authorized by the late Conscription Act of Congress." No one took him up on his offer, however, and in March 1864, Darrow volunteered, taking his $300 as a federal bounty instead of as a substitute fee. In contrast after the repeal of commutation, in October 1864, the district provost marshal at Dubuque, Shubael P. Adams, received a letter from Grant County, Wisconsin, offering "several men that want to go as substitutes" who would "go where they can get the most money . . . they want about $1000." D. S. Sigler, a veteran from Osceola, Iowa, wrote to Adams in December that he and another veteran were willing "to go on any quota." "We have served three years without bounty & now *want all there is going*." About two weeks later, Sigler added that he and his friend thought $700 each would be appropriate, but they would "go to the credit of the place from which we get the most Bounty—if we go at all."[47]

As these letters to Adams indicate, in the wake of commutation's repeal substitute prices increased by 100 percent or more. Though this dramatic increase might be thought to be more unfair to working and poor people than a fixed $300 exemption fee, such individuals

fact that some poor people got access through community funds or insurance clubs demonstrates. But he fails to acknowledge that these things were not contemplated by the law and that their use led to commutation's repeal.

[47] *Times*, May 26, 1863; Daniel Darrow, 21st Iowa Infantry, RG 94; and James M. Scott, Post Master at Glen Haven, Grant Co., Wisconsin, to S. P. Adams, Oct. 8, 1864, and Sigler to S. P. Adams, December 2, 17, 1864, Letters and Telegrams Rec'd, 3rd District, Iowa, Records of the Provost Marshal General's Bureau, Record Group 110, National Archives, Washington, D. C. (hereinafter cited as RG 110).

could not afford even $300 without help. Furthermore, the same methods that were used to give them access to commutation also worked to provide substitutes. In order to keep the cost to the community at a more manageable level, cities and counties worked harder to stimulate voluntary enlistments, offering their own bounties of $300 or $400 on top of the federal bounty. Still, some people no doubt suffered. Orlando Clark of Fayette County, Iowa, for example, a self-described "Poor man," was held to service under the draft in October 1864 when two men whose names were drawn ahead of his failed to report. Clark had to sell "most" of his farm property to raise the $800 necessary to hire a substitute in the market of October 1864.[48]

Clark was forced into this decision because in the fall of 1864 Iowa could no longer avoid the draft. The credits on previous quotas that had kept the state clear of the draft were now exhausted, at least according to the War Department. State officials saw things differently, and as a September date set for the draft neared, the exchanges of messages between state and federal officials became increasingly testy. But Iowa could no longer escape, and if the draft came to Iowa, there was reason to believe Dubuque would be one of the hardest hit locations. According to figures in the Des Moines *Daily State Register*, Dubuque County, Iowa's most populous county, had furnished 1,768 men for the Union Army, while the state's second largest county had sent 2,396. As of August 17, 1864, the city of Dubuque was 255 men deficient on its quotas; the portion of Julien Township outside the city added another thirty-eight to the deficiency. A month later, the city's deficiency had been reduced by only fifty and Julien Township's not at all.[49]

---

[48] Orlando Clark to S. P. Adams, November 16, 1864, Letters and Telegrams Rec'd, 3rd Dist. Iowa, RG 110. Geary, *We Need Men*, 89–97 and 140–66, argues that the repeal of commutation was unfair to workers most of all. But his evidence in fact shows members of the business class having just as much difficulty procuring exemptions after commutation's repeal as members of the working class did, something that had not been true while commutation was available. Furthermore, because his book is focused on the draft, Geary fails to appreciate the importance of local bounties in helping communities fill their enlistment quotas without drafting.

[49] For strained relationship between state and federal officials, see *Official Records*, series 3, vol. 4, 567, 596, 597, 636–38, 648, and 681. See *Des Moines Daily State Register*, June 1, 1864, for enlistments from Dubuque County and other counties; see also *Times*, August 17, September 14, 1864 for specific deficiencies. Although statewide surpluses kept the state draft-free until September 1864, it appears

Nevertheless, men in Dubuque reacted complacently to the impending draft that summer. After years of draft scares, according to Provost Marshal Adams, "a large majority of the people . . . had really come to believe that there would be no draft here." This "delusion" was "dispelled" when Adams received the order on September 21 to commence drafting. Wasting no time, Adams put the portion of Julien Township outside Dubuque city "in the wheel" the next day to fill a twenty-three-man deficiency. At this point, "several of the most prominent, and influential men of the County" approached Adams and asked him to suspend the draft in Dubuque County until the board of supervisors had time to meet and create a county bounty fund. Adams granted the delay for the rest of Dubuque County, but the Julien Township conscripts were held, and the draft continued in the other counties of Adams's district.[50]

Leading the delegation that waited on Adams was Dennis Mahony, who had temporarily retired from the newspaper business and had been elected sheriff of Dubuque County in 1863. In his report at the end of the war, Adams—as partisan a Republican as lived in the city—singled out Mahony as "the most active and efficient man in recruiting" after the commencement of the draft. With Mahony's encouragement, the county supervisors passed a $125,000 bond issue to fund a county bounty of $400 for each volunteer; the measure also extended the money to anyone drafted and entering the service as a result and to anyone who hired a substitute on his own. If townships and city wards wanted to offer additional bounties they could, though they were encouraged to limit the additional amount to $200 to avoid a bidding war.[51]

that the deficiencies of individual districts and subdistricts under the Enrollment Act were recorded; hence, when the draft came, the state's deficiency was apportioned to local communities according to their individual shortfalls. See, for example, exchange between Governor William Stone and the War Dept., *Official Records*, series 3, vol. 4, 284–85, 287, 288.

[50] Capt. S. P. Adams, Provost Marshal for 3rd District Iowa, "Historical Report," June 1, 1865, p. 5a; and Col. Thomas Duncan, Acting Assistant Provost Marshal General for Iowa, "Historical Report," Oct. 5, 1865, p. 11, reel 2, Historical Reports of the State Acting Assistant Provost Marshals General and District Provost Marshals, 1865, National Archives Microfilm Publication, M1163 (hereinafter cited as PMG Historical Reports [M1163]); and *Times*, September 23, 1864, for description of Julien Township draft.

[51] Adams, "Historical Report," 5b, reel 2, PMG Historical Reports (M1163); *Times*, September 22, October 4, 6, 8, 1864. There were two restrictions on relief

At first glance, given his opposition to the Enrollment Act as one of the Lincoln administration's "four acts of despotism," Mahony's leadership of the county bounty effort might be surprising. But Mahony recognized that the quota would have to be filled, and it would be better to have well-compensated volunteers than draftees torn from their families or forced to sell their property. The response of the *Times* is perhaps more surprising. In 1862, the *Times* had led the drive that culminated in a $50 local bounty, and in August and early September 1864, W. S. Peterson, the paper's new editor, regularly chastised Dubuque's city and county governments for not again establishing a bounty. But as soon as it appeared that the county would create a bounty, Peterson changed his tune. In an editorial on September 26, after noting the "inconsistency and impudence" of men who had long worked to "discourage enlistments" now working for a local bounty, he expressed his "hope that loyal men will give the whole movement a 'wide berth.'" Peterson had "no right to object" if individual citizens chose to form committees and raise private funds, "but against an appropriation by the Board of Supervisors we do most earnestly protest." For his part, the new *Herald* proprietor, Patrick Robb, took this opportunity to tweak the Republicans. Quoting Peterson's editorial, Robb noted that "Inasmuch as the movement referred to is the effort to fill our quota by volunteers, the above would seem very much like discouraging enlistments."[52] Robb stopped short of calling for Peterson's arrest, however.

Although it was a county bounty, Dubuque city seemed to be the major beneficiary. Every ward in the city filled its quota and escaped the draft, whereas other parts of the county were not so fortunate. The portion of Julien Township outside the city of Dubuque, for example, was drafted, in part simply because it had the bad luck to be the first subdistrict put into the wheel. Eventually, after allowing time for the bounty to work, five of the county's sixteen other townships were also drafted. One of these five was Taylor Township, the

---

for men who had hired substitutes. First, they had to put their names back on the draftable list for any future draft, and second, they would get only as much as they had paid for their substitute but not more than $400. This provision was put in the law in response to a concern raised in the *Times*; see *Times*, September 26, 1864. See also *Times*, November 19, 1864, for two men who took advantage of the provision.

[52] *Times*, August 19, 31, September 15, 1864, for pro-bounty/antidraft items; *Times*, September 26, 1864, for antibounty editorial; and *Herald*, September 27, 1864.

most reliably Republican subdistrict of the county, which failed to fill a deficiency of six men. In contrast, each of the city's five wards met a larger deficiency with the bounty; the largely Irish 1st Ward, for example, erased a deficiency of thirty-five using bounties. These two facts are not unrelated. Willing volunteers migrated from rural to urban areas seeking larger bounties, and Provost Marshal Adams managed quotas and enlistments to the benefit of Dubuque in particular. Thus, in addition to being an element of raising the Union Army, the Enrollment Act may have indirectly promoted urbanization and industrialization by mobilizing a workforce of rural-to-urban migrants.[53]

More immediately, the draft seems to have reinforced the strength of Dubuque's Democrats. The draft continued in the county throughout that fall's presidential election campaign; as late as November 19, nearly two weeks after the election, rejections of drafted men for physical disabilities and other reasons left Jefferson Township still two men short on its quota. Patrick Robb saw the draft as a powerful issue to use against Lincoln. In the weeks leading to the election, Robb could credibly assert that "another draft will surely come if Abraham Lincoln is re-elected, and still others, each succeeding one more cruel and remorseless than the last, until the last man shall be taken. Who will vote for an administration so bloody in its policy and purposes?" Not many, came the answer from Dubuque County. Despite an early prediction from Dennis Mahony that George McClellan, the Democratic nominee, "will not receive the Democratic vote," Lincoln, who had received 39 percent of the county's vote in 1860, received only 35 percent in 1864; in the city, his percentage dipped from 46 to 42.[54]

---

[53] *Official Records*, series 3, vol. 5, 732, 734; *Times*, October 4, 5, 7, 8, 9, 11, 12, 13, 15, 18, 28, 1864; Duncan, "Historical Report," pp. 9–11, reel 2, PMG Historical Reports (M1163); Murdock, *One Million Men*, 356; and, for Adams's favoritism toward Dubuque, see Thomas Duncan, AAPMG, to Adams, November 12, 1864; Capt. David Greaves, 21st Iowa Inf., to Nathaniel Baker, Iowa Adj. Gen., November 21, 1864; Lt. Col. S. G. Van Anda, 21st Iowa Inf., to N. Baker, November 2, 1864; and A. S. Blair, deputy provost marshal in Delaware Co., to Adams, January 26, 1865, all in Letters and Telegrams Rec'd, 3rd Dist. Iowa, RG 110. Even James Geary, who argues that Democratic ideas of a rich man's war and poor man's fight had no basis, sees wealthier localities drawing recruits from poorer areas; Geary, *We Need Men*, 13, 76, 171.

[54] *Times*, November 14, 16, 19, 1864 (for lingering draft); *Herald*, October 7, 1864; Mahony to Charles Mason, August 23, September 20, 1864 (reproductions), Dennis

Robb had been right. Safely re-elected, the Lincoln administration issued a new call for troops in December, with a draft set for February 15, 1865. On December 24, 1864, readers of the *Times* were greeted with a lead story full of Christmas cheer: "Prepare for the Draft." Ward meetings were held throughout the city that night to correct the lists of draft-eligible men. Few attended, however, and George Ballou at the *Times* concluded that despite the draft that had just occurred, "every man in the city is perfectly indifferent as to whether he is drafted at the coming draft or not." Ballou even endorsed the payment of "a liberal bounty" to help meet the city's quota. But this last draft scare of the war ended almost before it began. Three weeks before the scheduled draft date, Governor Stone told the *Times* to "announce that no more men are due from this State, under the pending call, and that we are relieved from the Draft."[55]

Recruiting for the Union Army thus passed through several discernible phases during the war. An initial voluntary rush to enlist quickly gave way to a more sluggish period that was met by adding an element of coercion via the Militia Act. After coercion proved its usefulness in the fall of 1862, the federal government moved to secure greater control over the system via the Enrollment Act. Although it simultaneously tried to make the bounty system more attractive to volunteers, under the Enrollment Act the federal government controlled the soldier-labor market with the provisions for substitution and, especially, commutation in the law. That failed, however, and the government had to repeal commutation, restoring a freer market for soldier labor. In Dubuque, furthermore, at each stage of the process there was emphasis on encouraging working-class and poor enlistments, along with the enlistment of young men who traditionally comprised the bulk of armies. This encouragement took several forms, including persistent draft scares, suggestions of the material benefits of enlisting, and assertions that the poor and

---

A. Mahony Papers, Center for Dubuque Area History, Loras College, Dubuque; and, for election data, William E. Wilkie, *Dubuque on the Mississippi* (Dubuque: Loras College Press, 1987), 231, and *Times*, November 10, 16, 1864. Dubuque was not unique in giving Lincoln a smaller percentage in 1864 than in 1860; see David Montgomery, *Beyond Equality: Labor and the Radical Republicans, 1862–1872* (New York: Alfred A. Knopf, 1967), 109. Montgomery found Lincoln's percentage of the vote declining in eight of nineteen major cities.

[55] *Times*, December 22, 24, 29, 1864; and *Semi-Weekly Times*, January 27, 1865.

working class had the most to gain by the successful prosecution of the war.

What remains is to get some indication of the results of this process in Dubuque. The question of who served in the Union Army is complex, and the necessary constraints of an essay like this leave room for only the most simplified discussion. A list of 1,321 soldiers from Dubuque has been compiled using various sources; these 1,321 men were then traced into the 1860 census, yielding a group of 595 who lived in the city in that year.[56] The group of 595 has been further subdivided into two groups: 371 "independent soldiers," men living on their own or with their own families, and 224 "soldier-sons" who lived as subordinate members of their parents' household.[57] This division is significant. In assessing the class background of soldiers, it is difficult to know how to handle sons. Clearly, they should not simply be included with their own personal data; they have not achieved their final occupation (if, indeed, they have any occupation) nor in most cases begun accumulating property. In the existing historiography, the solution generally has been to substitute parental data for sons who enlisted in the army. This is wrong as well, unless a similar substitution of parental data is made for sons who did not enlist. In the data for Dubuque that follow, parental data is substituted for *all* sons among *both* the soldiers and the overall city population.[58]

After dividing the populations into broad business and working

---

[56] The list of Dubuque's soldiers was compiled by beginning with a list of all soldiers from Dubuque County and eliminating those who could be identified in various sources as not from Dubuque city. Key sources include *History of Dubuque County, Iowa* (Chicago: Western Historical Company, 1880), 421–51 (the county list); Iowa Adjutant General's Office, *Roster and Record of Iowa Soldiers in the War of the Rebellion* (Des Moines: Iowa State Printer, 1908–1911); Compiled Military Service Records, RG 94, National Archives, Washington, D. C.; Records of the Provost Marshal General's Bureau, RG 110, National Archives, Washington, D. C.; and Iowa Adjutant General's Office, *Reports of the Adjutant General and Acting Quartermaster General of the State of Iowa for 1862, 1863, 1864–1865, and 1866* (Des Moines: Iowa State Printer, 1863, 1864, 1865, and 1866). For a more complete discussion of who enlisted from Dubuque, see Johnson, "An Army for Industrialization," chapter 5.

[57] By way of further clarification, independent soldiers include men who, as heads of household, had an elderly parent or parents living with them; soldier-sons include men who lived with their parents but the whole family lived as boarders in a private home, boarding house, or hotel.

[58] Some community-level studies of enlistment were cited earlier: Vinovskis, "Have Social Historians Lost"; Rorabaugh, "Who Fought for the North"; and Kemp, "Community and War." See also Steven J. Buck, " 'A Contest in which Blood Must

TABLE 2.1
VOLUNTEERS OF 1861 COMPARED TO ALL MALES 12 AND OVER

ALL MALES AGE 12 AND OVER IN DUBUQUE

	n	percent without	average property
BUSINESS CLASS	1222	29.1	$ 6,857.69
High Nonmanual	384	9.1	14,109.90
Low Nonmanual	838	20.0	3,534.49
WORKING CLASS	2791	66.5	583.80
Artisan	1232	29.3	951.24
Unskilled	1559	37.1	293.43
OTHER			
Farmers	176	4.2	6,398.90
Unclassifiable	10	0.2	3,535.00
none	558	—	1,563.26
TOTAL	4757		2,531.71

SOLDIERS	1st IOWA INFANTRY			OTHER VOLUNTEERS OF 1861		
	n	percent without	average property	n	percent without	average property
BUSINESS CLASS	30	37.0	$ 4,601.67	55	33.3	$ 6,202.73
High Nonmanual	6	7.4	15,783.33	15	9.1	12,706.67
Low Nonmanual	24	29.6	1,806.25	40	24.2	3,763.75
WORKING CLASS	49	60.5	803.06	105	63.6	497.76
Artisan	29	35.8	1,229.31	47	28.5	987.23
Unskilled	20	24.7	185.00	58	35.2	101.12
OTHER						
Farmers	2	2.5	5,700.00	4	2.4	13,225.00
Unclassifiable	0			1	0.6	0.00
none	4	—	25.00	3	—	3,500.00
TOTAL	85		2,222.35	168		2,719.43

Flow Like Water': Du Page County and the Civil War," *Illinois Historical Journal* 87 (spring 1994): 2–20.

TABLE 2.2
VOLUNTEERS OF 1862–1863

	n	*percent without*	*average property*
BUSINESS CLASS	54	27.8	$ 7,139.81
High Nonmanual	16	8.2	13,106.25
Low Nonmanual	38	19.6	4,627.63
WORKING CLASS	124	63.9	640.97
Artisan	54	27.8	1,270.00
Unskilled	70	36.1	155.71
OTHER			
Farmers	13	6.7	3,763.84
Unclassifiable	0		
none	3	—	4,233.33
TOTAL	194		2,740.31

classes with further subdivisions of each class into upper and lower groups, the overall pattern of enlistments in Dubuque was that sons from lower business-class (low nonmanual) and upper working-class (artisan) families and independent men from the upper and lower working class (artisan and unskilled) provided the bulk of the soldiers from the city. This conclusion takes into account mobility into the city between 1860 and enlistment. Volunteers who gave business-class occupations on their enlistment papers were much more likely to be found in the 1860 census than those with working-class occupations, 58.1 percent versus 48.7 percent.

In the context of war mobilization, however, the important data are those showing enlistments each year of the war. In August 1861, for example, Dennis Mahony asserted that the poor and working class had "done a reasonably fair share of service." How accurate was this claim? The enlistment data for 1861 offer a mixed answer (table 2.1).[59] In the 1st Iowa Infantry, men from low-nonmanual and artisan backgrounds were largely overrepresented, though for the low nonmanual this could be the result of their high level of persistence between 1860 and the time they enlisted. The artisans in the 1st Iowa

---

[59] For the sake of reducing the number of tables, tables 2.1–2.4 combine the independent and sons' data for the soldiers and (in table 2.1) the city.

TABLE 2.3
VOLUNTEERS OF 1864–1865

| | 100-DAYS MEN (1864) | | | OTHER VOLUNTEERS OF 1864–1865 | | |
	n	percent without property	average property	n	percent without property	average property
BUSINESS CLASS	35	50.0	$2,109.29	9	16.7	$10,122.22
High Nonmanual	11	15.7	4,463.64	1	1.8	0.00
Low Nonmanual	24	34.3	1,030.21	8	14.8	11,387.50
WORKING CLASS	33	47.1	1,497.73	43	79.6	595.93
Artisan	19	27.1	801.32	16	29.6	1,037.50
Unskilled	14	20.0	2,442.86	27	50.0	334.26
OTHER						
Farmers	2	2.9	8,000.00	2	3.7	0.00
Unclassifiable	0			0		
none	5	—	2,660.00	0	—	
TOTAL	75		2,034.00	54		2,161.57

owned much more property than artisans in the city, whereas the opposite was true for low-nonmanual men. High-nonmanual and un-skilled occupations were both underrepresented in the 1st Iowa; it was a poorer segment of the unskilled men who joined. This is proba-bly a function of the fact that the core of Dubuque's companies for the 1st Iowa was the city's prewar militia companies. More fraternal than military organizations, militia companies appealed primarily to low nonmanual men trying to rise in Dubuque society and to wealth-ier artisans, hoping to maintain their positions in a changing econ-omy. Most of the unskilled members of the 1st Iowa from Dubuque were probably recruited to fill out the 80 to 100 men needed to be mustered into the service.[60]

Enlistments in the remainder of 1861, broadly speaking, mirrored the city's male population, although allowing for differences in persis-

---

[60] For a discussion of militia companies, see Marcus Cunliffe, *Soldiers and Civilians: The Martial Spirit in America, 1775–1865* (Boston: Little, Brown, 1968), 215–54; and, for the companies in Dubuque, Oldt, *Dubuque Co.*, 253–55; *Times*, April 10, 1861; *Dubuque Express & Herald*, February 28, 1858; and *Herald*, Novem-ber 12, 1859, April 10, 1860.

TABLE 2.4
REENLISTMENTS

		RETURNERS			VETERAN VOLUNTEERS	
	n	*percent without*	*average property*	*n*	*percent without*	*average property*
BUSINESS CLASS	18	32.1	$ 7,419.44	11	16.7	$ 3,186.36
High Nonmanual	3	5.4	28,333.33	2	3.0	3,225.00
Low Nonmanual	15	26.8	3,236.67	9	13.6	3,177.78
WORKING CLASS	37	66.1	437.84	52	78.8	493.27
Artisan	17	30.4	811.76	22	33.3	950.00
Unskilled	20	35.7	120.00	30	45.5	158.33
OTHER						
Farmers	1	1.8	10,500.00	3	4.5	17,600.00
Unclassifiable	0			0		
none	2	—	25.00	1	—	50.00
TOTAL	58		2,763.79	67		1,694.78

tence rates, the working class was probably slightly overrepresented. Suggestive numbers here include the continuing imbalance in business-class enlistments, with high-nonmanual men under- and low-nonmanual men overrepresented, and the limited property ownership by unskilled volunteers. In 1861, it was clearly men from poorer unskilled backgrounds who enlisted, the only group for which that was true. Thus Mahony's comment that the poor and working class had done a "reasonably fair share of service" was accurate enough in 1861, but the evidence cannot sustain the implication that they had done *more* than their fair share.

Mahony might be said to have merely anticipated what was to come. Because very few men enlisted from Dubuque during 1863 and even fewer were found in the census, the data for 1862 and 1863 are combined, bringing together the periods of coercion and controlled soldier-labor market (table 2.2; compare to the top portion of table 2.1). In these middle years of the war, despite their higher persistence rates, business-class men as a whole and in each subgroup were underrepresented among the new volunteers from Dubuque. Those business-class men who volunteered in these years did own more property than the business class in the city, however. The working class also appears underrepresented, but taking low persistence rates into account erases that under-representation. Again in these years it was the poorer members of the unskilled group who joined the army, whereas slightly more prosperous artisans volunteered. Finally, in these years, farmers among the soldiers for the first and only time exceeded their percentage in the city as a whole, but the volunteers owned little more than one-half as much property as average. Thus the draft scare in all its elements, the effort to promote Irish enlistments, and the controlled market had the effect of increasing enlistments from the working class and poorer portions of the city's population. At the same time, business-class enlistments fell off from their 1861 levels.

Enlistments in the free market period, 1864–1865, followed essentially the same pattern, after separating another group of short-term soldiers from the whole (table 2.3). In May 1864, Iowa, along with other midwestern states, recruited a contingent of men to serve for a hundred days; these soldiers would see no combat but would be used in fortifications and for garrison duty, freeing the longer term soldiers currently occupied in these duties to fight. Interestingly, fully one-half of the hundred-days men from Dubuque came from the business class, though they were also the least wealthy group of business-class volunteers during the war. At the same time, the unskilled who enlisted for a hundred days were by far the wealthiest group of unskilled volunteers. There are several reasons for these patterns. First, the two Dubuque companies for hundred-days service, like those for the 1st Iowa, were built on a base of civilian militia companies. Second, because the service was for only a hundred days of garrison duty, the disruption to the men's civilian lives and the dangers of service were greatly diminished. Nevertheless, this service would immunize these volunteers from the "talking patriots" charge. Finally, when hundred-day recruiting slowed in Dubuque, war supporters invoked the draft to scare men into enlisting. Because a drafted man could not be guaranteed his choice of service, volunteering for a hundred days of guard duty was infinitely preferable to the alternative, which minimally might be a hundred days of combat service.[61]

In contrast to the hundred-days men, the other volunteers of

---

[61] *Times*, May 13, 14, 17, 1864.

1864–1865 were an overwhelmingly working-class group. Despite the lack of working-class persistence between the 1860 census and the date of enlistment, among the soldiers they far exceeded their percentage of the city's population. This was especially true of the unskilled. Working-class volunteers in 1864–1865, moreover, owned more property than their counterparts in the city. Business-class enlistments, in contrast, fell to their lowest levels of the war, although the low-nonmanual volunteers owned, on average, a large amount of property. From this it might be concluded that the free market for soldier-labor thus had not been beneficial to the working class; even the wealthier among them were forced to choose volunteering. But that conclusion would be incorrect. The enlistments of 1864–1865 continued the pattern established over the course of the war—as early as the volunteers after the 1st Iowa, allowing for differences in persistence, the working class and poor were starting to be over-represented among the soldiers. A more accurate conclusion, therefore, would be that working-class and poor men took advantage of the opportunity that the $400 county bounty and $300 federal bounty offered and went as well-compensated volunteers.

Data on reenlistments among Dubuque's soldiers further support this conclusion. Some scholars argue that the men who enlisted, especially early in the war, were uniquely endowed with patriotism and an ideological commitment to the cause that sustained them throughout their service; indeed, they were determined to see the war through to its end.[62] If this were true, it would be expected that reenlistments would mirror enlistments during the first year of the war, since most of those who had the opportunity to reenlist were volunteers from 1861. Some had served in a short-term regiment such as the 1st Iowa. Some had been discharged as disabled. Others were still in the army in late 1863, when the federal government offered them a $400 bounty (none had received more than $100, and some not that, when they originally enlisted), a thirty-day furlough home, and the title "veteran volunteers" if they would reenlist.[63] The data from Dubuque undermine the ideological commitment argument

---

[62] For the ideological commitment argument in reenlistments, see especially McPherson, *For Cause and Comrades*, 81–82.

[63] For "veteran volunteer" program, see *Official Records*, series 3, vol. 5, 650–51. James McPherson reports that around 136,000 of the roughly 236,000 men given the "veteran" option, took it; *Battle Cry*, 720.

and indicate that class was an important element in enlistment decisions.

Because 1861 was the year of the greatest business-class enlistments from Dubuque, the ideological commitment thesis suggests business-class soldiers should be well represented among the reenlistments. This was not the case, however (table 2.4). Among "returners," the business class was underrepresented compared to their percentage among the 1st Iowa and hundred-days volunteers. Men from high-nonmanual backgrounds were particularly underrepresented, and although as a group they owned a large amount of property in 1860, all but $1,000 of it was owned by one man, merchant Samuel F. Osborne, who served in the 1st Iowa and joined the 21st Iowa Infantry in 1862. In contrast, not only was the working class overrepresented among the returners, but those who returned came from the poorest backgrounds; working-class returners owned less property than comparable men in the 1st Iowa or, except for a $10 difference among artisans, the hundred-days men. The data are more striking among the "veteran volunteers." Given the opportunity to see the war through to its conclusion, only working-class soldiers responded from Dubuque; business-class soldiers chose to go home.[64]

A close examination of recruiting in Dubuque thus indicates that a strong class bias existed in Union Army enlistments. That bias was reflected both in the efforts to promote recruiting in the city and in the patterns of who enlisted. At the same time, however, this should not be taken as affirmation that the Civil War was "a rich man's war and a poor man's fight," but rather as an indication that it is time to discard that idea as a way of thinking about Civil War military service. As I have argued elsewhere, that service must be seen in the larger contexts of urbanization, industrialization, and proletarianization.[65]

---

[64] There is an "army class" issue involved here. Commissioned officers, who came from largely business-class backgrounds, generally did not participate in the "veteran volunteer" program; their commissions had no specific expiration dates. This might account for at least some of the lack of business-class "veteran volunteers." On the other hand, four officers from Dubuque are known to have been given the opportunity to become "veterans," and all four took a discharge instead. See Mortimer Hayden to Col. M. D. Green, September 13, 1864, in Hayden, 3rd Iowa Artillery, RG 94, National Archives; and David W. Reed, *Campaigns and Battles of the Twelfth Regiment Iowa Veteran Volunteer Infantry* (Evanston, Ill.: n. p., 1903), 195–96.

[65] For a short introduction to the argument, see Russell L. Johnson, "The Civil War Generation: Military Service and Mobility in Dubuque, Iowa, 1860–1870," *Journal of Social History* 32 (summer 1999): 791–820; and, for greater detail, Johnson, "An Army for Industrialization," esp. chapters 7 and 8.

Mobilization for the Civil War shared much in common with ongoing patterns of recruiting labor for industry, particularly in the way it promoted rural-to-urban migration. Once in the army, men experienced many elements of urban-industrial life, including disease environment, increased social distances, time discipline, bureaucratic organization, and homogenized skill levels. By understanding these elements more fully, military service will come to be seen as more than a brief interlude in a man's life and will gain its full significance. A more complete appreciation of the overall process of recruiting and who enlisted, therefore, is an important step in establishing the full significance of the Civil War in the nation's social, cultural, and economic development.

3

"If They Would Know What I Know It Would Be Pretty Hard to Raise One Company in York": Recruiting, the Draft, and Society's Response in York County, Pennsylvania, 1861–1865

Mark A. Snell

ON AUGUST 24, 1861, four months after Fort Sumter fell and one month after the Union Army met defeat at Manassas, fifteen-year-old Charles E. Gotwalt walked into a recruiting office on the corner of Market and Newberry Streets in York, Pennsylvania, and enlisted in Company A, 87th Pennsylvania Volunteer Infantry. By the time he was discharged on February 2, 1865, Gotwalt had fought in some of the bloodiest battles of the war, including the Wilderness, Spotsylvania Court House, and Cold Harbor. The 87th had just arrived at Petersburg, Virginia, in early June 1864, when Private Gotwalt was captured for the second time in three years. He survived the horrors of Andersonville, was liberated, and returned home. After more than three years of marching, fighting, and incarceration, Gotwalt was once again a civilian—and he had just celebrated his nineteenth birthday.[1]

---

[1] "Adventures of a Private in the Civil War," compiled by William A. Gotwalt. Typescript of an oral history in the collection of the Historical Society of York County, York, Pennsylvania. For charts, tables, and statistical methodology used in this essay, see my "A Northern Community Goes to War: Recruiting, the Draft, and Social Response in York County, Pennsylvania, 1861–65" (M.A. thesis, Rutgers University, 1987).

Gotwalt was one of more than ten thousand York County men who served in the United States military during the Civil War.[2] Because a descendant took the time to chronicle Gotwalt's Civil War experiences, we know his story and can see how the conflict affected him. Legions of other York County men also served, but we know little about them, or even if they were representative of their communities. Were most of York County's soldiers comparatively young, like Gotwalt? Did they come from all walks of society? Did the men who enlisted in 1861 along with Gotwalt bear any resemblance—from a socioeconomic perspective—to the men who were drafted in 1863, or who enlisted in the last year of the war? Did those citizens who stayed home support the war effort, and did that support change as the war progressed? Did enemy invasion have an impact—either adversely or otherwise—on the recruitment effort in the county?

In order to make these determinations, one must examine the relationship between the civilian communities in York County and the military units they raised and maintained. An important aspect of this study is the county's support of the war effort—especially from the perspective of supplying military manpower—and whether that support changed between 1861 and 1865. As the war continued and recruiting fell short of its goals, both the state and federal governments resorted to conscription. To determine if the conscripts were representative of their communities, here I undertake an analysis of their socioeconomic backgrounds in an effort to answer that age-old question of whether the Civil War had become "the rich man's war and the poor man's fight" (at least in York County).[3]

Situated on the west bank of the Susquehanna River with what was later to be known as the Mason-Dixon Line as its southern border, English settlers inhabited the area that became York County beginning in the late 1720s. They were followed in later decades by large

---

[2] John Gibson, *History of York County* (Chicago: F. A. Battey, 1888), 448. According to Gibson, more than 10,000 York county residents served in the Union forces. This number, however, includes men who served for very short periods, such as the three-month volunteers in 1861 and the men who served in "emergency" regiments during the Confederate invasions of 1862 and 1863.

[3] For a similar analysis, see Thomas R. Kemp's "Community and War: The Civil War Experience of Two New Hampshire Towns," in *Toward a Social History of the American Civil War: Exploratory Essays*, ed. by Maris Vinovskis (Cambridge, Eng.: Cambridge University Press, 1990), 31–77.

numbers of Germans, Welsh, and Scotch-Irish.[4] The county seat—
the Borough of York—was laid out in 1741 as the first Pennsylvania
town west of the Susquehanna River.[5] By 1860, the county had a
population of 68,200 in its thirty townships and several large boroughs and towns. York Borough was by far the most populated area,
with 8,605 residents in its five wards. The only other communities of
significant size were Hanover, located in the county's extreme south-
west corner, with a population of 1,630, and Wrightsville, on the bank
of the Susquehanna River, with 1,294 residents.[6] African Americans
comprised less than two percent (1,204) of the county's total population.[7]

York County's economy was rooted in agriculture, but by 1860, it
was feeling the limited effects of the industrial revolution, with the
railroad playing a major role in the county's gradual departure from a
rural economy.[8] By 1838, what would become known as the Northern
Central Railway linked York County's markets to nearby Baltimore
(about thirty miles south of the York County border) and from there
the rest of the South.[9] Because the county's economic interests were
connected with the South before the war, many of its citizens were
reluctant to voice any opposition to slavery and the way of life it
created. But York Countians had more in common with the South
than just a penchant for southern money. They also shared many of
the same social values and political ideals of their southern neighbors.

York County's voting record in presidential elections from 1800

---

[4] Georg R. Sheets, *The Setting of the Sun: The Story of York* (York, Pa.: Windsor
Publishing Co., 1981), 13–16.

[5] Ibid., 21, 45–50.

[6] U. S. Census Office, Population of the United States in 1860. For York County,
Pa., original unpublished returns. The county's townships in 1860 were: Carroll,
Chanceford, Codorus, Conewago, Dover, Fairview, Fawn, Franklin, Heidleberg,
Hellam, Hopewell, Jackson, Lower Chanceford, Lower Windsor, Manchester, Man-
heim, Monaghan, Newberry, North Codorus, Paradise, Peach Bottom, Shrewsbury,
Springfield, Spring Garden, Warrington, Washington, West Manchester, West Man-
heim, Windsor, and York Township. The boroughs and villages included Dillsburg,
Dover, Franklintown, Glen Rock, Goldsborough, Hanover, Lewisberry, Loganville,
Shrewsbury, Stewartstown, Wrightsville, and York.

[7] Ibid. A tabulation of the county's population statistics also appears in George R.
Prowell, *The History of York County* (Chicago: J. H. Beers, 1905), 1: 30; and Gibson,
History of York County, 588.

[8] John Denig, *The York Gazetteer and Business Directory for 1856* (York, Pa.: The
Eagle Press, 1856), 7–8, 17–30, 35.

[9] Ibid.

through 1860 reveals an unbroken pattern of countywide Democratic victories. Even after the Democratic party became increasingly associated with the advocacy of slavery, the majority of York Countians continued to cast their ballots for the Democrats.[10] There were a number of reasons for this loyalty, including tradition and the reluctance to jeopardize their southern trade, especially after the formation of the Republican party. But with the national affairs becoming increasingly tumultuous in the 1850s, many Yorkers saw the Democratic party as the only truly non-sectional party. In this time of crisis, the Democrats seemed likely to have the best chance of keeping the nation from being torn asunder.[11]

The local results of the 1860 presidential election came as no surprise to the citizens of York County. Of 11,761 votes cast in the county, 6,059 went to the Democratic candidates; 5,128 went to Abraham Lincoln, and John Bell of the Constitutional Union Party received 562 votes, thus giving the Democrats a county victory with almost 52 percent of the popular vote.[12] (Adams County, York's western neighbor, gave Lincoln 54 percent of the vote.[13])

Even after Lincoln's election and the subsequent secession of the

---

[10] G. A. Mellander and Carl E. Hatch, *York County's Presidential Elections* (York, Pa.: The Strine Press, 1972), 2–3. Voting statistics from 1800–1812 were provided by Professor Emeritus Charles Glatfelter, Gettysburg College, Gettysburg, Pa.

[11] Ibid., 6. Although the exact number of immigrants who settled in York County during the antebellum period is not known (and is beyond the scope of this study), a perusal of the 1860 census reveals a large number of foreign-born people living in the county at that time, with the Germans as the most predominant nationality. The Republican ties to nativism in the 1850s is a possible explanation why the Democrats reigned supreme in the county during that time. See David M. Potter, *The Impending Crisis, 1848–1861* (New York: Harper & Row, 1976), 241–43.

[12] *York Gazette*, November 13, 1860. The results of this election also were tabulated in Mellander and Hatch, *York County's Presidential Elections*, 6. A breakdown of the Democratic votes in the county has Stephen Douglas receiving 562, with the rest (5,497) going to the "Reading Ticket," which listed both Douglas and John C. Breckinridge. Although the strong Democratic tradition in the county before, during, and after the Civil War might indicate that voters were not necessarily interpreting their vote as a secession referendum, and that they would have voted Democratic regardless of the election issues, there is enough evidence from the local newspapers that secession was the point of contention receiving the most attention during the presidential election campaign.

[13] Matthew Gallman with Susan Baker, "Gettysburg's Gettysburg: What the Battle Did to the Borough," in *The Gettysburg Nobody Knows*, ed. by Gabor Boritt (New York: Oxford University Press, 1997), 149.

Deep South, many county residents favored compromise.[14] When "Southern Revolutionists" began seizing United States property in the South, York County's Democratic newspapers tried to justify and downplay these hostile actions, claiming that military installations such as Fort Sumter "were built to defend the country from foreign aggression, and as long as they are in the hands of the Southern people they are in possession of the members of one family. . . . Until the question [of Union] is settled the forts and arsenals will do very well where they are."[15] The firing on Fort Sumter abruptly silenced such talk.

In the spring of 1861, York County was as unprepared for the conflict as the rest of the nation. The existing militia was comprised of four companies—the Worth Infantry and York Rifles from York Borough, and the Hanover Infantry and Marion Rifles from Hanover—each with little or no military experience other than what they had gained at a few sporadic drills and holiday parades. When President Lincoln called for seventy-five thousand volunteers, all four militia companies immediately tendered their services and were promptly accepted by Governor Andrew Curtin.[16]

The two York companies saw immediate service guarding the bridges of the Northern Central Railway between York and Baltimore.[17] They were reinforced by the first three regiments of Pennsylvania Volunteers, which had been organized in Harrisburg and sent to Maryland on April 21. Returning to York on April 23, where they were joined by the two Hanover militia companies, the new military organizations began their formal military training on the public com-

---

[14] *York Democratic Press*, February 19, 1861. The Guthrie and Crittenden Compromises were attempts to appease the South by granting various concessions regarding slave laws and promises that the government would not interfere with slavery in states or territories where it already existed. Other conciliatory measures were proposed by committees not only in York but in a few other Pennsylvania counties as well. One such meeting in York called upon the state legislature to rescind the commonwealth's personal-liberty law, which made it illegal to kidnap a freedman and transport him over the state line for the purpose of re-enslavement. Likewise, the same law forbade any Pennsylvania justice of the peace from taking cognizance of any fugitive slave case. See Arnold Shankman, *The Pennsylvania Antiwar Movement* (Rutherford, N. J.: Fairleigh Dickinson University Press, 1980), 44.

[15] *York Democratic Press*, February 26, 1861.

[16] Prowell, *History of York County*, 355.

[17] Ibid.

mons, which was renamed "Camp [Winfield] Scott."[18] The commons traditionally served as the county fair grounds, so existing sheds, animal stalls, and other fair buildings were converted into barracks and administrative offices, and makeshift huts were thrown up to handle the overflow. Relations between the soldiers and the town's citizens were cordial. A recruit from nearby Lancaster County wrote home:

> The citizens of York have been very hospitable ever since our arrival. Many of the men were yesterday entertained at private residences, and the stores furnished many little articles of use and luxury for nothing or at cost price. . . . I am pleased to make a record of this patriotic feeling among the citizens as it stands in pleasant contrast with our treatment in Harrisburg, where many of the hotels or storekeepers . . . charged double price for articles of necessity or luxury.

As a result of York's hospitality, the Lancaster native concluded "the boys last night christened this place 'Camp Delight.' "[19] By the end of April, there were over five thousand volunteers living on the commons; two months later, the camp was quartering six infantry regiments and a battery of artillery.[20]

The communities throughout the county were very supportive of their soldiers during the war's first months. Their efforts were evident as early as April 22, when York's citizens sent provisions to the Pennsylvania troops guarding the Northern Central. The letter from the Lancaster County soldier about the state of affairs at "Camp Delight" also provides some indication of many Yorkers' early enthusiasm for the war. *The Hanover Spectator* reported "that many of our young men evince their patriotism by wearing Union neckties, composed of the 'red, white and blue.' " He also observed that "the ladies, God bless them! have also taken to wearing the National colors, which to our notion, heightens and adds to their attractions very considerably."[21]

York Borough went beyond cosmetic support when, on April 23, the grand jury recommended an appropriation of $10,000 from the county's funds to ensure that its "gallant volunteers and their families will be well taken care of." Together with contributions from Han-

---

[18] Ibid.

[19] *York Democratic Press*, April 30, 1861. The letter originally appeared in the *Lancaster Express* on April 24.

[20] Ibid.; Prowell, *History of York County*, 355.

[21] *Hanover Spectator*, May 10, 1861.

over, Wrightsville, and other townships and boroughs, over $16,000 was initially collected to defray unexpected costs that the volunteers' families might incur.[22] The county showed its support of the war effort in other ways as well. On April 22, an "immense meeting" was held in the courthouse to discuss the town's defense "during these troublesome times." Those in attendance resolved that "traitors" and those who gave comfort and aid to the enemy would be dealt with harshly, and that "the citizens of the several boroughs and townships . . . [should] arm themselves as home-guards for the protection of themselves, their neighbors, and their property." Official thanks were given to the "brave volunteers" and their families, and the earlier mentioned sum of $10,000 was recommended to be set aside for a family relief fund.[23]

The women also contributed their labors, forming what may have been York's first women's organization. In November, the members officially constituted themselves as "The Ladies' Soldiers' Aid Society." The initial committee was composed of the wives of some of York's most prominent citizens. These women organized other women, who in turn went about the tasks of collecting or making stockings, shirts, bandages, and other articles for the troops.[24]

In December 1861, the 900 members of the 6th New York Cavalry quartered for the winter at Camp Scott, renaming it "Camp Harris." Letters from some of the 6th New York's troopers to the editor of a York newspaper indicate that the Aid Society's endeavors were both effective and appreciated. A company commander wrote to *The York Gazette* to thank all of York's women "for the kind manner in which they have administered to the comforts of our troops." One particular undertaking especially impressed this New York officer. When the Aid Society heard that his men needed socks, they "kindly furnished them with one hundred (100) pairs of nice woolen socks, *knit with their own fair hands*." He concluded that "for such [a] kind, generous act of sympathy and patriotism their memory will ever be held most dear by both officers and soldiers."[25] Another New Yorker, this one

---

[22] *York Democratic Press*, April 30, 1861 (emphasis in original); broadside entitled "RELIEF AND PROTECTION of the Famlies [sic] of Volunteer Companies FROM YORK COUNTY," File 737, Misc. Civil War Papers, Historical Society of York County.

[23] *York Democratic Press*, April 30, 1861.

[24] Gibson, *History of York County*, 204.

[25] *York Gazette*, January 21, 1862 (emphasis in original).

an enlisted man, thanked the women for a home-cooked meal. "Will you permit the 6th N. Y. V. Cavalry, through the medium of a simple soldier," he asked the *Gazette's* editor, "to return thanks to the ladies of your town for their thoughtful and graceful kindness to us poor soldiers, in sending us such an ample Sunday repast yesterday evening. It's not the mere fact, but the evidence of kindness manifested in it that touches us so deeply. . . . The whole regiment unites in earnest thanks to the ladies of York, for their many kindnesses to us."[26]

Soon after the calls for three-month volunteers ended, the federal government required the state governors to furnish regiments for three-year service.[27] Again, there was no shortage of men eager to fight for the Union cause. The first three-year organizations in which county residents enlisted were part of Governor Curtin's Pennsylvania Reserve Corps (PRC), which was created by an act of the Pennsylvania Assembly. It consisted of the companies originally intended to make up the three-month regiments but that were in excess of Pennsylvania's quota.[28] There were fifteen regiments in the PRC, including thirteen infantry, one cavalry, and one artillery regiment.[29] The total number of companies within the Corps equaled 142, with York County "entitled" to furnish three of those companies.[30] The

---

[26] Ibid.

[27] Cited in William A. Itter, "Conscription in Pennsylvania during the Civil War" (Ph.D. dissertation, University of Southern California, 1941), 41, 47; James M. McPherson, *Ordeal By Fire: The Civil War and Reconstruction* (New York: McGraw-Hill, 1981), 165. The first call for three-year volunteers was on May 3, 1861, which required 42,034 state troops, 22,714 regulars, and 18,000 seamen. Congress later passed "An Act to authorize the Employment of Volunteers to aid in enforcing the Laws and protecting Public Property," which authorized the president to accept 500,000 volunteers for up to three years of federal service. This act became a law on July 22, 1861 (the day after the Union disaster at Bull Run).

[28] Cited in Edward G. Everett, "Pennsylvania Raises an Army," *Western Pennsylvania Historical Magazine* 39 (summer 1956): 100–1; and Itter, "Conscription in Pennsylvania," 45–47. The historian of the PRC, J. R. Sypher, said that "the bill was freely discussed and passed both branches of the legislature," apparently with bipartisan approval (Sypher, *History of the Pennsylvania Reserve Corps* [Lancaster, Pa.: Elias Barr & Co., 1865], 57). The men who enlisted in the regiments that comprised the PRC originally were signing up for three months' state service, but after the debacle at Bull Run, they were mustered into federal service for three years. According to Itter, "So confused was the arrangement, however, that some [soldiers] were never actually mustered into federal service, and at the expiration of their three month term of enlistment the state date of muster was held binding" (ibid., 47).

[29] Everett, "Pennsylvania Raises an Army," 100–1.

[30] *York Democratic Press*, May 28, 1861.

apportionment of the number of companies from each county was based, according to the PRC's official historian, "on the amount of population in the different counties; keeping in view the numbers already taken into United States service, [and] discriminating in favor of the agricultural counties as it is believed that sound policy dictates the importance of not interfering with their productive power."[31] York County's contribution to the Pennsylvania Reserve Corps consisted of two infantry companies (Company D, 30th Regiment, 1st Pennsylvania Reserves, and Company G, 41st Regiment, 12th Reserves) and one entire battery of artillery (Battery E, 43rd Regiment, 1st Pennsylvania Artillery; in addition, about twenty men from Battery A were recruited in York).[32]

York County also supplied most of the men in Companies D and I of the 76th Pennsylvania Volunteer Infantry (the "Keystone Zouaves"), which mustered into federal service on October 16, 1861, at Harrisburg's Camp Curtin.[33] The other three-year companies from York County mustered in during 1861 made up the greater part of the 89th Regiment, Pennsylvania Volunteer Infantry. Companies A, B, C, D, E, G, H, and K were manned almost entirely by soldiers who called York County their home.[34] The 89th was mustered into

---

[31] Ibid. This newspaper article also listed the following recruiting guidelines: "Each company will consist of 77 men, not over 45 nor under 18 years of age, of good physical strength and vigor. A company will consist of 1 Captain, 1 First Lieutenant, 1 Second Lieutenant, 4 Sergeants, 4 Corporals, 2 Musicians, [and] 64 Privates." On June 20, 1861, the authorized number of officers and men per company was changed to 101. Everett, "Pennsylvania Raises an Army," 103.

[32] Gibson, *History of York County*, 168–69; Sypher, *Pennsylvania Reserve Corps*, 64, 89–90, 103. Company D, 30th Regiment, was made up of soldiers from both York County and Lancaster County. Battery E, 1st Artillery, was detached from the corps throughout the war. Only Battery A and two of the other eight batteries assigned to the PRC were retained by the corps. I was not able to determine the total number of men who enlisted in these companies in 1861, as Gibson's *History* also lists the subsequent replacements that were assigned in later years, and the regimental history lists only those men present when the companies were mustered out. Even if it is assumed that the units had their total authorized strength when they were mustered in, there is still no way to determine how many men in Company D of the 30th Regiment were York County residents.

[33] Gibson, *History of York County*, 183–84; Frederick H. Dyer, *A Compendium of the War of the Rebellion* (reprint ed., Dayton, Ohio: Morningside Press, 1979), 1599.

[34] George R. Prowell, *History of the Eighty-Seventh Regiment, Pennsylvania Volunteers* (York, Pa.: Press of the York Daily, 1901), 2–12. Company F was comprised of soldiers from the Gettysburg area; Company I consisted of soldiers from New Oxford (Adams County) and the western area of York County.

the federal service in August and September of 1861. Company A was originally called the "Ellsworth Zouaves" in memory of Colonel Elmer Ellsworth, the first Union officer killed in the war. The Ellsworth Zouaves were organized as a militia company in York Borough in May 1861 and accepted for service with the 87th in August. The 87th's other companies were organized in August. Many of the officers and men who had been in York's three-month regiments formed the 87th's nucleus.[35]

As with many wars both before and since, the recruitment of young men in the early days of the conflict took on the appearance of a carnival, with patriotic speeches, parades, and flag raisings common sights throughout the county. On April 21, the *Hanover Spectator* reported that "the war feeling in this place ran at a fever pitch. . . . Speeches were made, and recruiting progressed quite rapidly, swelling the ranks . . . to the full number of men required." The *York Democratic Press*, which only a few weeks earlier expressed the strong desire for peace, proudly noted that the "Union feeling is intensely strong and the ancient Borough of York is not behind her neighbors in patriotism and zeal for the glorious cause." After describing the town's "gala appearance" with the widespread display of the American flag, the writer concluded that the "laws of the United States must be enforced, the orders of the government must be obeyed and the Flag of the Union must be respected at whatever cost."[36] James McPherson comments that this initial impulse of patriotism is known by the French as *rage militaire*, and that it usually wears off after the first few months of a war.[37]

The York County volunteers caught up in this *rage militaire* did not come from a cross section of society. An analysis of the socioeconomic backgrounds of the volunteers from Hanover indicates that the average enlisted volunteer of 1861 was 23.9 years old, a skilled laborer, single, a native Pennsylvanian, and had an estate worth $343, which at that time was equal to at least a half-year's wages.[38] If the value of the family estate of the soldiers who lived at home with their parents is included, then the average estate value is raised to $985.

---

[35] Ibid.

[36] *York Democratic Press*, April 23, 1861.

[37] James McPherson, *For Cause and Comrades: Why Men Fought in the Civil War* (New York: Oxford University Press, 1997), 16.

[38] McPherson, *Ordeal By Fire*, 357.

Comparing these values to the average family estate ($2,700) within the community, it is evident that the average enlisted man of 1861 came from the lower end of the socioeconomic scale.[39]

The officers from this community fared somewhat better in civilian life than most of their enlisted counterparts. These men usually were married and had children, were native born, averaged thirty-one years of age, had estates averaging $1,760, and most were skilled laborers who owned their own businesses.[40] Many of them not only served as officers in the three-month regiments, but continued their service by accepting commissions in either the three-year, nine-month, or twelve-month regiments. Their appointments were probably more influenced by politics than merit, for it would take a few hard-fought battles for the government to discover that an officer's quality was not determined by his political affiliation or social status.[41]

---

[39] United States Census Office, Eighth Census, 1860, Population of the United States in 1860, for York County, Pa., original unpublished returns. Hanover was chosen as the subject of this analysis because of the simplicity of matching names from the census with the list of this small community's volunteers. I arrived at these statistical averages by searching the census for the names of men who had enlisted in 1861, which I determined from 1861 company lists (both three-month and three-year units) printed in the county histories. Once I verified that the men on the census were the same ones listed in the county histories, I annotated their age, occupation, marital status, country or state of birth, and value of both their real estate and personal estate. Rank, company, and regiment were extrapolated from the county histories. To determine the soldier's age, I added one year to the age given on the 1860 census. If a soldier was a dependent son living at home with his parents, I listed the value of the parents' estate. The reason for listing the value of the parents' estates was to show the socioeconomic background of the individuals who depended on their families for support. The averages were determined by adding the numerical values together and dividing by the total soldiers or families surveyed (total families listed on 1860 census was 330, total enlisted soldiers positively verified was thirty-one).

[40] Ibid.

[41] The governor issued commissions in both the three-month and three-year companies and regiments. When vacancies occurred at the company level, the soldiers filled the void by voting for individuals from within the company. Officers from within the regiment voted for candidates to fill vacancies at the regimental level. The general commanding a department or army could appoint a board of officers "whose duty it shall be to examine the capacity, qualifications, propriety of conduct and efficiency of any commissioned officer of volunteers within his department or army, who may be reported to the board or commission, and upon such report, if adverse to such officer, and if approved by the President of the United States, the commission of such officer shall be vacated." Quoted in Itter, "Conscription in Pennsylvania," 47–48; and Stanley L. Swart, "The Military Examination Board in the Civil War: A Case Study," Civil War History 16 (September 1970): 227–28.

Another method of looking at Hanover's early volunteers is by determining the enlistment rates of men with different socioeconomic characteristics. We can accomplish this by comparing the men who served with those whose who stayed home.[42] Men who already had accrued property were less likely to enlist than those who were without property. Of the 170 service-age men who did not own property, twenty-three men (14 percent) enlisted. Of the 241 men who owned property, only thirteen (5 percent) enlisted. Age was a factor, as well. The greatest percentage of enlistees (14 percent) came from the 16–20 age group (all of these men were propertyless, but because most of them were apprentices learning a skill, they probably would not have remained that way for long). The 21–29 age group accounted for 9 percent (fifteen men) of Hanover's total enlistments in 1861; most of these men were skilled laborers (of which seven owned property and six did not).

The subgroup with the largest percentage of enlistments was the propertyless skilled laborers in the 30–39 age group. Thirty percent of the men in this category enlisted, compared to only 7 percent of the propertied skilled laborers in the same age group. Conversely, of thirty-four service-age men working as clerks or small shopkeepers, none from any age category enlisted. Of thirty-three men in the merchant/professional category, only 6 percent enlisted. These statistics indicate that in 1861, the three most important variables that determined the probability a man would enlist (from this community, at least) were: first, age; second, wealth; and third, occupational category.[43] It must be remembered, however, that even though a man owned property (which may have been worth as little as $25), it does not mean he was rich or even moderately wealthy. Even though 5 percent of the service-age men who owned property enlisted, their low estate values indicate that they were relatively poor.[44]

---

[42] The method used here was borrowed from an article written by W. J. Rohrbaugh entitled "Who Fought for the North in the Civil War? Concord, Massachusetts, Enlistments," *Journal of American History* 73 (December 1986): 695–701. Rohrbaugh's analysis is based on enlistments from 1861–1865, giving him a larger database for comparison.

[43] The results of Rohrbaugh's study revealed that 36 percent of the service-age men from Concord in the clerk/shopkeeper category (all ages) enlisted; in Hanover no one from this category enlisted.

[44] For a socioeconomic profile of all Union soldiers from 1861–1865, see McPherson, *Ordeal By Fire*, 357–59.

Unfortunately, it is nearly impossible to determine the partisan affiliation of those who enlisted because there were no voter registration requirements in York County. Although the politically aligned newspapers of that time certainly were biased, they are the only source available that might give some clue to the political composition of the county's military organizations. According to a report in the *York Democratic Press*,

> If we can believe the [regimental] newspapers, in nearly all the regiments in the field, votes have been taken that have shown a large preponderance in favor of the Democratic party. If we look at the political complexion of the companies and regiments raised in our own midst we can see this fact still more strongly evinced. Out of some fifty men from Spring Garden township, only about six are Republicans. Take the Worth Infantry, of which our citizens have always been so proud, and only about fourteen were Republicans. The 16th Regiment, commanded by Colonel Zeigel, a Democrat, was almost unanimously Democratic.[45]

Readers of that article might have believed that York County Democrats were more patriotic than the county's Republicans. A better explanation was that the Democrats were the majority party in York County. The Democratic party also appealed to men employed in artisan occupations, and as many of the early recruits were skilled laborers or apprentices, this also might explain why there were more Democrats in the ranks.[46]

The young men who rushed to their country's call in 1861 volunteered for any number of personal reasons, but the ones most apparent were excitement, patriotism, and the desire to achieve recognition within their communities. Men from the bottom of the economic scale had less to lose than men in the middle or at the top. It was simpler for a poor man to drop everything and enlist than it was for a man who had a stable job with a moderate income. It also was easier for a bachelor to embark on this patriotic venture than for a man who had to support a wife and children. No matter how poor a man was, the $12 monthly salary of an army private did not pay very many bills (despite the county's efforts to provide for the soldiers' families).

---

[45] *York Democratic Press*, October 1, 1861.

[46] James McPherson, *Battle Cry of Freedom: The Civil War Era* (New York: Oxford University Press, 1988), 30.

As the *rage militaire* subsided, it became evident that the war
would not end after a few battles, and regardless of why a man volunteered, attitudes began to change, and the eagerness to volunteer
dropped off sharply. Some of the county's three-month volunteers
already had seen enough and would not re-enlist for three years.
Many of the soldiers were so disgusted with army life that they would
not even remain for an extra ten days, which in one instance caused
a force to withdraw from an area prematurely and concede a strategic
piece of territory to the Confederates. A York soldier wrote from his
camp in western Virginia that "several regiments have just voted
upon the question of remaining ten days longer . . . amongst those
voting negatively was the Second [Pa.], so you may look for the [York]
'Rifles' home in a few days. The Sixteenth [Pa.] has not yet voted
upon it, but from the expressions of the men I do not think they will
remain."[47] Although recruiting slowed dramatically, the county still
managed to enlist enough men to fill the majority of Company A,
107th Pa. Volunteer Infantry, and Company I, 11th Pa. Cavalry (both
three-year regiments mustered in during the spring of 1862.)[48] Then
the War Department complicated matters by closing all state recruiting services on April 3, 1862, in anticipation of the war ending by
that summer.[49] It took the bloody encounter at Shiloh on April 6 and
7 and the early casualty returns from the Peninsula Campaign to
shake the northern government to its senses.[50]

On June 6, the recruiting service was rejuvenated. By month's end,

---

[47] *York Democratic Press*, July 30, 1861. This was a letter to the editor from a
soldier in the 16th Pa., written from a camp near Charlestown, Va. (now West Virginia.). The 2nd and 16th Regiments were part of a Union force under General
Robert Patterson that was supposed to prevent General Joseph E. Johnston's Confederate army from joining Beauregard's force near Washington. Not only did the
Confederates elude Patterson's army and eventually join Beauregard in time to defeat the Union forces at the Battle of Bull Run, but the vital rail junction at Harpers
Ferry was given back to the Confederates when Patterson was forced to retire because the ninety-day service terms of his soldiers had expired.

[48] Gibson, *History of York County*, 190–91.

[49] United States War Department, *The War of the Rebellion: A Compilation of the
Official Records of the Union and Confederate Armies*, 70 in 128 vols. (Washington,
D. C.: Government Printing Office, 1889–1901), series 3, vol. 2, pp. 2–3 (hereinafter
cited as *Official Records*).

[50] During the Seven Days, York's two infantry companies in the Pennsylvania Reserve Corps suffered twenty-five casualties. Sypher, *History of the Pennsylvania Reserves*, 566–67 and 705–6.

the federal government asked the states for 150,000 men.[51] This number increased in early July when Governor Curtin, Secretary of State William Seward, and New York governor Edwin Morgan appealed to Lincoln to raise the number to 300,000 troops; the president agreed.[52] Pennsylvania's quota was 30,000; York County was required to supply at least three companies of 100 men each.[53] If the quotas were not met in Pennsylvania and elsewhere, there would be conscription.[54] Anticipating a poor showing at the recruiting offices, Congress gave the president authority to determine the length of service (not to exceed nine months) of state militias when they were federalized. Even more important was a clause that allowed the president to interfere with the existing militia system of a state if its enrollment machinery was ineffective. On July 17, 1862, Lincoln signed the bill into law.[55]

York County's local governments responded with enthusiasm. The county commissioners appropriated $15,000 for "a fund sufficient to pay a bounty, that will secure the State's quota of volunteers—not less than fifty dollars to each volunteer who shall enlist in York County under the recent calls for additional troops."[56] Hanover also approved a "twenty-five dollar bounty for each recruit volunteering in this Borough, in addition to the amount paid by the County."[57] On August 4, Lincoln summoned 300,000 militia. If the individual states did not come up with their assigned quota by August 15, the federal government would require a special draft in those states.[58]

Pennsylvania did not meet its quota and so began enrollment for a

---

[51] *Official Records*, series 3, vol. 2, pp. 109, 183; James W. Geary, *We Need Men: The Union Draft in the Civil War* (DeKalb: Northern Illinois University Press, 1991), 8; Itter, "Conscription in Pennsylvania," 53.

[52] Itter, "Conscription in Pennsylvania," 53–54. The appeal for more troops by the secretary of state and the two governors was staged by Lincoln so that it would not appear that *his* Republican administration was directly asking for more men.

[53] *York Gazette*, July 29, 1862.

[54] Fred Shannon, *The Organization and Administration of the Union Army*, 2 vols. (Cleveland: Arthur H. Clark Co., 1928), 1: 71–73.

[55] Itter, "Conscription in Pennsylvania," 54. For the best description of Congress' role in the passing of the Militia Act of July 17, 1862, see Geary, *We Need Men*, 22–31.

[56] Ibid.

[57] *Hanover Citizen*, July 31, 1862; *Hanover Spectator*, August 1, 1862.

[58] *Official Records*, series 3, vol. 2, p. 293; Itter, "Conscription in Pennsylvania," 54.

militia draft. The current militia laws within the state were "extremely defective," according to Pennsylvania's adjutant general, who suggested to Governor Curtin that U.S. Marshals and deputies be used to complete a proper enrollment of all able-bodied men between the ages of eighteen and forty-five.[59] This plan was adopted, but early difficulties during the enrollment process delayed the draft until September 15. The draft was postponed again because of Robert E. Lee's first invasion of the North, itself resulting in a call for fifty thousand "emergency" volunteers to defend the state's borders. York County responded by supplying six emergency infantry companies, one cavalry company, and one artillery battery. Their term of service was uneventful, lasting only from September 12–24.[60]

The impending militia draft spurred York's communities to action, with a number of towns holding war meetings to encourage enlistments.[61] By inducing volunteering, the various townships hoped to receive enough enlistment credits to eliminate the need for a draft in their districts. Complicating matters, however, was a provision in the law that allowed men to enlist in the nine-month regiments, the same amount of time that a drafted man would serve.[62] Because the government's ultimate goal was to recruit men for three years' service, the enlistment of nine-months' men was a setback to the long-term war effort. Still, the enlistment of men for nine-months' service was perceived as more honorable than drafting them for the same period. The *Gazette*'s editor had this in mind when he described the easy duty of the nine-month enlistees:

> It seems quite probable now that the nine months' men will be used principally for garrison duty, and the elementary duties of a soldier's

---

[59] Quoted in Itter, "Conscription," 55.

[60] Ibid., 56; Gibson, *History of York County*, 200–1. When the Army of Northern Virginia attempted its first invasion of the North, which culminated with the Battle of Antietam on September 17, 1862, Governor Curtin issued a call for volunteers to serve for the duration of the invasion crisis.

[61] *York Gazette*, August 12 and September 9, 1862. The August 12 issue reported the proceedings of war meetings in Dover and Heidelberg Townships. The September 9 issue carried a story about a war meeting in Codorus Township, during which speeches were made in both German and English "for the purpose of raising the quota of troops of said township without a draft." The citizens of that township further "resolved to offer a bounty of $50, in addition to all other bounties, advance pay, etc."

[62] McPherson, *Battle Cry of Freedom*, 492.

life. Their labor will be light, their pay better than any other country ever offered; their turn of service during the winter months, when labor of all kinds is hard to be had, and their coming back home will be about June next; so their service will avoid all the extreme hot weather, and give them the pleasantest and healthiest months in the year. The aggregate of the pay will be a better sum per day than most men get at home-living.[63]

The men to which the article referred were the new soldiers comprising companies B, C, I, and K of the 130th Pa. Volunteer Infantry, which mustered in on August 9, 1862. The prophesy that they would be used principally for garrison duty proved to be far from accurate. Thirty-eight days after it mustered in, the 130th sustained heavy casualties in the attack on the "Bloody Lane" at Antietam.[64]

The militia enrollment was supervised by a local resident appointed the "Deputy Marshal of York County for the Enrollment of the Militia." He was assisted by forty-three other county residents appointed as enrollment officers, whose responsibilties included the enrollment of all able-bodied men between eighteen and forty-five within their assigned district (a township or borough).[65] York County's quota was 2,181 men out of the 7,894 enrolled. Included in the total enrollment were 1,904 soldiers who already were serving.[66] These prior enlistments (in three-year or nine-month regiments, not the emergency regiments) were credited to the townships and boroughs from which they enlisted, reducing the total number required from that district. If the total number of volunteers met or exceeded the quota for the district, the township or borough escaped the draft. If the number was less than the quota, a draft was held.[67]

When the draft lottery occurred on October 16, a total of 2,013 men were conscripted, but only 340 were actually mustered in. There were 341 exemptions, and 821 men furnished substitutes. As of De-

---

[63] York Gazette, September 2, 1862.

[64] York Democratic Press, August 15, 1862; Spangler, My Little War Experience, 18, 166. Company I of the 130th also had men from Montgomery County.

[65] York Democratic Press, August 28, 1862.

[66] Ibid., September 30, 1862.

[67] Commonwealth of Pennsylvania, "Special Instructions Relative to the Draft," September 6, 1862, Pennsylvania Historical and Museum Commission, Harrisburg, Pa. For an accurate description of the actual mechanics of the 1862 draft, see Shannon, Organization and Administration of the Union Army, 1: 278–80.

cember 2, 1862, 511 men still had not reported for service.[68] The *Gazette* announced that of those 511, "many have 'skedaddled,' while others still lurked around their homes."[69] During the Civil War, the term "skedaddled" meant fleeing to Canada or Europe.

The largest number of exemptions—151—was granted to the physically unfit. The next largest group of "exempts"—seventy-three—consisted of people having "conscientious scruples." Conscientious objectors were required to report to the draft commissioner and sign an oath stating "that he conscientiously scruples to bear arms, believes it unlawful to do so, whether in self-defense or in defense of his country, or otherwise howsoever"[70] In addition to deposing, conscientious objectors were required to pay "an equivalent sum for personal service."[71]

Hiring a substitute was a favorite way among York Countians to avoid service, but it was a financially costly measure, and it accentuated class differences. The November 4 issue of the *Gazette* carried an advertisement of a new business unknown to most residents, but one that quickly gained popularity:

U. STATES SUBSTITUTE AGENCY.

Persons drafted can procure *able-bodied substitutes, free from any draft*, by applying immediately at this office. 20 first-class Substitutes

---

[68] *York Gazette*, December 2, 1862. The following list of exemptions from the militia draft was reported: "School teachers, 13; Conscientious Scruples, 73; Invalids, etc., exempted by Surgeon, 156; School Directors, 2; Over 45 years, 17; Under 21 years, 8; Not Naturalized, 22; Assistant Postmasters, 2; U. S. Assistant [Tax] Collector, 1; Preacher, 1; By Order of Governor Curtin, 1; Excess of Quota, 15." The total number exempted was 341. War Department General Orders No. 121 required the enrollment of all men between the ages of eighteen and forty-five, but Pennsylvania's militia laws exempted from military duty all men under twenty-one years. Draft commissioners were given these instructions: "You will . . . when holding appeals, erase from the list, all persons who establish the fact to your satisfaction, that they are under twenty-one years. You can examine such persons under oath, when you are not otherwise satisfied." Commonwealth of Pennsylvania, "Special Instructions Relative to the Draft."

[69] Ibid.

[70] Commonwealth of Pennsylvania, "Depositions for Conscientious Objectors," Executive Office—Military Department, September 3, 1862. Existing records indicate that at least 151 men in York County filed for conscientious objector status during the 1862 draft. Conscientious Objector Depositions—1862, Department of Military Affairs, Office of the Adjutant General, Record Group 19, File 0507, Pennsylvania Historical and Museum Commission, Harrisburg, Pa.

[71] Commonwealth of Pennsylvania, "Special Instructions Relative to the Draft."

wanted immediately. Information furnished from headquarters gratis.
No charge till accepted. Don't get into speculators hands.
JACOB M. AUSTIN[72]

Judging by the number of men who furnished substitutes in lieu of
personal service (821), Mr. Austin probably had a very lucrative
trade. There is scant information available either about the men who
furnished substitutes or those who became substitutes, but with the
price of a "sub" in York County ranging anywhere from $200 to
$1,000, we can assume that men of moderate to high incomes were
probably the only residents who could afford one.[73] The *Gazette*
highlighted this point: "Almost every drafted farmer in the county
possessed of the means to procure a substitute, has done so regardless of expense. But the poorer class of laborers and mechanics, many
of them with large families depending on their daily labor for support, will be obliged to go into service, leaving the loved ones at home
unprovided for and unprotected."[74] Whether knowingly or not, the
editor was raising the issue of the Civil War becoming "a rich man's
war and a poor man's fight." If nothing else, his commentary was a
jab at the way President Lincoln was running the war.

   Most of the substitutes, along with the men who could not afford
one and had no legal exemption, were mustered into service and
became the 166th Regiment, Pennsylvania Infantry.[75] This unit consisted entirely of drafted men and substitutes from York County, except for a few of the staff officers who were appointed because of
their meritorious service in earlier regiments recruited in the
county.[76] The 166th was organized on the site of Camp Scott, now
dubbed "Camp Franklin" in honor of York native William B. Franklin, who was serving as a major general and corps commander in the
Army of the Potomac.[77] Some reluctant soldiers tried to desert from
Camp Franklin, but overall resistance was relatively light. On one
occasion, however, "shots were fired, . . . [and] during the disturbance several of the men succeeded in effecting their escape."[78] Ap-

---

[72] *York Gazette*, November 4, 1862 (emphasis in original).
[73] Prowell, *History of York County*, 378; *York Gazette*, October 28, 1862.
[74] *York Gazette*, November 23, 1862.
[75] Prowell, *History of York County*, 378; Gibson, *History of York County*, 172.
[76] Ibid.
[77] Ibid.
[78] *York Gazette*, December 2, 1862.

parently most of the drafted men were resigned to their fate, for the procedures of organizing the 166th remained uneventful. The regiment departed for Virginia on December 4, and operated in the Suffolk area through July 1863, seeing little action. During its term of service the 166th suffered only seventeen deaths: six from battle and eleven from disease.[79]

As mentioned, one of the main goals of the militia draft was to stimulate volunteer enlistments into existing regiments, so some of the locally recruited units sent officers back to York to set up regimental recruiting stations. Four recruiting offices opened in York during August: one each for the Regular Army, the 87th Pennsylvania, the 107th Pennsylvania, and an independent company.[80] Volunteers who enlisted in these units not only lowered their districts' quotas, but they also reaped rewards in the form of bounties, advance pay, and pension eligibility. Drafted militiamen had the option to become volunteers by changing their term of service from nine months to three years; by doing so they would be given the same monetary inducements as any other volunteer.[81] But most of the draftees could not be enticed, and recruiting for the three-year organizations picked up only slightly. For example, only twenty-six new recruits mustered into the 87th between August (when the draft was announced) and December (when the 166th was mustered in).[82] In terms of raising men to fill vacancies in the existing regiments, the militia draft in York County was a failure. On the other hand, the 166th never would have materialized without the draft, and it would have been much more difficult to have recruited the 130th Pennsylvania.

There are several reasons why York County residents were reluctant in 1862 to enlist for a three-year term. York had been a garrison town since the war's first days, so by the summer of 1862, the thrill of listening to military bands and watching soldiers march off to war had waned; the *rage militare* no longer raged. York also became the home of a U.S. general hospital in 1862, with wounded soldiers arriving by the train-load after large battles. Many young men who might

[79] Dyer, *Compendium*, 1620.

[80] *York Gazette*, August 12, 1862.

[81] Ibid., October 21, 1862; Shannon, *Organization and Administration*, 1: 285–86.

[82] Prowell, *History of the Eighty-Seventh Regiment*, i–xxv, lists the names of all the men who served in the regiment and the dates they mustered in.

have been anxious to don a blue uniform probably had second thoughts after seeing other boys lying in the hospital with shattered or amputated limbs. Further, barely a day went by when one of York County's newspapers failed to carry a story about a local soldier killed in battle or who had died from disease. Although most York residents still supported the war effort in spirit and materiel (the Ladies' Soldiers' Aid Society remained active throughout the war), it must have been difficult for a civilian not to develop a defeatist attitude, especially after the encounters of the Seven Days and Second Bull Run. The crisis of the Confederate invasion threat culminating with the Battle of Antietam was a bloody exclamation point to a trying summer.

York County's strong Democratic tradition undoubtedly added to the woes of the recruiting officers. Was it not Lincoln's "Black Republican" administration that caused these problems anyway? Why should the white men of the county sacrifice their lives for an administration that they had a difficult time supporting? Yorkers never were keen on freed people coming north to take their jobs, and after Congress abolished slavery in the District of Columbia in July and Lincoln announced the preliminary Emancipation Proclamation in September, it occurred to many citizens that the war had become a crusade to free the slaves. A headline in the *Gazette* announcing the abolition of slavery in the District of Columbia summed up the incredulous feelings of many York County citizens: "We can't Believe it—It is Impossible."[83]

Historian Fred Shannon attributed the paucity of enlistments in the eastern United States in 1862 to the absorption of the labor market by the war industries to such an extent "that the bounties as then offered, were insufficient to lure the men from their jobs. Hence the East had to draft."[84] Because York County's industrial base was relatively undeveloped (compared to Pittsburgh, Philadelphia, and the other major population centers), Shannon's thesis does not apply. More important was the perception that the Civil War actually *was* becoming the rich man's war and the poor man's fight, as the editor of the *Gazette* alluded in his mockery of the substitute provision. If poor white men were going to have to fight a war to free the slaves—a

---

[83] *York Gazette*, July 22, 1862.
[84] Shannon, *Organization and Administration*, 1: 292.

war that might not be over in the near future—they might as well do it for the shortest time possible, and nine months was a great deal shorter than three years. Some men already serving likewise were dismayed by the changing nature of the war. Private John Miller, a York resident in Company I, 76th Pennsylvania at Hilton Head, South Carolina, asked his brother to let him know "how recruiting went back home," and commented that "if they would know what i know it would be pretty hard to raise one Company in York." His conclusion was frightening, yet proved to be only an idle threat: "im afraid the niggar question will raise a rumpus in the army yet if I ever get home i'll shoot all the niggars i come across."[85]

Union military defeats added to the gloom. A terrible Union disaster at Fredericksburg, Virginia, in December further dampened home front morale. Spring 1863 saw another Union defeat at Chancellorsville and little progress in the western theater, where Vicksburg still had not fallen despite months of maneuvering. The Confederacy had not been subdued despite great losses in life. To complicate matters, the men drafted in 1862 would be discharged in June or July. Replacements had to be found for the casualties and discharges. The militia draft was an obvious failure; there would have to be a new conscription law passed if the Union armies were to remain in the field.

The remedy was a new law that removed conscription responsibility from the individual states and transferred it to the federal government. Signed by Lincoln on March 3, the Enrollment Act of 1863 was intended to stimulate volunteering by dangling the threat of a federal draft.[86] Troops were needed for the veteran regiments, not as members of new regiments under untried officers. The purpose of the Enrollment Act was to draft men for three years into existing regiments, such as the 87th or 76th Pennsylvania, or even better, get them to volunteer for the veteran regiments of their own choice. To underscore this point, a York County soldier serving in the 76th wrote to the *Hanover Spectator* to inform his civilian peers that "those who volunteer are generally the recipients of favors that are not granted to those who are drafted." He concluded with his own recruiting

---

[85] John Miller to George Miller, August 4, 1862, George Miller Papers, Historical Society of York County.

[86] Shannon, *Organization and Administration*, 1: 308.

pitch: "If there are in Hanover or vicinity any who desire to enter the service before the enforcement of the conscription act, we beg to remind them that they can do no better than by joining the 76th." [87]

Among the new draft law's provisions was a clause that allowed men either to furnish substitutes or pay a commutation fee of $300 to the U.S. government.[88] Because substitutes had cost as much as $1,000 in York County during the militia draft, the commutation clause was a welcome relief to many men who could not afford a substitute. Still, $300 was much more than many men could afford to pay.

To ensure proper management of the enrollment process and draft operations, the federal government relied on the Army's Provost Marshal General's Bureau. The local Provost Marshal Office (PMO) in Carlisle, Cumberland County, was responsible for all aspects of the draft process within Pennsylvania's 15th Congressional District (York, Cumberland, and Perry Counties). The PMO also administered the procurement of volunteers and the disposition of deserters in the 15th District.[89] The PMO began operations on May 9, 1863, under the leadership of Captain Robert M. Henderson, a Cumberland County resident.[90] Henderson also served as president of the enrollment board, comprised of himself, a surgeon, and a commissioner.[91] The surgeon was responsible for conducting the physical examinations of draftees, volunteers, and substitutes. The commis-

---

[87] *Hanover Spectator*, July 3, 1863.

[88] Cited in Itter, "Conscription in Pennsylvania," 67.

[89] Colonel William N. Grier, Historical Report of the Acting Assistant Provost Marshal General for the Western District of Pennsylvania; Harrisburg, Pa., March 20, 1866, Records of the Provost Marshal General's Bureau, Record Group 110, National Archives, Washington, D. C. (hereinafter cited as PMGB, RG 110). Pennsylvania was divided into two distinct draft districts: the eastern district, which included those counties east of the Susquehanna River, and the western district, where York County was located. The officer in charge of each district was known as an acting assistant provost marshal general, who was responsible for acting as a medium between the governor in Harrisburg and the provost marshal general in Washington. The two state districts were divided into subordinate districts, with the existing congressional districts forming the basis of the draft districts. Each district was headed by a provost marshal, who may have been either civilian or military, but was appointed with the rank of captain, regardless of status.

[90] Capt. R. M. Henderson, Historical Report for the 15th District of Pennsylvania; Carlisle, Pa., July 17, 1865, PMGB, RG 110 (hereinafter cited as Henderson, Report for 15th District).

[91] Henderson, Report for 15th District.

sioner, although initially having no specified duties, eventually became responsible for the accuracy and completeness of the district's list of enrolled men.[92]

On May 25, the 15th District was subdivided into forty-eight sub-districts, twenty-four of which were in York County. The board appointed enrolling officers (one per sub-district) the next day and directed them "to enroll all male citizens of the United States, and persons of foreign birth who have declared an oath [of] their intention to become citizens under and in pursuance of the laws thereof, between the ages of 20 and 45 years."[93] Henderson expected some resistance within his district, so he instructed his enrolling officers "to avoid all unnecessary harshness . . . [but] to be firm and fair in the discharge of their duties."[94]

As it turned out, the enrolling officers were not impeded by the residents of the 15th District but rather by the Army of Northern Virginia. In fact, Henderson was forced to move his operations to Harrisburg on June 24 to avoid the destruction of its records.[95] When the Army of Northern Virginia began its second invasion of the North in June 1863, President Lincoln and Governor Curtin frantically issued proclamations calling for fifty thousand Pennsylvania militia. The memory of previous rumors of Confederate invasion discouraged a rush to arms, and farmers were hesitant to leave their fields in the middle of the early harvest. There also was confusion at the militia recruiting stations, because many of the prospective militiamen thought they might be enlisting for long-term service due to the re-

---

[92] Murdock, *One Million Men*, 8.

[93] Henderson, Report for 15th District. York County's sub-districts were divided as follows: 1st: 1st & 2nd Wards, York; 2nd: 3rd & 4th Wards, York; 3rd: 5th Ward, York & West Manchester Twp.; 4th: Manchester Twp.; 5th: Conewago Twp.; 6th: Newberry & Lewisberry Twps., Goldsborough; 7th: Fairview Twp.; 8th: Franklin, Monaghan, & Carroll Twps.; 9th: Washington & Warrington Twps.; 10th: Dover Twp.; 11th: North Codorus, Jackson, & Paradise Twps.; 12th: Hanover Borough & Heidelberg Twp.; 13th: Manheim & West Manheim Twps.; 14th: Shrewsbury & Glen Rock Boroughs and Codorus & Shrewsbury Twps.; 15th: Springfield Twp., Loganville; 16th: York Twp.; 17th: Spring Garden Twp.; 18th: Hellam Twp. & Wrightsville Borough; 19th: Windsor & Lower Windsor Twp.; 20th: Chanceford Twp.; 21st: Lower Chanceford Twp.; 22nd: Hopewell Twp. & Stewartstown; 23rd: Fawn Twp.; 24th: Peach Bottom Twp.

[94] Ibid.

[95] Ibid.

cent call for three-year volunteers.[96] Despite the confusion, eight emergency infantry regiments and several independent cavalry companies and artillery batteries were organized in Pennsylvania.[97]

Among the units that sprang to the defense of the state was Company I, 26th Pennsylvania Emergency Regiment, whose ranks were filled primarily with Hanover men. On June 26, this untrained and ill-equipped regiment was deployed west of Gettysburg along the Chambersburg turnpike, where it was surprised and repulsed by the van of General Jubal Early's Division. Almost half of Company I was captured, including its commander.[98] Other companies were formed in York County, not just for the "emergency," but for six months' service. Two York companies of six-month soldiers were enlisted (Co. B, 1st Battalion, Pennsylvania Six Months' Infantry, and Co. A, 21st Pennsylvania Cavalry), and after their term of service expired in early 1864, most of the men re-enlisted for three years' service. Men from the county joined other six-month regiments as well, and some even re-enlisted when their 120 days' service expired.[99]

By the time of the Confederate invasion, York County residents had become accustomed to a war that had been dragging on for two years, with no end in sight. The prospect of a Confederate victory seemed more real every day. County newspapers hurled stones on a regular basis, with the Democratic organs blaming the war on the "Black Republicans" and the Republican papers charging the "Copperheads" with treason. The pride of the county, Major General William B. Franklin, had been relieved of his command in the Army of the Potomac in the flurry of events surrounding the Fredericksburg fiasco and the removal of Burnside as its commander. The Chancellorsville disaster only added to the gloom, with the crippled remnants of what had once been healthy, young Union soldiers arriving at

---

[96] Glenn E. Billet, "The Department of the Susquehanna," *Journal of the Lancaster County Historical Society* 66 (winter 1962): 6.

[97] Russell F. Weigley, "Emergency Troops in the Gettysburg Campaign," *Pennsylvania History* 25 (January 1958): 42–43.

[98] Prowell, *History of York County*, 403–4.

[99] Gibson, *History of York County*, 196–97; James M. Gibbs, comp., *History of the 187th Regiment Pennsylvania Volunteer Infantry* (Harrisburg, Pa.: Central Printing and Publishing House, 1905), 17–20. Company A, 21st Cavalry re-enlisted and became Co. A, 182nd P. V. I., and Company B, 1st Bn., became Co. B, 187th P. V. I.

York's military hospital. Topping it all off was Lincoln's announcement of the federal draft.

Despite it all, the people of York continued to contribute to the war effort. Calls for charity by the Ladies' Soldiers' Aid Society normally met with success, with money, clothing, toilet articles, and food items among the most common donations.[100] A soldier from Allentown who passed through York with the 128th Pennsylvania Volunteer Infantry in August 1862, commented on the goodwill and patriotism of the townsfolk. He wrote to his family that the citizens "gave three cheers for us," and he seemed elated that "many a young fair lady could be seen standing [in her] door with the stars and stripes in her hand." Before departing for Baltimore, the 128th was "marched to the Soldiers' Relief Association," where, according to this young soldier, "we took breakfast which was the finest received since we left home."[101]

After Second Bull Run and Antietam, the secretary of war issued urgent requests for volunteer surgeons to proceed to the battlefields to help minister to the wounded; on each occasion, a number of county physicians responded.[102] The Soldiers' Relief Fund also continued to solicit donations from the county's citizens for the care of widows, orphans, and crippled soldiers, as well as to provide for the welfare of the families of soldiers still serving. The various communities also showed pride in their men who went off to war by publishing in the newspapers the names of soldiers from their townships or boroughs who were serving, or by honoring them upon their return with parades, speeches, and banquets.

Many of York's businesses profited from the war by selling goods directly to the government, or by taking advantage of the constant flow of troops passing through York. Large quantities of flour from the P. A. & S. Small mills were supplied to the government, and newspaper advertisements attest to the numerous businesses that sold their wares or services to the troops.[103] For example, the classi-

---

[100] *York Gazette*, July 18, 1862. A list of donations and the names of the contributors usually followed a request for aid.

[101] Pvt. David W. Mattern to his family, August 20, 1862, in Carolyn J. Mattern, ed., "A Pennsylvania Dutch Yankee: The Civil War Letters of Private David William Mattern (1862–1863)," *Pennsylvania Folklife* 36 (autumn 1986): 4.

[102] *York Gazette*, September 2, 16, 1862.

[103] *Reminiscences of One Hundred Years—1809–1909* (York, Pa.: [n. p.], 1909), 6.

fied section of the November 4, 1862, issue of the *Gazette* included advertisements ranging from attorneys soliciting military pension claims services, to a store selling "MILITARY GOODS! such as War Blankets, Woolen Over-Shirts, Under-Shirts, Drawers, Blouses, Caps, &c., &c." There also was an advertisement for a substitute agent, one ad that hawked war bonds, and one that announced the publication (although a bit prematurely) of *The Pictorial History of the War for the Union*.[104]

By the early summer of 1863, few county residents actually had been hurt by the war, although wartime inflation had certainly cut into most people's pocketbooks. Families that lost sons or husbands to death or disabling injury in military service felt sharply the demands of war, but for the majority of Yorkers, the war was more of a nuisance than a life-altering experience. All this would change during the last week of June, when the Army of Northern Virginia brought the war right to their doorsteps. On June 27 at roughly 10 a.m., a Hanover farmer ran through the town yelling, "The enemy will soon be here. They are now in [the adjacent town of] McSherrystown."[105] Moments later the vanguard of General Jubal Early's forces entered Hanover, and for the first time in its history, an armed enemy was invading York County.

Rumors that the Rebels were approaching had circulated for days, and many residents had resorted to burying their household treasures in their gardens or yards to prevent their confiscation by Confederates.[106] Governor Curtin ordered residents of York and neighboring counties to remove their horses, cattle, and valuables to the eastern side of the Susquehanna River, and the county's banks followed suit by transferring money and documents to Philadelphia and New York. Many citizens left for safer areas.[107]

---

[104] *York Gazette*, November 4, 1862.

[105] Prowell, *History of York County*, 405. The Confederate troops were members of Lieutenant Colonel E. V. White's 35th Virginia Battalion. They entered Hanover via the Adams County hamlet of McSherrystown, which straddled Hanover's western border.

[106] Ibid.

[107] Ibid. The June 27 issue of Lancaster's *Daily Evening Express* reported that civilians from the west bank of the Susquehanna were seeking refuge in Lancaster County and that "an almost continuous stream of horses and cattle are passing over the Columbia bridge [connecting York and Lancaster Counties]." Quoted in Gerald A. Robinson, Jr., "Confederate Operations in York County" (M.A. thesis, Millersville State College, 1965), 40.

York County fortunately escaped the terror of a major battle, but it did not escape the occupation of its soil by Confederate troops. The sight of "Johnny Rebs" marching unopposed through the county and confiscating livestock and supplies was humiliating to many citizens and would not be lived down for many years. A few days before the Confederates entered his hometown, York resident James Latimer wrote, "There is the most extra-ordinary apathy with regard to this invasion. If the information we have is reliable we may have an attack on Harrisburg in a day or two, and yet nothing is being done here. We have sent *one* Company." Latimer noted that he enlisted for another company but it never organized due to a lack of volunteers. "If men wont go to the defense of their own State they don't deserve to be called patriot," he lamented. "I am ashamed of myself and my town."[108] Even an anonymous appeal by General Franklin, home on leave awaiting a new assignment, did little to motivate the men of York County to answer the call.[109] But what could be done? How could a few home guards and militiamen stop an enemy army that was yet to be decisively defeated in battle? Apparently, this was the prevailing attitude of most county residents who, rather than flee across the river as some of their neighbors had done, relied on the mercy of the Confederate soldiers for their safety.

When the Confederates entered the Borough of York on June 26, they exacted a requisition for food, clothing, shoes, and $100,000 in Union greenbacks. The *Gazette* reported that "every effort was made to fill the requisition," out of the fear, no doubt, that Early would take what he wanted anyway and then destroy the town for spite.[110] James Latimer noted that "Ward Committees were appointed to collect money, P. A. & S. Small furnished the groceries and flour, and the hatters and shoemakers were called on for the shoes and hats, with the understanding that the Boro' would assume the debt & repay the money & pay for the supplies." The residents scraped together all of the supplies and provisions they could, but collected

---

[108] James Latimer to Bartow Latimer, June 24, 1863, Historical Society of York County (emphasis in original).

[109] "The Crisis—An Appeal: A few practical reasons why the People of the Border Counties of Pennsylvania should respond to the last call of the President for Volunteers," in *York Gazette*, June 23, 1863. A manuscript version in Franklin's handwriting is in the W. B. Franklin Papers, Historical Society of York County.

[110] *York Gazette*, June 30, 1863.

only $28,000 in greenbacks. The Confederates hauled down the American flag flying in the town square and destroyed portions of the rail yard and some of the rolling stock, but generally there was little damage done within the borough. All in all, the Confederate invaders were well behaved. The only military engagements in the county were minor affairs at Wrightsville and Hanover.[111]

On the morning of July 30, Early and his command departed York under orders to rejoin the rest of the Army of Northern Virginia near Gettysburg. During the great battle that followed, Latimer reported that the sound of the cannon could be heard in York.[112] York's military hospital, closed during Early's occupation, was re-opened and began receiving hundreds of Gettysburg's wounded, so many that tents had to be set up to shelter them all.[113] Hanover also became the site of three small military hospitals, with the women of the town tending to the wounded and furnishing the hospitals with food and supplies.[114]

The invasion and subsequent Battle of Gettysburg had a profound effect on the citizens of York County. Livestock and supplies were confiscated, buildings in Wrightsville and Hanover were damaged by small arms and artillery fire, and the people were given a good scare, if nothing else. Some York County residents now became even more determined to defeat the Confederacy, whereas others were convinced that the slaughter should be stopped regardless of the Union's plight. The invasion created more issues and animosities about which the "Copperheads" and the "Black Republicans" would quarrel, and it gave the young men of the county additional reasons either to enlist or evade. To a farmer who had his animals or provisions commandeered, the war might have taken on a character of personal revenge; conversely, it might have convinced him that he had already suffered enough from the war, and to ask him or his sons to risk their lives in combat was asking too much. Likewise, the relatively decent conduct of the Confederate soldiers who occupied the Borough of York might have reinforced an attitude that the southern boys were not that bad after all; if they really wanted to leave the Union, why not let them? To others, however, the humiliation of having the flag disgraced and

---

[111] Ibid.

[112] James Latimer to Bartow Latimer, July 3, 1863, Historical Society of York County.

[113] Prowell, *History of York County*, 421.

[114] *Hanover Spectator*, July 10, 1863.

their soil occupied by an armed enemy was more than they could stand, and made them all the more anxious to enlist and put down the rebellion.

With the enrollment completed and the Confederate menace thwarted, "the order of the Provost Marshal General of July 22nd, 1863, to the Board of Enrollment, directing a draft to be made, was received and acknowledged August 1st, 1863," reported the draft board's Captain Henderson, "and the entire force of the Office was immediately employed in the necessary preparations to comply with the order."[115] Before a draft could be held, the quota for each of the sub-districts had to be determined by the enrollment board. After the quota for the 15th District was received, the board divided the district's quota among the sub-districts, based on the number of men enrolled, and then subtracted from each sub-district's quota the number of men who had volunteered since the last call for troops. If the number of volunteers (known as credits) equaled the quota, then there was no draft held in that sub-district. If the number of credits exceeded the quota, then those credits could be applied to any future drafts.[116]

In order to avoid a draft, town councils and concerned residents made concerted efforts to raise money that they could use to pay additional bounties, which they hoped would stimulate volunteering. They were not successful in their endeavors, however, and on August 20, the draft was held for all sub-districts. A total of 1,837 names were drawn.[117] Conscripts were to report in person within ten days to the PMO at Carlisle, where they would be given a physical examination. If the draftee was found physically fit, he was mustered in. If he was mentally or physically incapable of performing military service, he was issued a discharge certificate. The same process applied to substitutes, except that the "principal" was given a certificate of discharge if the substitute was accepted for service. If a draftee opted to pay the $300 commutation fee, he was required to report to the PMO to pay the fee in person, whence he too would be issued his discharge certificate.[118]

---

[115] Ibid.

[116] Itter, "Conscription," 78.

[117] Descriptive Books of Drafted Men and Substitutes Mustered into Service, August–October 1863, vol. 19, PMGB, RG 110.

[118] Henderson, Report for 15th District.

Commutation was the favored way to avoid service among York Countians in 1863: 613 men became $300 poorer rather than face the perils of the battlefield. Only 159 substitutes were furnished, as most men probably found it cheaper and easier to pay for commutation. There was a total of 1,633 exempts, including those who were medically unfit or were hardship cases, amounting to 89 percent of the quota. Of the remaining men drawn, 136 failed to report; only sixty-eight men actually were held to personal service.[119]

If the number of accepted substitutes is added to the number of drafted men held to personal service, the total credited to the county who actually mustered in was only 192 men (10.5 percent of the total names drawn).[120] The entire 15th District mustered in only 378 men out of 3,460 drawn (10.9 percent).[121] Compared to the state's total of 10,425 men mustered in (including substitutes) out of 82,314 drawn (12.7 percent), York's average of drawn vs. supplied was just under the commonwealth's average. York County also was under the national average of 12.3 percent (292,441 drawn vs. 35,883 draftees and substitutes mustered in).[122]

Unfortunately, the 1863 draft records for the 15th District contain the personal data (age, physical description, occupation, and birthplace) only for those men who either were held to personal service or who were exempted for medical reasons, with just the name, date and place enrolled, and reason for exemption listed for all others. According to these records, most of the sixty-eight men held to personal service were laborers (thirty-two semi/unskilled, twenty skilled), and their average age was twenty-six. Forty-eight of these men were native Pennsylvanians, thirteen were Maryland-born, and there was one each from Ireland, Prussia, Indiana, and Virginia. Seventeen of the men, or 25 percent of those held to service, were black.[123]

The descriptive records for ninety-nine of the substitutes survive,

---

[119] Descriptive Books of Drafted Men and Substitutes Mustered Into Service, August–October 1863, vol. 19, PMGB, RG 110.

[120] Ibid.

[121] Henderson, Report for 15th District.

[122] Murdock, *One Million Men*, 354, 356.

[123] Descriptive Lists, vol. 19, PMGB, RG 110. Of the fifty-nine "colored" men drafted in York County during 1863, seventeen were held to service, sixteen failed to report, ten had medical exemptions, ten had "other" exemptions, three already were serving, and three hired substitutes.

and are complete with all of the personal data properly annotated. These records reveal that the average substitute was twenty-four years of age, was either foreign-born or a from state other than Pennsylvania (only twenty-two of the substitutes listed were born in Pennsylvania), and fell into the "blue-collar" occupational group (skilled, semiskilled and unskilled laborers, and farmers). Of the foreign-born substitutes, twenty-five were German, fifteen were Irish, eight were Canadian (including New Brunswick), and the rest were from England, France, Italy, Spain, Cuba, Switzerland, and Hungary.[124]

Even if some of York County's poor were able to avoid service by paying the commutation fee, it remains true that most of the men who were held to personal service or who became substitutes were poor themselves. Historians have argued whether or not the commutation clause favored low-income draftees.[125] Fred Shannon holds that the clause was a "Concession to the Bourgeoisie" whereas Eugene Murdock and Hugh Earnhart argue that the $300 fee held down the price of substitutes and thus kept the hope of avoiding service within reach of the poor.[126] One thing is for sure: of the sixty-eight men held to personal service, only five could be considered "white-collar" workers (one lawyer, one clerk, two teachers, and a minister). The rest of the men were farmers, skilled laborers, or semi/unskilled laborers, and probably could not have afforded to pay the $300 even if they desired.

There were extralegal ways avoid the service, even if a man was too poor to pay the commutation fee or hire a substitute. The Union League of Lewisberry, a small, northern York County community, made a concerted effort to fill the quota by raising money to hire substitutes or by paying the commutation fee for its residents who

---

[124] Descriptive Books, vol. 19, PMGB, RG 110. It is not possible to ascertain how many of the substitutes (who were foreign born or born out of state) were "imported." Because their residence (at time of enlistment) was not noted in the descriptive books, it may be assumed that many of them were long-time residents of the community and became "subs" because they needed the money, not because a substitute broker went searching for newly landed immigrants. This may be especially true for the Germans, who may have been born overseas but emigrated at a very early age with their families. However, the high percentage of nonnative substitutes also suggests an interstate market in substitutes that was set up to protect the locals while providing a cheap source of substitute manpower.

[125] Murdock, One Million Men, 201.

[126] Shannon, Organization and Administration, 2: 1–45; Murdock, One Million Men, 201–3.

already had been drafted.[127] Purchasing "draft insurance" was another way legally to avoid service. The bylaws of the Washington Township "draft insurance society" stated it would "pay the fines [commutation fees] imposed on those of . . . [the] association who may be drafted, or pay substitutes to serve in the place of such conscripts." For the sum of $100, any man liable to be drafted could become a member with all the benefits that the association provided. If a member of the association was drafted and found exempt for medical or other reasons, he would "be clear from any claims from him by this company and all money paid in by him . . . [would] be refunded except ten dollars."[128] Regrettably, the names of those who belonged to this association have not survived, but the concept was obviously successful: of the eighty-one men drafted in the 9th subdistrict—which included Washington Township—only one was held to personal service.

If a man wanted to avoid conscription but could not afford to pay commutation, hire a substitute, or join a draft insurance society, the only other ways out were by "skedaddling" or fraudulently evading service. Of the 136 men who failed to report in 1863, a few were arrested and held to service but many were never found.[129] On September 21, two men who were drafted but failed to report were arrested in Manheim Township. The special officer who apprehended the culprits reported that "they resisted arrest, and endeavored to make their escape."[130] Similar arrests were made throughout the county not only during the 1863 draft, but also during subsequent drafts.

An easier way to avoid military service was to feign sickness. Levi Cooper, a resident of Peach Bottom Township (located along the Susquehanna River in the county's extreme southeastern corner), wrote a sarcastic note to Captain Henderson stating that he had "no doubt but a good many of the boys had the heart disease at the time

---

[127] J. E. McGrew to R. M. Henderson, December 22, 1863, Letters and Telegrams Received, 1863–1865, 15th District Provost Marshal's Office, PMGB, RG 110.

[128] Ibid.

[129] Descriptive Book of Arrested Deserters, May 1863–September 1865, PMGB, RG 110. Information in the Provost Marshal's records concerning arrests of men who failed to report is sketchy and incomplete, but existing evidence reveals that very few of these men were ever arrested and held to service.

[130] Special Officer Henry Heisner to R. M. Henderson, September 21, 1863, Letters Rec'd, PMGB, RG 110.

of the examination."[131] Thus, it is not surprising that the second largest number of exemptions in the county—456—were for physical disabilities or other medical problems.

One instance of fraud is worth mentioning just to show how men would compromise their integrity to avoid service. Alloise Gruber, a resident of Paradise Township in western York County, was drafted but failed to report. He subsequently "was arrested by a 'special officer' and upon his explanation that he had not received his [draft] notice was released from arrest and reported in person." According to Captain Henderson, "His explanation was satisfactory to the board—so far as to relieve him from the charge of desertion." Gruber then claimed exemption on the grounds that he was the only support of his widowed mother—all the more difficult to believe because he originally maintained that his draft notice was delivered not to his house but to his brother's home. Upon further investigation, the draft board found that Gruber had five other brothers, four of whom were between the ages of twenty and forty-five and all eligible for service. The board rejected his "sole-support" claim and ordered him to report for duty. After all of his lying and conniving, Gruber paid the commutation fee.[132]

As the tumultuous summer of 1863 faded into fall, the citizens of York went to the polls for the November gubernatorial election, which saw the re-election of Andrew Curtin. His Democratic challenger, Judge George Woodward, was described as being "every inch a Copperhead."[133] Not surprisingly, York County voters overwhelmingly supported Woodward, who received 8,069 votes, compared to

---

[131] Levi Cooper to R. M. Henderson, October 6, 1863, Letters Rec'd, PMGB, RG 110. Cooper wrote an earlier letter to Henderson, dated August 16, 1863, inquiring whether or not he could join the Invalid Corps, as he was one of the drafted men from Peach Bottom but was "not able to do military duty from the effects [sic] of a weak leg . . . [and was] near forty-five years of age." He also wondered if he would be able to get a furlough "to put in his crop of wheat and gather his corn." Apparently, Dr. Roland found him fit for service, however, because the descriptive lists for the 24th sub-district show that Cooper paid the commutation fee. Perhaps his gibe at the other shirkers with the "heart disease" was more out of envy than out of duty.

[132] R. M. Henderson to Lt. Col. J. V. Bomford, November 11, 1863, Letters and Telegrams Sent, May 1863–November 1865, vol. 3, 15th District Provost Marshal's Office, PMGB, RG 110.

[133] *Crawford Democrat*, June 30, 1863, quoted in Shankman, *Pennsylvania Antiwar Movement*, 133.

5,512 cast for Curtin.[134] Woodward's popularity among the majority of York County voters demonstrated their strong desire to end the war immediately, for Woodward called for a *status quo antebellum*. According to historian Arnold Shankman, few actually believed that Woodward could help bring an end to the war, but many felt that he could stop the draft in Pennsylvania.[135] With Curtin retaining power, conscription remained unthwarted.

The losses sustained by the Union Army during 1863 and the poor results of the first draft under the 1863 Enrollment Act left the generals in the field screaming for replacements. On October 17, President Lincoln issued a call for 300,000 more volunteers, which was followed by an order on February 1, 1864 to draft 500,000 men. A month and a half later, on March 14, an additional 200,000 men were ordered drafted to fill vacancies not only in the army, but also in the navy and Marine Corps. The draft was scheduled for April 15, 1864, but in the interim the draft districts were allowed to meet their quotas by inducing volunteering, which was to be stimulated by local and state bounties.[136] The 15th District Provost Marshal appointed special agents to procure volunteers, "but owing to the delay in confirming these appointments," Captain Henderson wrote, "the means of accomplishing the object failed, and therefore volunteers were generally procured by committees or individuals acting for Sub-districts."[137] Efforts to raise bounty money began in January, even without the help of "Special Agents." On January 8, the *Gazette* reported that "a considerable amount of money had been raised by the citizens of the borough of York" to exempt it from the draft.[138]

"On the 9th of January, a new arrangement of Sub-districts was made," Henderson recorded in his district's historical report, with

---

[134] Shankman, *Pennsylvania Antiwar Movement*, 136. The state totals were Curtin: 269,496; Woodward: 254,171. Soldiers were not allowed to vote unless they were physically present in their home county on election day; the law providing for absentee ballots had not yet been passed. Even had the York County soldiers been allowed to vote in the field during the 1863 election, their votes would not have been enough to give Curtin a county victory, but it would have made the county election results a little closer.

[135] Ibid, 132–33.

[136] Shannon, *Organization and Administration*, 2: 34.

[137] Henderson, Report for 15th District.

[138] *York Gazette*, January 8, 1864.

"each Township, Ward, or Borough forming one Sub-district; thus increasing the number from 48 to 95." The total number of sub-districts in York County thus increased from twenty-four to forty-three. The realignment gave each township or borough complete autonomy in recruiting men and in raising funds for bounties, thus effectively eliminating the fears of any given township's residents that another township or borough in the same sub-district might not pull its fair share of the load.

A man could collect a substantial amount of money for enlisting, depending on the regiment he joined and the amount of the local bounty. For example, the March 29 issue of the *Gazette* ran a recruiting advertisement for the Pennsylvania Reserve Corps (PRC), which urged readers to "AVOID THE DRAFT" by enlisting in the PRC and collecting a $400 bounty. The local bounty issue became very important after January 1864, when the War Department ordered all volunteers to be credited to the sub-district where they received their local bounty. This order caused a great deal of competition between districts and sub-districts before the law was repealed.[139] The provost marshal for the neighboring 16th District, of which Adams County was a part, wrote that "localities rich in patriotism but poor in means were drained of available material, to make up the numbers demanded of more opulent places."[140] Considering that the average local bounty was $250 in the 15th District during the call of March 14 and just $100 in the 16th District, it is safe to say that he was referring to the adjacent sub-districts in York County.[141]

York County's quota for the spring 1864 draft was 906, but many of the sub-districts avoided it altogether, having raised enough men to meet their quotas by the time the draft arrived. For example, both West Manchester and Jackson townships had supplied enough men in the previous draft to credit them with a surplus in the April draft. Consequently they were not required to furnish men this time around.[142] Other sub-districts were frantically recruiting volunteers,

[139] Itter, "Conscription," 106. Pages 105–112 give a complete account of Pennsylvania's bounty system.

[140] Historical Report for the 16th District, quoted in Itter, "Conscription," 107.

[141] United States War Department, *Final Report of the Provost Marshal General, 1863–1866* (Washington: Government Printing Office, 1866), 218.

[142] Undated newspaper clipping, File 737, Historical Society of York County. The January 6 issue of the *York Gazette* claimed the quota of the county to be 805 men, but contained the qualifier, "The quota, although subject to correction, is believed

and by late January, many had come close to their goal. One newspaper article stated that "a number of townships and Boroughs have put in considerable volunteers since the 31st of January. . . . The First Ward has raised 28 men thus far in February, and has consequently only 18 more to furnish. Since the 31st of January York Township has secured 28 volunteers, and is now only 15 short of the township's quota." The writer concluded that "other Districts have been raising men in the same proportion, and will be out of the Draft." He urged the other sub-districts "to move quickly [or] the draft on the 20th of March will fall heavily upon them."[143]

The descriptive list of volunteers credited to York County sub-districts from December 19, 1863, to June 2, 1864, provides some idea of the type of men who were recruited immediately preceding and during the time of the second federal draft. The list is incomplete, but of the forty-nine men described, thirty-six listed laborer as their occupation, three listed waiter, and one each listed driver, hostler, and seaman. Six of the volunteers on the list were skilled laborers: four carpenters, one cooper, and one wheelwright. Only one man held a white-collar job, and he was a lowly clerk.[144] Additional investigation reveals that almost half of the group was black (twenty-four of forty-nine), and of the twenty-five whites, only twelve were York County natives. The remainder included five who were foreign born and eight who claimed other counties or states as their place of birth. The average age of the volunteers was 26.5 years, but over a third of the group was under twenty-one. Seventeen men were in the 21–29 age group, ten were between 30–39, and five were forty or over.[145] The fact that over a third of the men in this group were under twenty-one and, based on their occupations, probably poor and propertyless, is not unusual; what is unusual is that almost half of this group was black, which is highly disproportionate when compared to the white/black ratio of the 1860 census.[146]

---

to be nearly correct." The confusion surrounding the exact number of men to be supplied is compounded by the 15th District historical report's lack of information on quotas.

[143] Ibid. The draft was not held on March 20, but was postponed until April.

[144] Descriptive Book of Recruits Mustered into Service, December 1863–April 1864, PMGB, RG 110.

[145] Ibid.

[146] Blacks made up less than two percent (1.77 percent) of York County's total population in 1860. Even if the county's black population greatly increased during

When the draft finally arrived, the names of 970 York County men were drawn. Incredibly, only seventeen men were held to personal service. As with the previous draft, the largest number of exemptions were the 399 men who paid the commutation fee, and the second largest group (two hundred) were those disqualified physically or mentally. Fifty-seven of the names drawn belonged to men who already were serving, and twenty-four men found substitutes. The remaining exemptions were granted for "other" reasons (too young or old, deceased, hardship, alien status, nonresident, and excess quota).[147] During this call, the entire 15th District drafted 1,573 men. Of those, thirteen failed to report, thirty-one furnished substitutes, 662 paid commutation, 317 were medically exempt, and 306 were exempt for other reasons. Only thirty-nine men were held to personal service in the three-county district.[148]

Descriptions are available for twenty of the twenty-four substitutes supplied by York County men, and as a group they look very similar to the substitutes furnished in the 1863 draft. Fourteen were foreign born, three were born in other states, one was from another Pennsylvania county, and only two were born in York. Only one substitute was a white-collar worker (clerk). One man was a farmer, four were skilled laborers, and the rest were semiskilled and unskilled. Four were between the ages of sixteen and twenty, thirteen were from twenty-one to twenty-nine, two were between the ages of thirty and thirty-nine, and one was older than forty. All of the substitutes were white.[149]

---

the three years since the census was compiled, the ratio of black enlistees vs. white enlistees when compared to the total county population would still be greatly out of balance. Some states, such as Massachusetts, would send recruiting agents to other northern states and into the Deep South to enlist freed blacks; the black recruits, in turn, would be credited to the district or sub-district that sent the agent on the recruiting mission. There is no evidence, however, that any of York County's sub-districts employed these questionable recruiting tactics: of the twenty-four black men who enlisted from December 1863 to June 1864, eleven were Maryland born (not unusual considering York County bordered Maryland), four were York natives, six were born in other Pennsylvania counties, and only three were from the South (Virginia, South Carolina, and Louisiana).

[147] Descriptive Book of Drafted Men and Substitutes Mustered into Service, May–July 1864, vol. 20, PMGB, RG 110. This list contained the name, residence, and reason for exemption.

[148] Henderson, Report for 15th District. Included in this total were names drawn in two supplementary drafts, which were "needed to fill the places of the men who were exempted" in the original draft. *York Gazette*, July 26, 1864.

[149] Descriptive Book of Drafted Men and Substitutes, vol. 20, PMGB, RG 110.

As with the 1863 draft, the first draft of 1864 saw most of the conscripts escape service, either by commutation or other means. And like the previous draft, the men held to personal service and the men who became substitutes or volunteered were forced to serve either because they were poor and needed the bounty (or substitute money) or because they could not afford to pay the commutation fee. From the number who legally avoided service and based on studies of other states and draft districts, York County probably had more than its fair share of poor men who were able to escape the draft. During the next draft, however, the repeal of the commutation clause forced many men to volunteer or be held to personal service who otherwise might have been able to avoid the perils of the battlefield.

To offset the terrific losses Union armies sustained in the spring and early summer of 1864, and to make up for shortages in the April draft, Lincoln issued another call for troops in July 1864, this time for 500,000 men. The major difference between this draft and the two previous federal drafts was that the commutation clause had been modified so that now only conscientious objectors could pay the $300 fee.[150] With commutation virtually eliminated, the price of substitutes skyrocketed to the exorbitant prices commanded during the 1862 militia draft, and many men who might have been able to avoid conscription now were forced to serve.[151]

The *True Democrat*, a York newspaper that began publication in June 1864 as the voice of the county's Union League, disagreed with the repeal of the clause. Nevertheless, the league decided to support the government's policy: "We do not propose . . . to discuss this question at present. As good citizens we shall counsel obedience to the laws, and acquiesce in any measure calculated to put down this revolt."[152] If nothing else, the clause's repeal would at least force more individuals to become actively involved in the recruiting process, or so thought the writer of the article. "By this bill every man liable to the draft is constituted an efficient recruiting agent. He must either assist in making up the quota of his district, provide a substitute, or go himself in person, if drafted."[153]

---

[150] Edward N. Wright, *Conscientious Objectors in the Civil War* (Philadelphia: University of Pennsylvania Press, 1931), 81–82.

[151] The June 28, 1864, issue of the *York Gazette* reported that "the price of substitutes was from $500 to $700 dollars."

[152] *True Democrat*, July 12, 1864.

[153] Ibid.

The county quota under the call for 500,000 men was 1,685. September 4 was the deadline for the sub-districts to meet their quotas.[154] The repeal of the commutation clause had a profound effect not only on York County, but on the entire 15th District. By the time the draft began, so many men had volunteered that only 515 names were drawn, which meant that the final adjusted quota for the three-county district was only 258 men (the number of names drawn was 100 percent in excess of the quota).[155]

There were several other reasons why the men of the county seemed more eager to volunteer. The editor of the *True Democrat* believed that "the fear of being drafted, together with the large bounty now being offered," created a tendency "in the minds of our young men the desire to volunteer."[156] In addition, the military tide finally turned: Lee and his army were under siege at Petersburg, and Atlanta fell to Union forces on September 2. But there was another important reason why men probably volunteered quicker than they had in the past: the threat of yet another invasion. This time, the Rebels who came to Pennsylvania were not as courteous as before.

On July 30, 1864, Confederate Brigadier General John McCausland demanded a ransom of $500,000 in greenbacks or $100,000 in

---

[154] *Hanover Citizen*, August 11, 1864; *True Democrat*, August 9, 1864.

[155] Henderson, Report for 15th District. Of the 515 men drawn from the entire district, 137 failed to report, sixty-nine furnished substitutes, two noncombatants paid commutation, and forty-two were held to personal service. There were also thirty-nine exempted for medical reasons, and 176 were exempted for "other" reasons. The Descriptive List of Substitutes for Drafted Men, September–December 1864, PMGB, RG 110, shows that, of the sixty-nine substitutes, fifty-two were credited to three York County sub-districts: Hopewell, Conewago, and Fawn Townships. These areas of the county were almost entirely agricultural, and no doubt the men who supplied the substitutes were probably owners of very large farms who were making quite a profit off the war. One resident of Fawn Township was so eager to avoid the recent draft that he failed to report. When apprehended, he claimed exemption "on account of loss of teeth." The draft board determined, however, that the teeth had all been pulled since the lottery was held. This toothless individual then offered to furnish a substitute, but the board determined he was to be held to personal service. Proceedings of the Board of Enrollment, March 31, 1864, vol. 2, p. 7, PMGB, RG 110.

[156] *True Democrat*, August 23, 1864. The August 9 issue of this paper reported that "West Manchester Township has agreed to pay a bounty of $225 to every recruit, until its quota is filled. A number of other townships are about to collect funds and make arrangements, for the purpose of getting out of the draft." *Final Report of the Provost Marshal General* lists $450 as the average local bounty in the 15th District during the July 1864 draft (p. 218).

gold from the town of Chambersburg, sixty miles west of York. The town could not raise the funds, so it was set ablaze as retaliation for the terrible devastation wrought by Union troops on the towns and farms in the Shenandoah Valley.[157] The destruction was complete. York County newspapers described the terrible scenes and appealed to the citizens of York for relief.[158] The thought of a Pennsylvania town going up in smoke, one so close to home, might have been just the motivation that was needed to scare or anger many men into enlisting who might not have otherwise done so. Perhaps the men of nearby Gettysburg had figured this out from their own experiences; enough men had enlisted in 1863 and 1864 to allow that embattled little town to escape all the federal drafts.[159]

The men who volunteered in the summer of 1864 could choose veteran regiments like the 87th or join one of the new twelve-month regiments, such as the 200th Pennsylvania Infantry.[160] A third choice was enlistment in one of the militia regiments that President Lincoln summoned for a hundred days of service in response to Jubal Early's raid into Maryland.[161] Regardless of the regiment they joined or for what reasons, the fact remains that the response was much greater

---

[157] Thomas A. Lewis, *The Shenandoah in Flames* (Alexandria, Va.: Time-Life Books, 1987), 92–93.

[158] *Hanover Spectator*, August 5, 1864; *True Democrat*, August 9, 1864; *York Gazette*, August 9, 1864. The *True Democrat* used this incident to stab its Copperhead competition: "Whether this act of fiendishness will have the effect of staying the toryism in the North and arousing the people to a determination to sweep out of existence those who can burn and destroy helpless women and children, or steep them still farther into advocating a cowardly peace, remains to be seen. For our part, we have little hope for the future so long as bold, bad, men—worse than open rebels—are suffered to stalk through the country, writing, publishing, and uttering the most infamous treason, and poisoning the rural population with premeditated falsehoods respecting the government and its actions, falsehoods which are without parallel in lying outside hell."

[159] Gallman, "Gettysburg's Gettysburg," 166.

[160] Most of the York County men who enlisted in the new one-year organizations were sent to the 200th Pennsylvania Volunteer Infantry, of which companies A, B, D, H, and K were comprised entirely of county residents. There were, however, York County men in the other companies of this regiment, as well as the 201st, 202nd, 207th, 209th, and 210th regiments (information furnished by Dr. Richard Sauers, formerly of the Pennsylvania Capital Preservation Committee). These regiments were organized in Harrisburg in August and September in response to the call for 500,000 troops. Dyer, *Compendium*, 1624–25.

[161] York's quota of militiamen for 100-days' service was 562 (*True Democrat*, July 19, 1864). Men who enlisted in the militia units were not counted toward a subdistrict's quota in the call for 500,000.

this time than during any call for troops since 1861. The August 23 issue of the *True Democrat* reported, "Recruiting has been quite brisk in this town and County for several weeks past. A large number of men . . . have joined volunteer companies, and . . . recruiting for them is still carried on . . . with every prospect that they will have their maximum number in a few days. Several army officers are in town recruiting for new organizations and are meeting with considerable success."[162] York County's response to Lincoln's most recent requests was admirable but, as the fall elections showed, it did not mark a significant change in its residents' collective stance on the war.

An important issue in Pennsylvania in the months preceding the elections was the question of whether or not soldiers stationed outside the commonwealth would be eligible to cast their ballots. Unionists were eager to adopt an amendment to the state constitution that would authorize soldiers in the field to vote. The Copperheads were caught in a quandary; they realized that the soldier vote could cause them to lose the election, but if they refused to support the amendment, they would be accused by their rivals of disloyalty and being ungrateful to the soldiers fighting the war.[163]

The "soldier vote" amendment was decided by a popular referendum on August 2. The Unionists scored a very narrow victory in York County: 4,265 voters supported the amendment; 3,884 were against it.[164] However, the outcome of the vote statewide was an overwhelming approval of the amendment, with 200,000 votes cast for and only 105,000 against.[165] The importance of this amendment would be measured in November, when the soldier vote insured a Lincoln victory in the Keystone State. In that election, York County lived up to its long Democratic tradition, collecting 8,500 votes for Democrat George B. McClellan compared to only 5,277 for Lincoln. York soldiers voting in the field cast 680 votes for Lincoln and 389 for McClellan.[166] The presidential election was so close in Pennsylvania that it took a couple of days for final tabulation. In the end, Lincoln tallied 296,382 votes to McClellan's 276,316, with the state's soldier vote giving Lincoln the edge.[167] Lincoln's victory demonstrated the resolve

---

[162] *True Democrat*, August 23, 1863.

[163] Shankman, *Pennsylvania Antiwar Movement*, 171–72.

[164] *True Democrat*, August 9, 1864.

[165] Shankman, *Pennsylvania Antiwar Movement*, 173; *True Democrat*, August 23, 1864.

[166] *True Democrat*, December 6, 1864; *York Gazette*, November 15, 1864.

[167] Shankman, *Pennsylvania Antiwar Movement*, 201–2. Lincoln received 26,712 soldier votes to McClellan's 12,349.

of the northern states to continue the war until total victory was achieved. More importantly, it signaled to Lincoln that most of his soldiers were staunchly behind him and would fight to the finish.

On Christmas Eve, 1864, Jacob Miller wrote to his brother in York, describing military life along the Mississippi River, near Memphis. As he closed, Miller mentioned that his regiment had recently received some replacements: "we got 75 new recruits last tuesday. they were all drafted men and substitutes. they think it rather ruff but cant be helped."[168] After three and a half years of civil war, the drain on the North's manpower pool had been tremendous, so that by the end of 1864, there were very few men remaining in the army who were fighting for love of country. The soldiers in the Union Army in late 1864 either were hardened veterans like Miller or raw recruits like the draftees and substitutes he described.

As 1864 drew to a close, most people in both the North and the South realized that the war would soon end. Petersburg remained under siege, and Sherman had completed his march to Savannah. The Confederacy's prospects were dismal, and the North's resolve was stronger than ever for unconditional victory. Yet winning the war continued to place a heavy toll on the Union armies. On December 19, the president issued what would be the final call for troops.

York County's quota under the call for 300,000 men—intended to fill the deficiency existing from the last draft—was set at 1,144.[169] As of January 31, little had been accomplished in the way of recruiting, but the *Gazette* attributed the county's slow reaction to the provost marshal general's "delay in assigning the correct quota."[170] By February's end, recruiting had accelerated. Many of the townships and boroughs already had secured their quotas, probably by the continued payment of high bounties and the prospect of impending victory.[171] Apparently the quota for York County, along with the rest of the 15th District, was met because Captain Henderson noted in the district historical report that no draft was held. Some confusion exists here, because records indicate that at least ten men were drafted between

---

[168] Jacob Miller to George Miller, December 24, 1864, George Miller Papers, Historical Society of York County.

[169] *True Democrat*, February 14, 1865.

[170] *York Gazette*, January 31, 1865.

[171] *True Democrat*, February 28, 1865. The average bounty paid in the 15th District during the December 1864 draft had risen to $500. *Final Report of the Provost Marshal General*, 219.

January and April 1865.[172] Henderson might have meant that the draft was cancelled—due to the surrender of the Confederacy— before any of the drafted men were mustered in, but his reports and records failed to mention this.

The men who volunteered or were drafted as a result of the final call probably never made it to a regiment before the war ended, or if they did, they had little chance of seeing any action. Those who had been in combat and lived through it to return home were not quite the same men who had left. Years or months of fighting—or worse yet, stagnating in a prison camp—had affected many of the county's young men. Some returned minus a limb, some came home with mental scars, many never returned at all. As a result of their ordeals, boys like nineteen-year-old Charles Gotwalt had matured far beyond their physical ages.

The civilians of the county likewise were touched by the war, albeit in a different way than the soldiers. Families had experienced the anxiety of sending loved ones to fight, not knowing if they would ever see them again. Invasion by an armed enemy, and the disgrace of surrendering the county seat and capitulating to their demands with- out a shot being fired in its defense would burn in the memories of its residents for generations. (When the Civil War Centennial was celebrated all across the country in the early 1960s, the City of York would not play up its role in the 1863 invasion.) York's military hospi- tal brought the reality of the war home to many citizens, as they witnessed crippled boys trying to recuperate. For the soldiers who were too seriously wounded to recover, a portion of one of York's cemeteries was donated for their burial—a constant reminder to York's residents of the high price of war.

The conflict also accentuated class differences in the county, as the poor were called upon disproportionately to fight for all the other

---

[172] Register of Quotas and Enlistments Credited to Sub-Districts, vol. 1, Records of the Provost Marshal General's Bureau, Record Group 110, National Archives. According to these records, between January and May 1865, York County was cred- ited with having 741 men enlist in volunteer organizations, thirty-nine joined the Regular Army, two enlisted in the navy, one signed up for the Marine Corps, eight were veteran volunteers, fifty-two men supplied substitutes, ten men were drafted and held to personal service, three paid commutation, and four men were listed as "miscellaneous," for a total of 860. These records also indicate that the county quota was 1,087. Even with this lower number, York County did not meet its quota if the statistics in this file are correct.

classes, and the black men whom many residents thought would be a burden to the taxpayers did more than their share. As the war continued, the volunteers became less representative of York County society. Although the majority of the men who enlisted or were drafted in the middle and latter parts of the war were young, their occupational data indicates that they were even less representative of their society than were the soldiers who enlisted in 1861. The draft took men without regard to wealth, race, social status, or ethnicity, but the various methods of legal evasion allowed many to escape service. Once the drafts were completed, the only citizens who had enlisted or were drafted and held to personal service were the poor, both white and black—and those few who were drafted and could afford to hire a substitute or pay commutation but acquiesced and enlisted anyway. The commutation clause allowed some poor men to avoid the service in 1863 and early 1864, but its repeal in the summer of 1864 crushed their hopes of escaping the battlefields.

Opposition to the draft was extremely mild when compared to New York's draft riots or the hostility exhibited in other areas of Pennsylvania, particularly the coal regions. Unlike the defiance that occurred in 1863, in Holmes County, Ohio, there was no organized resistance at all in York County, and those who refused to serve either paid commutation, hired a substitute, or "skedaddled."[173] Copperhead newpapers took a few shots at the Enrollment Act, but when quotas were announced the editors urged their readers to enlist or help in the recruiting effort.

By the time of the July 1864 draft, the recruiting game had become

---

[173] The most thorough account of the NYC draft riots is Iver Bernstein's *The New York City Draft Riots: Their Significance for American Society and Politics in the Age of The Civil War* (New York: Oxford University Press, 1990). For a discussion of draft resistance in the Pennsylvania coal fields, see Grace Palladino, *Another Civil War: Labor, Capital, and the State in the Anthracite Coal Regions of Pennsylvania, 1840–68* (Urbana: University of Illinois Press, 1990). A study of organized draft resistance in Holmes County, Ohio, is Kenneth H. Wheeler's "Local Autonomy and Civil War Draft Resistance: Holmes County, Ohio," *Civil War History* 45 (June 1999): 147–59. Wheeler argues that resisters in Holmes County, a rural, rather isolated region, were "culturally and ideologically hostile, at the very least, to federal conscription as a centralizing force. The Holmes County draft resisters believed that the Republican party and the Lincoln administration's policies threatened the world in which they lived. Thus, the resistance to conscription provides one example of opposition to the advance of modernization from within the Northern states, and places the context of worldwide encounters between traditional and modern ways." (158–59).

almost a matter of ritual to most of York County's townships and boroughs, so when the actual lottery occurred, only a few of the townships in the extreme southeastern and southern parts of the county were held to the draft. The bounty system was organized by local committees of citizens at the sub-district level, with money for local bounties raised by residents' donations, town council appropriations, and per capita taxes. The problems of bounty jumping and abuses of the substitute system by brokers do not appear to have been prevalent in the county, as no mention of these practices was noted in any of the local newspapers or in the 15th District provost marshal's final report.[174]

When county soldiers departed for the war, the local communities did their best to support and care for their families. As late as 1867, the "York Borough Soldiers' Relief Fund" still made payments to store owners for goods that had been supplied to the needy families of the soldiers. During the war, the fund also made cash payments to and for "Officers, Soldiers, Soldiers' wives and children, and widows and orphans, medicines and medical aid for wounded on the Gettysburg battle field."[175] The women of York County organized a relief organization for Union soldiers at the beginning of the war, and continued their successful management of it throughout the conflict. The culmination of their efforts was a benefit fair in February 1864, which raised money for the county's sick and wounded soldiers in the many military hospitals throughout the North. Despite their lack of enthusiasm for military service, the people of York County continued to

---

[174] Henderson, Report for 15th District. Captain Henderson made no mention of any problems incurred by substitute brokers abusing the system. In the "Letters Sent" file, he discussed an investigation into the facts concerning the case of a young soldier sent home "on sick furlough and was afterwards enlisted as a substitute or volunteer by parties in York." It is not known, however, whether or not this was the work of a broker or just some crafty individual (J. W. Patton to James Kindig, October 28, 1864, vol. 4, Letter's Sent, PMGB, RG 110). Another letter in the same file discusses the capture of two deserters in York, presumably bounty jumpers, but no mention is made whether or not they were York residents (R. M. Henderson to J. V. Bomford, May 25, 1864, vol. 4, Letters Sent, PMGB, RG 110). The historical report for the district lists 586 deserters as having been arrested in the 15th District, but the number of bounty jumpers included in that total is not annotated. Henderson apparently did not think bounty jumping, or for that matter, substitute brokering, was enough of a problem in his district tomention it in the final report.

[175] Committee Minutes of the York Borough Soldiers' Relief Fund, June 25, 1867, File 737, Historical Society of York County.

support their soldiers and the soldiers' families through 1865 and beyond.

Political factions attacked each other throughout the course of the war, but when it came to supporting the common soldier, both Unionists and Copperheads paid him due respect. The issue of equality for African Americans was another matter, however, and when the war took on the character of a struggle to free the slaves, many county residents began openly to oppose the conflict. The hostility generated toward emancipation, coupled with the severe losses sustained by Union forces in the winter of 1862 and the spring of 1863, had a negative effect not only on York County, but across the rest of the North. A series of federal drafts appeared to be the only way to stimulate volunteering from this point of the conflict until its end.

The war over, York's soldiers returned to parades, banquets, and ceremonies. Many of the county's communities celebrated with grand illuminations and torchlight processions, with everyone in the neighborhood set to "do it up right" for the returning heroes. "Certainly the surrender of Lee," as one paper put it, "is a victory such as we never had before to rejoice over."[176]

The citizens of York County had endured a great deal during the Civil War, perhaps even more than most other northern communities. Years later, old men throughout the county gathered at Grand Army of the Republic posts to reminisce about the war and the friends they left behind on the battlefields of the South; some even returned to the battlefields to dedicate monuments in memory of their fallen comrades.[177] The Union victory, however, did not usher in a new political era in York County. The strong Democratic tradition continued in the county for the remainder of the century until Teddy Roosevelt (1904) broke the stranglehold the Democrats enjoyed for so long. York County would send its sons (and daughters) to fight in other wars, and its people would be subjected to more drafts, but none of these events, not even the uproar over Vietnam, could compare to the trauma caused by the Civil War.

---

[176] *Hanover Spectator,* April 14, 1865.

[177] The 187th Pennsylvania is commemorated with two other Pennsylvania regiments on a monument located on the Monocacy battlefield, near Frederick, Maryland. The 130th Infantry is memorialized at Antietam; the 107th Infantry, 1st Reserves, 12th Reserves, 21st Cavalry, and 26th Emergency have monuments at Gettysburg.

2

Northerners and
Their Men in Arms

4

"Tell Me What the Sensations Are": The Northern Home Front Learns about Combat

Earl J. Hess

THE EXPERIENCE of combat in the Civil War was so different from anything the soldiers had seen in their civilian life that a yawning gulf of experience opened up to separate the army from the home front. Soldiers knew from their first encounter with battle what it was like to experience war. They heard the whistle of artillery and the singing of small arms fire; they saw the billowing smoke and the torn, mutilated bodies of comrades; they smelled the burning powder, the fresh odor of blood, and the rotting corpses on the battlefield; and they felt the physical sensations of near misses by Minié balls and the shocking pain of getting hit. No soldier had to wonder what it was like to be under fire after he had made the initial crossing over the gulf of experience, which was a rite of passage for the naive recruit.[1]

But what of the civilians left behind? Were soldiers the only ones who could know what it was like to be in battle? Were they the only ones in northern society who cared to learn what it was like? A great many if not the majority of northern civilians doubtless never bothered to ponder these questions. They were separated from the battle experience in the most basic way, and they probably were quite happy to ignore it. The North's large population meant that comparatively few northerners would be called on to join the army, and the fact that most of the fighting took place on southern soil meant that they could afford to continue life much as usual while the conflict raged. For many northern civilians, it was almost as if the war was

---

[1] Earl J. Hess, *The Union Soldier in Battle: Enduring the Ordeal of Combat* (Lawrence: University Press of Kansas, 1997), 19–21.

conducted in a foreign land. Samuel Chester Gale, a lawyer in Minneapolis, pondered this. "It is difficult for me and us in Minn. so far removed from the seat of action, to realize that we are in the midst of a great civil war[;] we see no devastating army—no dead and wounded, our industries go on much as usual."[2]

Yet the war thrust itself into the consciousness of many northerners who avidly sought contact with it. The media of the North— newspapers, illustrated weeklies, and the new art of photography— covered the war and the battle experience with a wide degree of effectiveness, ranging from the incompetent to the compelling.[3] For those civilians who were not content with media images and journalistic reporting, there were other ways to foster contact with the experience of war. Civilians eagerly sought information from friends and relatives in the army; they visited battlefields immediately after the firing stopped to observe the aftermath of war; they visited relatives in the army and insisted on being shown the fighting front. Still other civilians volunteered to work in military hospitals. A small minority of women disguised themselves as men to experience war firsthand. Many of these people who deliberately placed themselves in a position to see combat or its effects were mere tourists, motivated only by a desire to be entertained and to have a novel experience; still others were motivated by a desire to scavenge what material they could from the debris that littered the battlefields after a heavy engagement. Yet there were many northern civilians who not only were eager to learn about combat but also took the lessons to heart. Their experiences tied the home front a bit more securely to the armies that saved the Union. The gulf of experience was wide and difficult to cross, but it could be reduced by a sincere willingness of civilians to know what the soldiers were going through.

The desire to learn about war often was inspired by news of combat. William Henry Jackson, a Vermont artist, did not think much about the conflict until word of First Bull Run reached his little town

---

[2] Bell Irvin Wiley, *The Life of Billy Yank: The Common Soldier of the Union* (Indianapolis: Bobbs-Merrill Co., 1952; reprint, Baton Rouge: Louisiana State University Press, 1983), 360; and entry for June 27, 1861, Samuel Chester Gale Diary, Minnesota Historical Society, St. Paul.

[3] Earl J. Hess, "The Portrayal of Combat in Civil War Media," in *An Uncommon Time: The Civil War and the Northern Home Front*, ed. by Paul A. Cimbala and Randall M. Miller (New York: Fordham University Press, forthcoming).

of Rutland. "We had all grown used to thinking of the struggle between North and South as a clash of ideas instead of men," he wrote. The battle made Jackson realize that the war was now a contest of flesh and blood.[4]

Other civilians began to think about combat when they saw uniformed men parading through their streets. A New Yorker named G. B. Johnson assured his wife that *"when you see thousands* of men march through the streets on their way to the field of Battles as this city has witnessed this day *the war* begins to be a reality." Sidney George Fisher of Philadelphia witnessed the presentation of a flag to the 6th Pennsylvania Cavalry and noted the "stern reality" of the event. "It was no holiday parade, no playing soldiers, but what we saw was the preparation for actual war and the men before us were, we knew, in a few days to be marched away to a distant region, there to encounter danger and death."[5]

For Walt Whitman, who admitted to an insatiable desire for "more & more knowledge of actual soldiers' life," the sight of a cavalry regiment passing through the streets of Washington "had the look of *real war*." Whitman grew to become such a connoisseur of martial imagery that he was disappointed with the sight of unbloodied garrison troops. After watching the veteran IX Corps pass through Washington, he concluded it was "different to see a real army of fighting men, from one of those shows in Brooklyn, or New York, or on fort Greene." The dirty uniforms, weapons cleaned for bloody use, and the men's good spirits despite a night of soaking rain seemed to evoke a truer reality of war for Whitman.[6]

New York lawyer George Templeton Strong suggested that a gritty evocation of reality could jar civilians into thinking about war. He witnessed the funeral parade for Elmer Ellsworth, the first martyred

---

[4] William Henry Jackson, *Time Exposure: The Autobiography of William Henry Jackson* (New York: G. P. Putnam's Sons, 1940), 38.

[5] G. B. Johnson to wife, April 18, 1861, Steljes Collection, Harrisburg Civil War Round Table Collection, Archives, United States Army Military History Institute, Carlisle, Pa. (USAMHI); and entry for October 30, 1861, *A Philadelphia Perspective: The Diary of Sidney George Fisher Covering the Years 1834–1871*, ed. by Nicholas B. Wainwright (Philadelphia: Historical Society of Pennsylvania, 1967). 406–7.

[6] Walt Whitman to Louisa Van Velsor Whitman, February 12, 1864, June 30, 1863, and April 26, 1864, in *Walt Whitman: The Correspondence*, vol. 1: *1842–1867*, ed. by Edwin Haviland Miller (New York: New York University Press, 1961), 198, 114, 212.

hero of the North. Ellsworth was killed by a secessionist hotelkeeper in Alexandria, Virginia, when he tried to raise the Stars and Stripes in May 1861. Private Brownell, who in turn killed the hotelkeeper, rode beside the hearse driver with his bayonetted rifle. "This close juxtaposition of the murdered colonel with the bayonet that was red with his murderer's lifeblood forty-eight hours ago" violated the "solemn decencies" of a peacetime funeral. Yet the tableau was "significant—a stern symbol of the feeling that begins to prevail from Maine to Minnesota."[7]

The Ellsworth murder also became the first war incident that drew hordes of souvenir seekers. With Alexandria now in Union hands, many devoted patriots both in uniform and out had access to the Marshall House, where Ellsworth was killed. Lawrence W. Sandrino, a member of a New York regiment, was amazed at what the souvenir hunters had done to the house within a month after Ellsworth was killed. "[S]uch a looking house you or any [one] els never seen racked and torn to pieces. the floor and furniture torn to pieces. the stairs on which Elswort was shot is all carried away in pieces by visitors, the flag staf on which the rebels had their ensign flying, there is now the glorious stars & stripes. the staff is on the top of the house, the bottom of it cut allmost away." Sandrino took his own part of the loot. He sent to his mother a piece of the floor, a part of the whittled flag staff, a piece of the bed tick on which the murderer was laid after he was stabbed by Private Brownell, and a piece of wallpaper from the hotelkeeper's bedroom. Sandrino intended to send more relics to other relatives. He told his mother, "I do not know if they are of any good to you, but here they demand a good price."[8]

The public obsession with Ellsworth's death underscored a widespread realization that the military experience was alien yet interesting. There was a morbid fascination, to be sure, but there also was a genuine desire to learn more about it. Mary Christian Percy of Watertown, New York, wrote to her brother that "we are of an inquisitive turn just now—and have a famous appetite for details." Her curiosity was insistent. "Can't you tell us how you live—& how you employ

---

[7] Entry for May 26, 1861, *The Diary of George Templeton Strong: The Civil War, 1860–1865,* ed. by Allan Nevins and Milton Halsey Thomas (New York: Macmillan, 1962), 147.

[8] Lawrence W. Sandrino to mother, June 18, 1861, Ephraim Elmer Ellsworth Collection, Chicago Historical Society.

your time—whether you go out picketing—or foraging—in fact *what you do—& how you do it.*"[9]

Percy wanted to know about all facets of her brother's military experience, but many others zeroed in on the experience of battle. They asked for descriptions of combat and especially of the sensations one had upon entering it. Kansas farmer Samuel Reader assured his half brother that such information would "be read by us all with the greatest avidity." Ironically, much later in the war, Reader would himself experience what war was like when he served in a Kansas militia regiment and helped repel Sterling Price's attempt to invade the state. The inquisitive Mary Percy sought more specific knowledge than did Reader. "I want to talk with one who has been in a real bona-fide fight. I want him to tell me what the sensations are, whether one feels like running or fighting most."[10]

Letters from the home front to soldiers were often thrown away or lost because of the demands of active campaigning. Thus the historian is often forced to detect signs of civilian interest in war narratives by examining the opposite flow of mail, from soldiers to the home front. Soldiers often commented in their missives, "You wanted to know how we felt in the battle," or "you ask me to tell you all about the battle." Sometimes civilian curiosity could be intrusive. Major James Connolly of the 123rd Illinois answered his wife with a gentle lecture. "In your last letter you seem to think I don't give you enough description of battles armies, scenery, etc. If you were as tired of battles and armies as I am you wouldn't care to spend much time on them for they are very unpleasant things to be in and one does not like to reproduce memories of unpleasant things."[11]

Many soldiers were grateful that a gulf of experience existed between them and their loved ones at home. "Nothing gratifies me

---

[9] Mary Christian Percy to Henry, May 17, 1861, February 23, 1862, Augustus Cowan Papers, Illinois State Historical Library, Springfield.

[10] Samuel James Reader to Frank, August 11, 1861, in "The Letters of Samuel James Reader, 1861–1863," *Kansas Historical Quarterly* 9 (February 1940): 43; and Mary Christian Percy to Henry, September 30, 1862, Augustus Cowan Papers.

[11] John Burrill to parents, July 11, 1862, John Burrill Papers, *Civil War Times Illustrated* Collection, USAMHI; Charles E. Perkins to Sister, July 20, 1862, in "Letters Home: Sergeant Charles E. Perkins in Virginia, 1862," ed. by Ray Henshaw and Glenn W. LaFantasie, *Rhode Island History* 39 (November 1980): 118; and James A. Connolly to Mary, November 5, 1863, in *Three Years in the Army of the Cumberland: The Letters and Diaries of James A. Connolly*, ed. by Paul M. Angle (Bloomington: Indiana University Press), 136.

more than your absence," wrote W. H. Clune of the 6th Iowa after Shiloh. "No woman could behold the torn limbs, headless trunks and mangled corpses, but the dreadful scene of carnage would throw its dark and gloomy shadow over every future season of mirth and gayety."[12]

Yet the sentiments expressed by Connolly and Clune were not necessarily typical of all soldiers. In fact, many of them were only too happy to describe the most gory details of the battlefield and thus begin to satisfy home front desire to learn about combat. It was a way for them to regain contact with loved ones. A Massachussetts volunteer named John Barnard was amazed at the change in his writing habits in the army. "Before when I was from home I felt no inclination for writing and none to hear from home[,] now when a chance offers I must write." But circumstances often interfered. Busy with camp chores, soldiers often had to squeeze correspondence into their spare moments. "I do not have the opportunity of writing letters that a person does at home," complained Thomas H. Benton of Indiana. Jacob Behm of Illinois succinctly detailed a common problem. "It appears when I have time too [sic] write, I have nothing of importance too write, and when I could write a Letter of interest, I have no time too [sic] write."[13]

William H. Tebbetts would have heartily agreed with Behm. He wanted to write a full account of the Fort Donelson campaign, but his leaky tent refused to keep the rain out and he had "no convenience to write excepting" on his knee. Other men assured their home front correspondents that full descriptions would be forthcoming except for two essentials, paper and time. Faced with these difficulties, several soldiers simply referred their correspondents to newspaper accounts, "and you will know more than if I was to write all the time."[14]

---

[12] W. H. Clune to wife, April 13, 1862, W. H. Clune Papers, Iowa State Department of History and Archives, Des Moines.

[13] John Barnard to Sarah, December 23, 1862, John Barnard Papers, Manuscript Department, William R. Perkins Library, Duke University, Durham, N. C.; Thomas H. Benton to Sister, July 2, 1862, Thomas H. Benton Papers, Indiana Historical Society, Indianapolis; and Jacob Behm to Sister and Brother, December 21, 1863, Jacob Behm Papers, *Civil War Times Illustrated* Collection, USAMHI.

[14] William H. Tebbets to Sister, March 2, 1862, in "The Story of an Ordinary Man," ed. by Paul M. Angle, *Journal of the Illinois State Historical Society* 33 (June 1940): 232; Frank Malcolm to wife, August 24, 1864, in " 'Such is War': The Letters of an Orderly in the 7th Iowa Infantry," ed. by James I. Robertson, Jr., *Iowa Journal of History* 58 (October 1960): 335; Edward A. Acton to Mary, July 5, 1862, in " 'Dear

But when they did write letters home, soldiers had an opportunity to convey detailed, authentic information about the battle experience. Although some of them failed to capitalize on that opportunity because of their limited powers of observation and description, the truth was that soldier accounts are the most powerful body of writing about the experience of combat in the Civil War. Those men who referred their correspondents to newspapers did their comrades a disservice, for journalists consistently failed to inform the home front about the nature of combat. A civilian who had an honest, observant, and literate soldier in the army had the best chance of learning about the sensations of battle.[15]

Soldier letters not only conveyed information, they sometimes became relics of the battlefield. A letter written by a Confederate soldier was often found on the battlefield and sent home by a Unionist as a souvenir. Even more ghastly and vivid reminders of the destructive nature of combat were conveyed by bloodstained letters, written when the soldier was recuperating from a battlefield wound. Infantryman T. J. Tillison went a step farther when he sent home a lock of bloody hair from a comrade whose head wound proved fatal during the Atlanta campaign. Surgeon Abraham Welch, who was busy with the wounded for hours after a major engagement, sent a letter home in an envelope that was smeared in someone's blood. He explained, "It dropped from my pocket while performing an operation of amputating a leg at Fredericksburg."[16]

These letters, envelopes, and locks of hair brought the nature of conflict home to civilians. The home front also sought relics of a less personal nature. The sale of battle souvenirs was brisk in captured Confederate territory, as Lawrence Sandrino had already observed of

Mollie': Letters of Captain Edward A. Acton to His Wife, 1862," ed. by Mary Acton Hammond, *Pennsylvania Magazine of History and Biography* 89 (January 1965): 25; and Benjamin Stevens to Friends, April 13, 1962, in "The Civil War Letters of an Iowa Family," ed. by Richard N. Willis, *Annals of Iowa* 39 (spring 1969): 568.

[15] Hess, "Portrayal of Combat."

[16] James J. Cleer to father and mother, January 17, 1865, James J. Cleer Papers, Manuscript Department, William R. Perkins Library, Duke University, Durham, N. C.; James H. Rigby to Father, December 12, 1862, in "Three Civil War Letters of James H. Rigby, A Maryland Federal Artillery Officer," ed. by C. A. Porter Hopkins, *Maryland Historical Magazine* 57 (June 1962): 159; T. J. Tillison to Friends, June 7, 1864, Gregory A. Coco Collection, USAMHI; and Abraham Welch to Mary Ann, December 27, 1862, Abraham Welch Papers, Southern Historical Collection, University of North Carolina, Chapel Hill.

the Marshall House in Alexandria. Civilians who went south to work for the United States Sanitary Commission at Fort Henry, Tennessee, were also eager for artifacts. The soldiers obliged by selling Union grape shot and bullets as Confederate ordnance. They received $2.50 for the former and fifty cents for the latter.[17]

The numerous Sanitary Fairs held in the North's larger cities gave civilians an opportunity to examine and purchase battlefield relics closer to home, the proceeds being applied to soldier relief. Only lesser relics were sold. Items that were larger or unique were simply put on display to excite the interest of curious visitors. Weapons, ammunition, captured Rebel flags, and even the bloodstained uniform of Elmer Ellsworth were exhibited.[18]

The exhibits at Sanitary Fairs drew thousands of visitors, but it was also possible for a single soldier to draw a crowd of fascinated civilians when he returned home. Artilleryman Patrick H. White became an object of compelling interest when he arrived at his sister's home in Chicago following the battle of Shiloh. He still wore the clothes that saw him through the engagement. They held seventeen bullet holes—mostly his coat and the rear portion of his trousers were riddled—but he was not hurt. White was so tired that the first thing he did was fall asleep on the sofa, even though neighbors came streaming in to see him. His sister proudly displayed the torn coat and then pointed toward his pants. " 'And here are more bullet holes,' " she said, "turning me over as I laid on the lounge to keep that part covered."[19]

Relics of all kinds were a material way for civilians to gain some firsthand exposure to the battlefield, although in a delayed and indirect way. Another source of second-hand information included the rumor mill, but it was of a decidedly inferior quality. Rumors spread rapidly through the towns and cities of the North whenever some late-breaking news was on the horizon. Mary C. Percy of Watertown, New York, noted how rumors flew about "in this drowsy town," but

[17] Robert Price to Father, April 21, 1862, Robert Price Papers, Indiana Historical Society, Indianapolis.

[18] William Y. Thompson, "Sanitary Fairs of the Civil War," *Civil War History* 4 (March 1958): 51–67. See the photographs of Sanitary Fair displays in William C. Davis, ed., *The Image of War, 1861–1865*, vol. 1: *Shadows of the Storm* (Garden City, N. Y.: Doubleday, 1981), 400–4.

[19] Patrick H. White, "Civil War Diary of Patrick H. White," *Journal of the Illinois State Historical Society* 15 (October 1922–January 1923): 655.

she had the common sense to take them with a large grain of salt. A hospital worker in New York City, far from the fighting in Virginia, commented on the "wild & exciting reports" that were "coined from feverish & unreliable rumors." Ruth A. Whittemore of Owego, New York, often complained of hearing no news except that which was "too absurd to believe: you know there are busy-bodies every where that take particular delight in telling some thing wonderful. They will catch a word here and another there and then fill up the outline from their own excited imaginations and make out a story that any one else never heard or thought of."[20]

Charles Johnson recorded the flow of rumors in Pocahontas, Illinois. News of Shiloh circulated in the following form. "Hain't heerd 'bout the big fight on the 'Tenisy,' I reckon? That Gin'rl that hop'd [helped] the gunboats take them air forts down thar, whar they ketched so many sojers—Donels'n, and Henery, b'lieve they call 'em. I forgit his name—O yes, Grant. Well, 'he's got "whurp'd' " [whipped] mighty bad, him and his army—got his'n all cut up and lots of 'em tuck pris'ner. Some's sayin' they reckon he must 'a' been in licker to git 'whurp'd' that away. They fit two whole days, and if it hadn't ben for them air gunboats helpin', him and his whole army been tuck pris'ner, shore. They are sayin': 'Pears like Grant's awful lucky gittin' hop'ed from gunboats.' "[21]

In contrast to many rumors found in the issues of any major newspaper of the North, Johnson's re-creation of the Pocahontas rumor mill indicates that this bit of information about Shiloh was in the main accurate. But it was of value only if one wanted the most unrefined kind of information, such as who won and who lost at Shiloh. For any other type of knowledge, such as the nature of combat, the feelings of the soldiers, the physical nature of fighting with modern weapons and tactics, rumors were grossly inadequate despite their colorful and entertaining character.

Curiosity about all that related to combat spoke of a deep-seated

---

[20] Mary Christian Percy to Henry, March 9, 1862, Augustus Cowan Papers; New York Night Watcher's Club Journal, May 7, 1864, Illinois State Historical Library; Ruth A. Whittemore to Charles Ingersoll, December 1, 1861, in " 'Despotism to Traitors': The Rebellious South through New York Eyes," ed. by Walter Rundell, Jr., *New York History* 45 (October 1964): 336–37.

[21] Charles Beneulyn Johnson, *Muskets and Medicine, or Army Life in the Sixties* (Philadelphia: F. A. Davis, 1917), 24, 26.

longing among many civilians to make contact with war. There was here an aching impatience with the lack of information. Yet for many civilians, exposure to combat was a double-edged sword. Their curiosity was laced with personal significance if a loved one was exposed to the dangers of the battlefield. Letters from soldiers both eased and intensified the feelings of anxiety. "I spoke of the letters that came from the front," wrote George Daggett, who spent his adolescence in wartime Norwalk, Ohio. "They were frequent and regular at first, but later came at greater intervals and were fraught with tragic interest." Civilians were tied to the soldier experience by this string of correspondence; they could be relieved by good news and driven to a frenzy of worry by the absence of any letters. Daggett wrote movingly of this.

> Do you wonder that the children of that time grew prematurely old, who listened to the booming of cannon, and knew by the blanched face of their mother that, while it was celebrating a victory, it might also be sounding the death knell of a father? How often I have seen mother snatch a paper, and, without drawing a breath, scan the list of dead and wounded, and whenever we boys went for mail, how, when a letter was handed out with the well known writing . . . we would run like deer for home, to be met at the gate. All around us were sympathetic friends and neighbors, and during the long nights of suspense they gathered at the house to talk, and to pour oil upon the troubled waters.[22]

In this atmosphere of unease, civilians were often reminded of the dangers their loved ones tempted. The sudden discharge of a pistol by an Independence Day reveler startled Alice Grierson, whose husband was an Illinois cavalry officer. "[I]t made me think how dreadful it would be to have you face the deadly cannon of a battle field, and of the possibility that you may have to brave that danger." A Pennsylvania woman living in Chambersburg, quite near the scene of Lee's Gettysburg campaign, was upset by the report that a fearful battle was underway. "[T]he shock was so great that I got quite

---

[22] George Henry Daggett, "Those Whom You Left Behind You," *Glimpses of the Nation's Struggle: Papers Read before the Minnesota Commandery of the Military Order of the Loyal Legion of the United States, 1897–1902*, fifth Series (St. Paul: Review, 1903), 335, 337.

weak & immagined that I could already see My Samuel falling—I feel very uneasy about him—I cannot hear [about him] at all."[23]

When their worst fears proved true, civilians were faced with the ultimate challenge of the war. Many reacted stolidly and in ways guaranteed to sustain both their courage and their loved ones. A Michigan schoolteacher named Julia S. Freeman later remembered that news of her brother's wounding was brought by a little girl who interrupted a classroom recitation at precisely three o'clock on a September afternoon. She immediately left with a sister for Virginia to care for him. Marjorie Ann Rogers of Iowa described how similar news could absolutely crush the life out of a civilian. An acquaintance of hers told a woman that her husband had died in battle. Rogers recorded the reaction: she "did not speak or shed a tear, but stared at me as if I was not telling the truth. I never experienced anything like it in all the suffering I had seen." The widow eventually fainted, but later that day recovered enough to say, "I want to see my mother and then die." She had her wish. The mother arrived and a few days later buried her daughter. "Nothing could keep her," reported the friend who had brought the sad news, "she wanted to die and God let her die, and I was glad she could."[24]

In Chelsea, Massachusetts, Charles Currier described the feelings provoked by the war among civilians:

> It was our first thought in the morning: it clung to us by day, and hung phantom like over us at night; it turned our churches into depositories of hospital supplies, and made lint pickers of the worshippers. It was the constant recurrence of such events that had wafted to the winds, whatever of novelty or romance had been connected with earlier days of the strife, and settled thoughtful men into the conviction, that until it was fought to a conclusion, it must be made the absorbing business of the entire North. . . . Our only topic of discussion on the street, in office and store, nay, even in the pulpit, that of War! Grim, cruel war![25]

---

[23] Alice Grierson to Ben, July 7, 1861, Benjamin G. Grierson Papers, Illinois State Historical Library; and entry for July 2, 1863, Rachel Cormany diary, in *The Cormany Diaries: A Northern Family in the Civil War*, ed. by James C. Mohr (Pittsburgh: University of Pittsburgh Press, 1982), 339.

[24] Julia S. Freeman, *The Boys in White: The Experience of a Hospital Agent In and Around Washington* (New York: Lange and Hillman, 1870), 10; and Marjorie Ann Rogers, "An Iowa Woman in Wartime," *Annals of Iowa* 36 (summer 1961): 31.

[25] Charles A. Currier, "Recollections of Service with the Fortieth Massachusetts

Both civilians and soldiers fully realized that a gulf of experience separated them, that the home front could only with difficulty begin to understand what combat was like. But many soldiers were just as fully aware that they could not fully understand the emotional difficulties of being a civilian during wartime. The dreadful worry that attacked all civilians who had a loved one in the army was glimpsed by only the more perceptive of soldiers. "To them it was one long, dark night of suspense," recalled George P. Metcalf of the 136th New York. Colonel Bazel F. Lazear of Missouri wrote to his wife about it. "You have none of the excitement of the camp the march and the battle field to keep you up." No matter how hard they tried, combatants "could not fully enter into the sad, self-denying lives" that civilians led, according to another soldier.[26]

A great many civilians tried to understand combat by pestering soldiers for more letters, viewing relics at Sanitary Fairs, or pumping soldiers on leave for information; others sought to gain some familiarity with it by working in the hospitals, viewing battlefields, or even placing themselves under enemy fire. Of these types of encounters, the most common was the sight of the wounded, as thousands of civilians either volunteered as nurses or visited hospitals. Obviously not everyone who did this was motivated purely, or even primarily, by a desire to learn about combat. The major motivation was a humanitarian impulse or a patriotic zeal. Anna Morris Holstein spoke for many when she wrote of the wounded, "With all loyal women of the land, I worked zealously in their behalf; worked because there was irresistable impulse *to do, to act*. Anything but idleness, when our armies were preparing for the combat, and we knew not who should be the first to fall, who be called *widow*, or who *fatherless*."[27]

But nurses quickly came to realize that their work gave them a marvelous opportunity to learn more than they expected about the nature of combat. John Foster accompanied a group of hospital volunteers from Philadelphia's Ascension Church to Gettysburg. They arrived there only a week after the fighting. Foster learned with astonishment how battle affected the individual:

Infantry Volunteers," 4, Military Order of the Loyal Legion of the United States, Massachusetts Commandery Collection, USAMHI.

[26] George P. Metcalf Memoir, 159, Harrisburg Civil War Round Table-Gregory Coco Collection, USAMHI.

[27] Anna Morris Holstein, *Three Years in Field Hospitals of the Army of the Potomac* (Philadelphia: J. B. Lippincott, 1867), 10.

The wounds were of every imaginable description, and upon all parts of the person. There were wounds in the head, the breast, the abdomen, the legs, the feet, the hands; there were wounds of the flesh merely, and others affecting the vital organism; in some cases legs and arms were shot away so closely to the socket that it was impossible to gather up the cords, and the hurts were necessarily cauterized or left to fester and eat away the life; in others, the face would be partly shot away, leaving, perhaps, only a single eye or row of teeth; while in others still, simply an ear, or finger, or part of the nose would be missing.[28]

Foster moved a long way across the gulf of experience when he went to Gettysburg to care for the wounded, and other nurses felt the same way about their own encounters with the hospitals. "We often read of war and say it is sad," mused Mary A. Newcomb, "but one must see the battle-field and be with the wounded and dead to have an adequate idea of war." A hard-pressed volunteer nurse named Katherine Prescott Wormeley, who was suddenly presented with eighty more wounded to attend, confessed "this was like being on a battle-field. The men were just as they fell, in their muddy clothing, saturated with blood and filth."[29]

"I had never been so near death before," wrote Sophronia Bucklin of her first exposure to the hospitals. "The horror of its nearness had never chilled my heart till now." Only a small partition of thin, unpainted boards separated her sleeping quarters from the wounded. Bucklin was well within hearing of their groans on her first night in her sleeping quarters, where she dreamed "of battle fields strewn with horror; sounds as of blood trickling from many wounds; green grass and waving grain trodden by artillery; and the woods made the hiding places of ten thousand deaths."[30]

After spending a few days on a hospital transport, Harriet Whetten realized that she had journeyed far toward a realization of war. "Ev-

---

[28] John Y. Foster, "Four Days at Gettysburg," *Harper's New Monthly Magazine* 28 (February 1864): 386.

[29] Mary A. Newcomb, *Four Years of Personal Reminiscences of the War* (Chicago: H. S. Mills, 1893), vi; Katherine Prescott Wormeley to A., June 2, 1862, in *The Other Side of War with the Army of the Potomac: Letters from the Headquarters of the United States Sanitary Commission during the Peninsular Campaign in Virginia in 1862* (Boston: Ticknor, 1889), 99.

[30] Sophronia E. Bucklin, *In Hospital and Camp: A Woman's Record of Thrilling Incidents among the Wounded in the Late War* (Philadelphia: John E. Potter, 1869), 48, 51.

erything is so strange that nothing is strange, and it seems quite natural to me to be near the front lines of the grand army." She described caring for the wounded, crouching down between two injured men to write a letter for one of them, while a third man's wounded leg was dressed two feet behind her. "A fortnight ago I never could have believed that I could do these things, but the sense, the blessed sense, of doing good to these brave & patient men overpowers every thing." Working with the wounded was for Whetten "more like being—in fact, it was, on the edge of a battlefield."[31]

Those volunteers who gave not only of their time and labor but also of their heart and soul were the most fervent travelers across the gulf of experience. Katherine Prescott Wormeley was one of those people. "It is a piteous sight to see these men," she told her mother. "No one knows what war is until they see this black side of it. We may all sentimentalize over its possibilities as we see the regiments go off, or when we hear of a battle; but it is as far from the reality as to read of pain is far from feeling it." For Wormeley and those like her, working in the hospitals was a trip beyond an imaginative conception of battle into physical contact with its aftermath. "We who are here . . . dare not let our minds, much less our imaginations, rest on suffering; while *you* must rely on your imagination to project you into the state of things here."[32]

Walt Whitman, perhaps more than any other volunteer, used the hospital experience as a vehicle for understanding the meaning of battle. Drawn strongly to the wounded, he repeated the soldier's admission that written language was inadequate to describe the experience, writing his brother that he would "postpone till we come together again, any attempt to make you realize this whole thing." One had to go among the wounded "with personal feeling" and his "own way of investigation" to understand the appeal of these human relics of the battlefield. Whitman was a courageous explorer; he eagerly sought contact with the human drama of battle. The wounded opened "a new world somehow to me, giving closer insights, new

---

[31] Harriet Douglas Whetten to Hexie, May 19, 1862; and Harriet Douglas Whetten to Achee, July 3, 1862, in "A Volunteer Nurse in the Civil War: The Letters of Harriet Douglas Whetten," ed. by Paul H. Hass, *Wisconsin Magazine of History* 48 (winter 1964–1965): 139, 149.

[32] Katherine Prescott Wormely to mother, May 26, 1862, in *The Other Side of War*, 77–78.

things, exploring deeper mines than any yet, showing our humanity
. . . tried by terrible, fearfulest tests, probed deepest, the living soul's,
the body's tragedies, bursting the petty bonds of art." Identifying
strongly with the wounded, who represented young America in his
eyes, he tried hard to experience what they endured. "I sometimes
put myself in fancy in the cot, with typhoid, or under the knife."
Going farther, Whitman once wrote of his strong desire "to be present at a first class battle."[33]

The impressive and moving body of testimony from hospital volunteers of both sexes demonstrates how vividly working with the
wounded took civilians across the gulf of experience toward a genuine understanding of war. But it is important to note that these dedicated people came to understand war only because they sincerely
wanted to help the injured and they committed a substantial amount
of their time and energy to doing it. Hospital work was one of the
best ways for civilians to gain contact with battle; it made them participants by forcing them to clean, feed, and comfort those who fought
and suffered from war's effects. Few volunteers were so eager to
vicariously experience battle as Whitman was, but all of them came
to know what battle was like to a remarkable degree.

Civilians also gained a lesser kind of contact with battle when they
visited the battlefield. Fewer northerners than southerners had the
opportunity to do this, given that most of the engagements took place
in the upper South, yet a number of northern civilians traveled to the
war zone to visit loved ones in the army and encountered the devastation it wrought. Lovicy Ann Eberhart of Iowa journeyed to Rolla,
Missouri, where she met a woman whose husband had been hanged
by Rebel guerrillas for supporting the Union. She also encountered
a man whose eye had been shot out in battle, and another one with
an arm missing from a wound. She had gone south believing she
"knew all about the ravages of war" from reading newspapers and
perusing her husband's letters. "But, alas, I knew nothing of its horrors, devastation, and terror, until I passed over the grounds left des-

---

[33] Walt Whitman to Thomas Jefferson Whitman, January 16, 1863; Walt Whitman
to John Townsend Trowbridge, May 20, 1864; Walt Whitman to Nathaniel Bloom
and John F. S. Grey, March 19, 1863; and Walt Whitman to Louisa Van Velsor
Whitman, January 29, 1864, in *Walt Whitman: The Correspondence*, vol. 1, *1842–
1867*, 67, 224, 81–82, 193.

olate and barren by the foraging and destruction of the alternating armies."[34]

Written language failed Eberhart; spoken language often proved no more useful for other people. Sidney George Fisher of Philadelphia spoke with a Maryland civilian who had visited the field of Antietam immediately after the battle. "He could not find words to describe the frightful sufferings he witnessed." These civilians realized a truth told time and again by the soldiers, that "none but . . . those who have visited the battle field can have any idea of the sight it presented."[35]

When opportunity occurred, as it did at Antietam and Gettysburg, civilians flocked to the battle area. Those who came to help the wounded wrote vivid descriptions of their observations. By the time John Foster reached Gettysburg, the dead had been removed and the wounded had been gathered into hospitals. He was sensitive to the transformed terrain and described it as would a soldier, in terms that bespoke the disordered, demonic nature of battle. "Every tree was scarred and torn, a chilly blight resting upon its summer crown of beauty. . . . Here and there great girdles of fire blazoned the slopes, telling of slaughtered animals slowly consuming. Broken caissons, knapsacks, canteens, and small-arms were strewn on every path. Fences were prostrate, and blood sprinkled every tuft of grass which the feet of the contending armies had not trampled down." The sight of the battlefield clearly brought Foster closer to the experience of Civil War soldiers just as his work with the wounded had done.[36]

Foster was among a minority. Most visitors to Gettysburg came not to help the wounded but to gawk at war as if it were a circus brought to town for their amusement. They were the heirs of a long tradition in Western history; many people in classical Greece made the same visit to the many battlefields of that era as curious sight-seers and relic hunters.[37] Thousands of northerners flocked to Gettysburg after the battle, some of them to collect souvenirs, but most came to sal-

---

[34] Lovicy Ann Eberhart, "Reminiscences of the Civil War, 1861–1865," Lovicy Ann Eberhart Papers, Illinois State Historical Library.

[35] Entry for November 11, 1862, Sidney George Fisher Diary, in *A Philadelphia Perspective*, 441; and Jacob S. Kiester to Father, May 9, 1862, Jacob S. Kiester Papers, *Civil War Times Illustrated* Collection, USAMHI.

[36] Foster, "Four Days at Gettysburg," 381.

[37] Victor Davis Hanson, *The Western Way of War: Infantry Battle in Classical Greece* (New York: Oxford University Press, 1989), 202–3, 208.

vage equipment for personal use or sale. They cut the harnesses off dead horses and stole abandoned blankets and guns. The provost guard published warnings against this activity in the local newspaper but it failed to intimidate anyone. Quartermaster Captain W. Willard Smith estimated that between three and five thousand people roamed the twenty-five square miles of the battlefield every day. Guards counted as many as seventy-five wagons filled with booty leaving the area on one day alone, but less than half of them could be stopped. Most disturbing was the theft of weapons. Perhaps 40,000 rifle muskets were abandoned on the field by both armies, yet soldiers recovered only 24,178 of them. The rest found their way into the homes of local families.

To give these civilians some credit, they probably looked upon the battlefield as a golden opportunity to recoup some of the losses they suffered when soldiers in both armies took food and broke down fences for firewood. When Captain Smith sent armed men into the countryside in late July to search for and confiscate government property, they found huge amounts of wagons, guns, ammunition, and even horses. The civilians had hidden their booty in a variety of unusual places, and a few of them even offered resistance rather than allow the soldiers to take it.

These visitors had no interest at all in understanding the nature of combat. They callously took advantage of a sea of human suffering to feather their nests and raised the bitter hatred of the wounded and the hospital workers alike. There is something immensely poignant in their actions. Many of these relic hunters eagerly took the personal property of fallen soldiers. As one of them, John B. Linn, put it, "we returned picking up some letters, cards and cutting off some buttons for relics of the fight." Linn recalled that another man, ironically named Goodman, took an Enfield rifle. Linn's own scavenging knew no limits. He picked up a Bible that belonged to a dead soldier and found a letter written by a son to his soldier father that had bloodstains on it. He also took a letter written by a young girl to her lover in the army. These jackals got their comeuppance only when caught by a provost guard. They were forced to bury the dead or, if that task was already complete, to bury a horse as their punishment.[38]

---

[38] Eric A. Campbell, "The Aftermath and Recovery of Gettysburg, Part 2," *Gettysburg Magazine* 12 (January 1995): 99, 108–9.

Hospital workers found these men to be little more than "evil beasts." An anonymous volunteer described the visit of a local farmer to the hospitals. He only wanted to look on the wounded Confederates because he had "never seen a rebel." The volunteers gave him more than he bargained for. They guided him into a tent filled with wounded Confederate prisoners who were awaiting transport to northern prisons. One of them shouted, " 'Boys, here's a man who never saw a rebel in his life, and wants to look at you;' and there he stood with his mouth wide open, and there they lay in rows, laughing at him, stupid old Dutchman. 'And why haven't you seen a rebel?' Mrs. —— said; 'why didn't you take your gun and help to drive them out of your town?' 'A feller might'er got hit!'—which reply was quite too much for the rebels, they roared with laughter at him, up and down the tent."

This same hospital volunteer also recounted how the battle affected the population of Gettysburg and brought martial imagery into the consciousness even of small boys. They came to yell "Here, you rebel" at each other in play or in little fights. The children also played with percussion caps picked up from the piles of muskets left on the sidewalks. The XI Corps of the Army of the Potomac had retreated in headlong flight through the streets of Gettysburg on July 1, so there were hundreds of weapons littering the town. And, of course, most of the buildings in Gettysburg were converted into field hospitals, bringing the aftermath of war directly into the parlors of many civilians.[39]

The soldiers who were left behind on the battlefield also reacted to the casual tourists with feelings of disgust. They would have agreed with Jonathan P. Stowe, a wounded Massachusetts sergeant, who noted that many civilians came "in from all parts of country" around Antietam. They only came to "stare at us but do not find time to do anything." Artillery officer Charles Wainwright made the same complaint about visitors to Gettysburg. "Hundreds from the country around . . . came down in their waggons to see the sights, to stroll over the ground, and gaze and gape at the dead and wounded. But not one lifted a finger to help the tired soldiers remove the one or bury the other."[40]

---

[39] "Three Weeks at Gettysburg," in *Gettysburg Sources*, comp. by James L. McLean and Judy W. McLean (Baltimore: Butternut and Blue, 1987), 2: 156–58.

[40] Entry for September 21, 1862, Jonathan P. Stowe Diary, Jonathan P. Stowe Papers, *Civil War Times Illustrated* Collection, USAMHI; and entry for July 5, 1863,

Captain George A. Thayer of the 2nd Massachusetts observed many Gettysburg visitors and their reactions to the unburied dead. Such sights affected them very badly. The area around Spangler's Spring near Culp's Hill remained littered with the dead for some time after the battle. "To us, who were hardened to such things, the effluvia and the distorted bodies, swollen to blackness under the blazing sun, were becoming most intolerable to every sensibility. It required a very brief experience to divest these sightseers of desire to be more familiar with a battlefield. A few glances, and faces became deadly pale, as one faltered, 'Come, Bill, we have had enough of this.' "[41]

Obviously, the vast majority of these tourists had no desire to be under fire or to gain a deep, philosophical understanding of combat. Their shallowness was all too apparent to those hospital workers and soldiers who knew so well what war can do to bodies on the battlefield and to the awareness of those who survived it. The crowd of politicians and other civilians that hovered near the battle of First Bull Run and ingloriously fled when the Federal Army was defeated probably was motivated by the novelty and entertainment value of combat. Several of them were captured by the victorious Confederate army. None of them left much in the way of written accounts that shed light on whether or not they learned anything about the nature of combat.[42]

Although it is difficult to see that tourists truly wanted to learn about combat, despite the fact that they came into contact with its worst effects on the battlefield, other northern civilians gained contact with battle by visiting the armies and came away with a deep, considered understanding of it. Mostly, they went to the seat of war to visit friends and loved ones in the armies or to bring much needed supplies that would supplement the sometimes-meager government-issued rations and medical equipment. These people also came under fire when they decided to tag along during an active campaign.

Nadine Turchin was a remarkable woman. Born in Russia and mar-

A Diary of Battle: The Personal Journal of Colonel Charles S. Wainwright, 1861–1865, ed. by Allan Nevins (New York: Harcourt, Brace and World, 1962), 254.

[41] George A. Thayer, "Gettysburg, As We Men on the Right Saw It," in Sketches of War History, 1861–1865: Papers Read before the Ohio Commandery of the Military Order of the Loyal Legion of the United States, 1886–1888 (Cincinnati: Robert Clarke, 1888), 2: 40.

[42] William C. Davis, Battle at Bull Run: A History of the First Major Campaign of the Civil War (Baton Rouge: Louisiana State University Press, 1977), 239.

ried to John Basil Turchin, the only Russian to be commissioned as a general in an American army, she traveled with her husband's brigade during the Chickamauga campaign and came under fire. She did not try to write of her experiences until ten days later. "Although I had been very calm and determined even during the two days, I had not enough courage to recall my impressions." Nadine Turchin, who knew of the soldier's sufferings through long months of campaigning, did not take the experience of battle lightly.[43]

Dr. Simpson, a physician from Morgan County, Illinois, who worked as a contract surgeon with the 14th Illinois, was another thoughtful civilian who quite readily understood what war was about. He asked Lieutenant Colonel William Camm to take him to the skirmish line during the Federal advance on Corinth, Mississippi, for he wanted "to see how the ugly work was done, of which he got so much of in the hospital." Camm paired him with a private behind a tree while he took shelter with another skirmisher, close enough so he could keep an eye on the worthy doctor. Soon a Confederate soldier sneaked into the open to shoot at Simpson, but he was spotted by Camm, whose private killed the enemy. Later, when Simpson asked what the private shot at, Camm told him. Simpson "declared if he got back to camp with a whole skin he would gladly stay there."[44]

Another thoughtful civilian was Henry Goedeking of Belleville, Illinois, who visited the armies several times to help care for hometown boys wounded in battle. During the Vicksburg siege, he brought beer to his friends in the German 12th Missouri and eagerly studied the enemy lines through field glasses. Goedeking became acclimated to the sound of firing, claiming that he did not "feel quite right unless cannons are thundering all about him and there is a ball flying over him," in the words of his nephew.[45]

Chester Thompson was another serious-minded civilian who sought some kind of personal exposure to battle and came away with a new awareness of it. He watched the Federal attack at Fredericks-

---

[43] Entry for September 30, 1863, " 'A Monotony Full of Sadness': The Diary of Nadine Turchin, May, 1863–April, 1864," ed. by Mary Ellen McElligott, *Journal of the Illinois State Historical Society* 70 (February 1977): 66.

[44] Entry for May 27, 1862, "Diary of Colonel William Camm, 1861–1865," *Journal of the Illinois State Historical Society* 18 (January 1926): 875–76.

[45] Henry A. Kircher to "All!", June 7, 1863, in *A German in the Yankee Fatherland: The Civil War Letters of Henry A. Kircher*, ed. by Earl J. Hess (Kent, Ohio: Kent State University Press, 1983), 106.

burg from a distance and was amazed at the sight of long blue lines withering under Confederate fire. "I did not hear the groans of our men, who were wounded, but I did hear the shouts of the men when ordered to charge. I do not think I have any particular desire to see another battle, particularly if it was to be as hard an [sic] one for our men as the last has been." All of these women and men learned something about the reality of war from their vicarious exposure to it.[46]

The same probably cannot be said of other visitors to the armies who wanted to place themselves under fire. Hardened soldiers often found great amusement in the antics of casual visitors who had no idea what they were exposing themselves to when they asked to be led forward toward the enemy. Lieutenant Lyman Richardson of the 1st Nebraska met a Michigan cleric in the siege lines at Vicksburg, "perfectly green in war matters," who distributed religious tracts to the men. "He said if there was no danger he would like to look around a little. So just at dusk I took him down into the trenches & finally away up to the head of our sap behind the sap roller—which is only about fifty feet from the enemy's works. He heard two or three bullets whiz over our head—took a hasty peep at the enemys line—said very feelingly this is a *real* war, hadn't we better go back: So we returned—he will have some huge stories to tell when he gets back to Pontiac."[47]

There were probably many more civilian visitors to the Army of the Potomac, given its proximity to the national capital, than to any other field army of the Union, and they provided a never-ending source of amusement to the soldiers. Major General John Gibbon, a division commander in the II Corps, accompanied a group along the line of fortifications at Cold Harbor in early June 1864. Confederate artillery opened up on the small group. "You never saw such a demoralized set in your life as they were, nor a more grateful set when during a lull in the fire I proposed we should leave our advanced position."[48]

Another large group of tourists reached the Army of the Potomac

[46] Chester P. Thompson to Mother, December 20, 1862, Wendell W. Lang, Jr., Collection, USAMHI.

[47] Lyman Richardson to "Sarah & folks generally," June 28, 1863, Richardson Family Papers, Nebraska State Historical Society, Lincoln.

[48] John Gibbon to Mama, June 4, 1864, John Gibbon Papers, Manuscript Division, Maryland Historical Society, Baltimore.

with a delivery of Thanksgiving turkeys in November 1864. Colonel Theodore Lyman, a member of the army commander's staff, was given the job of showing them the siege lines at Petersburg. One man breathlessly asked Lyman "whether in my opinion he could be properly considered as having been 'under fire; because,' said he, 'I stood on the Avery house and could see the shells explode in the air, you know!' " Lyman began calling the civilians "turkies," because of their gift as well as for their ludicrous actions under fire. When one asked Lyman who "those men just over there" were during a visit to Fort Harrison, he replied they were Rebels. "God bless me!" exclaimed the man as he "popped down behind the parapet." Another civilian became very excited when a Rebel shell exploded overhead. Rushing to pick up a piece of it, he cried, "Oh! it's warm. Oh!! it smells of sulphur. Oh!!! let us go now." To Lyman, these people were sources of cheap if not contemptible humor. The sulfur smeller was delighted with his encounter with the shell as well as with "all other adventures, and was quite elated when his horse tumbled in a ditch and muddied him greatly."[49]

These comical visitors deserve to occupy the same category as those casual tourists who flocked to the battlefields at Antietam and Gettysburg earlier in the war. They had no serious desire to learn about combat and acted like giddy children when actually presented with evidence of real battle. Except for the hospital volunteers, everyone discussed thus far remained interested in battle, but they never joined the army or committed themselves to dealing with its aftermath. Thus they all, the serious thinkers like Dr. Simpson, the cynical opportunists like the scavengers of Gettysburg, and the "turkies" in Lyman's group, remained on the margins of combat. Their exposure was fleeting, and it produced widely varying impressions of battle. People such as Simpson probably related accurate information to their friends back home, whereas the "turkies" probably told wildly exaggerated stories about how they helped to capture Petersburg. Each one made what they wanted out of their exposure to combat.

Another group of northern civilians went much farther in their efforts to expose themselves to battle, even more so than the hospital

---

[49] Theodore Lyman to Wife, Nov. 27, 28, 1864, in *Meade's Headquarters, 1863–1865: Letters of Colonel Theodore Lyman from the Wilderness to Appomattox*, ed. by George R. Agassiz (Boston: Atlantic Monthly Press, 1922), 280, 282–83.

volunteers. Several hundred women disguised themselves as men and served for varying lengths of time in the northern army. They experienced the war as did a male soldier, albeit much less openly. There are precious few surviving accounts from these women soldiers that offer reliable evidence as to their motivation. Most seem to have been prompted to disguise themselves and join the war to seek adventure, to be near loved ones already in the army, or to break the narrowly defined roles assigned women in nineteenth-century American society.[50]

The only surviving letters written by a woman soldier, however, clearly indicate her desire to experience combat. Sarah Rosetta Wakeman actually began to impersonate a man before she joined the army in order to leave home and earn a living for herself. Some unidentified family problems led her to work as a coal handler on canal boats in upstate New York, in August 1862. She joined the 153rd New York a few months later, after meeting some soldiers. "They wanted I should enlist and so I did." Many long months of garrison duty in the Washington, D.C., fortifications followed. Even though Sarah, who had enlisted under the name Lyons Wakeman, had initially joined on the spur of the moment, she came to think a great deal about combat and wanted to experience it. "If I go into a battle," she wrote in April 1863, "I shall be alright. It is what I have wish for a good while." She did not worry about the danger and was not afraid to be under fire. "I don't believe there are any Rebel's bullet made for me yet. Nor I don't Care if there is." Wakeman got her wish during the Red River campaign and endured her first fire at the battle of Pleasant Hill on April 9, 1864. She never had a chance to write her family of that adventure. Wakeman developed chronic diarrhea soon after the campaign ended. She died on June 19, 1864.[51]

Wakeman and other women soldiers were the ultimate in civilian exposure to combat, for they transformed themselves into soldiers and put their lives in danger. Hospital volunteers also gained a much more intimate knowledge of battle than most civilians. These two

[50] Richard Hall, *Patriots in Disguise: Women Warriors of the Civil War* (New York: Paragon House, 1993).

[51] Sarah Rosetta Wakeman to Family, November 24, 1862, April 13, 1863, August 5, 1863, in *An Uncommon Soldier: The Civil War Letters of Sarah Rosetta Wakeman, alias Private Lyons Wakeman, 153rd Regiment, New York State Volunteers*, ed. by Lauren Cook Burgess (Pasadena, Md.: Minerva Center, 1994), 1, 9, 11–12, 28, 42.

groups made it most or all of the way across the gulf of experience that separated the home front from the soldier. Visitors to the battlefields and to the armies, and those civilians who relied on letters written by soldiers, could only hope to make it part way across the gulf. What did the home front make of their knowledge of battle? Comparatively nothing. There never developed a civilian version of a "Lost Generation" of Americans who were seared by the reality of modern combat to the point that they became disillusioned or entered into a crusade to end all wars. Each individual who caught a glimpse of what soldiers called "seeing the elephant" used the experience for whatever purpose was important to their personal lives.

5

"Listen Ladies One and All": Union Soldiers Yearn for the Society of Their "Fair Cousins of the North"

Patricia L. Richard

TUCKED IN between two advertisements, one for a milk maid and one placed by a nanny seeking employment, was a correspondence request sent by "M. Debray and Monte Cristo," soldiers stationed in Nashville, Tennessee. "Wanted—Two Young Gents, who sport brass coats and blue buttons wish to correspond with a couple of young, handsome and respectable ladies, with a view to fun, love or matrimony."[1] The soldiers paid for the *Chicago Tribune* ad by sending a "greenback" with their request. The payment ensured the advertisement ran from April 27 to April 31, 1863. The unique mode of communication spread among the soldiers, and by the end of May, the newspaper had published more than thirty soldiers' advertisements for correspondence. This phenomenon repeated itself in several northern newspapers and periodicals. Volunteers advertised for correspondents to brighten dull days, exchange ideas, and become prospective mates, but the soldiers' strongest motivation for placing the ads was to establish contact with respectable northern ladies. The wartime environment allowed few opportunities for the "boys in blue" to meet honorable women; they hoped to remedy their situation through correspondence requests.[2]

---

[1] M. Debray and Monte Cristo, "Wanted Correspondence," *Chicago Tribune*, April 27, 1863. It appears that the advertisers inverted the words intentionally for comic effect. For instance, Sergt. B. Stillwagon and Sergt. Harry Brooks described themselves as having "long curling eyes and small piercing black hair." *Chicago Tribune*, January 9, 1865.

[2] Soldiers were constantly asking family members to send them hometown news-

The ads for correspondence initiated by M. Debray and Monte Cristo sparked a craze in the military, mostly among Union troops fighting in the West, but also among New York volunteers. It also ignited enthusiasm among both men and women civilians. Although the majority of soldiers did not employ this novel method of meeting women, hundreds of people both in and out of the military did, and because of this, the ads reveal important aspects about soldiers and society during the Civil War. As the ads show, not all soldiers waited for the "cruel war" to end to establish personal relationships with respectable women. Before the war, these same men expected to begin a family while in their early twenties. When the war interrupted their domestic lives, familial goals were put on hold, but their desires to begin families did not disappear. Military life provided few opportunities for soldiers to establish a close relationship with a woman on any level. By placing the ads, soldiers hoped to remedy this paucity of womanly influence.

The ads provide a unique perspective into the courting world of nineteenth-century men and women. Some advertisers humorously described themselves as "seventy-five years old" with "hair like a porcupine's, and pug noses," but the majority of advertisers assured readers of their "unquestionable character and good education" and sought those "equally endowed." The ads expose not only the humorous and gentle sides of the soldiers, but more importantly, their humanity and desire for intimate relations. Finally, the women's participation in the ads, as both advertisers and correspondents, suggests an expanded perspective of the image of Victorian women. Certainly not all women viewed these ads as proper, but the women who participated in the craze most likely believed their behavior was nothing but respectable. Because of women's involvement in this unorthodox medium, these correspondence ads encourage us to rethink the notion of the "True Woman," which defined females as passive, submissive responders and gave nineteenth-century women few skills with which to discern a man's true character.[3]

---

papers. Some soldiers received metropolitan dailies such as the *New York Herald* or *Boston Transcript* by personal subscription, but most soldiers bought them from sutlers or newsboys. Soldiers shared the newspapers and literally wore them out through use. Bell Irvin Wiley, *The Life of Billy Yank: The Common Soldier of the Union* (Baton Rouge: Louisiana State University, 1952), 153.

[3] Bob Wilson, Frank White, Charley Lang, and Harry Case, "Wanted Correspondence," *Chicago Tribune*, January 28, 1865; "Sergeant A.," "Matrimonial," *New York*

Soldiers, civilians, and women utilized the correspondence ads to maneuver around Victorian etiquette and the complications of courting, which were magnified by the exigencies of war. Victorians formed their courting expectations on advice found in the voluminous etiquette manuals of the period, which declared that men and women typically expected to begin searching for life-long mates between the ages of twenty and twenty-four. The road to marriage for both men and women consisted of an intricate set of rituals interlaced by prescribed manners and morals, and a winnowing process based on the ability of the prospective mates to meet their suitor's social, financial, and religious standards. Prescriptive literature advised the sexes that before the search for a partner could begin they must turn inward and scrutinize their own suitability. Etiquette writers offered extensive lists for the conscientious person to follow, which included advice on cleanliness, eating, drinking, breathing, exercise, proper dress, ornaments, and hair and beard styles; and on "self-culture" defined as moral training, grace and movement, standing, sitting, and walking.[4]

Although it is difficult to determine how extensively Victorians observed the advice of etiquette writers, historian John F. Kasson suggests that few people slavishly followed the rules point by point, but most likely consulted manuals merely for guidance. Concerned with the rapidly changing social conditions around them, upper- and middle-class Victorians applied rules to every aspect of life in order to bolster their elite positions in an increasingly mobile society. The middle and upper classes used etiquette as a basis upon which to

Herald, February 12, 1864; and Karen Lystra, *Searching the Heart: Women, Men, and Romantic Love in Nineteenth-Century America* (New York: Oxford University Press, 1989), 122–24. On nineteenth-century women ideals, see Barbara Welter, *Dimity Convictions: The American Woman in the Nineteenth Century* (Athens: Ohio University Press, 1976); Nancy Cott, *The Bonds of Womanhood: "Woman's Sphere" in New England, 1780–1835* (New Haven, Conn.: Yale University Press, 1973); Carl N. Degler, *At Odds: Women and the Family in America from the Revolution to the Present* (New York: Oxford University Press, 1980); Mary P. Ryan, *Cradle of the Middle Class: The Family in Oneida County, New York 1790–1865* (Cambridge, Eng.: Cambridge University Press, 1981); and Barbara Leslie Epstein, *The Politics of Domesticity: Women, Evangelism and Temperance in Nineteenth-Century America* (Middletown, Conn.: Wesleyan University Press, 1981).

[4] Degler, *At Odds*, 6–8; and *How to Behave: A Pocket Manual of Republican Etiquette, and Guide to Correct Personal Habits* (New York: Fowler & Wells, 1856), 15, 42, 48, 81.

exclude people of lower classes or as standards by which social climb-
ers aped their betters on the social scale. The middle class especially
held tightly to these rules because the vicissitudes of the economy
left many of the group perched literally on the brink of financial ruin.
By adhering to prescribed manners, "they proved to society that they
were successful and polished." Kasson argues that Victorians were
also concerned with the larger issue of societal stability, brought on
by "a restless, highly mobile, rapidly urbanizing and industrializing
democracy." The shifting populace disrupted "traditional norms governing face to face conduct," which were grounded in the social context of the family and community. This "left a vacuum" of moral
"guidance on how to interact safely with others." To counter these
destabilizing forces, Victorians established rules of etiquette to
"teach each individual his social duties," and hoped this would but-
tress their crumbling social standards.[5]

Advice appeared in etiquette manuals, domestic novels, and even
cookbooks, guiding both sexes through the rituals, rules, and expectations of society. In her work on nineteenth-century womanhood,
Francis Cogan explains the complicated but necessary procedure involved in finding the appropriate mate. Through the advice literature,
writers encouraged a middle-class woman to maintain her personal
standards and seek a suitor "who truly was moral, intelligent, hardworking, and compatible." To find such a man, a woman needed to
follow the advice books' and the novelists' lists of courtship procedures. In the initial stages of courting, etiquette writers designated
gamblers, drunkards, and philanderers as men to avoid, even on the
superficial level of simple acquaintance. "Inappropriate men" also
included those who were "extremely different from the young
woman in social status, family background, or wealth," and those who
were "unrefined, uneducated, and tasteless." Authors recommended
women meet prospective mates through reputable friends, or by rely-
ing on their fathers and brothers to introduce them to co-workers or
college acquaintances. Above all, women were advised to use the

---

[5] Karen Rae Mehaffey, *Victorian American Women, 1840–1880: An Annotated
Bibliography* (New York: Garland, 1992), 65; John F. Kasson, *Rudeness and Civility:
Manners in Nineteenth-Century Urban America* (New York: Hill and Wang, 1990),
43, 53, 60, 258; and Karen Halttunen, *Confidence Men and Painted Women: A Study
of Middle-Class Culture in America, 1830–1870* (New Haven, Conn.: Yale University
Press, 1982), 193.

courting process to "determine the suitability" of their proposed mates and to winnow out those who were not compatible in intellect, piousness, health, wealth, or social status.[6]

Nineteenth-century men were just as conscious of prescriptive literature as the ladies. Perhaps the most popular author of behavior manuals for men was Lord Chesterfield. In his *American Chesterfield*, printed in 1857, he imparted his wisdom about the virtues and pitfalls of becoming a successful man. He encouraged gentlemen to maintain modesty and to have a genteel carriage and a pleasing countenance about them. He warned them to choose carefully their company and to employ their time wisely. Even though he believed women were "no more to be trusted than 'fresh-caught monkeys,' " he insisted that marriage was worth the hazards. Within a list of entertaining and somewhat curious advice for gentlemen choosing wives, he suggested that they "avoid fools and philosophers." Above all, Chesterfield encouraged the men to "know who you are marrying" by obtaining references. Historian Karen Halttunen explains Chesterfield's concern for references in her book *Confidence Men and Painted Ladies*. Halttunen argues that the fluidity of urban America made it more and more difficult for people to check the backgrounds of their new acquaintances, making references necessary. Nineteenth-century novels portrayed the grim results of ignoring advice by presenting plots that overflowed with duplicitous characters (usually male) as genteel figures that were eventually revealed to be corrupt fortune seekers. Chesterfield and other advisors stressed the need for both sexes to investigate their suitor's character, assuring their readers that research would prevent catastrophes resulting from improper introductions.[7]

Etiquette manuals also advised readers on appropriate conduct in public. In *How to Behave: A Pocket Manual of Republican Etiquette*, the author counseled men and women about how to act on the street,

---

[6] Frances Cogan, *All-American Girl: The Ideal of Real Womanhood in Mid-Nineteenth-Century America* (Athens: University of Georgia Press, 1989), 137–41.

[7] Lord Chesterfield, *The American Chesterfield* (Philadelphia: J. B. Lippincott & Co., 1857), 203–5, 211–13; Halttunen, *Confidence Men and Painted Women*, 51, 35; and Cogan, *All-American Girl*, 155. Advisors usually classified an introduction by someone less than a good friend as improper; they viewed a meeting between two people with no introduction by a third party as even more harmful, because neither had "honest" information they could have obtained from a mutual friend, to measure the other with.

at church, in a picture gallery, and at places of amusement. The manual also guided participants through a labyrinth of manners required during special occasions such as dinner parties, dances, holidays, weddings, and funerals. In general, historian John Kasson argues, men chaperoned single ladies in public to protect them "from an impertinent glance" or "an unwelcome compliment." Etiquette writers recommended that women assume the "ideal of uncompromising modesty." The female who did not heed their advice forfeited "all claims to consideration as a lady" when she attracted or sought the attention of the opposite sex. As a result, respectable women felt vulnerable in public. To avoid impropriety, women took shelter in their homes and only attended gatherings considered proper for their status. Therefore, the only opportunities for single women to pursue intimate relationships with men were through relatives and friends, and at certain mixed functions. In the winter, men and women socialized while attending apple bees, music societies, dances, skating, and the theater. In the summer, picnics usually included carriage rides, horseback riding, or brief train rides to a pastoral setting.[8]

A man and woman attending the same social gathering needed to be formally introduced to each other. It was "considered vulgar to approach someone in person" without a formal introduction by a third party who was known to both participants. Introductions could take place in person or by way of letter. In either case, Lord Chesterfield warned, "when a gentleman is to be introduced to a lady, her permission must first be privately obtained by the introducer." The introducer was not to take her job lightly, but was to incur responsibility for what would result from the association.[9]

Once an introduction was made, the newly introduced couple could exchange calling cards or "carte de visites" and the gentleman could request "to commence formal addresses" with the woman's

---

[8] *How to Behave*, 90–6; Kasson, *Rudeness and Civility*, 128–29; and Mehaffey, *Victorian American Women*, 84–85.

[9] Ibid., 67; Lord Chesterfield, *The American Chesterfield*, 222. The author of *How to Behave* believed that in certain situations two non-introduced people could talk to each other. Two people occupying the same seat in a railway car or a stage coach could converse without a proper introduction. This applied "to many other occasions" as well. But, he added, "you are not obliged . . . to know these extempore acquaintances afterwards." Gentlemen were also charged to offer their services to "any unattended lady who may need them," regardless of an introduction. "When the service" was "accomplished," he advised them to "bow and retire."

consent.[10] If a relationship blossomed, the couple began a period of courtship.[11] Although parents participated as spectators, there were definite rules and penalties enforced in the game of courtship. It was a romantic period filled with emotional thrills, during which couples regulated their own behavior and engaged in "erotic play, both in fantasy and in reality" with their mates. But couples also used the time to develop romantic attachments and test the depths of their feelings and commitment for each other, sharing their most personal desires during intimate meetings and through correspondence. "Suitors seeking courtship" and "men and women seeking positions" used letters as a form of introduction. Both sexes expressed inner needs and thoughts and utilized correspondence as an outlet for creativity.[12]

Victorians used letters for more than just courting, though. Letter writing was a popular pastime and the most frugal means of maintaining communication between family and friends. During the war, letters kept soldiers in touch with their relatives and were treated as the lifeline between home and camp. The volunteers related their rustic lifestyles and experiences in battle; families returned letters with the latest news concerning births, deaths, and marriages. Even under wartime conditions correspondents were encouraged to maintain decorum within their missives. In the spring of 1864, the soldiers recuperating at the Armory Square Hospital in Washington, D. C., were offered "lessons in form and composition of letter writing." The

---

[10] Mehaffey, *Victorian American Women*, 67–68. Calling and visits were done on certain days of the week, and for brief periods, usually lasting only fifteen to forty-five minutes. Calling cards gave the unique opportunity of allowing one to express interest in someone without "putting the pursued party in a precarious position."

[11] Ellen Rothman notes the difference between courtship and courting in her book *Hands and Heart: A History of Courtship in America* (New York: Basic Books, 1984), 23. "The word courtship applied to situations where the intention to marry was explicit (if not formally—and mutually—stated). Courting was the broader term used to describe socializing between unmarried men and women. Courting sometimes but not always led to courtship; few courtships began without a period of courting."

[12] Ibid., 119–22; and Karen Lystra, *Searching the Heart: Women, Men, and Romantic Love in Nineteenth-Century America* (New York: Oxford University Press, 1989), 158. Lystra explains that as marriage began to be based on "privatized experience of emotional openness and personal satisfaction with another . . . parents bowed out . . . because acceptance of the ideas and values of love and the self gave them little to act upon." Likewise, Rothman explains that parents who tried to "impose their will" found "their children subverting or resisting their control." Rothman, *Hands and Hearts*, 29. Also see Mehaffey, *Victorian American Women*, 66–67.

group met every Wednesday evening, but the volunteers were warned that only "ten" students "at one time" would be accepted. Teachers emphasized the intimate nature of letters and instructed their pupils to write with care because letters reflected one's character.[13]

Miss Leslie's Behavior Book, published in 1859, offered the soldiers another source from which to obtain the proper "dos" and "don'ts" of letter writing. Miss Leslie warned letter writers that within their missives they left "written evidence either of . . . good sense or . . . folly . . . industry or carelessness . . . self-control or importance." Thus to be a genteel letter writer required "controlled communication of proper sentiments." For courting couples, "letters should discuss interests, tastes, and character so that 'mutual Esteem and Respect' can develop." Above all, Miss Leslie instructed would-be correspondents that "a letter is of no use unless it conveys some information, excites some interest, or affords some improvement." Many nineteenth-century letter writers followed her advice by using correspondence as a vehicle to refine their penmanship, improve their grammar, or enhance their knowledge on a chosen subject.[14]

As can be seen in this brief look at Victorian standards for introduction and courting, even without the restrictive conditions of war, courting rituals were time-consuming and cumbersome. Although the rules were designed to aid both sexes in their search for the most appropriate mate, during the war, etiquette became yet another barrier to be overcome. Soldiers could not leave their posts to meet respectable ladies, and respectable ladies, at least not in large numbers, did not visit the field. This is neither to suggest that women were not present in the camps, nor that the women who were there could not be respectable. Thousands of women followed the units as laundresses and general helpers and would not have considered themselves to be anything but respectable. Although prostitutes followed the troops, few men would consider establishing an intimate

---

[13] During the Civil War, soldiers and civilians sent as many as 180,000 letters daily. Marilyn Mayer Culpepper, *Trials and Triumphs: Women of the American Civil War* (East Lansing: Michigan State University Press, 1991), 281; and *Armory Square Hospital Gazette*, March 26, 1864.

[14] Eliza Leslie, *Miss Leslie's Behavior Book: A Guide and Manual for Ladies* (Philadelphia: T. B. Peterson & Brothers, 1859), 164, 171–73; Halttunen, *Confidence Men and Painted Women*, 121; and Cogan, *All-American Girl*, 164.

relationship with these women beyond the sexual level.[15] Likewise, although Civil War dances were popular, only a minority of soldiers who were either on leave or posted in nearby camps attended them. These confining circumstances of war and the rules of etiquette allowed soldiers few opportunities to meet appropriate women.[16]

The small number of women the soldiers came into contact with did not satisfy their needs for an intimate relationship because they were either nurses (usually older and treated by the soldiers in a maternal manner), other soldiers' mothers and wives, prostitutes, or "secesh" women. Appointed as the superintendent of women nurses for the Union Army by Secretary of War Simon Cameron, Dorothea Dix was commissioned "to select and assign women nurses to general or permanent military hospitals." Elizabeth Leonard suggests in her study of northern women's war work that Dix had such strict requirements because she hoped to head off the public's concerns. She recognized the impropriety of young, single, female nurses in the midst of large groups of men, without the protection of home. Dix preferred that her nurses be between the "ages of thirty-five and fifty and of strong health and matronly appearance, and must display good conduct, or superior education . . . maintain habits of neatness, order, sobriety and industry, and present certificates of qualification and good character from two individuals."[17] Not all the female nurses

---

[15] See Jane E. Schultz, "The Inhospitable Hospital: Gender and Professionalism in Civil War Medicine," *Signs: Journal of Women in Culture and Society* 17 (winter 1992): 363–92, for more information about the type of women who followed the men to camp.

[16] Dances were especially popular during winter quarters. In her memoirs, Septima Collis, wife of General H. T. Collis, related that she witnessed several such dances and during the winter of 1863 in a camp near Washington, Major-General Warren gave a "magnificent ball." The event encompassed several hospital tents, and was decorated by a "sea of bunting," with clusters of wax candles and Chinese lanterns. Collis characterized it as "a scene of enchantment." Numerous bands added to the festive atmosphere. The gala occasion included a "superb supper" and was attended by an "immense number of fashionable people" who were transported by express train from Washington especially for the ball. Collis's experience, however, was an anomaly. Most army wives, according to historian Mary Elizabeth Massey, did not enjoy such elegant parties or camping conditions. In fact, few rank and file had the opportunity to participate in these parties. See Septima M. Collis, *A Woman's War Record, 1861–1865* (New York: G. P. Putnam's Sons, 1889), 34–36; and Mary Elizabeth Massey, *Women in the Civil War* (Lincoln: University of Nebraska Press, 1966), 70–71.

[17] Elizabeth Leonard, *Yankee Women: Gender Battles in the Civil War* (New York: W. W. Norton & Co., 1994), 7, 14–16.

gained their positions through Dix, so not all of the volunteers had to meet these rigorous standards, but the majority of women nurses did fit Dix's qualifications. Plain in looks and attire, and predominantly middle-aged, nurses were regarded by their patients as maternal figures. Female nurses comforted and aided the sick and wounded soldiers in the style of mothers, not wives. However intimate relationships between the nurses and volunteers were rare, they did occur. Still, even if all the single female nurses had begun courting soldiers, only a handful of Union soldiers would have enjoyed such relations because they outnumbered the nurses by approximately two hundred to one.[18]

Prostitutes and southern women, on the other hand, represented the repugnant females the soldiers encountered while in service. Cities designated as military centers became "mecca[s] for whores." In Bell I. Wiley's thorough study of Yankee soldiers, he describes Washington, Chicago, Cincinnati, Boston, and New York as teeming with "lewd" women, but notes that northern cities did not have a monopoly on debauchery. "In the wake of the invading forces" states Wiley, "moved an army of harlots, with the result that every occupied city became a haven of vice." Thousands of soldiers reveled in the sexual wares offered by the "strumpets," but the fact that these women willingly sold their bodies made them not worth considering as respectable mates or friends for gentlemen. John Kasson contends that women who welcomed and sought men's attention were not respectable, but objects of scorn. "Indeed, what most distinguished a prostitute was the way she attracted male attention by brightly colored attire . . . her freedom of movement in public," and the way in which she "linked easily with strangers."[19]

Similarly, southern or "secesh" women appeared as reprehensible as the prostitutes to the "boys in blue." Historian Stephen Ash argues that civilians in the occupied South, particularly the women, countered the "degradation of enemy occupation" by "flaunting their Confederate patriotism and their loathing of the invaders." Not only did southern women cheer for Jefferson Davis, but "they sang 'The

---

[18] Jane E. Schultz estimates that thirty-two hundred women worked as nurses and as many as twenty thousand worked as "hospital workers." See Jane E. Schultz, "The Inhospitable Hospital," 363.

[19] Wiley, *The Life of Billy Yank*, 257–58; and Kasson, *Rudeness and Civility*, 130–31.

Bonnie Blue Flag,' " and "they held their noses when passing Federal soldiers on the street." As long as the women were the offenders, the soldiers saw them as no physical threat and usually ignored them or occasionally goaded them on. But equally disrespectful behavior by the young or middle-aged men brought quick curtailment by the Federals. As the men "became more circumspect" in their actions, the "women grew bolder." The majority of southern women were aloof or treated the soldiers with contempt. As a result, "few Northerners recorded their impressions of the southern people without mentioning the virulence of the women." Most Union soldiers believed that southern women encouraged their men to fight the war "past rational calculation," and saw the women as more vicious than the southern men. Leander Stillwell wrote that "in my entire sojourn in the South during the war, the women were found to be more intensely bitter and malignant against the . . . United States . . . in general, than the men." Consequently, with the choices of maternal nurses, other soldiers' wives or mothers, prostitutes, or "secesh" women before them, it is no wonder the soldiers yearned for the company of the "noble women of the north."[20]

Stationed in Murfreesboro, Tennessee, "Brutus" of the 24th Ohio Regiment lamented about the kind of women he came into contact with during the war and how he might be saved from the affliction. He declared, "From cross old maids of doubtless age; from fleshy widows; from masculine women; from Southern sympathizers O' Lord deliver me . . . of Western girls with waving curls and teeth like pearls O' Lord, in thy bounty and mercy send me an unlimited supply."[21] Brutus and other soldiers yearned for contact with the virtuous and true women of the North. Brutus, however, was not seeking an exclusive correspondent but rather "an unlimited supply" of

[20] George Rable, *Civil Wars: Women and the Crisis of Southern Nationalism* (Chicago: University of Illinois Press, 1989), 166; Stephen V. Ash, *When the Yankees Came: Conflict and Chaos in the Occupied South, 1861–1865* (Chapel Hill: University of North Carolina Press, 1995), 42, 220; and Reid Mitchell, *The Vacant Chair: The Northern Soldier Leaves Home* (New York: Oxford University Press, 1993), 90–91, 96–97. Ash notes that in garrisoned towns the civilians and soldiers eventually established friendly relations. In fact, romance blossomed between some of the Federals and the southern belles. However, Ash warns that "amity between citizens and soldiers . . . should not be exaggerated. Many of the citizens continued to resent or even hate the occupiers."

[21] "Brutus," "Wanted Correspondence," *Chicago Tribune*, June 13, 1863.

"western girls" to rescue him from his plight. Soldiers may have been thinking about their mothers just before the battle, as the popular Civil War song suggests, but they desired a taste of home they could not get in letters exchanged with parents, siblings, other relatives, or male friends.[22] They longed for the dances, the church meetings, and the kinds of activities that presented the opportunities to associate with respectable, single women.

Correspondence offered the soldier his best hope of socializing with the "true women of the land." Most often the soldiers' female correspondents were their mothers, wives, sisters, or friends, but occasionally they would write to women from hometown Soldiers' Aid Societies who attached notes to the "delicacies" they sent to the "boys" at the front. Some single ladies who hoped to strike up a correspondence with a lonely soldier included notes boldly stating their age, build, and hair color, along with their names and addresses. While convalescing at Harewood Hospital in Washington, D.C., Edwin Horton received "a work bag full of little trinkets" with a letter from a lady "and a request to write." He "rote her" but assured his wife that he "dident put any love in it." Cleveland ladies placed their missives in the gloves they knit and sent their hopes in the form of a poem: "Brave Sentry, on your lonely beat/ May these blue stockings warm your feet/ And when from wars and camps you part/ May some fair knitter warm your heart."[23] "J. B." responded to the "Fair Sex" who pinned a note to the quilt he received from the Sanitary Commission by "heartily" thanking her and hoping for a "speedy reply" to his epistle. A Wisconsin soldier penned a similar letter of gratitude to the "dear little girl" who fashioned a comfort bag for a "boy in blue." An anonymous volunteer recuperating in a Nashville hospital acknowledged the "boldness" of his letter, but believed his purpose of thanking the "Ladies of Ohio" for the socks, slippers and

---

[22] The songs "Just Before the Battle Mother," and "Who Will Care for Mother Now?" were extremely popular among the troops during the war. See Irwin Silver, ed., *Songs of the Civil War* (New York: Oxford University Press, 1960), 153, 157.

[23] Culpepper, *Trials and Triumphs*, 250; Nina Silber and Mary Beth Sievens, eds., *Yankee Correspondence: Civil War Letters between New England Soldiers and the Home Front* (Charlottesville: University Press of Virginia, 1996), 50; and Anne L. Macdonald, *No Idle Hands: The Social History of American Knitting* (New York: Ballantine Books, 1988), 105.

handkerchiefs the society sent him pardoned his otherwise presumptuous actions.[24]

Thus since the beginning of the war, "bold" letters were passing from members of Soldiers' Aid Societies to volunteers with whom they were unacquainted. The propriety of this kind of correspondence was permitted because it was considered part of the women's patriotic duty. They wrote to the boys in order to boost morale. But the breakdown of social niceties during the war also allowed for such "familiar" letters to pass between the unacquainted correspondents without the taint of vulgarity, which most surely would have blemished the communication during normal circumstances. It is not difficult to believe, then, that soldiers involved in the correspondence craze felt similar letters between themselves and correspondents for whom they advertised were likewise sanctioned by the exigencies of the war that had loosened societal mores.[25]

Perhaps it was a letter like this that prompted M. Debray and Monte Cristo to advertise for correspondents in the *Chicago Tribune*. These two boys from Nashville ignited a correspondence craze among the western troops when they published their plea in April 1863. The typical ad included five components in no particular order: a request for correspondence, a physical description of the authors, a list of qualities they sought in their prospective correspondents, their purpose for advertising, and the authors' names and mailing addresses. The ads varied according to length and style. For instance, the soldier D. H. Jackson must surely have caught the eye of an Indiana girl when he advertised in the form of a poem:

---

[24] Anonymous to Ohio Ladies' Aid Society, October 8, 1863, Western Reserve Historical Society, Cleveland, Ohio; and "Touching Letters From a Wisconsin Soldier," *Sanitary Commission Bulletin* (Philadelphia) 39 (July 1, 1865): 1224.

[25] In a similar fashion, historian Kristie Ross believes that "lady volunteers" working on the hospital transports for the Sanitary Commission began to gain independence and autonomy through the confidence in their work and as a result desired greater freedom and power. Not only did their work broaden their views on women's subordinate roles, but, Ross argues, "the intimacy of life on the transports . . . forced the female volunteers to reconsider the everyday forms and behavior of both men and women." The spartan conditions on the boats, the exposure to wounded and dying men, and the cramped living quarters all "highlighted the artificially and socially contrived nature of the symbols and assigned attributes of gender." See Kristie Ross, "Arranging a Doll's House: Refined Women as Union Nurses," in *Divided Houses: Gender in the Civil War,* ed. by Catherine Clinton and Nina Silber (New York: Oxford University Press, 1992), 109.

Listen Ladies one and all,
to the sincere and earnest call.
For correspondence to cheer this life,
and afterwards to become a wife.
I am a Hoosier, when I am at home,
but this war has caused me to roam;
since July 1st of 1861,
I have been engaged in our country's fun.
Now ladies, who will be the first
a letter in the office to thrust,
and please don't fail in this kind action
to address your letter to D. H. Jackson.[26]

Although his method was unique, Jackson's message echoed that of hundreds of other soldiers who placed ads. Not all sought wives, but like M. Debray, Monte Cristo, and Jackson, advertisers utilized this novel medium to recreate the gaiety of civilian life, establish friendships, or simply brighten life in camp.

By placing correspondence ads in newspapers, soldiers hoped to relive some of the playful moments they enjoyed with women before they enlisted. "A young Artillery man" in Chattanooga solicited "correspondence with one or more of Illinois' bright eyed, rosy cheeked, free-hearted daughters." "Two of Abraham's chosen children" also voiced their "desire to correspond with an indefinite number of our fair cousins." Sergeants Stillwagon and Brooks of the 44th Indiana Volunteer Infantry simply missed the feminine touch. We "have been long exiled from female society," they explained, "and would now look to correspond with some of our fair cousins of the North."[27] The letter by an anonymous lieutenant who advertised in the periodical *Waverly* is perhaps the best example of the frivolous aims that some of the advertisers desired from the correspondence. "Dear Hattie," wrote the lieutenant, "Pardon the affectionate familiarity but you know its all in fun." Although he admitted in his missive that his advertised personal portrait differed "materially" from his "true" appearance, he thought "it was all for fun, therefore funningly gave a

---

[26] "Correspondence on the Brain," *Chicago Tribune*, August 12, 1863; and D. H. Jackson, "Wanted Correspondence," *Chicago Tribune*, June 4, 1864.

[27] "Two Artillery men," *Chicago Tribune*, January 8, 1864; and "Two of Abraham's," *Chicago Tribune*, September 10, 1863.

fictitious description as well as cognomen." Hattie apparently responded to his advertisement with similar light-hearted intentions. "Judging from your letter," the lieutenant noted, "I take you to be of . . . that class know[n] as 'romps'—a class by the way, which I rather admire." He enclosed a carte de visite of her "incognito" and asked Hattie, "when you answer this which I hope you will do without fail—be kind enough to give a correct description . . . of your own sweet self."[28]

Unfortunately, this is the only letter that survived between these two wartime correspondents. However, it provides tangible evidence that not only did some soldiers advertise with no more than entertainment as their aim, but that they did so with the belief that although their letters were silly, there was no impropriety in their participation. Both advice books, *How to Behave* and *The Ladies' Indispensable* assured their readers that casual acquaintances "last only for the time being. You are not obliged to know them afterwards, however familiar for the time." Letters exchanged between two informally introduced people, who wanted no commitment beyond the intimacy of the correspondence, allowed participants to act as if they occupied "the same seat in a railway car." There was "no reason . . . why [they] . . . should remain silent during the whole journey because they . . . [had] not been introduced." Their familiarity ended upon reaching their destination and neither was obligated to know the other afterwards.[29]

Other soldiers desiring correspondence with their "fair cousins of the north" were motivated by the dullness of camp life. The tedious nature of drills and the endless hours of waiting for orders wore on the soldiers' patience. Charlie Wallace asked for letters because "camp life is beginning to get tiresome and anything" to assuage the boredom "will be welcomed." A. J. Franklin, in Corinth, Mississippi, likewise desired correspondence "for the purpose of relieving the monotony of camp life, and whiling away some of the dull lonesome hours when off duty." At the end of the war, Captain J. C. P. and R. W. R. asked for correspondents to "greatly assist a veteran in passing

---

[28] "Anonymous," to Hattie, February 9, 1864, Special Collections, Carol M. Newman Library, Virginia Polytechnic Institute and State University, Blacksburg, Va.

[29] *How to Behave*, 68–70; and *Ladies' Indispensable Assistant* (New York: Nassau Street, 1852), 127.

away the hours which hang heavily upon us, since the rebels have been conquered and there is no more fighting for us to do." Soldiers convalescing also found the tedium of hospital life unbearable. One of "Uncle Sam's nephews" who "endured the hardships and encountered the dangers of several active campaigns" found "himself lying in garrison" and "growing tired of inactivity." In an unusually candid ad, two soldiers who had their legs amputated suggested that they had been "condemned and must pass the short remaining portion of" their "term of service in hospital." They boldly stated, "We are too young to be interesting, too poor to marry, and too lame to be elegant, but we do adore the girls, and would sell anything but our scars for long letters from pretty correspondents." They asked, "Shall we become insane from inactivity and be compelled to curse our wooden legs, or will someone take pity upon us and write to Fred Clayton and George Langford?"[30]

Boredom, the desperation for female companionship, and the frivolities of civilian life motivated other volunteers to seek novel methods to entertain themselves. A group of Massachusetts soldiers posted at Brandy Station, Virginia, in the spring of 1864, recreated a hometown dance. Not wanting to rely on the local ladies because they were too "rebellious," the men improvised by dressing up sixty soldiers as women. They chose the drummer boys to play the part of the females. The success of the masquerade was recorded when one soldier wrote home that "some of the real women went but the boy girls was so much better looking they left." These stories illustrate not only the ingenuity of the soldiers, but also the lengths to which they were willing to go to recreate activities from home. As noted by historian Reid Mitchell, the tales also indicate that these men "missed their home; they missed the social entertainment to which they had been accustomed; they missed women."[31]

---

[30] Charlie Wallace, "Wanted Correspondence," June 7, 1863; J. Henri Howi and Will Carpenter, May 15, 1863; A. J. Franklin, June 18, 1863; Fred Clayton and George Langford, April 4, 1864; and J. C. P. and R. W. R., April 26, 1865, all in *Chicago Tribune.*

[31] Mitchell, *The Vacant Chair*, 71–72. E. Anthony Rotundo noted that males involved in young men's organizations during the mid nineteenth century also engaged in this "gender-blurring" by having men play the female roles within their dramatic performances. He explained that this occurred during a time in life "when young men were living without maternal nurture and had to supply each other with some form of substitute." This was also at a time when these men were "most separate

The rules of introduction and courting could not be followed because soldiers did not have the time or opportunity. Placing ads, like holding an improvised ball, allowed soldiers to adapt to their restricted social environment, without pushing the boundaries of propriety too far. Letters to potential spouses or new-found female friends allowed them a taste of civilian life that they could not get in letters exchanged with their parents, siblings, or other relatives. The letters soldiers received from their wives, prospective mates, and sometimes simply friends who were women, filled a need for femininity these soldiers sorely felt. In an anonymous letter to Mrs. Esther Hawkes, a convalescing soldier expressed his need for womanly society and how her presence reified the concept of home for him. "I do wish you would come up and see me," he wrote. "You appear something like home to me and to all I guess that I know." Similarly, a "Western Soldier" confessed in a letter to a "New England Woman" with whom he was unacquainted that he had taken the liberty of reading two of her letters to other soldiers and "dared" to write to her in the unusual "circumstances" because he wanted to correspond with a lady from the "land of steady habits." He explained that correspondence from home "keeps up the spirits of the army," but they also wanted to "hear from those whom we have never seen—the good, true women of our land, whom we respect and honor."[32]

Not all advertisers desired simple friendship or a casual correspondence. Some volunteers undoubtedly resented the war's intrusion into their lives because it postponed careers and marriage plans. Many soldiers learned from relatives that their "girls" did not always wait for them to come marching home. Charles Clayton and William Cozen of the 12th Iowa Volunteer Infantry referred to themselves as "two veteran soldiers" who "have lately had the misfortune to lose their sweethearts and to supply their places wish to open correspondence." Cyrus and Harry Mortimer met with the same misfortune

---

from female company" and nervous about romantic intimacy, so "they used the stage to practice on each other." See E. Anthony Rotundo, *American Manhood: Transformations in Masculinity from the Revolution to Modern Era* (New York: Basic Books, 1993), 67.

[32] "Anonymous" to Esther H. Hawkes, December 24, 1863, Esther Hill Hawkes Papers, Library of Congress, Washington, D.C.; Lydia Minturn Post, ed., *Soldiers' Letters From Camp, Battle-Field and Prison* (New York: Bunce & Huntington, 1865), 201–4.

when "their girlfriends" sent "them word that they could not and would not wait for any pesky soldiers."[33] A "veteran" discharged from the service returned home to find he lost "his lover . . . while fighting his country's battles." Five soldiers from the 36th Illinois Regiment discovered that civilians had stolen their "Prairie Flowers" and blamed "the ruthless hands of a species of the Home Gents known as stay at Home Braves. Who will die for their country—if . . . they nest up in the loft while Betty kills the Bear." Other men left for war without girl friends. The "Gay Cavalier" and "Wild Rover" "were unfortunately called away before they had gained the affections of any of those dear ones, whose short and sweet epistles" were "so cheering to a soldier's life." Soldiers wanted correspondence to relieve their loneliness and boredom, but more than that, they wanted to meet someone of the opposite sex to establish a friendship. Like A. B. Franklin of the 1st Kentucky, many hoped "that a reciprocity of feeling" would "mellow acquaintance into friendship and prepare the way to matrimony."[34]

At first, the volunteers requested lady correspondents with "a view to fun, love, or matrimony."[35] As correspondence ads gained popularity, more soldiers placed advertisements focused on courtship and marriage. Mary P. Ryan explains in *The Empire of the Mother* that three social relationships existed between 1830 and 1860: "those of parents and children, husband and wife, and household and society." All soldiers had experienced the parent-child and household and society relationships. But in a culture that lauded domesticity and its core component the family, unmarried soldiers longed to establish households of their own. By placing ads, soldiers made a step in that direction. A cartoon appearing in *Harper's* in June 1863 reflects the expectations of northern society toward a soldier's marital status. A mustached volunteer is pictured leaning upon his rifle, as he converses with his beautiful sweetheart, Clara. With her head tilted down, she asks her soldier shyly, "Don't you think it an anomaly,

[33] Charles Clayton and William Cozens, "Wanted Correspondence," July 6, 1864; Cyrus and Harry Mortimer, August 24, 1863; and B. Stillwagon and Harry Brooks, January 9, 1865, all in *Chicago Tribune*.

[34] "Veteran," "Wanted Correspondence," July 18, 1865; Harry St. Clair, September 3, 1863; "Gay Cavalier" and "Wild Rover," "Wanted Correspondence," June 3, 1863; and A. B. Franklin, May 4, 1863, all in *Chicago Tribune*.

[35] M. Debray and Monte Cristo, "Wanted Correspondence," *Chicago Tribune*, April 27, 1863.

Tom, your preparing to fight for your hearth and home, while you have not a wife?" It seems obvious from the number of men advertising "with a view to matrimony" that the women were not the only ones who felt singleness was an "anomaly."[36] A captain from the 56th U.S. Infantry explained that "having been long in the service, [I] have but very limited acquaintances in the North, and would make this proposition with a view of selecting a partner for life." After giving a complete description of himself, a Wisconsin soldier stated that "on the whole [I] wish to quit a life of single blessedness and enter the portals of matrimonial felicity (after this cruel war is over)." Two other soldiers who believed they had "rejoiced in single blessedness long enough" desired "opening a correspondence with a few of Eve's fair daughters with the object" of changing "their present condition by assuming the vows of marital."[37]

The soldiers revealed their earnestness for serious correspondence by requesting that their correspondents meet specific requirements. Victorians admired intelligent, pious, chaste, moral, healthy women whose actions and dress were equally graceful and who commanded their households through efficiency and thrift. Rosy-cheeks, "high chests, plump arms, comely figures, and a graceful and handsome mien" described the ideal womanly form.[38] Soldiers requested many of these traits of the ideal woman in their advertisements. Almost all the soldiers specified a woman between the ages of sixteen and thirty-five who possessed a "fine figure" and a "good share of personal beauty." Soldiers serious about meeting a lifelong mate frequently noted the state they wanted girls to write from, usually Wisconsin, Illinois, Indiana, Michigan, or New York. They also desired a "respectable" and "refined" lady with a "pleasant disposition." Some

---

[36] Mary P. Ryan, *The Empire of the Mother: American Writing about Domesticity 1830–1860* (New York: The Institute for Research in History and The Haworth Press, 1982), 144–145; and *Harpers Weekly*, June 27, 1863.

[37] Captain C. S., "Wanted Correspondence," April 12, 1864; H. Clinton, March 7, 1864; and Charles Kelly and George Manning, June 6, 1864, all in *Chicago Tribune*.

[38] Nineteenth-century women commanded the domestic circle in management of household duties and raising their children. Women were educated to fulfill this role and to be companions to their husbands. They were not expected or encouraged to be educated for careers outside of the home. Cogan, *The All-American Girl*, 41. Percy Van Dyke desired an ideal woman, judging from his description. He advertised for "a young healthy, educated, and refined wife of an impassioned decided disposition; great beauty not absolutely essential, but a fine, well-developed figure indispensable." Percy Van Dyke, "Matrimonial," *New York Herald*, February 7, 1864.

soldiers were even more specific about what they did and did not want in a correspondent. A soldier stationed at Vicksburg warned that "rouge, slate pencils, bad spelling, and slang phrases, [are] inadmissible." Two soldiers from the 24th Ohio Volunteer Infantry were looking for well-rounded women when they asked for "ladies, who are pretty, intelligent, funny, religious, industrious, good singers, good dancers, good cooks, good Union girls and who will make good wives should they ever marry." Two officers from "Grose's Brigade" declared that they wanted to correspond with "two young ladies, who can get up early enough in the morning to dictate what shall be gotten up for breakfast and if Bridget be sick, will get it themselves without grumbling or burning their fingers." Peter Geisel and Joseph Reamer, stationed in Murfreesboro, Tennessee, wanted lady correspondents who "must be submissive but not look so," and who "must be for the Union, horse, foot, and dragoon," and "not [be] ashamed to be seen at work, and possess all other good qualities that constitute a lady."[39]

To ensure that their correspondents were physically attractive, they exchanged photographs and occasionally demanded them before a letter would be answered. Photographs, "shadows," or "likenesses" were very popular during the Civil War. Most volunteers carried photographs of family members or their "girls" into battle, so it was not unusual for these soldiers to petition their correspondents for a "shadow." In fact, letter writers had more reason to request likenesses because they had never met their correspondents, and they wanted to make sure they were not entering into a serious relationship that they would regret once they returned home. The "Ambrotypes" cost about a dollar each, so they were not cheap. Considering that the average volunteer earned $12 a month, the financial investment involved in corresponding is evidence of the seriousness of this phenomenon. A soldier "disabled in his-country's service" taking "this method of making his wants known," "respectfully requested" carte de visites from the ladies. A veteran on furlough in New York stated "carte-de-vistes [sic] must be enclosed," but assured the "fairer sex" he would return them "if so desired." A

---

[39] Charles Lynch, John S. Dayle and Jones M. Clarry, "Wanted Correspondence," November 24, 1863; "R. H. B.," August 27, 1863; John W. and Willie M., August 12, 1863; Osborn L. and Horace G., May 4, 1863; and Peter Geisel and Joseph Reamer, May 25, 1863, all in *Chicago Tribune*.

young soldier in "affluent circumstances" insisted that "all letters must contain carte-de-visites." Soldiers earnest about their propositions of marriage demanded the same honesty, seriousness, and commitment from the women responding to the ads. By asking for photographs and references, sincere volunteers hoped to maintain the standard of propriety required during typical courting practices.[40]

Soldiers felt the paucity of the company of respectable females and used the newspaper to aid them in their search, but the war did not limit the women's choices of potential mates nearly as much. Although enlistment took away the more patriotic men, it did not end social events. For instance, a young Michigan woman named Helen explained to her brother, George Aplin, that since the war had begun "the young people" of Thetford "get along just about as usual." Dances, picnics, skating, and outings continued in spite of the war, and the conflict even furnished ladies with new kinds of entertainment in the forms of fairs, amateur theatricals, and "calico balls," all in the name of raising money for the benefit of the troops. The war also produced a marrying craze in all areas of the North and South. Soldiers hurriedly tied the knot before being sent to the front, or volunteers sometimes entered "wedded bliss" while on leave. In general, the North was undermobilized in comparision to the South, but in northern communities such as Thetford, recruitment had created a scarcity of men. Within the same letter, Helen went on to explain that gatherings continued even though the "boys or young men [of the town] have left, (so many, that it is a great rarity to see one much more to speak to one.)." With so few men to compete with for the hand of a woman, she saw the implications for her brother. "So you see George," Helen suggested, "if you had remained here you would have a real pleasant time no doubt." Perhaps women in other small northern towns experienced a similar drought of men similar to that in Thetford and dreamed of dances with more young men. Whatever the reason for writing, the "noble women of the north" also participated in this unique mode of introduction.[41]

---

[40] Culpepper, *Trials and Triumphs*, 286; Percy Van Dyke, "Matrimonial," *New York Herald*, February 7, 1864; "Frank," "Matrimonial," *New York Herald*, January 22, 1864; and John Gephard, "Matrimonial," *New York Herald*, January 30, 1864.

[41] Massey, *Women in the Civil War*, 254–56; "Helen" to George Aplin, July 20, 1862, George Aplin Papers, Clements Library, University of Michigan, Ann Arbor. For more information about the undermobilization of men in the North, see Thomas R. Kemp, "Community and War: The Civil War Experience of Two New Hampshire

The number of women who responded to these requests and who actually struck up a correspondence with the "boys in blue" is uncertain, but we have a glimpse of women's courting preferences because the newspapers contain ads placed by the "gentler sex." Victorian women looked for particular traits in men, just as men did in women. The ideal male possessed sensitivity, "gentle" personal habits, intellect, moral values, an education, and industriousness. Most women desired men with fair complexions and handsome faces and figures, but they placed more importance on men's intellect, education, compatibility, economic status, and potential earning ability rather than on physical attributes. Although a handsome man could bring a woman aesthetic enjoyment, she was more likely to be concerned with future financial stability because she herself had limited earning potential. That is not to say that women did not aid their families' finances, but men were expected to be the primary economic providers.[42]

Undoubtedly some civilian men met the ideal, but most women held a patriotic place in their hearts for the volunteers. Their desires to acquaint themselves with noble mates were just as real as the soldiers', and in the first month of the correspondence craze Grace Greenwood and Gertie Hamilton of Ottawa, Illinois, placed their own ad. Wishing a correspondence with a "view to matrimony," they asked for "good-looking, intelligent" gentlemen between the ages of twenty and twenty-six who possessed "an income sufficient for all practical purposes." In 1863, only a handful of women placed ads but their numbers tripled in 1864 and 1865. More women, it seems, came around to the opinion that Lina Douglass and Gertrude Atherton of Coldwater, Michigan, expressed in April 1864. "Everybody is advertising for correspondents: why can't I? Was asked by a friend. So here we come. How many gentlemen will respond? Don't all come at once."[43]

Towns," in *Toward a Social History of the American Civil War*, ed. by Maris A. Vinovskis (Cambridge, Eng.: Cambridge University Press, 1990), 31–77.

[42] Cogan, *All-American Girl*, 143. See Karen Lystra's *Searching the Heart* for more about women's concerns with the earning potential of their prospective mates.

[43] Grace Greenwood and Gertie Hamilton, "Wanted Correspondence," May 25, 1863; and Lina Douglass and Gertrude Atherton, April 21, 1864, both in *Chicago Tribune*.

The women who placed ads were widows, those who considered themselves "desperate," those seeking correspondence for fun or mutual improvement, or those desiring marriage. But just because these women described themselves as "desperate" does not mean that they were not discerning. The widow Mrs. C.R.N. of Chicago portrayed herself as "not pretty but very lonely." She wished "to get acquainted with a few gentlemen to pass away lonely hours," adding that "Copperheads need not trouble themselves unless you intend to repent your sins and vote for Mr. A. L. in November." Alina Nancil, also of Chicago, noted that she was "a middle-aged widow lady" who "wished to make the acquaintance of a real gentleman, with intentions of matrimony." Annie and Mattie, two young widows of sixteen and twenty, directed their ad towards military men with "a view to matrimony." But, they noted, "no privates need apply."[44]

A couple of women considered themselves in a "desperate situation" and placed a correspondence ad because they felt they had no other choice. "Four charming young females" from Bloomington, Illinois, exclaimed that they had "been trying to get married these long years, and are now getting desperate," so they invited "the young males of America to open correspondence" with them. Georgina, a "pretty, educated, young, musician" from New York, felt "obliged to advertise for a husband." "Let the cry," she suggested, "be onward to marriage or to death." An unsigned ad from Mishawaka, Indiana, frankly stated this woman's situation. "I am getting on in years, I have never had a lover or gentlemen correspondent. I am desperate. Will someone take pity on the unappreciated?"[45]

Many women placed ads with the intention of gaining intellectual improvement and fun from the correspondence. Effie and Kittie from Lexington, Illinois, wanted to correspond with soldiers with the "object of fun and friendship." Writing from Indiana, Estelle, Imogene, and Irene wished "to open correspondence with same number of young gents, for pleasure and improvement." Gertrude and Leona,

---

[44] Mrs. C. R. N., "Wanted Correspondence," May 29, 1864; Alina Nancil, Aug. 29, 1863; and Annie and Mattie, April 21, 1864, all in *Chicago Tribune*.

[45] Clara Kenric, Maud Somers, Mable Morland, and Minnie Glenn, "Wanted Correspondence," *Chicago Tribune*, February 9, 1865; Georgina McCleanan, "Matrimonial," *New York Herald*, February 9, 1864; and "Anonymous," *Chicago Tribune*, May 9, 1864.

from Elkhart, Indiana, wanted to correspond with anyone, male or female, who had "fine literary taste and [an] education." Their object was "simply pleasure and improvement."[46]

Most of the women, however, hoped to meet prospective spouses, and the majority of the ads reflected this aim. Those who desired marriage were frank in their requests, stating "with a direct view to matrimony" or "object—matrimony." Other women were more detailed in their purposes. Julia and Hattie of Bloomington, Illinois, proclaimed our "object in view is love, but more particularly its consequences. None need answer this unless they are tall, handsome, have a mustache and smoke cigars and are willing to marry us." Edith and Maude from Chicago considered themselves neither beautiful nor wealthy, but they did have "an amount of common sense," and wished "to form a matrimonial alliance with gentlemen equally endowed." Nina and Nelly of New York, who were "thinking of launching out on the tempestuous sea of matrimony," wished "through the medium of the pen to learn more of the traits of the opposite sex." An unknown correspondent described herself as "an unorthodox lady, who is socially, intellectually, spiritually, and progressively companionable" and who "wants a husband who can meet her on the same base." Eve and Sue, from Beloit, Wisconsin, placed their request in the form of a poem: "By two lovely women, fair as the moon, Wanted—two husbands and that very soon . . . must NOT be enamored, of every new face—in fact, we would like to obtain if we can, what we never yet found, a reliable man."[47]

An interesting twist to the ads came in 1864. Because it was a leap year, by tradition, women could propose to men. The custom supposedly originated when St. Patrick, hoping to assuage St. Bridget's complaint that only men had the right to propose, offered to allow women the opportunity to propose once every seven years. Not satisfied, Bridget suggested that because it was leap year, women

---

[46] Effie Benton and Kittie Clayton, "Wanted Correspondence," June 25, 1864; Estelle, Imogene, and Irene, September 3, 1863; and Gertrude Brockway and Leona Cuyler, September 16, 1864, all in *Chicago Tribune*.

[47] Julia Mortimer and Hattie Bishop, "Wanted Correspondence," April 2, 1864, *Chicago Tribune*; Edith and Maude Wellington, July 1, 1863, *Chicago Tribune*; Nina and Nelly Marston, "Matrimonial," *New York Herald*, February 12, 1864; "Anonymous," *Chicago Tribune*, June 12, 1865; and Eve and Sue, *Chicago Tribune*, June 1, 1863.

should be able to propose every four years. St. Patrick agreed.[48] Whether Victorians took this practice literally or not, or whether the increase in the number of ads placed by females was merely a coincidence, almost three times the number of women advertised in 1864 as in 1863. An anonymous woman explained in her ad that this "year women have a right to say what they have a mind to." Many of the soldiers encouraged lady correspondents to take the initiative because of the custom. Three soldiers from the 13th Illinois Infantry wanted to correspond with "young girls" with the "view to fun and love and as it is Leap-Year, the girls must decide the rest." Three soldiers stationed near Athens, Alabama, wanted to "form matrimonial alliances" with the "marriageable daughters of the loyal North," but suggested, "Ladies take your choice as Leap Year gives you the unquestioned privilege to do so."[49]

Leap year or not, women's participation in correspondence ads, regardless of their declared purpose, was counter to the ideal of a middle-class Victorian woman. First described by Barbara Welter as a "True Woman," the ideal cast women as pious, pure, submissive, and domestic. But the most expected feminine virtue in a woman was submission. Men commanded the public realm and were the movers and doers. Women were restricted to the home and were expected, above all, to be passive, submissive followers of the men in their lives. Women's participation in the correspondence craze is therefore contrary to the concept of female gentility, as defined by Welter, and presents a problem for the historian. If women strictly followed the True Womanhood ideal, then it would seem that any woman who participated in the craze, whether with a response to an ad or as an advertiser herself, would fall short of the ideal, as her behavior would not be restricted to the home nor would it be consid-

---

[48] Over the years, to guard themselves against female pursuers, men insisted that women wanting to propose had to indicate "their intention by wearing a scarlet petticoat with a clearly visible hem." This gave the bachelors a warning and a sporting chance to get away. R. Brasch, *How Did It Begin? Customs and Superstitions and Their Romantic Origins* (New York: David McKay Co. Inc., 1966), 31–32.

[49] Mary E. Massey notes that the war caused rapid changes in conventions and that during 1864, leap year parties were held in which women planned and paid for men's entertainment. The more conservative citizens, of course, believed it "disgraceful" behavior for a lady. See Massey, *Women in the Civil War*, 259; Mrs. C. R. N., "Wanted Correspondence," May 29, 1864; Henry Harmless, Sergeant Williams and W. M. Napier, April 25, 1864; and Ralph Bangcliffe, Edward Mortimer, and John J. Louce, March 16, 1864, all in *Chicago Tribune*.

ered submissive. It is true that not all women and men condoned the correspondence craze, but because middle-class women willingly and boldly participated in the event it seems to suggest not that these women were an anomaly, but that nineteenth-century women had a broader concept of True Womanhood than historians first believed.[50]

Since Welter first voiced the True Womanhood thesis, in fact, it has come increasingly under attack. Scholars attempting to debunk the theory have argued that the image is too restrictive to encompass women of all classes and races. For instance, Joan Perkin explains that with the luxury of money, upper-class women usually ignored the tenets of True Womanhood. They had the ability to distribute patronage and were economically independent from their husbands. Confident in their own abilities and their own ideas, these women sensed few obligations to live under the constraints of middle-class morality. The lower classes also felt little pressure from the True Womanhood ideal. Working-class women were almost entirely beyond the reach of the civil law, because they had little or no property to protect and, when they did, they and their husbands had neither the resources nor the know-how to appeal to the courts. As a result, only women on the fringes of the middle class, anxious to attain status, and those firmly established as part of the middle class, eager to preserve their positions, felt any pressures to maintain True Woman concepts. For most lower-class women, the harsh economic realities that pushed them out of the home to earn money left them little time to worry about propriety.[51]

Other historians suggest that women more than likely chose aspects of the ideal rather than submitting to all of its principles. Ann Douglas, for example, disputes "the notion that women pursued this ideal wholeheartedly," but claims instead that women held on to certain tenets to maintain "influence inside the family, the church, and the social world." Karen Lystra extends Douglas's argument by proposing that neither Victorian women nor men absolutely followed their prescribed sex roles. Although definitions help us to understand past behavior, the essence of definitions are too restrictive and most likely would have been impractical. Men and women devised a sys-

---

[50] Welter, *Dimity Convictions*, 27–28.

[51] Joan Perkin, *Women and Marriage in Nineteenth-Century England* (Chicago: Lyceum Books, 1989), 101, 115.

tem for daily interactions that allowed them to blur gender boundaries while maintaining their distinctive sexual traits. In fact, Lystra
contends that Victorian "gender lines" were actually more fluid,
sometimes "redefined" and "more ambiguous than in the previous
century." On the other hand, Frances Cogan, in *The All-American
Girl*, argues that there were actually two ideals during the nineteenth
century from which women could choose, either the True Woman or
the Real Woman. The Real Woman ideal acted as the antithesis to
the True Woman in many ways, and each gained followers from 1840
to 1880. "Real Women," according to Cogan, "advocated intelligence, physical fitness and health, self-sufficiency, economic self-reliance, and careful marriage." Real Women were survivors, but they
were not selfish. They "remained good daughters, good sisters, wives,
and mothers because in their own eyes they were important to family
and to society." In a more recent study, Patricia Okker, in her work
on *Godey's* editor Sarah J. Hale, asserts that there were more than
two ideals. In fact, there were several competing definitions; women
chose principles to suit their own notions of womanhood. As an illustration, Hale and other editors relied on the tenet that women were
morally superior to men and used this as an offensive and defensive
weapon to both expand women's roles in public and defend bold
behavior that crossed gender lines. According to Okker, women
formed their own ideals of womanhood with their own understanding
of proper and improper behavior, within limits of course. Furthermore, Okker's study goes beyond simply suggesting that there were
opposing views of womanhood by offering an explanation for why
women may have felt comfortable about partaking in the craze.[52]

Okker submits that Hale cultivated the idea of a separate woman's
culture not only to generate a readership for her magazine, but also
to empower women through the principle of female moral superiority. Hale relied on the ideology of sexual difference, although she
continued to argue that women were not intellectually inferior, as a
rationale to expand women's influence beyond the home and into the
public realm. One of her techniques to create a different and essen-

---

[52] Ann Douglas, *The Feminization of American Culture* (New York: Alfred A.
Knopf, 1977), 7; Lystra, *Searching the Heart*, 123–24; Cogan, *The All-American
Girl*, 4, 75, 121–22, 133, 159; and Patricia Okker, *Our Sister Editors: Sarah J. Hale
and the Tradition of Nineteenth-Century American Women Editors* (Athens: University of Georgia Press, 1995), 15, 17, 27.

tially feminine atmosphere within the magazine was to establish a special relationship between herself and her readers. Described by Okker as having a "sisterly editorial voice," Hale spoke to her readers as confidential friends and encouraged them to respond with letters and to contribute poems and stories. Hale and other editors who used this sisterly editorial voice established a dialogue with their readers. Through this exchange and Hale's editorials and articles on moral superiority, women learned to take pride in their domestic work and to contribute to society outside of the home. Moreover, the experience of submitting their writings and opinions coupled with the intimate dialogue produced an environment in which women became accustomed to and comfortable with engaging newspaper and magazine editors. Confident about sharing their ideas within the public realm, it seems likely that this experience made participating in the correspondence craze appear less threatening. Undoubtedly there were some people who viewed all women's involvement in the craze as shocking, but the competing interpretations of womanhood actually afforded women a range of acceptable behavior. With such a broadened definition of the True Woman, and the knowledge that women had been contributing to periodicals and newspapers decades before the craze, it seems plausible that some women could have participated in the craze without loss of respectability.[53]

Self-assured and unashamed, many women joined the craze to seek the association of soldiers and even civilian men. Although civilians' odds of finding mates may have improved slightly during the war because of the single men who had volunteered, perhaps they viewed personal ads as a means of avoiding the "irksomeness of introduction, acquaintance and courtship" as two mechanics who advertised for correspondents expressed it. Civilians who advertised during the war included lonely businessmen, farmers, lawyers, or widowers looking for new spouses. The newcomer to town, or businessmen who merely wanted to make an acquaintance while in the city also utilized the ads.[54]

---

[53] Okker, *Our Sister Editors*, 15, 23–24, 31, 60–63.

[54] Historian Timothy Gilfoyle in his work on prostitution in New York City notes that by the 1840s, courtship rituals had changed so much because of the transient nature of the population, the importance of teenage peer groups, and the decrease of regulations by employers and churches. Many men began expressing their frustrations about the difficulty of meeting respectable women by advertising in the newspapers. "By the 1860s, 'personals' were a regular feature in New York newspapers.

Civilians seeking superficial companions placed ads for amusement and intellectual improvement. A middle-aged widower of Chicago asked to strike up correspondence with a "widow lady . . . with a view to confidential and paramount friendship." Charles Merton and R. T. Williams requested correspondence "to discuss with any number of ladies . . . such subjects as they may propose, either love, politics, or general literature." Charles Germayne, also of Chicago, began his ad with "Wanted-Flirtation." Germayne requested "the pleasure of an exchange of letters, . . . with some charming and delightful young lady, with view to mutual amusement."[55]

Most of the civilians, however, sought correspondents who would become their wives. A Chicago businessman "weary of going every evening from his business to his lonely bachelor rooms," wanted to form an "acquaintance" with a lady of refinement, "worthy to be called a wife: to welcome him . . . with a glad smile of joy to a home of mutual happiness." A young farmer from Steuben County, Indiana, desired a lady from "a respectable family and the possessor of at least $2,000." He added, "any young lady answering to the above description can procure a husband and home" by writing him. A New York "Gentleman" with "an ultimate view" to "matrimony" insisted his correspondent must be "the ideal of female loveliness." To him, this meant that she not be "over five feet in height," that she weigh "from 100 to 120 pounds," and possess "small feet and hands, brown hair, and brown or blue eyes." A Chicagoan, temporarily returned from California, asked to "form an acquaintance by letter . . . with the view of finding an agreeable companion" to return to the Golden State with him.[56]

Concerned with propriety, many assured prospective correspondents that the "strictest confidence" would be taken and the "strictest

---

In rural towns and villages where the market had less effect on the traditions, men had fewer problems meeting women. See Timothy Gilfoyle, *City of Eros: New York City, Prostitution, and the Commercialization of Sex* (New York: W. W. Norton, 1992), 102, 114.

[55] O. O. Oliver, "Wanted Correspondence," June 18, 1863; Charles Merton and R. T. Williams, March 22, 1864; and Charles Germayne, May 19, 1863, all in *Chicago Tribune*.

[56] J. Stafford, "Wanted Correspondence," *Chicago Tribune*, September 18, 1863; "Anonymous," *Chicago Tribune*, November 21, 1863; T. R. S., "Matrimonial," *New York Herald*, January 21, 1864; and Ralph McClure, *Chicago Tribune*, August 25, 1863.

discretion" would be kept. Louis Vancour and friend, from Springfield, Illinois, promised that "the advertisers" were "gentlemen" and would "treat all communications with the respect and confidence due from a gentleman to a lady." Eugene of Pekin, Illinois, pledged that "no deviations from the strict rules of propriety" would be "recognized," nor any "correspondence continued[,] without the knowledge and consent of parents or guardian." Willie Howard on the steamer *Baltic* assured his correspondents that "I will deal strictly honest and confidential with you." "Two young officers" of the 1st New Jersey professed to the "young ladies," that "all communications" would be "strictly confidential," but they would take "no notice" of "any communication unless accompanied by a carte de visite as proof of sincerity." Some "sincere" advertisers declared they were "of good moral character and steady habits" and desired the same qualities from the young ladies. Other correspondents seeking spouses required "Eve's fair daughters" to give their "real names." Aware of the commitment and proprieties that correspondence with "a view to marriage" necessitated, advertisers ensured confidentiality and morality, and asked for similar "steady habits," photographs, references, and real names from prospective mates as "proof of sincerity." Advertisers understood the "novel method" of the ads, but pleaded that circumstances "compelled" them "to resort to this medium."[57] However, they also realized the novelty of ads did not excuse them from the rules of etiquette. In fact, correspondents seeking matrimony were more likely to pursue and guarantee propriety because of the seriousness of their actions. It was not the act of courting that was anomalous, but their method of acquaintance. Correspondents bent a few rules of introduction, but maintained the broader precepts of

---

[57] Louis Vancour, "Wanted Correspondence," *Chicago Tribune*, December 10, 1863; Eugene, February 27, 1864, *Chicago Tribune*; Willie Howard, *New York Herald*, March 30, 1864; Harry Clarke & Edgar Effingham, "Matrimonial," *New York Herald*, February 12, 1864; and Charles Kelly or George Manning, "Wanted Correspondence," *Chicago Tribune,* June 6, 1864. See also August 25, 1863, May 2, 4, 5, 6, 1863, and June 16, 1863, *Chicago Tribune*; Willie Roberts & Eugene Curtis, "Wanted Correspondence," *Chicago Tribune*, June 16, 1863; Edgar Effingham, & Nina and Nelly Marston, "Matrimonial," *New York Herald*, February 12, 1864; and C. Hamilton, "Wanted Correspondence," *Chicago Tribune*, September 5, 1863. According to Rothman, men and women actively courting prized sincerity as a gauge by which to measure the intentions of each other and used it to uncover deceptive mates early enough in the courtship to avoid disaster. Rothman, *Hands and Hearts*, 42.

courting to preserve propriety and assure their correspondents of the sincerity of their missives. In essence, soldiers and civilians were willing to bend the code of propriety in order to maintain the decorum of meeting and courting respectable women.

The fact that the correspondents were concerned about the rules of propriety not only indicates sincerity of purpose, but also that the men and women seeking correspondents came from the middle class. Historians have shown that during the nineteenth century, only members of the middle class, or those on the fringes attempting to join the middling rank, were so anxious to follow the rules of etiquette so conscientiously. Assuring prospective mates of their own status and hoping to attract others of their class, advertisers left several signs of their middle-class identity. For instance, when the two officers from "Grose's Brigade" asked for women who would not grumble "if Bridget be sick," they signaled to all readers that they expected to have servants within their households. Not only was this a middle-class familial ideal, but their expectation that their potential wives would know how to make breakfast also hinted at middle-class feminine ideals that required women to be experts in the domestic art and managers of their households. Similarly, when a forty-six-year-old widower from New York sought a woman "willing to . . . make home pleasant and happy," he revealed his belief in the idea that women were meant to be the emotional and spiritual nurturers of the family. Indeed, his promise to "endeavor to make her a kind husband" suggested his acceptance of the companionate marriage, which depended upon the mutuality and friendship of the couple.[58] In turn, women seeking only the "boys in blue" showed these ladies' value in the manly ideal that the husbands should be the protectors of hearth and home. Certainly, volunteers who proudly declared their rank, described their injuries, or noted their time of enlistment within their ads identified with this ideal. Likewise, women who required their correspondents to "possess an income for all practical purposes," or a "moderate amount of . . . wealth" echoed society's belief that men were the economic providers and divulged their own concerns about maintaining their middle-class positions. Finally,

---

[58] Cogan, *All-American Girl*, 79–80; Rotundo, *American Manhood*, 132–33; Stephen M. Frank, *Life with Father: Parenthood and Masculinity in the Nineteenth-Century American North* (Baltimore: Johns Hopkins University Press, 1998), 24–25; *Chicago Tribune*, August 12, 1863; and *New York Herald*, January 19, 1864.

even advertisers not seeking permanent relationships communicated their middle-class status in their desires to begin a correspondence for the purpose of "mutual improvement." Moreover, the fact that these men and women had the leisure time to devote to the art of letter writing, and did not use letters simply as a means of communication, was yet another indication that they resided in the middle class. The irony is that the marks of class not only signaled potential correspondents, but they were also flags to more conservative middle-class readers who were not as convinced this "novel method" was a safe means of introduction, especially for members of their own class.[59]

Although it is difficult to gauge a response to activity of this nature because of the paucity of evidence, it is obvious that hundreds of men and women accepted this unique method of introduction simply by the record they left of their participation within the newspapers. Unfortunately, the only trace left of the public's opinion concerning the correspondence craze is the editorials of the *Chicago Tribune*.

The editors first responded to the ads in August 1863, at the height of their popularity. In an article entitled "Correspondence on the Brain," the editors reported the phenomenon, without commenting on its nature. They informed their readers that "a few months ago, an advertisement from a soldier, soliciting correspondence with young ladies was a curiosity. But the ailment has proved contagious in the army, and now this class of advertisements are inserted daily." The tone of the article was one of amusement with this new craze. In fact, it appears the editors believed these ads were harmless, as they stated that the "result will be a considerable increase in the revenue of the Post Office Department, and a brisk demand for marriage licenses when this cruel war is over." There was no stated concern about the impropriety of ladies or soldiers participating in this new medium of introduction.[60]

Two weeks later, the editors gave a less favorable report. When the ads continued to stream into the paper, the editors no longer saw these requests as amusing. The participants no longer appeared innocent but most probably were "young, indiscreet girls, and callow

---

[59] *Chicago Tribune*, May 25, 1863, and July 16, 1864; and Louise L. Stevenson, *The Victorian Homefront: American Thought and Culture, 1860–1880* (New York: Twayne, 1991), xx.

[60] "Correspondence on the Brain," *Chicago Tribune*, August 12, 1863.

boarding school misses." The editors claimed that "boys, young men, and females of questionable character" targeted the soldiers to "dupe" them. The soldiers did not receive missives from "respectable ladies" but from a "club of clerks . . . seated upon stools in a whole-sale house counting room." These "clerks" supposedly sent letters to the soldiers, pretending to be women, and enclosed photographs purchased from local photographers for twenty-five cents apiece. In their closing comments, the editors expressed their disdain for the indiscreet civilians and women who placed ads. The editors noted that the "folly" was no longer "confined to the boys in the army," but there were "many of this class of advertisement inserted by persons of either sex in the city." They admitted that a "few perhaps [were] in sober earnest," but the "great majority of them [were] from impure motives, by persons of questionable character."[61] Although there is no evidence of a "club of clerks" to fool the soldiers in this manner, it is interesting to note the different tones of the two editorials.

Initially, the editors viewed this as an innocent pastime, which they believed would fade away. Soldiers and civilians continued to send in ads, however, and the editors continued to publish the advertise-ments. By agreeing to publish the ads, the editors became the third party necessary for a proper introduction, and as the third party, the outcome of any relationship begun through the correspondence was the editors' responsibility. When the requests did not cease, the edi-tors felt it necessary to voice their concerns in a more direct article.

In a second article, the editors attempted to discourage any more people, in or out of the army, from participating in this "folly." The suggestion that men sat around forging signatures and buying fake photographs to fool soldiers seems a bit far-fetched. First, it is hard to believe grown men would have nothing better to do than write hundreds of letters to unsuspecting soldiers merely as a joke. Second, if men or disreputable women were involved, surely they had more profitable ends in mind than simply duping unwary soldiers. Of course, confidence men did devise elaborate ruses with which to in-veigle soldiers and swindle them out of their money. Agents for the United States Sanitary Commission reported that such widespread and systematic corruption thrived in all the major cities of the North where "sick, disabled, discharged or furloughed soldiers" passed

---

[61] "The Army Correspondence Mania," *Chicago Tribune*, August 24, 1863.

through on their journey home, and so certainly deception occurred on both sides of the correspondence, but these were most likely the minority, not the majority, as the editors suggested.[62]

Antebellum urbanites were susceptible to the games of the confidence man, and it does seem possible that the editors believed the unceasing flow of correspondence requests was just another elaborate racket. Karen Halttunen explains that "the proliferation of moveable wealth . . . and the growing confusion and anonymity of urban living, had made possible for the first time swindles . . . and other confidence games." It was the ad's quality of anonymity that the editors seemed most concerned with when they suggested that the correspondents were not the "young, indiscreet girls" they professed to be. Indeed, how would the soldiers know if their correspondents were propriety-conscious women, a "club of clerks," or worse, duplicitous women with vicious intentions? The editors believed the soldiers would not know until they were totally ensnared and powerless. By revealing that deceitful characters hid behind false names and identities intentionally to mislead their correspondents, the editors hoped to deter more innocent people from becoming involved. Perhaps the deceptive correspondents hoped eventually to arrange a meeting, at which point they would swindle their new confidants. Such a seducer advertised as "Favorite" in January 1864. Although the "handsome young lady of" eighteen clearly announced her intentions of matrimony, one has to wonder what devious designs prompted Favorite to ask for "the receipt of $1" to "secure an unlimited correspondence and if mutually agreeable a meeting."[63]

Favorite may have been a swindler, but her purpose seems a bit

---

[62] United States Sanitary Commission Document 26, June 28, 1861, 11; Vincent Coyler, *Report of Vincent Colyer on the Reception and Care of the Soldiers Returning from the War* (New York: G. A. Whitehorne, 1865), 10.

[63] "Favorite," "Matrimonial," *New York Herald*, January 20, 1864; and Halttunen, *Confidence Men and Painted Women*, 6–7. Halttunen's study provides answers to why the editors may have been suspicious of the correspondents from the newspapers. "A survey of New York police captains in the 1860s estimated that of 2,500 professional criminals in the city, 100 were confidence men operating games such as the 'Spanish Prisoner' racket; another 100 were 'damper sneaks,' men who posed as businessmen and engaged in elaborate negotiations or simply loitered around places of business to steal unguarded bonds of cash; and 25 were forgers. Police thus estimated that nearly one out of ten professional criminals in New York in the 1860s was a confidence man." Halttunen also notes that targets of the confidence men were just as easily males as females.

clearer than the correspondence practices of Hattie Burleigh. The true picture of what occurred between Hattie and her five soldier correspondents is ambiguous because the few surviving soldiers' letters reveal only fragments of their relationships. Martie, Willie, Charles, Albert, and Harvey all corresponded with Hattie between 1864 and 1865. How Hattie's correspondence with the soldiers began, or indeed, how she acquired their names and addresses remains a mystery. Seemingly, Hattie wrote to a couple of the men under the pretense of collecting "war stories" she intended to compile after the hostilities ended. Charles Field of the 108th New York thanked Hattie "for the kindness you would do me in giving me a place in your War Story . . . but I would respectfully decline as my adventures in the army are as naught." Lieutenant Harvey Lloyd asked Hattie "as far as sketches of camp life, adventures, skirmishes &c . . . are you going to write a book?" Martie, Willie, and Albert were simply happy to have a female correspondent. Martie believed himself "highly honored at securing" her as "a correspondent," and Willie assured Hattie he took "great pleasure in receiving" her "letters, as well as answering them." Albert found it "refreshing to unbend the mind from the affairs of war and read a kindly letter though it" was from one he "never knew and perhaps never" would, "except through the medium of the pen."[64]

What is clear is that Hattie was not entirely honest with her soldiers, especially when it came to her true identity. Although all her new friends eventually knew her as Hattie, she began her correspondence with Albert under the assumed name of "Miss Lizzie," and as "Iva May" with Harvey. When Charles asked Hattie about a correspondent of hers named "Willie" she "positively assert[ed]" she "had not a correspondent by the name, fictitious or otherwise." She asked Willie "never" to "reveal" her "Secret." He replied, "You speak as though you would be afraid that a certain friend should know of our

---

[64] Charles Field to Hattie Burleigh, August 27, 1864; Harvey Lloyd to "Iva May," June 1, 1864; Martie R. Connally to Hattie Burleigh, July 2, 1864; "Willie" to Hattie Burleigh, June 23, 1864; and Albert Jones to Hattie Burleigh, September 11, 1864, Hattie Burleigh Papers, Archives, United States Army Military History Institute, Carlisle, Pa. It is clear there are letters missing between Hattie and her soldier correspondents, because of references made to other letters. Unfortunately the only letters that survived consist of five from Martie, one from Willie, six from Charles, four from Albert and two from Harvey. (I am not certain, but I do not believe this is the same "Hattie" as the one previously mentioned.)

correspondence. May I be so bold as to ask if that friend has a right to object?" Interestingly, she sent Martie, Willie, and Albert photographs of herself, but did not favor Charles or Harvey with such items, even though Charles begged for a photo in every one of his letters. But, as the other men discovered, receiving a carte de visite was no guarantee that it was a true likeness of their correspondent. Martie wrote discouragingly, "I'm at a loss to know if you have sent me your true picture and name. Sometimes I think you have and other times something whispers that you have not." Willie apologized for his concerns. "In regards to the picture. . . . I am convinced tis of yourself. Pardon my doubts . . . I will entertain them no more." Albert, too, was uncertain about the authenticity of the photo. "Miss Lizzie . . . you assure me your name is incog. are you *sure* it is not the case with your visite, or the visite you sent me?"[65]

Although fictitious names and fake photographs may have been harmless between two people "sharing a seat on a railway journey," the dangers became real when deeper feelings were exchanged between the two. As Martie mentioned, it did not matter if Hattie's picture was true, because he wanted "a correspondence with some one who" would "write letters to cheer and enliven" him "in those dark and dreary hours." Therefore, "it matters not whether I ever see the person." Even though Albert initially likened their friendship to "the house that was built upon the sands," he hoped an "unwavering friendship" would be the result of their correspondence. With the exception of Harvey (perhaps only because other letters of his did not survive), all of Hattie's correspondents eventually expressed feelings for her beyond friendship and desired to meet her. Willie shared his hopes when he asked, "Hattie do [you] suppose you and I will ever meet, do you think from my picture you would know me, or care to meet me?" Hattie encouraged her correspondents in their feelings. Charles quoted her letter, "I too wish that Charlie were where you could 'look into his eyes,' for then I should have the satisfaction and pleasure of seeing . . . my 'authoress' correspondent." As a token of endearment, he promised to "select a few" of his "brown hairs" if in her next letter Hattie would "enclose a lock of" her

---

[65] Charles Field to Hattie Burleigh, August 27, 1864; "Willie" to Hattie Burleigh, June 23, 1864; Martie R. Connally to Hattie Burleigh, September 18, 1864; and "Willie" to Hattie Burleigh, June 23, 1864; Albert Jones to Hattie Burleigh, October 6, 1864, ibid.

"bonny brown and a piece of white or blue ribbon with which to tie" his. He signed his letters, "devotedly Charlie." When Albert informed Hattie he would be going home on leave, he suggested stopping to see her in New Hampshire. "But to give you a call, as I would on a friend in ordinary circumstances would be perhaps considered by *you* inadmissible. With me I am in favor of romance or any thing you are; therefore with regard to the affair I will allow you to dictate. I would ask you to be as lenient as your views of etiquette will allow." Perhaps the soldier most smitten with Hattie was Martie. Within a year of writing about friendship, Martie became "jealous of having any other person correspond" with her and began closing his letters with "a kiss" and "goodby my darling." He fantasized about spending the evening with Hattie in which they would "sail in" a "yacht" and "you say you would let me kiss you just as much as I please." He confided that if they did meet *"this individual* would be apt to fall in l—— with 'somebody.' "[66]

The correspondence between Hattie and her soldiers ended abruptly without a hint of how, or if, the relationships continued. Whether Hattie intentionally lied to the men is uncertain; perhaps she wrote because it was her "duty," as she explained to Harvey, or to pass some of her own dreary days, or even to be engaged in a "wicked" yet harmless adventure. What is clear is that this type of correspondence, grounded in ill-placed confidence, represented to the editors and to middle-class moralists a formula for disaster. Victorians understood that young men and women were "seldom tempted to outright wickedness," but that it was a seducer's facade of wealth, fashion, and a mild and courteous manner that enticed them. Although Favorite advertised with a touch of impropriety, at least her sly aims seemed obvious. Hattie's coy behavior with each of her correspondents was "gradual and unperceived," and therefore she represented to the editors the more dangerous of the two inappropriate women.[67] Confident that proper people could only become victims

---

[66] Martie R. Connally to Hattie Burleigh, September 18, 1864; Albert Jones to Hattie Burleigh, September 11, 1864; "Willie" to Hattie Burleigh, June 23, 1864; Albert Jones to Hattie Burleigh, October 6, 1864; Charles Field to Hattie Burleigh September 11, 16, 1864; and Martie R. Connally to Hattie Burleigh, October 26, November 27, 1865, and "From Fort McHenry," [no date], ibid.

[67] Harvey Lloyd to Hattie Burleigh, June 1, 1864, ibid; and Halttunen, *Confidence Men and Painted Ladies*, 5.

through such unguarded behavior, the editors took on the responsibility of uncovering the hoax. Overall, the editors' reaction confirms the unusual nature of the soldiers', women's, and civilians' actions involved in the correspondence, but their admonitions did not deter or slow down the stream of ads.

These ads are important to the historian for several reasons. First, they reveal that not all single people during the Civil War, whether soldiers, women, or civilian men, were willing to wait until the "cruel war" was over to find a mate. Soldiers bent social conventions to meet their needs for feminine contact by using the editors as the mutually known third party. In essence, they turned propriety on its head. Etiquette dictated that the introducer should know both parties being introduced. The editors did not know the prospective correspondents, but the advertisers and correspondents "knew" the editors. By publishing the soldiers' ads, the editors "introduced" them to women, and created a buffer between the two parties that lessened the vulgarity that a face-to-face introduction would have produced. Desperate for communication with the opposite sex, soldiers, women, and civilians improvised during a wartime situation that allowed neither the time nor the opportunity to follow all the rules of etiquette. By using the editors as a third party, the men and women who participated maintained at least a semblance of respectability.

Second, the ads provide unusual and candid insights into the expectations of men and women seeking prospective mates. The ads requesting "the companionship of a kind friend and a loving heart" or "gentlemen equally endowed" express the ideal of a companionate marriage. Obviously, advertisers meant to catch the eye of someone, so some ads appear a bit boastful. Advertisements for ladies of "a good reputation" and "unblemished characters" or "intelligent" and "affectionate" men represent traits honestly looked for in prospective mates.[68]

Most importantly, these ads present a new perspective on the women of the time. Women who participated in placing and answering ads most probably did not consider themselves to be anything but

---

[68] "Montague," "Matrimonial," *New York Herald*, March 2, 1864; Edith & Maude Wellington, "Wanted Correspondence," *Chicago Tribune*, July 1, 1863; J. C. Field, *Chicago Tribune*, June 18, 1863; and "Minnie and Grace," *Chicago Tribune*, April 6, 1864.

respectable. Surely a minority of women, such as Favorite, had less virtuous motives than simply finding a true friend or mate. But overall, the women who placed ads did so with the confidence that they were doing nothing wrong. Whether women were composing advertisements or answering requests to pass dreary days, for patriotic conviction, or even as a wicked adventure, their participation suggests that these women were more aggressive than the True Woman. Moreover, women's participation in the correspondence craze and Okker's argument that women carried on a dialogue between editors and readers broadens our understanding of women's seemingly bold actions during the war. Women may have been stretching the gender boundaries, or, as Okker suggests, they may have been operating well within their province of influence. The ads, therefore, establish a less restricted view of Victorian women, one that allowed them to act more assertively in their relations with men.[69]

M. Debray and Monte Cristo most assuredly did not understand the ramifications of their actions when they placed their ad in the *Chicago Tribune* on April 27, 1863. The correspondence craze their ad sparked sent a message to the people of that era and ours, that men and women will not be contained by conditions or by society's restrictions when it comes to courting. The war that caused these two soldiers to be in Nashville, Tennessee, kept them from the "handsome and respectable ladies" of the North. By 1863, they were willing to use correspondence to aid them in their search for "fun, love, or matrimony." Like M. Debray and Monte Cristo, many northerners sought and found innovative methods to replace social structures destroyed by the exigencies of war.

---

[69] Indeed, Lystra argues that women were quite aggressive in their courting relationships, and men more submissive than first believed. Although the nineteenth century had been defined by its separate spheres, Lystra believes "Victorians skillfully used their sex roles rather than slavishly followed them." In actuality, the "gender lines" were more flexible "than the static view of separate sphere has allowed." Lystra, *Searching the Heart*, 124.

6

Soldiering on the Home Front: The Veteran Reserve Corps and the Northern People

Paul A. Cimbala

DURING THE CIVIL WAR, the long-distance relationships between northern communities and their soldiers at the front allowed parents, brothers, and sisters to create idealized images of their local heroes while shielding them from some of the more unsavory aspects of the soldiers' life. The war, however, did not create an impermeable boundary between home folks and the reality of soldiering.[1] Soldiers came home on leave or to recover from their wounds and illnesses, for example, thus bringing their battlefield and camp experiences directly to their families and communities. But there were also other opportunities for many communities to interact with veterans in ways that often reinforced, but sometimes challenged, their perceptions of the familiar boys they had sent off to war. Convalescent hospitals,

---

[1] For example, see Earl Hess's essay in this volume. Also see the numerous collections of soldiers' letters home, including Judith A. Bailey and Robert I. Cottom, *After Chancellorsville: Letters from the Heart, The Civil War Letters of Private Walter G. Dunn and Emma Randolph* (Baltimore: Maryland Historical Society, 1998); and Stephen W. Sears, ed., *Mr. Dunn Browne's Experiences in the Army: The Civil War Letters of Samuel W. Fiske* (New York: Fordham University Press, 1998), as well as local studies such as J. Matthew Gallman, *Mastering Wartime: A Social History of Philadelphia during the Civil War* (Cambridge, Eng.: Cambridge University Press, 1990); Michael H. Frisch, *Town into City: Springfield, Massachusetts, and the Meaning of Community, 1840–1880* (Cambridge, Mass.: Harvard University Press, 1972); and Thomas H. O'Connor, *Civil War Boston: Home Front and Battlefield* (Boston: Northeastern University Press, 1997). For general studies of the wartime experience in the North, see J. Matthew Gallman, *The North Fights the Civil War: The Home Front* (Chicago: Ivan R. Dee, 1994); and Phillip Shaw Paludan, *"A People's Contest": The Union and Civil War, 1861–1865*, 2nd ed. (Lawrence: University Press of Kansas, 1996).

rendezvous points, prisoner-of-war camps, equipment depots, and other various provost marshal duties, including draft enforcement, all brought soldiers into direct contact with civilians in situations that were unique to the wartime experience and that did not have the warmth of familial relations shaping them. More often than not, the soldiers finding themselves in these circumstances were members of the Union Army's Veteran Reserve Corps.

The Invalid Corps, the original name of the Veteran Reserve Corps, came into existence in April 1863, as just one initiative of the United States Army to help alleviate the pressing need for front-line troops.[2] Semi-able-bodied veteran soldiers, men who in the past would have received discharges as unfit for field duty, filled its ranks as physicians transferred them from military hospitals to complete their terms of service behind the lines. The soldiers found themselves assigned either to a First Battalion company, which meant they could stand the rigors of guard duty and fire a rifle, or a Second Battalion company, which meant they were considered fit only for light duty, most likely at a military hospital.[3] The army assumed that if these men could no longer fight, they could certainly perform other duties and in the process free their more vigorous comrades to take their places at the front.

The officers of the Invalid Corps, disabled men who could prove good character, military competency, and past commendable service, had to make special application for the commissions that placed them

---

[2] General Orders, No. 105, April 28, 1863, Adjutant General's Office, War Department (AGO), Library, United States Army Military History Institute, Carlisle, Pa. (USAMHI). See Capt. J. W. De Forest to Brig. Gen. James B. Fry, November 30, 1865, in United States War Department, *War of the Rebellion: A Compilation of the Official Records of the Union and Confederate Armies*, 70 vols. in 128 (Washington, D.C.: Government Printing Office, 1880–1901), series 3, vol. 5, pp. 543–50 (hereinafter cited as *Official Records*) for a brief history of the corps' establishment in his final summary of its activities. For a general history of the Veteran Reserve Corps, see Stanley Michael Suplick, Jr., "The United States Invalid Corps/Veteran Reserve Corps" (Ph. D. dissertation, University of Minnesota, 1969). For a more recent survey, see Paul A. Cimbala, "Union Corps of Honor," *Columbiad* 3 (winter 2000): 59–91.

[3] Regiments generally consisted of six First Battalion companies and four Second Battalion companies. On March 21, 1865, all Second Battalion companies came under the command of the surgeon general. Even before that, the First and Second Battalion companies of any given regiment were rarely serving at the same posts. Capt. J. W. De Forest to Brig. Gen. J. B. Fry, November 30, 1865, *Official Records*, series 3, vol. 5, 559.

on an equal footing with officers in the regular army when it came to questions of seniority.[4] Importantly, Colonel James B. Fry, the provost marshal general, and his assistants who supervised the organization intended to create a "Corps of Honor" that would employ only the best available officers capable of maintaining a strict discipline over their men.[5] How well they succeeded would have much to do with how northern communities viewed the men of the corps, always so readily recognizable by the distinctive sky-blue uniform jackets and coats they wore.[6]

The Invalid Corps began accepting soldiers into its ranks in late May 1863; within six months, there were 491 officers and 17,764 men in sixteen newly organized regiments. By war's end, over 60,000 enlisted men and a thousand officers had served or were still serving in the ranks of twenty-four regiments and numerous unattached companies.[7]

In determining how accepting of their presence civilians would be, much depended on the personalities of and the extent of civility practiced by these rear-echelon troops, as well as the circumstances that brought them to the various northern communities in which they served. Soldiers represented the power of the Republican-controlled

---

[4] Col. R. H. Rush to Col. C. M. Prevost, Aug. 11, 1863, Letters Sent, vol. 1, 416–17, Veteran Reserve Corps, Provost Marshal General Bureau, Record Group 110, National Archives, Washington, D.C. (hereinafter cited as VRC, RG 110); W. McMichael to Capt. F. Wessels, Jan. 13, 1865, Regimental Records, 16th Regiment Veteran Reserve Corps (VRC), Records of the Adjutant General's Office, Record Group 94, National Archives, Washington, D.C. (hereinafter cited as AGO, RG 94). Fry remained the provost marshal general throughout the war. He received a promotion to brigadier general in September 1864. General Orders, No. 256, September 15, 1864, AGO, Library, USAMHI.

[5] Col. R. H. Rush to Col. C. M. Prevost, August 11, 1863, Letters Sent, vol. 1, 416–17; Col. R. H. Rush to Capt. T. Touty, August 28, 1863, Letters Sent, vol. 2, 68–69, VRC, RG 110.

[6] Enlisted men wore short cavalry-style sky blue jackets throughout the war. Officers initially wore sky blue frock coats. The uniforms were never very popular among the men and eventually officers were ordered to return to the standard dark blue frock coat. After the war, at least in the Washington, D.C. area, enlisted men were issued dark blue standard infantry blouses.

[7] Col. M. N. Wisewell to Brig. Gen. J. B. Fry, October 24, 1864, Reports of Operations, VRC, RG 110; Capt. J. W. De Forest to Brig. Gen. J. B. Fry, Nov. 30, 1865, Official Records, series 3, vol. 5, 566–67. For the points at which VRC units were stationed, see Janet B. Hewett et al., eds., Supplement to the Official Records of the Union and Confederate Armies, part 2, Record of Events (Wilmington, N.C.: Broadfoot Publishing Company, 1998), vols. 79 and 80.

federal government, which communities welcomed when they were concerned about the safety of lives and property and which they did not welcome if they perceived the presence as a threat to local autonomy. Well-behaved soldiers could become the recipients of the affection, good will, and charity of home folks longing after their own soldier-sons. Members of the corps could provide the means by which civilians eased their anxieties about the circumstances of their loved ones, acting as wholesome substitutes for their own boys away at the front. On the other hand, veterans turned rough and hard by their combat experiences sometimes exemplified the antithesis of the ideal that civilians held of their soldier boys. They could in fact be nuisances—or worse—who disrupted community life with their drunken shenanigans, thus providing occasion to force civilians to revise their views of the virtuous hero's life that their sons, husbands, and brothers were supposedly living. In the end, members of the Veteran Reserve Corps gave civilians many opportunities to witness soldiers' lives right in their own back yards. By no means did all civilians happily accept them as neighbors, but many loyal supporters of the Union cause looked warmly upon the boys in the sky-blue jackets because of what they did for their communities and the greater war effort.

From the outset, the Invalid Corps had an uphill battle to fight when it came to projecting its intended image as a "Corps of Honor." Throughout the war, there were soldiers who looked for an easy way to avoid dangerous duty. Before the establishment of the corps, hospitals often provided these men with a haven, and wounded and sick soldiers were able to prolong their absences from the ranks beyond a reasonable period of convalescence. In October 1863, for example, the *Detroit Advertiser and Tribune* printed a short piece on "Pretended Invalids in the Army," commenting on the "astonishing" number of men allegedly laid low by hernias and heart disease who were sequestered in Washington's military hospitals.[8] In September 1863, Captain Samuel Fiske, a former Connecticut preacher campaigning on the line with the Army of the Potomac, complained about this situation to the residents of Springfield, Massachusetts. "It has come to be a thing to be expected that those who are wounded or sent to the hospital sick, even slightly or temporarily so, are lost to

---

[8] *Detroit Advertiser and Tribune*, October 21, 1863.

the regiment for the rest of the war in nine cases out of ten," he wrote in the local newspaper. "Men are furloughed with the greatest ease from our hospitals and then stay at home, sending certificates from their easily persuaded family physicians for the extension of their furloughs." Even when put to use around military hospitals, these men were suspect, he complained, for those so detailed were sufficiently fit to return to share the rigors of campaigning with their old comrades. "As a matter of fact," he explained, "scarcely any of them rejoin their companies." Even the War Department recognized that invalids were apt to become "mere hangers-on of hospitals long after they were fit to resume the musket." The skulking, "invalided" soldiers, according to Captain Fiske, delayed victory by depleting the ranks of the armies of the United States.[9]

Patriots who agreed with Captain Fiske could easily misperceive the corps as an extension of this evil practice. Many front-line soldiers would happily provide additional evidence to confirm their fears. In December 1863, for example, Sergeant Gustave Magnitsky, formerly of the 20th Massachusetts Volunteer Infantry, protested his transfer to the Invalid Corps, arguing that he was perfectly fit to return to his old regiment. "I hate to be in the Invalid Corps, because there are too many imposters in it," he explained to his former commander, and, "I do not like to be considered one of them."[10] One could certainly find skulkers in the corps, but such a sweeping generalization was an unfair characterization. Colonel Fry, in fact, had designed the Invalid Corps to stop such abuses and to police the home front to make sure that men "who belong to the United States" did their duty.[11] It would be primarily through the home folks' increased familiarity with the invalids' duties that the corps would have the opportu-

---

[9] Dunn Browne to the *Springfield* [Mass.] *Republican*, September 21, [1863], in Sears, ed., *Mr. Dunn Browne's Experience in the Army*, 172–73. Fisk used Dunn Browne as his pseudonym when writing to the paper. For the government's view of the malingering problem, see the final report of the Veteran Reserve Corps, Capt. J. W. De Forest to Brig. Gen. James B. Fry, November 30, 1865, *Official Records*, series 3, vol. 5, p. 543.

[10] Sgt. G. Magnitsky to Commanding Officer 20th Mass. Vols., December 13, 1863, Letters Rec'd, VRC, RG 110.

[11] Fiske's words in Dunn Browne to the *Springfield* [Mass.] *Republican*, September 21, [1863], in Sears, ed., *Mr. Dunn Browne's Experience*, 173. For the intentions of the government in establishing the Invalid Corps, see Capt. J. W. De Forest to Brig. Gen. J. B. Fry, November 30, 1865, *Official Records*, series 3, vol. 5, pp. 543–44.

nity to shape its image as an honorable and useful organization—that is, if those civilians agreed with the government policies the men were implementing.

Two dangerous, very different kinds of situations tested the mettle of the Invalid Corps almost immediately after its establishment. They also provided northern civilians with opportunities to assess the new organization. In June 1863, in response to Confederate General Robert E. Lee's invasion of Pennsylvania, men from Invalid Corps rushed to the defense of Harrisburg, the state capital and a likely target of the rebel offensive, where citizens were in a state of "fearful excitement." Posted along the railroads and bridges of the city, over 500 men and officers from the corps maintained order and prepared to defend the town if Confederates approached the banks of the Susquehanna. As one officer noted, the arrival of less than a company of the corps "tended to restore confidence" among the people of Harrisburg. Furthermore, he believed, their performance was an excellent indication of the corps' "future usefulness."[12]

But farther east, the corps' debut was less auspicious and not universally welcomed. Shortly after the crisis in Pennsylvania passed, authorities in New York City called on the corps to assist in the suppression of the draft riot that erupted on July 13, 1863, and lasted several days. In this situation, the rioters perceived the men of the Invalid Corps to be an unwelcome, intrusive arm of federal authority. Rather than heroes, they were oppressors, and not very effective ones at that. On the first day of the riots, a detachment of seventy-five men from the Invalid Corps made its way by streetcar to the scene of the violence. Along the way, they encountered "crowds of men, women, and children gathered at the street corners" who "hissed and jeered them, and some even went so far as to pick up stones, which they defiantly threatened to throw at the car." Arriving at the scene, the soldiers fired a volley into the mob, which, according to the reporter for the New York Herald, enraged the crowd and prompted it to act "more like fiends than human beings." The soldiers turned and ran, discarding their weapons while "being pursued in hot haste by thousands." Squads of rioters cornered and savagely beat individual sol-

---

[12] Col. C. M. Prevost to Col. J. B. Fry, June 17, 1863, Letters Rec'd, VRC, RG 110. For a report on the chaotic state of things in the city, see the *Harrisburg Daily Patriot and Union*, June 17, 1863.

diers, whom they trapped in the narrow streets of the city. As *The New York Times* reported, "When the mob becoming satiated and disgusted with their foul work, he would be left sweltering in blood, unable to help himself." The *New York Herald* reported that the crowd beat one of the men that it had captured "almost into jelly, and, in fainting from loss of blood and exhaustion, the poor fellow was thrown into some alleyway, and left to take care of himself as best as he might." In another case, the mob disfigured a soldier, "cutting open his cheek and back part of his head." *The Times*' man concluded that the members of Invalid Corps, who had been hunted through the streets "like dogs," had been "shamefully maltreated." The events elicited some sympathy from witnesses; nevertheless, they did not hesitate to criticize the corps' poor performance, although they tended to place the greater blame on the officials who managed the efforts to disperse the rioters. As *The Times* noted, "the troops which were under arms yesterday were not handled with the slightest vigor, nor did they contribute in any marked degree to the restoration of the public peace." The Augusta, Maine, *Kennebec Journal* also criticized the authorities for not sending more troops to deal with the rioters and wrongfully assumed that the soldiers relied only on "moral force" when they resorted to firing blank cartridges, an erroneous assumption based on mistaken reports from *The Times*. Recovering from this fiasco, the Invalid Corps was back on duty for the second day of the riot with a detachment of men standing in reserve.[13]

At least one company of the corps won the respect of those citizens who were unsympathetic towards the rioters. This group of sixty-five men, commanded by Captain Thomas Graham, continued to partici-

---

[13] *The New York Times*, July 14, 1863, Trenton [N. J.] *Daily State Gazette*, July 15, 1863; *New York Herald*, July 14, 1863; *Chicago Evening Journal*, July 14, 17, 1863; *Rochester* [N.Y.] *Evening Express*, July 14, 1863; and *Augusta* [Me.] *Kennebec Journal*, July 17, 1863. *The Times* and papers such as the *Trenton Daily State Gazette* that relied on *The Times*'s account reported that the soldiers fired blanks into the crowd. The *Herald* and official correspondence stated that soldiers fired ball into the crowd. In addition to the papers cited here, see Col. Robert Nugent to Col. J. B. Fry, July 15, 1863, *Official Records*, series 1, vol. 27, part 2, pp. 899–901. For the larger context of the New York City riots, see Iver Bernstein, *The New York City Draft Riots: Their Significance for American Society and Politics in the Age of the Civil War* (New York: Oxford University Press, 1990).

pate in pacifying the city, marching through the disaffected area, and dispersing some of the rioters by their very presence. Graham and his men stood guard for long hours until finally returning to their base in Newark, New Jersey, on July 18. If the rioters did not care for them, "the respectable citizens" did, furnishing the invalid soldiers "bountifully with coffee and eatables." Graham was proud of the way his men conducted themselves under such stressful circumstances, and he believed that "they also feel proud in the good name they obtained by their Soldierly conduct and good behavior."[14]

Despite the unhappy events in New York City, the corps' initial publicity was generally favorable. Newspapers gave the Invalid Corps ample print to publicize its formation while keeping readers apprised of its development. The Trenton, New Jersey, *Daily Gazette*, for example, traced the good progress of the corps' organization through the spring, summer, and fall of 1863.[15] In December, an editorialist for that paper pronounced the members of the Invalid Corps stationed at that city's rendezvous camp "perhaps the most soldierly looking company we have had in Trenton."[16]

Other papers praised the intent of the organization, conveying to their readers a clear understanding of the purpose and usefulness of the corps. In September 1863, the *Philadelphia Inquirer* reminded its readers that the people of the United States were in Colonel Fry's debt for his efficient efforts in establishing "this 'Corps of Honor.' " Furthermore, continued the *Inquirer*'s editorialist, the nation should be most grateful to Fry for finding meaningful work for its heroes, a significant requirement if they were to maintain their manhood in the face of their personal misfortunes. "By its means the soldier who has given health and risked life perhaps shed his best blood, in defending his country, is kept from the cold charity of the world, and placed in an honorable position, where he is still usefully employed in serving his country," he wrote. "The light blue uniform is a mark of honor. It is an evidence that its wearer had done his duty in the field, and nine out of ten of the 'blue jackets' carries on his person an

---

[14] Capt. T. Graham to Col. R. C. Buchanan, July 20, 1863, VRC, Miscellaneous Papers, AGO, RG 94.

[15] *Trenton* [N.J.] *Daily Gazette*, May 19, 1863, June 1, 1863, June 13, 1863, August 27, 1863, September 25, 1863, October 7, 1863.

[16] *Trenton* [N.J.] Daily State Gazette, December 2, 1863.

honorable scar. The time will come when men will be prouder of his uniform than of the cross of the Legion of Honor."[17]

A *New York Times* editorialist seconded this opinion. "We do not know precisely to whom the nation is indebted for the idea of the organizing an Invalid corps, but his foresight and consideration entitle him to national gratitude," he reminded his readers. "It furnishes *employment* for a class of men whose sacrifices in their country's cause justly entitle them to the nation's gratitude; and who, in consequence of their services, should be spared the pain of becoming objects of national charity. They are willing *to work* for the country, but would refuse its alms. They only ask that the work assigned them be such as their physical condition permits them to perform." The writer, countering the fears of individuals such as Captain Fiske, made clear to the public that this particular purpose of the corps was by no means in conflict with the foremost national goals—defeating secession. The corps, he explained, by doing rear-echelon duty would allow "at least a score of thousands" of able-bodied men to serve at the front. "Thus will the country and the army be benefited, while the brave officers and soldiers who have sacrificed their limbs or their health in our service will be furnished with honorable employment as a reward for patriotic duty, faithfully discharged."[18]

When the government changed the organization's name to Veteran Reserve Corps in March 1864, a correspondent to the *Rochester Evening Express* repeated the earlier praise and predictions of the continued usefulness of the corps. The men of the corps, he wrote, "have been a little restive under the impression that has gone abroad that they were mere pensioners, and only fit to parade the streets. Many of these men, minus a leg, an arm, or carrying with them the scars of many a hard fight, are still anxious to be placed where they can be of the most use to their country." Furthermore, he explained, "although unable to endure the marches and privations of an active campaign, [they] still desire to be placed in positions where, when occasion requires it, they can earn further and more enduring laurels."[19] Later that summer, the paper printed a hometown soldier's letter full of praise for the corps. Because of its source, it lent military authority

---

[17] *Philadelphia Inquirer*, n.d., reprinted in *Trenton* [N.J.] *Daily Gazette*, September 25, 1863.

[18] *The New York Times*, September 9, 1863.

[19] *Rochester* [N. Y.] *Evening Express*, March 31, 1864.

to the editor's earlier good opinion of the organization while emphatically contradicting rumors that had been circulating in Rochester about the corps' "demoralization, [and] untrustworthiness." Referring to the units of the 16th Regiment then stationed at Elmira, New York, the soldier noted that they were a "splendidly drilled and officered regiment . . . and are acknowledged by all to be an efficient and trustworthy regiment." Contrary depictions "were all canards."[20]

Nevertheless, some civilians remained suspicious of a military organization that the Republican government would station near their towns, in their cities, and away from the front. In October 1863, some "Nervous people" of Detroit expressed concern about the purpose of "Those Invalid Soldiers" newly arrived in their town. There had been what Republicans labeled a riot in Detroit earlier that month and apparently the Democrats were worried about the purpose of the presence of the military men. One can only imagine Detroit Democrats wondering if a Lincolnian police state had descended upon them. The local editor reassured his readers, while taking a jab at those apprehensive Democrats, that most of the men had already been dispersed into the hinterlands.[21]

Thus from the Invalid Corps' formation, editorialists alerted civilians to the heroic nature of the organization and its members' previous sacrifices for the Union, as well as the organization's potential usefulness. But as the Detroit Democrats had indicated, not all northerners would be convinced of the corps' benevolent nature, let alone its predicted effectiveness. The "invalids," as many continued to refer to the men of the corps throughout the war, would be left to make their own case in the communities where they found themselves on duty.

Of course, not all northerners had opportunities to witness the "invalids" in action, a circumstance that in itself probably contributed to some of the less-favorable caricatures of the corps that circulated during the war. The corps' duties, however, brought a significant number of the men into contact with the residents of many communities. For example, by November 6, 1863, there were over two thousand men of the Second Battalion working in Washington, D. C.'s hospital wards, not to mention the men of the several regiments that

[20] Ibid., August 10, 1864.
[21] *Detroit Advertiser and Tribune*, October 27, 28, 1863.

were guarding government buildings, bridges, and military posts surrounding the capital, as well as patrolling the city's streets.[22] Residents of Columbus, Ohio, came into contact with VRC men from
nearby Camp Chase, where the soldiers guarded prisoners of war.
So, too did the people of Indianapolis, where VRC men could go on
leave from Camp Morton, another prisoner of war camp. Chicagoans
could make the acquaintance of the men stationed at Camp Douglas,[23] and Trentonians were not alone in having opportunities to witness the work of the corps at the local rendezvous camp. Well-
populated towns and cities such as Portland, Maine; Concord, New
Hampshire; New Haven, Connecticut; Boston, Massachusetts; New
York City; and Pittsburgh, Pennsylvania, also had rendezvous camps
where various detachments of the corps guarded recruits and draftees.[24] Members of the corps took advantage of the local social life
near their posts, attending the theatre, prayer meetings, temperance
gatherings, and, if they happened to be stationed in Washington,
presidential receptions.[25] Civilians near various military hospitals,
prisoner of war camps, and rendezvous camps, therefore, had ample
opportunity to watch the corps on and off duty.

From their posts, the "invalids" contributed to the safety and well
being of the communities in which they were stationed. In February
1864, for example, men from the corps who were guarding the railroad "Long Bridge" over the Potomac at Washington assisted hurt
soldiers after a train accident there, prompting one editorialist to
alert residents of the capital that they deserved "Great praise" for
their ministrations.[26] More dramatic, perhaps, for the residents of the
district, was the VRC's march into the breech to man the defenses
around Washington in July 1864, when Confederate General Jubal

---

[22] Col. Richard H. Rush to Col. James B. Fry, November 6, 1863, Annual Reports,
VRC, RG 110.

[23] General Orders, No. 190, May 3, 1864, AGO, Library, USAMHI.

[24] Col. M. N. Wisewell to Brig. Gen. James B. Fry, October 24, 1864, Annual
Reports, VRC, RG 110.

[25] Entries for January 2, 10, 23, 28, 1865, as well as various additional entries
throughout the year, William H. Beedle Diary, Library of Congress, Washington,
D. C.; Charles F. Johnson to Mary Johnson, March 15, 1864, Charles F. Johnson
Papers, Archives, USAMHI.

[26] *Daily National Intelligencer*, February 8, 1864. See also the *Washington Evening Star*, February 6, 1864.

Early threatened the capital city.[27] More routinely, the corps maintained order in the nation's capital. Men from several regiments patrolled roads and streets leading into the city in an effort to crack down on smuggling, checked passes of soldiers attending the local theaters and frequenting the local bordellos, and stood guard at houses of ill repute while surgeons examined the resident prostitutes.[28]

In July 1864, the corps once again came to the aid of Harrisburg, Pennsylvania, taking up a posting there to guard the city in the event that the Confederates then operating in Maryland advanced.[29] Later, in February 1865, three companies of the 16th Regiment VRC patrolled the city's streets.[30] Farther west in Indianapolis, members of the 17th Regiment patrolled the streets, assuring peace and quiet for the residents.[31] Performing their provost marshal duties, they broke up "three camps of disreputable characters in the suburbs of the city" during the spring of 1864.[32] In August, the corps dealt with another disorderly situation that offended upright, God-fearing residents. "A bevy of dismally abandoned females" had congregated near one of the area's military posts, where at one point "they, with their soldier chevaliers succeeded in raising quite a rumpus," provoking a general free-for-all. "The battle raged for a few minutes, but the Veteran Reserve Corps coming up at a critical moment, on the double quick, dispersed the assailants." The "invalids" captured "the squad of cyprians, and one of their male attendants, who were escorted with the honors of war to the county jail," reported Colonel W. R. Holloway,

[27] Col. G. W. Giles to Col. M. N. Wisewell, July 22, 1864; Lt. Col. R. E. Johnston to Col. M. N. Wisewell, October 1, 1864; Col. G. W. Giles to Capt. J. W. De Forest, October 10, 1865, Letters Rec'd, VRC, RG 110; Lt. Col. R. E. Johnston, "History of the 9th Regt V. R. C. continued," October 1, 1864, Letter and Endorsement Book, 9th Regiment VRC, AGO, RG 94; Capt. J. W. De Forest to Brig. Gen. J. B. Fry, November 30, 1865, *Official Records*, series 3, vol. 5, 553.

[28] Col. M. O. Mansfield to Capt. J. W. De Forrest, October 17, 1865, Letters Rec'd. VRC, RG 110; David Herbert Donald, ed., *Gone for a Soldier: The Civil War Memoirs of Private Alfred Bellard* (Boston: Little, Brown and Company, 1975), 254.

[29] Capt. S. W. Purchase to Brig. Gen. Fry, October 20, 1864, Letters Rec'd, VRC, RG 110.

[30] Special Orders, no. 111, Acting Assistant Provost Marshal General, Pennsylvania, February 28, 1865, Regimental Papers, 16th VRC, AGO, RG 94.

[31] Capt. J. W. De Forest to Brig. Gen. J. B. Fry, November 30, 1865, *Official Records*, series 3, vol. 5, p. 564.

[32] *Indianapolis Daily Journal*, May 11, 1864.

the satisfied publisher and editor of the local Republican newspaper, the *Indianapolis Daily Journal*.[33]

Communities along the northern border also had opportunities to come into contact with the "light blues" as they did their duty to protect the northern people from rebel marauders who attempted to rob their banks and disrupt their routines. In December 1863, fearful of enemy incursions, the army stationed companies from the 11th Regiment at Fort Porter, Buffalo, New York, "to protect that important work, from rebel sympathizers, or rebels from Canada."[34] In October 1864, members of the Veterans Reserve Corps rushed to Saint Albans, Vermont, to help the citizens chase down a band of Confederate raiders who had crossed the Canadian border and robbed three of the town's banks.[35] Men from the corps, in the wake of this raid, also took up posts elsewhere along the Canadian border, including Rochester and Buffalo, New York, to prevent similar occurrences.[36] During 1865, Company G of the 2nd Regiment took up its station at Saint Albans and Island Pond, Vermont, where it patrolled the border, enforced a passport system, and guarded important roads leading into Canada.[37]

Such duty won the appreciation and hearty approval of loyal citizens. In July 1864, the 8th and 15th Regiments received orders to leave Camp Douglas to report to Washington to assist the troops there in defending the capital while hundred-day men were to replace them at the prisoner-of-war camp. This shuffling of troops dismayed Chicagoans, who had come to respect the VRC provost guard as a "model organization" that "so efficiently guarded" a potentially dangerous prison population. A member of the Board of Trade, sup-

---

[33] *Indianapolis Daily Journal*, August 13, 1864. Holloway wrote favorably about the VRC until he sold his interest in the paper and retired in December 1865. *Indianapolis Daily Journal*, December 29, 1865.

[34] Lt. Col. G. Jennings to Col. J. E. Farnum, September 20, 1864, Letters Rec'd, VRC, RG 110.

[35] Maj. William Austine to Col. Van Buren, October 23, 1864, *Official Records*, series 1, vol. 43, pt. 1, pp. 455–56; *Hartford Connecticut Courant*, October 20, 1864; *Rochester* [N. Y.] *Evening Express*, October 21, 1864.

[36] Bvt. Brig. Gen. A. S. Diven to Maj. Gen. John A. Dix, November 8, 1864, *Official Records*, series 1, vol. 43, pt.1, pp. 580–81. For a concise treatment of the problems resulting from the border tensions and their solutions, see Paludan, *A People's Contest*, 280–81.

[37] Lt. Col. F. Blaydolf to Brig. Gen. J. B. Fry, October 17, 1865, Letters Rec'd, VRC, RG 110.

ported by other influential citizens, and no doubt well aware of the limits of Chicago's own under-staffed police force, worked to retain the VRC men. "The prominent objection" to removing the VRC regiments, explained a newspaper correspondent, "lies in the fact that the safety of Chicago requires at Camp Douglas a garrison of veteran soldiers." In his mind, as well as those of the concerned citizens, the VRC men fit the bill.[38]

In Indianapolis, the corps won the vigorous support of editor Holloway, not only for its efforts to preserve order in the city under difficult conditions performing duties "far more arduous than is generally supposed," but also for its good behavior, "strict military discipline," and courtesy.[39] When Colonel A. A. Stevens of the local VRC detachment received the brevet rank of brigadier general, Holloway praised the man, noting that "since he has been stationed among us, [he] has discharged his duties to the satisfaction of the authorities and with courtesy to all who have come in contact with him."[40] Indeed, Major Charles Johnson, an Invalid Corps officer, believed that most of the citizens of Indianapolis were just as pleased with his organization as was the newspaper man. "The Corps here stands very high," he once told his wife, "and the light blue coat is the pass port into society, especially if it has a double row of buttons down the front." By way of proof of the citizens' recognition of the corps' honorable reputation, he mentioned that the local theater management required patrons to leave a security deposit if they wished to use the establishment's opera glasses, but "that security has *never* been asked of an officer of the Invalid Corps while it is demanded of every other arm of the service."[41]

Farther south in Greenupsburg, Kentucky, the corps also impressed local citizens with its usefulness. In October 1863, an Invalid Corps detachment arrived in the town for provost marshal duty, took up residence in the courthouse, and quickly won the hearts of the people. Confederate guerillas had been "prowling around" nearby, and there was a general fear that they would soon plunder the town. The arrival of the soldiers, credited by the civilians with "being the

---

[38] *Chicago Evening Journal*, July 6, 11, 12, 1864.

[39] *Indianapolis Daily Journal*, March 22, 1864.

[40] Ibid., March 13, 1865.

[41] Charles F. Johnson to Mary Johnson, March 15, 1864, Charles F. Johnson Papers.

best behaved soldiers they ever saw," provided residents with "a great relief" and elicited "the warmest gratitude to the soldiers who have come so opportunely to their relief."[42]

Rebel raiders elicited genuine concern from Union citizens living along the northern and southern borders of the loyal states. But for those people living along the various routes to the front, draftees, substitutes, and bounty men, ever ready to take their chances with desertion, were more likely to disturb the peace of their communities. The intent of some of these ne'er-do-wells was quite clear when they were apprehended in Connecticut with burglar's tools and stolen property on their persons.[43] Frequently, the Veteran Reserve Corps had to deal with these men.

Reports from the commanders of the various VRC regiments always included figures of the number of deserters that their units guarded at one time or another. On occasion, VRC men participated in disciplining their charges. In December 1864, at Camp Burnside, for example, VRC officer Colonel A. A. Stevens "arranged everything most admirably" for the public execution of three deserters by members of his command. The Indianapolis newspaperman Colonel Holloway was most impressed with the way the corps conducted its solemn business, and although the execution was not a public affair, he reported it in detail. Among those allowed to witness the "terrible lesson" were about a hundred bounty jumpers.[44]

Less frequent than guard duty and more frequent than executions were the times when VRC men actually participated in the recapture of deserters. A detachment from the 6th Regiment was stationed in Sandusky, Ohio, where its men patrolled the city streets, its wharves and its railroad depots, arresting deserters who might disrupt the peace of the town. In return, the mayor complimented the detachment "as being the most efficient and orderly detachment ever stationed in that City." Men from that same regiment also participated in a more rigorous campaign to capture deserters in Allen County, Ohio. In the fall of 1864, detachments stationed at various points in the county arrested around a hundred deserters.[45] In December,

---

[42] Capt. C. W. Grier to Maj. W. W. Lidell, October 20, 1863, Letters Rec'd, VRC, RG 110.

[43] *Hartford Daily Courant*, January 19, February 25, 1865.

[44] *Indianapolis Daily Journal*, December 24, 1864.

[45] Capt. G. Nagle to Capt. J. W. De Forrest, October 17, 1865, Letters Rec'd, VRC, RG 110.

another detachment of VRC men traveled from Indiana into a part of Crawford County, Illinois, controlled by "a band of deserters and desperadoes," capturing ten deserters and two of the individuals who had been harboring them.[46]

Also during the winter of 1864–1865, the 16th Regiment patrolled a large swath of rugged territory in south-central Pennsylvania, stretching north from Fayette County on the state's southern border up through Westmoreland, Huntingdon, Blair, and Cambria Counties and north into Centre and Clearfield Counties. They, too, arrested numerous deserters, but as with their comrades in the 6th Regiment, they were also concerned with sweeping up troublesome draft resisters and bringing them into the service. Prior to this campaign Private Hiram Tilley, a member of the 16th, informed his parents that "our boys have quite a repetation [sic] for subduing" Copperheads, and rightly so.[47] By the time the 16th Regiment began to wind down its duties in Pennsylvania, it had captured and forwarded to the front 2,783 deserters from regiments already in the field and 3,717 draft dodgers, as well as 3,447 convalescents who may or may not have been all that eager to return to their units.[48] The activities of the 16th Regiment were not unusual. In the fall and winter months of 1864, Provost Marshal General Fry used VRC men to help control draft resisters in New York State, Indiana, Illinois, and elsewhere.[49]

In situations such as these, VRC men often interacted with local citizens, and at times entire communities, on terms that would have been familiar to their comrades who had served in New York City

---

[46] *Indianapolis Daily Journal*, December 29, 1864.

[47] Hiram Tilley to parents, September 1, 1864, Hiram Tilley Letters, Pearce Civil War Documents Collection, Navarro College, Corsicana, Texas.

[48] Bvt. Lt. Col. F. A. H. Gaebel, "Report of the History and Operations of the 16th Regt. V. R. Corps," enclosed in Bvt. Lt. Col. F. A. H. Gaebel to Capt. J. W. De Forest, October 19, 1865, Letters Rec'd, VRC, RG 110; *Trenton* [N. J.] *Daily State Gazette*, December 17, 1864; *Rochester* [N.Y.] *Evening Express*, December 19, 1864. For the larger context of anti-war sentiment in Pennsylvania, see Arnold M. Shankman, *The Pennsylvania Antiwar Movement, 1861–1865* (Rutherford: Fairleigh Dickinson University Press, 1980); and Grace Palladino, *Another Civil War: Labor, Capital, and the State in the Anthracite Regions of Pennsylvania, 1840–1868* (Urbana: University of Illinois Press, 1990).

[49] Lt. Col. G. Jennings to Col. J. E. Farnum, September 1864, Letters Rec'd, VRC, RG 110; Col. James B. Fry to Maj. Gen. Joseph Hooker, October 3, 1864, *Official Records*, series 1, vol. 39, pt. 2, p. 61; Capt. J. W. De Forest to Brig. Gen. J. B. Fry, November 30, 1865, *Official Records*, series 3, vol. 5, p. 565; *Trenton* [N. J.] *Daily Gazette*, April 1, 1864; and *Indianapolis Daily Journal*, December 29, 1864.

during July 1863. They acted as a strong and sometimes covert arm of the government, assisting federal authorities in ferreting out "disloyal" individuals.[50] In Indiana, for example, VRC men policed rumors of Copperhead conspiracies, frequently sent out details to arrest "disloyal" citizens, and participated in a raid to shut down a printing and bookbinding establishment where they found incriminating evidence of disloyal activity.[51]

The recusant communities responded as an oppressed minority not only because they might have opposed the draft and the war, but also because they objected to such a violation of their liberties and were jealous of their local prerogatives.[52] Thus, the VRC men in their efforts to enforce military service also confronted civilians who were aiding and abetting its resistance. When members of the 6th Regiment took up duty in Allen County, Ohio, not only did they search for draft dodgers and deserters, but also "scoured the District" to arrest "all persons who presumed to defy the authority of the Gov'mt" by encouraging resistance to military service. On one occasion, when two men from the 6th were transporting a deserter to Lima, Ohio, they were attacked by fifteen men who freed the prisoner.[53] In several of the Pennsylvania counties patrolled by the 16th Regiment, the federal authorities could not find willing citizens to serve draft notices; the VRC men took up the slack. As with the 6th Regiment, the 16th Regiment also encountered armed resistance to the draft and arrested 184 "disloyal Citizens" in Clearfield, Centre,

---

[50] Charles F. Johnson to Mary Johnson, August 8, 13, September 28, 1863, Charles F. Johnson Papers; and Maj. F. A. H. Gaebel to Maj. R. T. Dodge, February 2, 1865, Letters Rec'd, VRC, RG 110.

[51] *Indianapolis Daily Journal*, August 22, 1864; and Capt. J. W. De Forest to Brig. Gen. J. B. Fry, November 30, 1865, *Official Records*, series 3, vol. 5, p. 561.

[52] For a general discussion of the Union draft as well as resistance to it and its enforcement, see James W. Geary, *We Need Men: The Union Draft in the Civil War* (DeKalb: Northern Illinois University Press, 1991). Kenneth H. Wheeler makes an important case for the argument that a desire to protect local autonomy played a role in resistance to the draft. See his article "Local Autonomy and Civil War Draft Resistance: Holmes County, Ohio," *Civil War History* 45 (June 1999): 147–59. See also Peter Levine, "Draft Evasion in the North during the Civil War, 1863–1865," *Journal of American History* 67 (March 1981): 816–34. Judith Lee Hallock, "The Role of Community in Civil War Desertion," *Civil War History* 29 (June 1983): 123–34 lends statistical evidence to how community stability or lack thereof influenced the rate of desertion from two locations on Long Island, New York.

[53] Capt. G. Nagel to Capt. J. W. De Forest, October 17, 1865, Letters Rec'd, VRC, RG 110.

and Columbia Counties.[54] As P. Gray Meek, the editor of a Centre County Democratic newspaper warned, this fate might await anyone. "No individual is safe, no citizen has any assurance that the sanctity of his home will not be invaded by the hirelings of Federal authority."[55] Indeed, Major Frederick A. H. Gaebel, commander of the 16th Regiment, executed the arrest order for Meek, who was charged with "counseling persons to assault and obstruct the Military forces of the United States in performance of service in relation to the Draft."[56]

Those individuals and communities who helped draft dodgers and deserters would have reacted to any representatives of the central government in a similar manner, but in many of these cases it was the Veterans Reserve Corps who ran into their violent resistance. One may assume that they easily transferred their hatred of the government to those men who enforced its policies. In July 1863, Private Hiram Tilley observed that the efforts of the detachments of the 16th Regiment to enforce the enrollment for the draft were not especially welcomed in some communities near Scranton. Some of the coal miners they encountered "did not like us very well." "[T]hese places are inhabited by prety rough people," he told his parents. "I guess if one or two soldiers was to attempt this business alone they would not get back to Head quarters to report."[57]

Loyal unionists might applaud the Veterans Reserve Corps' efforts at reining in draft dodgers and deserters—these men were never *true* Union soldiers to begin with—but one wonders if they had ever given much consideration at the outset of the war to the type of damage that good Yankee soldiers might visit upon their communities. On furlough in cities, a noticeable number of men tended to do their best to enjoy themselves, frequenting drinking establishments and prostitutes, and at times engaging in "the most disgraceful and ob-

---

[54] Bvt. Lt. Col. F. A. H. Gaebel, "Report of the History and Operations of the 16th Regt. V. R. Corps," enclosed in Bvt. Lt. Col. F. A. H. Gaebel to Capt. J. W. De Forest, October 19, 1865, Letters Rec'd, VRC, RG 110.

[55] *Bellefonte* [Pa.] *Democratic Watchman*, December 16, 1864. The editorialist did not specifically mention the 16th Regiment or the Veteran Reserve Corps, but these were the "hirelings" doing the arresting in Columbia County and elsewhere in the region.

[56] Maj. R. I. Dodge to Maj. F. A. H. Gaebel, February 24, 1865, Western Division, Pennsylvania, Provost Marshal General Bureau, Record Group 110, National Archives, Washington, D.C.; and *Bellefonte* [Pa.] *Central Press*, March 3, 1865.

[57] Hiram Tilley to parents, July 10, 1863, Hiram Tilley Letters.

scene exhibitions of rowdyism."[58] On their way to the front, some new soldiers took whatever opportunities they could find to have one last fling. Returning home from war, many of the survivors of prolonged hardship became unruly when faced with delays in receiving their discharge papers.

Throughout the corps' existence, residents of many towns where soldiers congregated depended on a provost guard of "invalids" to maintain the peace in the face of disorderly soldiers out to have some fun. In May 1864, men from the 4th Regiment VRC protected farmers who came to town to stroll the streets of Charleston, Illinois, from iron-knuckled attacks by some hundred-day men.[59] Also during 1864, Auburn, New York, residents watched VRC patrols try to maintain discipline among volunteer soldiers. The citizens from Pottsville and Schuylkill Haven, Pennsylvania, "frequently called upon" companies of the 14th Regiment VRC "to protect property threatened by mobs composed of soldiers at home on furlough."[60] But residents near the rendezvous camps were particularly oppressed by the antics of large numbers of soldiers on their way to or from the war.

In 1864, troop movements disrupted the peace and quiet of the residents of Indianapolis. Soldiers passing through the town "do not always observe a very strict behavior, and many of them take the occasion to drink and become intoxicated and rude. It is often extremely difficult to preserve order among them," thus "rendering the work of the provost guard arduous and difficult, and the treatment they have received has been sometimes very aggravating."[61] Still, the citizens there relied on the VRC to do its best to maintain order among these crowds, as they did when, in April 1864, the provost guard arrested liquor dealers who peddled their wares to sojourning soldiers or when the guard arrested an entire company of rowdy soldiers and put them to work cleaning up the rendezvous camp. As the editor of the *Daily Journal* explained, "Veteran soldiers as well as others must yield obedience to authority, and those from other States, while passing through here, form no exception."[62] Selling li-

---

[58] *Harrisburg Daily Patriot and Union*, February 13, 16, 20, 1864.

[59] Capt. John Gifferman to Capt. C. P. Horton, May 20, 1864, Regimental Papers, 4th VRC, AGO, RG 94.

[60] *Rochester* [N. Y.] *Evening Express*, March 29, 1864; and Lt. Col. Carlisle Boyd to Col. M. N. Wisewell, May 7, 1864, Letters Rec'd, VRC, RG 110.

[61] *Indianapolis Daily Journal*, April 25, 1864.

[62] Ibid., April 15, 29, 1864.

quor to soldiers—with its "evil consequences"—was a recurring problem in Indianapolis, but the VRC men who provided the city with a provost guard continued to do their best to contain it.[63] No doubt the actions of the "invalids" in such cases reinforced the *Daily Journal's* editor's respect for the corps.

Cities and towns in the path of the ebb and flow of the war experienced similar situations to those that troubled Indianapolis. Located on a rail line, Elmira, New York, was well positioned to have problems with, as a local editorialist called them, "foreign soldiers" passing through the town. The depot camp there was crowded, discipline was loose, bars provided ample supplies of liquor, and the number of soldiers in town increased faster than the trains could take them away to the front. On February 25, 1864, such conditions led to what one VRC officer remembered as "a little disturbance in town." Troopers of the 1st Veteran Michigan Cavalry arrived only to discover that there was no transportation available to move them along and that there was no room for them in the barracks. With no legitimate place to go, "they were let loose in the town by their officers." The troopers quickly found the local drinking establishments and "soon elevated by potations of whiskey," they became eager to tear apart the town. The Michiganders destroyed property near the station, engaged in a gunfight with soldiers trying to restrain them, and generally ran amuck until elements of the 12th and 16th Regiments VRC stationed in the town arrived on the scene. The "invalids" restored order when they "at once marched to the various scenes of disturbance and arrested all the Michigan Cavalry men that could be found" and then "scoured the town and stopped any further demonstration from the enemy."[64] Private George Dale of the 16th Regiment later remembered that the affair "ended in . . . quite a battle." Such rear echelon duty was not without risk. Dale suffered from an accidental gunshot wound that cost him his arm, an operation that, the *Elmira Advertiser* informed its readers, the "poor fellow bore . . . with utmost fortitude."[65]

---

[63] Ibid., August 29, 1864.

[64] Lt. Col. L. Eastman to Lt. Col. Moore, February 25, 1864; A. Meyer to Lt. H. Montgomery, March 3, 1864, Regimental Papers, 16th VRC, AGO, RG 94; and *Elmira Advertiser*, February 26, 1864, reprinted in *Rochester Union and Advertiser*, February 27, 1864.

[65] *Elmira Advertiser*, February 26, 1864 reprinted in *Rochester Union and Advertiser*, February 27, 1864. Despite paying the soldier a public compliment, the re-

Once more at the end of the war, Elmira experienced the problems of being on a rail line used by thousands of soldiers. Returning volunteers caused various disturbances as they passed through the town on their way home, but members of the 1st Regiment VRC were on hand to restore order. Members of the 1st Regiment also acted as military police in Rochester, New York, where they reined in disorderly soldiers from the disbanding regiments staying there.[66]

The VRC men who supervised the coming and going of troops at Elmira at the end of the war delayed their own return home to oversee the mustering out of the volunteer regiments. They were not alone. The 13th Regiment VRC stationed in Boston oversaw the mustering out of 27 volunteer organizations, totaling 7,920 men; at Readville, Massachusetts, its detachments supervised the mustering out of 3,468 men.[67]

Always shorthanded, regiments such as the 13th stretched their reserves of manpower and patience to accomplish one of their last assignments. The 3rd Regiment VRC, for example, guarded several rendezvous camps in New England, including New Haven and Hartford, Connecticut; Augusta, Maine; and Brattleboro and Burlington, Vermont. "The large number of volunteer organizations being disbanded at these Rendezvous has severely tested the endurance, faithfulness, and discipline of the Reg't.," an officer reported. "It has performed double duty for weeks. The returning soldiers were many of them disorderly and did not readily endure restraint. . . . Riots were sometimes organized involving the entire camp in mutiny and the duty of quelling these was upon a small force of the 3rd V.R.C." On June 22, 1865, Vermont troops broke up property and caused a general disruption of the peace in Burlington until men from the 3rd Regiment quelled the disturbance. Only a few days later, on June 26, Vermont soldiers rioted again in Burlington, but a detachment from

---

porter mistakenly identified Dale as a member of the 11th VRC. See Hewett et al., eds., *Supplement to the Official Records*, part 2, 80: 32. Dale gave a brief account of his history in his entry to William Oland Bourne's left-handed writing competition. See G. W. Dale to W. O. Bourne, December 26, 1865, box 2, William Oland Bourne Papers, Library of Congress, Washington, D.C.

[66] Capt. J. W. De Forest to Brig. Gen. J. B. Fry, Nov. 30, 1865, *Official Records*, series 3, vol. 5, p. 560.

[67] Ibid., 563.

the 3rd Regiment restored "perfect order" after shooting two of the returning soldiers and arresting others.[68]

Citizens who benefited from the order brought by a detachment of VRC men were profuse in their praise for their protectors. Detachments of the 6th Regiment stationed at Crestline, Ohio, guarded the town's railroad depots while about fifteen thousand troops passed along the lines en route home. The town council there "tendered them a public vote of thanks for their prompt and efficient aid in preserving the peace and protecting the property of the town." In general, "The Regiment for the past year has received some very flattering compliments from Private and Public sources News papers &c of the Gentlemanly and Soldierly deportment shown during its stay in the various places where they have been Stationed."[69] In Indianapolis, Colonel Holloway reminded his readers of the importance of the corps in maintaining order among the troops and in the city. "Since this Corps has been on duty, an unusual number of veteran soldiers, recruits, and troops from other States have been constantly in the city, rendering the work of the provost guard arduous and difficult, and the treatment they have received has been sometimes aggravating." Often unaccompanied by officers, the sojourning soldiers did "not always observe a very strict behavior, and many of them take the occasion to drink and become intoxicated and rude." Understandably, "it is often difficult to preserve order among them," but the corps did its best. "The Provost Guard, composed of troops of the Veteran Reserve Corps, are frequently censured by unreflecting persons for the strict manner in which they perform the duties assigned to them. A comparison to the order of the city now with what it was a few months ago, demonstrates conclusively the general efficiency of the provost work, and much praise should be awarded them for their diligence," he reminded his readers. "Nearly one-third of our population is now military, and the Provost Guards are an imperative necessity. They protect us and we should sustain them."[70]

The corps, however, had to be careful when enforcing discipline

---

[68] Lt. Col. G. Mallory to Brig. Gen. J. B. Fry, October 20, 1865, Letters Rec'd, VRC, RG 110.

[69] Capt. G. Nagle to Capt. J. W. De Forrest, October 17, 1865, Letters Rec'd, VRC, RG 110.

[70] *Indianapolis Daily Journal*, April 25, 1864.

on home-state troops lest they appear too eager to embarrass the returning veterans by assuming the worst before it happened. In Trenton, New Jersey, where the VRC generally had a good reputation in the Republican press, it overstepped the borders of propriety when, in June 1865, it prepared for the arrival of New Jersey soldiers. "On Tuesday evening, our citizens were greatly surprised at seeing two or three hundred men of the Veteran Reserve Corps marched through the city, and distributed in squads of twenty or thirty in different quarters," the *Daily State Gazette* reported. "A great parade of loading their pieces was made, and if one might judge from appearance an immediate attack was apprehended on the city. Various surmises were made as to the object of this unusual parade . . . but the prevailing opinion was that the troops were ordered out to guard the Governor, and men undertook to circulate a report that the returned volunteers had threatened a riot and to fire the city." The editor believed that this assumption was an insult to the orderly New Jersey soldiers returning from the war, one promulgated by Copperheads trying to disgrace the men. Still, the earliest returning soldiers, who felt slighted by the lack of fanfare upon their arrival in the state capital of Trenton, did not seem to hold their Democratic governor in high esteem. Given what the VRC faced elsewhere, the precaution just might have been warranted.[71]

First and foremost, the "invalids" were veteran soldiers, sharing much of the same urges as the volunteers they attempted to discipline. What made them heroes on the home front was that most of them controlled their baser urges, or had good officers who could do it for them. Still, the men and officers of the corps were not always successful; there were times that the "invalids" reminded citizens of the looser yet harder ways of soldiers that camp life and battle nurtured.

In February 1864, an anonymous "Union Man" from Easton, Pennsylvania, complained that VRC men were causing all sorts of trouble in his town. "Now these men are under no regulations," he explained, "but are permitted to be out at all hours of the night, and

---

[71] *Trenton* [N. J.] *Daily State Gazette*, June 15, 1865. On the perceived slighting of returning veterans by the Democratic state administration and the soldiers' view of New Jersey's Democratic governor Joel Parker, see *Trenton* [N. J.] *Daily Gazette*, June 7, 8, 9, 10, 13, 1865; and William Gillette, *Jersey Blue: Civil War Politics in New Jersey, 1854–1865* (New Brunswick: Rutgers University Press, 1995), 311.

every few days we have reports of a citizen having beaten and ro[b]bed, others waylaid and beaten by Soldiers." He suggested that such boisterous and apparently fit men might be of service at the front. "I would Suppose, if they [are] able to play the roudy every night on the Streets [and] Knock down citizens, they [are] fit for the field, and I have no doubt Some twenty thousand are at this time playing old Soldier in different parts of the country."[72] Captain Samuel Yoke, the provost marshal stationed at Easton, investigated. He concluded the charges were unfounded, coming from "a class of citizens in this place . . . who entertain a particular dislike to any person clothed in the uniform of the U. S. army and take the advantage of every opportunity to provoke and irritate them and no doubt would be pleased to have their private grievances settled by the department and if possible affix the blame upon the government."[73] However, if in this case the accusation was a false one, in others they had substance.

At times, the "invalids" were guilty at most of trying to break the humdrum routine of military regimentation or of frolicking about in ways that would not have been unusual in a camp setting but breached civilian notions of public decorum. During August 1863, men from Camp E. V. Sumner passed their spare time loitering about the Wenham, Massachusetts, train station, prompting complaints from local citizens.[74] In May 1865, soldiers of the 16th Regiment stationed at Harrisburg took to skinny-dipping in the river while in full view of the residences of some of its citizens. More serious was the habit the men of the 16th had of randomly firing their guns, probably because they were simply feeling exuberant over the war's end. This activity prompted a complaint from the mayor.[75]

On other occasions, officers proved that they, too, could fall short of being the gentlemen that were critical for supervising the army's Corps of Honor. During the summer of 1864, one of its officers besmirched the corps' reputation by playing the Lothario with the wife

---

[72] A Union Man to J. B. Fry, February 11, 1864, Letters Rec'd VRC, RG 110.

[73] Capt. Samuel Yoke to Maj. C. C. Gilbert, February 20, 1864, enclosed in A Union Man to J. B. Fry, February 11, 1864, Letters Rec'd VRC, RG 110.

[74] General Orders, No. 18, September 3, 1863, Regimental Order Book, 15th VRC, AGO, RG 94.

[75] Special Orders, No. 95, May 18, 1865, Regimental Order Book; Capt. R. Theune to Lt. Col. F. A. H. Gaebel, May 26, 1865, Regimental Papers, 16th VRC, AGO, RG 94.

of a Columbus, Ohio, man. The newspaper reports made their way back to Washington, thanks to a concerned citizen.[76]

In January 1864, Colonel S. D. Oliphant explained to headquarters that several of his men had committed an assortment of crimes, provoking the civil authorities to demand that he turn them over for prosecution. One of his men had committed bigamy, another had stolen a pocketbook, and a third was accused of "larceny of an overcoat, which was pledged for whiskey—poison at one of these very houses from which the liquor was taken & ordered to be returned."[77] As with soldiers in general, the "invalids" who most frequently caused trouble for themselves, their officers, and the communities in which they were stationed strayed from the narrow path with bottles in their hands. In October 1863, Captain G. W. Merrick, an assistant provost marshal general, complained to the Invalid Corps commander at Chambersburg, Pennsylvania, about his men. He had arrested and jailed three "invalids" from his command "who were found in the Street, near midnight, intoxicated and engaged in riotous conduct, making indiscriminate attacks upon all who passed by."[78] On another occasion, four privates had been drunk and engaged in fighting with citizens in the streets of Harrisburg, "using at the same time blasphemous and abusive language, thereby disturbing the peace of the good citizens of the city." [79]

At times, lax discipline encouraged such bad behavior. In August 1863, Captain Henry Kerr allowed his men the freedom to move about the town of Williamsport, Pennsylvania, when they were not on duty as long as they answered three roll calls a day.[80] But by December of that year, complaints had reached Washington that Kerr and his subordinate officer, Lieutenant Von Schirock, were not doing their utmost to control their undisciplined and rowdy men. Colonel

---

[76] Rev. E. P. Goodwin to E. M. Stanton, July 23, 1864, and enclosures, Letters Rec'd, VRC, RG 110.

[77] Col. S. D. Oliphant to Col. R. H. Rush, Jan. 25, 1864, Letters Rec'd, VRC, RG 110.

[78] Capt. G. W. Merrick to Commanding Officer, Invalid Company No. 17, October 20, 1863, Regimental Papers, 16th VRC, AGO, RG 94.

[79] Charges and Specifications against Privates Robert Marshall, John Middleton, Peter R. Cassiday, Henry D. Carpenter, [n.d.], Regimental Papers, 16th VRC, AGO, RG 94.

[80] Capt. H. C. Kerr to [—], August 27, 1863, Company Order Books, A to D, 16th VRC, AGO, RG 94.

Moses N. Wisewell, the officer in the provost marshal general's office then in charge of matters pertaining to the corps, informed Colonel Fry that reports painted a disturbing situation. The men, he explained, "do as they please and go where they please that through the neglect of the com[man]d[in]g officers, substitutes for drafted men have been allowed to desert and make good their escape." Furthermore, "Men placed on guard at the clothing-room [sic] have been found so intoxicated as to be unable to attend to their duty—that they are allowed to leave camp without a pass and wander about the country and return as they choose. Citizens in Williamsport have made complaints of the men being intoxicated and disorderly upon the streets night and day, and people in the country also complain of the depredations of the men—robbing them and destroying their property." Unlike some other complaints, he was convinced that these accusations had substance. "When we hear reports derogatory to officers coming as they do through different channels it is fair to assume the immediate commander must be cognizant of the fact."[81]

So not all of the corps' men lived up to its high standards, thereby straining relations with the civilian population, but the corps did its utmost to maintain discipline. In the vexing matter of public drunkenness, local commanders took extraordinary steps to locate and shut down the grog shops responsible for the bad behavior of the men. Officers of the 16th Regiment, which was stationed throughout several counties in the Harrisburg area, did their best to curtail the problem. On March 1, 1865, Major Frederick A. H. Gaebel, then in command of the regiment, ordered his men to stay away from the Conrad House in Philipsburg, Pennsylvania, promising that "every man found in the Bar Room will be arrested forthwith and brought to the Guard House."[82] Later, when stationed in Harrisburg, the regimental officers continued to deal with the same problem, but resorted to covert activities to track down proprietors who persisted in selling liquor to soldiers against orders. "Send to this Office at once 2 or 3 Sharp and intelligent Soldiers, who can dress in citizens clothing," one officer requested of another. He planned to send them under cover into the various taverns to observe their proprietors'

---

[81] Col. M. N. Wisewell to Col. C. M. Prevost, December 4, 1863, Regimental Papers, 16th VRC, AGO, RG 94.

[82] Circular, March 1, 1865, Company Order Books, A to D, 16th VRC, AGO, RG 94.

marketing practices.[83] Such measures went far in curtailing the availability of alcoholic beverages; nevertheless, as one veteran of the corps remembered, "we managed to get it some way."[84]

Throughout its history, the Veteran Reserve Corps was intent on swiftly disciplining officers and men who brought such disrepute to its ranks.[85] Sergeant G. W. Drake, stationed with the Invalid Corps in Greensburg, Pennsylvania, in October 1864, was reduced to the ranks "for theft from a citizen." Other malefactors in the VRC received punishment or were dismissed from the service.[86] But for the wrongly accused, the disciplinary process provided opportunities to test the support they believed they had cultivated in the communities in which they had worked. Those who had good relations with civilians were likely to receive the requested assistance. In February 1864, John A. Hopper, who apparently had clashed with other officers in his regiment, was charged with drunkenness and summarily discharged from the service. Hopper turned to his old neighbors in Scranton, Pennsylvania, for help, and they were happy to oblige him because of his good service to them. Scrantonians petitioned Abraham Lincoln on Hopper's behalf, explaining to the president that "his brave and uncompromising efforts saved us much life and property in our troublesome days when Copperheadism was rampant." Furthermore, "the citizens feel a deep interest in his wellfare because of his *undoubted* Loyalty and the unswerving manner in which he maintained law and order, at the frequent risk of his life." Assuring Lincoln that the charges were generated by malice alone, they explained "that the charge of *drunkenness* &c. is very unjust and unfounded and cannot be alleged but by his Enemies." A second group of petitioners also assured Lincoln that Hopper was a victim of the malicious whims of other officers and that "when commanding here appeared to us to be a good and efficient officer." Hopper's case drew significant support from the community; the second petition held the

---

[83] Capt. R. [Henne?] to Capt. F. Randlett, June 5, 1865, Regimental Papers, 16th VRC, AGO, RG 94.

[84] Donald, ed., *Gone for a Soldier*, 252.

[85] Col. R. H. Rush to Col. C. M. Prevost, August 11, 1863, Letters Sent, vol. 1, 416–17, VRC, RG 110.

[86] Capt. T. Leddy to Col. C. M. Prevost, October 17, 1864, Regimental Papers, 16th VRC, AGO, RG 94.

signatures of a hundred men, including Baptist, Presbyterian, and Methodist Episcopal clergymen.[87]

Veteran Reserve Corps men and officers frequently participated in solemn public functions that indicated much about how other members of the military and the civilian population felt about the organization. Significantly, four companies of the 12th Regiment acted as an honor guard while the assassinated president's body lay in state at the Capitol and then acted as an escort to the train depot. An honor guard of VRC officers and noncommissioned officers accompanied President Abraham Lincoln's body on its journey to Springfield, Illinois, and its final resting place.[88] More important, as far as the corps' relationship with local communities was concerned, were the local processions held in honor of the slain president in which men from the organization played visible roles.[89] When communities staged memorial services for less august but still important local heroes, the "invalids" were on hand to lend dignity to the occasion.[90]

The imposition of discipline on individuals who insulted the Union cause also provided opportunities for the VRC men to participate in serious public ceremonies that reinforced their role as active champions of the war effort. In 1864, VRC men stationed at Indianapolis participated in parades that were designed to humiliate the offenders. On November 2, substitute agents in league with bounty jumpers, as well as the jumpers themselves, marched between a row of

[87] John M. William et al. to Abraham Lincoln, February 27, 1864, and M. J. Hickock et al. to Abraham Lincoln, February 1864, Letters Rec'd, VRC, RG 110. Also see John A. Hopper to Abraham Lincoln, June 20, 1864, Letters Rec'd, VRC, RG 110.

[88] Lt. Col. M. O. Mansfield to Capt. J. W. De Forest, October 18, 1865; Maj. G. Bowers to Brig. Gen. J. B. Fry, Oct. 18, 1865, Letters Rec'd, VRC, RG 110. For illustrations of the VRC honor guard in the presidential funeral procession, see *Harper's Weekly*, May 13, 1865, and the Currier and Ives colored lithograph "The Funeral Procession of President Lincoln, April 25, 1865 Passing Union Square," 1865, in the Harry T. Peters Collection, the Museum of the City of New York.

[89] For example, see *Rochester* [N. Y.] *Evening Express*, April 20, 1865; *Indianapolis Daily Journal*, April 21, 1865; Circular, April 19, 1865, Regimental Papers, 5th VRC, AGO, RG 94 (which directed the 5th VRC to take part in the funeral procession in Indianapolis); and Maj. F. A. H. Gaebel to Capt. J. W. De Forest, October 19, 1865, Letters Rec'd, VRC, RG 110 (which notes that a company of the 16th Regiment participated in the ceremonies at Harrisburg, Pennsylvania).

[90] *Trenton* [N. J.] *Daily State Gazette*, June 6, 1864; and *Indianapolis Daily Journal* September 21, 1864.

bayonet-wielding VRC men, in step to the music of the "Rogue's March," provided by the regimental band. About two weeks later, the men repeated the "rare and unique" entertainment before sending about 100 more bounty jumpers off to the front. "[A]nd may they have a happy time," wished an editorialist for a local paper.[91]

But just as solemn occasions were a part of wartime life, so, too, were the public celebrations and the social affairs that united communities and reaffirmed their common cause. The "invalids" played roles in these events, while adding some entertainment to the lives of the civilians residing near their camps.[92] In areas of larger concentrations of VRC men, citizens could count on the soldiers to provide them with some martial displays that diverted them from the ordinary affairs of life. Residents of Davenport, Iowa, could watch the men from the 11th Regiment who guarded prisoners at the Rock Island, Illinois, barracks conduct dress parade on the frozen river that stood between them.[93] In Indianapolis, the population enjoyed the muster and music of the 17th Regiment, rewarding each band member in September 1864 with "a handsome three dollar military cap . . . as a testimonial of the appreciation of their services by the people and the Committee."[94] At the end of May 1865, when the last contingent of the 22nd Regiment left Indianapolis to be reunited with the rest of the regiment at Columbus, Ohio, the editor of the *Daily Journal* reminded his readers of the regiment's positive contributions to the local social scene. "Persons who have availed themselves of the benefit of the free concerts in the Circle, will miss the band, and the

---

[91] *Indianapolis Daily Journal*, November 2, 17, 1864.

[92] Michael H. Frisch notes that the various amusements in which the people of Springfield, Massachusetts, engaged, similar to those noted above and below, were not examples of populations "captivated by the abstract glory of war," but were more similar to social safety valves that allowed the people to relieve some of their anxieties about the war. The VRC, which contributed its share to the behind-the-lines military pomp, thus assisted in contributing to the mental health of the communities in which its men were stationed. Thomas H. O'Connor also notes that even at times of celebration, the war was never far from the minds of Bostonians. J. Matthew Gallman notes the importance of public rituals for expressing shared values and the power of public displays, which suggests that in some locales, the VRC was a helpful presence for facilitating the values of the Union cause. See Frisch, *Town Into City*, 60; O'Connor, *Civil War Boston*, 99, 150; Gallman, *Mastering Wartime*, 83–116; and Gallman, *The North Fights the Civil War*, 120–21.

[93] Addison W. McPheeters, Jr., to R. P. McPheeters, January 26, 1864, McPheeters Family Papers, Archives, USAMHI.

[94] *Indianapolis Daily Journal*, September 7, 1864.

citizens generally will regret the departure of the 22nd," he wrote. "We hope the citizens of Columbus will extend to them the cordial greeting which their good behavior merits."[95]

The VRC further integrated itself into the public lives of local civilians by participating in various moments of community celebration. In February 1864, when the 10th Connecticut returned home and paraded through the streets of New Haven, members of the 3rd Regiment "were on hand, as usual, with their drum corps," and in August, VRC men, including the 17th Regiment's "excellent band," participated in Indianapolis's public welcoming-home ceremonies for returning hundred-day volunteers.[96] In September 1864, the 17th Regiment helped the city celebrate the victory in Mobile harbor by firing a one-hundred-gun salute.[97] Celebrations broke out throughout Indianapolis when news of Richmond's fall arrived in the town, and the 22nd Regiment's band was on hand to participate, serenading various establishments with rousing renditions of "Red, White and Blue" and "Hail Columbia," "creating unbounded enthusiasm" along the way.[98] In the wake of Richmond's fall and again when Confederate General Robert E. Lee surrendered, VRC men from Camp Coburn marched in military parades in Augusta, Maine.[99] In May 1865, members of the 10th Regiment guarded the reviewing stands as the Union's victorious armies marched in the Grand Review.[100]

The Fourth of July, a particularly important celebration of the Union cause during the war and in its immediate aftermath, found citizens in some locales watching members of the corps march in their parades. In 1864, Lois Bryan Adams witnessed "a grand review of the troops belonging to the Invalid Corps," noting that the event "passed off in fine style, and was witnessed by thousands of delighted spectators." The men also gave them a "faint idea of the smoke and smell of battle" by firing off several cannon rounds. [101]

---

[95] *Indianapolis Daily Journal*, May 30, 1865.

[96] *Hartford* [Conn.] *Evening Press*, February 20, 1864; and *Indianapolis Daily Journal*, August 30, 1864.

[97] *Indianapolis Daily Journal*, September 7, 1864.

[98] Ibid., April 4, 1865.

[99] *Augusta* [Me.] *Kennebec Journal*, April 7, 14, 1865.

[100] Maj. G. Bowers to Brig. Gen. J. B. Fry, October 18, 1865, Letters Rec'd, VRC, RG 110; and Cimbala, "Union Corps of Honor," 84 (photograph).

[101] Adams sent regular columns to the *Detroit Advertiser and Tribune*. These remarks, dated July 4, 1864, appeared in the July 11 issue. Her columns are reprinted

In 1865, Fourth of July parades had the additional significance of being victory celebrations. In Trenton, New Jersey, Lieutenant Colonel Benjamin Runkle, the commanding officer of the 21st Regiment VRC, understood that the day's importance went beyond the scope of antebellum celebrations. The day was now an occasion transformed by the outcome of the war. Along with honoring American independence and "the sacrifices of our heroic Ancestors," celebrations would commemorate the "memory of our gallant comrades who are sleeping beneath Southern sod." Furthermore, it would be a day for honoring "those who maimed and wounded still live," as well as the "Country redeemed, regenerated, and disenthralled."[102] Of course, his command and VRC soldiers elsewhere throughout the North were still on hand to add martial flavor to the occasions even if their fit comrades were hastily shedding their uniforms for civilian garb.

Members of the corps paraded through the streets of Evansville, Indiana, and then joined their neighbors at a celebratory ball.[103] The people of Augusta, Maine, watched three companies of the 3rd Regiment march along with the local Knights Templar, school children, the Maine Coast Guard, various decorated wagons, wounded soldiers transported by other wagons, the fire department, local officials, and Camp Coburn's brass band.[104] In Trenton, New Jersey, citizens placed Lieutenant Colonel Runkle in charge of organizing the local parade, including its military and civilian units. At sunrise on that great national holiday, the VRC employed two field pieces to fire "A NATIONAL SALUTE" on the parade grounds of the Trenton barracks. Two field pieces spewed out thirty-six rounds, one for every state of the Union, welcoming the town's first postwar Independence Day celebration. The officers of the 21st Regiment closed the day's celebrations with a "rounds" of a different kind at a "collation" they hosted at their barracks where "toasts were offered, speeches made, and everybody enjoyed themselves 'prodigiously.' "[105]

---

in Lois Bryan Adams, *Letters from Washington, 1863–1865*, ed. by Evelyn Leasher (Detroit: Wayne State University Press, 1999), with these remarks appearing on page 171.

[102] General Orders, No. 23, June 26, 1865, Regimental Papers, 21st VRC, AGO, RG 94.

[103] Jonathan Turley to Brother, July 3, 1864, Jonathan Turley Papers, Indiana State Library, Indianapolis.

[104] *Augusta* [Me.] *Kennebec Journal*, June 30, July 7, 1865.

[105] *Trenton* [N. J.] *Daily State Gazette*, June 28, 29, July 4, 6, 1865.

Civilians who interacted with the Veteran Reserve Corps on these occasions or benefited from the diligence of its men at other times showed their appreciation in various ways, making life a bit more enjoyable for the "invalids." Along the way, the women of the communities provided the boys with a good dose of mothering. The people of Greenupsburg, Kentucky, where the VRC had protected the community from rebel raiders, offered them "every convenience possible," vying "with each other in administering to their comfort." But the sick "invalids" found that "the ladies are constant to them as nurses."[106] During the summer of 1863, the citizens of Pottsville, Pennsylvania, "especially the ladies," were "unremitting in kindness & attention" to sick members of the VRC stationed there, although the local commander worried that the community was spoiling his fit officers and men.[107]

In the January 16, 1864, issue of the *Indianapolis Daily Journal*, the soldiers of the 5th Regiment publicly gave thanks to "the 4th Ward Ladies" for fifty-three pairs of woolen mittens. The men resolved "that our hearts, no less than our hands, are warmed by this generous manifestation of sympathy, and that in after years, the memory thereof shall be a nucleus around which will gather many pleasing thoughts of the fair donors. . . . That it gives us unfeigned pleasure to assure our citizen friends, that the principles which led us to the field, are none the less dear to us as 'Invalids,' and that by every means in our power, we will seek to give them prominence."

The most common way by which communities and especially the local women showed their appreciation to the VRC men in their midst was by feeding them. In June 1865, Mary Seymour presented the VRC men at the Hartford, Connecticut, depot camp with a "splendid feast of strawberries,"[108] but more substantial dinners were common. In October 1863, Invalid Corps members thanked the Soldiers' Aid Society and the citizens of Detroit for a "splendid dinner." "It was pleasing to us to behold so many smiling faces and to think those who have served their country in the battles for the preservation of the Union, have not been forgotten by our lady friends," they

---

[106] Capt. C. W. Grier to Maj. W. W. Lidell, October 20, 1863, Letters Rec'd, VRC, RG 110.

[107] Maj. S. D. Oliphant to Col. R. H. Rush, September 5, 1863, Letters Rec'd, VRC, RG 110.

[108] *Hartford Evening Press*, June 22, 1865.

gratefully wrote. "May they prosper in their present cause, and be a comfort to many a poor soldier who has left home and friends to fight for that blessed Flag." Furthermore, the men expressed additional thanks to "the ladies who so frequently visit us at our quarters."[109] Private Hiram Tilley of the 16th Regiment also enjoyed a similar kindness. In 1863, while stationed at Scranton, Pennsylvania, where both officers and men of the corps "are apparently much respected by all," he and his comrades enjoyed a good bit of hospitality. "We are told that the ladies are going to bring us our supper tonight[,] a sort of donation I suppose," he wrote to his family. Such an action, however, did not strike him as being out of the ordinary. He explained that "hardly a day passes but what something good to eat is sent to our quarters by some of the people who live here."[110] When Tilly's company moved to Williamsport in Lycoming County, Pennsylvania, to enforce the enrollment for the draft, he discovered that he had acquired an even better berth. "[W]e hope that our company will stay here a good long time, for I guess we have struck the best people so far," he informed his family. "We thought the Scranton people were good and so they were, but these people have done them all out. They gave us a dinner to day which was fine, with enough left over for another day."[111]

The holidays especially prompted the locals to do their best to make the VRC men feel at home. On Thanksgiving Day 1864, the men of C Company, 21st Regiment, received a "sumptuous dinner" from the women of Trenton, New Jersey. Furthermore, the ladies themselves attended the dinner and "with their lovely and smiling faces" added much to the event by "doing their utmost to cause us to realize to the fullest extent, the importance of the occasion, fully succeeded in their efforts, causing our minds to wander to our homes, where perchance our wives, mothers and sisters, were doing a similar Christian duty toward faithful Union soldiers that may be encamped in their vicinity."[112]

The women of Indianapolis and Baltimore matched the female Trentonians in the hospitality they offered to the "invalids." On

---

[109] *Detroit Advertiser and Tribune*, October 12, 1863.

[110] Hiram Tilley to Mother, July 16, 1863, Hiram Tilley Letters; and Col. Frank P. Cahill to Col. J. B. Fry, December 11, 1863, Letters Rec'd, VRC, RG 110.

[111] Hiram Tilley to Mother, August 21, 1863, Hiram Tilley Letters.

[112] *Trenton* [N.J.] *Daily State Gazette*, November 26, 1864.

Thanksgiving Day 1864, members of the 17th Regiment stationed at the state arsenal in Indianapolis enjoyed an "abundant dinner" thanks to the women of the city. "Such kindnesses are bright spots in a soldier's life, and coming as they did on this occasion, from those to whom they are comparatively strangers, are fully appreciated and will be gratefully remembered."[113] The previous year, W. G. Dunn, who had been transferred into the corps about a month before Thanksgiving, wrote of his holiday experience in Baltimore, where he was stationed at the Jarvis General Hospital. "Thanksgiving day passed off very pleasantly," he noted. "The ladies of the Union Relief in this City gave the soldiers in this Hospital an excelent dinner." Later in December, Dunn looked forward to "a grand dinner" on Christmas and New Years, also provided by the women of the Union Relief of Baltimore.[114]

With the end of the war, the men of the Veteran Reserve Corps faced the prospects of returning to civilian life. The nation was intent on mustering out its army, and General Ulysses S. Grant saw no need to maintain an organization of invalids. Some officers, desirous to secure the fruits of Union victory while remaining gainfully employed, found their way into the Bureau of Refugees, Freedmen, and Abandoned Lands. There they continued to serve their nation in its efforts to reconstruct the states of the erstwhile Confederacy. Most enlisted men were eager to go home and by the end of 1865 had received their discharges. By the end of the summer of 1866, the army had consolidated those men who continued in the corps into four Veteran Reserve regiments, where they served until the War Department finally disbanded them in March 1869. But as the North turned to peace and shed itself of the extraneous trappings of war, the "invalid" officers, mindful of their limited prospects in the peacetime economy, called on the support of their friends in one last effort to retain a place in the national service. In August 1865, they embarked on a lobbying effort to keep the corps alive, circulating petitions in the hopes that the support the documents generated would convince the War Department at least to wait until Congress convened later in the year and considered their collective fate. The campaign provided

---

[113] *Indianapolis Daily Journal*, November 26, 1864.

[114] Walter G. Dunn to Emma Randolph, November 28, December 23, 1863, in Bailey and Cottom, eds., *After Chancellorsville*, 21, 23.

those individuals who appreciated the corps' wartime work for the Union cause with one last opportunity to express their appreciation of the organization's efforts.[115]

Local, state, and national politicians wrote letters in favor of at least delaying a decision about the corps' future. Petitions and letters arrived at the War Department from diverse sources: citizens of Grand Rapids, Michigan; the secretary of state and other officials from Springfield, Illinois; a resident of Grinnell, Iowa; and a United States senator from Vermont, among numerous others.[116] Congressman Leonard Myers of Philadelphia argued that those who wished to stay in the service should be given positions in the regular army. "These men are veterans in deed and have helped to save the Country in its darkest hour," he wrote. "Their officers are generally brave, tried, & faithful Union men."[117] J. G. Fell, the president of the Union League, also believed that if the VRC were to be disbanded, the government should find places in the regular army for those men of the corps who wished them. "These men were volunteers in the true sense," he wrote. "They were on the right side at the right time for the right reasons, and will infuse into the Army the kind of spirit

[115] General Orders, No. 116, June 17, 1865; General Orders, No. 155, October 26, 1865; General Orders, No. 165, November 24, 1865; General Orders, No. 56, August 1, 1866; General Orders, No. 92, November 23, 1866; General Orders, No. 24, July 24, 1868; General Orders, No. 16, March 11, 1869, AGO, Library, USAMHI; Edwin Stanton to Andrew Johnson, November 22, 1865; and Circular No. 53, December 1, 1865, AGO, *Official Records*, series 3, vol. 5, 510, 568. For examples of the lobbying effort, see Lt. Col. John H. Gardner and others to E. M. Stanton (August 1865), and a copy of the "Strictly Confidential" circular dated November 3, 1865 and signed by Col. James C. Strong enclosed in Maj. F. A. H. Gaebel to Capt. J. W. De Forest, November 10, 1865, Letters Rec'd, VRC, RG 110. See Cimbala, "Union Corps of Honor," 80–85 for a discussion of the last days of the Veterans Reserve Corps; also see this essay for a brief discussion of the motivation of individuals who wished to remain in the VRC. The latter topic is explored in greater detail in Paul A. Cimbala's "Officers of the Veteran Reserve Corps: Motivation and Expectations of Veteran Soldiers during the American Civil War and Reconstruction," paper presented at the conference The Veteran and American Society, Center for the Study of War and Society, University of Tennessee, Knoxville, Tennessee, November 12, 2000.

[116] N. L. Avory and others to E. M. Stanton, August 1865; Sharon Tyndale and others to E. M. Stanton, August 21, 1865; J. B. Grinnell to E. M. Stanton, August 24, 1865; and Solomon Foot to E. M. Stanton, August 19, 1865, Letters Rec'd, VRC, RG 110.

[117] Leonard Myers to E. M. Stanton, August 16, 1865, Letters Rec'd, VRC, RG 110.

which it has so much needed."[118] A. H. Laflin, congressman from New York, argued that because the nation owed these patriotic soldiers who had been disabled in the service of their country a debt that it could never repay, it should retain them in the service. "I speak the general voice of the [congressional] District and that I believe of the whole nation."[119]

The corps' old friends at the *Indianapolis Daily Journal* provided additional examples of the high opinion of the "invalids" that those who had come to know them during the war had of them. Colonel Holloway wrote directly to the provost marshal general's office and then used the columns of the paper to further the cause.[120] In the August 25, 1865, issue, the editor argued that the consolidation of the VRC was being done for selfish reasons because the officers in Washington simply did not like the organization. Note well, he informed his readers, that these Washington desk soldiers had had "easy positions at home, and were constantly surrounded by all the comforts of life." On the other hand, at the same time, the men they wished to separate from the service had been "absent in the field, suffering all the privations and hardships of a soldier's life, until either stricken down by disease or pierced with rebel bullets," and finally recovered sufficiently to do further service in the corps. His solution for financing the corps' continuance was simple: muster out the excessive numbers of generals and their staffs and keep the "gallant and meritorious" VRC officers in service to do their jobs. It was not only the right thing to do, Holloway argued, but it would also be less expensive than maintaining all that extraneous brass!

Throughout the fall, Holloway and the *Indianapolis Daily Journal* argued for the VRC's cause, proclaiming the good service its men had performed for the nation, while reminding its readers and Congress of the debt they owed to the men who could no longer perform their old peacetime jobs because of their genuine sacrifices for the Union. Even as the consolidation process was taking place, the paper urged Congress to find positions for the soldiers who wished to remain in the service. But despite all good intentions and efforts, Con-

---

[118] J. G. Fell to E. M. Stanton, September 6, 1865, Letters Rec'd, VRC, RG 110.

[119] A. H. Laflin to E. M. Stanton, August 24, 1865, Letters Rec'd, VRC, RG 110.

[120] W. R. Holloway to Brig. Gen. James B. Fry, August 25, 1865, Letters Rec'd, VRC, RG 110.

gress and the army consolidated and eventually disbanded the VRC.[121]

In December 1865, the officers who remained in Indianapolis received their orders to return to their homes. Holloway paid them one last tribute. "These soldiers and gentlemen have, during their residence among us, made hosts of warm friends by their uniform good conduct, and in whatever quarter their future lots may be cast, they will carry with them the good wishes of our citizens." Saying farewell, the editor, no doubt speaking for the entire loyal community of Indianapolis, wished them "prosperity in whatever station they may be called on to fill."[122]

By the time these men left Indianapolis, they and their comrades in other cities and towns across the North had completed significant service in the Union cause. Guarding rendezvous camps, patrolling streets, rushing into the breech when rebels advanced on northern cities, they proved themselves to be every bit the soldiers that some cynics did not expect them to be. To be sure, some of the men and officers of the corps failed to live up to the expectations of their superiors and embarrassed the organization in some northern communities. They certainly did not win the good will of the dissenters in the northern population who were on the receiving end of the actions of the corps. But by integrating themselves into the public and social lives of the northern communities in which they were stationed, the "invalids" provided opportunities for loyal northerners to show their appreciation to the soldiers in the light-blue uniforms for the sacrifices that they had made. In such circumstances, their presence helped shape the way communities experienced the war.

---

[121] *Indianapolis Daily Journal*, October 14, 19, 31, November 30, 1865.
[122] Ibid., December 7, 1865.

7

Saving Jack: Religion, Benevolent Organizations, and Union Sailors during the Civil War

Michael J. Bennett

IN HIS WORK *For Cause & Comrades: Why Men Fought in the Civil War,* James M. McPherson contends that, as products of the Second Great Awakening, "Civil War armies were, arguably, the most religious in American history."[1] Many soldiers, he contends, marched off to war with Bibles in their pockets. Not so for Union sailors, who "with few exceptions" were more prone to throw their Bibles aside.[2] Overall, most men who served as Union sailors in the Civil War seemed to lack the religious dedication McPherson attributes to their brothers in arms. Unlike the soldiers' experience, sailors' time in the navy during the Civil War lessened, rather than encouraged, genuine and expedient reliance upon prayer, conventional religious practices, and faith in God. Much of the blame for failing to save "Jack" falls upon the navy, which took actions that effectively discouraged religious expression aboard ships and helped turn the irreligious impulses of its recruits into fixed patterns of behavior. The navy failed to provide enough chaplains and Bibles, worked sailors on Sundays, and abandoned a prewar policy of mandatory attendance at Sunday services. Stirred by charges of Sabbath desecration and a perceived erosion in religious sentiment among an already irreligious set of men, the United States Christian Commission launched a vigorous

---

[1] James M. McPherson, *For Cause & Comrades: Why Men Fought in the Civil War* (New York: Oxford University Press, 1997), 63.

[2] Journal entry for September 8, 1861, in Amos Burton, *A Journal of the Cruise of the U.S. Ship Susquehanna* (New York: Edward O. Jenkins, 1863), 75–76; James M. Merrill, "Men, Monotony and Mouldy Beans—Life on Board Civil War Blockaders," *American Neptune* 16 (January 1956): 54.

campaign to reclaim sailors' souls. The commission sent ministers, Bibles, and religious tracts to ships on the blockade and gunboats on the Mississippi. Their efforts raised the morale and awakened the religious sensibilities of some sailors, but arrived with too little, too late.[3] The commission could not overcome the spiritual vacuum of Union ships.

Social scientists, psychologists, and historians have identified religion, whether defined as prayer, a belief in God, or ritualized practice, as a critical resource in helping men confront the hardships of military life and the horror of combat. Samuel A. Stouffer's groundbreaking 1949 work, *The American Soldier*, confirmed for many what historians, sociologists, and clergy had already believed for generations—that "there are no atheists in foxholes."[4] Stouffer and his staff discovered that 84 percent of infantrymen and 71 percent of enlisted men in other branches of the service responded that prayer "helped a lot" "when the going got tough" in World War II.[5] Moreover, war also seemed to intensify religious convictions. Seventy-nine percent of enlisted men with combat experience, compared to 54 percent of men without combat experience, responded that their army service had increased their faith in God.[6]

Union troops also showed a sincere reliance upon prayer, faith, and religion to deal with the death, destruction, and inhumanity of the Civil War. Civil War historians have uncovered ordinary soldiers' attachment to religious practice. Soldiers used religion to overcome

---

[3] There exists no detailed analysis of the problem of religion and the Union sailor in the Civil War. Those works that address the subject do so only superficially and take the general position that Union sailors benefited from divine services administered by a navy that sincerely cared about the plight of their souls. This likely reflects the more modern approach taken by the navy with regard to its sailors and a lack of inquiry into sources left by sailors and chaplains. See Robert M. Browning, Jr., *From Cape Charles to Cape Fear: The North Atlantic Blockading Squadron during the Civil War* (Tuscaloosa: University of Alabama Press, 1993), 211; William Still, "The Common Sailor: The Civil War's Uncommon Man, Part I, Yankee Blue Jackets," *Civil War Times Illustrated* 23 (February 1985): 32–33; Dennis J. Ringle, *Life in Mr. Lincoln's Navy* (Annapolis: Naval Institute Press, 1998), 88–89.

[4] James McPherson contends that Father William Thomas Cummings coined the phrase in a field sermon on Bataan in 1942. See McPherson, *For Cause & Comrades*, 63, 204, n. 3; See Frances C. Steckel, "Morale and Men: A Study of the American Soldier in World War II" (Ph.D. dissertation, Temple University, 1990), 311.

[5] Samuel A. Stouffer et al., *The American Soldier*, vol. 2, *Combat and Its Aftermath* (Princeton, N.J.: Princeton University Press, 1949), 178.

[6] Ibid., 186–87.

the hardships of army life and the psychological shock associated with combat. Based upon the letters and diaries of ordinary soldiers, James M. McPherson, Earl J. Hess, and Warren B. Armstrong strongly argue that not only did religion help soldiers survive the war, but that it also ultimately made them "better" soldiers. Religion, in both simple and complex forms, they contend, gave northern soldiers the courage to fight and the confidence to handle the physical and psychological effects of military service and combat.[7]

Religion's resiliency among soldiers stemmed from two factors. First, Union soldiers enlisted with a strong core of religious beliefs and practices. Charles J. Stille wrote that Union soldiers were "young men of character, intelligence and courage such as had never made up the rank and file of any army."[8] Second, whether or not Union soldiers were the most religious in history, northerners, unwilling to see their sons, husbands, and brothers succumb to the evils of camp life and the despair of war, insisted that religious access not be lost as millions of men left home for the first time. As a result, even though away from their small towns and living in an army camp, Union soldiers regularly possessed access to the rudimentary articles of religious expression. The army provided for chaplains; Christian organizations sent literature and ministers into camp. The army erected chapels under tent awnings in order to give men a sanctuary from the army, if even for a short time. In these makeshift chapels, chaplains conducted weekly Sunday services and weekday prayer meetings. The open space of camps and their proximity to civilian

---

[7] James McPherson contends that like the experience of soldiers in World War II, religion served "the important function of increasing his resources for enduring the conflict-ridden situation of combat stress." Even if men only became "Army Christians," it still made them better soldiers. See McPherson, *For Cause & Comrades*, 76; Earl J. Hess reaches the same conclusion in *The Union Soldier in Combat: Enduring the Ordeal of Combat* (Lawrence: University Press of Kansas, 1997), 194; Warren B. Armstrong, *For Courageous Fighting and Confident Dying: Union Chaplains in the Civil War* (Lawrence: University Press of Kansas, 1998), x; Gerald F. Linderman, *Embattled Courage: The Experience of Combat in the American Civil War* (New York: The Free Press, 1987), 102–7.

[8] Lemuel Moss, *Annals of the United States Christian Commission* (Philadelphia: J. B. Lippincott & Co., 1868), 42; Gardiner H. Shattuck, Jr., *A Shield and A Hiding Place: The Religious Life of the Civil War Armies* (Macon, Ga.: Mercer University Press, 1987), 22; McPherson, *For Cause & Comrades*, 63; Charles J. Stille, *History of the United States Sanitary Commission: Being the General Report of its Work during the War of Rebellion* (Philadelphia: J. B. Lippincott & Co., 1866), 20–21.

society also lent soldiers an opportunity for their own private devotions or a chance to attend local church services.[9]

The role of religion and its importance for Union sailors during the war was more uncertain. Unlike the hallowed glow applied to northern soldiers, wartime attitudes characterized Union Jacks as anything but religious or moral. Part of the image problem arose from lingering prewar stereotypes that routinely labeled sailors as immoral and irreligious. Historian Marcus Rediker contends that sailor irreligiosity began with seventeenth-century English merchant sailors. This tradition was apparently passed on to their American counterparts.[10] Before the war, social commentators railed about the natures of American seamen. Reformers fretted over the state of their souls. In 1842, Charles Rockwell leveled a host of charges against navy sailors, calling them "reckless, profligate, intemperate, profane creatures of impulse."[11] In fact, the notion of sailor irreligiosity proved so pervasive during the war that Mary Osborne chastised her brother for joining the navy instead of the army. "I hope as you have turned sailor instead of soldier," she wrote, "that you will not be contaminated with vice."[12]

Union sailors did seem less susceptible to religious expression and less inclined to use religious practice to fortify themselves during the war. The recorded observations of 118 common sailors, four navy chaplains, four surgeons, and thirteen officers from every major naval squadron, as well as the delegate reports of the United States Christian Commission, strongly indicate that Union sailors exhibited little

---

[9] Theresa Rose McDevitt, "Fighting for the Soul of America: A History of the United States Christian Commission" (Ph.D. dissertation, Kent State University, 1997), 97.

[10] Marcus Rediker provides an excellent starting point for analyzing the origins of sailor irreligiosity in the Anglo-American merchant marine, in *Between the Devil and the Deep Blue Sea: Merchant Seamen, Pirates, and the Anglo-American Maritime World 1700–1750* (Cambridge, Eng.: Cambridge University Press, 1987), 167–68, 173–77. For works of fiction, based on fact, which illustrate the irreligiosity of sailors, see Daniel Defoe, *Robinson Crusoe* (London: W. Taylor, 1719; reprint, New York: New American Library, Inc., 1960); Richard Henry Dana, Jr., *Two Years Before the Mast: A Personal Narrative of a Life at Sea* (1840; reprint, New York: World Publishing Company, 1946); Herman Melville, *White Jacket or The World in A Man-of-War* (New York: Harper and Brothers, 1850; reprint, New York: Quality Paperback Book Club, 1996).

[11] Charles Rockwell, *Sketches of Foreign Travel and Life at Sea*, 2 vols. (Boston: Tappan and Dennet, 1842), 2: 293; Harold D. Langley, *Social Reform in the United States Navy, 1798–1862* (Urbana: University of Illinois Press, 1967), 43–67.

[12] Mary Osborne to Joseph B. Osborne, September 8, 1864, Osborne Family Papers, Manuscripts Division, Library of Congress, Washington, D. C.

interest in conventional expressions of religious practice and spiritual matters during their time in the navy. Furthermore, until early 1864, sailors' experiences in the wartime navy seemed to lessen, rather than increase, their adherence to spiritual beliefs and participation in religious practices. This conclusion is also based upon the comparatively little space that sailors gave the subject of religion in their letters, diaries, and journals. If Union tars thought about life, death, salvation, prayer, God, or their souls, they rarely recorded such thoughts.

Although no one kept statistics on their moral and spiritual standards, many Union sailors joined the navy already in a state of "quiet unreligiosity."[13] In 1861, a "religious sailor" proved difficult to describe. At the top of the spectrum, the term likely denoted someone who faithfully subscribed to a mainstream Christian denomination, attended church every Sunday, prayed daily, and lived a moral life. At the low end, a Christian sailor could be someone who had accepted Christ as his savior and promised to lead a good life. Religious sailors naturally noted, in shock, the low levels of sailor religiosity and the small number of Christians among their shipmates. Seaman C. W. Fleyne complained to Dr. William Thoms, head of the New York Nautical School, an organization dedicated to the technical and moral education of seamen, that out of eleven officers and a hundred crew aboard the U.S.S. *Commodore*, there was "not one Christian among them."[14] One sailor serving on the gunboat *Daylight* counted one Christian in a crew of two hundred.[15] Chaplain Joseph Stockbridge, chaplain on the *Lancaster*, counted only three "professed Christians" among his crew.[16] He reported that in 1863, out of a wartime force of 51,500, there were only "hundreds of professedly religious sailors."[17] Levels of religiosity, from complex to simple, proved so low among

---

[13] Reuben Elmore Stivers, *Privateers & Volunteers, The Men and Women of Our Reserve Naval Forces: 1766 to 1866* (Annapolis, Md.: Naval Institute Press, 1975), 353–54.

[14] C. W. Fleyne to Dr. William F. Thoms, August 21, 1864, William F. Thoms Papers, Letters from Union Sailors, New York Nautical School, 1853–1864, Manuscripts Department, New-York Historical Society, New York City.

[15] Edward P. Smith, *Incidents of the United States Christian Commission* (Philadelphia: J. B. Lippincott & Co., 1871), 469.

[16] Clifford M. Drury, *The History of the Chaplain Corps, United States Navy*, vol. 1, *1789–1939* (Washington, D. C.: Government Printing Office, 1949), 101.

[17] Joseph Stockbridge to Navy Department, May 18, 1863, Officers' Letters, Official Correspondence, U.S. Navy, 1853–1884, Manuscripts Division, Huntington Library, San Marino, California (hereinafter referred to as Official Navy Correspondence).

Union tars that the appearance of five, ten, or twelve religious sailors in a company of 150 was often enough to announce the presence of a Christian crew.[18]

The relationship between religious beliefs and sailors proved, in many ways, an enigma. Without question, the Union navy had its share of sailors who lacked dedication to mainstream religious beliefs and practices.[19] A great many sailors likely resented and ignored the teachings and strictures of organized churches and clergy. Many, in the estimation of the Reverend William Rounesville Alger, possessed a "lack of piety."[20] Some hard characters, such as Seaman John G. Morrison, exhibited an open hostility to religious intrusion. After encountering a street preacher in Cairo, Illinois, Morrison scoffed, "What gammon it [religion] is. It is only time and money wasted."[21] However, the attitudes of most Union sailors, even ones labeled irreligious by chaplains and religious sailors, did not fall into such neat categories as religious or profane. Part of the problem in ascertaining the attitudes of Union sailors toward religion was that sailors were a complex set of men from more diverse cultural, religious, and economic backgrounds than soldiers. They exhibited a complex range of attitudes concerning religion, from sincere personal belief to doubt, ignorance, disbelief, distance, and skepticism. Moreover, many Union sailors decried accepted displays of piety and brought unpopular Catholic ideals and alien rituals as well as elements of Protestant evangelicalism into the navy's traditional Protestant enclave.[22]

Furthermore, it is difficult to obtain a clear picture of Union sailor attitudes toward religion because, although outwardly not religious, sailors often borrowed religion and Christian beliefs when it served their interests. For example, many Union sailors marked themselves with tattoos of crosses and crucifixes on their forearms and chests.

---

[18] Langley, *Social Reform in the United States Navy*, 279–80.

[19] Willard L. Sperry, ed., *Religion in the Post-War World*, vol. 2, *Religion of Soldier and Sailor* (Cambridge, Mass.: Harvard University Press, 1945), 49–52; Marcus Rediker asserts that strong notions of irreligiosity and skepticism had their roots in sailor plebeian culture and anticlericalism. See Rediker, *Between the Devil and the Deep Blue Sea*, 173–79.

[20] William Rounesville Alger, "Effect of Sea Life on Land Life," *The Boatswain's Whistle* 1 (November 9, 1864): 5. *The Boatswain's Whistle* is a newspaper contained in the Americana Catalogue, Huntington Library.

[21] Entry for February 23, 1862, Civil War Diary of John G. Morrison, 1861–1865, Naval Historical Foundation Collection, Washington Navy Yard, Washington, D. C.

[22] Drury, *The History of the Chaplain Corps*, 100.

Although traditionally viewed as an outward sign of religious fervor, Union sailors—aware that certain churches demanded a proper land burial—tattooed themselves with religious symbols in order to increase their chances of securing a shore burial.[23] During the Civil War, sailors used religion to channel their dissatisfaction with the navy, especially when they believed naval practices violated Christian principles. Religion then arose in the form of a complaint. Sailors paid particular attention to Christian practices that worked in their favor such as Sabbath observance, fair treatment, and objections to physical abuse. When officers trampled upon traditional Christian practices and sensibilities, sailors complained—not because they were religious, but because religion gave them a potential ally against the trampling.[24]

In attempting to explain Union sailors' religious shortcomings, it is unclear whether they were irreligious before they went to sea or whether ships transformed good men into sailors. Many of the same conditions suspected in the past of curbing spirituality and religious practice among sailors proved prevalent on Union ships. To date, no historical study has systematically analyzed whether the sea drew men of a profane bent or if ships "dechristianized" sailors. Nevertheless, the United States Navy between 1861 to 1865 appears to offer a fertile area to begin the study of this issue for two important reasons. First, northern military strategy forced the navy to recruit over 100,000 naval volunteers, over 80 percent of whom had not been sailors before.[25] Second, the nature of the Union service—especially

---

[23] Descriptions of tattoos are from physical descriptions of men contained in rendezvous reports between 1861 and 1865 in Enlistment Returns, Changes, and Reports, 1846–1942, Weekly Returns of Enlistments at Naval Rendezvous, January 6, 1855–August 8, 1891, vols. 17–41, Records of the Bureau of Naval Personnel, Record Group 24, National Archives, Washington, D. C.; William P. Mack and Royal W. Connell, *Naval Ceremonies, Customs, and Traditions* (Annapolis: Naval Institute Press, 1980), 288.

[24] John Swift to Rosie Whiteside, December 3, 1863, in Lester L. Swift, ed., "Letters from a Sailor on a Tinclad," *Civil War History* 10 (March 1961): 50.

[25] *Report of the Secretary of the Navy, With an Appendix Containing Reports From Officers, December 1865* (Washington, D. C.: Government Printing Office, 1865), xiii. Based on a sample of 4,571 sailors out of the total 118,044 men who enlisted at United States Navy Rendezvous between April 15, 1861 and April 22, 1865, only 19 percent listed their prewar occupation as "sailor," "seaman," "waterman," "mariner," or "boatman." The sample was assembled from Enlistment Returns, Changes, and Reports, 1846–1942, Weekly Returns of Enlistments at Naval Rendezvous, January 6, 1855–August 8, 1891, vols. 17–43, Records of the Bureau of Naval Personnel, Record Group 24 (hereinafter referred to as Sailor Sample).

the blockade—exacerbated the debilitating effects of ships by forcing most sailors to spend six months to a year aboard ship without going ashore. At no time in previous history had men been compelled to remain aboard ship for so long a period.[26] The immersion of over 100,000 novices into extended isolation on ships offers a rare glimpse into how religious beliefs adapted, changed, or withered as new sailors adjusted to life and war aboard ship.

A number of conditions did discourage religious beliefs and practices aboard Union ships. Merely living on a ship at sea was dangerous. Unlike soldiers, sailors faced the prospect of death from violent gales, drowning, and ship accidents every single day. William Rounesville Alger argued that northern sailors came to believe in their own invincibility after winning too many battles with the sea. "Too constant contact with phenomena calculated to awaken awe and submission," Alger opined, "hardened sailors to the power of God." [27] Reformers thought the disgusting physical conditions aboard ships ultimately fouled sailors' souls. Men accustomed to wide open spaces, a cool climate, and freedom of movement experienced tremendous difficulty adjusting to cramped, filthy, vermin-ridden conditions of ships. Instead of romantic, carefree adventures, men discovered ships to be rough, confining, and depressing environments in which to work and live. Seaman Joseph Collins called his ship "an awful dirty hole." Many simply could not endure the reeking, putrid atmosphere of the berth and gun decks.[28]

Other realities made Union ships spiritual vacuums. Because of a lack of space, there were no chapels and no privacy for personal devotions. Owing to transportation costs and difficulties, Bibles and

---

[26] Edward F. Merrifield, "The Seaboard War: A History of the North Atlantic Blockading Squadron, 1861–1865" (Ph.D. dissertation, Case Western Reserve University, 1975), vi; Still, "The Common Sailor," 35; Merrill, "Men, Monotony, and Mouldy Beans," 57–58; Horatio L. Wait, "The Blockade of the Confederacy," *The Century Magazine* 34, new series (October 1898): 919.

[27] Alger, "Effect of Sea Life on Land Life," 5.

[28] Peter Karsten, *The Naval Aristocracy: The Golden Age of Annapolis and the Emergence of a Modern American Navalism* (New York: The Free Press, 1972), 73; Merrill, "Men, Monotony, and Mouldy Beans," 49–51; Browning, *From Cape Charles to Cape Fear*, 209–10; Alger, "Effect of Sea Life on Land Life," 5; Joseph Collins to Mother & Father, December 10, 1862, James B. and Joseph T. Collins Papers, Manuscripts Department, New-York Historical Society, New York City; George E. Clark, *Seven Years of a Sailor's Life* (Boston: Adams & Company, 1867), 171.

other religious literature proved scarce until 1864. Yet although the effects of a lack of chapels and literature were points of debate in explaining the religious vacuum of a ship, ministers, politicians, sailors, and their families did agree on one overriding factor in the production of irreligious sailors—isolation. Minister William Rounseville Alger believed the isolation weakened the sailor's religious impulses by "exempting him from society."[29] Once a ship went to sea, water effectively severed sailors geographically and institutionally from the potential influence of society's primary religious institutions— churches and ministers. Sailors noticed the effects of such exemption immediately. "I am deprived of the influence of society in a measure," Osborne wrote to his sister Mary.[30] They also became acutely aware of the absence and the opportunity to go to church. "We have no church to go to no social meetings no meetings for singing same as we have in New York," lamented William C. Miller.[31]

More importantly, however, the isolation of a ship separated sailors from the secondary sphere of religious influence—families and friends.[32] Family, particularly female family members, traditionally played a key role in reinforcing religious beliefs and practices.[33] The transition to a ship represented the first time that many men had ventured outside the reach of these circles. Mary Osborne worried that her brother would be doubly susceptible to religious erosion and the "dangers of the inexperienced sailor" because he could not "hear from home + friends as often as you did in the Army."[34] Sailor isolation was exacerbated by the fact that sailors did not receive mail as regularly as soldiers did. Steamers brought mail to ships semi-regularly but were not consistent. Men often went for weeks without receiving any mail.[35] Freed from the religious network of churches and

[29] Alger, "Effect of Sea Life on Land Life," 5.

[30] Joseph Osborne to Mary Osborne, October 16, 1864, Osborne Family Papers.

[31] William C. Miller to Brother William Thoms, December 14, 1861, Thoms Papers.

[32] Rediker, *Between the Devil and the Deep Blue Sea*, 173.

[33] Nancy F. Cott, *The Bonds of Womanhood: "Women's Sphere" in New England, 1780–1835* (New Haven: Yale University Press, 1977), 126–59.

[34] Mary Osborne to Joseph B. Osborne, September 8, 1864, Osborne Family Papers.

[35] Thomas Copernicus Wright to Jane Wright, September 30, 1864, Civil War Papers–Union, Manuscripts Division, Missouri Historical Society, St. Louis, Missouri.

families and placed in an environment where traditional recourses to religion failed to exist, sailors often lived in a religious vacuum in which they more easily abandoned religious practice and behavior.

Socialization into the society of the ship also inhibited the development of religious sentiments among sailors. In those first few weeks in the navy, men, unsure in their new environments, sought to prove their toughness and masculinity as they assimilated into crews. Reliance upon religion, particularly prayer, was not an admirable trait in the all-male atmosphere of a ship. The successful, admired sailors were ones who were able, through their own skill and self-reliance, to weather storms, win fights, hold large quantities of liquor, and overcome any hardship.[36] According to sailors' lore, only a ship destined to sink should contain sailors who pray.[37] Moreover, northern crews tended to be populated by "hard characters" and "bad men," who, through mockery, threats, and physical violence, often seized control of the moral tenor of crews.[38] George Clark called his mates "as hard a set as one would care to be among."[39] Evangelical or "Bible-thumping sailors" provided more amusement than effective religious instruction. Many old salts laughed at and mocked any expression of religion.[40] Isolated from land and desperate to fit into shipboard life, most men quickly jettisoned outward practices and utterances of religion. In fact, during the war, Union tars admitted that they often were afraid to voice religious sentiments and participate in religious services in the presence of other sailors.[41]

Critical to and symbolic of this "dechristianization" process was the overpowering use of swearing, profane jests, and ribald songs by old salts and hard characters. Union sailors swore constantly and used God's name in vain with abandon, especially on Sundays. The practice upset religious sailors and officers. Thomas McNeil complained that many of his crewmates used God's name in vain with great frequency. William Miller fretted, "We have go to stop on board and listen to profane songs + jests." Such rough talk not only offended

---

[36] Alger, "Effect of Sea Life on Land Life," 5.

[37] Rediker, *Between the Devil and the Deep Blue Sea*, 169.

[38] James Birtwistle to Dr. William F. Thoms, November 8, 1862, Thoms Letters; I. E. Vail, *Three Years on the Blockade: A Naval Experience* (New York: The Abbey Press, 1902), 156.

[39] Clark, *Seven Years of a Sailor's Life*, 170–71.

[40] Stivers, *Privateers & Volunteers*, 354.

[41] Smith, *Incidents of the United States Christian Commission*, 453–55.

proper societal mores but also possessed distinct anti-church overtones. Profanity had traditionally been the vocabulary of blasphem-
ers.[42] In fact, Union sailors swore so much that officers began
punishing men for uttering profanities and Congress banned swearing in 1862. Sixteen-year-old George Yost, serving on the *Cairo*, marveled at the audacity of the navy's prohibition. "Captain [Thomas]
Selfridge made us a little speech in which he declared his intention
of enforcing a rule heretofore unnoticed which was to not allow any
profane swearing." Yost was incredulous. "[A]nd whoever broke this
rule was to be severely punished," he marveled in his diary.[43]

An old maritime religious tract had warned sailors that "a tongue
that swears does not easily pray."[44] To the religious few, the stream of
profanity must have seemed to be a fitting medium for the immoral
environment in which they now lived. Although isolated from land,
Union sailors on both the blockade and river squadrons managed to
import every conceivable form of vice and immoral behavior onto
their ships. Below deck, men regularly drank to dissipation, assaulted
each other with fists and knives, stole from each other, caroused with
prostitutes, and worse.[45] The immersion into a violent, immoral envi-

---

[42] Rediker, *Between the Devil and the Deep Blue Sea*, 167.

[43] Thomas McNeil to William Thoms, November 5, 1862, Thoms Papers; William
C. Miller to Brother Thoms, December 14, 1861, Thoms Papers; entry for September 12, 1862, George R. Yost Diary, Manuscripts Division, Illinois State Historical
Library, Springfield, Illinois; entry for October 31, 1863, in Kent Packard, ed., "Jottings by the Way: A Sailor's Log—1862 to 1864," *Pennsylvania Magazine of History
and Biography* 71, part 1 (April 1947): 151; Stivers, *Privateers & Volunteers*, 353–54.
In fact, the problem of swearing became so embarrassing and so disruptive for the
navy that officers began handing down harsh punishments for it and Congress statutorily banned the habit in 1862. See *An Act for the Better Government of the Navy
of the United States*, July 17, 1862, 37th Cong., 2d sess., in *Statutes at Large of the
United States of America*, vol. 12, part 2 (Washington, D. C.: Government Printing
Office, 1863), 602.

[44] Rediker, *Between the Devil and the Deep Blue Sea*, 167.

[45] General Order No. 158 of Rear-Admiral David D. Porter, January 18, 1864, in
United States War Department, *Official Records of the Union and Confederate Navies in the War of the Rebellion*, series 1, 27 volumes (Washington D. C.: Government Printing Office, 1894–1917) (hereinafter cited as *Official Records Navies*), 25:
701; Browning, *From Cape Charles to Cape Fear*, 212; entry for June 25, 1863,
Thomas Lyons Journal, Journal Kept on Board U.S. Steam Gun Boat Carondolet
and Lafayette, January 8, 1863 to January 20, 1863, Manuscripts Division, Library
of Congress; Still, "The Common Sailor," 34–36; entry for November 1, 1865, Journal of Chaplain Donald C. McLaren, July 25, 1865 to October 24, 1867, P. H. W.
Smith Collection, Manuscripts, New Jersey Historical Society, Newark, New Jersey;
Sperry, *Religion in the Post-War World*, 59–60.

ronment cowed the few professedly religious and nominally religious sailors.[46] Almost immediately confronted with an immoral environment the likes of which many had never seen, and hostility toward religious practice, Christian sailors quickly sank into spiritual ineffectiveness and despair. Many were so disheartened that they wanted to leave the ship.[47] "I have never been so impressed with the dreadful reality of sin as I have been here," wrote Seaman Joseph Bloomfield Osborne to his girlfriend from the decks of the *Vanderbilt*.[48] Yet religious sailors could not avoid the atmosphere of sin. They had to live and work in the middle of a vice-ridden atmosphere that they never would have been exposed to on land. Such unwanted exposure to an immoral environment led Thomas McNeil to lament that"there is a grate many temptations on the water."[49]

The confluence of all of this led many sailors to characterize their new environment in depressing, dark terms. Although some men likened it to prison, most sailors intuitively compared life aboard ship to the worst place they could possibly imagine—hell.[50] Franklin E. Smith called living on a ship "a perfect hell."[51] Another sailor likened his naval experience to the "devil's own purgatory."[52] For a group of purportedly irreligious men, the borrowing of a spiritual term to describe their plight is a curious choice, but one packed with meaning. From the sailors' perspective, life aboard ship proved not many removes from the place where the damned suffered misery, torment,

---

[46] James E. Valle, *Rocks & Shoals: Order and Discipline in the Old Navy, 1800–1861* (Annapolis: Naval Institute Press, 1980), 15.

[47] James Birtwistle to William F. Thoms, November 8, 1862, Thoms Papers; Andrew H. Foote to Henry H. Halleck, February 25, 1862, *Official Records Navies*, 22: 632; Francis B. Butts, "Reminiscences of Gunboat Service on the Nansemond," in *Personal Narratives of the Events in the War of Rebellion, Being Papers Read Before the Rhode Island Soldiers & Sailors Historical Society*, 3d series (Providence, R.I.: N. B. Williams, 1884), 7; diary entry, n.d. (September 1861), Diary of John B. Wirts, Special Collections, University of California at Los Angeles, Los Angeles, California; Valle, *Rocks and Shoals*, 15–16.

[48] Joseph B. Osborne to Louise Landau, October 3, 1864, in Merrill, "Men, Monotony and Mouldy Beans," 57.

[49] Thomas McNeil to William F. Thoms, November 5, 1862, Thoms Papers; Stivers, *Privateers & Volunteers*, 354.

[50] Anonymous, "Life On a Blockader," *Continental Monthly* 6 (July 1864): 50; Ringle, *Life In Mr. Lincoln's Navy*, 50.

[51] Franklin E. Smith to Family, December 26, 1861, in Merrill, "Men, Monotony and Mouldy Beans," 49.

[52] Entry for July 2, 1863, Fayette Clapp Diary 1862–1863, Western Historical Manuscripts Collection, Ellis Library, University of Missouri, Columbia, Missouri.

and endless punishments. Hell represented total turmoil, wickedness, and conditions destructive to the system. To Christians, hell was the total and permanent isolation from God. Surgeon Fayette Clapp, serving on the Mississippi Squadron and witnessing the miseries of sailors remarked, "A boat, where the world is the boat—or vice versa, may be made more disagreeable than Hades."[53]

By April 1861, the United States Navy knew three things about religion and the special needs of sailors at sea. First, the service possessed a collective wealth of experiences that confirmed that ships tended to become religious vacuums once they left port. Second, the navy also understood that religion helped sailors overcome the isolation of the seafaring life and the hidden wounds generated by hardship and combat. Third, the navy knew that chaplains aboard ship functioned as the primary means of guaranteeing the exercise of free and regular religious practice among sailors and the preservation of the Sabbath. Navy clergy led divine services, held morning and evening prayers, and provided guidance to the spiritual lives of sailors.[54] Chaplains also shouldered the responsibility for the moral and spiritual education of sailors, many of whom were young or unexposed to any previous religious education. In fact, in 1854, the House of Representatives had rejected an effort to remove chaplains from the navy. One of the overwhelming justifications for retaining clergy was Congress's explicit recognition that a ship became devoid "of all means of moral and religious culture" when at sea. In concluding that the navy needed chaplains to preserve religious practice aboard its ships, the House concluded: "The navy have still stronger claims than the army for the supply of chaplains: a large portion of the time our ships-of-war are on service foreign from our own shore. . . . If you do not afford them the means of religious service while at sea, the Sabbath is, to all extents and purposes, annihilated, and we do not allow the crews the free exercise of religion."[55]

Any plans the navy possessed, however, for preserving acknowledged methods of religious rhythm aboard ship during the Civil War unraveled because of a shortage of clergy. The service started the war with only twenty-four chaplains, but in December 1861, retirements

---

[53] Entry for August 29, 1863, Clapp Diary.

[54] Drury, *The History of the Chaplain Corps*, 1–2.

[55] U.S. Congress, *Chaplains in Congress and in the Army and Navy*, House Report No. 124, 33d Cong., 1st sess., March 27, 1854 (serial 743), 2: 7–8.

shrank their number to nineteen.[56] During the war, the number of chaplains never exceeded nineteen. Meanwhile, the number of sailors in the navy leaped from 7,600 to 51,500.[57] In 1861, there was, on average, one chaplain for every 320 sailors. By 1865, the ratio of chaplains to sailors had fallen to one chaplain for every 2,450 men.[58] Because of this shortage, the navy placed most of its chaplains at navy yards, not on ships, reasoning that chaplains could assist more sailors at a naval station than on a ship. The ramifications of this decision proved enormous. For most of the war, Union sailors had no chaplains on their ships when they put out to sea for months at a time. As of April 1864, the whole force of sailors on the blockade from Fortress Monroe in Virginia to the mouth of the Rio Grande in Texas served without the guidance of a single chaplain.[59] The Mississippi Squadron featured one chaplain, who was stationed at the naval base in Cairo, Illinois.[60]

For their part, chaplains did not rush to serve in the navy. Many failed to volunteer because of the harshness and isolation of naval service, particularly on the blockade.[61] Navy chaplains also sensed a resistance to their enlistment from senior officers and from the navy itself. Those few chaplains willing to serve often were turned away by captains. Sailors dryly noted that captains often had difficulty "hunting up" chaplains they approved.[62] Strangely enough, facing an obvious shortage of chaplains, some administrative officials believed the navy already had too many. Gustavus Vasa Fox, assistant secretary

---

[56] Drury, *The History of the Chaplain Corps*, 94; charts showing numbers of chaplains, vessels, and men in the United States Navy, 1861–1865, 1906, July 12, 1924, Naval Personnel, Misc. Material, NV, Chaplains in the Navy, 1855, subject file, U.S. Navy, 1775–1910, Record Group 45, National Archives, Washington, D.C.

[57] Still, "The Common Sailor," 25.

[58] Drury, *The History of the Chaplain Corps*, 95.

[59] "Second Annual Report of the U.S. Christian Commission for the Army and Navy," April 1864, in United States Christian Commission, *United States Christian Commission for the Army and Navy: Work and Incidents* (Philadelphia: U.S. Christian Commission, 1862–1865), 231; Moss, *Annals of the U.S. Christian Commission*, 337.

[60] "Third Annual Report of the U.S. Christian Commission for the Army and Navy," January 1865, Mississippi Squadron, in ibid., 101.

[61] Bell I. Wiley, " 'Holy Joes' of the Sixties: A Study of Civil War Chaplains," *Huntington Library Quarterly* 16 (May 1953): 290–91; "Religious Instruction in the Army," *Princeton Review* 35 (July 1863): 386–99.

[62] Entry for September 8, 1861, George Adams Bright Journal, George Adams Bright Papers, Manuscripts Division, Huntington Library.

of the navy, actually objected to a proposal to appoint more chaplains. In a letter to the superintendent of the Naval Academy, George S. Blake, Fox groused, "We have more chaplains in the navy than can be used, and are about to appoint a few more." When the proposal for more chaplains received approval, the new appointments inexplicably found themselves assigned to the academy, not aboard ships.[63]

Whatever public statements Congress and the navy made about chaplains, privately, the service and its senior officers did not want them aboard ships. Traditionally, a chaplain serving shipboard proved to be a difficult fit.[64] The mere presence of a clergyman served as a nettlesome reminder of the awkward reconciliation between the realities of war and the demands of Christianity. Although many northern clergy proved zealous supporters of the cause, at root, a chaplain's message of peace and mercy seemed incompatible with the purpose of war.[65] Sailors too possessed their own reservations about chaplains. They regarded them as bad luck because they believed the devil owed them spite, which, many believed, could only bring trouble to the ship and the crew.[66]

Chaplains also posed practical problems. On a ship at sea, every sailor had two or three tasks to perform. Chaplains did not. Nothing aggravated sailors and officers more than watching a chaplain stroll the decks while the rest of the men worked. To make matters worse, when chaplains did work, they seemed only to interfere. Sailors noticed that the mere presence of a chaplain on board dampened the potential for debauchery—for officers and sailors. Men also sensed the chaplain's presence and had to think twice about the content of their acts with a clergyman around.[67] If sailors forgot that the chap-

[63] Gustavus Vasa Fox to George S. Blake, September 30, 1862, in Robert M. Thompson and Richard Wainwright, eds., *Confidential Correspondence of Gustavus Vasa Fox, Assistant Secretary of the Navy, 1861–1865*, 2 vols. (New York: De Vinne Press, 1918–1919), 2: 389.

[64] Armstrong, *For Courageous Fighting and Confident Dying*, 44.

[65] Rollin Quimby, "The Chaplains' Predicament," *Civil War History* 8 (March 1962): 26; George Fredrickson, "The Coming of the Lord: The Northern Protestant Clergy and the Civil War Crisis," in *Religion and the American Civil War*, ed. by Randall M. Miller, Harry S. Stout, and Charles Reagan Wilson (New York: Oxford University Press, 1998), 110–30.

[66] Rockwell, *Sketches of Foreign Travel and Life at Sea*, 392.

[67] Entry for October 24, 1865, McLaren Journal; William J. Clark to Mother, January 28, 1862, William Clark Letters, Manuscripts Division, Historical Society of Pennsylvania, Philadelphia, Pennsylvania.

lain was aboard, he appeared all too happy to remind them. Chaplains routinely criticized men for bad habits, bad language, and bad living and filed written reports with the navy on all that they witnessed. Although chaplains were statutorily required to file reports, this kind of moral overseeing created a good deal of tension and won few friends aboard ship. Officers and sailors resented the prying of the chaplain's eyes into their daily lives. [68] Chaplains raised so much trouble by their omissions and commissions that sailors loved to retell the yarn about two sailors, one old and one new, sitting around the scuttlebutt, when the young one asked the older, "What does the chaplain do?" "He does nothing six days a week," the other soldier scolded, "and disturbs the peace on Sunday."[69]

True to the moral of the yarn, chaplains did most of their disrupting on Sundays. They did this in two ways. First, chaplains vociferously objected to any activity, particularly work, performed on Sundays. Throughout the war, chaplains rebuked captains, privately and publicly, for working sailors on Sunday. This criticism placed captains in an awkward situation because their primary duty was the proper operation of a vessel. Captains would not sacrifice the safety of their ships or suspend naval operations to keep the Sabbath holy. Captains ruled absolutely and resented any intrusions into their authority. Moreover, captains historically had not permitted a religious-driven calendar or holidays to alter a ship's work schedule.[70] Chaplains, on the other hand, firmly believed that Sunday was their day and, of course, the Lord's. Sunday clashes naturally ensued. After witnessing Sabbath violations on the *Potomac*, Joseph Stockbridge preached the following Sunday on the "duty of properly observing the Sabbath." Furious about a public rebuke and challenge to his authority from the chaplain, the captain issued Stockbridge a written reprimand.[71] When the chaplain on the *Raze Independence* sermonized on his ship's Sunday violations, the captain cut him off in mid-sentence and closed the service.[72] During the Civil War, captains rou-

---

[68] *An Act to Increase and Regulate Pay of the Navy of the United States*, 36th Cong., 1st sess., June 1, 1860, in *Statutes at Large*, vol. 12, 24.

[69] Drury, *The History of the Chaplain Corps*, 108.

[70] Rediker, *Between the Devil and the Deep Blue Sea*, 174.

[71] Joseph Stockbridge to Navy Department, May 18, 1863, Official Navy Correspondence.

[72] Ibid.

tinely threatened, muzzled, and confined chaplains to their rooms to keep them out of the way.[73]

The second difficulty surrounding navy chaplains was that their denominational affiliations proved ill-matched to the men they sought to serve. Although naval regulations vaguely commended chaplains to "instruct in the principles of the Christian religion," the Episcopal faith had been official Sunday service aboard ships and the dominant religion among chaplains.[74] By 1861, the nation's religious affiliations had greatly diversified.[75] Baptists and Methodists had replaced Episcopalians as the republic's dominant faith. In addition, waves of Catholic immigrants from Ireland and Germany had also radically altered the religious landscape.[76] In 1854, the three largest religious groups in the United States were Methodists (4,209,333), Baptists (3,130,878), and Roman Catholics (2,040,316). Episcopalians numbered 625,213.[77] In fact, foreign-born sailors constituted 44 percent of Union naval volunteers, many of them from heavily Catholic places in Ireland and Germany.[78] The composition of the navy's chaplain corps only partially reflected these changes. Of the twenty chaplains who served between 1861 and 1870, there were eight Episcopalians, seven Methodists, four Baptists, and one Presbyterian.[79] The navy had no Catholic chaplains. In fact, there was not a Catholic chaplain in the navy until 1888.[80]

---

[73] Thomas G. Salter to Gideon Welles, July 18, 1864, Gideon Welles Papers, Rare Books and Manuscripts, Huntington Library.

[74] *Regulations for the Government of the United States Navy 1865* (Washington, D.C.: Government Printing Office, 1865), 102.

[75] Karsten, *The Naval Aristocracy*, 73.

[76] Dorothy Denneen Volo and James M. Volo, *Daily Life in Civil War America* (Westport, Conn.: Greenwood Press, 1998), 39–40.

[77] Denominational figures are from tables originally published in the *Christian Almanac* and appended to *Chaplains in Congress and in the Army and Navy*, 5, 9–10.

[78] Ella Lonn concluded that although the foreign influence varied from ship to ship, she estimated that anywhere between one-fourth and one-half of vessels' crews were foreign born. See Ella Lonn, *Foreigners in the Union Army and Navy* (Baton Rouge: Louisiana State University Press, 1951), 637, 640; Based upon the Sailor Sample, 44 percent of all Union sailors were foreign born. The largest single ethnic group was the Irish at 20.4 percent, followed by the English at 10.19 percent, Canadian at 4.72 percent, Germans at 4.02 percent.

[79] A Chart Showing Religious Affiliations of United States Navy Chaplains From 1778 to September 1939, in Drury, *The History of the Chaplain Corps*, 255.

[80] Drury, *The History of the Chaplain Corps*, 100. According to Drury, there were no Jewish chaplains in the navy during the Civil War.

More importantly, events in the 1850s had made the navy particularly sensitive to the divisiveness that chaplains could generate among
religiously mixed crews. In 1853–1854, some Baptist and Presbyterian chaplains had touched off a furor called "The Prayer Book Controversy" when they openly objected to the use of the Episcopal
liturgy aboard ship. These same chaplains had delivered sermons to
crews—containing Catholic and Episcopal sailors—that attacked
Catholic and Episcopal teachings on infant baptism and apostolic
succession.[81] These events had triggered a minor religious war aboard
certain ships, angering Catholic and Episcopal sailors and creating
hostilities among Protestant sailors of other denominations. Many of
these wounds had not healed by 1861.[82] To make matters worse,
many of the chaplains who had precipitated the controversy were still
in the navy or applied for reinstatement when the war arrived. This
fact, coupled with the regulation adopted in 1860 that allowed chaplains to use the formal service of their avowed denominations, convinced the navy that chaplains were a divisive force.[83] With such a
potentially volatile mix of religious views among Union sailors, the
navy and its captains were not about to let chaplains destroy crew
cohesion by aggravating religious divisions. It was not surprising then
that those few chaplains that did make it aboard ships found their
influence checked and the content of their sermons curtailed by already wary captains.[84]

The absence of chaplains shaped the religious lives of Union sailors
in a number of ways. The largest consequence was that their absence
let captains assume firm control over the distillation of religion
aboard ship. From 1861 to early 1864, captains dictated the content,
format, and regularity of religious practice on most Union vessels,
from prayers to weekly divine services. Suspicious of the potential
pitfalls that religion presented, Union captains adopted a traditional,
conservative approach that maintained the formalities of religious

---

[81] Thomas G. Salter to the Secretary of the Navy, April 26, 1854, Letters of the
Brazil Squadron, Official Navy Correspondence; Commander Samuel Mercer to
Secretary of the Navy, April 25, 1854, Letters of the Brazil Squadron, Official Navy
Correspondence.

[82] Joseph Stockbridge to Honorable Hannibal Hamlin, March 20, 1861, in Drury,
The History of the Chaplain Corps, 98, n. 18.

[83] *An Act to Increase and Regulate Pay*, Statutes at Large, vol. 12, 24.

[84] Joseph Stockbridge to Navy Department, May 18, 1863, Official Navy Correspondence.

practice while downplaying theological, spiritual content. The practice of religion outwardly remained the same. Captains retained the Episcopal rite as the official liturgy of the Sunday services, called the "divine service." Their continued adherence to the Episcopal rite was partially understandable; over 40 percent of officers were Episcopalian. The Episcopal service, derived from the Book of Common Prayer, had also been the official liturgy of the navy since its inception.[85] Although captains led their sailors through the same prayers chaplains had used in the past, they refashioned their tenor. In the hands of captains, Sundays and divine services became exercises in naval obedience rather than religious education and a source of comfort and strength.[86]

On Sundays, Union captains bound together the weekly physical inspection and the performance of weekly divine services. The scheduling of the two back-to-back, however, was mandated by naval regulations, which required that weekly inspection precede the divine service.[87] Although the mechanics of inspection and Sabbath services remained the same, with the captain overseeing both as political, military, and now religious authority, the compulsive nature of the captains' power, epitomized by the inspection, spilled into Sunday services.[88] Inspection commenced at 9:30 a.m., with officers forming sailors into a line on the port side of the quarterdeck. Standing orders required that sailors on Sundays dress in their best uniforms and be fully clean.[89] As their names were called, sailors had to pass through a gauntlet of Marines and officers standing on the starboard side of the quarterdeck. Sailors removed their caps respectfully while senior officers examined their appearance.[90] If a sailor or his uniform proved

[85] Drury, *The History of the Chaplain Corps*, 69, 100–1; Karsten, *The Naval Aristocracy*, 73.

[86] Karsten, *The Naval Aristocracy*, 87–88.

[87] Still, "The Common Sailor," 32; Rowland Stafford True, "Life Aboard a Gunboat," *Civil War Times Illustrated* 9 (February 1971): 37; entry for March 18, 1862, Log of Charles A. Poole, Manuscripts, G. W. Blunt White Library, Mystic Seaport Museum, Mystic, Connecticut; entry for February 1, 1863, Clapp Diary.

[88] Karsten, *The Naval Aristocracy*, 87–88; Stivers, *Privateers & Volunteers*, 354; William Keeler to Ann Keeler, July 14, 1864, in Robert W. Daly, ed., *Aboard the USS Florida: 1863–65: The Letters of Paymaster William Frederick Keeler, U. S. Navy to his Wife, Anna* (Annapolis, Md.: Naval Institute Press, 1968), 185–86.

[89] Stivers, *Privateers & Volunteers*, 354–55.

[90] John D. Milligan, ed., "Navy Life on the Mississippi River," *Civil War Times Illustrated* 33 (May–June 1994): 67–70; entry for February 1, 1863, Clapp Diary;

unclean, Marines stopped the offending man at the mast, where officers berated him. Sailors listened to comments like, "Jones why are your shoes not blacked?" and "You are a filthy beast, a disgrace to your shipmates." Officers then ordered crewmates to strip and scrub dirty sailors hard with brushes, sand, and hickory brooms.[91]

All of this constituted a less than inspiring prelude to the divine service, which followed promptly at 10:00 a.m. At the tolling of the church bell, sailors hoisted the church pennant upon the flagstaff and assembled on the port side of the quarterdeck in their best suits, hats doffed.[92] Enlisted men sat cross-legged or "sailor style" on the hard planks of the deck. Officers usually sat on the other side of the deck on campstools. Fresh from inspection, the captain led the divine service. The liturgy varied, depending upon the captain, but usually started with the captain rumbling through a few chapters from the New Testament. He would then recite the formal liturgy from the Book of Common Prayer.[93] Sailors remained quiet, looked at the sea, and responded to the end of each prayer with quiet amens.[94]

Ambivalent in their role as chaplain and untrained in the nuances of theology, captains' sermons hammered away on a few basic

---

entry for March 18, 1862, Poole Log; entry for April 16, 1865, Frank S. Judd Diary, Manuscripts Department, Historical Society of Pennsylvania; Symmes E. Browne to Fannie E. Bassett, April 27, 1862 in John D. Milligan, ed., *From the Fresh Water Navy: 1861–64, The Letters of Acting Master's Mate Henry R. Browne and Acting Ensign Symmes E. Browne* (Annapolis: Naval Institute Press, 1970), 69.

[91] Still, "The Common Sailor," 32.

[92] Charles C. Coffin, *My Days and Nights on the Battlefield* (Boston: Estes and Lauriat, 1887), 255; William F. Hutchinson, M. D., "Life on the Texan Blockade," in *Soldiers' and Sailors' Historical Society of Rhode Island, Personal Narratives of Events in the War of Rebellion, Being Papers Read Before the Rhode Island Soldiers' and Sailors' Historical Society*, 3d ser. (Providence: N. B. Williams, 1883), 12; entry for November 23, 1862, James E. Henneberry Diary, Research Collections, Chicago Historical Society, Chicago, Illinois.

[93] Entry for February 1, 1863, Clapp Diary; entry for March 8, 1863, in James A. Barnes and Elinor Barnes, eds., *Naval Surgeon Blockading the South, 1862–1866: The Diary of Samuel Pellman Boyer* (Bloomington: Indiana University Press, 1963), 77. In all likelihood, captains and Episcopal chaplains used the Book of Common Prayer of 1789 (First American Prayer Book); see Chester S. Zinni, Jr., *A Concise of the Book of Common Prayer: 1549 to 1979* (New York: Nomis Publications, Inc., 1981), 31.

[94] Entry for July 24, 1864, William Wainwright Log, Manuscripts Department, G. W. Blunt White Library, Mystic Seaport Museum; Edward A. Pierson to Mother, March 12, 1862, Edward A. Pierson Papers, Manuscripts Division, New Jersey Historical Society; Clark, *Seven Years of a Sailor's Life*, 190; entry for February 10, 1866, McLaren Journal.

themes. One recurring notion was to remind sailors that their mothers, sisters, and wives were at home praying for them and watching over their conduct.[95] The references to women were not intended as romantic gestures on the captain's part. In Civil War America, men equated women with religion and a moral life. Reid Mitchell, in *The Vacant Chair: The Northern Soldier Leaves Home,* writes, "Women provided the moral influence that kept men from temptation and on the path of virtue." In fact, the association proved so strong that the mere ringing of church bells could immediately conjure up feminine images for soldiers.[96] Sailors made the same connection. William Wainwright commented that thoughts of church stirred up images of sharing prayer books with "rosey cheeked girls" and the chance of accidentally touching hands in moments he described as "electric."[97] Captains invoked the feminine image to harken sailors to a religious, moral, and orderly life by reminding them of the connection. John Rodgers, the first commander of the Mississippi Squadron, even contemplated bringing sailors' wives aboard in order to instill religion into his men.[98]

The use of the feminine image by captains to imbue religion in their sailors also reflected their underlying discomfort with the role of chaplain. Religion to northerners largely remained the province of women and was commonly thought to possess the ability to soften and civilize—undesirable traits in both soldiers and sailors. Thus, captains feared that religion would weaken the fighting spirit of their sailors. In order to negate such a danger, captains altered beyond recognition the religious content of their services. As one captain readily admitted, "If it did no good, it could do no harm."[99]

In order to contradict any feminine qualities associated with their religious role, captains often herded their men to services using profanity.[100] After discovering a sailor missing from his divine service,

---

[95] Joseph Watson, "Life On Board a Blockader: Being the Reminiscences of a Paymaster in the U.S. Navy, 1863," 379–80, Rare Books and Manuscripts, Huntington Library.

[96] Reid Mitchell, *The Vacant Chair: The Northern Soldier Leaves Home* (New York: Oxford University Press, 1993), 73–74.

[97] Entry for July 24, 1864, Wainwright Log; Clark, *Seven Years of a Sailor's Life,* 250–51.

[98] John D. Rodgers to Dear Sir, June 30, 1861, in John D. Milligan, *Gunboats Down the Mississippi* (Annapolis, Md.: Naval Institute Press, 1960), 9.

[99] Entry for June 22, 1862, Bright Journal.

[100] Drury, *The History of the Chaplain Corps,* 71.

one captain erupted, "Put this man in double irons, d—n him! I'll teach him to come to his prayers."[101] Swearing during sermons and prayers was not uncommon. One captain in giving a sermon on hypocrites called them "damn rascals."[102] Another captain, leading a service before the assault on Fort Fisher, when informed that his ship would not be in the fight that day, ended the service abruptly. Throwing down his prayer book violently, he exclaimed, "Well! I'll be G-d d—d if I'm going to pray if we aren't going to fight."[103] His sailors erupted in laughter. Although profanity may have protected a captain's masculinity, it did tend to make a mockery of services. Further, the use of profanity and its antireligious overtones left no misunderstanding as to the captain's true thoughts on the subject and only encouraged sailors to treat religion as an undesirable exercise.

Obedience constituted another popular theme of captain-styled divine services. Commander Rodgers admitted that one of the purposes of the inspection and divine service was to "break down the spirit" of his men.[104] For this purpose, the prayers of the Episcopal service seemed to mesh nicely with captains' underlying message of obedience and control. Many officers, arguably, had no problem booming out prayers to sailors that harkened them "to submit . . . to my governors . . . to order myself lowly and reverently to all my betters and to do my duty."[105] The import of these prayers, when combined with the intrusive and demeaning nature of the inspection before services, was not lost on the men. Sailors felt that religion was being used to break and relegate them to positions of insignificance.[106] In the unlikely event that sailors overlooked the message of obedience and subordination emanating from captain-style divine services, they often reinforced the lesson by ordering such backbreaking work as coaling and loading stores immediately after the service. Landsmen Amos Burton, who had joined the navy in 1860, noticed the change almost immediately. In September 1861, he

---

[101] Watson, "Life on Board a Blockader," 380.

[102] Ibid.

[103] Entry for December 24, 1864, Diary of Calvin G. Hutchinson, Hutchinson Papers, Rare Books and Manuscripts Division, Huntington Library.

[104] John D. Rodgers to Dear Sir, June 30, 1861, in Milligan, *Gunboats Down the Mississippi*, 9.

[105] Karsten, *The Naval Aristocracy*, 74.

[106] Ibid., 84.

wrote, "How difficult our Sabbath now is to what it was a few months ago."[107]

When the captain held divine services, Union sailors seemed to make an attentive congregation. Certainly, the inspection before helped to temper their spirits. The fact that the captain controlled every facet of their lives and that he was giving the sermon likely played a large role in commanding their undivided attentions. Certainly the craving for social excitement also led religious and irreligious sailors to be very attentive listeners on the Sabbath.[108] Whatever the reason, coal heaver William Wainwright observed that sailors proved better behaved and more attentive than civilian churchgoers. "I have never seen so much quietness and attention paid to the word of God as I have seen on board this ship."[109] Surgeon Edward Pierson remarked that sailors attending a divine service after battle, with faces "black as your hat from the Powder" and grumbling amen at the end of each prayer, "was the most solemn sight I ever witnessed."[110] Chaplain Donald McLaren recalled that the war increased the intensity and attentions of both sailors and chaplains at Sunday services.[111]

Overall, sailors laughed at and resented the captain acting as chaplain aboard ship. On a deeper level, however, Union sailors rejected the captain as a religious figure. Sailors viewed captains' assumption of religious duties as the ultimate intrusion into a final, personal sphere.[112] In addition, seamen quickly saw through their captains' thinly disguised motives and lack of piety. Some sailors laughed to themselves watching a captain "pretend to be very pious" or "put on a parson's face, as far as he knew how."[113] In their eyes, putting on a parson's face did not make a person religious. William Wainwright complained, "There is no more religion in him [Captain Winslow] then there is in my old boat."[114] Worse yet, the captain's performance

---

[107] Entry for September 8, 1861, Burton, *A Journal of the Cruise of the U.S. Ship Susquehanna*, 75; Entry for January 10, 1864, George Durand Diaries, Manuscripts Department, New-York Historical Society, New York City.

[108] Rockwell, *Sketches of Foreign Life and Travel at Sea*, 2: 394.

[109] Entry for July 3, 1864, Wainwright Log.

[110] Edward A. Pierson to Mother, March 12, 1862, Pierson Papers.

[111] Entry for September 17, 1865, McLaren Diary.

[112] Karsten, *The Naval Aristocracy*, 87–88.

[113] Entry for March 13, 1864, in Packard, "Jottings by the Way," part 2 (July 1947), 265; Watson, "Life on Board a Blockader," 380.

[114] Entry for December 13, 1863, Wainwright Log.

delivered little in the way of entertainment value. As one sailor complained, "It is tiresome tho, as the Captain is rather long." Wainwright concluded that divine services held no attraction for him because "I dont like to go to hear a man that cant preach any better than myself."[115] Finally, captains' use of the Episcopal liturgy also likely ground against the consciences of religious sailors who did not adhere to the Episcopal faith. Methodist, Baptist, and Congregationalist sailors objected to the formality of the Episcopal service. Catholic sailors—many of them Irish—increasing in number as the war progressed, arguably challenged the captains' use of the Episcopal service on both religious and political grounds.[116]

Entrusted with the spiritual care of their sailors, captains and the navy took other measures that discouraged religious expressions among sailors. First, the navy did not provide sufficient numbers of Bibles so sailors could read and pray in their own manner. In 1864, with the number of Union sailors at an all-time high, the navy purchased seventy-five Bibles.[117] Second, although navy regulations mandated that divine services be held "whenever circumstances and weather allow," captains regularly failed to hold divine services weekly, if at all.[118] Some captains routinely omitted services if they felt there was pressing work. Others dropped services if they did not care to have them.[119] One sailor commented that divine services were "uncommon at sea."[120] James E. Henneberry marveled that his boat, the *Essex*, did not have a religious service until November 1862.[121] Surprisingly, religious and nonreligious sailors expressed ill feelings over the lack of regular services. In their letters and diaries, they meticulously recorded the absence of church on Sundays and holy

---

[115] Ringle, *Life in Mr. Lincoln's Navy*, 89; entry for November 26, 1863, Wainwright Log.

[116] Drury, *The History of the Chaplain Corps*, 101; Charles O. Paullin, *Paullin's History of Naval Administration, 1775–1911* (Annapolis, Md.: Naval Institute Press, 1968), 303; Melville, *White Jacket*, 195; Karsten, *The Naval Aristocracy*, 73–74.

[117] Merrill, "Men, Monotony and Mouldy Beans," 54.

[118] Entry for November 23, 1862, Henneberry Diary.

[119] Joseph Stockbridge to Navy Department, May 18, 1863, Official Navy Correspondence; Log Entry, May 10, 1863, Poole Log; entry for May 3, 1863, Wainwright Log.

[120] Entry for March 18, 1865, Edwin R. Benedict Diary, 1864–65, Special Collections Department, Robert W. Woodruff Library, Emory University, Atlanta, Georgia; entry for October 4, 1863, in Barnes and Barnes, eds., *Naval Surgeon*, 167.

[121] Entry for November 23, 1862, Henneberry Diary.

days.[122] Obviously, some irreligious sailors used a lack of services to vent their general unhappiness over the navy—given the choice, even irreligious sailors would rather pray than work. "At 10 A.M., instead of divine service, we hauled up along the bank and took in 40 cords of fence rails," John G. Morrison groused, "and instead of praying we fiddled (on the rails)."[123]

Protestant or Catholic, religious or not, nothing raised sailors' ire like working on the Sabbath. Union sailors used to chant the following rhyme when they toiled on Sundays: "Six days shalt thou labor and do all thou art able. On the Sabbath Day holystone the deck and scrub the cable."[124] Whatever level of religiosity, most sailors—whether based upon religious belief, cultural tradition, or self-interest—had internalized the belief in and the cultural practice of not working on Sundays. For Americans in the nineteenth century, Sundays meant rest, relaxation, and religion. The sacredness of the Sabbath and its crucial role in preserving the rhythm of an individual's holy life extended back to the seventeenth century.[125] Although captains had already substantially dampened the religious spirit of the day, sailors still wanted to retain the rest and relaxation parts. Granted, the Union navy could not have waged a six-day-a-week blockade or suspended river operations on Sundays. For the most part, sailors accepted the reality that fighting and some operational work had to be done on the Sabbath. Nevertheless, sailors did vehemently object to work performed on Sunday they believed unnecessary, non-essential, or unduly burdensome.[126] One sailor growled that scrubbing the decks and polishing all of the ship's brass work on Sunday was nothing short of "shameful."[127] Fifteen-year-old Charles Mervine, after helping loose, make, and shake out the sails one Sabbath, complained, "Such is a sailors Sunday. I wonder if the Hon. Sect'y of the Navy allows such work as this to be carried on."[128] The

---

[122] Entry for October 12, 1862, Yost Diary; entries for May 3, November 26, December 25, 1863, Wainwright Log; entry for May 10, 1863, Poole Log; Joseph B. Osborne to Louise Landau, October 17, 1864, Osborne Family Papers.

[123] Entry for January 4, 1863, Morrison Diary.

[124] Entry of October 4, 1863, Barnes and Barnes, eds., *Naval Surgeon*, 168.

[125] Robert H. Abzug, *Cosmos Crumbling: American Reform and the Religious Imagination* (New York: Oxford University Press, 1994), 111–12.

[126] Entry for April 14, 1862, Poole Log; entry for February 1, 1863, Lyons Journal.

[127] Entry for January 10, 1864, Durand Diaries; entry for November 6, 1864, in Packard, "Jottings By the Way," part 2, 276.

[128] Ibid.

few chaplains that did manage to make it aboard observed—to their dismay—that Sunday morning was often one of the "busiest mornings of the week in cleaning ship insides out."[129]

The overall result proved dispiriting to common sailors. To a man, sailors admitted that Sundays became the most lonesome day of the week. Edwin R. Benedict summed up the melancholy effect the day played upon sailor emotions. "The day was a rather lonesome one," he noted in his diary, "as nearly all Sabbaths in the Navy are."[130] One of the reasons for the abject loneliness of the day was that sailors directly associated Sundays and church with home. Gazing upon the white wooden churches that centered each of the small towns that his boat passed down the Mississippi moved John Swift to write, "I feel an indescribable longing to spend one Sunday evening at home."[131] Swift was not alone. It was on Sundays that sailors wistfully recalled women, friends, and community.[132] Sailors recalled watching people wrestle with itchy collars and whispering to friends. Some, probably few, even missed passing the collection plate.[133] It was not that sailors were avid churchgoers. Sundays and divine services represented vivid memories of home, family, and women. In violating these focal points of weekly Christian cultural and religious practice, many men likely felt that the navy was personally abusing them and further isolating them from home.

Without question, some sailors broke the Sabbath in their own right by gambling, singing, and music playing.[134] Nonetheless, the impact of being forced to work on a day traditionally reserved for rest demoralized the men and squandered an opportunity for the navy to foster religious feeling, or at least raise morale, by playing upon the day's vivid connection to home and family. To many men, captains had refashioned the calendar based upon work rather than religion.

---

[129] Joseph Stockbridge to Navy Department, May 18, 1863, Official Navy Correspondence; entry for January 10, 1864, Durand Diaries.

[130] Entry for March 7, 1865, Benedict Diary.

[131] John Swift to Rosie Whiteside, December 3, 1863, in Swift, "Letters from a Sailor on a Tinclad," 50.

[132] Reid Mitchell contends that Union soldiers immediately associated church with women. See Mitchell, *The Vacant Chair*, 73.

[133] Entries for November 29, 1863, July 24, 1864, Wainwright Log; entry for April 14, 1862, Poole Log.

[134] Joseph B. Osborne to Louise Landau, October 17, 1864, Osborne Family Papers; Joseph Stockbridge to Navy Department, May 18, 1863, Official Navy Correspondence.

In the process, Sundays became less sacred and more depressing. Seaman Edwin R. Benedict lamented, "Another Sabbath day so sacred in many localities (but far different here)."[135] Charles A. Poole wrote that while scrubbing the decks and polishing the brasswork one Sunday, "I could not help thinking of the difference between my Sundays now and when I was at home. The same work has to be done today that is done every day."[136] Religious sailors regarded such measures as a callous disregard for their consciences and a government "wink" to men of "bad conscience."[137] Men ambivalent about religion and the Sabbath still clutched to the cultural and the calendar's treatment of Sunday as a day of rest. Even men of bad conscience did not want to work on Sundays. In short, the captains' harshening of an unpopular Sunday service coupled with increased labor on the Sabbath managed to offend just about everyone, hindered morale, and squashed religious sentiment among sailors on the day most favorable for nurturing it.

The special needs of Union sailors when it came to religious instruction and the obstacles encountered in attempting to meet those needs—a lack of chaplains, the heavy presence of Catholic and other non-Episcopal sailors, and the dispirited response to a religious program headed by the captain—goaded the navy into making changes. Since 1799, sailors had been compelled to attend divine services aboard ship no matter what their faith or lack of faith.[138] As much as the navy valued conformity and the Episcopal leanings of its officers, it placed a higher premium on recruiting sailors and winning the naval war. In order to increase harmony and decrease tension over religion, the navy decided to abandon its policy of mandatory attendance at divine services in favor of a voluntary form of religious practice. On July 17, 1862, Congress passed *An Act For the Better Government of the Navy of the United States*, which "earnestly recommended" but did not compel sailors to attend divine service. The act also deleted the requirement for daily morning and evening prayers.[139] The navy had likely adopted these policy changes, in large part,

---

[135] Entry for February 19, 1865, Benedict Diary.

[136] Entry for April 14, 1862, Poole Log.

[137] Joseph Stockbridge to Navy Department, May 18, 1863, Official Navy Correspondence.

[138] Ibid.; *An Act For the Better Government of the Navy of the United States*, April 23, 1800, in Drury, *The History of the Chaplain Corps*, 100–1.

[139] *An Act for the Better Government of the Navy of the United States*, July 17, 1862, in *Statutes at Large*, vol. 12, 601.

as a concession to the increasing number of Catholics, Baptists, and Methodists joining the service since the 1850s. In fact, in 1860, the navy had begun excusing Catholic soldiers from divine service in order to, in the words of then-secretary of the navy Isaac Toucey, "respect the religious convictions of the Catholics."[140] Moreover, the navy's action also reflected a universal trend taking place throughout the northern military. The Lincoln administration had made a conscious effort to defuse any semblance of religious tensions by making concessions to all religious groups, even unpopular ones. Lincoln appointed Catholic and Jewish chaplains in the army even though, before the war, the chaplain law provided only for appointment of Protestant denominations.[141] The underlying message conveyed by these measures was simple—while engaged in a civil war, "all Christians are made one."[142] Religious factions were expected to subordinate their divisions for the good of the Union, and the government would do its part by granting members of differing denominations some measure of autonomy. It was in this spirit that the navy's decision to drop mandatory attendance should be seen.

The navy's adoption of voluntary attendance at divine services immediately altered the spiritual practices of sailors and religious environment of Union ships. At 10 a.m. on Sundays, sailors now had a number of options. Men could attend the official Episcopal service, not attend services, or worship as they wished. Catholics took advantage of the change by performing their own services, using their own prayers from their own prayer books.[143] Black sailors also benefited from the new atmosphere. Continuing a tradition that had its roots in the prewar maritime culture of African American seamen, the navy encouraged some measure of religious autonomy for black sailors.[144]

---

[140] Isaac Toucey to Captain William S. Hudson, February 20, 1868, box 298, Living Conditions, Customs, 1860–1939, Navy Subject File; *Chaplains in Congress and in the Army and Navy*, 5.

[141] Abraham Lincoln to Arnold Fischel, December 14, 1861, and Abraham Lincoln to Archbishop John J. Hughes, October 21, 1861, in Roy P. Basler, ed., *The Collected Works of Abraham Lincoln*, 9 volumes (New Brunswick, N. J.: Rutgers University Press, 1953), 4: 69; 5: 559–60.

[142] Smith, *Incidents of the United States Christian Commission*, 168–69.

[143] Entry for December 3, 1865, McLaren Diary.

[144] W. Jeffrey Bolster, *Black Jacks: African American Seamen in the Age of Sail* (Cambridge, Mass.: Harvard University Press, 1997), 123–25. The navy permitted the enlistment of free blacks before and during the war. On September 20, 1861, the navy officially accepted former slaves called "contrabands" into the blockade

Aboard ship, black sailors conducted their own services.[145] If close enough to shore or in port, officers allowed African American sailors to go ashore and attend their own church services—a concession not granted to white sailors.[146] Even the navy's sacred burial traditions gave way in light of the new policy. Where once sailor funerals had been headed by the captain and subject to navy—not religious—procedures, funerals now became subject to the religion of the deceased.[147] Captains now permitted Catholic sailors to be buried using the Catholic burial rite instead of the traditional naval ceremony. If possible, officers sought out a priest to conduct the liturgy and secured burial plots in Catholic cemeteries.[148]

Christian sailors used their newly found freedom to construct a decentralized, less formal style of worship. They did this by organizing small prayer meetings aboard ship. Officers permitted men to hold these gatherings on their own time, wherever they could. Highly informal, prayer meetings usually consisted of a few sailors gathering on the open deck or in cramped and uncomfortable corners of the

---

squadrons. Contraband sailors were accepted into the Mississippi squadron on April 30, 1862. (See Gideon Welles to C. H. Davis, April 30, 1862, in *Official Records Navies*, vol. 23, 80–81.) Increasing religious diversity was not the only threat to the Episcopal divine service. The increasing number of African American sailors presented the navy with a religious problem of a different kind. Even though black sailors shared Christian denominations with white sailors, many whites viewed the black practice of Christianity as a different sort of religion, "black religion." This characterization of black Christianity as a separate form of worship also fit neatly into racial attitudes favoring segregation. In fact, seeking to isolate blacks from white social systems, the Mississippi Squadron had adopted an official policy of segregation, which sequestered blacks into their own eating, working, and drill groups on board ship. Although it is doubtful that black sailors were denied attendance at formal divine services, they were likely not fully integrated into white religious practices. See Mitchell, *The Vacant Chair*, 59; Reid Mitchell, *Civil War Soldiers: Their Expectations and Their Experiences* (New York: Viking, 1988), 119–20; U.S. Navy, *Internal Rules and Regulations for Vessels of the Mississippi Fleet in the Mississippi River and its Tributaries* (Cincinnati: Rickey & Carroll, 1862–1863), 7–13. In fact, a popular photograph of a divine service shows black sailors sitting, in their own group, on the deck of a ship at the outer most fringes of a congregation of sailors. See Still, "The Common Sailor," 32–33.

[145] Entry for June 15, 1863, Lyons Journal.

[146] Entry for November 17, 1862, Henneberry Diary; entry for May 30, 1863, Durand Diaries.

[147] Mack and Connell, *Naval Ceremonies, Customs, and Traditions*, 174, 180; James Glazier to Parents, July 31, 1863, Glazier Collection, Rare Books and Manuscripts, Huntington Library.

[148] Entry for August 26, 1863, Wainwright Log.

ship. Sometimes, the meetings merely consisted of men huddled together while on night watch reciting simple prayers. In these meetings, sailors recited prayers, read scripture, wooed converts, and unburdened themselves of their troubles.[149] An article appearing in the June 1863 issue of the *Sunday School Times* described how one sailor, after finding only one Christian in his crew of 200, started a meeting on the *Daylight*: "The next day about ten o'clock he got his hymn-book and Bible, and took charge of the 'right wing' of the ship to begin his meeting. It was a very solemn service; an invitation was given to all those who felt their need of Christ to express it; twelve men knelt and asked the two to pray for them. Several of these found the 'pearl of great price.' "[150] After July 1862, prayer meetings became the most popular form of religious expression among sailors. Interest in these meetings proved so great that Christian sailors often gathered as many as four to seven times a week. On one ship, prayer meetings were held every night for ten months. As the war progressed, the numbers at prayer meetings easily outpaced attendance at regular Sunday services. Religious seamen seemed to respond to the democratic, less formal, and heart-felt nature of these meetings. As a result of these prayer meetings, "Many sinners were awakened," commented Joseph Stockbridge.[151]

Although many sinners may have been awakened, most of them fell back to sleep. Despite the outgrowth of prayer meetings, their impact proved limited. Overall, the most significant impact of the jettisoning of compulsory attendance was that, in mid-1862, most sailors stopped going to service on Sundays.[152] Seaman James E. Henneberry, serving on the Mississippi Squadron, noted that shortly after voluntary attendance commenced, only one-half of the crew on his boat attended divine service one Sunday.[153] On both the Mississippi and blockade squadrons, attendance progressively dwindled

---

[149] Robert McClure to Dr. William F. Thoms, November 28, 1861, and Thomas McNeil to Dr. William F. Thoms, November 5, 1862, Thoms Papers; Joseph Stockbridge to Navy Department, May 18, 1863, Official Navy Correspondence; Chaplain Report, U.S.S. *Lancaster*, Bay of Panama, October 27, 1862, Official Navy Correspondence.

[150] Smith, *Incidents of the United States Christian Commission*, 469.

[151] Drury, *The History of the Chaplain Corps*, 101; Joseph Stockbridge to Navy Department, May 18, 1863, Official Navy Correspondence.

[152] Ibid.

[153] Entry for November 23, 1862, Henneberry Diary.

among sailors and officers.[154] Some Sundays there were only a handful in attendance.[155] A lieutenant serving on a James River gunboat sadly observed in shock that only one sailor answered the church bell on a Sunday after the adoption of voluntary attendance.[156] Predictably, irreligious sailors happily stopped attending services. Catholics and evangelical Protestants possessed theological reasons for not attending. Men who had never formed the church-going habit, or who were not religiously inclined, quickly concocted all kinds of excuses for not going. Sailors rationalized that they received nothing out of the service, or could not hear the captain, or that it was too hot, or they were too busy.[157] William Wainwright offered a glimpse into the Sunday morning decision process for sailors not inclined toward religion: "I started on deck with the intention of going to church. but before I got on deck my mind changed. I have no doubt but it would be better for me to go but has [sic] long as I dont take any interest when I do go. I think I might as well stay away."[158]

The navy's intentions in allowing voluntary attendance at services were practical in scope and represented a balance between extreme positions on religion. By abandoning compulsory attendance, the navy had merely acknowledged the religious diversity of its crews by allowing for a divergence in practice. However, the government's attempt to let irreligious and religious sailors decide for themselves which form, if any, of religion to practice in a harsh environment lacking clergy and churches effectively discouraged most formal religious practice. As Chaplain Edmund C. Bittinger phrased it, "Sailors like soldiers will only do what is required of them."[159] Clergy and religious leaders quickly pinned growing sailor irreligiosity to the abandonment of compulsory attendance at divine services. The near collapse of sailor attendance at Sunday services prompted chaplains and northern religious groups to protest. In fact, the furor surround-

---

[154] Entry for March 13, 1864, Wainwright Log.

[155] Drury, *The History of the Chaplain Corps*, 101–2; Joseph Stockbridge to Navy Department, May 18, 1863, Official Navy Correspondence.

[156] Moss, *Annals of the United States Christian Commission*, 327.

[157] Entries for March 13, July 3, 24, September 18, 1864, Wainwright Log; Joseph Stockbridge to Navy Department, May 18, 1863, Official Navy Correspondence; Drury, *The History of the Chaplain Corps*, 100–1.

[158] Entry for November 29, 1863, Wainwright Log.

[159] Edmund C. Bittinger to Navy Department, March 10, 1862, in Drury, *The History of the Chaplain Corps*, 100.

ing navy and army actions with regard to the Sabbath had initially prompted leaders of various religious groups in New York City to meet with President Lincoln on November 13, 1862. They called upon him and the heads of all military departments to ensure a better observance of the Sabbath. Lincoln agreed to do something.[160] Although he did not re-institute compulsory attendance, on November 15, 1862, Lincoln issued a general order demanding that Sunday labor in the navy "be reduced to the measure of strict necessity." Lincoln assured northerners that the measure had been taken to protect the sacred rights of Christian sailors and as a sign of deference to the "best sentiments of a Christian people."[161]

Lincoln's order did little to reinvigorate the Sabbath and religious practice among sailors. "The repeal requiring the presence of the Ship's company at divine service has given a strong impetus to Sabbath desecration," complained Chaplain Stockbridge to the Navy Department in May 1863.[162] Moreover, Chaplain Stockbridge reported that a host of new sailor "customs" had arisen since the institution of voluntary attendance at services. These customs seemed to turn the traditional nature of the day on its head. Not only did sailors stop going to services, they began engaging in all sorts of activities that openly defied the spiritual tenor of the day. Sailors now openly and lustily worked, gambled, danced, and played music on Sundays.[163] Aside from work, Sundays used to be rather quiet aboard ship. Now, Seaman Joseph Osborne observed, Sunday nights had grown "lively."[164] Captains seemed to view the new voluntary religious practice policy as a vindication of their earlier attempts to work sailors on Sunday. They now forsook holding services altogether and

---

[160] Basler, ed., *Collected Works of Abraham Lincoln*, 5: 498, n. 1. An account dated November 13, 1862, in the *New York Tribune*, recorded that "Messrs. Fred. Winston, David Hoodley, Foster, Booth, and another gentleman, representing religious bodies in New York City, called upon the President and the heads of departments today to urge upon him the propriety of enforcing a better observance of the Sabbath in the army. The interviews are represented as agreeable and satisfactory."

[161] *Order for Sabbath Observance*, General Order, November 15, 1862, in ibid., 5: 497–98.

[162] Joseph Stockbridge to Navy Department, May 18, 1863, Official Navy Correspondence.

[163] Ibid.

[164] Joseph B. Osborne to Louise Landau, October 17, 1864, Osborne Family Papers.

worked sailors harder than ever. Chaplain Joseph Stockbridge warned that unless the navy adopted some "counter-action" to stem the erosion of sailor attendance, "our Sabbath is gone."[165]

One could argue, as some citizens did before the war, that the navy had no right or constitutional basis for administering religion to men, many of whom did not want it anyway.[166] However, from a practical standpoint, the navy knew, based upon centuries of accumulated sea experience and its own short history, that sailor morale declined in a ship atmosphere overcome with immorality and irreverence. Although the extreme situations of Union sailors during the Civil War made the preservation of religious practice more difficult, such conditions also made them more necessary. What Union sailors needed were tailored religious services and moral instructions designed to lift men's spirits and provide some semblance of hope and a link to shore.[167] Officers noticed that collective services and prayers seemed to help sailors, even if they did not want them. An officer serving on the *Lackawanna* admitted that "the service of the Church had always an excellent influence" on Union sailors.[168]

Moreover, the navy's compromises on religion made the situation worse by denying sailors even the traditional, improvised methods of spiritual recourse aboard ship. The cumulative effect of its actions was that sailors did not, as readily as soldiers did, use religion to buoy their morale under trying conditions.[169] According to James McPherson and Earl Hess, most soldiers fell back on religion to get them through the war, but sailors lacked that response in any organized

---

[165] Joseph Stockbridge to Navy Department, May 18, 1863, Official Navy Correspondence.

[166] The constitutionality of the government's providing of chaplains for the military is an issue far from settled. See Israel Drazin and Cecil B. Currey, *For God and Country: The History of a Constitutional Challenge to the Army Chaplaincy* (New York: Ktav Publishing House, 1995).

[167] *Chaplains in Congress and in the Army and Navy*, 7–8; Stivers, *Privateers & Volunteers*, 353.

[168] Still, "The Common Sailor," 32; James Thayer to William F. Thoms, October 31, 1861, Thoms Papers; entry for November 2, 1864, in Packard, "Jottings By the Way," part 2, 275; Arthur M. Schlesinger, ed., "A Blue Bluejacket's Letters Home, 1863–1864," *New England Quarterly* 1 (October 1928): 562; Merrill, "Men, Monotony and Mouldy Beans," 51.

[169] "The History of The Christian Commission," in William C. Wilkinson, *A Free Lance in the Field of Life and Letters* (New York: Albert Mason, 1874), 270–71.

form. Chaplains reported that the navy's good-intentioned, wrong-headed measures ultimately "demoralized" sailors.[170] By early 1864, sailors' letters and journals rang with this demoralization. Many complained of chronic depression, fatigue, and lack of purpose in their service. The majority of sailors' letters frequently reveal thoughts of discouragement, depression, and unhappiness. A handful committed suicide.[171] Living in the religious vacuum in which the navy helped to create, many other sailors wilted, then fell back on alcohol and other forms of escape to get them through their war.[172]

The navy's problems in addressing the spiritual needs of sailors eventually prompted religious organizations to expand their efforts to reach sailors by launching a campaign to bring religion aboard ships of the blockade and gunboats of the Mississippi. Before the war, reform-minded organizations such as the Missionary Society for Seamen and American Seaman's Friend Society had labored hard to bring religion to and improve the living conditions of American sailors.[173] Groups like these had been in the forefront of the fight to abolish flogging as a means of punishment in 1850 and the prohibition of alcohol on ships in 1862.[174] Sailors were also a set of men that reformers had targeted as lacking woefully in religion. In order to help ameliorate this situation, the American Bible Society and the Missionary Society for Seamen supplied scriptures and religious tracts to merchant mariners for years, and had constructed floating chapels in places like New York harbor to minister specifically to seamen where they lived.[175]

---

[170] Joseph Stockbridge to Navy Department, May 18, 1863, Official Navy Correspondence.

[171] Joseph Osborne to Louise Landau, October 2, 1864, in Merrill, "Men, Monotony and Mouldy Beans," 50; Stivers, Privateers & Volunteers, 345; Merrill, "Men, Monotony and Mouldy Beans," 51; entry for September 23, 1864, Wainright Log; entry for October 25, 1864, in Packard, "Jottings By the Way," part 2, 275; entry for March 2, 1864, in Lawrence Van Alstyne, Diary of An Enlisted Man (New Haven: Tuttle, Morehouse, & Taylor, 1910), 276.

[172] Valle, Rocks and Shoals, 18; General Order, Navy Department, July 17, 1862, in Official Records Navies, vol. 7, 584.

[173] Langley, Social Reform in the United States Navy, viii, 67.

[174] Ibid. The grog ration and the bringing of spirits aboard ship was abolished on September 1, 1862, General Order of Gideon Welles, July 17, 1862, Official Records Navies, vol. 7, 584.

[175] Drury, The History of the Chaplain Corps, 97; Annual Reports of the Protestant Episcopal Church Missionary Society for Seaman, 1851–1891 (New York: White & Ross Printers, 1965), 7–47.

The Civil War caused these reform organizations to intensify their efforts and spawned new ones. Fearing an erosion of morals due to the uprooting of millions of men from their homes and families, members of the Young Men's Christian Association (YMCA) organized the United States Christian Commission on November 15, 1861, in New York City. Organizers formed the commission to inspire soldiers and sailors to live "faithful, consistent Christian lives" when away from home in the service. Unlike the United States Sanitary Commission, the Christian Commission's purpose was unabashedly religious. Its members, called "Christians," attracted strong religious support from Methodist and Episcopal churches.[176] The work of the commission was to be carried out by 4,886 centrally commissioned agents, called "delegates." These delegates promised to function as "moral police amid these national convulsions." Although the army was their first priority, the commission eventually saw the expanse of naval volunteers as a unique opportunity to reach a group of men once thought physically and morally unreachable.[177]

The commission did not intend merely to preach at sailors. The organization realized that it first had to meet the men's temporal wartime needs before the sailors would listen to a religious message. The commission molded its approach around the traditional view of charity as a religious obligation and primarily "alleviative in nature."[178] This approach represented an ideological break with the tradition the navy chaplains and captains had emphasized in the past. Commission preachers believed their primary responsibility to be the alleviation of the suffering and hardship of sailors, not sermonizing on the message of salvation. Commission delegates hoped that if they tried to help sailors' bodies, they might also save their souls.[179]

In order to "hunt out" Christian sailors, commission members developed a four-pronged plan of operations. First, they distributed clothing, fresh fruits and vegetables, and drinks among ordinary sail-

---

[176] Robert H. Bremner, "The Impact of the Civil War on Philanthropy and Social Welfare," *Civil War History* 12 (December 1966): 301.

[177] McDevitt, "Fighting for the Soul of America," 9; U.S. Christian Commission, *Work and Incidents*, 83.

[178] Bremner, "The Impact of the Civil War on Philanthropy and Social Welfare," 301.

[179] Douglas R. Oxenford, "Ideology, Ecclesiastics and the Seafarer: A Pilot Study" (M.A. Thesis, The Ohio State University, 1983), 3, n. 3; McDevitt, "Fighting for the Soul of America," 152.

ors. It was not uncommon for a delegate to arrive aboard a ship toting such hard-to-get items as oranges, apples, jams, and lemonade. Second, delegates planned to establish personal contact with sailors by making individual visits. Personal contact with psychologically and physically ailing sailors, they believed, was pivotal to achieving success.[180] Third, commission delegates volunteered to lead Sunday services and prayer meetings aboard ship.[181]

Lastly, in trying to understand the religious problems of sailors, the commission concluded that the greatest factor impeding religious practice and spirituality among sailors stemmed from isolation. As a result, the fourth and final part of the commission's attack was to attempt to re-connect sailors to northern society and the reinforcing influences of families. To accomplish this, the commission adopted two critical approaches, one old and one new, to counterbalance sailors' religious isolation. The first measure the commission took was to hire dispatch boats to make bimonthly rounds through the squadrons distributing thousands of Bibles and bundles of religious tracts and inspirational literature.[182] An officer on the receiving ship *North Carolina* reported that the commission sent so many Bibles that every member of the crew had at least one copy.[183] The inspirational literature, easy to read and sensibly written, played upon religious themes, good stories, and temperance morals. Such titles as "Come to Jesus," "The Little Captain," and "Where Is Jesus?" were designed to spark religious curiosity before delegates arrived and maintain it after they left.[184]

The second measure that the commission took was to do whatever it could to revive, maintain, or instill a home influence in sailors' lives. The commission hoped to establish a "living electric chain between

---

[180] George M. Fredrickson, *The Inner Civil War: Northern Intellectuals and the Crisis of Union* (New York: Harper & Row, 1965), 107.

[181] Drury, *The History of the Chaplain Corps*, 97; entry for August 28, 1864, Samuel Pollock Diary, Manuscripts Division, Illinois State Historical Library.

[182] U.S. Christian Commission, *Work and Incidents*, 101, 115, 121, 163–64, 231.

[183] Drury, *The History of the Chaplain Corps*, 97; Moss, *Annals of the United States Christian Commission*, 687; U.S. Christian Commission, *Work and Incidents*, 120–21; McDevitt, "Fighting For the Soul of America," 151, n. 166; Ringle, *Life in Mr. Lincoln's Navy*, 89.

[184] Stivers, *Privateers & Volunteers*, 354; Moss, *The Annals of the United States Christian Commission*, 707.

the hearth and the tent, which could only be met by persons from home, with hearts to sympathize, tongues to cheer, and hands to relieve."[185] This chain would not be established by abstract references to mother and family as captains had done in their sermons. Instead, the commission took highly practical approaches to establishing and maintaining the bond between sailors and shore. Whenever possible, delegates distributed secular and religious newspapers from sailors' hometowns.[186] More importantly, delegates encouraged sailors to write home. Letter writing was expensive for sailors, many of whom suffered from poverty. The navy did not provide men with pencils, paper, envelopes, and postage to write home. Sutlers often charged as much as forty cents for a single sheet of paper and an envelope.[187] Commission delegates brought along writing supplies for sailors and mailed their letters free of charge.[188] If a man was unable to write because of an injury or illiteracy, the commission member would write the letter for him. By subsidizing the exchange of letters, the commission enlisted the assistance of family and friends, particularly women, in the campaign to save sailors from Satan's reach on board ship.

Not surprisingly, the navy was skeptical. Although commission chairman George H. Stuart extended the commission's offer of assistance in 1861, commission delegates did not begin visiting sailors until 1864. Only when sailor morale plummeted aboard ships did the navy let commission delegates aboard ship. In Stuart's opinion, Secretary of the Navy Gideon Welles had looked with "jaundiced eye" on its offer to assist with the spiritual lives of sailors. According to Stuart, Welles had only cautiously accepted the commission's offer to assist in 1861, by saying the navy would accept only "legitimate

---

[185] U.S. Christian Commission, *Principles and Position of the United States Christian Commission* (San Francisco: Towne & Bacon, 1864), 1. Reid Mitchell contends that links to home and the family were central to soldiers' understanding and surviving the Civil War; see Mitchell, *The Vacant Chair*, xiii.

[186] McDevitt, "Fighting for the Soul of America," 195; U.S. Christian Commission, *Work and Incidents*, 72; Reverend H. Loomis, *Christian Work Among Soldiers* (Yokohama, Japan: Fukuin Printing Company Ltd., 1908), 10.

[187] Still, "The Common Sailor," 34; U.S. Christian Commission, *Work and Incidents*, 189, 71–72, 83; Smith, *Incidents of the United States Christian Commission*, 298, 444.

[188] U.S. Christian Commission, *Work and Incidents*, 71–72.

means to promote the welfare (present and future) of all who are in the service."[189]

According to the commission, the navy feared that too much religion would make sailors "effeminate" and deprive them of courage.[190] Furthermore, although many denominations were represented among the commission's delegates—including Methodists, Baptists, and Congregationalists—they were heavily Protestant and not at all timid. Most preachers were evangelical and of the "blue flame sulphureous order," as one sailor commented.[191] In order to gain access to sailors, the commission bent to the will of the navy and to the demographic realities of the men who served as sailors. As the navy had already done, the commission buried denominational and doctrinal differences for the cause of the Union and promised to adhere to its guiding principles of "Catholicity," "Nationalism," and "Voluntariness."[192]

Once begun, visitation work proved extremely difficult. The task of reaching sailors was logistically problematic because delegates had to travel to sailors where they lived—on ships and boats of the blockade and Mississippi River fleets. Reaching soldiers was not so difficult. In army camps, the commission established "stations" where the men could come and worship, visit, and receive literature.[193] Although delegates did establish permanent stations in places like the Brooklyn Navy Yard and the Navy Yard at Charleston, these places were merely pass-through points, where if recruits had time—much

---

[189] Gideon Welles to George H. Stuart, December 16, 1861, in U.S. Christian Commission, *Work and Incidents*, 107. President Lincoln also seemed to view the commission as a double-edged sword. George Stuart invited the president to speak at its first meeting of the year on February 12, 1863, in Washington, D. C. The president, calling the matter "not *very* important," still felt the matter of his appearance weighty enough that he asked the cabinet whether he should attend. Only one cabinet member, Secretary of the Treasury Salmon P. Chase, recommended that the president attend. He did not. See Abraham Lincoln to Alexander Reed, February 22, 1863, and Abraham Lincoln to William H. Seward, February 18, 1863, in Basler, ed., *Collected Works of Abraham Lincoln*, 6: 114–15, 110.

[190] U.S. Christian Commission, *Principles and Position of the United States Christian Commission*, 10.

[191] John Eliot Parkman to Elizabeth Parkman, December 11, 1864, John Eliot Parkman Papers, vol. 1, Manuscripts Division, Massachusetts Historical Society, Boston, Massachusetts; Fredrickson, *The Inner Civil War*, 107.

[192] U.S. Christian Commission, *Principles and Position of the United States Christian Commission*, 10–13.

[193] Wiley, *The Life of Billy Yank*, 269.

less the inclination—they grabbed a handful of literature and went on their way.

In order to reach the men where they lived, captains sometimes permitted commission ministers to preach to sailors on the berth deck, which was one of the few places aboard ship that sailors could relax and sleep. The berth deck was also the favorite place for sailors to steal, drink, and beat and knife one another. Delegates often read prayers aloud to sailors as they lay in their hammocks. It must have proven an unusual sight for rough and tumble sailors to have a minister read prayers to them as they went to sleep. One delegate recalled, "I stood by the swinging hammocks, and read to them from the Book of Books, concerning God's wonderful love to them."[194]

To their displeasure, delegates found ships made poor churches. The noise, the crowded conditions, and constant buzz of activity made holding services difficult.[195] Furthermore, jumping from boat to boat under the scrutiny of captains and wading into hostile environments loaded with nonbelievers required tough men. J. D. Wyckoff reported that he visited quite a few gunboats on the Mississippi River before he encountered any religious sailors. On more hospitable ships, he met one or two religious sailors among crews of 150–200 men.[196]

Despite all of these obstacles, commission delegates seemed to bring certain positive elements to religious services that too many captains had not, namely fervor, piety, and most of all sincerity.[197] John Eliot Parkman noticed the difference immediately when the Reverend W. L. Tisdale preached to sailors one Sunday:

> A man of excellent intentions I have no doubt, but badly clothed and clammy, with a tendency to burst as he warms to his work. He preached on the berth deck and as it was no more than six inches above his head it proved a wonderful Sounding board as he hurled and writhed in the telling points of his discourse—He has gone, but the deck still rumbles and my head is cracking.[198]

Surprisingly, Union sailors seemed to accept grudgingly the efforts of commission delegates. Without question, they mocked the "Holy

---

[194] U.S. Christian Commission, *Work and Incidents*, 101.

[195] Ibid., 151.

[196] Smith, *Incidents of the United States Christian Commission*, 454.

[197] Fredrickson, *The Inner Civil War*, 107.

[198] John Eliot Parkman to Elizabeth Parkman, December 11, 1864, Parkman Papers.

Joes" that came across their decks for their religious fervor and bois-
terousness. Sailors likely cringed and growled when ministers bela-
bored the evils of drink, wanton women, and tobacco, or handed
them less empathetic tracts such as "Hell and its Miseries."[199] Nevertheless, unlike their objections to navy distilled religion, Union sailors
did not complain about commission visits. For a number of reasons,
sailors believed commission ministers to be sincere in their mission
and accepted them as a genuine source of religious and spiritual comfort. One of the reasons for sailor empathy was that commission delegates received little compensation for their work. Sailors seemed
genuinely impressed that someone would board a ship to work for
less than they did.[200] In addition, for men already feeling put upon
and abused, the free distributions of foodstuffs, reading materials,
and mailing supplies were most appreciated. John Swift, who had not
been to church in some time, expressed gratitude for the literature.
"I have one of their bibles which does as well," he wrote.[201] Sailors
also greatly tacitly thanked the commission for the free writing supplies and postage by engaging in the very act of writing home. As
Sunday conjured up the strongest feelings for friends and families, it
was not surprising that whole crews often feverishly used the day to
write letters to friends and family back home.[202]

Most importantly, commission delegates adapted their demeanor
and the content of their services and visits to meet the specific religious needs of Union sailors. Through sympathy and humanitarianism in both its charitable distributions and religious services, the
commission touched some of the hearts and minds of crews aboard
ships.[203] Christians incorporated these values into the content of their
liturgies. Gone were the invocations to obedience, captains' railings
about lowliness and hypocrites, and dry readings from chapters of
the New Testament. In their place, commission ministers used "kind
words" and invoked images of Christ as the Good Shepherd who
would "bring us through our *Warings* to honorable peace" and would

---

[199] Ibid.

[200] McDevitt, "Fighting for the Soul of America," 157.

[201] John Swift to Rosie Whiteside, June 2, 1864, in Swift, "Letters from a Sailor on
a Tinclad," 55.

[202] Entry for May 23, 1865, Judd Diary; John Swift to Rosie Whiteside, June 2,
1864, in Swift, "Letters From a Sailor on Tinclad," 55; George A. Bright to John
Bright, November 17, 1861, Bright Journal.

[203] Wilkinson, *A Free Lance*, 288–91.

shield them in "Every hour of Danger Battling with the Foes of our government."[204] Other ministers restyled familiar psalms to accommodate the unique situation of the sailor. "Thou shall not be afraid for the Terrors by night nor the *Shell that Flieth by Day*," assured Minister E. B. Turner to sailors on the *Onondaga*. Fully aware that seamen loved to sing, the commission also employed hymns tailored to sailors' special circumstances and trials. Hymns such as "Look Aloft," "A Home Beyond the Tide," and "Far At Sea" echoed familiar themes of loneliness, storms, and temptations.[205] A particular favorite, the "Sailor's Hymn," called out:

> Tossed upon life's raging billow
> Sweet it is, O Lord to know
> Thou didst press a sailor's pillow
> And canst feel a sailor's woe.[206]

Minor incidents reveal the subtle impact the commission made on individual sailors. The Reverend J. D. Wyckoff, a Congregationalist pastor who performed services for sailors on the receiving ship at Cairo, recalled a story concerning Seaman John Jones. Wyckoff had noticed that during the meetings, Jones had not participated in the service. Afterward, however, Wyckoff recalled that Jones approached him and sheepishly asked for a copy of the *New York Observer* and a Bible for "a mate." Wyckoff thought this strange but complied with Jones's request. As Wyckoff turned to leave, Jones again approached the minister and with his right hand extended, partly closed and inverted so as to conceal the contents of his hand from his crewmates said, "I want to do something for Christ; won't you take this for the Commission?" As Jones hurried away, Wyckoff looked down into his hand and saw five dollars.[207]

On June 14, 1864, the steamboat *Eclipse* exploded on the Mississippi River killing and severely injuring many on board. Amid the frightful burns and broken bones, one sailor, who had been severely scalded, recognized the voice of a commission delegate from meet-

---

[204] Fredrickson, *The Inner Civil War*, 107; entry for July 24, 1864, Journal of Levi Hayden, vol. 1, May 27, 1864 to January 31, 1879, Levi Hayden Papers, Division of Rare Books and Manuscripts, New York Public Library, New York City.

[205] United States Christian Commission, *Hymn-Book For the Army and Navy* (Cincinnati: U.S. Christian Commission, n.d.), 14–16.

[206] Ibid., 15–16.

[207] Smith, *Incidents of the United States Christian Commission*, 453–54.

ings on the receiving ship at Cairo. Even though he admitted that he was not a religious man and that he had, in fact, been afraid to participate in the Cairo meetings, the sailor cried out that he wanted "to see the Christian Commission man." When the commission delegate responded, the man said to him, "I've been a great sinner, but I'm seeking repentance and forgiveness. I'm not ashamed to ask Christians to pray for me now."[208] These incidents, although individual in nature, do speak to the type of collective impact the commission made on religious and nonreligious sailors alike. Seaman John Swift summed up the contribution that the Christian Commission had made to sailors' lives. "[T]here is a Society in this Country," Swift wrote his sister, "which supplies all who are fighting under its flag, with food for body & soul."[209]

The commission's efforts also seemed to awaken the religious consciences of some sailors.[210] Observers recalled that the commission's services worked a positive effect on the men. Levi Hayden concluded that they created an atmosphere of "Pathos Love and reverence for the Deity unity and good fellowship" even in sight of the enemy.[211] Other sailors acknowledged that they felt the "benison" and comfort of these prayers all day long.[212]

Proof of this awakening was the increase in voluntary attendance at divine services that often followed a dissemination of literature and visits by the commission's delegates. Both the commission's delegates and the navy's officers credited the distribution of literature for the dramatic rise in formal service attendance by sailors. On ships where only a few of the crew had previously attended divine service, after a distribution of literature and a visit by delegates, over a hundred would appear at the ringing of the church bell.[213] When an officer notified the commission that only one sailor attended a divine service one Sunday, it sent a round of literature. The very next Sunday, 100 men attended the service. As a result of the literature, the officer marveled, "There is a great change among the crew."[214] Some men

[208] Ibid., 454–55.

[209] John Swift to Rosie Whiteside, June 2, 1864, in Swift, "Letters From a Sailor on a Tinclad," 55.

[210] Drury, *The History of the Chaplain Corps*, 97.

[211] Entry for July 24, 1864, Hayden Journal.

[212] Still, "The Common Sailor," 32; Ringle, *Life in Mr. Lincoln's Navy*, 139.

[213] U.S. Christian Commission, *Work and Incidents*, 120–21.

[214] Moss, *Annals of the United States Christian Commission*, 327.

even altered the tenor of their lives by signing "temperance contracts" under which they agreed to forego alcohol, swearing, "wicked companions," and the "wild life."[215]

Yet, in 1865, as the war drew to an end, the commission sadly concluded, "Work for Christ on our gunboats, and among sailors generally, is very peculiar work . . . it might be termed difficult."[216] The commission's conclusion denotes the frustration and mixed results the organization ultimately achieved among Union sailors. To be certain, the commission did achieve some successes. Its literature purportedly reached 580 ships and over 34,000 officers and enlisted men.[217] In many small ways, the commission's efforts also alleviated some of the hardships suffered by sailors aboard ship. What is unclear is how much of an impact the commission made in planting the seeds of religious practice and faith into the souls of a group labeled "irreligious." Ministering to men not prone to expressions of religion and denominationally divided, with almost no chaplains and isolated on a ship, was a daunting task at best. Moreover, the commission's work among sailors was further hampered by its late start in 1864 and the isolation of ships from land and from each other, thus making collective, sustained religious awakenings extremely difficult. Not surprisingly, despite the commission's efforts, no large-scale revivals took place among sailors during the Civil War comparable to those that swept the ranks of their army counterparts.[218]

The troubled tale of religious expression among Union sailors, ignored until now, reveals much about the difficulties of maintaining spiritual practice and belief on the church-free, cosmopolitan environments of ships. Not only does their story uncover a different religious history for northern sailors during the Civil War, the obstacles they encountered provide a prototype for examining how the religious ideals and practices of both sailors and soldiers weather when released from the reinforcing influences of families, clergy, and orga-

---

[215] Drury, *The History of the Chaplain Corps*, 101; Chaplain Report, U.S.S. *Lancaster*, October 27, 1862, Official Navy Correspondence; entry for November 1, 1865, McLaren Journal; Charles Kember to Dr. William F. Thoms, August 4, 1861, Thoms Papers.

[216] U.S. Christian Commission, *Work and Incidents*, 101.

[217] Stivers, *Privateers & Volunteers*, 353.

[218] James Moorhead, *American Apocalypse: Yankee Protestants and the Civil War 1860–1869* (New Haven: Yale University Press, 1978), 65–69; Wiley, "Holy Joes," 287.

nized church communities. Their story is an important one as it shows how naval volunteers, many of whom were not traditionally religious, struggled with the spiritual vacuum of ships, the antireligious tendencies of the institutional military, and the varied religious and irreligious beliefs and backgrounds of their fellow shipmates. Recognizing the religious problems faced by men when they go to the sea should cause historians to reassess their views about the nature and scope of stereotypical notions concerning sailor irreligiosity and broaden our understanding of the spiritual complexities faced by men when they head off to war, be it on sea or on land, far away from the reach of clergy, family, and friends.

8

In the Lord's Army: The United States Christian Commission, Soldiers, and the Union War Effort

David A. Raney

AIDED BY A CRUTCH, the aged warrior hobbled to the front of the platform to address a throng of curious and admiring well-wishers. The multitude of nearly ten thousand had gathered in Ocean Grove, New Jersey, on an August afternoon in 1884 for a reunion of the United States Christian Commission and other Civil War benevolent organizations. Speaking only with the greatest of effort and in a voice that faltered, the old hero thanked the Christian Commission for the extensive good it had performed on the field and in the hospital during the late war. "I had special opportunities," said he, "to know of service rendered, of consolations administered by the side of death-beds; of patient, unwavering attentions to the sick; of letters written to the mourning parents of noble sons." The general's voice cracked and tears began streaming down his cheeks. Ulysses S. Grant could go no further. Overcome with emotion, he was helped to his seat amid thunderous applause. Sadly, Grant's public appearance that day was his last; in less than a year, throat cancer claimed the life of one of America's most celebrated war heroes.[1]

The Christian Commission to which Grant referred was formed in November 1861, by representatives from several northern branches of the United States Young Men's Christian Association (YMCA).

---

[1] *New York Tribune*, August 4, 1884; *Philadelphia Record*, August 3, 1884; *Jersey City Evening Journal*, August 5, 1884; Robert Ellis Thompson, ed., *The Life of George H. Stuart* (Philadelphia: J. M. Stoddart, 1890), 312–13; William S. McFeely, *Grant: A Biography* (New York: W. W. Norton, 1981), 495–96.

YMCA leaders viewed the Civil War as an unparalleled opportunity to convert young men to Christ; the field of battle would become a field of ministry. Under the aegis of the Christian Commission, the YMCA sought to coordinate its efforts to minister to the needs of Union soldiers. Although Christian Commission workers believed that it was their Christian duty to provide for the wants of soldiers on both sides of the conflict, especially on the battlefield, their efforts concentrated on the "boys in blue."

Members of the Christian Commission realized that the needs of the troops were temporal as well as spiritual. It would be difficult if not impossible for evangelists to attract the Union's fighting men to Christ if their physical needs were not met. Thus, the Christian Commission's varied activities were, at their base, directed toward preparing soldiers to receive Christ as their Savior. Although the Christian Commission has been remembered largely as an agency that distributed Bibles and other religious reading material to Union forces, it also engaged in activities ranging from supplying fresh food to the troops to teaching black soldiers, all in an attempt to bring them to the Lord. As George H. Stuart, the organization's chairman, suggested, "there is a good deal of religion in a warm shirt and a good beefsteak."[2]

On April 15, 1861, President Abraham Lincoln issued a proclamation calling forth "the militia of the several States of the Union to the aggregate number of 75,000" in order to quell an insurrection "too powerful to be suppressed by the ordinary course of judicial proceedings." Within days troops began to assemble in Washington, the first arriving from Pennsylvania on April 18. William Ballantyne, a local bookseller and later the chairman of Washington's branch of the Christian Commission, along with his associates from the Washington YMCA, quickly began to minister to the spiritual and physical needs of the troops. Recalling the evangelistic efforts he and his colleagues undertook among the incoming soldiers, Ballantyne remarked, "Time hung heavy on their hands, and they had nothing to read. We took all the tracts we had in stock, and used them up. Having a large number of the *Family Christian Almanac* of a former year on hand, I had the young men in the store cut out the calendar part, and

---

[2] Thompson, ed., *The Life of George H. Stuart*, 129.

stitch a brown paper cover over the reading portion, which made an excellent tract, and so distribute them. The men were also supplied with [New] Testaments, and the Rev. J. G. Butler, pastor of the English Lutheran Church, preached to them."[3]

The Washington branch of the YMCA sprang into action as thousands of soldiers poured into the city. Soon after troops began to arrive, the association divided the city into districts; each district was administered by chosen members of the YMCA chapter. Those in charge of the districts were responsible for meeting the spiritual wants of the soldiers within their respective fields.[4]

The YMCA of Chicago also recognized promptly the necessities of the hour. On April 25, 1861, the Chicago Association called a meeting of clergymen to discuss a proposal to send delegates to preach to troops stationed in Cairo, Illinois. Several Chicago pastors and laymen were sent to Cairo including Dwight L. Moody, who later became famous as the revivalist preacher who founded the Moody Church and the Moody Bible Institute in Chicago. During the last part of May, Moody and an associate named B. F. Jacobs instituted a series of meetings with the soldiers in their camp near Cairo; the gatherings elicited a great deal of interest among the soldiers stationed there. An edition of thirty-five hundred hymnbooks was printed to supply a seemingly insatiable demand for religious reading material, and "the meetings at the camp continued to increase in interest until as many as eight or ten were held each evening, and hundreds were led to seek Christ."[5]

On April 18, the 6th Regiment Massachusetts Volunteer Infantry arrived in New York for a stopover on its way to Washington. Vincent Colyer of the New York YMCA visited the regiment that day in order to discern and provide for the needs of the troops. A young artist who went on to neglect his prospering studio in favor of philanthropic work within the Union ranks, Colyer was astonished to find that the soldiers had already been supplied with New Testaments and other items. Apparently, women from Concord, Massachusetts, had pre-

---

[3] Lemuel Moss, *Annals of the United States Christian Commission* (Philadelphia: J. B. Lippincott, 1869), 68–69, 69n; James M. McPherson, *Battle Cry of Freedom: The Civil War Era* (New York: Oxford University Press, 1988), 274.

[4] Moss, *Annals*, 83.

[5] Ibid., 76.

empted the representatives of the New York YMCA by providing the volunteers with welcomed reading material before they left Boston.[6]

Shortly after the first Battle of Bull Run, Colyer left New York for Washington. He arrived on July 24. Visiting the hospitals in the city, which were choked with wounded soldiers from the recent engagement, Colyer observed:

> In going through one of the wards where some thirty suffering soldiers were lying on their cots, I took a large package of tracts, opened it, and allowed each man to choose for himself. . . . As each wounded man chose a book, he would raise himself up on his cot and inquire of his neighbor what book he had chosen; and having ascertained he would then select some other, and remark, "when we have read each our own we will exchange." While they were thus engaged, a number of the wounded who were seated out on an open verandah enjoying the cooler air, espying through an open window the package and what was going on within, sent several of their number hobbling in to make a selection for them.[7]

Colyer remained in Washington to work in the camps and hospitals. He was struck by how much the wounded soldiers in particular appreciated conversation, reading material, and letters written on their behalf to loved ones at home. His efforts were aided significantly by fellow laborers from the New York YMCA as well as representatives from other benevolent associations. Local societies and churches began to provide Colyer and his fellow workers with increasing quantities of supplies, and governmental authorities on the state and national levels generally cooperated with their activities.[8]

Colyer realized quickly that the efforts that had been "undertaken in Christian sympathy as a temporary task, would have to be kept up and extended as a permanent duty." The temporary task of meeting the spiritual needs of the nation's soldiers began to assume massive proportions, and it became apparent to him that the mission could be accomplished only if the Christian forces of the country were mobilized under central leadership. With this in mind, Colyer wrote to his colleagues at the New York YMCA on August 22, 1861, to advo-

---

[6] Ibid., 69n–70n; Richard C. Lancaster, *Serving the U. S. Armed Forces, 1861–1986: The Story of the YMCA's Ministry to Military Personnel for 125 Years* (Schaumburg, Ill.: Armed Services YMCA of the USA, 1987), 1.

[7] Moss, *Annals*, 92–93.

[8] Ibid., 93–94.

cate calling a convention of YMCA chapters in the loyal states to consider forming a "general commission." Reaction to his suggestion was favorable, and on September 23, the New York Association created a committee, chaired by Colyer, that was charged with the responsibility of pursuing the matter. Colyer corresponded with a number of army chaplains to obtain their views about how the proposed convention could best achieve its objectives. He received more than sixty replies, indicating broad support for his agenda. Colyer also visited with the leaders of several YMCA chapters in the East to elicit their support for a convention. Once again, the response was overwhelmingly positive; the proposition met with approval everywhere he traveled. The "National Committee of the Young Men's Christian Associations of the United States" was formed as a result of Colyer's vigorous efforts. The new committee possessed the exclusive right of calling the convention that would assemble the much-anticipated "general commission." The National Committee was based in Philadelphia. George H. Stuart, a wealthy merchant who was the primary force behind the creation of that city's YMCA chapter, was selected as chairman of the group.[9]

Shortly after the creation of the YMCA's National Committee in the autumn of 1861, the group asked Colyer to formulate a written statement outlining the need for the "general commission" that he had originally recommended to his colleagues at the New York YMCA. He obliged. In his letter, he asked the National Committee to call a convention "at the earliest practicable day, to consider the spiritual wants of the young men of our army, in order that the same may be provided for by the appointing of a 'Christian Commission,' whose duty it shall be to take entire charge of this work." Continuing his justification for the creation of a "Christian Commission," Colyer wrote:

> The government has now over 250,000 men enlisted, the far greater majority of whom are young men, and not a few of them members of our Associations. These young men are risking their lives for their country, exposed to constant hardships, and subjected to all the temptations and debasing influences of camp life. They are liable to sickness and prolonged suffering from wounds in hospital, and to sudden death upon the battle-field. To meet the great wants of these young men,

---

[9] Ibid., 95–96.

under circumstances which so urgently call upon our Christian sympathies and gratitude (for they are assembled in defense of our homes, our rights, and our government), no adequate exertion has yet been made.[10]

Although Colyer made several references to the physical needs of the soldiers, he nonetheless maintained that evangelism should be the commission's overriding concern. Indeed, his communication to the National Committee included several letters from army chaplains who were excited by the prospect of a new vehicle that would help to steer young men to the Lord. "May God bless you in your labor of love and charity," penned J. R. Carpenter, chaplain of the First Regiment of District of Columbia Volunteers. "I believe the seed of truth sown during this war will be the means of awakening many souls to Christ." Also included was a letter from Warren H. Cudworth, chaplain of the 1st Regiment Massachusetts Volunteer Infantry. Writing in response to Colyer's earlier correspondence about the proposed commission, Cudworth asserted, "I rejoice in the Lord at your 'labor of love.' In my opinion this is a work second only in importance to the appointment of the highest officers in command. Blessings upon you and your true yoke-fellows everywhere for trying to introduce more of the Spirit of God into our ranks. Camp life abounds with temptations, and the soldier's calling is demoralizing in the extreme."[11]

On October 18, 1861, the National Committee decided to call a convention to form the commission that Colyer and his associates sought. On November 14 delegates from YMCA chapters throughout the North met at the headquarters of the New York Association and, after two days of meetings, appointed twelve men (later expanded to fifty) as members of the new "Christian Commission." George H. Stuart was selected as the permanent chairman of the organization.[12]

The newly formed Christian Commission wasted little time in formulating its objectives. In a December 11 letter, Stuart wrote of the commission's intent "to take active measures to promote the spiritual and temporal welfare of the soldiers in the army, and the sailors and

---

[10] Ibid., 96; *A Memorial Record of the New-York Branch of the United States Christian Commission. Compiled Under the Direction of the Executive Committee* (New York: John A. Gray & Green, Printers, 1866), 10–11.

[11] Moss, *Annals*, 97.

[12] Ibid., 99–106.

marines in the navy, in co-operation with chaplains and others." On January 13, 1862, the commission's executive committee issued a circular that outlined an eight-point program to meet the needs of the Union troops. The goals expressed in the circular ranged from furnishing religious reading material to aiding the formation of religious associations in the several regiments. Above all, the Christian Commission was to employ its efforts to bring soldiers to a personal relationship with Jesus Christ. "We propose to encourage in them whatever is good," the circular announced, "and keep fresh in their remembrance the instructions of earlier years, and to develop, organize and make effective the religious element in the army and navy." The commission recognized the opportunities for evangelism that the war offered, and the organization intended to exploit such avenues fully. "The field is open to us," wrote the executive committee. "We can have free access to their immortal souls—the chaplains desire and call for our aid—the Government wish it—and the men ask for and receive religious reading and teaching, with an eagerness most touching. Thousands, who at home never entered the house of God, and had none to care for their souls, now in imminent peril, desire to know of Him who can give them the victory over death, through our Lord Jesus Christ."[13]

The cornerstone of the Christian Commission's efforts was its extensive use of unpaid agents as delegates. The commission typically selected delegates from among the ranks of evangelical clergymen, although a substantial number of laymen were also commissioned for work in the field. Because the commission remained an interdenominational organization throughout the war, any member of an orthodox Protestant church was welcome to apply for service. The commission did not solicit the assistance of Unitarians, Roman Catholics, and others outside the fold of evangelical Christianity. Of the approximately five thousand delegates who served during the war, only a handful were women. During the early and often chaotic stages of its existence, the commission allowed delegates to serve for various periods of time, but as the war dragged on, each delegate was expected to serve for at least six weeks. In 1862, the year in which

---

[13] Ibid., 108–9; United States Christian Commission (USCC), *Documents of the Christian Commission: 1862* (Philadelphia: Gwalt & Brown, Book and Job Printers, 1862), 27–29.

the commission began its benevolent operations, the organization sent 356 delegates to the field; by the close of the war, 4,859 had labored on behalf of the group.[14]

Prior to heading for the field, delegates signed a certificate, or "commission," that highlighted the wide variety of services that they were expected to perform:

> His work will be that of distributing stores where needed, in hospitals and camps; circulating good reading matter among soldiers and sailors; visiting the sick and wounded, to instruct, comfort, and cheer them, and aid them in correspondence with their friends at home; aiding Surgeons on the battle-field and elsewhere, in the care and conveyance of the wounded to hospitals; helping Chaplains in their ministrations and influence for the good of the men under their care; and addressing soldiers and sailors, individually and collectively, in explanation of the work of the Commission and its delegates, and for their personal instruction and benefit, temporal and eternal.[15]

The certificate also instructed delegates to observe all military regulations and to "abstain from casting reflections upon the authorities, military, medical and clerical." The commission was acutely aware that infractions of its self-imposed rules might lead to cool relations with officers, surgeons, and chaplains that could jeopardize its work.[16]

Cool relations did prevail for a time between the commission and army chaplains. Major General O. O. Howard, a staunch supporter of the Christian Commission, delivered a public address on February 22, 1863, in which he opined that "the chaplaincy system of the army has proved a failure." Howard's comments, caustic as they were, reflected a widespread realization that army chaplaincy was not meeting the expectations, lofty or otherwise, of men within the ranks. Commanding officers decried a severe shortage of chaplains, and stories abound of chaplains who neglected their duties, lied to the men in their care, and even committed theft. Brigadier General David

---

[14] William H. Armstrong, *A Friend to God's Poor: Edward Parmelee Smith* (Athens: University of Georgia Press, 1993), 46–49, 87; USCC, *Fourth Annual Report* (Philadelphia: n. p., 1866), Exhibit F.

[15] Sydney Ahlstrom, *A Religious History of the American People* (New Haven, Conn.: Yale University Press, 1972), 678–79. Commission of Duncan C. Milner, Duncan C. Milner Collection, Folder 64, Illinois Historical Survey, University of Illinois Library, Urbana.

[16] Commission of Duncan C. Milner, Illinois Historical Survey.

Bell Birney lamented the "wretched broken-down men that often seek refuge in an army chaplaincy." Colonel Robert McAllister wrote in a letter to his wife that he wished the regimental chaplain would resign. "He is of no earthly use to us here. He has not held a prayer meeting or don[e] anything for the good of the regiment. . . . He is disliked by all." A private complained that his chaplain "lied to me about carrying the mail & does nothing at all but hang around his tent & sort the mail. He never goes around any amongst the men & I think he is nothing but a confounded humbug & nuisance." As early as September 1861, a Gettysburg newspaper reported:

> We are sorry to say that several Chaplains have already shown them-
> selves to be very bad Christians, and that they are not proof against
> temptation. In this connection we are reminded of an incident which
> occurred a few days ago. A Chaplain belonging to a regiment in the
> vicinity of Washington, and who was also Postmaster of the regiment,
> was known to have robbed the mails, an officer went to the encamp-
> ment to arrest him. As he approached the *good* man's tent he thought
> he heard the voice of prayer—he stopped and listened, and then cau-
> tiously looked in, when he saw the guilty Chaplain and a soldier on
> their knees. The officer withdrew, and arrested him the next day in the
> street.[17]

A report on military chaplains issued in Ohio by a committee of the Presbyterian Synod of the Western Reserve concluded that although many chaplains were "excellent and faithful and self-denying," most were a disappointment. The committee observed that "the uniform testimony of men, who have had the best opportunities of forming a correct opinion, is, that a majority of the Chaplains are unworthy of the place they hold; that by their incompetency, or the gross neglect of their duties, they prove themselves faithless servants of the State, and do incalculable injury to the profession of the ministry and to the Christian religion."[18]

Howard's remarks about the chaplaincy system, coupled with numerous reports of chaplain malfeasance, inspired the New York

---

[17] James O. Henry, "History of the United States Christian Commission" (Ph.D. dissertation, University of Maryland, College Park, 1959), 190; James I. Robertson, Jr., ed., *The Civil War Letters of General Robert McAllister* (New Brunswick, N.J.: Rutgers University Press, 1965), 286; Armstrong, *A Friend to God's Poor*, 62; *Gettysburg* [Pa.] *Adams Sentinel*, September 11, 1861.

[18] Armstrong, *A Friend to God's Poor*, 62.

branch of the Christian Commission to propose a scheme for securing the voluntary enlistment of a minister for each brigade of the
army. Each volunteer was to serve without compensation for two or
three months, and the Christian Commission was to defray the ex-
penses associated with the minister's service. Even though the proposal was intended to supplement rather than to replace the work
of chaplains, many of the chaplains viewed the idea as an affront.
Predictably, conscientious chaplains resented the suggestion that
they were derelict in the performance of their duties. They attacked
the volunteer minister plan as a usurpation of a chaplain's prerogatives and faulted Howard's assessment for its sweeping nature and
lack of judgment. A chaplain in the Army of the Potomac intimated
that the Christian Commission's objective was to thrust itself into a
position of prominence by denigrating the work of others.[19]

As relations between chaplains and the Christian Commission
soured, Howard thought it best to clarify his views about the chaplaincy system. In a speech delivered at the second anniversary of
the Christian Commission, in January 1864, he seemed to echo the
sentiments of many chaplains who blamed inadequate numbers
rather than incompetence for the system's difficulties:

> I know of many chaplains, very many, who are working constantly for
> the cause of Christ. I know that the chaplain in a regiment is the man
> whom all the men look up to; and if he is a good man they love him
> and trust him. They give him their money; they go to him in trouble;
> they go with their confidence, and he is *the* man of the regiment. But
> all I have to say is that I mourn, often, that in my command there are
> so few chaplains at all; and where there are no chaplains, there the
> Christian Commission can work effectively. Instead of there being a
> rivalry between the Christian Commission and the chaplaincy, those
> who are really the servants of the Lord work together as brethren
> should, arm in arm, hand in hand, heart in heart. They work together,
> they pray together, they preach together, they labor together in every
> way for the good of the soldier and for the cause of their common
> Master.[20]

Howard's call for cooperation between chaplains and the Christian
Commission reiterated what had been the organization's intent from

---

[19] Henry, "History of the United States Christian Commission," 190–95.

[20] *Major-General Howard's Address at the Second Anniversary of the U. S. Christian Commission* (Philadelphia: Caxton Press of C. Sherman, Son & Co., 1864),
13–14.

its inception, that those working under the auspices of the commission were to assist chaplains in the performance of their duties and to avoid criticizing or otherwise undermining their work. In this spirit, the commission abandoned its volunteer minister proposal and redoubled its efforts to work amicably and efficiently with chaplains. The commission continued to provide chapel tents and religious reading material to chaplains. Delegates further aided them by conducting religious services, visiting the sick and wounded, and performing other needed tasks. Edward P. Smith, a delegate who went on to become the commission's field secretary, regarded the cultivation of good relations with chaplains as a prerequisite to accomplishing his mission. His exertions bore fruit, and in May 1863, a group of chaplains from the Army of the Cumberland met with Smith in Murfreesboro, Tennessee, and passed the following resolution: "*Resolved*, that we hail with gratitude to God, the advent of the Delegates of the U. S. Christian Commission among us; that they have our thanks for the supply of religious reading furnished us; and that we assure them that we shall be happy to cooperate with them in sowing the good seed in this vast field of labor."[21]

The best-remembered function of the Christian Commission was its distribution of religious reading material to the troops, and with good reason. In its circular of January 13, 1862, the Commission's executive committee listed as its first goal "furnishing to them [soldiers] religious tracts, periodicals and books." The commission made this objective a priority, as it was one of the most efficient methods by which a large number of soldiers could be exposed to the Christian message.[22]

The Christian Commission worked closely with the American Bible Society and the American Tract Society to distribute Christian literature to Union soldiers. Organized in 1816 and 1823, respectively, the Bible and Tract Societies sought to promote Christian knowledge and win souls to Christ by disseminating religious reading material throughout the United States. In its first four years of work, the American Bible Society distributed nearly 100,000 Bibles; by the early 1820s, the American Tract Society had printed 777,000 tracts and was publishing a bimonthly magazine, a Christian almanac, and

---

[21] Armstrong, *A Friend to God's Poor*, 62–63.
[22] USCC, *Documents of the Christian Commission: 1862*, 27.

a series of children's books. After the outbreak of the Civil War, the Bible and Tract Societies organized massive fundraising drives and, through coordinated efforts with the Christian Commission, were able to put thousands of Bibles, tracts, and edifying books into the hands of northern soldiers.[23]

In the years 1862 and 1863, the American Bible Society donated to the Christian Commission Bibles worth $10,256 and $45,071.50, respectively. In 1864, Bible Society donations to the commission reached $72,114.83 in value; its 1865 donations were worth $52,382.66. Although it is difficult to determine the value of the tracts donated to the Christian Commission by the American Tract Society, it is safe to say that the group gave the commission untold millions of pages of tracts.[24]

The generous donations made by the Bible and Tract Societies enabled the Christian Commission to place the Word of God or some form of Christian literature into the hands of thousands of northern soldiers. From 1862 to 1865, the commission distributed 1,466,748 Bibles, Testaments, and portions of Scripture; 1,370,953 hymn and psalm books; 18,126,002 religious weekly and monthly newspapers; 39,104,243 pages of tracts; and 296,816 bound library books. Even this massive effort, though, did not put an end to the constant dearth of reading material that beset the Union forces. The Reverend J. M. Barnett, a commission delegate who was busy supplying soldiers in Hillside, Pennsylvania, with warm underclothing, reading materials, and words of ministry on January 15, 1863, soon discovered the severity of the reading matter shortage:

> In one street of the camp, I was asked by a soldier for a paper, and stopped to give it to him, when, in a moment, a hundred others gathered around, stretching out their hands and eagerly saying, "Give me a paper!" "Give me one!" "Give me one, too!" My stock was quickly exhausted, and even after I told them that they were all gone, they still followed, beseeching me for something to read.[25]

Although the Christian Commission distributed more religious reading material than secular literature, the commission realized early the evangelistic potential of winning the confidence and friend-

[23] Ahlstrom, *A Religious History*, 424–25, 680.
[24] USCC, *Fourth Annual Report*, Exhibit G.
[25] Ibid., Exhibit F; USCC, *First Annual Report* (Philadelphia: n. p., 1863), 51–52.

ship of fighting men by giving them popular books to read. In addition, many secular works touched upon topics of morality and therefore paved the way for religious ministry. Like many of the commission's activities, establishing loan libraries composed largely of secular books exhibited a potential for saving more souls. Hence, the commission's executive committee announced on January 13, 1862, that a primary goal of the organization would be "furnishing, as far as possible, profitable reading, other than religious, and, wherever there is a permanent military post . . . establishing a general library of such works."[26]

Chaplain Joseph Conable Thomas of the 88th Regiment Illinois Volunteer Infantry was the driving force behind the establishment of the Christian Commission's loan library system. Shortly after joining his regiment in September 1862, Thomas was disturbed to find his fellow soldiers paying excessive sums for literature of an inferior quality. Determined to supplant this "trash" with better reading material, Thomas set out to secure quality periodicals for his men at reasonable costs. His successful efforts on behalf of his regiment gained the notice of General George H. Thomas, who in September 1863 appointed the chaplain general reading agent for the Army of the Cumberland. In this capacity, Chaplain Thomas convinced the publishers of several prominent periodicals, including *Atlantic Monthly*, *Harper's Magazine*, and *The New York Times*, to supply their wares at half their regular subscription price. The Christian Commission was initially reluctant to support Thomas's efforts, primarily because they involved collecting money from soldiers, but it eventually endorsed the plan after generals Thomas, Grant, and Howard urged it to do so.[27]

The Christian Commission warmed to Chaplain Thomas's methods, and in January 1864, it secured a commitment from numerous publishers to supply books to the commission at half their retail price. Thomas, who went on to become the commission's general library agent, sifted through about one hundred publisher catalogs to compile a list of books that would be suitable for the nascent loan library system. In selecting books, Thomas was guided by the following prin-

---

[26] USCC, *Documents of the Christian Commission: 1862*, 28.

[27] Carrol H. Quenzel, "Books for the Boys in Blue," *Journal of the Illinois State Historical Society* 44 (autumn 1951): 221–22.

ciples: "None but the best works; none but the best, most suitable and cheapest editions; secular works as well as religious; utility rather than variety." Public donations of books supplemented the works obtained from publishing houses. Each library typically consisted of 125 volumes, among them works of history, biography, science, fiction, and religion. The library of Thomas's 88th Regiment included Washington Irving's biography of George Washington, George Bancroft's *History of the United States*, and Sir Walter Scott's *Ivanhoe*. Libraries were loaned to hospitals, camps, and vessels on the condition that a surgeon, chaplain, or other authority figure would act as a librarian who would take responsibility for the collection and report back to the commission on its use. By 1865, the number of loan libraries in Union facilities had increased to approximately four hundred, of which twenty-five were on large war vessels, fifty at forts and military posts, and the rest in regiments and hospitals.[28]

The loan library system was endorsed by a number of prominent military figures including the commander-in-chief of the Union forces. On December 21, 1864, William Ballantyne, chairman of the Christian Commission's Washington branch, wrote to Abraham Lincoln, seeking the sanction of the president's name for giving "a Library of new & choice books as a Holiday Present to every Gunboat in the Navy & to every Brigade in the Army; for this purpose it [the Christian Commission] makes its appeal to the public for 300,000 volumes." Replying on December 30 to Ballantyne's request, Lincoln stated that the proposal promised "much usefulness" and had his "hearty approval." General Grant saw in the loan libraries "nothing . . . to oppose, but on the other hand everything to commend," and General Burnside took "great pleasure" in supporting the system.[29]

The evangelistic value of the Christian Commission's loan libraries can hardly be overstated. Chaplain W. Allington of Hospital 14 in Nashville, Tennessee, observed in November 1864 that "the library has begotten content, lessened rambling through the city, created devotional feeling, increased the number of our religious services, and attendance thereon; in short, renders hospital life, to all con-

---

[28] Ibid., 224–29; Moss, *Annals*, 716–24; USCC, *Fourth Annual Report*, 84–85.

[29] William Ballantyne to Abraham Lincoln, December 21, 1864; Abraham Lincoln to William Ballantyne, December 30, 1864, Abraham Lincoln Papers, Library of Congress microfilm edition (Washington, D. C.: Library of Congress, 1959), reel 89, series 1, items 39444–5; Quenzel, "Books for the Boys in Blue," 226.

cerned, more happy, and duty more pleasant." Chaplain B. L. Brisbane of the 2nd Wisconsin Cavalry stationed in Alexandria, Louisiana, reported in June 1865 that his library "is doing immense good. It is the best thing the Christian Commission has done for the service. . . . It has a deep and abiding influence—intellectually, morally, and spiritually. Each regiment should have a good and faithful chaplain, a good library, a chapel tent, and a horse and light, well-made wagon. The chaplain could do more good with these than by preaching." In October of the same year, Brisbane declared proudly, "a number of souls lately converted. . . . I ascribe much to the library." Similarly, Chaplain J. S. Rand of Library 99 in Hempstead, Texas, indicated in November 1865 that "the soldiers have employed much of their time in reading, instead of card-playing. We have a chapel tent, in which we keep the library, and have prayer-meetings every evening. We have some clear conversions." The commission was keenly aware that its loan libraries possessed a significance that extended far beyond providing entertainment for northern soldiers.[30]

Bibles and other reading material weren't the only items that the Christian Commission distributed to Union soldiers. Out of concern for the physical needs of these men as well as a desire to save their souls, the commission undertook a massive effort to distribute warm underwear, socks, slippers, sheets, pillows, writing materials, and fresh food to the troops. The commission's annual report for 1863 solicited from the public foods ranging from oatmeal and farina to pickles, jams, and dried fruits. The commission also urged the public to send "Good brandy, Madeira wine, Port wine, [and] Cordials. Domestic wines are excellent in winter, apt to spoil in summer."[31]

The solicitation and distribution of alcoholic beverages was a strange practice for a number of Christian Commission delegates, many of whom were temperance advocates. The exigencies of war, however, led them to administer whiskey, brandy, and wine as "stimulants" and in some cases to employ blackberry cordials as a treatment for diarrhea. They pointed to Proverbs 31:6 as a justification for their actions: "Give strong drink unto him that is ready to perish." Well aware of the tenuous position that he occupied, one delegate was happy to report that "in no case has any complaint been whispered that any of the cordials . . . go down the wrong throats."[32]

---

[30] USCC, *Fourth Annual Report*, 85–88.

[31] USCC, *Second Annual Report* (Philadelphia: n.p., 1864), inside back cover.

[32] Armstrong, *A Friend to God's Poor*, 51.

From 1862 to 1865, benevolent associations and the public donated $2,839,445.17 worth of stores to the Christian Commission's
central and branch offices. While distributing these gifts of food,
clothing, writing materials, and miscellaneous articles, commission
delegates continually sought avenues by which they could minister to
the spiritual needs of the troops. Commission workers who handed
out much-desired items recognized that their Christian message became more effective; grateful soldiers were willing to listen to the
kind words of their benefactors. B. F. Bradbury of Bangor, Maine,
visited the hospitals of Falmouth, Virginia, shortly after the battle of
Fredericksburg, and recalled, "my chief work was in visiting various
regiments, and bestowing nice articles of diet, clothing, &c., for the
sick in the hospitals; and in cases where there was no faithful chaplain, we almost always read the Scriptures, sang and prayed, and said
a few words to them. . . . In this labor, we were always kindly received, and frequently expressions of deep gratitude were heard from
the suffering ones." Bradbury marveled at "how interested they are
when you speak to them of Jesus, how ready, in many cases, they are
to be led to the Savior."[33]

Hospitals provided the Christian Commission with a golden opportunity to reap a bountiful harvest of souls. Throughout the war, commission delegates sought to bring comfort to the wounded and dying
while at the same time preparing them for the next life. Time was of
the essence; everywhere soldiers were passing on without the assurance of salvation. J. N. McJilton, secretary of the commission's Maryland branch, explained the purposes of the organization's hospital
work in a January 1864 letter to commission chairman Stuart. "In the
hospitals near the battle-fields," McJilton wrote, "the delegates of the
Commission engaged most earnestly in their work. While employed
in the relief of the physical suffering of their charge, they were fully
mindful of the necessities of the soul. They read the Scriptures and
other religious books to the men, and conversed and prayed with
them, encouraging them in every possible way to consider their
safety, not only as it regarded the comforts of the present, but the
realities of the future world."[34]

The Reverend Edward Payson Goodwin, a commission delegate

---

[33] USCC, *Fourth Annual Report*, Exhibit G; USCC, *First Annual Report*, 36–37.
[34] USCC, *Second Annual Report*, 157.

from Columbus, Ohio, also echoed the evangelistic importance of hospital work. Writing to his wife on June 17, 1865, from the hospitals of City Point, Virginia (located outside Petersburg), Goodwin requested, "pray much for me that this new Endeavor may have blessed results.—That I may go in th[e] fulness [sic] of God's blessing, have needful strength & health, & prove an Efficient workman in th[e] vineyard of th[e] Master."[35]

Many delegates often coordinated their ministry with the work of surgeons while keeping in mind the commission's admonition to respect the authority of army medical personnel. In December 1862, a corps of commission delegates was sent under the authority of Surgeon General William A. Hammond to Hammond General Hospital at Point Lookout, Maryland. G. L. Shearer, head of the delegation, reported that the hospital contained approximately two thousand patients, eleven hundred having arrived recently as a result of the clash at Fredericksburg. The surgeon in charge received the delegation cordially, provided them with quarters and food, and appointed them "acting medical cadets" to facilitate their work among the patients. The delegates then dressed wounds, engaged the men in conversation, wrote letters to loved ones on behalf of the soldiers, and generally acted to comfort the hospital inmates.[36]

The delegation did not limit its efforts to providing temporal aid to the sick and wounded soldiers. The workers went on to distribute a large quantity of Bibles, tracts, and other religious reading material to the men in an attempt to reach them with the Christian message. The delegates also held evening meetings in the chapel. Describing the delegation's worship services, Shearer wrote: "A passage of Scripture was explained; songs of praise and fervent prayers ascended; the soldiers frequently leading in prayer, to the edification of the assembly. The services were solemn and impressive; men renewed their vows to God; thoughtless souls were aroused, some were conversed with, who were seeking the Lord with tears, and the faith of many was strengthened. . . . Numbers were asking the way of salvation."[37]

Soldiers who were sick or wounded had special needs that could

---

[35] Edward Payson Goodwin to Mrs. Edward Payson Goodwin, June 17, 1865, Edward Payson Goodwin Papers, Small Collection 571, Illinois State Historical Library, Springfield.

[36] USCC, *First Annual Report*, 53.

[37] Ibid., 54.

not be met through the regular channels of army provision. Their diet, for example, had to be altered in order to supply them with necessary nutrients. Stale hardtack, raw beans, and tainted meat were hardly suitable for men who were recovering from life-threatening maladies. To meet this need, the Christian Commission sanctioned the creation of "special-diet kitchens" that would prepare food for soldiers who could not subsist on regular army rations. Annie Wittenmyer, a commission agent from Iowa, was placed in charge of the effort to supply the needs of these patients.[38]

Wittenmyer's kitchen work was inspired in part by a chance encounter with one of her brothers in a Missouri hospital on a cold January morning. The sixteen-year-old boy, afflicted with typhoid fever and acute dysentery, had rejected the unappetizing breakfast that had been offered to him. "On a dingy-looking wooden tray" she remembered, "was a tin cup full of black, strong coffee; beside it was a leaden-looking tin platter, on which was a piece of fried fat bacon, swimming in its own grease, and a slice of bread." She went on to ask, "could anything be more disgusting and injurious to fever-stricken and wounded patients?" This and other shocking experiences led her to conclude that "thousands of our brave men have died of debility, who, if nourished with suitable food, at the proper time, might now have been in the front ranks of our army."[39]

Despite separate management, Wittenmyer's kitchens were a part of the hospitals they served and thus subject to control by military authorities. Soldiers in need of a special diet were allowed to select food items from a list prescribed by a ward surgeon. Meals were then prepared in an adjoining kitchen, with many of the supplies furnished by the Christian Commission. Female kitchen managers, whom Wittenmyer selected with an eye toward culture, social standing, and Christian character, supervised all facets of food preparation.[40]

According to Wittenmyer, she encountered no opposition to her efforts. The president, secretary of war, and surgeon general endorsed her activities, as did General Grant. At her request, Grant and two staff members visited kitchens near City Point, Virginia, to see firsthand the work being done on behalf of the sick and wounded.

---

[38] USCC, *Third Annual Report* (Philadelphia: n.p., 1865), 24, 41–46.

[39] Ibid., 41, 43, 46; Annie Wittenmyer, *Under the Guns: A Woman's Reminiscences of the Civil War* (Boston: E. B. Stillings & Co., 1895), 72–73.

[40] Wittenmyer, *Under the Guns*, 217–18, 260–63.

Dressed in a slouch hat and plain clothing to avoid recognition by the troops, Grant observed the distribution of a meal and even toured some of the wards to watch the soldiers eat. Impressed by what he saw, Grant later remarked, "Those men live better than I do." While the general was passing through one of the wards, an inmate mistook him for a Christian Commission delegate. "Say, Christian," the patient exclaimed, "won't you bring me a pair of socks?" "I'll see that you get a pair," Grant replied. The general saw to it that the man got his socks.[41]

Wittenmyer established over one hundred "special-diet kitchens" during the war; many remained in operation during the summer of 1865 as troops were mustered out of the service. The facilities prepared untold quantities of milk, chicken soup, beefsteak, fish, omelets, and potatoes for the consumption of sick and wounded men who might have perished on standard army provisions. Reflecting upon the effectiveness of the kitchens, Wittenmyer observed that by 1864, "hundreds of precious lives have been saved, and very many souls have been brought to the knowledge of Christ through this instrumentality." Like Christian Commission delegates who performed other tasks, kitchen workers were concerned preeminently with the spiritual dimension of their work.[42]

Burying the dead afforded Christian Commission delegates yet another opportunity to spread the Christian message. The Reverend B. B. Hotchkin of Pennsylvania recounted a sober incident after the December 1862 battle at Fredericksburg: "I saw a party of soldiers going out to bury the dead. I followed. They were about to put nine bodies, wrapped in their blankets, into a trench, and cover them up. I said, 'Boys, you ought not to bury these men like dogs. No, no! Shall we have services?' 'Yes.' The men gathered up, and we had services, and gave them a Christian burial." Hotchkin's graveside ministry undoubtedly gave the men who were present an opportunity to reflect on their own mortality and spiritual condition, thereby fostering an environment in which future evangelism might enjoy a greater chance of success. Similarly, the Reverend G. J. Mingins understood that the singular experiences of war often made men more receptive to spiritual overtures:

---

[41] Ibid., 213–14, 263–64.

[42] Ibid., 264–67; Armstrong, *A Friend to God's Poor*, 112; USCC, *Third Annual Report*, 44–46.

One day we were burying some poor fellows who had fallen in the battle of Antietam, and a soldier was helping us. He told us how he had passed through the fierce conflict unharmed; "for which," said he, "I thank God." "Thank the rebels for being such bad marksmen," said a man near us. The soldier, looking him in the face, said: "I ain't no Christian, God knows. After what we passed through I ought to be a better man. You may think as you like; I think God saved me, not the rebels' bad shooting."

Reflecting on the exchange, Mingins proclaimed, "here was ground to work upon."[43]

The Christian Commission also promised education as a means to further its evangelistic aims. Chaplain Little of a West Virginia regiment operating in the Shenandoah Valley during the opening months of 1865 used materials obtained from the commission to construct a chapel that doubled as a schoolhouse. In the evenings the soldiers gathered there for preaching and prayer meetings, and during the day the chapel became a schoolroom. According to Edward P. Smith, who by 1865 had become the commission's field secretary, "forms and rude desks were arranged around the walls, and then from morning till night, from one to two hundred 'boys in blue' sat with their books, and slates, and pens, and spelt, and read, and wrote under the direction of their Professor and his ample corps of assistants." Chaplain Little parlayed the popularity of his basic lessons into an opportunity for evangelism; when the "school day" ended, preaching and prayer soon followed.[44]

Instruction and conversion were not restricted to white soldiers. In the Army of the James, the large number of black troops eager to learn encouraged the general in command to propose building schoolhouse facilities for these soldiers if the Christian Commission agreed to provide the books and instructors. Sensing another opportunity to win souls, the commission accepted the general's proposal and furnished the requisite resources. "The school houses," declared the commission's annual report for 1864, "serve the double purpose of schools and chapels, and added benefits thus accrue to the men."[45]

The commission stepped up its program to educate black troops

---

[43] USCC, *First Annual Report*, 26, 62.

[44] USCC, *Fourth Annual Report*, 91.

[45] USCC, *Third Annual Report*, 31.

as the war drew to a close. In February 1865, it sent twenty teachers in a single day to serve in black army units. Its work in the XXV Corps in Virginia was extensive; coordinating its efforts with chaplains, the commission promoted educational activities in each regiment of the corps. The government supplied lumber for school buildings; the commission furnished instructors, books, and supplies; and the prospective students provided the labor. "Negroes in blue could be seen every where, carrying huge logs upon their shoulders for the schoolhouse, till, as if by magic, thirty neat and commodious edifices attested the eagerness of the colored men to learn to read and write." The commission also assisted educational programs targeted toward "contrabands" (slaves who had come into Union lines), but its role diminished as armies were disbanded and other groups such as the American Missionary Association became more active in the field.[46]

Throughout its brief history, the Christian Commission continually sought and usually received the approbation of military and governmental figures as well as the men it served. As early as December 11, 1861, the commission's chairman wrote to Abraham Lincoln asking for the president's blessing upon the group's intent "to take active measures to promote the spiritual and temporal welfare of the soldiers in the army, and the sailors and marines in the navy, in cooperation with chaplains and others." Lincoln penned a favorable reply the next day: "Your christian and benevolent undertaking for the benefit of the soldiers, is too obviously proper, and praise-worthy, to admit any difference of opinion. I sincerely hope your plan may be as successful in execution, as it is just and generous in conception." Lincoln reiterated his support for the commission's goals and actions in a February 22, 1863, letter to Alexander Reed, the organization's general superintendent. Respectfully declining an invitation to attend a commission meeting in Washington, Lincoln asserted:

> Whatever shall be sincerely, and in God's name, devised for the good of the soldier and seaman, in their hard spheres of duty, can scarcely fail to be blest. And, whatever shall tend to turn our thoughts from the unreasoning, and uncharitable passions, prejudices, and jealousies incident to a great national trouble, such as ours, and to fix them upon the vast and long-enduring consequences, for weal, or for woe, which are to result from the struggle; and especially, to strengthen our reli-

---

[46] Armstrong, *A Friend to God's Poor*, 110–12.

ance on the Supreme Being, for the final triumph of the right, can not but be well for us all.[47]

Other significant figures in the government and armed forces also responded favorably to the aims of the Christian Commission. In a December 13, 1861, letter to commission chairman Stuart, Secretary of War Simon Cameron wrote, "This Department is deeply interested in the 'spiritual good of the soldiers in our Army,' as well as in 'their intellectual improvement and social and physical comfort,' and will cheerfully give its aid to the benevolent and patriotic of the land who desire to improve the condition of our troops." Likewise, General George B. McClellan sent Stuart a letter stating that plans to provide for the pressing needs of men in the ranks "meet my cordial approval, and will, if carried out in the proper spirit, prove of great value."[48]

Despite ringing endorsements from Lincoln, Cameron, and McClellan, the Christian Commission initially met a cool public reception. Many benevolent groups such as the Tract and Bible Societies were clamoring for support at the beginning of the war, as was the well-known United States Sanitary Commission. This atmosphere led the public to view aid requests made by philanthropic newcomers such as the Christian Commission with considerable wariness. Perceiving the public mood, commission secretary Archibald M. Morrison reported in a July 12, 1862, letter to Stuart that "there is a great confusion in the public mind, here in New York, among the numerous agencies busied in similar operations, and all making their appeal and claim to the public in behalf of the army. Each party canvasses the ground on its own behalf, and men are disinclined to take up any more."[49]

An attorney from Rochester, New York, eventually relented to his wife's repeated attempts to solicit contributions from him for the work of benevolent organizations such as the Christian Commission. Initially considering his donation a waste of money, he changed his mind after a stint in the army:

---

[47] Moss, *Annals*, 108n–9n; Roy P. Basler, ed., *The Collected Works of Abraham Lincoln* (New Brunswick, N. J.: Rutgers University Press, 1953), 6: 114–15.

[48] United States War Department, *War of the Rebellion: A Compilation of the Official Records of the Union and Confederate Armies*, 70 vols. in 128 (Washington, D.C.: Government Printing Office, 1880–1901), series 3, vol. 1, pp. 742–43; USCC, *Documents of the Christian Commission: 1862*, 5.

[49] Moss, *Annals*, 117.

While at home my wife was constantly asking me for one, two or five dollars for soldiers' aid societies, of which she was a member. I never caught her in a foolish act before; but I believed that this was such, and though I gave her money, I laughed a good deal over it with my partner (whose wife was also engaged in the work with mine), and entered the sums in my accounts as "To Foolishness, Dr., $5." I fell in battle. The first man who came to my aid was a member of the Christian Commission. The next aid I received was from a Commission man. I began to look at this thing and to think. To-day I was hungry, and along with their Bibles and tracts they brought me food. O, sir, the Christian Commission is doing *a great work*. I have already written to my partner to sign himself, not *five* dollars, but *twenty* dollars, for what we once laughed at as our "wives" foolishness![50]

The public was not alone in its initial coolness toward the Christian Commission. Early in the war, friction existed between the commission and a number of governmental and medical officers. Because the commission was slow to complete its organizing process, it wasted valuable time in establishing its legitimacy in the eyes of the government. As a result, and because many other groups and individuals were clamoring for governmental favors, Secretary of War Edwin M. Stanton and General Henry Halleck originally placed restrictions on the commission's activities. Delegates were routinely denied passage through military lines and thus were prevented from performing their duties. In addition, many surgeons were initially annoyed by the presence of commission workers among their patients. Commission agents, the medical men griped, had no professional training or medical experience; consequently, they had no business rambling about the army's hospitals.[51]

Christian Commission efforts in the field in late 1862 and early 1863 brought the organization the legitimacy it sought. After carrying out a number of effective benevolent activities after the battles of Second Bull Run, Antietam, Fredericksburg, and Murfreesboro, the commission earned newfound respect from the government, the military, and the public. Fundraising became more productive, surgeons became less bellicose, and the authorities lifted the restrictions they had placed on the commission's work.[52]

---

[50] Records of the United States Christian Commission, Central Office, Letters Sent, 1862–1866, Record Group 94, National Archives, Washington, D. C.

[51] Moss, *Annals*, 124–25, 136–39.

[52] Ibid., 124–26.

Army surgeons were among the first to recognize the value of the Christian Commission's service. Commission delegates typically were practical, and their gifts of clothing, food, reading material, and encouraging words helped to alleviate the widespread suffering among sick and wounded soldiers. Surgeons soon realized that the commission's ministry had medicinal value. In a letter to commission chairman Stuart dated November 11, 1863, the Reverend S. Hopkins Emery of Quincy, Illinois, wrote about the religious services he performed for the soldiers in Quincy hospitals. "The physicians in charge," Emery declared, "testify that it has been an advantage to the men in every particular. Prayer, or some sweet hymn of praise, is oftentimes better than medicine."[53]

Military leaders also could not ignore the commission's good works. After meeting with the Reverend E. S. Janes of the commission's executive committee, Secretary of War Stanton issued a memorandum on January 24, 1863, that stated, "Bishop Janes is authorized to state that he has received assurance from the Secretary of War, that every facility consistent with the exigencies of the service will be afforded to the Christian Commission, for the performance of their religious and benevolent purposes in the armies of the United States, and in the forts, garrisons, and camps, and military posts." The commission was free to ply its trade.[54]

Because Christian Commission delegates often worked closely with army medical personnel, commission workers soon became familiar with the practices of the United States Sanitary Commission. The Sanitary Commission was formed in the summer of 1861 as a service organization intended to complement the army's medical bureau. Henry W. Bellows, the Unitarian minister of New York's All Souls Church, was the primary force behind the agency's founding, and he led the group throughout the war. Frederick Law Olmsted, a landscape architect, was appointed general secretary of the organization, and George Templeton Strong, a New York lawyer, was selected as its treasurer. From its inception, the Sanitary Commission concerned itself with problems in the Union army, ranging from sanitation and drainage to faulty diet and preventive medicine.[55]

---

[53] Ibid., 125–26.

[54] Ibid., 131.

[55] Ahlstrom, A Religious History, 679; William Quentin Maxwell, Lincoln's Fifth Wheel: A Political History of the United States Sanitary Commission (New York: Longmans, Green & Co., 1956), 10.

Although the goals of the Christian and Sanitary Commissions overlapped frequently and their agents in the field often coordinated relief work, the two groups routinely competed with each other for resources and quarreled incessantly over ideology and methods for solving problems. The two organizations agreed to a limited degree of cooperation in December 1862, but the consensus quickly broke down. Issues of faith often dominated the relationship between the two agencies: the Sanitary Commission had little use for what it regarded as the excessive and misplaced religious fervor of the Christian Commission, and the Christian Commission mistrusted the strong secular undercurrent in the Sanitary Commission. Members of the Christian Commission were troubled by Bellows's refusal to believe in the divinity of Christ. The commissions also differed sharply in the tactics they employed to serve needy soldiers. Christian Commission delegates regarded their work as a spiritual enterprise that required personal contact with the troops and strove, in the words of the group's second annual report, to "enhance the value of both gifts and services by kind words to the soldiers as *a man*, not a machine." The Sanitary Commission insisted that relief work could be performed best by paid professionals who maintained order by distributing stores and service through proper military channels. Consequently, Sanitary Commissioners derided the Christian Commission's "sentimentality" and purported lack of attention to rules and organization. The Sanitary Commission's use of paid workers stood in sharp contrast to the Christian Commission's reliance on volunteer delegates. Walt Whitman, who became a Christian Commission delegate in January 1863, expressed his distaste for Sanitary Commission workers in a letter to his mother:

> As to the Sanitary Commissions & the like, I am sick of them all, & would not accept any of their berths—you ought to see the way the men as they lie helpless in bed turn away their faces from the sight of these Agents, Chaplains &c. (*hirelings* as Elias Hicks would call them—they seem to me always a set of foxes & wolves)—they get well paid, & are always incompetent & disagreeable—As I told you before the only good fellows I have met are the Christian Commissioners— they go everywhere & receive no pay.[56]

---

[56] Maxwell, *Lincoln's Fifth Wheel*, 192–93; George M. Fredrickson, *The Inner Civil War: Northern Intellectuals and the Crisis of the Union* (New York: Harper & Row, Publishers, 1965), 105–8; USCC, *Second Annual Report*, 18; Armstrong, *A Friend to God's Poor*, 49, 73.

George Templeton Strong, an Episcopalian who served as the Sanitary Commission's treasurer, did not share Whitman's views about the two organizations. In an April 10, 1863, diary entry, Strong recounted a meeting that he and others from the Sanitary Commission had with a Christian Commission delegation. Strong complained about the Christian Commission's lack of cooperation with his organization in a matter concerning supplies. The diarist asserted:

> There is an undercurrent of cant, unreality, or something else, I do not know what, in all their talk, that repels and offends me. This association, calling itself a "commission" when it is no more a commission than it is a corporation, or a hose company, or a chess-club, or a quadratic equation, and thus setting out under false colors and with a lie on its forehead, seems to me one of the many forms in which the shallowness, fussiness, and humbug of our popular religionism are constantly embodying themselves.[57]

Strong was not the only Civil War figure to become annoyed by the activities of the Christian Commission. In April 1864, while General William T. Sherman was in the midst of military operations in eastern Tennessee, Christian Commission delegates asked to transport Bibles and religious tracts via the railroads. "Rations and ammunition are much better," the general was said to have retorted. On another occasion, Sherman attacked an 1864 congressional act that authorized northern governors to recruit southern blacks to fill military enrollment quotas. Criticizing the law in a July 14, 1864, letter to General Halleck, Sherman opined, "before regulations are made for the States to send recruiting officers into the rebel States, I must express my opinion that it is the height of folly. I cannot permit it here and I will not have a set of fellows hanging around on any such pretenses. We have no means to transport and feed them. The Sanitary and Christian Commissions are enough to eradicate all traces of Christianity out of our minds much less a set of unscrupulous State agents in search of recruits."[58]

Despite Sherman's peremptory comments and actions, he was not entirely unsympathetic to the Christian Commission's agenda. In the

---

[57] Allan Nevins and Milton Halsey Thomas, eds., *The Diary of George Templeton Strong* (New York: Macmillan, 1952), 3: 310–11.

[58] Lloyd Lewis, *Sherman: Fighting Prophet* (New York: Harcourt, Brace and Company, 1932), 352, 392.

years following the war, General Howard enjoyed telling a story in which commission worker Edward P. Smith inadvertently raised Sherman's ire. On a Sunday morning in May 1864, Sherman sat in a cottage in Kingston, Tennessee, plotting his next move against General Joseph E. Johnston, his Confederate counterpart. Sherman's thoughts were interrupted suddenly by the ringing of a church bell. Thinking that the disturbance was the work of whimsical soldiers, the general ordered a patrol to find and arrest the perpetrators. The detachment traced the sound to a Baptist church where Smith had been preparing for a service. Smith had rung the bell to notify others of the approaching assembly and, while descending from the belfry, experienced some difficulties. His pants became snagged on a nail, and one leg of his garment ripped to his waist. Shortly thereafter Sherman's soldiers arrived on the scene, and a corporal ordered Smith to "fall in." Bewildered, Smith asked why he was being detained.

"To take you over there to General Sherman's headquarters," replied the corporal.

"Can't go in this plight," pleaded Smith. "Take me where I can fix up."

"Them's not the orders," the corporal barked. "Fall in."

Smith was received at Sherman's headquarters by his chief of staff, General John M. Corse. Corse asked Smith why he had been ringing the church bell. Smith replied that he had done so to announce Sunday services at the church. Corse relayed the information to Sherman, who, glancing at the hapless clergyman, appeared genuinely surprised by the explanation.

"Sunday, Sunday!" exclaimed Sherman. "Didn't know it was Sunday; let him go."[59]

Shortly after the war, when commission chairman Stuart asked Sherman for his assessment of the group's efforts, the general admitted, "at times I may have displayed an impatience when the agents manifested an excess of zeal in pushing forward their persons and services when we had no means to make use of their charities." He added that with the opportunity to "look back on the past with com-

---

[59] Armstrong, *A Friend to God's Poor*, 96–97; Oliver Otis Howard, *Autobiography of Oliver Otis Howard, Major General United States Army* (New York: Baker & Taylor, 1907), 1: 535–36.

posure," he was pleased to share his belief that the commission's program was "noble in its conception, and applied with as much zeal, kindness, and discretion as the times permitted."[60]

Although many rank and file soldiers appreciated the efforts of groups like the Christian Commission, some did not. One disaffected soldier lamented "the vast amount of mistaken or misguided philanthropy that was expended upon the army by good Christian men and women, who, with the best of motives urging them forward no doubt, often labored under the delusion that the army was composed entirely of men thoroughly bad, and governed their actions accordingly." Another recalled that "tracts upon the wickedness of dancing, attending theatres, sleeping in church, extravagance in dress, and similar matters, were extensively circulated among the troops," and he opined that "it was evident that the dealers had shrewdly cleared their shelves of the unsalable rubbish which had been accumulating for years." Resourceful troops often found novel uses for the religious literature that was made available to them. One soldier who was vying for tracts that were being distributed by a chaplain demanded, "I don't want them little things: give me some of those big papers with the flag on them. I am going on picket, and want some to put my rations in." Others declared tracts "first-rate to kindle fires" and "just what I want to light my pipe with."[61]

Troops occasionally jeered commission workers. As a group of delegates carrying carpetbags passed, one soldier asked them if they had any lemons to sell. "No, my friend," one of the men responded solemnly, "we belong to the army of the Lord." "Oh, ye—es," the soldier shot back, "stragglers! stragglers!"[62]

Although noteworthy and frequently amusing, anecdotes involving indifference or hostility toward the Christian Commission are rare and do not represent the general attitude of the Union troops toward the organization. Most soldiers who came in contact with the commission appreciated both its temporal and spiritual efforts. Troops everywhere appreciated gifts of reading material, wounded soldiers

---

[60] Thompson, ed., *The Life of George H. Stuart*, 342–43.

[61] David M. Hovde, "The U. S. Christian Commission's Library and Literacy Programs for the Union Military Forces in the Civil War," *Libraries & Culture* 24 (summer 1989): 300; Henry N. Blake, *Three Years in the Army of the Potomac* (Boston: Lee and Shepard, 1865), 310.

[62] Armstrong, *A Friend to God's Poor*, 56.

welcomed palatable meals, and dying men derived comfort from hearing commission delegates reassure them with messages of salvation. The observations of Private Wilbur Fisk of the 2nd Regiment Vermont Volunteer Infantry were typical:

> This Christian Commission has become to be respected by all the boys. Even those who care but little about its benefits personally speak well of it, and think it a very good thing. The idea of an enterprise of such infinitude being carried on and supported by voluntary contributions from those who are interested in our welfare mainly because we belong to the common brotherhood of mankind, and have souls to save, as well as bodies to preserve, carried with it such a weight of argument for the sincerity and power of that christian principle which begets this spirit of benevolence, that no man attempts to gainsay or resist it.[63]

General George G. Meade suggested in a letter to commission chairman Stuart that nobody appreciated the organization's efforts more than the army's top officers. "I assure you," Meade wrote shortly after the Battle of Gettysburg, "no one looks with more favor upon the true Christian, who ministers to the spiritual wants of the dying or the physical wants of the wounded, than those who are most instrumental in the line of their duty in causing this suffering; hence you may rest satisfied that in this army your agents and assistants will receive every co-operation, and be treated with all the consideration due the important and noble work they are engaged upon."[64]

Perhaps General Grant did the best job of summing up the army's attitude toward the Christian Commission. "To the Commission," said Grant, "the army felt the same gratitude that the loyal public felt for the services rendered by the army."[65]

On February 10, 1866, in Washington, the United States Christian Commission held its final business meeting. Acknowledging that the circumstances that created the need for the organization had passed, the assembly formally closed the activities of the Commission. In doing so, the group adopted a resolution thanking God for terminating the rebellion and for opening the country to the influences of

---

[63] Emil Rosenblatt and Ruth Rosenblatt, eds., *Hard Marching Every Day: The Civil War Letters of Private Wilbur Fisk, 1861–1865* (Lawrence: University Press of Kansas, 1992), 212.

[64] USCC, *Second Annual Report*, 52.

[65] Moss, *Annals*, 126.

education and religion. Furthermore, the delegation expressed its "devout gratitude to God, for His blessing upon the officers and delegates of the Commission in their efforts to relieve the sufferings of our soldiers and seamen—and to impart to them—and especially to the sick and dying—that instruction and consolation in the religion of Jesus, which is beyond price."[66]

From 1862 to 1865, the Christian Commission's 4,859 delegates preached 58,308 sermons, held 77,744 prayer meetings, and wrote 92,321 letters for sick and wounded soldiers. In addition, they distributed untold millions of Bibles, tracts, hymn books, religious papers, and library books to troops suffering from a severe shortage of reading material. Commission delegates also buried the dead, comforted the wounded, and provided special meals for soldiers too sick or feeble to survive on standard army rations. These efforts were made possible by donations of cash, publications, services, food, and other stores worth over $6 million. The chief objective of the commission was, in the words of General Howard, "to save the soul, to conserve souls that were professors of Christ, and to snatch like brands from the burning those who have fallen into vicious practices." Through Christian charity, commission members sought to lead countless men in blue to the Lord. And for men facing imminent death on the battlefield, commission workers mused, the need for spiritual guidance was particularly urgent.[67]

---

[66] USCC, *Fourth Annual Report*, 204.

[67] Moss, *Annals*, 292–93; Maxwell, *Lincoln's Fifth Wheel*, 191; *Major-General Howard's Address at the Second Anniversary of the U. S. Christian Commission*, 12.

9

Carrying the Home Front to War: Soldiers, Race, and New England Culture during the Civil War

David A. Cecere

Sunday I attended divine service . . . conducted by some abolitionists . . . from . . . Massachusetts and there was so much talk about the confounded niggers that I came out disgusted and by the way if any one comes to you asking for contributions for the niggers, tell them you have a son in the army who needs your help more than they do. The niggers are used much better than the soldiers, and there is not a soldier who does not hate the sight of a nigger. [1]

Thus wrote Sergeant George Turner to his father in June 1862. Six months earlier, while stationed at Hilton Head, South Carolina, in 1861, Turner had described to his cousin the "sport" that white soldiers derived from the presence of African American "contrabands" in the Union camp: "They sing and dance until our sides are nearly bursting with laughter and then . . . an empty barrel is brought before the audience, [and] we then offer one of the niggers five cents, to butt the head in with his wooly pate . . . and in goes barrel head, nigger head, and half his body." Two years later, Turner again wrote to his cousin: "When you hear nay one remark that nigger soldiers will not fight, please request them to come down here and judge for themselves. The 54th Mass Infantry 'colored' is as good a fighting

The author wishes to thank his advisor, J. William Harris, for all of his invaluable assistance in bringing this article to fruition. He also wishes to thank W. Jeffrey Bolster, Lucy E. Salyer, Randall M. Miller, Paul A. Cimbala, and his graduate student colleagues at the University of New Hampshire History Department, all of whom helped to make this essay a better piece of scholarship.

[1] George M. Turner to Father, June 19, 1862, in *Yankee Correspondence: Civil War Letters between New England Soldiers and the Home Front*, ed. by Nina Silber and Mary Beth Sievens (Charlottesville: University Press of Virginia, 1996), 85.

regiment as there is." Writing from Jacksonville, Florida, to his aunt in May 1864, Turner summed up his three years of interracial encounters: "The plan of having negro soldiers is very well in some cases; but when it comes to putting the whites and blacks on the same footin, I come to the conclusion it is about time to quit soldiering, in fact I do not have any great love for a nigger." Turner's reactions to African Americans evolved in their complexity: initially, they were entertainers; then blacks became a source of resentment; later they proved themselves stalwart soldiers; and finally they were competitors. This development is representative of many Yankee Civil War soldiers' tangled experiences with blacks and matters of race.[2]

This essay will explore the cultural mechanisms responsible for the change and continuity within Yankees' racial understandings, analyzing how and why white soldiers learned, unlearned, and refused to learn about race. Numerous scholars have described white soldiers' inconsistent and often contradictory racial reactions to blacks. This study builds upon that body of scholarship by examining the untidy relationship among the cultural knowledge Yankees derived from the home front, their understandings of race, and their interracial experiences, thereby revealing the functional nature and real-life consequences of this dynamic. In order to work from a relatively coherent root culture, this study will focus on the racial attitudes of a selection of several native Yankee soldiers who represent some of the most common cultural traits of antebellum New England. A close reading of their letters home brings to light the forces that gave shape and meaning to the evolution of their racial attitudes. Aside from the

---

[2] George M. Turner to Cousin, December 15, 1861; George M. Turner to Cousin Ursula, July 28, 1863; George M. Turner to Aunt Susan, May 2, 1864, in ibid., 85, 86, 87. Bell I. Wiley noted that "it seems doubtful that one [northern] soldier in ten at any time during the conflict had any real interest in emancipation per se." James M. McPherson sought to modify Wiley's conclusions, noting that "if 'emancipation per se' meant a perception that the abolition of slavery was inseparably linked to the goal of preserving the Union, then almost three in ten Union soldiers took this position during the first year and a half of the war." This support of abolition was usually grounded in a desire to deprive traitorous southerners of their "property" and thereby cripple the South's war effort; the property themselves were rarely objects of Yankee humanitarianism. Bell Irvin Wiley, *The Life of Billy Yank: The Common Soldier of the Union* (New York: Bobbs-Merrill, 1951; reprint, Baton Rouge: Louisiana State University Press, 1978), 40–44. James M. McPherson, *What They Fought For, 1861–1865* (Baton Rouge: Louisiana State University Press, 1994), 56.

convenience of using such a geographic focus, it is useful to view this region as the epitome of northern distinctiveness during the Civil War era. Certainly, in the minds of the Civil War generation, Yankeedom most strongly reflected the social, cultural, and economic trends that set the northern states apart from the South.[3]

The most profound difference between North and South was, of course, slavery. The "peculiar institution" was the foundation of the antebellum South and, as Lincoln noted in his second inaugural address, it was "somehow" responsible for secession and its consequences. For this reason, historians of race during the Civil War usually write about the South.[4] However, there is a northern side to

---

[3] Silber and Sievens, eds., *Yankee Correspondence*, 4. Although limited attention has been given to the wartime cultural meanings and development of northerners' racial perceptions, compelling historical research has linked racial themes with the prewar North: Eric Lott, *Love and Theft: Blackface Minstrelsy and the American Working Class* (New York: Oxford University Press, 1993); David R. Roediger, *Wages of Whiteness: Race and the Making of the American Working Class* (New York: Verso Press, 1991); Shane White, *Somewhat More Independent: The End of Slavery in New York City, 1770–1810* (Athens: University of Georgia Press, 1991); W. Jeffrey Bolster, " 'To Feel like a Man': Black Seamen in the Northern States, 1800–1860," *Journal of American History* 76 (March 1990): 1173–99. Randall Jimerson and Reid Mitchell described some of the widespread racial notions and reactions evidenced among northern soldiers: Randall C. Jimerson, *The Private Civil War: Popular Thought during the Sectional Conflict* (Baton Rouge: Louisiana State University Press, 1988), chapter 4; Reid Mitchell, *Civil War Soldiers: Their Expectations and Their Experiences* (New York: Touchstone, 1988), 117–26. For the most part, however, scholars dealing with northern racism immediately before and during the war have emphasized political, legal, and economic institutions, abolitionists, and the reactions of soldiers or elite segments of white society to the Emancipation Proclamation per se: Leon F. Litwack, *North of Slavery: The Negro in the Free States, 1790–1860* (Chicago: University of Chicago Press, 1961); Phillip Shaw Paludan, *"A People's Contest": The Union and Civil War, 1861–1865* (New York: Harper & Row, 1988), chapter 9; James M. McPherson, *The Struggle for Equality: Abolitionists and the Negro in the Civil War and Reconstruction* (Princeton, N.J.: Princeton University Press, 1964); Forrest G. Wood, *Black Scare: The Racist Response to Emancipation and Reconstruction* (Berkeley: University of California Press, 1968); McPherson, *What They Fought For*; George M. Fredrickson, *The Inner Civil War: Northern Intellectuals and the Crisis of the Union* (Urbana: University of Illinois Press, 1965), chapter 8; Joseph T. Glatthaar, *The March to the Sea and Beyond: Sherman's Troops in the Savannah and Carolinas Campaigns* (New York: New York University Press, 1985), chapter 3.

[4] One of the many fine works of scholarship where Civil War racial history is crafted as a southern story is J. William Harris, *Plain Folk and Gentry in a Slave Society: White Liberty and Black Slavery in Augusta's Hinterlands* (Hanover, N. H.: Wesleyan University Press, 1985). Joel Williamson argues that "the primary roots of race relations in modern America can be found in the Southern past," and that

this story of race and war. Unlike the South, the North had no singular institution to structure race relations during the antebellum era.[5]
The typical antebellum New Englander rarely encountered an African American, let alone a slave.[6] Whereas white southerners struggled with the wartime demise of slavery, Union soldiers marching
southward groped for responses to the black faces they encountered.[7]
But they did not grope blindly. Because military indoctrination did
not break down and rebuild soldiers' mentalities, each New England
army company was a mobile, blurred reflection of its community. In
short, soldiers carried their home front culture with them into what
amounted to a foreign land, the South, where they drew upon their
portable culture to help them cope with unprecedented experiences.[8]

"[t]here is a Southern story to be told in race relations, and it can told with a relatively narrow focus on the South. . . . [or] as the Southern portion of a national
story." It is my intent to expound upon the northern portion of this national story.
Joel Williamson, *A Rage for Order: Black-White Relations in the American South
since Emancipation* (New York: Oxford University Press, 1986), viii–ix. This research
is also a response to Maris Vinovskis's challenge to social historians "to rediscover
the effect of the Civil War on nineteenth-century society." Maris A. Vinovskis, ed.,
Toward a Social History of the American Civil War: Exploratory Essays (Cambridge,
Eng.: Cambridge University Press, 1990), xii.

[5] It is probable that the common antebellum northerner gave little deliberate
thought to complex issues of slavery and race; evidence suggests that they did, however, absorb the racial images provided by black face minstrelsy. Lewis O. Saum,
The Popular Mood of Pre-Civil War America (Westport, Conn.: Greenwood Press,
1980), 164–67, 169–74. Also see Lott, *Love and Theft*, passim; and Roediger, *Wages
of Whiteness*, passim.

[6] According to both the 1850 and 1860 U.S. Censuses, .8 percent of New England's population was black, with the following break-down by state in 1860: Maine
.2 percent, New Hampshire .2 percent, Massachusetts .8 percent, Vermont .2 percent, Connecticut 1.9 percent, Rhode Island 2.3 percent. U.S. Department of Commerce, Bureau of the Census, *Negro Population in the United States, 1790–1915*,
reprint ed. William Loren Katz (Washington: Government Printing Office, 1918;
reprint, New York: Arno Press, 1968), 51.

[7] For similar arguments regarding racial adaptation, see T. H. Breen, "Creative
Adaptations: Peoples and Cultures," in *Colonial British America: Essays in the New
History of the Early Modern Era*, ed. by Jack P. Greene and J. R. Pole (Baltimore:
The Johns Hopkins University Press, 1984), 197; and Eric Foner, *Nothing But Free-
dom: Emancipation and its Legacy* (Baton Rouge: Louisiana State University Press,
1983), 73.

[8] Reid Mitchell emphasized the adaptive capabilities of Civil War soldiers, asserting, for example, that "to these nineteenth-century northerners there could be no
such thing as a purely masculine world. If those who were to bear the feminine
values of nurture were absent, then the soldiers themselves had to embody them."
Reid Mitchell, *The Vacant Chair: The Northern Soldier Leaves Home* (New York:
Oxford University Press, 1993), 21–25, 71–75, chapters 2 and 3; Gerald F. Linder-

Thus armed by the home front, Yankees served at the front line of racial adaptation. Wartime racial interaction evoked stark commentary in letters and diaries, which suggests that such experiences challenged Yankees' prewar racial assumptions. The result was a dialectic in which white New Englanders' daily lives employed social and cultural forces to transform their understandings of race.[9]

Examination of these soldiers' letters reveals that their racial perceptions fall into two broad phases. The first phase, in the early years of the war, is marked by two-dimensional understandings of African Americans: blacks were subhuman, simple-minded, amusing pets, often the butt of jokes. In the second phase of the war, these Yankees formulated new, more complex responses to daily encounters with slaves, contrabands, freedpeople, and African American soldiers. As

man, *Embattled Courage: The Experience of Combat in the American Civil War* (New York: The Free Press, 1987), 34–37, 41–43; James I. Robertson, *Soldiers Blue and Gray* (Columbia: University of South Carolina Press, 1988), 122–24; and Paludan, "*A People's Contest,*" chapter 1. Regarding the ability of war to create a common sociocultural experience among a generation of soldiers, see Fred Anderson, *A People's Army: Massachusetts Soldiers and Society in the Seven Years' War* (Chapel Hill: University of North Carolina Press, 1984). In addition, evidence suggests that military service and conscription cut across the northern class structure and offered a fair representation of northern male society, making the Union army a reasonable microcosm of male New England. James M. McPherson, *Battle Cry of Freedom: The Civil War Era* (New York: Oxford University Press, 1988), 603–5; and Thomas R. Kemp, "Community and War: The Civil War Experience of Two New Hampshire Towns," in Vinovskis, ed., *Toward a Social History of the American Civil War*, 58–70, 48n.

[9] Historians such as Joseph Glatthaar have examined the reformulation of northern culture regarding race, but their work has focused on the rather special case of white officers and black soldiers serving in the Union's segregated African American regiments. For the duration of the war, according to Glatthaar, black soldiers and their officer corps generally set aside their differences and worked together for the good of the Union and African Americans. Considerable mutual respect developed between most of these white officers and black soldiers, but the end of the war meant the end of their unique alliance. Although his analysis is persuasive, Glatthaar's focus on the approximately 7,000 white officers who volunteered to serve in all-black units was necessarily a biased sampling, representative of neither white Union soldiers in general or those from New England. Joseph T. Glatthaar, *Forged in Battle: The Civil War Alliance of Black Soldiers and White Officers* (New York: The Free Press, 1990), 82, 93, 229–30. See also Dudley T. Cornish, *The Sable Arm: Black Troops in the Union Army, 1861–1865* (New York: Longmans Green & Co., 1956; reprint, Lawrence: University Press of Kansas, 1987); Robertson, *Soldiers Blue and Gray*, 208–14; and Thomas C. Holt, "Marking: Race, Race-making, and the Writing of History," *American Historical Review* 99 (February 1995): 8, 10. Reid Mitchell detailed northern soldiers' descriptions of the South as "unredeemed . . . strange and un-American." Mitchell, *Civil War Soldiers*, 94–101, 107.

assumptions formulated in racial isolation in New England collided
with interracial encounters down South, Yankees blended their new
experiences into their pre-existing world view: slavery is cruel, but
there is no rush to emancipate; slavery should be abolished, although
it has no black victims; the future of freed African Americans is dubious, but nonetheless they should not be re-enslaved.[10]

Early in the war, roughly from 1861 to 1862, the everyday lives of
New England soldiers revealed a collection of racial stereotypes
based on prejudices against skin color and assumptions about primor-
dial African American characteristics. Such stereotypes were rooted
in eighteenth-century developments, when white Americans increasingly justified slavery by formulating a pejorative assessment of
blacks. During the antebellum era, white revulsion to African American equality was connected to perceived differences in social background and intellectual capability between the races. These white
prejudices were popularized by antebellum dramas and novels whose
underlying message was that blacks could not, in the foreseeable
future, overcome their racial and cultural shortcomings enough to
benefit the American sociocultural mix. Blacks threatened to retard
progress, or so the thinking went. New England soldiers frequently
exhibited and reproduced this larger understanding of blacks as "outsiders." These antebellum racial prejudices, usually formed in the

---

[10] The premise here that race is a "culturally constructed system of meanings" is
particularly influenced by J. William Harris, "Etiquette, Lynching, and Racial
Boundaries in Southern History: A Mississippi Example," *American Historical Review* 100 (April 1995), esp. 388–91. Also see George M. Fredrickson, *The Arrogance
of Race: Historical Perspectives on Slavery, Racism, and Social Inequality* (Middletown, Conn.: Wesleyan University Press, 1988), 3–14. For additional insight into
culture as process, see Anne C. Rose, *Victorian America and the Civil War* (Cambridge, Eng.: Cambridge University Press, 1992), esp. 5–16. Similarly, McPherson
argues that Union soldiers' opinions regarding slavery and its relation to the war's
aim were "[i]n a state of flux." McPherson, *What They Fought For*, 57. Yankees'
responses were inconsistent because there was nothing homogenous about the racial
perspectives they experienced during the antebellum era. See James Brewer Stewart, *Holy Warriors: The Abolitionists and American Slavery* (New York: Hill and
Wang, 1976); Ronald G. Walters, *The Anti-Slavery Appeal: American Abolitionism
after 1830* (Baltimore: The Johns Hopkins University Press, 1976); Larry E. Tise,
Proslavery: A History of the Defense of Slavery in America, 1701–1840 (Athens:
University of Georgia Press, 1987), esp. 261, 285, and chapter 10; and Wood, *Black
Scare*, 13–14. Forrest Wood argues that "[o]nly when race-related issues threatened
to affect [Northerners'] lives directly did they overtly act upon their racism"; he
also suggested that there was an "empirical" element of observation inherent to the
formation of their racial attitudes. Wood, *Black Scare*, 10, 15.

absence of firsthand interracial experience, formed the cultural lens through which Yankee Civil War soldiers saw and judged blacks they met during the war.[11]

In practical terms, soldiers tended to distinguish between the institution of slavery, which was in their minds the foundation for the traitorous rebellion, and the black victims of the institution. Writing from on board the steamer *South America*, off Lookout Point, Maryland, a New Hampshire sergeant described a "little negro boy" that a colonel from Pennsylvania "had." The boy "amused us very much yesterday with his tricks. . . . He could imitate plaining, sawing wood, the buzzing of a bumblebee, the drawing of a cork from a soda bottle . . . and a variety of other necromantic tricks." Sergeant Enoch Adams, of Durham, New Hampshire, did not question the colonel's right to "have" the boy; only his entertainment value was of consequence. Although in 1861 Adams had credited himself, as a Union soldier, with loosening "every fetter from the trembling slave," his language in 1862 suggested that he thought of this child more as a possession than a person. He avoided dealing with the human realities of slavery—that is, the untidy affair of slaves themselves—by reducing African Americans to caricatures. Adams continued his letter by describing a mock conversation acted out by the boy "ventriloquist," who mimicked a southern tavern keeper, thereby creating a "perfect illusion." The passage concluded on another subject with a brief description of a Pennsylvania surgeon's "little black dog . . . Floyd . . . [who] stole a sick man's dinner." Taken as a whole, Adams's anecdotes coldly expounded upon the pets on board the steamer; the dog is granted a name, whereas the boy remains a nameless "darkey."[12]

White soldiers often tapped into antebellum-era minstrel images by describing what were supposedly racially inherent talents and physical abnormalities of African Americans, who provided amusement in the midst of dull camp life. Minstrel shows, which depicted

---

[11] Winthrop D. Jordan, *White Over Black: American Attitudes toward the Negro, 1550–1812* (New York: W. W. Norton, 1968), 308–11; George M. Fredrickson, *The Black Image in the White Mind: The Debate on Afro-American Character and Destiny, 1817–1914* (New York: Harper Row Publishers, 1971; reprint, Hanover, N. H.: Wesleyan University Press, 1987), 17; and William L. Van Deburg, *Slavery and Race in American Popular Culture* (Madison: University of Wisconsin Press, 1984), 24.

[12] Enoch G. Adams to Sarah S. Adams, November 26, 1861, April 8, 1862, in Adams Family Papers, Special Collections, Dimond Library, University of New Hampshire, Durham. Also see Wiley, *Billy Yank*, 109–23.

the southern black as an object of entertainment for whites, were the most significant and widespread form of popular culture prior to and during the Civil War. Such theatrical productions portrayed blacks as primitive outsiders and often demonstrated an almost pathological tendency to ridicule and exaggerate racially distinctive features to the point of debasing slaves to mere burlesques of humanity. Minstrelsy portrayed a wide variety of dehumanizing images: blacks appeared as childlike dullards, culturally inferior, comical, and socially inept. In a letter to his sister dated February 1862, Charles Brewster, a Massachusetts sergeant, described a "darkey" who made great "sport" for a squad by "singing and dancing." Brewster continued: "One great sport is to get them [the contrabands] butting each other with their heads. . . . They look so comical, just like sheep butting at each other." Whereas Enoch Adams had associated the slave boy with a dog, Sergeant Brewster explicitly equated freed slaves with domesticated animals, a comparison found in popular almanacs in preceding decades. Even a self-described "staunch abolitionist" unwilling to "recognize . . . property in human flesh and blood" might still perceive the physical attributes of African Americans with condescending amusement and fascination: "One of them has got feet that are about 24 inches long and they turn out both ways and such a comical looking Nigger you never saw." Contempt for the abstract belief in human property did not necessarily translate into compassion for slaves or recognition of their humanity.[13]

Many northern soldiers tended to revel in the convenience of black servants, who provided whites with cheaply acquired leisure, the "power" of command, and the curious oddity of black faces. Writing to his brother in January 1862, George Barnard, scion of a wealthy mercantile family of Boston, described his "little nigger" servant,

---

[13] Charles H. Brewster to Mary Brewster, February 26, 1862; Charles H. Brewster to Martha Russell Brewster, March 5, 1862, in *When This Cruel War is Over: The Civil War Letters of Charles Harvey Brewster*, ed. by David W. Blight (Amherst: University of Massachusetts Press, 1992), 89–90, 93–94. White, *Somewhat More Independent*, 67–68; Van Deburg, *Slavery and Race in American Popular Culture*, 18, 40, 42. Wiley, *Billy Yank*, 175–77; and Robert C. Toll, *Blacking Up: The Minstrel Show in Nineteenth-Century America* (New York: Oxford University Press, 1974), 73, chapter 3. Head-butting, although comical-looking to whites, was actually a traditional form of African martial arts. W. Jeffrey Bolster, *Black Jacks: African American Seamen in the Age of Sail* (Cambridge, Mass.: Harvard University Press, 1997), 119–20.

William, as "a source of great amusement." He would dance, sing, and laugh "all day long," and provided the regiment with "such fun" that they "would be sorry to lose him." This portrayal is reminiscent of minstrelsy skits that depicted slaves as carefree and born to serve whites. Indeed, Barnard attended a camp "negro minstrel concert" in March 1863, and his off-handed mention of the event suggests that it was a commonplace occurrence. In January 1862, Barnard "had the nig's head shaved with a razor . . . which made him look quite comical." He then engaged William in sparring matches and proudly announced that his contraband "is a great sparrer for his size but when people of twice his size attack him he rushes at them and butts them in the stomach with his little black head which doubles them up." Barnard delighted in describing the antics of his pet: "William is scooting about with his head shaved, sleeves and pants rolled up, making a very funny looking little nig; at present he is lying on his back singing 'Dixie.' " "I don't know what I should do without him." From this self-absorbed perspective, the two were almost a team, surviving everything from mundane camp life to bouts of lice and sharing the care packages sent from his family. In July 1862, William and Barnard together "tore open" such a parcel, after which "William seized upon a small bundle and seeing 'For William' marked upon it, immediately took possession of it, sqealing [sic] and prancing about like a young Hottentot." By dispensing baubles and lording over his human possession, Barnard played out some of his otherwise impotent elitist attitudes—such as his call for a military dictatorship to prosecute the Union war effort.[14] A frustrated non-entity in the national arena, Barnard—one of tens of thousands of nameless Union soldiers whose fate seemed to rest with a faceless, remote government—derived a measure of satisfaction and empowerment from his quasi-ownership of a black servant, who, he assumed, enjoyed their relationship as much as he did.

Barnard also employed a white boy, an "orderly" named Fuller. Although his two servants occupied a roughly similar status in his

---

[14] George M. Barnard to Inman Barnard, January 3, 1862; George M. Barnard to Father, March 28, 1863; George M. Barnard to Inman Barnard, June 7, 1862; George M. Barnard to Mother, January 17, 1862; George M. Barnard to Mother, July 26, 1862; George M. Barnard to Inman Barnard, April 12, 1862; George M. Barnard to Father, October 20, 1862, George M. Barnard Papers, Massachusetts Historical Society, Boston. See also Jimerson, *Private Civil War*, 77.

view, an implicit acknowledgment of racial difference still existed. Fuller was afforded a greater portion of dignity, apparently never having been belittled like a living toy. On the contrary, in typical Victorian fashion, Barnard instructed Fuller to give William a reading lesson every day, clearly establishing a hierarchy of competence, with Fuller in the active role of teacher. It is interesting to note that this was a hierarchy that Barnard altered by lifting up William to Fuller's level; both boys shared the ignominy of sleeping under Barnard's bed. However, Barnard noted that "when anybody comes in after dark they say that they can see nothing but the darkey's eyes and teeth." Both were "good boys," but race tended to distinguish Fuller from William.[15]

Romantic literature such as Harriet Beecher Stowe's *Uncle Tom's Cabin* was a source for some of the most famous models for understanding African Americans and informed the racial assumptions of one John Henry Jenks, a well-to-do shoe merchant from Keene, New Hampshire. Unlike minstrelsy's portrayal of blacks, Stowe's African American characters enjoyed unique, but not inferior, racial traits that complemented those of Anglo Saxons. Blacks theoretically possessed feminine qualities of gentle selflessness: they were affectionate, docile, forgiving, emotional. In May 1864, Sergeant Jenks wrote from Louisiana to his wife about "a little [black] girl . . . I love to talk with, she is a regular Topsey . . . after she told me [her name] she asked me to give her a pair of shoes." Jenks assumed that this slave girl, "*Amelia*," was the life-model for Stowe's character, a brash young slave whom a New England woman attempted to reform. His regiment's historian also described slaves as "our Uncle Tom" or "a genuine . . . Aunt Chloe." Jenks, at least, was aware of his assumptions' origin; after he spent the night in a "negro shanty" in March 1863, he excitedly wrote to his wife that the experience "brought impressively to my mind the reading of 'Uncle Toms Cabin.' Little did I then think I should spend the night with them." With Stowe's novel in mind, Jenks sympathetically interpreted this encounter as evidence that African Americans were downtrodden, held in check beneath the weight of slavery. Condescending descriptors such as

---

[15] George M. Barnard to Inman Barnard, January 3, 1862, Barnard Papers. See also Daniel Walker Howe, "Victorian Culture in America," in *Victorian America*, ed. by Daniel Walker Howe (Philadelphia: University of Pennsylvania Press, 1976), 9, 12, 18–19.

"charming" and "wooly-headed," modifiers reminiscent of Stowe's writing, marked his curiosity.[16]

New England soldiers also encountered blacks as laborers, which resulted in a different interracial dynamic. Writing to his wife in December 1862, from on board the steamer *Illinois*, Marshall Stearns was typical of northern soldiers who reveled in the cheers of southern African Americans. He described as a "treat" the shoreline crowded with "darkeys [who] swing their hats bonnets hankerchiefs [and] jump up and turn around & jump up again," just like the sensationally popular "Jim Crow" song-and-dance routine developed by antebellum minstrel Thomas D. Rice. Shortly after settling into his station at Baton Rouge, Stearns was "detailed to take charge of the Contrabands" there. These former slaves, now held as "contraband" of war, would eventually perform a variety of tasks for the army, working "on the entrenchments, in the storehouses, on levees and as teamsters." Although his assignment included an opportunity to command a detachment of white soldiers as well as the contraband laborers, Stearns hoped to "get out of this job," having "never had a desire to boss a gang of darkies." Uncomfortable with directing black ditch-diggers instead of courageously fighting alongside his friends from Massachusetts, Stearns enlisted the aid of his company captain and regiment's colonel to get him off the hook, but to no avail.[17]

In a short time, Stearns's extensive interaction with blacks altered

---

[16] John H. Jenks to Almina Crawford Jenks, May 4, 1864, March 10, 1863, in Jenks Family Papers, Special Collections, Dimond Library, University of New Hampshire, Durham. Also see H. F. Buffum, *A Memorial of the Great Rebellion: Being a History of the Fourteenth Regiment New Hampshire Volunteers . . . 1862–1865* (Boston: Franklin Press: Rand, Avery & Company, 1882), 352. George Fredrickson has described Stowe's novel as the quintessential example of romantic racialism, a northern nineteenth-century "doctrine which acknowledged permanent racial differences but rejected the notion of a clearly defined racial hierarchy." A different version of romantic racialism influenced the assumptions of highly educated officers like Colonel Thomas W. Higginson of Boston, Massachusetts. Fredrickson, *Black Image in the White Mind*, 102, 107–8, 110; Thomas Wentworth Higginson, *Army Life in a Black Regiment* (Boston: Lee and Shepard, 1869); Mitchell, *Vacant Chair*, 52–54, 68; and Harriet Beecher Stowe, *Uncle Tom's Cabin, or Life among the Lowly*, ed. by Ann Douglas (1852; New York: Penguin Books, 1986), 66–68.

[17] Marshall S. Stearns to Sula Hillard Stearns, December 14, 23, 1862; Marshall S. Stearns to Brother, January 9, 1863, in Ethel Jackson, "What the Stearns Family Was Like, 1968," 62; Stearns Family Papers, Special Collections, Massachusetts State Library, Boston. See also Toll, *Blacking Up*, 28; and Jimerson, *Private Civil War*, 121.

his racial attitudes. In January 1863, his letter hinted at sympathetic paternalism regarding his new-found "family" of over twelve hundred contrabands, who were "a sight to behold[;] some are lame blind crippled[,] from the real African to 7/8 white children with light hare [*sic*] & blue eyes and fair complection [*sic*] and are Slaves." The cruel realities of slavery were being presented to Stearns *en masse*. For his personal comfort he took on "a Mulatto woman to cook for us [his detachment]." He also had "a waiter that is very near white and as smart as needs be[;] I hope it will be so that I can carry him home with me." "[H]e was a slave but he is so white you would not dream that his mother was anything less than a white woman."[18] These excerpts demonstrate the complexity of Stearns's interracial encounters: skin color momentarily is equivalent to intelligence; slave and free seem chronologically to overlap; "white" blacks were enslaved as readily as "full" blacks.

As these Yankees' firsthand knowledge of race increased, blacks gradually became a more complex racial "other" against whom whites could define themselves.[19] Starting around 1862, they drew upon the white home front's cultural models for understanding the world and began to observe blacks in the language of class and free labor, military service, family, miscegenation, and Christianity.[20]

Trying to disentangle the institution of slavery from moral or humanitarian considerations, class-conscious soldiers viewed contrabands with a utilitarian eye. They saw in abolition an economic opportunity legally to acquire cheap "servants," a term traditionally

[18] Marshall S. Stearns to Sula H. Stearns, January 4, 1863, December 23, 1862, Stearns Family Papers. See also Earl J. Hess, *Liberty, Virtue, and Progress: Northerners and Their War for the Union* (New York: New York University Press, 1988), 101.

[19] Soldiers' descriptions also implied a white need to formulate a future social role for African Americans: if they were no longer slaves, then what was their position in society? Indeed, the popular term "contraband" was a dehumanizing label indicative of former slaves' ambiguous legal and social status during the war. Eric Foner argued that "in all postemancipation societies, the pivot on which social conflict turned was the new status of the former slave." Foner, *Nothing But Freedom*, 1.

[20] Joan Wallach Scott, *Gender and the Politics of History* (New York: Columbia University Press, 1988), 2, 6–7. See also Nancy F. Cott, "On Men's History and Women's History," in *Meanings for Manhood: Constructions of Masculinity in Victorian America*, ed. by Mark C. Carnes and Clyde Griffen (Chicago: University of Chicago Press, 1990), 205–11; and Stephen M. Frank, " 'Rendering Aid and Comfort': Images of Fatherhood in the Letters of Civil War Soldiers from Massachusetts and Michigan," *Journal of Social History* 26 (fall 1992): 7–8.

associated with a black, slave-like underling, separate and distinct from the superior position of a white "independent" wage earner. This servant category dovetailed with minstrelsy's emphasis on the subordinate sociocultural status of African Americans. Men such as Enoch Adams, a "Black Republican of the deepest dye," were well-steeped in the related tenets of free labor, according to which poverty or economic failure were caused by individual, not social, shortcomings, an ideology applied to both African Americans and whites. Individuals were expected to begin at the bottom of the economic ladder and work their way up, with neither special privileges nor any fetters to keep them down. However, New England racial conceit assumed that the freedpeople lacked the capacity for self-directed work and therefore needed the friendly guidance of paternal Yankee employers.[21]

Rather than perceive contrabands that "flock across from Virginia by the hundreds" as pastoral entities from the supposedly pre-industrial South, soldiers such as Adams viewed them as plentiful menial laborers newly available for simple contractual employment.[22] To "have" such "black servants" was to "live in great style." Adams's

---

[21] Enoch G. Adams to Sister, April 11, 1865, Adams Family Papers. See also McPherson, *Battle Cry of Freedom*, 497; Roediger, *Wages of Whiteness*, 44–47; Toll, *Blacking Up*, 67–68; and Eric Foner, *Free Soil, Free Labor, Free Men: The Ideology of the Republican Party before the Civil War* (New York: Oxford University Press, 1970), 23–24, 261–62. For a related discussion concerning northerners' application of free labor to the postwar South, see Eric Foner, *Reconstruction: America's Unfinished Revolution, 1863–1877* (New York: Harper and Row, 1988), esp. chapter 4. See also Lawrence N. Powell, *New Masters: Northern Planters during the Civil War and Reconstruction* (New Haven, Conn.: Yale University Press, 1980), 5.

[22] Enoch G. Adams to Sarah S. Adams, October 21, 1863, Adams Family Papers. Such perceptions are related to James W. Hurst's assertion that antebellum law encouraged the assumption that "[h]uman nature is creative, and . . . it is socially desirable that there be broad opportunity for the release of creative human energy." Hurst also cited the increasing influence of market forces and the contract in social organization. Adams's act of "property confiscation" was probably partially based on an understanding that "slavery had proved to be a system which did not fulfill the property function of generating a constantly expanding reach of human creative power." Although whites tapped into these concepts in order to rationalize emancipation and structure their employment of contrabands, racism encouraged northern soldiers blithely to exploit their new-found servants rather than allow them to participate in the market as free economic agents fully endowed with the liberty, energy, and creativity that whites supposedly exercised. James Willard Hurst, *Law and the Conditions of Freedom in the Nineteenth-Century United States* (Madison: University of Wisconsin Press, 1956), 5–6, 14, 25.

frequent self-references throughout his letters—comments on his appearance; others' envy of his beautiful wife; his superior military talents; his personal popularity; the exceptional aptitude of his contraband servant, as contrasted with others' servants—suggest that he was concerned about his social standing and his ability, or lack thereof, to rise up in the world and in military rank. As a member of the New Hampshire branch of the illustrious Massachusetts Adamses, Enoch Adams lived in the shadow of presidents, diplomats, cabinet members, and industrialists, with only a degree from Yale and employment as a teacher to speak for him. Quasi-ownership of a contraband was, perhaps, a small panacea for his worries of inadequacy, an ornament that would affirm to the world and himself that Adams was somehow worthy. Writing to his mother in October 1863, he described his "many marks of respect and esteem" in camp, including having "a contraband for a waiter"; unlike the entertaining, nameless "darkey" aboard the *South America* in 1862, Adams acknowledged this boy's name, "Robert Chewn." Adams described him as "an excellent boy, about 14 years of age. . . . [who] just escaped from the jaws of Slavery." His new servant was "very handy, one of the best boys I ever saw." Such compliments were based on Robert's ability to clean Adams's cottage and cook, as the role of a servant-waiter was often considered the appropriate application of a contraband's skills. Such an arrangement also spared Yankees the indignity of doing womanly chores, a practical concern that troubled many soldiers; it was problematic to overlap the manly affair of war with the feminine duty of washing one's own socks.[23]

Such adaptations of gender could overlap with understandings of race and class. In September 1863, Adams coaxed his wife into joining him at Lookout Point, Maryland. He promised her that "you will suffer none if you come out here. I can have a black girl to wait on you for her board, and you can take her back with you when you return home, if you desire." Pragmatically, once Adams's wife joined him, he would no longer need a black servant, yet employment of an underclass servant would be a minor status symbol for the Adamses.

---

[23] Enoch G. Adams to Sarah S. Adams, May 23, 1862, October 16, 1863, Adams Family Papers. See also Mitchell, *Vacant Chair*, 82; and Roediger, *Wages of Whiteness*, 97, 118–19.

Also, a girl would be the obvious choice for tending to Mrs. Adams's genteel needs, as only a female could properly fulfill such a duty. Finally, the girl's race made it feasible to compensate her with only board and to cart her off northward at some future date. Indeed, at the simplest economic level, contrabands were commodities, war-booty for whites. Adams inquired of his mother in September 1863: "Do you want my contrabands? Do you want me to bring you home a black boy and girl if I should happen to have a chance to come?"[24]

Conceptions of manhood also affected whites' assessments of African Americans. In March 1864, Adams wrote: "There is a negro regiment here [at Lookout Point, Maryland]. They perform their duty well indeed, and elicit the praise of every one." This black regiment performed the same duty—guarding Confederate prisoners—for which Adams was responsible.[25] Although similar to his praise of his servant, Robert, the distinction is that war was a place where "boys" became "men," and for African American men in the Civil War, this was especially true. A man was assertive, defended and expanded his way of life, and acted in his own behalf. Prior to the war, male slaves were denied these attributes by southern law and custom. But because manhood was equated with the power to kill and destroy, Yankees often viewed African American soldiers in this masculine light. There were finer distinctions, however, that informed this middle-class northern conception of manhood. Physical violence could be masculine, but true manhood also demanded self-discipline and civilized morality, and there is no evidence that Adams attributed these

---

[24] Enoch G. Adams to Mary Elizabeth Libbey Adams, September 9, 1863; and Enoch G. Adams to Sarah S. Adams, September 18, 1863, Adams Family Papers. For a revealing discussion on race, gender, and class, see Evelyn Brooks Higginbotham, "African American Women's History and the Metalanguage of Race," *Signs* 17 (winter 1992): 251–74.

[25] Enoch G. Adams to Christopher Pearse Cranch, March 1[?], 1864; Enoch G. Adams to Sarah S. Adams, November 24, 1863, December 3, 1863, Adams Family Papers; and United States War Department, *The War of the Rebellion: A Compilation of the Official Records of the Union and Confederate Armies*, 70 vols. in 128 (Washington, D.C.: Government Printing Office, 1891), series 1, vol. 33, p. 930 (hereinafter cited as *Official Records*). Adams's acceptance of black soldiers was not entirely beyond the antebellum norm. In 1857, New Hampshire Republicans passed legislation allowing African Americans to enroll in the state militia. See Foner, *Free Soil*, 285. Adams's letter implored Cranch (a cousin by marriage) to assist him in obtaining a promotion, an obsessive preoccupation for Adams. *Dictionary of American Biography* (New York: American Council of Learned Societies, 1930), 2: 501–3.

characteristics to the black soldiers he encountered.[26] On the contrary, in the same year that he was complimenting black soldiers, Adams wrote:

> Conundrum. Sambo, why are the Rebel defences around Richmond like Robinson Crusoe? Ans. 'Case dey are both de works of *De Foe*.[27]

In spite of some development in his racial perceptions, minstrel images lingered in Adams's mind.[28]

Conceptions of class, gender, and blackness also influenced white notions regarding the relative capabilities and future of freedpeople. Sgt. Brewster no longer judged them as playthings or as "sheep," but as hirelings within his competitive world. In January 1862, Brewster informed his mother that he had obtained "a bright looking mulatto [boy], 17 years old." There was an element of economic practicality motivating his acquisition: "I was on the lookout for a servant as I am allowed $13 dollars extra for subsistence and $2[.]50 for clothing per month if I have a servant, and it does not cost half that to keep him." Having learned that the boy had been whipped with little provocation by his slave-master, Brewster tempered his self-interest with indignation and went to great lengths to conceal the escaped slave from his former owner. It can be assumed that Brewster provided room and board for his servant's labor, but he implied that the boy's true payment was the "easy life . . . he has now"; his duties were "to keep wood cut for one fire and brush my Clothes & Boots and keep my sword bright." Brewster's attitude reflects the low economic status of unpaid household labor and the assumption that contraband servants enjoyed the romanticized life of a child. By completing menial do-

---

[26] Jim Cullen, " 'I's a Man Now': Gender and African American Men," in *Divided Houses: Gender and the Civil War*, ed. by Catherine Clinton and Nina Silber (New York: Oxford University Press, 1992), 77–79, 91; Mitchell, *Vacant Chair*, 11 and chapter 1; Howe, "Victorian Culture," in Howe, ed. *Victorian America*, 18–19; and Hess, *Liberty, Virtue, and Progress*, 42–43.

[27] Enoch G. Adams to Sarah S. Adams, July 28, 1864, Adams Family Papers. Any emphasis within subsequent quotations has been maintained from the original documents.

[28] Toll, *Blacking Up*, 86, 65. For a similar situation, see the series of letters from Sergeant George M. Turner to Family, from December 1861 to May 1864, in Silber and Sievens, eds., *Yankee Correspondence*, 84–87. It is noteworthy that Turner, too, alluded to "Minstrel Concerts" when describing contrabands.

mestic tasks, this contraband was judged "perfectly honest, and I *reckon* he is a *right smart nigger.*"[29]

This racial attitude was informed by a popular mentality defined by minstrelsy's juxtaposition of white labor and blackness. In Brewster's case, his prewar efforts at attaining coveted economic independence had produced few tangible results—prior to the war, he was a wage-earning shop clerk. With a dependent widowed mother and two sisters back home, Brewster, a free-soil Republican, was determined to rise up in the world and support his family. One way to accomplish this was to acquire the services of a black hireling, which perhaps alleviated his anxiety over being a white hireling himself. In short, to own others' labor was preferable to being the labor owned. Demonstrated aptitude at household chores meant an African American was simultaneously less economically threatening, a credit to his people, and functioning at a level commensurate with his capabilities—a "right smart nigger." Brewster wrote to his sister that one contraband "washes clothes for the boys and I guess makes quite a good thing of it," while another was designated the "smartest and brightest darkey" ever seen because of his exceptional "singing and dancing." Moreover, by perceiving blacks' apparent ineptitude at operating as free men, New England soldiers like Brewster could find hope for themselves by judging them an underclass of lackeys, at a pathetic socioeconomic level to which whites would never descend by virtue of their race. Writing in March 1862, Brewster explained that his regiment was compelled to give up its contraband servants by a "pro-slavery" Union officer. The following incident ensued:

> Three of [the expelled contrabands] arrived back [in the Union camp]. they had been within ten miles of the Pennsylvania line, but a white man stopped them and questioned them so closely that they got scared and turned round and came back. we gave them a good dressing down and scolded them well for their cowardice, and tonight they are going to start again. I told mine not be taken alive, and if anybody undertook to [capture him,] kill him if he could, but they are most of them poor cowards, and I don't [doubt] but they are just as well off. I don't know

---

[29] Charles H. Brewster to Martha R. Brewster, January 15, 1862, February 9, 22, 1862, in Blight, ed., *When This Cruel War Is Over*, 77–78, 81–82, 87–88. See also Jimerson, *Private Civil War*, 77; and Jeanie Attie, "Warwork and the Crisis of Domesticity in the North," in *Divided Houses*, 248.

[that] they are . . . capable of taking care of themselves[,] it don't seem possible that men would get so near to freedom and then turn back to a certain doom as they do.[30]

Brewster believed that these timid child-men were ill equipped to control their own destinies. Although sympathetic and even willing to advise a contraband to murder a white man, Brewster, nonetheless, judged blacks as incapable of successful action independent of direct white guidance.[31]

Because of such incidents, lack of firsthand experience with black soldiers easily resulted in skepticism about their reported contributions on the battlefield. In May 1864, Brewster doubted newspaper accounts "of the terrible fighting that [General] Burnsides negroes have done" because "a few days ago they had not been into a fight at all and I don't believe they have now." Soldiers were willing to believe only what their eyes saw. In spite of this, Brewster's letter hinted at potential ties of comradeship between white and black troops: "Our men are much opposed to taking [Confederate] prisoners since the Fort Pillow affair, that has cost the Rebels many a life that would otherwise have been spared."[32] Brewster probably identified with the

---

[30] Charles H. Brewster to Mary Brewster, February 26, 1862, March 8, 1862, in Blight, ed., *When This Cruel War Is Over*, 89–90, 95–97. Eric Lott argues that white antebellum wage-earners began developing a class-consciousness based in part on an abhorrence of becoming "blacker" with every threatening advance of bourgeois industrialization. Lott, *Love and Theft*, 67, 69, 71. See also David W. Blight, "Introduction," in Blight, ed., *When This Cruel War Is Over*, 8–10, 12, 17; Roediger, *Wages of Whiteness*, 13–14, 49, 86; and Toll, *Blacking Up*, 67.

[31] Brewster's combination of sympathy and rejection is partially explained by Alexander Saxton's analysis of minstrelsy. He argued that a white audience could potentially identify with minstrel characters' emotions and even sympathize with their laughable attempts to become "human," but that the audience "at the same time feasted on the assurance that they [blacks] could not do so." John H. Riggs of the 7th Vermont Regiment would have agreed with Brewster's belief in the freedpeople's inability to function assertively, writing that if "the government did not furnish rations for them [contrabands] they would die." John Harpin Riggs to Father, December 12, 1862, in Silber and Sievens, eds., *Yankee Correspondence*, 96. See also Alexander Saxton, "Blackface Minstrelsy and Jacksonian Ideology," *American Quarterly* 27 (March 1975): 27–28; and Toll, *Blacking Up*, 66–69, 71, 88.

[32] In April 1864, forty miles north of Memphis, Tennessee, a Confederate force of fifteen hundred cavalrymen under Maj. Gen. Nathan Bedford Forrest stormed and took Fort Pillow, defended by 550 Federals, nearly half of whom were black soldiers. Two-thirds of the African American troops were killed, whereas 36 percent of the white defenders died. After the engagement, Washington accused Forrest of committing numerous atrocities against black soldiers who had surrendered. Although

blacks murdered at Fort Pillow, because the next sentence in his letter addressed the general issue of African Americans in the Union army. Indeed, he was curious and open-minded enough to wish he "could see them in battle once, and know for certain whether they would fight or not." Still admitting a month later that he "may be mistaken" about black troops because "we see but little of them," Brewster assessed the issue with a veteran's eye for utility: "I imagine that they [black soldiers] do not amount to any certain sum in a fight and in such tough battles as we have it will not do often times to put in troops which you cannot depend upon." Nonetheless, he allowed that African Americans "add considerably to the strength of the army for they can do many of the duties in the rear which white soldiers once had to do." In October 1864, Brewster's opinion significantly shifted from his 1862 assessment of blacks. He grudgingly wrote to his mother that "praises of the negroes and the late operations at the front are in everybodys mouth, and they all agreed that they fought nobly. The Hospitals at Portsmouth and over to Hampton are full of their wounded and mangled bodies."[33] The potency of confirmed casualties could persuade a skeptical Yankee that African American troops were not just ditch-diggers or "sheep," but comrades-in-arms whose courage and mettle were worthy of praise.

Other Yankee soldiers remained inflexible in their assessment of black troops. Writing to his father in January 1863, from Fredricksburg, Barnard railed against the government forming " 'Nigger' Regiments," because such an endeavor would only antagonize white soldiers and make "trouble." Newspaper accounts made little impact on the opinion, often based upon local hearsay, that African Americans made poor soldiers: "It [black cowardice] is hushed up as much as possible and great puffs appear about them in the papers but even the 54th [Massachusetts Regiment] it is said did not behave well and [at] the Fort (Pillow) it is acknowledged that they ran as soon as

---

considerable evidence exists that Forrest's men did execute some black soldiers, the exact extent of the incident is clouded. Northern contemporaries were well aware of this famous engagement and its racial implications. Consequently, the resolve of African American troops was stiffened and many whites began to develop a more positive assessment of black soldiers. Glatthaar, *Forged in Battle*, 156–57.

[33] Charles H. Brewster to Martha R. Brewster, May 24, October 12, 1864; Charles Brewster to Mattie Brewster, June 11, 1864, in Blight, ed., *When This Cruel War Is Over*, 304, 316, 332. See also Jimerson, *Private Civil War*, 93; and Silber and Sievens, ed., *Yankee Correspondence*, 14–15.

there was any danger of the steel." Barnard's only concession was that African American troops might "do well" after long discipline.[34]

The diversity of wartime experiences created a mosaic of racial reactions. In 1862 Barnard and Brewster had agreed about blacks; in their letters they described them as jester-like entertainers of whites. In 1863, near the end of his service, Barnard's opinion about African Americans had changed little. By 1864, Brewster's firsthand interracial experience exceeded Barnard's in both breadth and depth, resulting in a greater potential for reformulation of his racial understandings—a process that existed within the fabric of soldiers' daily lives and was structured by specific historical contexts.

Soldiers with extensive interracial experiences and sympathetic intentions did not necessarily become uncompromising advocates of equal opportunity for black soldiers. Writing to his wife in January 1863, Marshall Stearns, too, noted the tendency of a "Niger regt" merely by its existence to "provoke" white Union officers. He did not include himself in this disgruntled cohort. On the contrary, he wrote that he "would let them [the black regiment] fight & I must say that they drill full as well as we did one month ago." Although sympathetic to the plight of the slave and supportive of black troops being sent into combat, Stearns was not an ideologue. He put a positive spin on black soldiers being restricted to construction work: "We have 3 regts of colored people here. They are useing the pick & shovel every day now building forts. We are going to let Jeff [Davis] & co know that we can build as strong places as he can." As a carpenter, currier, and tanner, Stearns probably felt that the humble, backbreaking tasks of pick and shovel were genuinely praiseworthy—as hard work was held in high regard by northerners, particularly those such as Stearns who had worked their way up to the level of a skilled artisan. In April 1863, Stearns was offered a captain's commission in an African American regiment, but he declined the offer because he would "rather go with men that I know." Personal attachment to his

---

[34] George M. Barnard to Father, January 6, 1863; George M. Barnard to Father, April 27, 1864, George M. Barnard Papers. Edward F. Hall of the 3rd New Hampshire Regiment expressed similar reservations about using African Americans as soldiers; he was convinced that their role should be limited to digging trenches and field cooking. Edward F. Hall to Wife and Son, July 15, 1862, in Silber and Sievens, eds., *Yankee Correspondence*, 90–92. See also Jimerson, *Private Civil War*, 88, 96–97.

fellow volunteers from Massachusetts overcame the enticements of promotion and a raise in pay. Moreover, his support for black combat soldiers was perhaps mitigated by his constant exposure to African Americans as contraband laborers, whom he perceived as drone-like "Beese" that he had "to hive."[35]

While serving in Maryland and Louisiana, Sergeant John Henry Jenks projected onto blacks Yankee values pertaining to family and economic advancement. By soliciting blacks' opinions on "the subject of slavery . . . [and their] desires for freedom," he tried to understand their lives, as well as impress upon them his purpose for being among them. Writing to his wife in March 1863, Jenks detailed his visit to a "*niggar* shanty" near Poolesville, Maryland, "occupied by a negro woman about 50 years old, her son who had fits, and a man about 35." Jenks wished he "could tell you my feelings as I sat there . . . at the dead of night . . . talking to that poor ignorant slave [woman]." He described the industry of the male slave, who after completing "the toils of the day for his Master [made] brooms chairs and baskets to sell to procure tobacco, Sunday clothes for himself and wife, and some of the luxuries of life, such as sugar." Jenks drew from free labor ideology and interpreted this slave as a black entrepreneur with material aspirations. By exemplifying key values of northern economic culture, this slave's behavior encouraged Jenks to theorize that "such men can take care of themselves."[36] Knowledge of a tenacious slave struggling to improve his family's circumstances also appealed to his Yankee notions about manly assertiveness; the situation conformed to the idealized New England family in which the ambitious father was the leader-provider for his dependent wife and children.

Soldiers could also recognize slaves' abilities to absorb information, draw conclusions, and value freedom, all elements fundamental to economic advancement. In Louisiana, Jenks contrasted the negative influences of that state with the more benign circumstances of the

---

[35] Marshall S. Stearns to Sula H. Stearns, January 21, March 28, April 8, 1863; Marshall Stearns to Jo Calender, April 14, 1863, Stearns Family Papers. See also Foner, *Free Soil*, chapter 1; and Glatthaar, *Forged in Battle*, 41–42. For an interesting collection of letters by a New England soldier who chose to serve in a black regiment, see the Jewett Papers, Manuscripts and Special Collections, Boston Athenaeum.

[36] John H. Jenks to Almina C. Jenks, May 22, 1864, March 10, 1863, Jenks Family Papers. See also Jordan, *White Over Black*, 310; Fredrickson, *Black Image in the White Mind*, 108; and Foner, *Free Soil*, 16–17.

border states, implying that environment, not race, was the key to intelligence and capabilities. His regiment's history echoed this environmentalist tone: "In Louisiana a different and a lower class of the African race was encountered. . . . The bright ones were brighter, but the mass was of a lower grade than in Maryland and Virginia." In a May 1864 letter to his wife, Jenks wrote that

> The negroes [in Louisiana] are very ignorant, much more so than they were in M[arylan]d. Still they know how to prize their freedom; their Massas told them before we came, we were awful critters, and would kill them all, or send them off, and they thought we were not white. . . . They have very little confidence in the white man now, are very suspicious they are to be wronged, that is the most ignorant. Some of them it is difficult to make understand your meaning.[37]

Because Yankees viewed education as the cornerstone of social progress, it is not surprising that Jenks attempted to correct the understanding of the "ignorant" slaves. However, he later implied that freedpeople were satisfied and fulfilled by taking "in washing for a living," again exhibiting the assumption that such domestic chores were ideally suited to blacks. Jenks, like so many of his compatriots, expressed a kaleidoscope of marginally compatible racial opinions that could lead him both to praise and belittle blacks. In the end, Jenks's hopes for black Americans were bolstered by his observations of the slaves' personal aspirations. While visiting a liberated New Orleans slave family in May, he described "two noble fig trees, under which they sit when evening shades warn them of nights approach, and tell of the past, sad past, and the golden hopes of the future, which they can see in the distance, with no fears mingled with their joy, when this war shall be over, and they know they are no longer to be slaves."[38] Jenks was inspired by their ability to persevere, and he carefully chose his words while describing their confidence. It is atypical that he stopped to strike out and correct his choice of words. Apparently, he thought it important to capture accurately the certainty of the freedpeople's optimism and implicitly to support their aspirations. Jenks also acknowledged the self-awareness

---

[37] John H. Jenks to Almina C. Jenks, May 4, 1864, Jenks Family Papers; and Buffum, *History of the Fourteenth Regiment, NH*, 347–48.

[38] John H. Jenks to Almina C. Jenks, May 22, 1864, Jenks Family Papers. See also Foner, *Free Soil*, 264–65; and Wood, *Black Scare*, 4.

with which they reflected on their lives, with a complex mixture of sadness and joy. These were people with dreams, not unlike himself.

Yankee faith in progress inspired Jenks to envision a "colony" of New Englanders moving to the South after the war. With firm confidence and no apparent dread of living among the freedpeople, Jenks predicted "rivers . . . lined with mills of all kinds and the skill of the mechanick . . . seen in every village, and prosperity plenty and happiness . . . stamped upon these oppressed states." Such expectations regarding the superiority of northern society and skills were common among Republicans and Free Soilers of the 1850s. In the short-term pursuit of prosperity, many men considered seeking an officer's commission in a black regiment. Jenks, for example, expressed no qualms about serving with blacks, but he recognized the strict functional value placed upon them by men in power: "I dont doubt but what I could get a Com[mission], but I want to get out of this [war] as soon as possible, and the Negro regt[s] will have to be the last in the field."[39] Although this option remained available to Jenks, he did not exercise it, as he wished to fulfill his duty to the Union and rejoin his family as soon as possible.

Separated from loved ones and yearning for home, New Englanders' perceptions of African Americans could be expressed in terms of family and domesticity, which were at the core of northern culture and often foremost in the minds of Yankees. Certainly, Jenks viewed blacks in terms of his own longing for his family. Embodying sentimental humanitarianism, he described the shattered slave families he encountered near Poolesville, Maryland, in March 1863: "[A 50 year-old woman's] husband lived four miles distant she has had 14 children 7 of them have died, the rest are within a radius of 12 miles. Her daughter was in another shanty and had lots of little ones; her husband ran off 2 months ago: he did not live on the same plantation with her. The other [35 year-old] negro Henry was married to a girl

---

[39] John H. Jenks to Almina C. Jenks, September 6, 1863, July 22, 1863, Jenks Family Papers. See also Foner, *Free Soil*, 43, 52, 64, 72; and Bell Irvin Wiley, "Billy Yank Down South," *Virginia Quarterly Review* 26 (autumn 1950): 561. Extensive interaction with African American soldiers could also result in no alterations of racial attitudes, as with Colonel Thomas W. Higginson. Higginson, *Army Life*, 251, 244–45, 259–60, 261, 262; Mitchell, *Vacant Chair*, 58–59; and Fredrickson, *Black Image in the White Mind*, 119.

12 miles off, had 5 children."[40] Slavery's profound disrespect for the family unit was anathema to the New England mind. Perhaps talking with this woman encouraged Jenks to envision his own wife, separated from him and raising their two young children in his absence. Jenks was an affectionate father and husband, frequently expressing concern for his distant family's well-being and his heartfelt desire to be re-united with them.[41] In May 1864, he wrote from New Orleans of another slave family: "I could not [but] feel that amid all the disolutions of war, the sundering of family ties, the deserted hearth stones, the vacant chair, the intense solicitude for absent friends, and the deep settled grief for those bourne on the list of dead, there are many hearts made happy, many ties made sacred, and many a hearth stone surrounded with happiness and love through this same *monster War*."[42] In spite of the suffering brought upon New England families by the war, Jenks was comforted in knowing that slave families could be reborn, in part because of the North's sacrifice. This lonely merchant-shopkeeper from New Hampshire who did not survive the war to rejoin his own family granted blacks the same humanity of emotions and sanctity of familial bonds that he would have granted to whites.[43]

---

[40] John H. Jenks to Almina C. Jenks, March 10, 1863, Jenks Family Papers. See also Mitchell, *Vacant Chair*, xiii; Robertson, *Soldiers Blue and Gray*, 102–4, 110; and Jordan, *White Over Black*, 368–69.

[41] For a fascinating examination of the tension between military service and family during and after the war, see Megan J. McClintock, "Civil War Pensions and the Reconstruction of Union Families," *Journal of American History* 83 (September 1996): 456–80. Again, the influence of Stowe's novel can be felt, as she emphasized the evil ability of the slave trade to dismember black families. Stephen Frank argued that "separation from toddlers and infants was a source of distress and even guilt for some [soldier-]fathers." Frank, "Images of Fatherhood," 20.

[42] John H. Jenks to Almina C. Jenks, May 22, 1864, Jenks Family Papers. Some of the imagery employed by Jenks was adapted from the sentimental ballads popularized during the war. For example, see Richard Crawford, ed., *The Civil War Songbook: Complete Original Sheet Music for 37 Songs* (New York: Dover, 1977), 118–20; and Robertson, *Soldiers Blue and Gray*, 83–88. Charles Boyle of the 15th Connecticut Infantry, with similar sentimentality, also witnessed the Union war effort as instrumental in reuniting African American slave families. Charles Boyle to Sisters, December 25, 1863, in Silber and Sievens, eds., *Yankee Correspondence*, 104–5.

[43] Mitchell, *Vacant Chair*, xi–xiv. Meschack P. Larry, of Maine, made a similar empathetic connection between slavery and soldiering: "I agreed to obey orders and therefore no one is to blame but myself if I do not like them[;] can a slave say the same[?]" Meschack Purington Larry to Sister, Feb. 16, 1863, in Silber and Sievens,

Other "family" experiences were marked by paternalism, such as when black servants failed to live up to the elitist expectations of a Boston Brahmin. In August 1862, George Barnard wrote to his mother asking her to keep an eye out for "a gentleman's servant," preferably "a good, strong honest white boy between 17 and 40," because "my darkey [William] has turned out as all darkies do, eventually, and after having almost exhausted my patience he has cleaned out as he said to see his Mother." Vexed by his once-amusing servant's turn toward self-determination, this indignant tone suggests a paternal sense of betrayal because William's maternal bonds were deemed fraudulent. If Barnard had still judged him an outsider, the boy's departure would have had little impact; friends, not strangers, are damned as traitors. William had apparently become a quasi-friend whose loyalty, from Barnard's perspective, was a given, yet this ungrateful servant-companion had bolted. This explains the bitter hostility of Barnard's July 1863 letter: "I must have a faithful, intelligent servant and I have been obliged to use my sword on my infernal nigger." Neither faithful nor intelligent—nor good, strong, or honest—the returned William, or perhaps some other nameless African American, suffered Barnard's ire. "All darkies" were unreliable and inadequate, and thus undeserving of a place even at the family servants' table, not a surprising attitude for a haughty man of wealth who believed that in regards to the less fortunate, "indiscriminate kindness is not much better than no kindness at all."[44]

Other soldiers viewed African American families with compassion and empathy. From the outset of his military service, Marshall Stearns promised his neighbors back in Northfield that he would take care of the "N. boys" under his command. Such a departing pledge was oft-repeated throughout the North, as Civil War officers such as

eds., *Yankee Correspondence*, 98. Colonel Higginson noted the strength of African American familial bonds, arguing that fighting for "homes and firesides" was a "powerful stimulus" for black soldiers. Higginson, *Army Life*, 245–47, 257–59.

[44] George M. Barnard to Mother, August 8, 1862; George M. Barnard to Father, July 4, 1863; George M. Barnard to Inman Barnard, December 9, 1863, George M. Barnard Papers. This incident is representative of one of the "tragic contradictions within American Victorian culture," the "conflict between didacticism and racism, between assimilation and rejection of others." Howe, "Victorian Culture," in Howe, ed., *Victorian America*, 24. Barnard's reaction echoed slaveowning southerners' dismay over the wartime defection of their "loyal" black servants. Jimerson, *Private Civil War*, 69–71.

Stearns endeavored to care for their men and keep them alive and whole.[45] True to his word, Stearns converted part of his headquarters into a makeshift hospital where he nursed back to health numerous ill and wounded soldiers from his company. Stearns instinctively adapted this nurturing role to his "undesirable" command of hundreds of contraband laborers near Baton Rouge. In February 1863, Stearns was dismayed by the poor condition of his black charges as they arrived in camp. "I have just had a call from 15 of the Poor fellows one wanted a shirt another pants & some of them needed a full suit & blankets." Even worse was the "horrid sight" of a "whipped darkey" and other "ragged ones that came into the Qtrs. I have had some worse than raged [sic] for I had one come in that had on nothing." As a result of his observing this collective suffering, Stearns became committed to their well-being and to "living up to the president Proclomation [sic] in respect to" the former slaves. His complaints about his assignment gradually faded, but tongue-in-cheek references to the condition, activities, and size of "my family" of contrabands became more common. Such quasi-familial bonds could prove quite resilient; immediately after Stearns's regiment was mustered out, two members of his contraband family turned up on the doorstep of his Northfield home. His mulatto cook, Mrs. Kline, and her young son Joe had volunteered to travel North at Stearns's expense. The two apparently stayed on with the Stearns family for a few years as servants, well liked by both the household and the community.[46]

In the fall of 1864, Charles Brewster was an army recruiter in Virginia, where he also aided in maintaining the correspondence between black soldiers and their wives. "I read thier [sic] letters from and write letters to thier [sic] husbands . . . at the front," he once

---

[45] Mitchell, *Vacant Chair*, 80–83. For a related compelling discussion of gender and military service, see Samuel J. Watson, "Flexible Gender Roles during the Market Revolution: Family, Friendship, Marriage, and Masculinity Among U.S. Army Officers, 1815–1846," *Journal of Social History* 29 (fall 1995): 81–106. For an overview of gender and masculinity, see Clyde Griffen, "Reconstructing Masculinity from the Evangelical Revival to the Waning of Progressivism: A Speculative Synthesis," in Carnes and Griffen, eds., *Meanings for Manhood*, 183–204.

[46] In Ethel F. Jackson, "Three Centuries of the Stearns Family, 1600–1900, 1939," 49–50; Marshall S. Stearns to Sula H. Stearns, February 1, April 8, 1863; Marshall Spring Stearns to Jo Calender, April 14, 1863; Jackson, "What the Stearns Family Was Like, 1968," 72–73, Stearns Family Papers.

explained, "so that I expect I shall be adept at writing love letters."[47] Such firsthand experience forced Yankees to view African Americans as people with emotional bonds, and not simply as either military men or as the comical flotsam and jetsam of war.

The issue of miscegenation rarely surfaced in New Englanders' letters home, but when it did these soldiers were not sexually threatened by freedmen. Neither were they anxious about the African American remaining on his own side of the line supposedly drawn by God and science to preserve the purity of the white race. However, a letter's audience, mother or wife, certainly was a constraining factor on soldiers' expressions of sexual-racial tensions. Nonetheless, the progeny of interracial relationships left these soldiers struggling with the meaning of skin color, a racial conundrum resulting in profound ambivalence.

In New Orleans, in May 1864, John Jenks commented on "lots of young [black] women round with beautiful little babes almost white. . . . I think they feel proud of a white babe and take great pains to show it, they dont pay much attention to the black soldier when they can get white." Although this is not an unusual observation of Civil War–era New Orleans, the absence of further commentary seems noteworthy. Apparently not appalled by racial mixing, he casually noted the situation, complimented the infants, then bypassed an opportunity to condemn either immoral white soldiers or licentious black women. Possibly, his temperate reaction was again influenced by the romantic racialism of *Uncle Tom's Cabin*, which depicted mulatto characters such as George Harris as a combination of the finer qualities of both races. In June 1864, Jenks conversed "with a colored woman and her *almost* white daughter."[48] Again, the racial feature was important enough to be noted explicitly, but it was neither criticized nor approved. Nonetheless, the fact that she was described as "*almost* white," rather than as "*almost* black," is telling; because the qualifier possessed the emphasis, black was perceived to be her racial starting point, with "white" as the "*almost*" achieved goal of moving up the racial ladder. Her daughter had fallen short of the mark, but the daughter's new position was an ambiguous racial limbo.

[47] Charles H. Brewster to Martha Brewster, October 27, 1864, in Blight, ed., *When This Cruel War Is Over*, 335.

[48] John H. Jenks to Almina C. Jenks, May 4, 22, 1864, Jenks Family Papers. See also Fredrickson, *Black Image in the White Mind*, 117.

Prior to the war, Marshall Stearns "did not believe in white Ni-gers." His surprise at their existence led him to draw comparisons when writing to his wife in January 1863, when a mulatto woman "came in last week whiter than you are & did not show the Nig in the least." He also described an African American infant who was as white "as you ever saw (at least I never see one [whiter])." As skin color became a blurred issue, so did assumptions regarding supposed race-determined capabilities. For instance, Stearns chose to delegate a task based on the whiteness of an African American: "I scend [sic] this [letter] in a hurry by a slave going to N Orleans he is as white as I am & I will wish him to put it in the [post] office."[49] This nameless slave was apparently white enough to be trusted; his appearance be-lied his mixed ancestry. And how could it not be? How could Stearns, day after day, treat a white-looking man like a black slave? Although Stearns struggled with this question, he never arrived at a coherent understanding of the social or cultural meaning of a "white Niger." He, and other Yankees like him, muddled on, trying to adapt and respond to a world that was rapidly being changed by a war for Union *and* emancipation.

Emancipation, which was in turn often linked with providential Christianity, formed still another context for the expression of racial perceptions. Many soldiers naturally attributed emancipation to God's will. Writing to his mother in November 1861, Enoch Adams, the son of an itinerant minister of the Second Great Awakening, an-ticipated Congress's acting as the Lord's agent by abolishing slavery, after which "Ethiopia shall stretch out her hands unto God." This abstraction reflects the assumption that women and African Ameri-cans, as a people, shared childlike qualities of passivity. When reality struck in April 1862, Adams declared in another letter: "You doubt-less have heard of the abolition of slavery in the District of Columbia. Glory to God! Verily the world moves." Referring to the enactment of the Emancipation Proclamation, in January 1863, he wrote: "Slav-ery is forever abolished on this Continent. God has broken the chains of the slave. Be still, and know that I am God." Quoting from Psalms 46:10, Adams attributed abolition to a providential God, whose might "makes wars cease" and safeguards His chosen "though the earth

---

[49] Marshall S. Stearns to Sula H. Stearns, January 10, 21, 1863, Stearns Family Papers.

should change," reassuring themes for a white Union soldier coping with emancipation. His scripture choice suggests that God, through His Union agents, freed the slaves in order to terminate the war; emancipation was only a means to a greater end, preserving the Union. A year later Adams re-expressed his interpretation of emancipation, while emphasizing the importance of human initiative. "Lincoln's Christmas Present" began:

> From the North Pole to the Isthmus
> There will not be a slave,
> Rebellion by next Christmas
> Will be silent in his grave,
>
> And our Liberty's assaulters
> Will find it is the same
> With us as Vesta's altars
> We forever keep the flame.[50]

Alluding to the triumph of freedom over the "slave power," the demise of rebellion was contingent upon emancipation, whereas the liberties assaulted belonged to Adams and white America, not slaves. His "Death of the Rebellion," written in April 1865, made similar claims:

> Fit tyre of race Caucasian
> That liberates a world!
>
> . . . .
>
> No more shall fetters broken
> Emit their horrid clanks,
> But instead shall be outspoken
> The living voice of thanks.
>
> . . . .
>
> And the hydra-headed terror,
> Is crushed 'neath feet of braves,
> And the land is purged of error,
> As the land is purged of slaves.[51]

Here, Adams implied the existence of a racial hierarchy, with whites in the active, dominant role. His assumption of this power relationship and his expectations regarding black reactions were perhaps in-

---

[50] "Lincoln's Christmas Present," December 1864, Adams Family Papers.
[51] "Death of the Rebellion," April 1865, ibid.

spired by antebellum-era imaginative magazine pieces popular in the North, in which hapless black literary characters would prostrate themselves before their emancipators and proceed to repay their saviors for services rendered.[52]

The form that Adams used to express himself, poetry, is as significant as the meanings embedded in his verses. Poetry was a cultural medium of enormous import in antebellum society, especially for New England, whose poets dominated the art. Poetry was part and parcel of everyday life in New England. It was recited at public events, memorized by school children, appended to political oratory, and devoured by the general reading public as quickly as it could be published. Writing verse was both a prestigious affair and a polite accomplishment within the reach of the average literate Yankee. Thus when these young military men found themselves provoked, inspired, perplexed, or frightened, they often instinctively expressed themselves through poetry. One finds that soldiers' letters are replete with poems that are usually didactic, often uplifting, and sometimes moving.[53]

Other soldiers' biblical allusions suggest a more compassionate and sublime understanding of the relationship between God and abolition, which was deemed a moral end unto itself. In May 1864, John Jenks linked emancipation with his patriotic duty to flag and comrades. He saw no "point of leaving *them* [Confederates] alone, for their hands are already red with the blood of those who have stood up for their Countries flag." Continuing, he stated that "there are millions here, anxiously looking to us to redeem them from bondage, worse then [*sic*] that of the Children of Israel." Rather than Adams's pathetic image of "Ethiopia," Jenks identified slaves as a worthy, noble people who, with human leadership and God's assistance, had

---

[52] Enoch G. Adams to Sarah S. Adams, November 26, 1861, April 27, 1862, ibid. See also Saum, *Popular Mood of Pre-Civil War America*, 3–4, 13–15; Fredrickson, *Black Image in the White Mind*, 113–15; Foner, *Free Soil*, 9, 98–102; Hess, *Liberty, Virtue, and Progress*, 28–30; and White, *Somewhat More Independent*, 62–63.

[53] Lawrence Buell, *New England Literary Culture: From Revolution Through Renaissance* (Cambridge, Eng.: Cambridge University Press, 1986), chapter 5; *The Columbia Book of Civil War Poetry: From Whitman to Walcott*, ed. by Richard Marius (New York: Columbia University Press, 1994), xiii–xiv. For another example of a soldier's poetry, see Erastus W. "Rat" Everson to Salome B. Everson, November 25 and December 17, 1862, in Everson Papers, Rare Books and Manuscripts, Boston Public Library.

endured enslavement and would escape bondage. This perception reflected the evangelical Christian humanitarianism endemic to romantic racialism, which characterized blacks as natural Christians. Although Jenks believed that African Americans were human beings whose hopes were worthy of fulfillment, his humanitarianism did not translate into fiery abolitionism. In June 1864, he encountered a mansion in Louisiana with "several rows of neat Negro houses, painted, looking like a pleasant little village. . . . [with] several hundred negroes, which will probably be free. . . . [Their owner] is a good true Union man. It is encouraging to see a few *such* men true to their Countries flag."[54] Jenks believed that cruel slavery was evil, but he did not acknowledge the abstract injustice of *all* slavery.

The Civil War was the first opportunity for extensive face-to-face interaction between African Americans and a wide range of male New England. This study suggests a shift in patterns of interaction and in underlying assumptions about race, which was caused by a collision between white soldiers' unprecedented interracial wartime experiences and their prewar racial assumptions. The force of daily encounters with—or at least observations of—blacks eroded and modified Yankees' two-dimensional racial notions, thereby blending the image of a comical, simple-minded, even subhuman African American with more complex racial models, the nature of which varied from one New Englander to another. Dehumanizing attitudes were not wholly discarded, but there was no longer a unified predominant viewpoint. Often, hostility rather than ambivalence marked white adaptation, but even this response suggested a more complex understanding of blacks. Because Yankee soldiers carried the home front to war, they were able to expand their repertoire of racial perspectives and reactions by using sociocultural terms and models derived from the paradigms that gave meaning to New England life.

---

[54] John H. Jenks to Almina C. Jenks, May 5, June 9, 1864, Jenks Family Papers. See also Fredrickson, *Black Image in the White Mind*, 104–6. The imagery that Jenks employed, as well as the overall spiritual tone of his letters, is consistent with the evangelical merchant-shopkeepers described by Paul E. Johnson, *A Shopkeeper's Millennium: Society and Revivals in Rochester, New York, 1815–1837* (New York: Hill and Wang, 1978), 4–8, 136–38.

3
From War to Peace

10

"Surely They Remember Me": The 16th Connecticut in War, Captivity, and Public Memory

Lesley J. Gordon

ON NOVEMBER 30, 1864, twenty-year-old Sergeant Major Robert H. Kellogg of the 16th Regiment Connecticut Volunteers became a free man. Since early May 1864, he and most of the rest of his regiment had been confined in Confederate prisons at Andersonville, Georgia, and Florence, South Carolina. After his exchange, he went home to Connecticut for a short furlough to recuperate and regain his strength, but he soon had to return to duty at Camp Parole, Annapolis, Maryland, to help process the thousands of other fellow prisoners returning north after months of incarceration. Through much of January 1865, as the war wound down, he witnessed the release of many other prison survivors like himself. Kellogg began to write about his experiences, drawing heavily from a personal diary he had kept in prison. Promised up to $1,000 for his account, Kellogg worked on his book feverishly, mailing stacks of manuscript pages to a publisher in Hartford. Printed in March 1865, *Life and Death in Rebel Prisons* was one of the first of many Andersonville memoirs published over the next three decades.

There were other factors than money at work in motivating Kellogg to make his personal story public. Convinced that few at home understood the appalling conditions he had withstood, he felt driven to share his experiences. Part of Kellogg's liberation was no doubt the freedom to tell his story openly. He was by no means an objective chronicler, depicting Confederates as cold, immoral people who deliberately caused the deaths of thousands of helpless men. In October 1865, he would testify in the Henry Wirz trial, helping to convict the hapless commandant of Andersonville for war crimes. But in January 1865, only two months after his release, Kellogg was anxious to inform the northern populace of the terrible ordeals he and his comrades had withstood. His publisher, L. Stebbins, explained that the purpose of the book was to "spread the facts of this subject through the entire North" in order to "raise a storm of indignation" against the Confederacy. Kellogg dedicated his account to dead prisoners' families and reminded readers of the peaceful lives he and other soldiers had left behind to go to war. He wanted to bring the prison experience home.[1]

During their captivity, most northern prisoners had very little communication with their families and friends and lost that crucial connection between soldiers and civilians. There were occasional smuggled newspapers and wild rumors of exchange, but for most prisoners, their suffering was not merely physical; they endured the mental anguish of not communicating with their loved ones. As a Hartford newspaper observed, "the greatest trial of captivity is having nothing from home."[2] Prisoners certainly did not stop thinking of their families and friends hundreds of miles away. In fact, reflecting on home, imagining what might be happening there, and thinking about the lives they left behind, seems to dominate surviving diary entries.[3]

This essay narrates the story of one northern regiment in war and

---

[1] Kellogg dedicated his book "To the Widows, Children, Fathers, Mothers, Brothers and Sisters, of the Thousands of Brave Men Who Have Left Their Homes in the Morning of Life, Sundered Family and Social Ties; Abandoned Cherished Enterprises and Business Schemes, for the Purpose of Maintaining the Laws of Freedom Inviolate, And in the Faithful Performance of Their Duty, Have Been Captured By the Enemy, And Gone Down to Untimely Graves, Through Unparalleled Sufferings, Is This Volume Most Respectfully Dedicated." In Robert H. Kellogg, *Life and Death in Rebel Prisons: Giving a Complete History of the Inhuman and Barbarous Treatment of our Brave Soldiers by Rebel Authorities, Inflicting Terrible Suffering and Frightful Mortality, Principally at Andersonville, Ga, and Florence, S.C., Describing Plans of Escape, Arrival of Prisoners, with Numerous and Varied Incidents and Anecdotes of Prison Life* (Hartford, Conn.: L. Stebbins, 1865). See also Robert Hale Kellogg Diary, Connecticut Historical Society, Hartford, Conn. (hereinafter cited as CHS); and Lesley Jill Gordon-Burr, "Storms of Indignation: The Art of Andersonville as Postwar Propaganda," *Georgia Historical Quarterly* 3 (fall 1991): 587–600.

[2] *Connecticut Courant*, July 23, 1864.

[3] Reid Mitchell in particular has explored the important role images of home played in the minds of northern soldiers, but he says very little about prisoners. See Reid Mitchell, *The Vacant Chair: The Northern Soldier Leaves Home* (New York: Oxford University Press, 1993). This author especially focused on the unpublished

captivity, paying particular attention to the regiment's impressions of home before, during, and after their imprisonment. By utilizing a select number of unpublished diaries and letters, as well as a scattering of published accounts, it begins to explore how some soldiers, stripped of their ability and opportunity to fight, and dying from starvation, disease, and exposure, struggled to see their suffering as part of the larger Union war effort. Made helpless by their captivity, they strove to keep their identity as loyal northern soldiers and maintain their commitment to the war effort. Veterans of the unit sought to redefine their helpless and dehumanizing incarceration into something courageous and necessary to northern victory. They later publicly presented their regiment's terrible imprisonment as stoic resistance to the enemy's war-making capabilities on par with performing heroically in battle.

This essay is just one part of a larger story of soldiers lost in the margins of war, first transferred from active service to garrison duty, then kept in the South's most notorious stockade. The 16th Connecticut participated in only one large-scale engagement during their entire service, the battle of Antietam. After a mere two weeks in uniform, the green regiment broke under enfilade fire just south of Burnside's Bridge, sustaining nearly 25 percent casualties. In 1863, the unit was placed on garrison duty, first in eastern Virginia and then in coastal North Carolina. Stationed at Plymouth in January 1864, with a scattering of other small units, the regiment was far removed from the major operations of the war. When they were captured on April 20, 1864, they felt they had been forgotten and left vulnerable by the Union military hierarchy. When remnants of the regiment finally came home in June 1865, they arrived in Hartford earlier than anyone expected and a hasty welcome had to be organized. One member later wrote: "The Sixteenth was always called an *unfortunate regiment*, for if there was any special hardship to endure the regiment was sure to be called on to experience it; either by accident or otherwise. It was our bad luck."[4]

The 16th Connecticut did not begin its service with any prophetic signs that it would be so unfortunate. In fact, there were high expec-

---

diaries of six men from the 16th Connecticut: Robert Kellogg, Oliver Gates, Joseph Barnum, Samuel Grosvenor, Charles Adams, and Ira Forbes.

[4] Bernard Blakeslee, *The History of the Sixteenth Connecticut Volunteers* (Hartford: Case, Lockwood and Brainard Co., Printers, 1875), 108–9.

tations for the new regiment to perform well and reflect favorably on
its home communities in prosperous Hartford County when it was
formed in the summer of 1862. The regiment included members of
some of the oldest and wealthiest families in the state, as well as
recent arrivals from Germany and Ireland. Most were young, unmarried, and inexperienced, but anxious to go to the front. Volunteers
included farmers, mechanics, teachers, and artisans. Their reasons
for joining were similar to those of other Union troops. Some felt
strongly that the Union had to be preserved, a few were abolitionists
and sought an immediate end to slavery. Many were devout Christians who saw a religious purpose in the war. There was also social
pressure to enlist and the belief that war would be an exciting adventure. Sometimes idealistic motivations mixed with practical ones; certainly, the promise of bounties and steady pay was attractive to many
men.[5]

Before leaving Hartford, the unit encamped near the state capitol
at "Camp Williams." There was a steady stream of visitors, and men
easily obtained furloughs to go home. One private's mother came to
see her son nearly every day after he enlisted.[6] Twenty-year-old Elizur D. Belden described doing very little in camp, except enjoying
the dancing, music, and female guests. On August 26, just before the

---

[5] W. A. Croffut and John M. Morris, *The Military and Civil History of Connecticut
During the War of 1861–1865* (New York: Ledyard Bill, 1869), 227–29; *Catalogue
of the 14th, 15th, 16th, 17th, 18th, 19th, 20th, and 21st Regiments and the Second
Light Battery Connecticut Volunteers; and the 22d, 23d, 24th, 26th, 27th, 28th Regiment Connecticut Volunteers for Nine Months, Compiled from Records of the Adju-
tant-Generals Office 1862* (Hartford: Press of Case, Lockwood and Company, 1862),
47–67; "Muster and Descriptive Rolls, 16th Regiment Connecticut Volunteers," Records of the Military Department, Connecticut Adjutant General's Office, RG 13,
Connecticut State Library, Hartford, Conn. (hereinafter cited as CSL). James M.
McPherson has explored this best in his recent book, *For Cause & Comrades: Why
Men Fought in the Civil War* (New York: Oxford University Press, 1997). Examples
of motivation for different members of the regiment include Robert H. Kellogg to
Father and Mother, September 10, 1862, Kellogg Papers, CHS, where Kellogg
states, "We must free the blacks or perish as a nation." In Samuel Richards to B. B.
Lewis, August 31, 1863, Archives, United States Army Military History Institute,
Carlisle, Pa. (hereinafter cited as USAMHI), Richards reasons that it is time southern masters switched places with their black slaves; Ira Forbes concluded in March
1864 that the "more I know about slavery, the more I abhor and detest it." See Ira
Forbes Diary, March 17, 1864, Yale University Library, New Haven, Conn. (hereinafter cited as YU).

[6] John B. Cuzner to Ellen Van Dorn, August 27, 1862, John B. Cuzner Papers,
CHS.

regiment left for the front, he maintained that so many civilians poured into camp that "the blue coats of the boys could hardly be seen by the crowd of visitors."[7] However, Bernard Blakeslee recalled those first few days of soldiering as "a shock to most of the men" and a "complete revolution in their method of life," despite the many visitors and festive atmosphere.[8] On August 15, Colonel Frank Beach arrived and tried to instill some semblance of military discipline and conformity on the men, with little success. When Beach angrily blasted the troops for their shortcomings, the new volunteers scoffed at him, vowing to "fill his back full of bead."[9] Just before the regiment was to report to the front, the men rushed home for one last visit. A newspaper reported that those who remained in camp had home brought to them: "Those who could not get away were visited by their friends and sweethearts who brought them delicacies, etc."[10]

The journey south offered more lessons in military discipline. The men scoffed at having to stay in the lower deck of the ship and complained bitterly that officers seemed to have better rations. Resentment toward Colonel Beach, a West Pointer and son of a prominent Hartford banker, only continued. He seemed arrogant and arbitrary. John Edward Shipman, a twenty-nine-year-old Hartford printer in Company C, wrote a friend that Colonel Beach frequently struck the men with his sword: "a favorite game with him." According to Shipman, Beach and other officers plundered goods the men were given by a generous farmer, and one day the colonel "took a chicken away from a man who had bought it," only afterward offering to pay for it. "Many of the men," Shipman wrote, "swear they will shoot him if he ever goes into action with us."[11]

The march to the front brought harsher realities. It was a long, tiring journey through Virginia into western Maryland. The dust was thick and men fell repeatedly out of the ranks to rest, unable to keep up the pace. On September 3, the regiment finally received guns, and soon after had their first real drill with arms. But they were wholly

---

[7] Entries for August 19, 23, 26, 1862, Elizur D. Belden Diary, CHS.

[8] Blakeslee, *History of the Sixteenth Connecticut Volunteers*, 5.

[9] Quoted from William Relyea, "The History of the 16th Connecticut Volunteers," 4, CHS; see also Blakeslee, *History of the Sixteenth Connecticut Volunteers*, 6; Croffutt and Morris, *Military and Civil History of Connecticut*, 228–29.

[10] *Hartford Courant*, August 27, 1862.

[11] J. Edward Shipman to Friend Hubbard, September 14, 1862, Lewis Leigh Collection, USAMHI.

unprepared for combat when, two weeks later, on the bloodiest single day of the war, they were called into action.[12]

On the afternoon of September 17, 1862, the 16th Connecticut was rushed into the fray just below Burnside's Bridge. Faced with severe enfilade fire, the regiment broke in a wild panic. Elizur Belden recorded in his diary: "The bullets flying thick and fast, men falling all around. I turned with the rest and made for the fence over which I clim[b]ed."[13] Private John B. Cuzner wrote his fiancée Ellen soon after the battle and claimed that there were a few members of the regiment who "did not frighten," but he was not one of them: "As for myself, I am a big coward."[14] The day after the battle, a mere twenty-five men reported present for duty. For the next several days, armed guards kept watch over the regiment's camp to prevent more desertions.[15]

In the days and weeks that followed Antietam, as the regiment took stock of its humiliating baptism of fire, members of the 16th continued writing letters home, trying to describe what they had experienced. Kellogg wrote to his father: "We were murdered. A green Regt. placed unsupported in a cornfield in the immediate vicinity of a cunning fire—and as it were left to take care of itself."[16] Eventually these painful individual memories of Antietam would be replaced by a generalized and very public one of honor and courage. But for now, the men of the 16th Connecticut had many more months of service to endure.[17]

---

[12] Entries for September 3, 4, 1862, Elizur Belden Diary, CHS; entry for September 3, 1862, Charles Lee Diary, Charles Lee Papers, CHS. The date that the regiment received their guns is not entirely clear, nor do all accounts agree on when the men began to learn to use them. Charles Lee states that they began drilling with their Whitney rifles on September 3 and learned to load and fire them on September 9; but Elizur Belden cites September 4 as the day they began to drill with them.

[13] Entry for September 19, 1862, Elizur Belden Diary, CHS.

[14] John B. Cuzner to Ellen Van Dorn, September 21, 1862, John B. Cuzner Papers, CHS.

[15] Garrett B. Holcombe to Sister, September 23, 1862, Antietam National Battlefield, Sharpsburg, Md. (hereinafter cited as ANB); see also entry for September 18, 1863, Robert H. Kellogg Diary, CHS.

[16] Robert H. Kellogg to Father, September 20, 1862, Robert H. Kellog Papers, CHS.

[17] A more complete account of the regiment's Antietam experience is Lesley J. Gordon, " 'All Who Went Into That Battle Were Heroes': The 16th Regiment Connecticut Volunteers Remember Antietam," in *The Antietam Campaign*, ed. by Gary W. Gallagher (Chapel Hill: University of North Carolina Press, 1999): 169–91.

Some had already had enough. Others seemed to change their minds weekly, and some were even more determined to see the war to its end. John Cuzner, who admitted to being a coward at Antietam, insisted a few days after the battle that he was content to stay in uniform: "You can tell any one that thinks I am tired of soldiers life," he wrote his fiancée, "it is no such thing[.] if they told me I could go home to day[,] I would not[.] that's as true as I write it[.] I have got a good Rifle and know how to use it as well as most people and I don't mean to have it idle while my term lasts."[18] William H. Drake wrote a cousin in late September: "The boys are about sick of the fun and I don't think you could enlist 10 men out of the Reg. To day if back home. One thing I know they could not get this chap again."[19] Austin D. Thompson agreed. He wrote home to Electra Churchill that he too had lost his taste for war: "The soldiers life is a rough tough life, and for my part I care not how soon the war is finished."[20] But five days later, Thompson felt differently: "I like soldiering first rate when I can get under some good shady tree and write letters to friends."[21] Thompson also noted an extra skittishness on the part of the regiment: "Some of the boys seem to be a little afraid when they hear the cannons roar. I don't know as I blame them much for they are dangerous things to have around, especially when they are loaded and fired at any one."[22]

After the debacle at Antietam, the 16th Connecticut would face very little gunfire at all. They sat out the battle of Fredericksburg in December 1862, and in February 1863, they were transferred from the Army of the Potomac to Suffolk, Virginia, where they saw only sporadic fighting during the Confederacy's failed siege of the town. Their discontent with soldiering did not abate; in fact, kept out of the major action and kept far from home, morale weakened. Austin D.

---

[18] John B. Cuzner to Ellen Van Dorn, September 21, 1862, John B. Cuzner Papers, CHS.

[19] William H. Drake to Cousin, September 29, 1862, Civil War Letters, Box II, CHS.

[20] Austin D. Thompson to Electra Churchill, October 3, 1862, Austin D. Thompson Papers, CHS.

[21] Austin D. Thompson to Electra Churchill, October 8, 1962, Austin D. Thompson Papers, CHS.

[22] Austin D. Thompson to Electra Churchill, October 16, 1862, Austin D. Thompson Papers, CHS; see also Gordon, " 'All Who Went Into That Battle Were Heroes,' " 177–80.

Thompson maintained in late December 1862 that he had "lost all patriotism." "You go through the whole Regt. and if you find one [member] that says he is not sick of living in the way that you do, you may have my head for a football." Thompson complained that the officers continued to hoard the best meat, living "fast," while the men in the ranks did all the work. To make matters worse, the regiment had yet to be paid.[23]

Just before their transfer to Suffolk in February 1863, the regiment nearly staged a mutiny. The paymaster told members of the regiment that he had no evidence that the 16th ever had been formally mustered into service or even existed. Irate members of the unit organized a committee to draft a letter to the governor of Connecticut. "We were willing to serve our term of enlistment," William Relyea recalled, "but we wanted our pay and unless that was forthcoming or some proper reason was given why we did not receive it, we should consider our contract with the government null and void." Their letter to the governor affirmed that they did not "wish to shirk our duty in any way," but that "if we were an unknown quantity and have not been properly mustered into the service of the United States we should request the Governor to recall us as we had been out of the state longer than the law allowed them to keep us." If in fact they were not really soldiers, they would willingly go home and resume their civilian lives. Governor William Buckingham responded by accusing the regiment of mutiny and threatening to have the entire regiment remustered with no pay for the time already served. Lawyers were retained, and it looked like the 16th Connecticut's next real combat experience was going to be a legal one rather than on the battlefield. An officer eventually quelled the regiment's discontent by making a personal visit to Washington, pay was issued, and, as the regiment's chronicler William Relyea described, "the boys were made happy."[24]

Moved from Suffolk, Virginia, to a camp near Portsmouth during the summer of 1863, the 16th settled into relatively pleasant quarters. It was even further removed from several key campaigns, including

---

[23] Austin D. Thompson to Electra Churchill, December 27, 1862; officers living "fast" comes from Austin D. Thompson to Electra Churchill, January 11, 1863. See also Austin D. Thompson to Electra Churchill, October 23, 1863; and Austin D. Thompson to Electra Churchill, January 4, 1863, Austin D. Thompson Papers, CHS.

[24] Relyea, "History of the 16th Connecticut," 92–94, CHS.

Gettysburg, Vicksburg, Chickamauga, and Lookout Mountain. Men built winter cabins, a church, and a hospital. Military discipline was lax; there were poker games, theatrical productions, and plentiful liquor available. Mail was steady, and men anxiously kept up with the news from home, poring over letters from loved ones and friends. Captain Joseph Barnum counted each and every letter he received from his wife and the ones he sent her, making special note in his diary.[25] Many civilians visited camp, including officers' wives and Hartford newspaper reporters. Lieutenant Colonel John Burnham's mother came to Portsmouth for several weeks and helped care for sick in the hospital. As one historian has noted, "these visits tended to bring the war very close to the home folks."[26] But they also served to bring home to the soldiers. Peddlers were frequent visitors to camp. "We can get almost anything we want here from peddlers," Harrison Woodford wrote to his mother. "We can get ice cream, lemonade, pies & cakes, cherries, onions, fried fish, beer & almost anything else."[27] Leander Chapin sent his mother a pair of pants and three shirts: "I have clothes enough now to last for several months."[28] Life for the 16th Connecticut was about as comfortable as it could be.[29]

Despite their comfortable quarters, relaxed discipline, and frequent civilian visitors, men of the 16th Connecticut, like Civil War soldiers everywhere, complained. They complained about bad food, unfair officers, and continual sickness. They did not like the work they did: building breastworks and going on sporadic raids was rarely very exciting. Kellogg described their status as "nomads," so cut off did the men feel from the rest of the Union Army and main theaters.[30] Devout Christians worried about the spiritual state of the

---

[25] Joseph H. Barnum Diary, CHS.

[26] Quote from John Niven, *Connecticut for the Union: The Role of the State in the Civil War* (New Haven: Yale University Press, 1965), 321. Additional evidence of visitors to the camp (especially wives) includes entry for January 6, 1864, Joseph Barnum Diary, CHS; Kellogg, *Life and Death in Rebel Prisons*, 205; Austin D. Thompson to Electra Churchill, December 19, 1863, Austin D. Thompson Papers, CHS.

[27] Harrison Woodford to Mother, June 19, 1863, typescript copies of originals, Harrison Woodford Papers, CHS.

[28] Leander Chapin to Mother, November 25, 1863, Leander Chapin Papers, CHS.

[29] More on Portsmouth is found in Austin D. Thompson to Electra Churchill, November 30, 1863; and December 6, 1863, Austin D. Thompson Papers, CHS.

[30] Kellogg speculated that being sent to North Carolina was an "act of spite engen-

unit, with so much idle time on their hands. And although they were far removed from the worst fighting, men of the 16th wondered if in fact the northern people appreciated the sacrifice of the men in blue.[31]

In January 1864, orders came for the 16th Connecticut to abandon its comfortable quarters at Portsmouth, Virginia. Learning that their unit was going to be detached from Edward Harland's 2nd Brigade and sent to North Carolina, the men balked. Showing the same stubborn defiance they had displayed nearly a year earlier over their lack of pay, they refused to vacate their quarters for another regiment to occupy. They burned the entire encampment, leaving it, in the words of one private, "a mass of ruins."[32] It had served as their home away from home and strangers were not going to enjoy its comforts. Nearly all the regiment's commissioned officers were arrested for allowing the camp's destruction. Upon hearing news of the officers' arrest, several men stepped out of ranks and refused to move out of camp as ordered. A Delaware Battery took position opposite the regiment and readied to take aim. Outrage ran up and down the ranks and the men vowed to charge and take the battery if in fact it opened fire. After several tense moments, cooler heads prevailed and the 16th Regiment Connecticut Volunteers marched out of Portsmouth onto railroad cars and soon headed for Plymouth, North Carolina. Color corporal Ira Forbes described "an alarming amount of drunkenness" on board the small boats taking them further south.[33]

Plymouth was an important strategic position, located on the south bank of the Roanoke River. It anchored the northernmost point of Federal occupation on the North Carolina coastline, serving as a supply depot for Union land forces stationed there. The actual town of Plymouth bore deep scars from the war. Most residents had fled, and many residences and businesses were burned-out ruins. A soldier described it to his mother: "Plymouth is one of the many places in

---

dered by the sorely disappointed people who displaced us and who were especial friends of the General commanding the department." See Kellogg, *Life and Death in Rebel Prisons*, 140.

[31] Ira Forbes contends that there was a high level of religiosity in the regiment at Portsmouth. See entries for January 9, 11, 1864, Ira Forbes Diary, YU.

[32] Leander Chapin to Gilbert Chapin, January 31, 1864, Leander Chapin Papers, CHS.

[33] Quotation from entry for January 21, 1864, Ira Forbes Diary, YU. See also Relyea, "History of the 16th Connecticut," 138–39, CHS.

the South that can ascribe its desolation to the rebellion. Formerly it was a very pretty place for a Southern village."[34] But now, it was desolate and damaged by Confederate raids and Union occupation.

The 16th Connecticut was stationed just outside the town with the 101st and 103rd Pennsylvania and 85th New York Volunteer Infantry, portions of the 2nd Massachusetts Heavy Artillery, the 24th New York Independent Battery, a squad of the 12th New York Cavalry, and two companies of the 2nd North (Loyalist) Carolina. Four gunboats patrolled the river, protecting the small garrison from enemy attack. All told, there were about twenty-eight hundred men at Plymouth under the command of Brigadier General Henry W. Wessells. Most men were veterans, and except for the 16th, all the infantry units had seen a lot of hard fighting. One member of the 16th remarked that "all of these regiments were but the remnants of noble regiments that had been decimated by battle and disease."[35]

From January until April 1864, the 16th Connecticut kept busy manning forts, posting sentries, mounting guard duty. There were frequent detachments sent out on scouting expeditions, and for three weeks in March, the unit went to New Bern to help build fortifications. But it returned to Plymouth to resume garrison duty outside of town. A steady stream of slaves, Unionist civilians, and Confederate deserters came over the lines to seek refuge in the federal garrison. A contraband Sunday school was set up nearby, and some members of the 16th visited and even taught classes. Mail came regularly, officers' wives continued to visit, and baseball, wicket, and card games were common distractions. Hometown newspapers were not hard to obtain, keeping the men abreast of local news and events. The Temperance Society sponsored formal debates on resolutions such as whether "intemperance is a greater evil than war" and "the present war will be productive of more good than evil." The men again built comfortable quarters, putting floors into their tents and building brick fireplaces. Trips to town were frequent, and in March, several members of the regiment were allowed to go home on furlough so they could vote in Connecticut's gubernatorial election. Their duty,

---

[34] Leander Chapin to Mother, February 14, 1864, Leander Chapin Papers, CHS.

[35] Relyea, "History of the 16th Connecticut," 160; also James G. Barrett, *The Civil War in North Carolina* (Chapel Hill: University of North Carolina Press, 1963), 213; Philip Katcher, *Lethal Glory: Dramatic Defeats of the Civil War* (London: Arms & Armour Press, 1995), 149–50.

as at Portsmouth, was not especially difficult or taxing, but the war dragged on and men complained that they were not getting enough to eat.[36] A private wrote to his mother: "I do not think we will have any fighting to do, nothing more than a little skirmish occasionally. There is not force enough here to do any amount of fighting. We are simply [a] garrison."[37] Except for Antietam, the 16th Connecticut's wartime service had proven more monotonous than dangerous. Many began to count the days until their three-year term would be over. For some, their early idealism was giving way to disillusionment and frustration. Samuel Derby wrote to his wife Elizabeth on April 1, 1864, that "this war has altered a good deal since we left the state then it looked more like a war for the union but now it looks like a war for political capital and money for some are making . . . fortunes out of this war."[38]

The regiment had changed as well. Its ranks had been reduced ever since Antietam, and in 1863, an increasing number of conscripts arrived to bolster its strength. In July 1863, when rumors began to spread that the draftees were coming, Austin D. Thompson reflected: "The latest news is that the 16th is going to be filled up with drafted men. Some of the boys do not like it very much but however I do not see as they can help themselves."[39] These new arrivals always seemed set apart and treated differently from the original volunteers who had formed the regiment nearly two years earlier.

Among that core group of original volunteers, there did remain those committed to the war and doing their military duty no matter what form it took. Austin Thompson explained that he would very much prefer coming home to staying in the army, but could not bear the public shame if he came home dishonorably: "But if I can stand it through to the end, I had much rather do it, than go home with a

---

[36] Details of Plymouth from Paul C. Helmreich, ed., "The Diary of Charles G. Lee in the Andersonville and Florence Prison Camps, 1864," *Connecticut Historical Society Bulletin* (January 1976): 13–14; Barrett, *The Civil War in North Carolina*, 213; Ira Forbes Diary, YU.

[37] Leander Chapin to Mother, February 2, 1864, Leander Chapin Papers, CHS.

[38] Samuel Derby to Elizabeth Derby, April 1, 1864, in "Samuel Derby's War Letters," ed. by James M. Kuras, *New Hampshire College Journal* 1 (spring 1993): 8.

[39] Austin D. Thompson to Electra Churchill, July 17, 1863, Austin D. Thompson Papers, CHS. Ira Forbes simply called them "new recruits." See entries for February 2, 7, 9, 1864, Ira Forbes Diary, YU.

name that some of the boys have."[40] Private Leander Chapin wrote to his brother Gilbert in March 1864:

> Your advice in begging me to keep out of danger sounds harsh coming from a friend of his country. I know how you feel and highly appreciate your motive but I beg of you not to write in such a way. It is productive of no good, rather harm. Shall I not do my duty wherever I am called to go? It is much safer to go right along even though the enemy's balls are dealing death on all sides than it is to seek a better place. Experience proves this. Let me die a hero rather than live a coward.[41]

One year earlier, Chapin had told his mother that the war saved him. "I came near dying at home at any rate I cared so little for my life I was tempted time and time again to make way with myself." He was convinced that if he had not enlisted, "I would by this time have been in another world."[42] Now, exactly twelve months later, Chapin chided his mother for hoping the regiment would be sent to a safer place—the16th Connecticut already was far removed from the action and at a well-fortified spot. Chapin wanted letters from home that were happy and free of worry. His family's constant complaining and fretting only unnerved the young soldier, and in his mind, made him "unfit for the duties of my place."[43]

The type of soldiering the 16th Connecticut had so far endured did not match their initial expectations, nor did it match the experiences of many other units close to the front. But Leander Chapin and other original members of the unit found something they had not discovered in their predictable prewar lives: comradeship and a sense of identity larger than themselves. Chapin told his brother in March 1864, "Where my regiment goes there I go."[44]

One month later, Chapin found his words tested when the harsh realities of war suddenly turned on the regiment yet again. On April 17, 1864, Confederate Brigadier General Robert Hoke attacked Plymouth with a large combined land and naval force, outnumbering

---

[40] Austin D. Thompson to Electra Churchill, August 17, 1863, Austin D. Thompson Papers, CHS.

[41] Leander Chapin to Gilbert Chapin, March 19, 1864, Leander Chapin Papers, CHS.

[42] Leander Chapin to Mother, March 19, 1863, ibid.

[43] Leander Chapin to Gilbert Chapin, March 19, 1864, ibid.

[44] Ibid.

the Federals nearly four to one.[45] When the Confederate ram *Albermarle* successfully made its way by the Union fleet protecting the Federal position, the Yankee troops faced attacks from all sides. The 16th Connecticut, numbering four hundred men, was positioned at Fort Williams, at the center of the Union breastworks. From the early evening of April 17 until the morning of April 20, the regiment withstood nearly constant cannonade fire and battled back several infantry charges upon their entrenched works. Captured Union gunboats pounded the bluecoats' position unmercifully. Men were scared. Lieutenant Colonel Burnham tried to soothe the regiment's nerves by ordering the band to play patriotic songs. At first, this seemed to work. Robert Kellogg remembered: "Brave hearts became braver, and if the patriotism of any waxed cold, and the courage of any faltered, they here grew warmer and stronger until the pride of country had touched the will, and an indomitable principle had been kindled that virtually declared the man a hero until death." But before long, a Confederate battery took aim at the musicians and shells began to drop over their heads. At this moment, Kellogg wrote, "the musicians retired precipitately, the bass drummer throwing his sticks in one direction and his drum in another, leaving the defense of the breastworks to the boys with the rifles."[46]

On April 20, 1864, the Confederates demanded surrender. Union General Wessells refused. He later reported: "I was now completely enveloped on every side, Fort Williams an inclosed work in the center of the line, being my only hope. This was well understood by the enemy, and in less than an hour a cannonade of shot and shell was

---

[45] Numbers vary, but Wessells listed his casualties at 2,834 men killed, wounded, and missing; a member of the 24th New York claimed only sixteen hundred of Wessell's men actually participated in the fight. A Richmond newspaper reportedly counted Wessell's loss to be "2,500 men, 28 pieces of artillery, 500 horses, 5,000 stands of small arms, 700 barrels of flour. . . and most important, the strong position of Plymouth." Hoke's numbers vary from 10,000 to 12,000. See Barrett, *The Civil War in North Carolina*, 220; United States War Department, *The War of the Rebellion: A Compilation of the Official Records of the Union and Confederate Armies*, 70 vols. in 128 (Washington, D.C.: Government Printing Office, 1880–1901), series 1, vol. 33, 301 (hereinafter cited as *Official Records*); Wayne Mahood, *The Plymouth Pilgrims: A History of the Eighty-Fifth New York Infantry in the Civil War*, ed. by David G. Martin, rev. ed. (Hightstown, N.J.: Longstreet House, 1991), 168.

[46] Kellogg, *Life and Death in Rebel Prisons*, 29; a slightly different account of this is included in Relyea's "History of the 16th Connecticut," 172, CHS.

opened upon it from four different directions. This terrible fire had to be endured without reply, as no man could live at the guns." Wessells finally decided that he had no more options. "This condition of affairs could not be long endured, and in compliance with the earnest desire of every officer I consented to hoist a white flag, and at 10 a.m. of April 20 I had the mortification of surrendering my post to the enemy with all it contained."[47] "General this is the saddest day of my life," Wessells reportedly observed to Hoke. Hoke responded: "General Wessells, this is the proudest day of mine."[48]

"The 'rebs' took us all," recorded Samuel Grosvenor in his diary on April 20, and indeed, nearly the entire regiment was captured except for one company and a scattering of men on detached service.[49] Surrendering was done "with no willing grace," maintained Sergeant Major Robert Kellogg, "yet it could not but be attended with the consciousness that we had tried the virtue of resistance to the utmost."[50] Oliver Gates similarly explained that "we could not do much against such odds so we were obliged to surrender."[51] The men were exhausted. Kept awake with little sleep and little food for three days and under nearly constant artillery fire by the enemy, the end of the fight had to have come as somewhat of a relief.

Marched inland, the regiment was unsure of their final destination. But food was plentiful, and Confederates allowed them to take frequent rests. Although the men were pleasantly surprised by the kind treatment initially afforded them by their captors, it was clear that life had changed. Kellogg remembered: "Instead of the calls to which we had been wont to listen and the labor we had been accustomed to perform, we were but passive beings, subject to the will of the conqueror."[52]

---

[47] H. W. Wessells, to John J. Peck, August 18, 1864, *Official Records*, series 1, vol. 33, 299.

[48] Quoted in Katcher, *Lethal Glory*, 157.

[49] Entry for April 20, 1864, Samuel Grosvenor Dairy, CHS. Not all of the 16th Connecticut was captured. On April 17, Company "H" escorted women and other civilians from Plymouth to Roanoke Island. They would continue in active service as the 16th Connecticut even though they numbered only about 100 men. There are accounts claiming that the Confederates shot black Union soldiers "in cold blood," refusing to take them prisoners. See Oliver Gates Diary (May 1864), CHS.

[50] Kellogg, *Life and Death in Rebel Prisons*, 33.

[51] Oliver Gates Diary (May 1864), CHS, punctuation added.

[52] Kellogg, *Life and Death in Rebel Prisons*, 34.

Several members of the regiment wrote hasty letters to their families at home, reassuring them that they were safe, and predicting that they would be quickly exchanged. Kellogg wrote his father a short note and told him not to worry. "The rebs treat us very kindly and as a whole [are a] fine set of men & good soldiers," Kellogg confessed. "I can but laugh at the ridiculous plight we are in."[53]

The Confederates stopped in Tarboro and a crowd of curiosity-seekers came out of their homes to gaze upon the enemy. Kellogg described prisoners singing " 'Home Sweet Home' and 'Sweet Hour of Prayer,' and many other beautiful hymns, richly suggestive of homes on earth and home in heaven."[54] Singing helped to bolster their spirits and keep the men cheerful as they continued their journey further south.

On May 3 and 4, 1864, the men of the 16th Connecticut entered Andersonville prison. Robert Kellogg scribbled into his diary: "As we entered the place a spectacle met our gaze which almost froze our blood—our hearts failed us as we saw what *used to be* men now nothing but mere *skeletons* covered with filth & vermin. God protect us! He alone can bring us out of this awful mess."[55] "Oh horrors of horrors!" Samuel Grosvenor wrote, "I only got so as to look into the stockade where I am likely to stay quite a while when my heart goes sick and my blood curdles in my veins."[56] Ira Forbes wrote, "of all places of distress and misery and suffering which I have ever seen this is the worst."[57]

The Confederacy erected Andersonville near the town of Anderson, deep in Georgia, eleven miles northwest of Americus. After two years of war and the Federal policy of refusing prisoner exchanges, the Confederates desperately needed a new location to handle the growing number of Union captives overwhelming Richmond's prisons. Andersonville, first opened on February 24, 1864, initially mea-

---

[53] Robert H. Kellogg to Father, April 20, 1864, Robert H. Kellogg Papers, CHS; also Kellogg, *Life and Death in Rebel Prisons*, 37; entry for April 20, 1864, Ira Forbes Diary, YU.

[54] Kellogg, *Life and Death in Rebel Prisons*, 39.

[55] Entry for May 3, 1864, Robert H. Kellogg Diary, CHS, underlines from original. Apparently, most of the regiment entered the prison over two days, May 3–4, although those who remained behind to care for the wounded did not enter the prison until June. See also entries for May 3, 4, 1864, Ira Forbes Diary, YU.

[56] Entry for May 4, 1864, Samuel Grosvenor Diary, CHS.

[57] Entry for May 3, 1864, Ira Forbes Diary, YU.

sured about sixteen and a half acres. Later, it was enlarged by ten more acres. About the time the 16th arrived, in early May 1864, 12,213 inmates crowded into the open-air stockade. By the time Andersonville closed its gates for good, forty-one thousand men had been imprisoned there; nearly one-third of this number made the prison their final resting place.[58]

An estimated four hundred members of the 16th Connecticut were imprisoned at Andersonville; nearly one-third of them died there.[59] At first glance, the experiences of the 16th Connecticut did not seem especially unique from those endured by their fellow inmates. Like most, they suffered from exposure, contagious disease, and lack of adequate sanitary facilities, tainted water, improper diet, and inadequate medical care. Diarrhea, dysentery, and scurvy tormented the regiment. Relatively healthy when they arrived, members of the 16th soon grew weak and severely ill.

But because so many of the same regiment were at Andersonville at the same time, members of the 16th strengthened their sense of regimental identity during their long incarceration. They relied heavily on one another for survival. Organized into groups of ninety, the 16th Connecticut soldiers continued to share their living quarters with their comrades, often sticking to the same company affiliations they shared from the start of their enlistment. Diaries attest to the necessity for friends to help weaker prisoners persevere despite the prison's horrific conditions.[60]

A band of raiders within the prison wreaked havoc on new arrivals, and the 16th Connecticut, with their overcoats and blankets still intact, offered easy targets. Sergeant Major Kellogg wrote, "we as a regiment presented a united front, and were therefore too strong for

---

[58] William Marvel, *Andersonville, The Last Depot* (Chapel Hill: University of North Carolina Press, 1994); Ovid L. Futch, *History of Andersonville Prison* (Gainesville: University Press of Florida, 1968), 17.

[59] Not all members of the captured 16th Connecticut arrived at Andersonville at the same time, and commissioned officers were sent to Macon instead and soon exchanged. Numbers vary regarding prisoners and deaths. Kellogg estimates 300 men from the regiment were imprisoned at Andersonville, of which nearly one-third died. Other accounts give higher estimates. See, for example, *Dedication of the Monument at Andersonville Georgia October 23, 1907 in Memory of the Men of Connecticut Who Suffered in Southern Military Prisons 1861–1865* (Hartford: State of Connecticut, 1908), 32; Kellogg, *Life and Death in Rebel Prisons*, 61.

[60] These generalizations are drawn from the diaries examined for this essay, including the accounts of Kellogg, Gates, Grosvenor, and Forbes.

them." For a unit that had stayed relatively safe and removed from most of the hardest fighting of the war, the change must have been a shock. Kellogg admitted: "It required no little vigilance and sacrifice to adapt ourselves to all these circumstances of our prison life."[61]

Members also kept special tabs on how each other fared. Although the unit itself was broken down by the prison's system of organization, word traveled fast about new arrivals, those who entered the hospital, and those who died. Robert Kellogg, Oliver Gates, Samuel Grosvenor, Henry Adams, Charles Lee, and Ira Forbes all carefully recorded deaths within the regiment. On June 20, Lee described the death of Corporal Bosworth: "This is the first death which has occurred in our regiment since we came here and we have none at all in the hospital. But we are all liable to be taken down and die in a few days."[62] Diarists often referred sadly to the families left fatherless, mothers left childless, and the wives made widows.[63] Ira Forbes was with Leander Chapin when he died on July 20, 1864. The young soldier, who had told his mother that joining the army saved his life, and who had chided his younger brother for wanting him to quit the service, died in Forbes words "easily." Chapin apparently was "out of his head for quite a while before he died," and left "no word for his friends at home." But Forbes observed that Chapin had told him just a few days before his death that "he had strong hopes of returning home."[64] Oliver Gates also recorded Chapin's death, adding, "we had a short and appropriate service over his remains previous to his being carried out for burial."[65] Robert Kellogg usually mentioned that a proper service for the regiment's dead occurred before the bodies were taken to the gate to be buried outside the stockade. Years after the war it was a point of pride among survivors that no member of the 16th Connecticut "lacked reverent burial."[66]

The dehumanizing nature of their imprisonment weighed heavily on the minds of several members of the regiment. It seemed so unmanly, so cowardly, for them to be made so helpless. As one member

---

[61] Kellogg, *Life and Death in Rebel Prisons*, 67–68.

[62] Helmreich, ed., "Diary of Charles G. Lee," 19.

[63] For example, see entry for July 17, 1864, Ira Forbes Diary, YU; entry for August 12, 1864, Oliver Gates Diary, CHS.

[64] Entry for July 20, 1864, Ira Forbes Diary, YU.

[65] Entry for July 20, 1864, Oliver Gates Diary, CHS.

[66] *Dedication of the Monument at Andersonville, Georgia*, 12.

explained: "They do not ask to be free from all participation in the strife, but they do long to walk forth from their *cankerous* dens, even though it may be to meet the sulphurous smoke of the cannon, in the fiercely contested battle, for there, at least would be *glorious action.*"[67]

Members of the 16th struggled to find meaning in their captivity and affirm their commitment to the war.[68] Corporal Charles Lee wrote on July 4, 1864: "This is the anniversary of our national independence and instead of celebrating it in Connecticut as I have done every year of my life except last year, I am a prisoner of war shut up in this nasty bull-pen with no immediate prospect of getting out. Yet I am perfectly willing to suffer it all, if it does anything towards saving the union."[69] On August 11, 1864, Robert Kellogg reflected: "Two years ago today I entered Uncle Sam's service and I can honestly say now that I am not sorry that I enlisted, even if I am 'in durance vile.' "[70] Oliver Gates was not so sure. Marking the date that he entered the service he confessed: "Sometimes I regret having enlisted for so long a time as three years to leave a wife and a little girl at home so long but my Country needed my services and thus far [I] have tried to do a Soldier's Duty faithfully and in an active service of two years we have necessarily seen more or less hardship but nothing can compare with this imprisonment[.] no human suffering can exceed what we witness here." He declared: "When I came in here three months ago I was a strong healthy man and could endure almost anything as I thought but now I am but the wreck of my former self almost a Cripple."[71]

It was doubly painful to be kept in such horrific conditions with

---

[67] Kellogg, *Life and Death in Rebel Prisons*, 76.

[68] Scholars have debated whether in fact Civil War soldiers grew disillusioned with the war's ideals, but few have examined the attitudes of prisoners. See Gerald Linderman, *Embattled Courage: The Experience of Combat in the American Civil War* (New York: The Free Press, 1987); McPherson, *For Cause & Comrades*; Earl J. Hess, *The Union Soldier in Battle: Enduring the Ordeal of Combat* (Lawrence: University Press of Kansas, 1997). See also Reid Mitchell's insightful essay "Not the General but the Soldier," in James M. McPherson and William J. Cooper, eds., *Writing the Civil War: The Quest to Understand* (Columbus: University of South Carolina Press, 1998), 80–95.

[69] Helmreich, ed., "Diary of Charles G. Lee," 20.

[70] Entry for August 11, 1864, Kellogg Diary, CHS; also Kellogg, *Life and Death in Rebel Prisons*, 215.

[71] Entry for August 10, 1864, Oliver Gates Diary, CHS.

little or no word from loved ones. Some men tried to imagine what was happening hundreds of miles away in Connecticut. They contrasted their awful plight with that of their friends and families at home whom they knew had plenty to eat, warm beds, and clean clothes. Sundays and holidays were times when prisoners' thoughts especially drifted northward. "We awoke Sunday morning," Robert Kellogg recalled, "to find our thoughts *homeward bound*, as usual. We wondered what they were doing, thinking and saying there, and it really seemed to do us good to think and dream of home."[72] One particular Sunday in July, a devoutly Christian member of the regiment wrote in his diary that he would "greatly rejoice to be at home with my dear friends, and enjoy with them the sacred ordinances of the Sanctuary."[73]

Many believed that their friends and families had no idea how miserable conditions were at Andersonville. Hartford newspapers took several weeks to report the regiment's captivity, and when it did, it simply stated that they were transferred to Georgia and treated well. Letters from home occasionally made their way to the men, but most prisoners' families were unaware of their loved one's plight.[74] Kellogg described how he and his comrades "thought of our friends at home and wondered how they would feel if they knew we were in such condition." He tried to imagine how his parents would feel seeing their "only son seated on the ground, selling beans by the pint and loudly extolling their excellent qualities."[75]

Thoughts of family and friends gave prisoners a reason to persevere. First Sergeant Oliver Gates reluctantly considered having to take "Confederate medicine" in order "to save [my] life for I have some Loved ones at home to live for my Wife and little Girl."[76] He filled his diary with frequent references to his family, hoping that he would one day see them again. Another soldier affirmed that they "receive great consolation from the assurance which we all feel that our loved ones at home remember us at the Throne of Grace which

[72] Kellogg, *Life and Death in Rebel Prisons*, 136.

[73] Entry for July 3, 1864, Ira Forbes Diary, YU.

[74] *Hartford Daily Courant*, May 6, 1864; Kellogg, *Life and Death in Rebel Prisons*, 188, 236. Ira Forbes noted that on September 1, 1864: "Some of our men have received letters from home to day." Ira Forbes Diary, YU.

[75] Kellogg, *Life and Death in Rebel Prisons*, 67; quotation from 187–88.

[76] Entry for June 19, 1864, Oliver Gates Diary, CHS.

they assemble themselves in the House of prayer and worship and also in their individual homes."[77]

But prisoners also worried that their friends and families might forget them. With so little news from home it was easy to give in to these fears. On June 2, 1864, Ira Forbes reflected: "To night I am feeling well, and am thinking of home and dear ones far away. Surely they remember me. Thank God for such amiable friends as I have."[78] The thought of dying so far from home also tormented the men. As one soldier grew weak, he told Kellogg: "If I could only live just to see my wife and mother, I could die happy; but to die *here*, far away from home and be buried here, —I tell you Robert it is tough."[79]

Prisoners also worried that the U.S. government had forgotten them. It was hard for them to believe that political and military leaders were not doing all they could to free them. Ira Forbes observed that "not a few of the men" were "much inclined to think that the Govt is forgetting us, if not forgetting us, neglecting us."[80] Kellogg believed that the Confederates helped to stir this "cruel suspicion" that "we were abandoned by our government and our friends." This suspicion, Kellogg maintained, was more difficult to accept than the actual "sickness, hunger and exposure and the thousand petition ills which beset us."[81] There were constant rumors of exchanges and a growing concern that the Union's use of black soldiers had affected prisoner exchange. Oliver Gates at first refused to believe such stories, but by late August, he had changed his mind. He admitted that before his capture he had been supportive of the federal policy toward arming blacks, but after more than three months at Andersonville, Gates bitterly wrote: "For my part I am sorry that she [the Union] ever armed a nigger as a Soldier for I think if she had not[,] Prisoners would have received proper care and the exchange would have been continued." He confessed that "the idea that the Prisoner is patriotic enough to say that he is willing to stay here a Prisoner

---

[77] Entry for July 3, 1864, Ira Forbes Diary, YU; see also Kellogg, *Life and Death in Rebel Prison*, 75–76.

[78] Entry for June 2, 1864, Ira Forbes Diary, YU; one month later he felt confident his friends and families were praying for the men to come home.

[79] Kellogg, *Life and Death in Rebel Prisons*, 240.

[80] Forbes does not distinguish whether the men he describes included members of the 16th, but he does record that he and "Sergeant Lee" believed that it was a wrong impression. See entry for July 12, 1864, Ira Forbes Diary, YU.

[81] Kellogg, *Life and Death in Rebel Prisons*, 75.

until the nigger is recognized as a Soldier as subject of exchange equal with the white man is entirely false." Gates stated that all white prisoners had a "perfect hatred" toward blacks and "that the government would be the gainer by giving three for one in exchange if she accounts human life in the proper scale." Getting out of prison alive was his only concern.[82]

In July 1864, a petition circulated the stockade to be sent north and plead for the government to do more to obtain their release. Robert Kellogg and Ira Forbes convinced fellow members of the 16th not to sign it. To Kellogg, the petition seemed an acknowledgment that Union military and political officials *could* release them but for some reason chose not do so. This was an assumption about the northern people and government he refused to make.[83] Ira Forbes was "disgusted with the entire affair." "Should it be carried through," he predicted, "I cannot see how it can fail to produce discord among our people and involve our Administration in some considerable difficulty, which would be highly pleasing to the rebels." Believing it would only disgrace the prisoners who signed it, Forbes concluded: "It can do no good but will do much harm."[84] The petition was sent north, although it is unclear how much direct effect it had on changing the United States government's position. There was also increasing public pressure to resume exchanges.[85]

Oliver Gates also turned his anger on northern men whom he believed remained at home profiting from the war, rather than serving their country. He reasoned, "Could the men at home that are making

---

[82] Entry for August 23, 1864, Oliver Gates Diary; see also entry for July 12, 1864, CHS. The use of federal black troops did in fact directly affect these prisoners because when the Confederacy refused to treat black soldiers as regular prisoners of war, the federal government halted all exchanges. This was also a calculated move by Grant to break the Confederacy's fighting power, predicting that exchanged southern soldiers would return to the ranks. William Marvel is extremely critical of the federal policy and partly blames the Union for the awful conditions at Andersonville. See Marvel, *Andersonville*, x–xi, 25–26.

[83] Kellogg, *Life and Death in Rebel Prisons*, 159, 182–83, 188–89.

[84] Entry for July 20, 1864, Ira Forbes Diary, YU. Kellogg states that the majority of prisoners were in favor of the petition, but he managed to convince everyone in his "ninety" not to sign it. See Kellogg, *Life and Death in Rebel Prisons*, 188.

[85] Historian William B. Hessletine argues that in fact these prisoner petitions, in addition to "stories of barbarities of Southerners led the officials responsible for the prisons to adopt a policy of retaliation while the people of the North clamored for exchange." See William B. Hessletine, *Civil War Prisons: A Study in War Psychology* (New York: Frederick Unger Publishing Co., 1930), 223.

money out of the war see what a vast amount of suffering they are helping to prolong by not giving their services to the country—they would help to close this war by trying to liberate us if not be enlisting by encouraging others to do so. Every man in the south is a Soldier both old and young, rich and poor. Now their whole business is war. If the war is carried on by the North in this way it would be over in a month."[86]

But the war dragged on, and so too did their incarceration. As weeks turned to months, life in this horrific place took its toll on regimental unity and numbers. The filth, medical neglect, disease, and hunger weakened even the healthiest soldier, and the 16th Connecticut began to see its ranks dwindle. For some, basic human instincts of self-preservation took over. Augustus Moesner volunteered as a clerk so that he could obtain extra rations. Hiram Buckingham and Andrew Spring also accepted paroles to work outside the stockade.[87] Other members of the regiment looked on this behavior with disdain. Learning about Buckingham and Spring, Oliver Gates bitterly hoped that neither would ever be exchanged. Later, he found himself accepting the same offer so that he could work in the hospital and not languish in the overcrowded stockade. In the final pages of his wartime diary he admitted how his feelings changed toward those he had originally condemned. "Terrible we looked upon them [those who accepted paroles] then as the next thing to traitor but afterward we were glad to accept the same condition ourselves and we have learned to be more Charitable to others while we are ignorant of the nature under which they act." Gates was convinced that staying out of the pen saved his life.[88]

In September 1864, Andersonville was emptied of most of its inmates. Surviving members of the 16th Connecticut were soon transferred to another prison in Florence, South Carolina. Conditions

---

[86] Entry for May 31, 1864, Oliver Gates Diary, CHS, punctuation added.

[87] N. P. Chipman, *The Tragedy of Andersonville: Trial of Captain Henry Wirz the Prison Keeper* (Sacramento, Calif.: published by the author, 1911), 225; entry for August 10, 1864, Robert H. Kellogg Diary, CHS. Buckingham was a steward in the hospital and Spring worked in the cook house.

[88] Gates accepted the parole after the transfer to Florence. See entry for June 22, 1864, Oliver Gates Diary, CHS, "an Explanation" written on the final pages of Diary III. Kellogg also expressed anger at "men foolish enough to go outside today, taking parole & going to work on the stockade." See entry for May 23, 1864, Robert Kellogg Diary, CHS.

were not much better at Florence, although the change of location initially cheered the prisoners' spirits. When Ira Forbes got to Florence he quickly found a portion of the regiment had already arrived: "Have seen several of our boys. They are greatly pleased with the change, but disappointed that it was not an exchange."[89] For the next several weeks, hunger and sickness continued to take its deadly toll. Confederates eagerly offered prisoners their freedom if they took an oath of allegiance to the South. Hundreds did, although it appears that none of the 16th Connecticut became "galvanized Yankees." Some began to believe that in fact they had been entirely forgotten by the United States government and the people at home.[90]

The prison ordeal for most remaining members of the regiment lasted until December, when freedom finally came and survivors were transferred to a parole camp at Annapolis, Maryland. The feeling of joy and relief was indescribable. On board a ship headed north, Ira Forbes gazed up at the U.S. flag: "It never appeared more beautiful than it does today."[91] As portions of the unit were released, Hartford newspapers began to publish many names of the regiment's dead and report on the condition of those paroled. On December 10, 1864, one article hinted at the mental state of the survivors as much as their broken physical health: "A majority of the men look comparatively well, but nearly all have the scurvy. Their appearance is no evidence of their real condition. Many of them are mere wrecks of hale, hearty men, and no doubt will soon sink away."[92] One week later, a letter to state governor William A. Buckingham was published by a man named Robert R. Corson, who had just returned from Camp Parole in Annapolis. He told the governor: "I have seen many sad sights in the hospitals and on the battlefields, but there is nothing that makes my heart so sick as the story of these poor boys' sufferings, from their own lips."[93]

Men were given a thirty-day furlough to go home, but in light of their physical conditions this seemed ridiculously short and many resented having to return to the war at all. Company "H," which

---

[89] Entry for September 18, 1864, Ira Forbes Diary, YU.

[90] Entry for November 8, 1864, ibid.

[91] Entry for November 30, 1864, ibid.

[92] *Hartford Weekly Courant*, December 10, 1864; see also December 24, 1864.

[93] Robert R. Corson to William A. Buckingham, December 7, 1864, in the *Hartford Weekly Courant*, December 17, 1864.

had continued in active service, welcomed back some of its long-lost members. John Cuzner returned to duty in late January and was amazed to discover his health rebounding so quickly. It was hard to believe that only one month earlier he thought he would die; now he wrote, "I feel as well as I ever did." But a few months later he was seriously ill with typhoid fever.[94] In fact, many entered the hospital soon after returning to service, their health still weakened by their long imprisonment.[95] Few had any stomach for continuing to serve either. Sergeant Jacob Bower felt depressed after having to return to the regiment so soon, finding army life tedious and his fellow comrades prone to excessive drinking.[96] He, like many others, counted the days until his three-year enlistment was up or the war ended, whichever was sooner. The month-long furlough to Connecticut only made their homesickness worse. "I never since I enlisted longed so much for next August," Cuzner wrote, "as I have since I came home. When my time is out[,] I shall not be thinking well, I have to report at such and such a time but will go and come when I please."[97] Even when the war ended in April 1865, the 16th Connecticut still waited for orders to go home. Discipline was nearly nonexistent, and the days seemed endless.

Finally, the 16th Connecticut went home in late June 1865. A mere 130 men marched the streets of Hartford on the official day of mustering out before a shocked and saddened crowd of onlookers. The regiment had arrived earlier than anticipated, and the official welcoming ceremony was hastily arranged. Lieutenant Colonel John H. Burnham read a farewell addressed to his fellow soldiers, concluding: "Although a less amount of glory in the field has fallen to our lot than to some others, no regiment from the State has been subjected to so much suffering."[98] Prominent Hartford citizen Ezra Hall also spoke,

---

[94] John B. Cuzner to Ellen Van Dorn, January 29, 1865; May 15, 1865, John B. Cuzner Papers, CHS.

[95] Besides Cuzner, Kellogg was listed as in the hospital in May, and Oliver Gates also battled typhoid soon after his release. See Robert H. Kellogg, Compiled Service Record of Union Soldiers, Records of the Adjutant General's Office, Record Group 94, National Archives, Washington, D. C. (hereinafter cited as AGO, RG 94, NA); Oliver Gates Diary, CHS.

[96] Entries for February 17, March 6, 18, 23, May 11, 1865, Jacob Bower Diary, USAMHI.

[97] John B. Cuzner to Ellen Van Dorn, February 9, 1865, John B. Cuzner Papers, CHS.

[98] John Burnham, quoted in Blakeslee, *History of the Sixteenth Connecticut Volunteers*, 115.

warmly greeting the regiment. "Heroes of many a hard-fought battle and worthy veterans of a redeemed country!" He recalled the summer day in 1862 when the 16th Regiment Connecticut Volunteers first left for war: "It was hard to leave your situations, your homes, and those you loved. And a sharper pang would steal along your feelings as you thought the step might take you forever from the dear New England hills and all you held dear." But love of country superseded love of home and family, Hall affirmed, and "you went out from your homes to camp." He proclaimed: "No braver regiment ever went out from our city or state." After recounting the "sad day" at Antietam, their unforgettable capture at Plymouth, and their "martyred dead" at Andersonville, Hall declared: "Go bear your honors and your trophies to your homes, and, around your own hearths be as great and good as you have been in war."[99]

Survivors of the 16th Connecticut did return to their homes to try to begin life anew. Members scattered across the state, rejoining families, seeking work, and resuming their civilian identities. Jacob Bower recorded his first day as a full-fledged citizen by stating: "At home once more and free feeling happy."[100] But happiness was not always lasting. Oliver Gates came home in time to witness the death of his young daughter. He himself nearly died in January 1865 from a severe bout of typhoid. Attempting to resume his prewar mason job, Gates struggled to make ends meet. In 1897, while at work at a construction site, his left arm was nearly ripped off when his clothes tangled in a piece of machinery. Unable to work, he lived for the next ten years mainly off the modest pension provided by the U.S. government for the lingering effects of rheumatism he suffered while imprisoned at Andersonville.[101] Ira Forbes graduated from Yale in 1870, but like Gates, his health never entirely recovered from his imprisonment and he grew increasingly erratic in his behavior. In 1911, he was admitted to an insane asylum, committed by two comrades from the regiment, George Q. Whitney and John Gemmill. The previously pious Forbes had grown "profound, abusive and obscene," "abusive and threatening to [his] wife," denouncing his friends and

---

[99] Ezra Hall quoted in ibid., 111–14.

[100] Entry for June 30, 1865, Bower Diary, USAMHI.

[101] Oliver Gates Pension File; Abbie Gates (widow) Pension File, Civil War and Later Pension Files, Records of the Veterans Administration, Record Group 15, National Archives, Washington, D. C.

relatives. Forbes died nine months later, at the age of 68.[102] Robert Kellogg worked as a drug store clerk, but felt alone and isolated in an unfamiliar city. When a local deacon died, Kellogg felt numb, unable to feel the "solemnity of the occasion. Death seems to have lost its solemnity in me since 'Andersonville.' "[103] He soon married and left Connecticut for Ohio where he found work with an insurance company.

With time, the public and private memories of the 16th Connecticut changed. In 1907, Robert Kellogg sent a short note to his good friend George Q. Whitney, who had been amassing materials for a detailed history of the regiment. "Were we really ever in Andersonville?" Kellogg scribbled on the back of a business card.[104] As the years and decades passed, the raw realities of Andersonville did indeed seem like a horrible dream. Kellogg, Whitney, and many others deliberately set out to reconfigure their painful and humiliating past into something courageous and brave. They maintained their regimental identity and kept close correspondence with each other, recalling their three-year service. Like other Civil War veterans, members of the 16th took increasing pride in simply having survived the war. But these men, haunted by the helpless suffering they endured and the many dead they left buried in Georgia, sought to give meaning to their torment and leave no doubt that their painful ordeal had been for a larger purpose: saving the Union.[105]

This postwar recasting of the regiment's "bad luck" past took several forms. The first involved the regimental flag. During the 1870s, a story began to circulate that at Plymouth, when it became clear that

---

[102] Information on Forbes, including the actual application for his asylum committal, is found in the George Q. Whitney Collection, RG 69:23, Box 7, Connecticut State Library (hereinafter referred to as CSL). It is unclear what a modern-day diagnosis of Forbes's condition would be, but one cannot help wonder if his imprisonment played a role in his deteriorating mental health.

[103] Entry for October 26, 1865, Robert H. Kellogg Diary, CHS. Kellogg along with a few other members of the 16th Connecticut testified at the Henry Wirz trial. See Chipman, *The Tragedy of Andersonville*, 164–66, 251–52; 327–31.

[104] Robert H. Kellogg to George Q. Whitney, George Q. Whitney Collection, RG 69:23, Box 5, CSL.

[105] Historians have paid increasing attention to the memory of the war and the active role veterans played in changing the public memory of the war. Memory of prisoners has gotten less attention, except by scholars of Andersonville who quickly dismiss much of postwar accounts of the prison as exaggerated and overly politicized. See, for example, Linderman, *Embattled Courage*, 275, 277; Hess, *Union Soldier in Battle*, 187–88; Marvel, *Andersonville*, 323–24.

there was no hope of escape, regimental color guards tore the unit's flags into shreds and distributed them to members. Hastily burying the flagstaffs in the ground, men hid pieces of flag in their clothes. Later, some of these fragments, saved as one writer described "like holy relics through humiliation, torture, and albeit the anguish of crucifixion," were collected and sown into a white silk flag with a center design made of the old flag's scraps. In 1879, the new flag was displayed during a solemn public ceremony in Hartford. According to one account, "when these veterans [of the 16th Connecticut] came marching by, the shouts that greeted them, expressive of mingled pity and praise, as this strange symbol of heroism and suffering came to be understood, were enough to make a hero of anybody and a martyr too."[106] Indeed, the inspiring flag-saving story helped to make heroes and martyrs out of the hapless regiment. It is this dramatic tale that veterans themselves recounted repeatedly in the postwar years. It is still repeated publicly today.[107]

However, there seems some reason to doubt the accuracy of this account. There are no references whatsoever describing members salvaging the flag in any of the diaries consulted by this author. Robert Kellogg recounted returning to Plymouth in April 1865 to find the flagstaffs. "Going to the place where our color staffs were buried we dug for a long while but without finding them. We were afterward told by a lady resident that the Rebels found them soon after taking

---

[106] The flag's full inscription reads: "The device of this flag is composed entirely from remnants of old colors of the 16th Regiment Connecticut Volunteers. The colors were torn into shreds by the officers and men and concealed upon their person in order to save them from the enemy at the Battle of Plymouth, N.C. April 20th, 1864, where together with the whole Union force at the post, after three days of fighting, the regiment was compelled to surrender. Many of the men bearing these relics were taken to southern prisons where, under untold privations, they still sacredly watched over and kept their trusts, successfully returning them to their native state." This flag is now at the state capitol building in Hartford, Conn. See Samuel G. Buckingham, *The Life of William A. Buckingham* (Springfield, Mass.: W. F. Adams Publishers, 1894), 252; also Guy Lemieux, "The Connecticut Hard Luck Regiment Lives Again," unpublished typescript in possession of the author.

[107] Veterans of the 16th Connecticut repeated this story frequently. See, for example, "Address" George Q. Whitney Collection, RG 69:23, Box 4, CSL. More recent examples include the mayor of Sharpsburg, Maryland, narrating the flag story during a public ceremony in 1995 honoring a local church with a stained glass window depicting the famous "Prisoner of War flag." See Christopher Yeager, "Presentation," September 17, 1995, copy in possession of author. A regimental history of the 85th New York claims that they too stripped their flag and tore it into shreds to be distributed among the men. See Mahood, *The Plymouth Pilgrims*, 185.

possession of the town." But he made no mention of the scraps being preserved.[108] Even Ira Forbes, the color corporal who allegedly hid strips of the flag faithfully during his seven-month-long captivity made absolutely no mention of the regiment's flag in his detailed diary. Instead, Forbes recorded proudly receiving a piece of the 101st Pennsylvania flag when already at Andersonville.[109] In addition, an account published by a southerner in the 1890s further casts doubt on the truthfulness of the dramatic story of flag-saving. Frank P. O'Brien, an Alabama artilleryman who fought at Plymouth, attested in an 1893 *Blue and Gray* article that one of his comrades snatched a flag from the hands of a color corporal. O'Brien recalled: "The brave fellow begged for possession of his colors. It proved to be the battle-flag of the 16th Connecticut, and when this was denied him, he asked that a piece be given him as a memento." The captors supposedly agreed and cut a corner from the bottom of the flag and gave it to the color bearer. Years later, after a chance meeting between the former Confederates and veterans of the 16th Connecticut, O'Brien claimed to have helped return the flag to Connecticut in 1888. A Hartford newspaper flatly denied that this was the Sixteenth's actual battle flag but affirmed, "the good feeling of the Alabama veterans in returning it is as greatly appreciated by the 16th as if it were a flag which had been torn by shot and shell in the rage of battle."[110]

There were other ways to bolster the 16th Connecticut's wartime record. As Civil War veteran activities grew more popular during the 1880s and 1890s, surviving members of the regiment were eager to participate. They wanted to reclaim the military identity that members of the 16th had defined during their actual service. Now old, graying civilians in peacetime, that martial past seemed increasingly appealing. The 16th Connecticut selected the day of their first and

---

[108] Entry for April 18, 1865, Robert Kellogg Diary, CHS. Nor does Kellogg recount this story in his published book.

[109] Forbes stated that the 101st had "been in several engagements—at Williamsburg, Fair Oaks, in the 'Seven Days' fight before Richmond, on the Blackwater, at Kingston [sic] and finally at Plymouth, where it ended its career gloriously." See entry for March 31, 1864, Ira Forbes Diary, March 31, 1864, YU.

[110] Frank O'Brien, "The Story of a Flag and the Strange Bringing Together of Its Captors and Defenders, As Related by One of the Former," *Blue and Gray Magazine* 2 (August 1893): 143–45; newspaper account from the *Hartford Times* quoted in O'Brien's article. A biography of Connecticut state governor William A. Buckingham claims that the flag the regiment tore up and preserved was its state flag. See Buckingham, *Life of William A. Buckingham*, 252.

only large-scale battle experience in the war, September 17, as the date of their annual reunion. Like Civil War veterans North and South, these reunions were not meant to dwell on past humiliations or failings; instead, these yearly events were opportunities to reunite old comrades, mourn the dead, and take pride in military service. Wives, children, and grandchildren attended, enjoying rousing speeches, music, and bountiful food. Hartford newspapers began referring to the regiment as the "Fighting" "Brave" and "Gallant" "16," making special note of each year's reunion.[111]

In 1894, the 16th Connecticut joined other state units to raise funds and place a monument at the Antietam battlefield. Erecting the monument at the spot near where the unit broke and ran, veterans made no public mention of their disappointing performance under fire. The Reverend Charles Dixon described the 16th Connecticut as full of "noble men whose hearts glowed and burned with patriotic fire."[112]

But if their unheroic role at Antietam could be recast as heroic, so too could their dehumanizing captivity at Andersonville. The flag anecdote had already helped to draw attention to the unit's prison ordeal, but some members were determined to do more. Veteran leaders of the 16th Connecticut were encouraged by the success of other northern states to win public support and funds to build Andersonville monuments. In 1905, Robert Kellogg and George Q. Whitney began to persuade other veterans and state leaders to build a shrine to Connecticut men imprisoned at Andersonville. Although the monument was to honor all Connecticut soldiers who suffered in all southern prisons, the effort was led by members of the 16th. In an address to the military committee of the state legislature, one of the veterans explained the need to build the monument immediately: "There are many aged fathers, mothers and other near relatives of those who suffered and died there whose declining years would be in a measure smoothed to know that their State had given some little

[111] See, for example, *Hartford Times*, August 1, 1908, August 29, 1913; *Hartford Courant*, September 17, 1907; *Hartford Post*, August 29, 1912; Hartford newspaper clipping [1931], Robert H. Kellogg Papers, CHS.

[112] "Invocation" by Rev. Charles Dixon, in *Souvenir of Excursion to Antietam and Dedication of Monuments of the 8th, 11th, 14th and 16th Regiments of Connecticut Volunteers October 1894* (Hartford: n.p. 1894), 54. More on this is in Gordon, " 'All Who Went Into That Battle Were Heroes.' "

show of appreciation of the much that those who were personally dear to them had done to her honor and credit."[113] The state appropriated $6,000 to build the monument and appointed a commission of five men to oversee the project. Four of the five men appointed to the state commission were former members of the 16th Connecticut: Frank Cheney, George Q. Whitney, Norman L. Hope, and George Denison.[114]

The commission carefully selected the memorial's design, seeking "a figure which should represent a very young man, in Civil War uniform to the smallest details, and whose expressions should be that of courage and heroism that are developed in suffering,—strong, modest, hopeful." They wanted to portray "a typical soldier-boy of the northern people, and his bearing that of one who has learned poise by endurance."[115] Bela Lyon Pratt, a student of Augustus Saint-Gaudens, was named the sculptor. The man chosen as a model for "Andersonville Boy" was the 16th Connecticut's former Sergeant Major Robert Kellogg. The bronze figure depicts a young, beardless private, stripped of his gun and equipment, standing with his left foot forward and his kepi in one hand by his side. More civilian than soldier, only his uniform marks him as a warrior. At the base of the statue are the words: "In Memory of the Men of Connecticut Who Suffered in Southern Military Prisons." The *Boston Transcript* characterized the statue as "a simple figure of a private infantry soldier, disarmed and helpless, standing with a sober foreknowledge of the very probable fate before him." He seemed "a mere boy, a typical New England lad" fresh from school and the New England town in which he resided. The paper described him as "manly and modest, he is one of the kind who take things as they come, without bravado and without posing. But there is something in the genuineness, the simplicity, the rugged naturalness of the boy's bearing which makes

---

[113] "Address to Chairman and Gentlemen of Military Commission," George Q. Whitney Collection, RG 69:23, Box 4, CSL. George Q. Whitney was apparently the author of these statements.

[114] Whitney, Hope, and Denison were all imprisoned at Andersonville; Cheney, former lieutenant colonel of the regiment, was shot in the arm at Antietam and discharged in December 1862. He was a beloved member of the unit and very active in veteran activities. The final member, Theron Upson, was in a Connecticut artillery unit. See Frank Cheney, Compiled Service Record of Union Soldiers, AGO, RG 94, NA; *Dedication of the Monument at Andersonville*, 17.

[115] *Dedication of the Monument at Andersonville*, 23.

it seem safe to predict that he will be constant and faithful to the end."[116] A modern observer has noted that the statue has "little that identifies his terrible ordeal as a prisoner at Andersonville."[117] Indeed, this statue, an idealized young Robert Kellogg in bronze, conveys male strength, individual self-restraint, and dignity. Meant to represent the experience for all Connecticut prisoners of war, it instead idealizes the youthful innocence of men untouched by the hard realities of either war or captivity.

The Connecticut state legislature appropriated another $7,500 in 1907 to complete the monument and fund transportation of any living ex-prisoners interested in attending the dedication ceremony. Eighty-three men accepted the offer to return to Georgia, and on October 21, 1907, these veterans, along with twenty other guests including family members and some state officials, boarded trains bound for the South. Two days later, on October 23, 1907, "Andersonville boy" was formally unveiled by three daughters of men in the 16th. It was an emotional moment. Men cried as they remembered their terrible ordeal in the stockade and the death of so many of their comrades, but returning to the site of so much suffering no doubt helped heal some of the old wounds. Former Lieutenant Colonel Frank Cheney, who himself was not imprisoned at Andersonville, thanked the state of Connecticut for "having so generously provided the ways and means for carrying out our sacred duty." Cheney described the "Soldier Boy of Andersonville" as "the ideal young soldier, as he stood for all that is noble and loyal and enduring, when he offered himself and his life, if need be, for our loved country." "We leave him here," Cheney stated, "feeling that he is a son or brother, loved and lost in the service of his country, and that he is now with our comrades at rest."[118] Robert Kellogg also spoke. Standing beside the bronze likeness of his younger self, the sixty-three-year-old veteran addressed the small crowd. Forty years was a long time, and he was not there to dwell on the troublesome memories of that distant time. Nor did he feel as he had in 1865, that he needed to focus on

---

[116] Quoted in ibid., 71.

[117] See David F. Ransom, "Connecticut's Monumental Epoch: A Survey of Civil War Memorials." *Connecticut Historical Society Bulletin* 58 (1993): 231.

[118] *Dedication of the Monument at Andersonville*, 27. Cheney also expressed his disappointment with the fact that the monument was unfinished because the pedestal had yet to arrive from the north, but the ceremony went on as scheduled.

spreading "storms of indignation" among his listeners. Instead, he pronounced his and his comrades' imprisonment at Andersonville "a lesson in patriotism. To this retired and beautiful spot will thousands resort in the long years to come, to learn again and again lessons of heroic sacrifice made by those who so quietly sleep on those long rows of graves." Kellogg referred to the prewar lives he and his comrades left to "voluntarily" enter military service. He stressed the "passive part" the prisoners played in winning the war, and reaffirmed his regiment's unity during its long trial. "Maintaining their company and regimental organization as closely as possible, they took counsel with one another, and with grim determination made ready for an unequal combat. It was to be a daily struggle with false and discouraging reports of exchange and with heart-breaking yearnings for home; a prolonged contest with exposure, hunger, sickness and death, amid surroundings repulsive beyond description. But they set themselves to meet it." He refrained from any bitterness toward the Confederates, but did deem all his Connecticut comrades as disciplined, unselfish, and loyal: "Solicitations to enter the military service or civil employment of the Southern Confederacy were turned aside with scorn by them, though acceptance meant instant release from the fate that now so clearly stared them in the face." Prisoners died "not in the heat and excitement of the battle," but "in the loneliness of a multitude, with a comrade only by their side, within an enemy's lines and under a hostile flag." Kellogg proudly reported that a southerner stood nearby and listened to his speech and judged his words entirely true. Kellogg's only regret was that more people from Connecticut did not share in the ceremony.[119]

But plans were already in the works for a replica of "Andersonville Boy" to be erected on the grounds of the Connecticut state capitol.

---

[119] Kellogg's address in *Dedication to the Monument at Andersonville*, 34–37; also 23. Luther Dickey, a member of the 103rd Pennsylvania who was captured at Plymouth with the 16th Connecticut and imprisoned at Andersonville, also noted that dying in battle had been well celebrated and recognized publicly, but suffering and dying in prison was little acknowledged. In 1910, he wrote: "In the judgement of the writer, the men who languished and died in the military prisons of the South, after enduring the horrors and miseries of these places for months were not surpassed in indomitable courage and heroic devotion to duty by any who fell in charging the ranks of the enemy, and that these men did fully as much as those who comprised the armies of Grant and Sherman." See Luther Dickey, *History of the 103rd Regiment of Pennsylvania Veteran Volunteer Infantry 1861–65* (Chicago: L. S. Dickey, 1910), 289.

Not long after the ceremony in Georgia, George Q. Whitney, representing the 16th Connecticut, gave a formal address to dedicate the monument. Whitney unabashedly proclaimed that "no one has ever disputed that our record was a credit to the state and an honor to every man who has shared its fortunes." He ended his speech by assuring the crowd, "You need never be ashamed that you have in this way helped to honor those who honored their country in peril."[120] Kellogg wrote to Whitney that having the duplicate in Hartford finally brought the regiment's prison experience, as well as those of other Connecticut soldiers, home: "A duplicate Monument on the Capitol grounds at Hfd will round out the whole memorial plan in a noble way. With *that* there, the one in the Cemetery at Andersonville will never be forgotten."[121] He later added, "The thought of our 'Andersonville Boy' standing in Connecticut soil, where it may be seen by Conn. People fills my heart with rejoicing." Kellogg also hoped that the duplicate monument would serve as a lesson for future generations and a meeting place where "children would play, and lovers meet, and old soldiers rest and think."[122]

"Andersonville Boy" does not reveal anything about the real story of the 16th Connecticut, nor any other northern regiment for that matter. It says nothing about the stinging humiliation of being routed in battle or the disillusionment of being regulated to the backwater of the war; nor does it convey anything of the deep powerlessness these men felt as captives surrounded by death and disease, worried that their family, friends, and the U.S. government had forgotten them. But this monument does lend insight into how these northern veterans began to view the war's meaning and their role in it many decades after its end.

---

[120] "Address" by George Q. Whitney, George Q. Whitney Papers, RG 69:23, Box 4, CSL. See also Robert H. Kellogg to George Q. Whitney, May 25, 1907, George Q. Whitney Papers, RG 69:23, Box 5, CSL.

[121] Robert H. Kellogg to George Q. Whitney, May 10, 1907, emphasis in original, George Q. Whitney Papers, RG 69:23, Box 5, CSL.

[122] Robert H. Kellogg to George Q. Whitney, March 17, 1909, ibid.; Robert H. Kellogg to George Q. Whitney, August 4, 1910, ibid.

11

"Honorable Scars": Northern Amputees and the Meaning of Civil War Injuries

Frances Clarke

THREE YEARS after losing his arm during an infantry charge, Charles Coleman reflected on the joys of soldiering. Along with his fond remembrance of waving crowds, splendid landscapes, and idling time away by the campfire, Coleman reminisced about his final battle which left him a "one armed man for life." "Some may think this ought not to be mentioned with the pleasures of a soldiers life," he wrote, yet for Coleman, losing an arm had its own rewards. Surrounded by "kind surgeons" and "tender nurses" who tried their utmost to save his limb, he explained that "everything was procured for my comfort. . . . I was sent home free of expense" and later "fitted with an artificial arm." Moreover, he continued, a benevolent government "paid my board, transportation, and for my arm, and is now paying me eight dollars per month." He concluded that "the pleasure in all this consists in knowing that my feeble efforts for the benefit of our common country are remembered and appreciated and . . . I cannot but feel happy to think that I lost my arm in so good a cause and for so just a government."[1]

According to Coleman's narrative, "the great principle of love of country" led him to enlist, and supportive friends and loving parents "buoyed [him] up in the trials and hardships consequent upon the

My thanks to Michael Johnson, Dorothy Ross, Ronald Walters, Carolyn Eastman, Tom Foster, and Rebecca Plant for their comments and suggestions.
  [1] Charles Coleman, competition 1, entry 49, William Oland Bourne Papers, Manuscript Division, Library of Congress, Washington, D. C. Hereinafter, competition and entry numbers are cited as follows: 1:49. In the quotations taken from these manuscripts, I have retained original emphasis and misspellings throughout.

life of a soldier." Coleman expressed sentiments that historians James McPherson and Reid Mitchell have pointed to as central in motivating and sustaining northern soldiers during the Civil War—devotion to home and nation.[2] Most antebellum northerners adhered to the classical republican assumption that the maintenance of self-government depended on a virtuous male citizenry, capable of exercising independence, self-control, and civic responsibility.[3] "Self-government" thus referred to both the legal and political institutions of republican government, and to male citizens' personal conduct that underpinned and enabled those institutions. As Mitchell notes, northern patriotism also derived much of its force and content from an understanding of the Union as a family writ large, a legacy bequeathed by the Revolutionary generation that male citizens felt duty-bound to defend. By this logic, secession was at once an attack on republican government, a betrayal of filial obligations, and an illegitimate and dangerous expression of male identity.[4]

Some historians argue that the beliefs and values initially motivating northern soldiers were dramatically eroded by the harsh reality of combat and by the changing nature of warfare and weaponry.[5] Coleman's narrative does not support such interpretations. Returning home a maimed veteran, Coleman had ample knowledge of the unromantic aspects of battle, yet as he discussed the meaning of his lost limb, he framed his sacrifice in terms of the "good cause" and "just government" for which he had fought. Highlighting the "benevolent" public and private response to his injury, Coleman underscored the justice of his wartime patriotism by invoking a "common country" that had proven itself worthy of the sacrifices made on its behalf.

He was not alone in narrating his war injury in a way that both

---

[2] Reid Mitchell, *The Vacant Chair: The Northern Soldier Leaves Home* (New York: Oxford University Press, 1993); and James M. McPherson, *For Cause & Comrades: Why Men Fought in the Civil War* (New York: Oxford University Press, 1997).

[3] Earl J. Hess, *Liberty Virtue, and Progress: Northerners and Their War for the Union*, 2nd ed. (New York: Fordham University Press, 1997), chapter 1.

[4] Mitchell, *The Vacant Chair*, 14. Also McPherson, *For Cause & Comrades*, 18–19.

[5] Gerald F. Linderman, *Embattled Courage: The Experience of Combat in the American Civil War* (New York: The Free Press, 1987), most clearly articulates the position that a gap between expectations and reality led to disillusionment among northern soldiers. In contrast, both Hess, *Liberty, Virtue and Progress*, and McPherson, *For Cause & Comrade*, argue that soldiers' patriotic and ideological convictions remained largely intact.

validated and drew meaning from northern understandings of the Civil War. Along with roughly four hundred other maimed soldiers, Coleman entered one of two left-handed penmanship competitions staged in New York in 1866 and 1867 for the benefit of northern veterans who had lost a limb during the war. Providing far more than a sample of their left-handed writing, most authors took the opportunity to detail their understandings of the war and to meditate on the meaning of injury and sacrifice. Like Coleman, many of those who took pen in hand did not dwell on the extent of their physical loss. Instead, they claimed to have sacrificed their right arm willingly, in the cause of national union. "Were such a thing possible, as the restoration of my arm, I would not have it restored. I consider it an honor and am proud of it," one entrant declared. Another claimed, "if i had a dozen arms like it was i would [have] given them all soner than have the states torn from this glorious Union which our forefathers fought for."[6]

Although not all northern amputees were this sanguine about their loss, it is important to recognize that the Civil War took place within, and helped to create, a context of meaning that enabled many of these men to consider their injuries as unambiguously "honorable scars." Instead of examining this context, scholars who have studied Civil War amputees tend to anticipate the literature on post–World War I war wounds, which interprets the loss of a limb as a mark of feminization or humiliation.[7] Erin O'Connor, for instance, examines the medical discourse surrounding the phenomenon of phantom limbs, in which some amputees claimed to feel painful or twitching sensations in their lost body parts. She suggests that the "fraudulent body language" of the amputee rendered him "effeminate," akin to

---

[6] Henry C. Allen, 1:15; William Compton, 1: 236, William Oland Bourne Papers.

[7] On the treatment of crippled Word War I veterans and the links between emasculation and war wounds, see Seth Koven, "Remembering and Dismemberment: Crippled Children, Wounded Soldiers, and the Great War in Great Britain," *American Historical Review* 99 (October 1994): 1167–202; Joanna Bourke, *Dismembering the Male: Men's Bodies, Britain and the Great War* (London, Eng.: Reaktion Books, 1996), chapter 1; and Robert Weldon Whalen, *Bitter Wounds: German Victims of the Great War, 1914–1939* (Ithaca, N. Y.: Cornell University Press, 1984), chapter 3 and passim. Whalen notes that maimed Word War I German veterans "were seen to be, and felt themselves to be, freaks." Indeed, artistic representations of the war frequently used the disabled veteran as a pathetic and grotesque figure, symbolizing pointless destruction.

the hysterical female.[8] In contrast, Lisa Herschbach begins her study of the artificial limb industry in the postbellum North by noting that amputation represented both "manly heroism and effeminate dependency."[9] Yet both authors claim that prosthesis resolved the threat to manhood caused by amputation, in the process reconstructing the maimed veteran as an industrial laborer, by eliding the distinction between man and machine.

In assessing this discourse, it is notable that the majority of amputees never even attempted to have a prosthetic device fitted, although the federal government provided artificial limbs to Union soldiers free of charge.[10] Moreover, many of those men who were fitted with prosthetic limbs later reported to pension officials that they soon abandoned them either because they were useless or painful, or both.[11] It is possible that some amputees returned home unaware of

---

[8] Erin O'Connor, "'Fractions of Men': Engendering Amputation in Victorian Culture," *Comparative Studies in Society and History* 39 (October 1997): 744–47. O'Connor's argument deals with the medical discourse on the meaning of amputation that arose between 1851 and 1914, rather than specifically with Civil War amputees.

[9] Lisa Herschbach, "Prosthetic Reconstructions: Making the Industry, Re-Making the Body, Modelling the Nation," *History Workshop Journal* 44 (autumn 1997): 24–25. Historians of the post–World War I prosthetic limb industry have also argued that the reconstruction of the human body based on principles of engineering was a dramatic achievement of this war, symbolically erasing the suffering of the maimed and reconstructing the male body along utilitarian lines. See, for example, Roxane Panchasi, "Reconstructions: Prosthetics and the Rehabilitation of the Male Body in World War I France," *differences: A Journal of Feminist Cultural Studies* 7 (fall 1995): 109–40.

[10] Congress passed an act in July 1862 guaranteeing artificial limbs for maimed Union soldiers. An allowance of $50 for an arm or foot and $75 for a leg was specified, though commissioned officers were ineligible for such benefits until 1868. Laurann Figg and Jane Farrell-Beck, "Amputation in the Civil War: Physical and Social Dimensions," *Journal of the History of Medicine and Allied Sciences* 48 (October 1993): 463. Dixon Wecter, *When Johnny Comes Marching Home* (Boston: Houghton Mifflin Co., 1944), 214 notes, however, that a government report published in 1866 noted orders for only 3,981 legs, 2,240 arms, 9 feet, and 55 hands; an unofficial newspaper estimate several years later gave a similar figure, suggesting that only a minority of amputees claimed the artificial limbs to which they were automatically entitled.

[11] In my survey of more than a hundred Civil War amputees' pension files, I found only one man who expressed satisfaction with his prosthetic limb. Instead, many of these amputees claimed a commutation fee in lieu of a prosthetic device. From 1870 on, amputees were eligible to claim either the cost of a new prosthesis or a commutation fee of equal value. It is possible that some of those who claimed the commutation fee continued to use a prosthetic device supplied prior to 1870, but many others

the government's offer to replace their missing parts. In other cases, amputation had been performed so close to the shoulder or hip joint that fitting a prosthetic device was impossible. Yet it seems clear that many amputees did not wish to hide their injuries. Indeed, one recent study examining photographs of 151 limbless Civil War veterans reveals that the majority of men pictured effectively drew attention to their missing arms or legs by taking up empty sleeves or trouser legs and attaching them to other parts of their clothing.[12]

Amputees could express pride in their mutilated bodies in large part because nineteenth-century definitions of white manhood did not revolve around the physical proportions and attributes of the male body. As Anthony Rotundo and other historians of manhood note, the extension of the capitalist marketplace before the Civil War had drawn northern men into a new world of ceaseless striving. Many began directing their energies toward "self-improvement" and "self-discipline," believing that hard work rather than talent was the key to social advancement.[13] Definitions of improving and mastering the self rested on a revised understanding of the relationship between mind and body, requiring above all the control of bodily desires and passions through the development of a strong character and resolute will.[14] Because manhood was understood to rest on self-discipline rather than physicality, white men's identities were couched in terms of difference from those who purportedly lacked self-discipline, namely women and those they considered "lesser races."[15] According

---

doubtless made do without. It should also be noted that although only twenty-two men in this survey specified their postwar occupations to pension officials, none of these were industrial laborers. The majority worked in offices, as bookkeepers, real estate agents, pension attorneys, postmasters, or salesmen. Prosthetic limb manufacturers clearly recognized this fact, as advertisements for their products frequently pictured an artificial arm holding a pen.

[12] Figg and Farrell-Beck, "Amputation in the Civil War," 467–68.

[13] Anthony Rotundo, *American Manhood: Transformations in Masculinity from the Revolution to the Modern Era* (New York: Basic Books, 1993), chapter 1.

[14] Ben Barker-Benfield, "The Spermatic Economy: A Nineteenth-Century View of Sexuality," in *The American Family in Social Historical Perspective*, ed. by Michael Gordon (New York: St. Martin's Press, 1973), 336–72, explores the way Victorian commentators drew connections between male economic and sexual behavior.

[15] Gail Bederman, *Manliness & Civilization: A Cultural History of Gender & Race in the United States, 1880–1917* (Chicago: University of Chicago Press, 1993) has discussed the changing importance of the male body to definitions of male gender identity in the nineteenth century, as well as the connections between understandings of race and ways of conceptualizing white manhood. On the importance of self-

to many who wrote left-handed manuscripts, the disciplined character of northern men had been crucial to their military victory. These
amputees drew from the language of manly self-discipline as they
recounted their wounding and subsequent attempts to master injuries, suggesting that through their response to suffering they personi-
fied the ideal citizen soldier. Rather than negating their identities as
men, injury for some amputees constituted the evidence of manhood.

For others, a disciplined response to injury had the potential to
inspire and thus redeem their society. These men were born during
the decades of evangelical fervor that followed the Second Great
Awakening, in which the remote God of Calvinism had been replaced
by a gentler and more comprehensible Savior who suffered to save
humankind.[16] Some amputees took the suffering Christ as their
model of manhood, figuring power as an inner strength and conceptualizing their own sacrifices in sentimental and providential terms.
Their positive assessments of the value of suffering reveal a markedly
different attitude to wartime pain and injury than that described by
historians such as George Fredrickson. According to Fredrickson,
northern elites who concerned themselves with the plight of the
wounded came to reject spontaneous popular benevolence in favor
of a new "tough-minded" affirmation of efficiency, order, and bureaucracy.[17] In contrast, the narratives written by these several hun-

---

discipline among Union soldiers, see Mitchell, *The Vacant Chair*, 46. Some northern
troops clearly failed to conform to dominant definitions of white manhood, instead
seizing on army life as an opportunity for drinking, swearing, extra-marital sex, or
gambling—forms of behavior that most civilians deemed immoral or improper. The
majority, however, understood self-discipline as both a political and a personal imperative, that which defined them as rational, adult, citizens fighting against an
overly passionate, irrational, and effeminate South. For a discussion of northern images of southern effeminacy, see also Nina Silber, "Intemperate Men, Spiteful
Women, and Jefferson Davis," in *Divided Houses: Gender and the Civil War*, ed. by
Catherine Clinton & Nina Silber (New York: Oxford University Press, 1992), 285.

[16] Randall M. Miller, Harry S. Stout, and Charles Reagan Wilson, eds., *Religion
and the American Civil War* (New York: Oxford University Press, 1998), 4. For an
examination of the changing image of God throughout the nineteenth century, see
Susan Curtis, "The Son of Man and God the Father: The Social Gospel and Victorian Masculinity," in *Meanings for Manhood: Constructions of Masculinity in Victorian America*, ed. by Mark C. Carnes and Clyde Griffen (Chicago: University of
Chicago Press, 1990), 73.

[17] George M. Fredrickson, *The Inner Civil War: Northern Intellectuals and the
Crisis of the Union* (New York: Harper Torchbooks, 1965), 108, chapters 6–7. See
also Lori D. Ginzberg, *Women and the Work of Benevolence: Morality, Politics, and
Class in the Nineteenth-Century United States* (New Haven, Conn.: Yale University
Press, 1990), chapter 5, who also suggests that benevolent women replaced the senti-

dred amputees suggest that war served rather to increase the efficacy of a sentimental and religious language for many northern soldiers. Perhaps because they had already proven their manhood in battle, soldiers were comfortable weeping over the strains of songs that idealized motherhood and domesticity. As they discussed the benevolent response of civilians toward their suffering, amputees praised such activities precisely because they were voluntary, reaffirming the seemingly spontaneous love and affection of familial bonds.[18] If self-controlled manhood was necessary for the survival of republican institutions, suffering held equal political importance in the North, where many viewed the voluntary sacrifices of a citizen army, and the sympathy such sacrifice evoked, as a guarantee against a potential nation of self-interested and atomized individuals.[19]

Civil War amputees were among those who suffered greatly for

---

mentality of earlier generations and instead exalted the virtues of efficiency, rationality, and order. In contrast, Anne Rose, *Victorian America and the Civil War* (Cambridge, Eng.: Cambridge University Press, 1992), in her introduction disputes Fredrickson's characterization of the Civil War as the transitional moment for middle-class northerners, arguing that trends in intellectual and social life that he attributes to the war, such as bureaucracy and individualism, were largely in place by the 1850s. I would add that all three authors underestimate the continuing influence of sentimentalism, both within and outside the middle classes. The memoirs of female nurses, for example, are replete with sentimental tales of heroic deaths, bereft mothers, and grieving widows, and these writers invariably portrayed their own sympathetic response to the wounded as formative in men's recoveries and distinct from the callous rationality of male doctors. Moreover, as historian Patrick Kelly argues, northern benevolent workers were quite adamant that the bureaucratic structures they had created should be disbanded along with the armies at the end of the war. Members of the Sanitary Commission, he notes, overwhelmingly endorsed voluntarism, hoping to keep sick and disabled veterans in their homes and communities through the provision of pensions and limited assistance in finding employment. See Patrick Kelly, *Creating a National Home: Building the Veterans' Welfare State 1860–1900* (Cambridge, Mass.: Harvard University Press, 1997), chapter 1.

[18] For soldiers and civilians alike the war revived rather than challenged the potency of spiritual beliefs, witnessed by religious revivals among the troops and by public pronouncements depicting the war as a Divine Judgment on the North for tolerating slavery or worshipping secular pursuits. Anne Rose notes, however, that this wartime evangelicalism rested on a weak foundation. Although northerners "recalled religion for consolation" during the war, she argues that religious discussions tended to employ comforting generalities lacking in the intellectual rigor that characterized earlier religious debate. More importantly, Rose suggests that the sectional crisis contributed to the long-term secularization of northern culture, simultaneously revealing "the depth of Americans' involvement in civil issues" and enhancing "the authority of public institutions as tools for defining national objectives." Rose, *Victorian America*, 61–66.

[19] Phillip Shaw Paludan, "Religion and the American Civil War," in Miller et al., eds., *Religion and the American Civil War*, 28.

their commitments. The unique set of narratives submitted by hundreds of these men as they competed at left-handed penmanship provides the rare opportunity to examine how wartime injury and sacrifice were understood and given meaning during and immediately after the Civil War. These documents reveal that antebellum assumptions regarding manhood, citizenship, and suffering continued to shape the identities of northern soldiers wounded in battle. For many of these men, Union victory had validated prewar beliefs and values, enabling them to incorporate bodily loss into a sense of personal and masculine identity.

Of the 2,200,000 northern men who served in the Union army and navy, at least 21,753 survived the amputation of a limb.[20] Clearly, something had to be done to aid these maimed patriots, yet northerners worried over the extent and form public aid should assume. Their responses were colored by prewar attitudes toward the needy, which tended to blame those in poverty for their own plight, as well as by new concerns about the potentially debilitating effects of army life on male individualism. Afraid of augmenting the growing numbers of dependent poor, northerners generally agreed that the best course was to help veterans help themselves. To this end, numerous ventures aimed at employing disabled soldiers sprang up in northern cities during the war. In New York, Boston, and Philadelphia, messenger services staffed entirely by amputees provided work for a small number of men, and in several large northern cities, men could register at employment agencies operated by the Sanitary Commission, which promised to match employer and employee free of charge.[21] Others found employment with the federal government,

---

[20] Joseph K. Barnes, ed., *The Medical and Surgical History of the War of the Rebellion* (Washington, D. C.: Government Printing Office, 1883), part 3, vol. 2: *Surgical History*, 877, notes that Union surgeons reported performing 29,980 amputations; of this number, 21,753 men survived. Barnes further records that soldiers were roughly one-and-a-half times more likely to face upper rather than lower extremity amputations, but he concedes that these figures underestimate the number of Civil War amputations. The collection of medical statistics during the war, he explains, was neither uniform nor complete, particularly during the early war years. Moreover, amputations performed on officers were never recorded, nor were those executed by family physicians, or those occurring after soldiers were discharged from service for wounds received during the war.

[21] On the Sanitary Commission's attempts to find work for disabled veterans in Cleveland and Ohio, see Dr. J. S. Newberry, *U.S. Sanitary Commission in the Valley of the Mississippi During the War of the Rebellion, 1861–1866*, Sanitary Commission No. 96. (Cleveland: Fairbanks, Benedict & Co., 1871), 511–17.

which gave preference in civil offices to appropriately trained and honorably discharged veterans. Yet these measures never came close to finding work for all who sought it, and the government provided nothing comparable to the rehabilitation hospitals and training schemes that catered to veterans injured in subsequent wars.[22] Moreover, even this limited assistance was short-lived. By mid 1866, the army had closed its remaining hospitals, and employment offices had ceased operations, leaving disabled veterans largely to fend for themselves.

One northerner who concerned himself with the plight of maimed veterans was newspaper editor William Oland Bourne. The son of a staunch abolitionist, Bourne spent most of his life assisting the needy. In the decade before the war, he had been active in educational and labor reform. When the Central Park Hospital in New York opened its doors to sick and injured soldiers in the summer of 1862, Bourne signed on as a volunteer.[23] Over the next two years, he became a regular visitor around the wards, befriending the men and conducting religious services. In his diary, Bourne recorded details of those who came under his care and, having kept in touch with many of his former patients, he had an intimate knowledge of the difficulties soldiers faced in adapting to civilian life. To help ease this transition, he began publishing *The Soldier's Friend* in December 1864, filling its pages with details of bounty and pension laws, information on newly formed veterans' organizations, and a range of other useful information, alongside his own patriotic verse.[24]

Concerned primarily with finding work for disabled soldiers, Bourne led by example, hiring amputees to hawk *The Soldier's Friend* in the railway cars and streets of New York. From the earliest editions, he lectured those missing a limb on the benefits of self-help. "[M]ake up in mind what you have lost in body," he advised, claiming, "Your will can carry you farther on one leg than you can travel

---

[22] Wecter, *When Johnny Comes Marching Home*, 186. The Lincoln Institute, a precursor to the Veterans' Administration, did provide some training for amputees in telegraphy, typewriting, and bookkeeping according to Figg & Farrell-Beck, "Amputation in the Civil War," 474.

[23] *The New York Times*, June 7, 1901.

[24] *The Soldier's Friend*, December 1864, 2. Monthly editions of this newspaper were published in New York between December 1864 and June 1868. After this date, weekly editions were issued until publication ceased in September 1869.

without it on two."[25] If the will was more important to manhood than bodily integrity, Bourne implied that it could only be demonstrated by vaulting oneself into white-collar employment. "There are hundreds of good clerks who have lost a right hand, but who are to[o] inert to learn to write with the left," he stated.[26] To remedy this situation, he published details of a penmanship competition in June 1865, offering premiums of $1,000 to "the Left-Armed Soldiers of the Union" as "an inducement to that class of wounded . . . to fit themselves for lucrative and honorable positions."[27] By the time judging began in February 1866, Bourne had received some 270 manuscripts, a response so enthusiastic that he organized a further round of prizes, adding an additional 120 entries the following July.[28]

It soon became apparent that enthusiasm was not spread uniformly among left-armed veterans. Only a few commissioned officers chose to write manuscripts, for example, and others were perhaps dissuaded by the mildly condescending tone of uplift that infused the entire enterprise.[29] Competing at penmanship was also out of the question for most black soldiers, since the vast majority had only

---

[25] "Work for Disabled Soldiers," *The Soldier's Friend*, March 1865, 1.

[26] "Four Rules for Discharged Soldiers," ibid.

[27] Ibid., June 1865, 2.

[28] These documents provide necessarily limited data. Because they were written in the immediate postwar period, it is impossible to determine the extent to which the identity of these writers altered as the century progressed, nor do they offer more than a glimpse at how the loss of a soldier's limb affected family members. Although the pension files of Civil War soldiers can sometimes provide detailed accounts of postwar lives, in the case of amputees this source presents several difficulties. On one hand, some of the men who entered Bourne's competition failed to give full names or particulars of their enlistment, making it impossible to know whether they applied for a pension. Moreover, the pension files of amputees are generally far less detailed than those for men with less obvious forms of injury. Because pension applicants initially had to prove that the disability or death of a soldier was related to military service, the most extensive files were those requiring thorough investigation. For amputees, a single appearance before a medical board was usually enough to secure a pension. An act passed in June 1866 stipulated the pension rates for fourteen specific types of disability, providing $15 a month for the loss or total disability of an arm or leg. *United States Statutes at Large*, 14: 56–58. On changes in Civil War pension legislation, see John William Oliver, *History of the Civil War Military Pensions, 1861–1885*, Bulletin of the University of Wisconsin, no. 844, History Series, no. 1 (1917).

[29] Major General Oliver Otis Howard, who lost his right arm at Fair Oaks, for example, refused Bourne's entreaty to join the competition, although he did agree to judge the manuscripts. O. O. Howard to H. W. Bellows, February 27, 1868, box 5, William Oland Bourne Papers.

recently escaped from slavery, under which an education was legally denied them. But even among literate African Americans, Bourne's competition was irrelevant. Will Thomas, one of the two black soldiers who put pen to paper, noted, "I dont expect to secure a position as *clerk*, that being proscribed on account of my *color*."[30] As Thomas recognized, black soldiers injured in the line of duty faced a unique set of difficulties in civilian life that a penmanship competition was ill designed to address.

Those who did enter received instructions broad enough to provide much scope for individual variations. Bourne advised contestants that manuscripts should include personal and military details, together with a "brief" literary specimen either "original or selected," and readers of *The Soldier's Friend* learned further that "essays on patriotic themes, and especially narratives of the writer's experience in the service . . . are preferred." From the outset, contestants also knew that they were writing for an audience, as Bourne planned to exhibit the manuscripts and use the proceeds to publish a memorial volume that each entrant would receive.[31] Thus, writers probably had potential audiences in mind as they fashioned identities through their narratives, just as they continued to construct identities in the light of public expectations after manuscripts were written.

In the glare of a public spotlight some were taciturn, providing a few sparse sheets listing personal details and names of battles, whereas others sought center stage with manuscripts that ran to dozens of pages. Colonel W. Davis, the highest ranking participant and one of the more prolific writers, submitted a third-person narrative that detailed his impressive ancestry and various prewar accomplishments, but most entrants were more modest.[32] More than a dozen men copied lines of poetry or political speeches (Lincoln's being the favorite), and several opted out of the role of narrator entirely, instead allowing transcribed military reports or discharge papers to speak on their behalf. Quite a few amputees clearly felt that, as victors in war, they should have a say in the way peacetime society was organized and took the opportunity to lecture their readers on politics. But the vast majority chose to recount their military histories,

---

[30] William Thomas, 1:93, William Oland Bourne Papers.

[31] *The Soldier's Friend*, March 1865, 1. The proposed memorial volume, however, was never published.

[32] W. W. H. Davies, 1:268, William Oland Bourne Papers.

starting with enlistment and ending with discharge from military service, and only a minority specified prewar occupations or detailed
postwar lives.

By virtue of making the effort to write with their left hands in the
first place, all entrants were automatically participating in an exercise
that defined them as hardworking and worthy of employment. For
some, this was precisely the point. John Koster, for example, hoped
that a potential employer might read his manuscript, explaining to
his readers that "I have no business," and being "by trade a Paper
Maker, I would like a Position as foreman of a Mill."[33] Likewise,
William Kipling wrote at the end of his manuscript, "If this should
meet the eye of any kind person who can get me some permanent
employment I shall feel thankful."[34] Whereas Kipling implied that he
would be satisfied with any paid work, Bourne had more specific
employment prospects in mind for his contestants. The fact that he
chose to focus his efforts on left-handed amputees reveals that he
construed the loss of a right arm as the greatest hindrance to gaining
"lucrative and honorable" work, which he understood as clerical
rather than agricultural or manual employment. If Bourne's own notion of the gainfully employed and "honorable" amputee focused on
what he did for a living, however, those who entered his competition
fashioned their own understandings of what it meant to be a member
of "The Left Armed Corps."

In Bourne's estimation, manuscripts should be judged not according to their content, but on the quality of their penmanship. In contrast, many of his competitors insisted that amputees represented a
singular class of veterans, who should be considered in light of their
military service and sacrifice rather than their aptitude for clerical
work. Frequently voiced criticisms emphasized the class bias inherent in a penmanship competition, which effectively rewarded those
who had achieved a level of training denied to many. What of those
"who have not had opportunities to acquire an education?" inquired
Joseph Eoyolf.[35] And what of those, complained Charles Jackson,
who must work all day and "have to sit up evenings with their eyes
half closed, to do their writing?"[36] Even if they could not best their

---

[33] John Koster, 1:124, ibid.
[34] William Kipling, 1:231, ibid.
[35] Joseph Eoyolf, 1:207, ibid.
[36] Charles Jackson, 1:221, ibid.

more privileged competitors with a pen, these men nonetheless demanded recognition of their place in the Left Armed Corps. Although the majority probably entered with hopes of winning the generous prize money on offer, this desire only explains the pains entrants took over the form of their manuscripts; it cannot adequately account for their contents.[37] Extending their discussions well beyond the "brief" writing sample that Bourne mandated, these writers created a site in which they could explore the meaning of wartime service and injury, in the process delineating their own roles in national salvation before a grateful public.

In addition to the desire to win or to demonstrate a resolute work ethic, Bourne's competition seems to have appealed to many because it enabled them to claim a particular form of identity—not as soldiers who happened to have lost a limb, but as members of a unique group whose injuries bore witness to their service on the front lines of battle. In Delmer Lowell's estimation, the loss of a limb revealed the difference between that "class of persons who pretended to love the Union" and those who "stood up boldly to defend it."[38] Amputees, in other words, could act as spokesmen for all patriots, because their wounds demonstrated the courage of their convictions. And, echoing the sentiments of numerous manuscript writers, Frank Otis deemed it "the duty of *every* member of the left arm'd corps . . . to add something to the collection."[39] Taking this duty very seriously indeed, at least seven of the forty-five men who wrote for both competitions had already won a prize the first time around and were thus ineligible for further premiums. It was their "duty" to present their histories, many suggested, because they bore the visible memory of war. Referring to the proposed memorial volume that would feature their narratives, one writer declared "truly such a book will be prized next to the Bible itself."[40] Through these histories, he implied, readers could

---

[37] To Bourne's original offer of $500 in premiums, the United States Sanitary Commission and the Committee of Awards added an extra $500. This sum was divided into first, second, third, and fourth prizes of $200, $150, $100, and $50 respectively, and the remaining sum was distributed among seven prizes for second-class penmanship, four prizes for ornamental penmanship, and twelve prizes for literary merit. In the second competition, Bourne awarded ten premiums of $50, each bearing the name of a Union general.

[38] Delmer Lowell, 1:228, William Oland Bourne Papers.

[39] Frank George Otis, 1:62, ibid.

[40] W. MacNulty, 1:238, ibid.

seek inspiration, solace, and meaning. Suffering had sanctified their message.

As they detailed their military histories, most penman focused on the tangible results of battle to give meaning to their sacrifices, expending far more ink detailing the collective trials and successes of the Union army than on their own pain and suffering or their time in the hospital. Reaching the point in their stories at which they were injured, manuscript writers continually drew attention to the context in which they had received their wounds, marking their positions as men injured in the thick of the fight, and thus connecting their injuries to eventual military success. Dozens of writers, for example, emphasized that they were injured while in the act of firing their weapons, and many added the seemingly obvious point that their severe wounds forced their removal from the front lines. Representing a typical account of injury, Louis Boos wrote, "In the act of firing the 17th time I was hit by [the] enemy, the ball passing through my wrist at the pulse and my arm dropped powerless. . . . I became reconciled to my misfortune on hearing of the glorious achievements of the Army of the Potomac under Grant."[41] Others followed Boos in attributing meaning to their injuries by reference to subsequent events. Conrad Dodge described his wounding as a moment of collective victory at the expense of personal sacrifice, explaining that as a shell tore through his arm, "a fearful pain, agonizing beyond expression ran through my frame . . . but as I fell the glorious flag of my country was planted in triumph upon the enemy's works, and the hated banner of treason torn down and debased. Oh! in spite of the agony I suffered a shrill of extacy ran through me to know that victory was won, and a feeling of exultation and pride filled my heart, which made my sufferings seem immesurably less."[42] Similarly, Conrad Dippel wrote of coming to consciousness after losing his arm, "without coat and without blanket, amidst acres and acres full of wounded and dying men." But as he was loaded onto an ambulance, he looked out the window to see a group of rebel prisoners "guarded by U.S. colored troops in double file. This gave me really the greatest satisfaction and I forgot all my sufferings in reflecting how quick Providence turns the luck of man and does justice to every one."[43] Highlighting

---

[41] Louis Boos, 1:10, ibid.

[42] Conrad Dodge, 1:128, ibid.

[43] Conrad Dippel, 2:29, ibid.

their own contributions to victory while minimizing the unpleasant details of personal suffering, these men sought to reaffirm the selfless aims they believed had led them to war.

Drawing their readers' attention to the larger significance of military triumph, amputees directly addressed a public discourse that had the potential to invalidate the sacrifices of individual soldiers. During the war, northern civilians had sharply criticized the treatment of wounded soldiers, and amputation was frequently portrayed as a matter of bad luck or medical negligence. Newspapers regularly carried stories of overzealous surgeons lopping off limbs for the merest flesh wound, or operating in a drunken stupor on the wrong body part. In addition, many in the North were justifiably outraged at the failure to provide facilities for the wounded.[44] Particularly during the early war years, before the Ambulance Corps and a system of division hospitals had been established, wounded men might lay on the battlefield for days. Those who could walk sometimes wandered from hospital to hospital seeking admission. According to George Fredrickson, northerners came to wonder if this carnage had any purpose, or if perhaps soldiers might be simply "cattle herded to slaughter."[45] A few of those who submitted manuscripts gave voice to similar disillusionment as they sketched the poor treatment they had received. Minnott Tolman recounted being placed aboard a steamer "under the controll of a Dutchman for a Surgeon, who took better care of himself than he did of the wounded men, and as a consequence . . . the wounds became gengreenous and did not do well," resulting in the amputation of his arm.[46] Likewise, another man reported receiving a "poor amputation by an intoxicated surgeon."[47]

Yet it is striking that those who penned manuscripts generally did not seek to elicit public sympathy at the expense of their medical providers. In fact, of those men who mentioned hospital experiences, only eight saw cause for complaint, whereas four times as many praised the surgeons who had amputated their limbs, noting their kindness and "skill."[48] After providing the names of his surgeons, for

---

[44] George Worthington Adams, *Doctors in Blue: The Medical History of the Union Army in the Civil War* (New York: Henry Schuman, 1952), 4–5.

[45] Fredrickson, *The Inner Civil War*, 82.

[46] Minott Tolman, 2:74, William Oland Bourne Papers.

[47] B. D. Palmer, 2:28, ibid.

[48] According to Adams, it was far more common for soldiers to perceive surgeons as incompetent or brutal "quacks." Adams, *Doctors in Blue*, 55–56.

example, Edgar Worth hoped they might see his manuscript so he could thank them "for the best amputation I have ever seen."[49] As Worth and his fellow left-armed writers were aware, Civil War soldiers often died as a result of amputation; the fact that they survived their operations gave some proof of the efficacy of their medical treatment.[50] More frequently, writers drew attention to the severity of their wounds, implicitly taking issue not only with the prevalent image of superfluous amputations, but with the equally numerous stories of men who refused to part with their limbs yet survived, contrary to their surgeon's dire predictions. Emphasizing the inevitability of his amputation, Elbert Fuller wrote, "I had the misfortune of receiving a severe wound in the elbow joint which rendered amputation absolutely necessary in order to save my life . . . but I have the proud satisfaction of knowing that I have done my country some service . . . and I have cheerfully given my own righ[t] arm . . . in defence of the American Flag."[51] Likewise, George Warren explained that "they examined [my arm] and told me it could not be saved as the bones wer too badly shattered. I then gave it up willingly for I had the asurance that it could not be given for a nobler or better cause."[52]

Demonstrating the severity of an injury was no trifling concern. Those men quoted above did not just lose an arm, they *gave* one, and if this sacrifice was to be meaningful it could hardly be the result of a botched or unnecessary operation. Even in the sketchiest accounts

---

[49] Edgar Worth, 1:174, William Oland Bourne Papers. Others were thankful that recently discovered anesthetics were employed during their surgeries. John Bryce titled his manuscript "How I felt under Cloriform," recounting the dream he had while "Dr. Bliss" worked on his arm. "[I] set sail as a vessel sailing through the air," he wrote, and "had a narrow River to Cross which seemed very Deep. . . . I felt no pain During the cutting of my arm. It seemed Pleasant while in the stupor." John Bryce, 1:199, William Oland Bourne Papers. Martin S. Pernick, *A Calculus of Suffering: Pain, Professionalism and Anesthesia in Nineteenth-Century America* (New York: Columbia University Press, 1985) details the introduction of anesthetics to the United States in 1846, noting that the surgeon general standardized the use of anesthetics in the Union Army after 1862, and that the vast majority of Union troops were unconscious during their operations, 181–83.

[50] Barnes, ed., *Medical and Surgical History*, part 3, vol. 2: *Surgical History*, 877, records a 26.3 percent overall fatality rate for recorded amputations, a figure encompassing enormous differences in the survival rates that pertained to different types of amputations. On one end of the scale, the loss of a hand or fingers led to a 2.9 percent fatality, whereas amputations attempted at the hip had a fatality rate of 83.3 percent.

[51] Elbett Fuller, 1:215, William Oland Bourne Papers.

[52] George Warren, 1:260, ibid.

of injury, writers invariably detailed their shattered bones and severed arteries. Describing the specific location of wounds in "bones" or "joints" implicitly differentiated their injuries from less serious soft-tissue wounds that may or may not have required amputation, in the same way that endorsing a surgeon's skill substantiated the necessity of amputation.

As they specified their own contributions to military success, dozens of amputees also emphasized the response to soldiers' sufferings on the part of northern civilians. They presented injury not as an individual event, but as part of a larger story of voluntarism and sacrifice among northerners that had been crucial to the war's outcome. John Foster remembered the daily visits of Miss Gibson, a "ministering angel" who "showed us many attentions appreciated only by a soldier away from home and friends." Praising northern women whose unpaid labor supplied wounded soldiers with clothing, food, and bandages, he went on to note that "in all the hospitals I received every comfort that one could need and I might say more than one could expect."[53] Similarly, Lewis Kline wished to "say a word in favor of the Ladies who have so nobly stood up for their Country, and although not carrying a Gun they did more than many soldiers who did."[54] Others followed James Smith in arguing that "scarcely a family in the country" escaped the impact of war. Instead of particularizing his own sacrifice, Smith offered a "tribute" to those northerners "who

---

[53] John Foster, 1:242, ibid.

[54] Lewis Kline, 2:25, ibid. According to both men, the sympathetic response of female nurses and civilians played a vital role in the recovery of the wounded. After experiencing the decidedly un-domestic conditions of battle, female caregiving could reassure and remind injured men that sacrifices were appreciated, and that the world beyond the battlefield remained intact. Henry Palmer described lying in his bed, thinking on "man's total depravity," when he felt the "warm pressure of a soft hand" and looked up to see a "Samaritan woman, in whose eyes shone woman's goodness of heart. . . . I then felt that the Ladies of Philadelphia were teaching the world that there is *yet* upon earth, *Christianity*." Henry Palmer, 1:73, William Oland Bourne Papers. The symbolic significance of being tended to by a female nurse, particularly a middle-class "lady," is underestimated by those historians who note that soldiers' gratitude far outweighed the contributions of actual women, who formed a relatively small number of those tending the wounded. In a culture that placed the greatest value on home and family, female acceptance of war aims and recognition of male sacrifice was crucial. In fact, several amputees apparently not cared for by women nonetheless devoted entire manuscripts to their work among the wounded. Although amputees valorized the work of middle-class white nurses, only a single writer mentioned the new responsibilities his wife was compelled to undertake as a result of his injury.

aided us in every conceivable way," suggesting that the suffering accompanying mass death linked soldiers and civilians together with a bond of mutual sympathy.[55]

The many amputees who wrote in praise of benevolent civilians bear out James McPherson's recent contention that the Civil War did not create the sort of antagonism between soldier and civilian that scholars have pointed to as characterizing twentieth-century war narratives.[56] Northern volunteers, he argues, felt no indiscriminate resentment toward those remaining at home but instead reserved condemnation and hostility for civilians they considered unpatriotic.[57] James Holder's narrative was one of returning home in 1864 to confront those who "forgot they had a Country" and instead railed "against the cause in which I had been so recently engaged in the most terrible and desperate maner." Yet he also returned "to receive the smiles and caresses of all good, loyal citizens of the neighborhood in which I had resided." These "loyal people" later elected him country recorder.[58] Such narratives reminded audiences that patriotism required an on-going recognition of the sacrifices made by injured soldiers, and writers censored those who failed to respond appropriately. Charles Dodge chided the civilian who "far from the scene of danger . . . regard[s] the mingled horrors of a battlefield, much as he would some spectacular drama . . . but is less inclined to raise the blazing cross of honor; which he has generously granted—to gaze upon the wound that won it."[59] Through a judgmental mode of address, amputees positioned themselves as moral arbiters of their society with an authority that came directly from their wounds.[60]

---

[55] James H. Smith, 1:233, William Oland Bourne Papers.

[56] See, for example, Paul Fussell, *The Great War and Modern Memory* (London: Oxford University Press, 1975). On the gendered aspects of soldiers' anger and disillusionment toward civilians in World War I, see Sandra M. Gilbert, "Soldier's Heart: Literary Men, Literary Women, and the Great War, *Signs* 8 (spring 1983): 422–50.

[57] McPherson, *For Cause & Comrades*, 141–42, 168. Here, McPherson takes issue with Linderman's argument in *Embattled Courage*, which suggests that Civil War soldiers experienced much the same sense of disillusionment with war goals and disgust at simple-minded civilian patriotism witnessed in later wars. Accounting for the higher desertion rates in the later years of the war, McPherson points to conscripts, substitutes, and bounty men who entered the war in greater numbers during this period and were not motivated by the same convictions that sustained those who enlisted in 1861 and 1862.

[58] James Holder, 1:36, William Oland Bourne Papers.

[59] Charles Dodge: 1:47, ibid.

[60] My thanks to Ronald Walters for making this point.

The patriotic sacrifice evidenced by their wounds was, for some writers, inseparable from the stalwart manhood they believed had been crucial to military success. Several narratives centered on dramatic examples of courage under fire and endurance in the face of injury. Men wrote of whistling on their way to hospital, or laughing at the sight of their injuries. Two or three soldiers hopped off the operating table and went straight out to watch the progress of a battle, and one proudly recounted laying without flinching while a Confederate surgeon amputated his arm without the aid of anesthetics. These accounts are stated without lengthy comment or description, presenting the amputee as a man of action and self-control who has already illustrated his manliness through injury and recovery. Drawing from a form of rough democratic manhood that rejected emotional display and social refinement in favor of physical courage and endurance, these men constituted their identities in opposition to the dominant way of formulating male identity that defined and shaped, but was not limited to, the nascent middling classes.

By revealing their ability to withstand hardship and endure pain, amputation offered some men firm proof of their manhood. Declaring that amputation "was necessary, to constitute *me* a perfect man," Henry Allen explained, "I wanted to bring a mark home with me to show that I had been w[h]ere danger came near me. I have that mark, and so conspicuous, that all can see it. I am proud of it. No man can say, that Allen was a coward and hid from danger."[61] Those amputees who affected a rugged stance toward injury and suffering were most likely drawn from the ranks of wage-earning laborers. For men like Henry Allen, who entered the war as a mechanic, the need to acquire a "conspicuous" mark as testimony to manly heroism and self-control had become increasingly pressing by the mid nineteenth century, as they watched their independence and autonomy eroded by the emergence of large-scale industrialization in the North.[62] However, as will be noted later, writers employing a language of rugged manhood were far outnumbered by those who framed their in-

---

[61] Henry C. Allen, 1:15, William Oland Bourne Papers.

[62] Allen's pension file lists him as a mechanic before the war; a death certificate dated 1911 notes that he later became a salesman. Henry C. Allen, Civil War and Later Pension Files, Records of the Veterans Administration, Record Group 15, National Archives, Washington, D.C. (hereinafter cited as Civil War Pension Files, RG 15).

juries in sentimental and providential terms. More importantly, even in these accounts presenting the wound as a mark of bravery, the context in which a wound had been received remained central.

When Allen described his wound as an "honorable scar," he referred simultaneously to his daring under fire and to the cause for which he fought. Rhapsodizing over the war wound, Phil Faulk made this connection clear, declaring that "veteran scars are enduring, priceless momentoes of glory won in the deadly breach at the cannon's mouth, and in the heat of the fierce charge. They . . . speak of deeds of noble daring performed, where none but true and brave could venture. They proclaim your patriotism in language more eloquent than human tongue. They picture the price of liberty and union, and are richer ornaments than the purest gold."[63] These "veteran scars," according to Faulk, were not "priceless" simply because they demonstrated bravery, but because they symbolized bravery animated by patriotism. By the late nineteenth century, veterans on both sides of the conflict would come together to celebrate a manly courage detached from the political issues involved in the war.[64] But as Faulk discussed the meaning inherent in his amputated limb, his pride came from the belief that injured northerners were "standing up nobly, voluntarily in defence of [our] country's free government." Continuing on in this vein for several pages, Faulk expressed in the most profuse and florid prose what numerous amputees put more simply. "I went because I thought it my Duty to go and I served three years for my country," stated George Dale. "I stood up for my rites

---

[63] Phil Faulk, 2:91, William Oland Bourne Papers.

[64] In the introduction to *Manliness & Civilization*, Bederman notes that as avenues for advancement in the market place narrowed, and as white males found their authority and control over public space eroded by the activism of women, working class, and ethnic groups, increasing numbers of men began to emphasize bodily differences between women and men, celebrating aggressiveness, physical force, and male sexuality. It is impossible to know what Civil War amputees made of these developments, but there is evidence to suggest that many continued to conform to the older notions of self-disciplined manhood that they endorsed in their manuscripts. Although by 1893, the federal government was spending an enormous 41.5 percent of its annual income on roughly a million Civil War pensioners, only 9,000 amputees ever applied for the pensions to which they were automatically entitled. Statistics on government expenditure for pensions can be found in Theda Skocpol, *Protecting Soldiers and Mothers: The Political Origins of Social Policy in the United States* (Cambridge, Mass.: Harvard University Press, 1992). For the number of amputees applying for a pension, see William H. Glasson, *Federal Military Pensions in the United States* (New York: Oxford University Press, 1911), 138, 157.

untill I lost my rite arm" and was "willing to sacrifise my life for such a great cause as we were engaged in."[65] It was this "great cause" that most amputees pointed to as they validated their sufferings and demanded that civilians do likewise.[66]

Demonstrating their unflagging support for the war, the majority of amputees continued in military service after losing an arm. Of those who survived amputations, well over two-thirds remained on duty as members of the Invalid Corps (later renamed the Veteran Reserve Corps), whereas around fifty-eight hundred sought an immediate discharge.[67] Specifically designed to reward only those who were "meritorious and deserving," the VRC was organized into two battalions. Those missing a limb were assigned to the Second Battalion, authorized to carry swords and revolvers. They were sent to perform hospital or clerical duties or to guard warehouses, offices, and supply depots.[68] To underscore further their roles as honorable patri-

[65] George W. Dale, 2:30, William Oland Bourne Papers.

[66] Representations of the wound as a "decoration" or "ornament" to the male body drew on a long history. Tattoos had long been popular among certain groups of men in Europe and the United States, notably those in the military, for example, not least because they symbolized a bearer's ability to withstand pain. Likewise, Robert A. Nye describes how European men courted the dueling scar as a symbol of manhood prior to World War I (*Masculinity and Male Codes of Honor in Modern France* [New York: Oxford University Press, 1993]). As one scholar points out, the meanings attributed to physical appearances have altered markedly over time. Those whose bodies differed from the norm have for centuries been seen through a complex and changing dialectic of fascination, fear, disgust, and sensuality—from the eroticization of the disabled in medieval festivals to the sexualization of the tubercular sufferer's emaciated body in the Victorian era. Only in the modern period with the introduction of mass-produced standards of physical perfection, he argues, have the disabled become "the aesthetically neutered objects of benevolence and assistance." Harlan Hahn, "Can Disability be Beautiful?" *Social Policy* 18 (winter 1988): 26–32.

[67] Statistics on men entering the Invalid Corps were drawn from Byron Stinson, "Paying the Debt," *Civil War Times Illustrated* 9 (July 1970): 20–29. Recruiting invalid soldiers for use in wartime was not new; an Invalid Corps had been established during the Revolutionary period, following earlier European precedents. On the development of the VRC, see Stanley Michael Suplick, Jr., "The United States Invalid Corps/Veteran Reserve Corps" (Ph.D. dissertation, University of Minnesota, 1969), chapter 1.

[68] Provost Marshal General James B. Fry ordered the posting of handbills advertising the Invalid Corps as a "corps of honor" in June 1863. Convalescent soldiers with limbs intact were generally assigned to the First Battalion of the corps, which performed provost and guard duty. United States War Department, *The War of the Rebellion: A Compilation of the Official Records of the Union and Confederate Armies*, 70 vols. in 128 (Washington, D.C.: Government Printing Office, 1880–1901), series 3, vol. 3, 337. Although soldiers sometimes viewed the VRC as the repository

ots, many companies of soldiers in the Second Battalion were also put to work guarding prisoners, conscripts, stragglers, and deserters.[69]

Only a handful of the four hundred men who entered Bourne's competition wrote of their wounds in terms of the pain of injury, the tedium and misery of hospital life, or the devastating effects of bodily dismemberment.[70] Instead, many gave meaning to bodily loss by defining it in terms of a noble cause, a collective national sacrifice, and an honorable victory. For these men, war wounds presented an opportunity to exemplify self-governing manhood in civilian life and thereby continue to sustain the republican institutions they fought to preserve.

Military service was understood by many soldiers as both an education in self-discipline and a triumphal vindication of those who put this education to use. Instead of describing soldiering as the cause of their injuries, it was for many amputees the very reason for their successful efforts at rehabilitation. Some discussed this education in terms of military discipline. Louis Boos, for instance, explained that he initially thought his officers "very despotic," but later came to learn that "discipline will improve a young man, will give him an experience of hardships, troubles and sufferings, which he would hardly meet with in a life time outside the Army."[71] In a second manuscript written several years later, Boos was still reflecting with "feelings of pride and wonder at the many trials" he had passed through which had enabled him "to bear the crosses of . . . life upon coming home to live as a private citizen."[72] For Rufus Robinson, army life also revealed unknown potential. Addressing his disabled comrades, he noted, "Our experience has taught us that we little knew what could be achieved by us physically, until we entered the field as soldiers, and the same rules applies to us mentally."[73] Whereas some men's self-discipline helped them cope with bodily loss, others attributed their fortitude to the particular trials of losing an arm. William McLeod argued that amputation was a great benefit for men like

---

for incompetent officers and malingering convalescents, wounds received in battle excluded amputees from such indictments.

[69] Suplick, "The United States Invalid Corps," 126 ff.

[70] I counted only four statements of unqualified regret over the loss of an arm.

[71] Louis J. Boos, 1:10, William Oland Bourne Papers.

[72] Louis J. Boos, 2:19, ibid.

[73] Rufus L. Robinson, 1:71, ibid.

himself. "A good many of the maimed ones went into the army as I did, under age, and when they had been to school but little," he explained, but those who lost an arm were now forced "to cultivate their minds." He suggested that "the mental discipline they have received . . . but above all, the self-knowledge they have acquired, will in a great measure compensate, if not entirely repay them for the parts of their bodies they left on the different fields of strife."[74]

Discussing their efforts at writing, amputees further endorsed the positive benefits of army life by suggesting that penmanship was analogous to military service in its demand for long hours of bodily training, mental discipline, and persistence. Like many others, T. J. Cavanaugh recounted spending his every leisure moment trying to master penmanship. Just as General Grant had succeeded after suffering countless setbacks, he explained, so he dropped his pen "time and time again in despair," finally offering his manuscript as tangible proof that "perseverance will accomplish wonders in writing, as well as in War."[75] Believing that self-discipline and perseverance had won the war, these men sought to demonstrate their continuing commitment to the virtues of self-discipline through their writing and in their postwar lives.[76]

For many northerners, the remarkably quick and relatively peaceful disbanding of the Union army provided a dramatic affirmation of the self-disciplined nature of northern manhood. This rapid demobilization, according to historian Gerald Linderman, proves that soldiers returning home "were willing, even anxious to thrust into shadow all things martial" because they felt "a pervasive sense of the war as loss."[77] Although numerous men who penned left-handed manuscripts applauded their return to civilian life, this reflected a

---

[74] William McLeod, 2:100, ibid.

[75] T. J. Cavanaugh, 1:169, ibid.

[76] Historian Tamara Thornton notes that the concept of penmanship as an act of self-mastery was common in the Victorian era. She describes the way penmanship pedagogy during this period was understood as "a process of character formation, both in the literal sense of making letters and in the figurative sense of constructing a self." Although the eighteenth-century student learned to write by passively transcribing model alphabets or phrases, writing instruction in the following century reformulated writing as a mastery of the will over the body, emphasizing the importance of hand position, body posture, and physical movement. Tamara Plakins Thornton, *Handwriting in America: A Cultural History* (New Haven: Yale University Press, 1996), 43, 50.

[77] Linderman, *Embattled Courage*, 271.

confirmation rather than rejection of what they believed to be the attributes of the volunteer soldier. William Penn Sands, for instance, saw "the quietude with which a million of veteran soldiers, have laid aside their arms, and renewed the peaceful vocations of life" as a testament to "the intelligence of our Army."[78] And, like many other amputees, Fred Barker noted proudly that at the end of the Grand Review he "immediately put on a suit of citizen's clothes and started for school."[79] Statements such as these implied that the writer maintained the self-discipline and independence soldiers took with them to war; they were not permanently brutalized by their experiences.

As they recounted their effortless adaptation to both civilian and military pursuits, these manuscript writers explicitly praised the American ideal of a voluntary army in contrast to the standing armies of Europe. Northern volunteers, they argued, went to war after reasoning that their cause was a just one, in distinction to European soldiers who responded only to compulsion or financial rewards. Because their service to the Union was freely and intelligently given, they purportedly lost none of their individualism by surrendering their independence to the military. Proudly contrasting the armed forces of the Union with those of Europe, Joseph Gelray insisted that the latter were "like a vast machine," its officers the "only thinking men." How different it was in America, he claimed, "where so few make war their trade" and where the "citizen soldiery" is "a living, breathing, thinking patriot."[80] Focusing their narratives on braving the battlefield and surviving the rigors of military discipline only to resume their civilian occupations with the same courage and persistence in the face of injury, amputees rendered themselves exemplary American citizen soldiers.

The fact that their manuscripts would be displayed to the public probably added to the sense some writers had of themselves as inspirational examples of citizen soldiers. A number of penmen expressed a belief that the Union victory had taught European nations a lesson, in terms of both the durability of the republic and the strength and persistence of a volunteer army of republican men. They imagined

---

[78] William Penn Sands 1:6, William Oland Bourne Papers.
[79] Fred Barker, 1:150, ibid.
[80] Joseph Wiley Gelray, 1:108, ibid.

their wounds as the physical memory of the war, and their postwar lives as an embodiment and continuation of the lessons taught by the war. As keepers of the war's memory, amputees wrote of their duty to manifest a spirit of independence and self-discipline in their efforts to find paid employment. "We are the living monuments of the late cruel and bloody Rebellion" wrote Jonathan Allison, and now we "prepare to act another part in the great drama of life" by deciding on a livelihood "as becomes soldiers or good citizens."[81] For Allison, volunteering for war and fulfilling one's duty as a "good citizen" by seeking a livelihood were inseparable. Similarly, Phinicas Whitehouse addressed maimed soldiers: "If there remains a spark of that patriotism that prompted you to seize the musket, or a semblance of that manhood you exhibited on the field of battle . . .you will rather seek at once for permanent, honorable employment."[82] These amputees exhibited little sympathy for those who failed to manifest the appropriate spirit of self-help. Coming upon a one-legged soldier begging for his livelihood, Henry Allen explained, "I made up my mind that he was an indolent fellow before he went to war. There is no man who has lost an arm or a leg . . . but can earn a good support with the limbs left him."[83]

Claiming that amputation did not necessarily imply dependence on public aid was clearly a way for some writers to distance themselves from the image of the helpless cripple. But the injunction that amputees find permanent work was also bound up in differentiating northern soldiers from their counterparts in Europe. For European amputees, the traditional form of compensation was either institutional care or a license to beg on the King's highway.[84] Several manuscript writers went to some lengths to prove that the citizen soldier would accept no such dependence. J. Cavanaugh denied that any men with "empty sleeves" were "among the thousands of vagabonds clothed in Soldiers garb, that fill the streets." If you "meet one of that class," he maintained, "he generally has some employment and

---

[81] Jonathan McKinstry Allison, 1:67, ibid.

[82] Phinicas P. Whitehouse, 1:136, ibid.

[83] Henry C. Allen, 1:15, ibid.

[84] Judith Gladys Centina, "A History of Veterans' Homes in the United States, 1811–1930" (Ph. D. dissertation, Case Western Reserve University, 1977). See chapter 1 for a history of the European response to injured soldiers.

is clean and sober," because "most of them lost their arms at the front."[85] The fact that these northern amputees had volunteered for war, Cavanaugh implied, was proof enough that they were too independent to beg for their living.

The portrayal of the northern amputee as an exemplary citizen soldier was shared by those who attended the exhibition of left-handed manuscripts. House Speaker Schuyler Colfax told a crowd gathered at the opening of the second exhibit that these manuscripts "proved how American energy could triumph over adverse circumstances." After viewing the manuscripts, author Fanny Fern was moved to write a tribute in the *New York Ledger* praising this tangible evidence that the northern soldier could remain "self helpful and courageous" even when "so hacked and hewed to pieces that not half his original proportions remain."[86] Believing that Europeans could benefit by viewing this display of self-discipline, independence, and perseverance, conference organizer William Bourne, together with several veterans groups, conferred with the secretary of state over the possibility of sending the exhibition to Paris.[87]

Framing patriotic manhood in terms of self-discipline and self-help, however, had the potential to make failures of those who were unable to earn an independent living. Wounded in both legs and both arms, John Thompson wrote, "I suppose there is no language fully adequate to describe the extent of inconvenience. . . . To be compelled just in the prime of life (when teaming with anticipations of future prosperity and pleasure) to consent to be a permanent cripple for life . . . is a matter of no small moment. . . . We lose in a great measure our place in society."[88] Although Thompson was physically

---

[85] J. Cavanaugh, 1:169, William Oland Bourne Papers. Stories of maimed veterans begging in the streets also failed to elicit much sympathy from William Bourne, who stated that a blind veteran seeking alms and wearing a placard that declared his war service was a disgusting sight. "If he *is* a soldier," Bourne argued, the government has provided for his "liberal provision . . . enough, surely to render such mendicancy inexcusable." *The Soldier's Friend*, November 1865, 4.

[86] Broadside Concerning Contest, folder 1, box 1, William Oland Bourne Papers.

[87] *The Soldier's Friend*, June 1866, 2.

[88] John M. Thompson, 2:63, William Oland Bourne Papers. For eleven months, Thompson lived with pieces of shrapnel lodged near his hip joint, experiencing the "severest pain conceivable" as they worked their way to the surface of his skin. He died in 1874, apparently of blood poisoning from his wounds, one of the many uncounted casualties of the Civil War. See the pension file of John M. Thompson, Civil War Pension Files, RG 15.

unable to work, there were also amputees whose inability to find paid employment took an emotional toll. In his manuscript, Dorus Bates advised fellow left-armed soldiers "never get the blues," telling them "you will have to go but a short distance to find some poor fellow that is more unfortunate than yourself." But Bates was unable to take his own advice. A boyhood friend later described him as "full of life hope and ambition . . . up to the time he lost his arm." After this, "his constant theme was regret at the necessity of being placed on the retired list of the army as it must necessitate his being thrown out of the line of promotion." He was married in 1877, and the following year saw the birth of his first child, but Bates remained unemployed and finally committed suicide two years after his daughter was born.[89]

Paid employment was a necessary precondition for manly independence, and independence had traditionally been an attribute that defined white manhood. Thomas Perrine believed that the loss of an arm reduced him to the level of a slave—removing his control over women by lessening his powers of attraction and rendering his political rights as a white man mute by extending them to African Americans. One section of his manuscript reads:

> Awful day! that took away
> My arm and sweetheart too:—
> An empty sleeve, an empty heart—
> 'Twould make a darkey blue.
>
> These negroes all, Judge Taney said,
> "A White man's rights do lack."
> The rebels left no right to me—
> I might as well be black.[90]

Perrine pointed to the possibility of framing amputation as the loss of sexual and racial privileges. It is thus significant that he was one of very few manuscript writers to represent his injuries in this way, whereas a far larger number of amputees presented their sacrifice as maintaining and enabling those same rights by upholding the Union.

Underscoring their belief that the Union was saved through both bodily sacrifice and military action, many left-handed writers utilized the multiple meaning of "arms"—as individual limbs, weapons, or

---

[89] D. E. Bates, 1:7, William Oland Bourne Papers. See also Dorus E. Bates's pension file, Civil War Pension Files, RG 15.

[90] Thomas Perrine, 1:50, William Oland Bourne Papers.

parts of the military attached to the body of the Union. John Bryson wrote, "Victory has crowned our arms at last!. . . / Those traitor hands were powerless to *destroy* / This glorious Union, which *our fathers gave* / . . . And though thou'st stabbed us to the very core, . . . / Our Union will arise, secure in every part."[91] Similarly, Alfred Whitehouse reminded his audience that "The right arm's gone / the nation yet remains / Tho many perished, / yet we are saved, / The right, will triumph over wrong, / Tho it leave us but one left arm strong."[92] Both by shouldering arms and through the redemptive sacrifice of their right arms, they claimed to have ensured the integrity of the Union. Only by doing so, these writers argued, could they protect the rights they enjoyed as members of that Union. Charles Edwin Horne made this connection clear when he explained, "When we think of the rights and privileges defended and forever preserved for those who make home so happy, can we for a moment regret even the loss of our strong right arm. . . . The strong right arm of the government is yet in its full vigor."[93] Or, as another put it, despite losing a right arm, he maintained his "right to cast a vote."[94] Their rights—as family members and political participants—had been assured, in other words, by taking up arms and, finally, by sacrificing an arm.

Here, these writers skillfully employed the symbolic resonance that amputation held during the Civil War. During debates over secession, in time-honored political tradition, commentators utilized corporeal metaphors to describe the polity. Suggesting that the nation was a singular body, northerners rendered secession analogous to amputation. New York lawyer George Templeton Strong illustrated this connection when he wrote in his diary that secession "would do fatal mischief to one section or another and great mischief to both. Amputation weakens the body, and the amputated limb decomposes and perishes. Is our vital center North or South," he worried. "Which is Body and which is Member?"[95] Had those in

---

[91] John Bryson, 2:23, ibid.

[92] Alfred Whitehouse, 2:73, ibid.

[93] Charles Edwin Horne, 1:179, ibid.

[94] Julius Wood, 1:115, ibid. On the importance of political participation in defining white male identity during this era, see Paula Baker, "The Domestication of Politics: Women and American Political Society, 1780–1920," *American Historical Review* 89 (June 1994): 630.

[95] Allan Nevins and Milton Halsey Thomas, eds., *The Diary of George Templeton Strong* (Seattle: University of Washington Press, 1988), 158.

Bourne's competition employed a logic parallel to that used by Strong, they should have figured amputation as a "fatal mischief" to the individual. Instead, the force of their analogy lay in the inversion of this logic—where national dismemberment was not equivalent to individual amputation, but precluded by it.

William Bourne took the lead from his entrants, likewise suggesting that individual dismemberment could be equated with national unity and with the protection of white manhood. When visitors in New York and Washington came to view the work of the Left Armed Corps, they entered a hall where the manuscripts were displayed on long tables running the length of the room. Looking to one side, they read large banners proclaiming "The Arm and Body you may Sever, But Our Glorious Union Never," and "We lost Our Right Hand for Our Rights, And 'tis the Left Hand now that Writes," whereas those on the opposite wall declared "Our Disabled Soldiers Have Kept the Union from Being Disabled," and "See the Conquering Heroes Come. The Left Hand. The Empty Sleeve. All Americans Together Not a Fetter in the Clime."[96] Here, the Union had been saved not only by those who accepted personal disability to stave off national dismemberment, but also by the extension of freedom to African Americans. Even those white soldiers who refused to accept equality with blacks would have easily grasped his point. The free soil movement that arose among white men in the antebellum North was centered on fears that the extension of slavery into free territories would eventually debase white manhood, undermining individualism and devaluing labor.[97] By maintaining the Union, they argued, "The Empty Sleeve" protected a nation of free men.

Although northerners saw the Union as an inseparable body, they just as frequently described this body politic through familial metaphors that linked the strength of the nation to that of the family.[98] Conflating personal, national, and familial identity, many amputees discussed their right arms as family members, sacrificed to maintain

---

[96] *The Soldier's Friend*, March 1866, p. 1.

[97] Eric Foner, *Free Soil, Free Labor, Free Men: The Ideology of the Republican Party Before the Civil War* (New York: Oxford University Press, 1970).

[98] This connection had military implications that are discussed by Megan J. McClintock, "Civil War Pensions and the Reconstruction of Union Families," *Journal of American History* 83 (September 1996): 460, who argues that the provision of more generous pensions for bereaved families and injured soldiers played a crucial role in encouraging voluntary enlistment in the North.

the integrity of home and nation. Dozens of writers, for example, portrayed their missing limbs as a lost family member or a departed and sadly mourned "best friend."[99] Ira Borshears began his manuscript by describing the "innocent childhood" of his right arm, his "companion and helper." As his limb "grew apace with the days and years," it became an "apt scholar and learned the use of many things." Now, having "served its owner and his country well," his limb "sleeps in death," its "virtues and untimely loss" now "recorded, by the inheritor of its labors, the lone Left Hand."[100] Likewise, Henry Palmer attributed a consciousness to his amputated limb, describing its loss in terms of individual death, his right arm bequeathing "unto the left arm, all the properties of which it died, seized and possessed. The seal of this last Will and Testament was the bloodseal of amputation—Patriotism, Love of Country, and Equal Rights were the subscribing witnesses to the instrument—The body from which the arm was severed, was the Executor—In Heaven's Court the Will was proved, allowed and recorded."[101]

Personifying their limbs and rendering their loss in terms of a death scene allowed these writers to grieve without relating grief to a permanent condition, inherent in the nature of their injuries, for the mourning and melancholy associated with funerals were liminal states. In their portrayal of grief, writers often explicitly made this transition from initial sadness or revulsion to reconciliation and acceptance of their loss. Phinicas Whitehouse was one of several men who signaled this transition in an ode to his lost arm:

> I look at this, the feeble thing before me—
> The piteous wreck of what was once an arm—
> And can you wonder, if a cloud comes o'er me?
> If smiles are vain, and kind words cease to charm.
>
> The cloud *does* come at times, but does not tarry;
> It passes over, and again 'tis fair;

---

[99] All of these poems to lost limbs drew heavily on sentimental imagery. For example, the first stanza of Allen Hayward's poem titled "Amputated" reads: "It was the hand that long ago my mother held/ And mated with its fellow with the evening prayer. . . . Tis the hand/ that held sweet, dying Minnie's till her arm was cold/ And linked to Death and then was not ashamed/ To dash away a brothers tears." Allen Hayward, 1:74, William Oland Bourne Papers.

[100] Ira Borshears, 1:64, ibid.

[101] Henry Palmer, 1:73, ibid.

Ungrateful I, to murmur, or to carry
A heavy burden, which I need not bear.

What matters it, one arm its task has ended?
'Tis well, it may be, why should I repine?
For Life's stern conflicts I am still defended,
While, true and faithful, one stout arm is mine.

With that, and Heaven to aid me, let me labor
With cheerful heart, whate'er my lot may be;
And though may rust the rifle and the sabre,
May that lone arm a final "victory" see![102]

Such representations of injury not only marked the writer as one who had accepted loss, but also called for a particular form of sympathetic identification. Portraying themselves as a grieving friend or relative asked readers to draw upon their own experiences of bereavement and comprehend the loss of a limb in terms of empathy rather than condescension.

That many amputees conceptualized loss in terms of a sentimental death scene is testimony to the power that providential notions of suffering continued to hold for many who lived through the Civil War. There is, in fact, little evidence among these manuscripts to support claims made by historians that disillusionment resulted from such massive suffering, or that sentimentality was diminished by the brutal nature of the war. Although the value of sacrifice for manuscript writers had been clearly established through military victory, many invested their continual sufferings with the spiritual power to transform society. As several scholars have noted, the most pervasive and compelling narrative trope used by sentimental writers in the Victorian period was that of religious conversion, where the mute sufferings of an innocent victim worked to redeem the world, confirming the acquisition of grace through their calm resignation, and eliciting tender feelings of sympathy in the unregenerate.[103] Historians have linked the rise of sentimentality to the development of a middle class in the eighteenth century, suggesting that the bourgeoisie sought to differentiate their own high-minded and "civilized" virtue from what they understood to be the coarse manners of the less

---

[102] Phinicas P. Whitehouse, 2:8, ibid.

[103] Lewis O. Saum, "Death in the Popular Mind of Pre–Civil War America," *American Quarterly* 26 (December 1974): 477–95.

privileged and the barbarity of other races.[104] Over time, the sentimental novel came to be associated with middle-class women writers
and condemned as trite, trivial, and overly emotional.[105] During and
immediately after the Civil War, however, the appeal to emotions and
celebration of domesticity and evangelical piety that characterized
the sentimental novel were the prerogative of neither women nor
those in the middle class. Indeed, the majority of left-handed manuscript writers presented themselves through what could be termed
"sentimental manhood," exemplifying the traits of both pathetic victim and brave soldier. Specifying his pitiable condition alongside his
manly achievements, Charles Horne wrote, "Home, doubly dear
since so nearly lost, to thee I inscribe these few unlettered lines—so
feebly written by a trembling left hand . . . may no murmuring breath
escape the lips of him, who even with the fearful loss of his right arm,
helped to achieve such glorious results."[106] Resigning himself to his
loss, Horne laid claim to the redemptive power of suffering.

Presenting manhood in terms of mute anguish and the heroic mastery of obstacles, these manuscripts drew from sentimental literature's validation of suffering and from the Romantics' attempts to
portray the lives of the humble and lowly as sublime.[107] "Real greatness has nothing to do with a mans sphere," George Dale stated. The
man who "bears the most heavy burden chearfully . . . whose reliance
on truth, on virtue, on god is most unfaltering" was truly great, he
claimed, and these men were invariably "buried in obscurity."[108] Like
Dale, most writers made no direct mention of their personal burdens,
only implicitly suggesting that their injuries gave them access to the
most potent form of earthly power by rendering their lives closer to
that of the suffering Christ. "Sacrifice is necessary to happiness,"
wrote Henry Chaffee, and only those who could "throw aside . . .
love of wordly things" were able to "possess the *heavenly*."[109] Trans-

---

[104] See, for example, G. J. Barker-Benfield, *The Culture of Sensibility: Sex and Society in Eighteenth-Century Britain* (Chicago: University of Chicago Press, 1992).

[105] Jane Tompkins, "Sentimental Power: *Uncle Tom's Cabin* and the Politics of Literary History," in *The New Historicism Reader*, ed. by H. Aram Veeser (New York: Routledge, 1994): 206–28.

[106] Charles Edwin Horne, 1:179, William Oland Burne Papers.

[107] Meyer Howard Abrams, *Natural Supernaturalism: Tradition and Revolution in Romantic Literature* (New York: W. W. Norton & Co., 1973), 391–92.

[108] George Dale, 2:30, William Oland Bourne Papers.

[109] Henry Chaffee, 1:156, ibid.

forming suffering into an opportunity to exemplify Christian fortitude, they represented the acceptance of injury as a mark of true
"greatness." More often than not, this acceptance was demonstrated
tacitly, and the disposition to view injury in providential terms left
little room for bitterness or irony. After serving throughout the entire
war, Alfred Tuttle had his arm shot off outside Appomattox Court
House, one day before Lee's surrender. If the irony of this situation
struck Tuttle, it did not find its way into his text. Instead, he merely
noted, "I have great reason to be thankful that I did not meet the
fate of thousands of my comrads, whose bones lay bleching on southern Battle Fields."[110] Given the carnage they witnessed, it is not surprising that many amputees perceived their glass half full, and
thanked a merciful God. Constituting themselves as true believers,
many noted that earthly sufferings were transitory anyway and, as
one writer put it, "this body entire shall rise from the grave."[111]

Suffering also held political implications for many writers, who
voiced the long-held and widespread view that blood and sacrifice
were necessary for national redemption. William Livermore believed
that antebellum Americans had come to view liberty "as a boon not
a bond." But the suffering accompanying war, he claimed, revealed
to citizens that there was "no trust so awful as moral freedom and all
good civil freedom depends upon the use of that."[112] This equation
of liberty and suffering derived from Scottish common sense philosophers, who suggested that the capacity to suffer the consequences of
one's choices was inherent in the nature of freedom. To do away
with suffering, according to this reasoning, would ultimately lessen
freedom by rendering choices meaningless.[113] Liberty could be maintained only if men chose between right and wrong and accepted the
"grand and terrible responsibility of freedom," Livermore argued.

Making similar arguments by drawing on the biblical imagery of
the apocalypse, other amputees viewed the war as a visitation of
God's wrath, followed by the inauguration of a new era. Looking on
the thousands who bore "honorable scars," John Stewart asked,
"Why this amount of suffering?" His answer lay in "God's truth,"
that "Nations (as individuals) that sin must suffer." Portraying the

---

[110] Alfred B. Tuttle, 1:247, ibid.
[111] Quoted in James Holder, 1:36, ibid.
[112] William B. Livermore, 1:59, ibid.
[113] Pernick, A Calculus of Suffering, 62.

antebellum North as a profane nation of "money worshipers," Stewart's narrative examined the transformations wrought by wartime suffering. "[B]enevolence and disinterestedness [were] enshrined in the American character," he wrote, as "Womanhood" was "laid in death from excessive sympathy and labor," and as men rushed to uphold "the principal of self government" and sweep away forever the curse of slavery.[114] Another manuscript writer using less apocalyptic and more sentimental imagery suggested that "the widow and the orphan, the empty chair at the fireside, and the empty sleeve in the old blue uniform . . . with mute eloquence . . . will remind us through such sacrifice as these are the blessings we now enjoy purchased."[115] Given that they had witnessed firsthand the fragility of the Republic, it is unsurprising that they believed such reminders necessary.

Civil War amputees constantly reiterated in their narratives that they were engaged in a mighty endeavor, a "vast upheaval, shaking the foundations of all established things."[116] Arguing that the issues at stake were so important and the parts they played so crucial, they figured the "honorable scar" as the necessary precondition for national salvation and an inspirational reminder of the sacrifices inherent in self-government. Portraying through their penmanship the same control over their recalcitrant bodies they believed they had demonstrated in wartime, manuscript writers sought to exemplify the principles of self-governing manhood that underpinned their political commitments. Believing themselves God's chosen instruments, they looked forward with faith to the eventual reunion of their bodies in "that land, where their are no armless soldiers."[117]

---

[114] John Stewart, 1:93, William Oland Bourne Papers.
[115] John A. Ludford, Jr., 1:11, ibid.
[116] Ibid.
[117] Henry Chaffee, 1:156, William Oland Bourne Papers.

12

The Impact of the Civil War on Nineteenth-Century Marriages

Megan J. McClintock

MUCH OF THE recent scholarship on the Civil War explores the social and cultural dimensions of America's bloodiest conflict, particularly the connections between the battlefield and the home front. In
their studies of Civil War soldiers, for example, James McPherson
and Reid Mitchell explore the influence of home, family, and community on the wartime experiences of the men who fought for the
North and the South.[1] Because regiments were locally raised and
trained, men often served alongside neighbors and family members.
Letters and the more immediate communication brought by returning soldiers and visitors to friends and family in camp sustained the
links between community and the military. Newspaper coverage kept
civilians apprised of their native sons in uniform.[2]

This interaction between the home front and the battlefield shaped
how soldiers perceived the war. In their correspondence and diaries,
soldiers described the war as a defense of home and family and the

For their helpful comments and assistance, I wish to thank Peggy Pascoe and Julie
Shapiro. An earlier version of this essay was presented at the 1998 Annual Meeting
of the American Society for Legal History.

[1] James M. McPherson, *For Cause & Comrades: Why Men Fought in the Civil
War* (New York: Oxford University Press, 1997); and Reid Mitchell, *Civil War Soldiers* (New York: Viking Penguin, 1988).

[2] Michael H. Frisch, *Town Into City: Springfield, Massachusetts, and the Meaning
of Community, 1840–1880* (Cambridge, Mass.: Harvard University Press, 1972),
56–61; Emily J. Harris, "Sons and Soldiers: Deerfield, Massachusetts and the Civil
War," *Civil War History* 30 (June 1984): 160; Thomas R. Kemp, "Community and
War: The Civil War Experience of Two New Hampshire Towns," in *Toward a Social
History of the American Civil War: Exploratory Essays*, ed. by Maris A. Vinovskis
(Cambridge, Eng.: Cambridge University Press, 1990), 40–43; and Reid Mitchell,
The Vacant Chair: The Northern Soldier Leaves Home (New York: Oxford University
Press, 1993), 24–30.

preservation of domestic unity as the larger meaning of the conflict. To be sure, the men who went to war in the 1860s were motivated by duty, honor, and patriotism, but ties to community pulled men into the conflict and love of family helped many of them endure military service.[3]

Conversely, ties to home could undercut a soldier's commitment to the war. News that family members were struggling to make ends meet or wanting for basic necessities distressed soldiers and diminished their morale. Many men in uniform longed to be home, and desertions on both sides increased as the war dragged on and home front conditions deteriorated.[4]

The evidence suggests that married men experienced the conflict between familial and patriotic duties more acutely than single men. Letters between Union soldiers and their wives reveal the strains of separation and deprivation. Wives of soldiers suffered from depression and loneliness while awaiting news of their husbands, and men found military duty intolerable when it prevented them from caring for their wives and children. Even receiving a long-anticipated note did not always alleviate anxiety: disagreement and misunderstandings were inevitable when men were absent from home for a prolonged period and letters were the sole method of communication. Straitened circumstances aggravated already frayed marital relationships. Women wrote their husbands asking for help and even demanded they return home, but soldiers were often unable to aid their families without deserting.[5]

But the impact of the Civil War on marriage reached far beyond the poignant wartime experiences of soldiers and their wives to influence definitions of marriage in the nineteenth century. Recognizing the hardships suffered by bereaved families, in July 1862, Congress established a pension program for dependents of deceased Union soldiers. As increasing numbers of men died of war-related

---

[3] McPherson, *For Cause & Comrades*; and Mitchell, *Civil War Soldiers*.

[4] Ibid.

[5] Eugene H. Berwanger, ed., " 'absent So long from those I love': The Civil War Letters of Joshua Jones," *Indiana Magazine of History* 88 (September 1992): 205–39; Albert Castel, "Dearest Ben: Letters from a Civil War Soldier's Wife," *Michigan History* 71 (May/June 1987): 18–23; McPherson, *For Cause & Comrade*, 95, 111, 134, 138; Mitchell, *Civil War Soldiers*, 71; Mitchell, *The Vacant Chair*, 19–20, 29–30; and Bell Irvin Wiley, *The Life of Billy Yank: The Common Soldier of the Union* (Indianapolis: Bobbs-Merrill Co., 1951), 289–91.

injuries and illnesses in the postwar decades, their widows applied for pensions. The adjudication of their claims made marriage an issue of public policy, not just private experience.

For example, on November 18, 1887, Assistant Secretary of the Interior Hawkins issued a decision in a contested Civil War pension case that had reached his office on appeal. The widow in question, Mary Stacey, had filed for a pension in 1886, alleging that she had been married to James Stacey, a captain in the Union army. A few days before Mary filed her application, Delila Stacey, who also claimed to be the soldier's widow, had submitted a similar application. According to Delila, she and James had married following his divorce from Mary. Mary's story disputed Delila's account, asserting that no divorce had taken place. Agents at the Bureau of Pensions investigated the case and determined that James Stacey had followed the proper divorce proceedings and that Delila was his legal widow. Hawkins upheld the bureau's decision and rejected Mary's claim.[6]

Stacey's case is just of one tens of thousands of pension claims filed by widows in the post–Civil War decades. In their applications, women frequently included heartbreaking stories of the hardship they experienced after the loss of their husbands. Many of these tales of wartime loss were complicated by inadequate evidence of legal

---

[6] U. S. Government Printing Office, *Decisions of the Department of the Interior, in Cases Relating to Pension Claims* (Washington, D. C.: Government Printing Office, 1887), 1: 435–37. The Bureau of Pensions was created by executive order in the early 1830s. It was first an office under the secretary of war. Congress created the position of a commissioner of pensions in 1833. When Congress created the Department of the Interior in 1849, the Bureau of Pensions became part of that department and the secretary of the interior was given supervisory and appellate power over the commissioner. The primary functions of the Bureau of Pensions were examination and adjudication of claims and the payments of benefits. Widows' applications were examined by clerks in the Widow Division. Cases requiring further investigation were sent to the Special Examination Division. Special examiners residing in districts throughout the country investigated the facts of the case, primarily by interviewing parties with some knowledge of the claimant. Definitions of marriage were made by commissioners who issued instructions and regulations that guided the decisions of the clerks. Presumably individual clerks were in a position to weigh the evidence and make a judgment about a widow's marital status. Special examiners made recommendations to the commissioner based on their findings, and the commissioner ultimately made the decision about the validity of a claim. Secretaries and assistant secretaries of the interior made policy when they ruled on an appeal. Gustavus A. Weber, *The Bureau of Pensions: Its History, Activities and Organization* (Baltimore, Md.: Johns Hopkins University Press, 1923), 27, 28, 40, 43, 46, 47.

marriage to a Union soldier or, to take the example of Mary Stacey, complicated relational histories that ultimately disqualified the applicant from receiving a pension. But even in straightforward and successful claims, the federal government determined what constituted a legal marriage. In deciding who was the legal widow, what guided Bureau of Pensions agents and the assistant secretary? Did they follow state standards, or their own departmental standards? What can Civil War pension applications tell us about the impact of the conflict on marriage in the nineteenth century, particularly the relationship between state and federal powers in defining marriage?

Widows of Union soldiers received benefits under existing pension laws for the first fifteen months of the conflict, but by the summer of 1862 the weaknesses of the system and the discrepancies created by those old laws had become obvious. The act of 1862 granted a monthly pension to the widow of any member of the military who died after March 1861 from a war-related injury or disease. To be eligible for a pension, a widow had to establish two things: that her husband's death was attributable to his military service, and that she had been his wife. Thus, proof of a valid marriage was required in an application for a widow's pension. In determining whether there was a legal marriage, the Bureau of Pensions could have referred to state law. The application of state law, however, would not have been straightforward; neither would it have led to uniform results.

In the 1860s, laws governing the creation of marriage varied significantly from state to state. Although, in hindsight, the beginnings of a general movement away from common-law or informal marriage and toward requirement of formal marriage might be discerned, most jurisdictions still readily recognized informal marriage. A few jurisdictions, however, generally rejected common-law principles and required formal marriage.

The legal regulation of marriage by the states was further complicated because in a number of states the law did not recognize marriages among slaves and Native Americans. So, for example, in some states open and notorious cohabitation was sufficient to establish a lawful marriage if the cohabitants were free, but not if they were slaves. In other states open and notorious cohabitation in the absence of the required formalities did not establish a valid marriage. In still other states, cohabitation was sufficient to create a lawful marriage for all who engaged in it. It is against this background of varying state regulation of marriage that the Bureau of Pensions was required to act.

In preparing their claims, applicants for a Civil War widow's pension could turn to the Bureau of Pensions for guidance. On July 21, 1862, one week after passage of the new law, Commissioner of Pensions Joseph H. Barrett issued instructions and procedures for procuring a pension. According to Barrett, "[t]he legality of the marriage may be ascertained by the certificate of the clergyman who joined them in wedlock, or by the testimony of respectable persons having knowledge of the fact, in default of record evidence."[7] Regulations in effect in later years restated the preference for record evidence, but allowed applicants unable to supply such evidence to substitute eyewitness testimony to the marriage ceremony, baptismal records of the children, or testimony of witnesses to the cohabitation of the parties as husband and wife.[8]

The ready acceptance of alternatives to public and official evidence of nuptials was consistent with widely held beliefs about the nature of marriage. After the Revolution, the majority of antebellum courts accepted informal or common-law marriage. Arguing that marriage was a natural right, judges declared that laws governing the creation of marriage were merely directory, not mandatory. In other words, although the laws might direct people to create a marriage through various formalities, these formalities were not in fact required. In the view of most nineteenth-century judges—and ultimately the United States Supreme Court—unless the legislature expressed an intention to abolish common-law marriage, informal marriage continued to exist and those who conducted themselves in a way that created a common-law marriage were as lawfully married as those who followed the formalities set forth in the statutes. In their opinions, nineteenth-century judges favored legitimizing behavior that reflected popular understandings of what it meant to be married over enforc-

---

[7] Instructions included in Henry Clay Harmon, *A Manual of the Pension Laws of the United States of America* (Washington, D. C.: W. H. and O. H. Morrison, 1862), 96.

[8] U.S. Congress, House of Representatives, *Select Committee on the Payment of Pensions, Bounty, and Back Pay*, House Report 387 (serial 1983), 46th Congress, 3rd session, 1880, 421; *Regulations Relating to Army and Navy Pensions* (Washington, D.C.: Government Printing Office, 1881), 10; and Sen. Daniel Vorhees (Democrat, Ind.), statement, *Congressional Record*, 47th Congress, 1st session, Jan. 16, 1882, 409.

ing the formalities of legal marriage. In keeping with this sentiment, many legislatures eliminated formalities required to create a marriage.[9]

The administration of pension laws conformed to this legal and cultural approach to the definition of marriage. At least in the immediate postwar years, pension administrators were not overly concerned with the formalities of matrimony. The pension files reflect this lax approach to the question of legal marriage. In their applications, many widows testified to the difficulty of obtaining "record" evidence of marriages, particularly those solemnized in the antebellum era. Having accounted for the absence of formal documentation, these widows then established their marriages by cohabitation and reputation.

Although the policies followed by pension administrators were consistent with popular understandings of what it meant to be married, they were not sensitive to the variations in the laws of the states. Not all states were equally solicitous of common-law marriage. Not all states would so easily dispense with proof of formalities, and different formalities might be required by different states. The practices of the pension bureau did not reflect concern for or interest in the specifics of state law. Instead, they tracked popular sentiments regarding marriage, were consistent with the dominant view within the legal community, and resulted, for the most part, in the liberal award of pensions.

These patterns are particularly visible in cases involving former slaves. The enlistment of African American soldiers in 1863 made marriage practices among slaves an issue of federal pension policy. Slave codes did not prohibit slaves from marrying, but slave unions were not recognized by state law.[10] The legal instability of slave marriages was exacerbated by sale of spouses, forced separation, and

---

[9] Helen I. Clarke, *Social Legislation: American Laws Dealing with Family, Child, and Dependent* (New York: D. Appleton-Century Co., 1940), 77–79; Lawrence M. Friedman, *A History of American Law* (New York: Simon and Schuster, 1973), 179–80; Michael Grossberg, *Governing the Hearth: Law and Family in Nineteenth-Century America* (Chapel Hill: University of North Carolina Press, 1985), 69–81; Hendrik Hartog, "Marital Exits and Marital Expectations in Nineteenth-Century America," *Georgetown Law Journal* 80 (1991): 95–129; Otto E. Koegel, *Common Law Marriage and Its Development in the United States* (Washington, D. C.: John Byrne & Co., 1922), 105; and Stuart J. Stein, "Common-Law Marriage: Its History and Certain Contemporary Problems," *Journal of Family Law* 9 (1969): 278.

[10] Grossberg, *Governing the Hearth*, 129–32; and Herbert Gutman, *The Black Family in Slavery and Freedom, 1750–1925* (New York: Pantheon, 1976), 270, 295.

death. Slave marriages and family life varied tremendously, depending upon region, size of plantation, and the sexual ratio of the slave population. Slaves practiced long-term monogamy, serial monogamy, and, less frequently, polygamy.[11]

Acknowledging that women who had been in relationships with men who had been slaves before they entered the service were not able to provide evidence of legal marriage, Congress approved a law in July 1864 that created a special standard of proof for former slave unions.[12] Testimony that the applicant and the deceased soldier had cohabited as husband and wife for at least two years prior to his enlistment made an African American widow eligible for a pension. Women who resided in states in which they could legally wed were still required to submit the "usual evidence."[13]

By 1866, difficulties experienced by African American applicants for widows' pensions in meeting the existing evidentiary requirements led Congress to repeal the 1864 law and replace it with new provisions. Senators were most concerned with two groups of widows: those who could not produce evidence of two years' cohabitation prior to their husband's enlistment because they had been separated by sale or by war; and those who resided in states where they could have legally married but had not.[14] In its final version, the 1866 act allowed all African American women to qualify as "widows" for purposes of receiving a pension "without other evidence of marriage than proof, satisfactory to the Commissioner of Pensions, that the parties had habitually recognized each other as man and wife, and lived together as such."[15]

With no required period of cohabitation and no distinction be-

---

[11] Margaret A. Burnham, "An Impossible Marriage: Slave Law and Family Law," *Law and Inequality* 5 (1987): 197–201; Donna L. Franklin, *Ensuring Inequality: The Structural Transformation of the African-American Family* (New York: Oxford University Press, 1997), 12–18; Ann Patton Malone, *Sweet Chariot: Slave Family and Household Structure in Nineteenth-Century Louisiana* (Chapel Hill: University of North Carolina Press, 1992), 4–67; Brenda E. Stevenson, *Life in Black and White: Family and Community in the Slave South* (New York: Oxford University Press, 1996), 159–256; and Brenda Stevenson, "Distress and Discord in Virginia Slave Families, 1830–1860," in *In Joy and in Sorrow: Women, Family and Marriage in the Victorian South, 1830–1900*, ed. by Carol Bleser (New York: Oxford University Press, 1991), 117–18.

[12] See discussion of proposed legislation in *Congressional Globe*, 38th Congress, 1st session, June 24, 1864, 3233.

[13] Act of July 4, 1864, 13 Stat. 389 (1864).

[14] *Congressional Globe*, 39th Congress, 1st session, May 18, 1866, 2667–70.

[15] Act of June 6, 1866, 14 Stat. 58 (1866).

tween marriages that had occurred in free or in slave states, the 1866 law incorporated into pension policy differences between African American and white American family structure and marital relations. Studies of postwar black families indicate that although many former slaves welcomed the opportunities to legitimize their slave unions afforded by the Freedmen's Bureau and new southern state laws, not all did. Many former slaves continued marital relations without legal formalities, seeing the emphasis placed on marrying with official sanction as another example of white interference with their families. Some former slaves did not turn to the courts to divorce for the same reason. Pension policy was flexible enough to accommodate the importance former slaves continued to place on the substance, rather than the legal formalities, of marital relationships.[16]

In 1873, the evidence required of African American widows was further amended to include "proof that the parties were joined in marriage by some ceremony deemed by them obligatory" as an alternative to evidence of cohabitation. Congress also took steps to limit the application of this alternative standard of proof of marriage: the soldier in question must have enlisted prior to passage of the 1873 law.[17]

Although the actions of Congress may be readily justified and commended, they recognized women as married who, under the laws of the states most concerned with the matter, may not have been so recognized. Southern laws varied in their treatment of slave marriages in the postbellum years. Some states required formal solemnization, some states required registration of slave unions, and some deemed slave marriages legitimate if the parties continued to cohabit as man and wife after emancipation.[18]

---

[16] See Ira Berlin and Leslie S. Rowland, eds., *Families and Freedom: A Documentary History of African-American Kinship in the Civil War Era* (New York: The New Press, 1997); Catherine Clinton, "Reconstructing Freedwomen," in *Divided Houses: Gender and the Civil War*, ed. by Catherine Clinton and Nina Silber (New York: Oxford University Press, 1992), 306–19; Laura F. Edwards, " 'The Marriage Covenant is at the Foundation of all Our Rights': The Politics of Slave Marriages in North Carolina after Emancipation," *Law and History Review* 14 (spring 1996): 81–124; and Franklin, *Ensuring Inequality*, 28–43.

[17] Act of March 3, 1873, 17 Stat. 570 (1873). This law also included Native American widows in its provisions.

[18] Joel Prentiss Bishop, *New Commentaries on Marriage, Divorce, and Separation* (Chicago: T. H. Flood & Co., 1891), 286–88; Edwards, " 'The Marriage Covenant is at the Foundation of all Our Rights,' " 91–92; and Grossberg, *Governing the Hearth*, 133–36.

Thus the pension laws concerning African Americans are perhaps the clearest instance of independent federal law governing the creation of a marriage. Although it is apparent that the federal law would conflict with some state laws—indeed, it was in part dissatisfaction with the results that might be reached under a traditional state law analysis that motivated the Congress to adopt a special federal standard governing the creation of marriage—members of Congress appear to have enacted this law without concern that they were usurping power traditionally entrusted exclusively to the states.

Although the federal government's involvement in marriage regulation may be understood as part of the vast expansion of federal powers during and immediately after the Civil War, it is in an area that has been overlooked in the literature on state-federal relations in the postwar era. The wartime enlargement of the presidency has received extensive attention; so too have the establishment of an income tax and national banking system.[19] The Reconstruction era witnessed unprecedented federal protection of individual civil rights, and these developments have also been well documented.[20]

As the author of a recent study of national "soldiers' homes" for Union veterans argues, however, the expansion of federal powers in the second half of the nineteenth century was not limited to the political and economic arenas, but encompassed social welfare provision as well.[21] In providing for Civil War widows, the federal government expanded its regulatory powers still further into the "private" realms of family and marriage.

Independent federal regulation of marriage, most markedly for African Americans, continued well after the war ended. Some pension applications fit well within the existing laws, such as free blacks who had married prior to emancipation. For instance, Frances Wells married her husband William in Massachusetts and lived with him sev-

---

[19] See, for example, J. Matthew Gallman, *The North Fights the Civil War: The Home Front* (Chicago: Ivan R. Dee, 1994); Morton Keller, *Affairs of State: Public Life in Late Nineteenth-Century America and Society* (Cambridge, Mass.: Harvard University Press, 1977); and James A. Rawley, *The Politics of Union: Northern Politics during the Civil War* (Hinsdale, Ill.: The Dryden Press, 1974).

[20] The scholarship on Reconstruction is extensive. For a comprehensive, one-volume treatment, see Eric Foner, *Reconstruction: America's Unfinished Revolution, 1863–1877* (New York: Harper & Row, 1988).

[21] Patrick J. Kelly, *Creating a National Home: Building the Veterans' Welfare State, 1860–1900* (Cambridge, Mass.: Harvard University Press, 1997).

eral years before he enlisted with the 54th Massachusetts Infantry.
She relied on witnesses who could attest to her cohabitation with her
husband and their reputation as married to establish her claim in
1872. This evidence, she reminded pension administrators, was in
compliance with the 1866 law.[22]

African American claimants who had formed their relationships
years after the end of slavery raised more troublesome issues regarding the interpretation and application of pension statutes. Were these
post-emancipation relationships to be measured against white norms
of legal marriage or against the standard drawn up for slavery-era
unions? What had been the intent of Congress in 1866 and in 1873?
In two rejected pension cases appealed to the Department of the
Interior, these questions received different answers.

In 1887, Assistant Secretary of the Interior Hawkins considered an
appeal submitted by Fanny Curtis, whose application for the accrued
pension of her husband, Frank, had been rejected by the Bureau of
Pensions. In her original claim, Curtis stated that she and the deceased soldier were first cousins. He was ill and "in need of a wife's
care" when he proposed marriage to her in 1884. Curtis rejected his
offer of "regular" marriage because of their close familial relationship. Instead, Curtis and Frank simply agreed to live together as husband and wife. There followed a marital relationship: the couple
cohabited, held themselves out as married, and shared maintenance
of the household. When Frank's health deteriorated, Curtis nursed
him "as a good wife should."

As did applicants for widows' pensions, widows who claimed accrued invalid pensions had to prove legal marriage. In reaching his
decision in Curtis's appeal, Hawkins reviewed the laws governing African American marriages and concluded that Congress intended
them to apply only to claimants who had been slaves or had lived in
states where they could not legally wed. "It would be preposterous,"
he stated emphatically, to believe that Congress would allow disregard of state marriage laws. Because the parties in this case could
have contracted a legal marriage, and since the laws of the District

[22] Documents, July 15, 1865, January 3, 1868, and February 27, 1872, Frances
Wells's Pension File, Widows' Certificate Series, Civil War and Later Pension Files,
Records of the Veterans Administration, Record Group 15, National Archives, Wash-
ington, D.C. (hereinafter cited as Civil War Pension Files, RG 15). See also Caroline
Jones's pension file in ibid.

of Columbia did not recognize a common-law marriage, Hawkins upheld the Bureau's earlier decision and Fanny Curtis did not receive Frank Curtis's accrued pension.[23]

In 1891, then Assistant Secretary Bussey came to a different conclusion. The case in this instance concerned the rejection of a pension claim on the grounds that the applicant, Maria Myers, had never been the legal wife of the soldier, and thus was not his widow. Although Myers became the wife of Corporal Jerry Myers according to the laws of Nebraska in 1875, Myers was not free to marry. She had been previously married, under slavery, to Wesley Tarwater, with whom she continued to cohabit until 1870. In that year, Tarwater's first wife reappeared after a prolonged separation and persuaded him to leave Myers. Myers and Tarwater did not obtain a divorce.

This complicated series of relationships raised issues unique to slave marriages, the most important of which concerned their binding nature. Bussey argued that slave unions ceased to exist when the parties were permanently separated. According to this line of reasoning, Tarwater's first marriage had been dissolved at the time he married Myers. He was free to marry Myers and their continued cohabitation after emancipation transformed their slave union into a binding and legal marriage. Thus their failure to obtain a legal divorce when Tarwater rejoined his first wife created an impediment to subsequent marriages. Because Myers's marriage to the deceased soldier was invalid, Bussey upheld the rejection of her claim.

Despite his negative report in Myers's appeal, Bussey did assert that since the soldier in question enlisted in the service prior to March 3, 1873, the validity of his marriage to the claimant in 1875 was not affected by "the law of the place where they resided at the time of such marriage." Instead, as long as there was no impediment to their marriage, African American widows could submit evidence of cohabitation or of a ceremony "deemed by them obligatory," as could those claimants who had married under slavery.[24]

---

[23] *Decisions of the Department of the Interior*, 1: 324–27. In 1888, Curtis's case once again came before Assistant Secretary Hawkins. Although this ruling affirmed the 1887 decision that only slave unions were exempt from adherence to local law, Hawkins restored Curtis's pension on the grounds that D.C. law did not explicitly prohibit common-law marriage and therefore her marriage was valid. Ibid., 2: 159–61.

[24] Ibid. (1891), 4: 398–405. Bussey used as guidance section 4705 of the 1874 *Revised Statutes* on pensions that repeated the language of the 1873 law. *Revised Statutes*, 58 Stat. 916 (1874).

Did Bussey's interpretation of the statutes regarding African American marriages amount to a federal definition of marriage, at least for African Americans? In another 1891 decision, Bussey insisted that Congress did not intend to enact a law of marriage for African Americans or to regulate marital rights. Both were properly left up to the states. Congress intended instead "to establish grounds for *title to pension*" for African American widows and to do so lawmakers needed "to be governed by *pre-existing conditions*," which in this case was slavery. Slave marriages, according to Bussey, followed slave custom and were based on the master's consent, mutual consent, or a community-sanctioned ceremony, and were not legal or solemnized according to local law.[25]

This line of reasoning raises a puzzling question: why would African Americans who married years after the end of slavery and who thus had little need to be lifted from "the neglect of the State" to the "care of the Nation" be exempt from following state law in establishing their pensionable status?[26] If, as Bussey asserted in 1889, the statutes addressing African American marriages were designed to deal with the "anamolous domestic relations among" slaves and to "give legal protection and public sanctity" to informal slave unions, on what grounds could those statutes be applicable to post-emancipation marriages?[27] In addition, although Congress could have written a statute that said pensions would go to African American women when certain specific conditions—such as cohabitation—were satisfied, it had not done so. Instead, the standard qualification—widowhood—applied to African Americans as well as white Americans. This left the bureau no way to grant African American women pensions save by determining that they had been married.

Bussey's insistence that pension laws did not amount to federal regulation of marriage but merely defined the conditions that made a widow eligible for a pension confirm that, at least by 1891, there was some conscious concern about federal involvement in the marriage question. This concern is more obviously reflected in the 1882 amendment to federal pension law that specifically required that

---

[25] *Decisions of the Department of the Interior* 4: 362–71.

[26] See Bussey, ibid., 4: 368.

[27] Ibid., 3: 7, 260.

marriage be proven in accordance with local law.[28] Did this statute ratify existing practice in the Bureau of Pensions, as Bussey asserted in an 1890 pension appeal case, or did it signal increased attention to state law and a departure from previous administration of pension laws?[29] An examination of pension files reveals what was actual practice regarding definitions of marriage.

In most cases, widows applying for a pension were able to supply some official documentation of their marriages. The Bureau of Pensions favored record evidence, such as marriage licenses and certificates, and county, court, and church records. When this evidence was unavailable, which it frequently was, applicants explained their inability to supply documentation and submitted instead the testimony of the official who had presided at the wedding or the testimony of witnesses to the marriage ceremony.[30] Widows occasionally sent in a record of the wedding in the family Bible as well.[31]

There were a significant number of widows, however, who had no record of their marriages. These widows included testimony of witnesses to their cohabitation with the soldier and to the reputation of their relationship; and they received pensions.[32]

It is noteworthy that, except in a very few claims submitted by African American women, in no cases that I have seen did a widow testify to a common-law marriage; all described an actual marriage ceremony, even if they could offer no proof. Yet the occurrence of a

---

[28] Act of Aug. 7, 1882, 22 Stat. 345 (1882). African-American marriages mentioned in the 1873 statute were exempt from this statute.

[29] *Decisions of the Department of the Interior* 4: 135.

[30] For examples of files in which the widow submitted testimony of the minister or other official, see the pension files of Eliza Smith, Margaret Grumling, Elizabeth Wrigh, Susan Thompson, Jerusha Bradley, Helen Robbins, Sarah Hostetler, Mary Sharp, Isabel Haney, and Margaret Ann Murray, Widows' Certificate Series, Civil War Pension Files, RG 15. For testimony of witnesses to the wedding ceremony, see the pension files of Elizabeth Dodd, Rebecca Sarver, Jerusha Cady, Mary Fitzpatrick, Anne Moody, Mary Jane Trumbill, Martha Ege, Janet Robinson, Anne Laub, Laura Cromwell, Gatsey Donald, Rutecle McBee, Margaret Britt, and Martha Kern in Widows' Certificate Series, Civil War Pension Files, RG 15.

[31] See pension file of Martha Mays, Widows' Certificate Series, Civil War Pension Files, RG 15.

[32] For examples of evidence of cohabitation, see the pension files of Rachel Day, Christiana Kastler, Lucy McFadden, Elvina Clemons, Mary Delane, Caroline Derrick, and Isabella Cherry, Widows' Certificate Series, Civil War Pension Files, RG 15.

marital ceremony would not satisfy the laws of all states. State laws
reflected varying concerns about those officiating at ceremonies and
the manner in which they were conducted. Thus, the presence of
testimony that a ceremony had taken place would not necessarily
show compliance with state law.[33]

In the applications submitted in the first decade after the war,
there are no references by either claimants or government employees
to state law. There may not have been much need to refer to local
law, as most cases were straightforward. Perhaps more importantly,
in the war and immediate postwar years, public sympathy was
strongly in favor of caring for widows and their testimony was not, in
the vast majority of cases, questioned. Whatever the cause, in the
first years after the war, widows' claims were for the most part not
closely examined and applications for pensions were routinely
granted without objection.[34]

By the mid-to-late 1870s, however, mention of state laws begins to
appear in particular cases: those in which there was suspicion that
the widow had either secretly remarried or was cohabiting with a
man as his wife. Because remarriage terminated a widow's pension
or her rights to one, a widow who concealed her remarriage or who
lived with a man without marriage would be able to retain her pension or perhaps qualify for one. Of course, as the years went by,
widows began new relationships, providing the Bureau of Pensions
with more complicated marital histories, but concerns about fraud
and the skyrocketing costs of the program also fueled the increased
scrutiny of widows' private lives.[35]

These cases raised the ambiguity of the marital state in a way that

---

[33] Grossberg, *Governing the Hearth*, 94.

[34] The most common exception to the ease with which claims were allowed were
those filed by former slaves. Complicated marital histories and stereotypes about
sexual promiscuity led to investigations by pension agents.

[35] By the 1870s, members of Congress and pension administrators were preoccu-
pied with the opportunities and incentives for fraud in the Civil War pension system.
These concerns are reflected in numerous congressional documents. See U.S. Con-
gress, House of Representatives, *Annual Report of the Commissioner of Pensions*,
House Exec. Doc. 1 (serial 1449), 41st Congress, 3rd session, 1870; ibid. (serial
1680), 44th Congress, 1st session, 1875; U.S. Congress, Senate, *Report to Accom-
pany Bill S. 637*, Senate Report 24 (serial 1667), 44th Congress, 1st session, 1876;
U. S. Congress, House of Representatives, *Annual Report of the Commissioner of
Pensions*, House Exec. Doc. 1 (serial 1850), 45th Congress, 3rd session, 1878; and
U. S. Congress, House of Representatives, *Annual Report of the Secretary of the
Interior*, House Exec. Doc. 1, (serial 2190), 48th Congress, 1st session, 1883.

earlier applications had not. Did cohabitation as husband and wife without legal formalities constitute marriage? Did pregnancy and childbirth equal marital relations with the father of the children? In the absence of a ceremony and divorce to delineate the beginning and end of a relationship, how was the marital state to be identified? To answer these questions, and to police the pension rolls, pension bureau agents inquired into state laws, which in the late nineteenth century were progressively more rigid as to what constituted legal marriage and were increasingly hostile to common-law unions.[36]

A look at three complicated cases suggests that although pension agents did begin to look to state law in the late 1870s, the outcome was far from consistent. The first case concerns Sarah Bassham, who married as a slave in 1851, in Tennessee. Her first husband enlisted and died during the war. Bassham applied for a pension some years later. In 1875 the Bureau of Pensions conducted an investigation of her claim, in which a special agent interviewed her friends, family, and neighbors. At issue was the nature of her relationship with one Thomas Springer, with whom she had had three children. Were they actually married? If they were, Bassham was not eligible for a pension. According to both Bassham and Springer, they were not. They had never formalized their relationship and, although they lived in adjoining rooms, they had never spent a night together and did not hold themselves out as married. Other testimony taken by the investigator confirmed Bassham's and Springer's accounts. In a letter to the commissioner of pensions, special agent John Wager concluded that because "pension law grants pension[s] to those who have lived similarly" to Bassham, she was not entitled to a pension. In other words, Wager argued that because African American widows whose marital relations with a Civil War soldier were as ambiguous as Bassham's had received pensions, it was only logical to conclude that Bassham's arrangement with Springer was a marriage. Moreover, Wager continued, the laws of Tennessee legalized "such modes of living as mar-

---

[36] Although the Supreme Court validated common-law marriages in 1877, in *Meister v. Moore*, and most judges continued to endorse it, state legislatures bowed to public pressures to increase marital regulation. As a result, by the late nineteenth century, almost every state had passed laws requiring formal marriage. Grossberg, *Governing the Hearth*, 88–92; William Leach, *True Love and Perfect Union: The Feminist Reform of Sex and Society* (New York: Basic Books, 1980), 152; and Stuart J. Stein, "Common-Law Marriage," 280.

riages."[37] But despite this seemingly strong case against Bassham, and Wager's recommendations, she was awarded a pension in 1877.

In an 1878 case, pension agents again consulted state law to determine the marital status of Emily Carrick. Carrick had been receiving a pension for several years when her benefits were terminated in 1878 on suspicion that she had remarried, a charge that she denied. The agent in charge of the case submitted extensive testimony, including that of Carrick's brother and son, that Carrick had married Thomas Fike in Buffalo, New York, two years earlier. The special agent consulted the laws of Ohio, where Carrick and Fike were then residing, and reported that "cohabitation or the practice of living together as man and wife" did not constitute marriage. Curiously, however, Carrick ultimately lost her pension on grounds of marriage by cohabitation.[38]

Another ambiguous relationship confronted pension officials in 1881, when a pensioner named Elizabeth Sible was dropped from the rolls for alleged remarriage. The investigation that led to the loss of Sible's pension revealed that, according to the examiner's report, Sible had lived as the wife of Charles Haight for a period of two years and the couple had been recognized as married in the community. Although a search had failed to uncover proof of formal marriage, the examiner believed that there was sufficient evidence "to conform to the requirements of the New York State law to establish a legal marriage between them."[39]

What can we make of these cases? In the first, the Bureau of Pensions apparently set aside state law to award a pension; in the second, pension agents ignored state law to terminate a pension; and in the third, state law strengthened the government's case against a pensioner. Did the inconsistency in the pension bureau's use of state law reflect the range of interpretations of marriage statutes? What was meant by cohabitation? Was there ambiguity concerning the proper balance between state and federal authority on marriage? Did the Bureau of Pensions manipulate state law at will to bolster the desired decision? Or can the variant interpretations of the law be explained

---

[37] Testimony, Nov. 4, 5, 1875, and letter, Nov. 12, 1875, Sarah Bassham Pension File, Widows' Certificate Series, Civil War Pension Files, RG 15.

[38] Report, October 16, 1878; and report, October 26, 1878, Emily Carrick Pension File, ibid.

[39] Report, January 22, 1881, Elizabeth Sible Pension File, ibid.

by the different men who reviewed these complicated cases and the different contexts in which they worked? What these cases show is that there was no uniform policy concerning adherence to state law in pension claims.

In 1882, Congress provided the Bureau of Pensions with a clear directive: in pension cases, marriage would be proven according to local law.[40] This statute reflected a new attention and deference to state law that was missing previously in the adjudication of pension claims.

Why was this law passed in 1882? Why not earlier? And why was it necessary at all? One factor was so that as widows formed new relationships, state law provided pension agents with guidance as they struggled to determine a widow's marital status. In cases in which local law did not give pension agents the ability to drop a widow from the rolls for contracting a common-law marriage, a clause of the 1882 law authorized pension agents to terminate a widow's pension for "open and notorious adulterous cohabitation."[41] This language reflected the growing concern among policymakers that widows attempted to retain their pension benefits while forming new relationships. In addition to the alleged immoral behavior of widows, the number of applications filed by widows increased dramatically in 1880 and remained relatively high into the 1890s.[42] The greater attention paid by pension officials to state law was perhaps a result of the concern with fraud and rising costs that came with the surge in applications.

A larger context of the 1882 law cannot be overlooked, however: the marriage reform movement that was well underway in the United States by the late 1870s and early 1880s. Scholars have located the origins of this movement in the growing rate of divorce and changing status of women and identified the range of voices that joined the pro-marriage regulation faction: Protestant clergy, educators, feminists such as Elizabeth Cady Stanton, and Republican reformers such

---

[40] Act of August 7, 1882, 22 Stat. 345 (1822).

[41] Ibid.

[42] In 1879, the Bureau of Pensions received 9,767 dependent applications, most of which were widows' claims. In 1880, 25,602 dependent claims reached the pension bureau. See U. S. Congress, *Annual Report of the Commissioner of Pensions*, House Exec. Doc. 1 (serial 1911), 46th Congress, 2nd session, 1879; and ibid., House Exec. Doc. 1 (serial 1960), 46th Congress, 3 session, 1880.

as Theodore Roosevelt. Although the marriage reform movement failed to produce uniform divorce or marriage laws, its impact was felt in state legislatures across the country. In addition to deterring common-law unions, state statutes tightened the regulation of marriage through requiring licensing and registration and restricting access to divorce.[43]

In light of the late nineteenth-century reform activity focused on marriage and divorce, the timing of pension legislation that underscored the supremacy of state laws in determining legal marriage is intriguing. Did the 1882 law add the weight of the federal government to efforts to shore up legal marriage? Did the National Divorce Reform League, which was the most prominent reform organization concerned with the issue, have some influence on pension policy in the 1880s? There is no direct evidence that I have found of any cross fertilization between federal policy and social reform in this instance, but reform has influenced federal social policy at other times, such as during the Progressive Era and Civil Rights Movement. The possibility that the federal government, through pension policy, played a role in deterring common-law marriage in the late nineteenth century merits further examination.

Once the 1882 law went into effect, did pension agents defer to state law in their determinations of marital status? Is there evidence of a change of policy as well as law? Pension files, including those that reached the desk of the assistant secretary of the interior on appeal, indicate that after 1882 local statutes were routinely authoritative in marriage determinations.

Hannah Lightfoot's protracted application is a case in point. Lightfoot lost her pension on the grounds that she was not the legal widow. Lightfoot testified that she married James Lightfoot in Alabama in 1846, with the consent of their owners and they cohabited until her husband's enlistment. Parts of Lightfoot's story were disputed by Laura Callahan, who filed a contesting claim alleging that she married James Lightfoot two or three years prior to the war and it was she, not Lightfoot, who was living with him at the time he enlisted.

---

[43] Grossberg, *Governing the Hearth*, 83–102; Lynne Carol Halem, *Divorce Reform: Changing Legal and Social Perspectives* (New York: The Free Press, 1980), 27–51; Leach, *True Love and Perfect Union*, 150–52; and Roderick Phillips, *Putting Asunder: A History of Divorce in Western Society* (Cambridge, Eng.: Cambridge University Press, 1988), 458–514.

The special investigator reported in 1886 that James abandoned Hannah Lightfoot in 1859 or 1860, and lived with Callahan as his wife until his death. Although the investigator believed that Lightfoot deserved the pension in return for her loyalty and hardship, Alabama law dictated that Callahan was the legal widow because she was living with James at the time slavery ended and continued to do so after the end of the war. The investigator concluded that, according to local law, the decision to suspend Lightfoot's pension was correct.[44]

After 1882, local law held sway in the Department of the Interior as it did in the Bureau of Pensions. In two cases that Assistant Secretary Hawkins considered in 1887, he noted in his reports that, as Congress had directed in the 1882 law, he had followed local law in reaching his decisions.[45]

This pattern continued, as indicated by several opinions issued by Assistant Secretary Bussey in 1890. These cases concerned the claimant's or soldier's marital status at the time of their marriage. If one or both of the parties had been previously married, but no definitive proof of divorce or the death of the former spouse could be obtained, was the claimant's marriage to the soldier valid? Was she, in fact, a widow?

Elizabeth Felber's claim illustrates these complex relationships. Both she and her deceased husband had been previously married. Felber could offer no proof of her first husband's death; moreover, her second husband, the Civil War soldier, had a living wife at the time that he married Felber. Confronted with Felber's murky marital status, the Bureau of Pensions had rejected her claim. Felber appealed. In reaching his decision, Bussey referred to the laws of Ohio, where Felber and the soldier had wed. Because Ohio was a common-law state, Bussey reasoned, once the impediments to Felber's second marriage were removed by the presumed death of her first husband and by the soldier's divorce from his first wife, Felber and the soldier were legally married. Bussey reversed the previous decision and granted Felber her widow's pension.[46]

---

[44] Report, May 24, 1886, Hannah Lightfoot's pension file, Widows' Certificate Series, Civil War Pension Files, RG 15.

[45] *Decisions of the Department of the Interior* 2: 56–57, 173. The first of these two cases, that of Thankful Morse, was a Revolutionary claim.

[46] Ibid., 4: 329–337. For cases that contain similar facts, see ibid., 3: 293–96; and ibid., 4: 67–77, 380–83.

Although the validity of Felber's marriage to a Civil War soldier was in doubt, the fact that she had participated in a formal marriage ceremony with him was not. Remarriages of Civil War widows were frequently informal, however. Convinced that widows were entering into illicit relationships to avoid termination of their benefits, members of Congress attached a clause to the 1882 law that authorized the Bureau of Pensions to terminate a widow's pension for "open and notorious adulterous cohabitation." Decisions by assistant secretaries of the interior gave no clear direction as to the application of this clause. Some decisions stated that the act had retrospective effect and if cohabitation occurred at any time during a woman's widowhood, she lost her right to a pension.[47] In other decisions, assistant secretaries argued that the application of the act was limited to behavior that came after its passage.[48]

If governed by the latter interpretation, pension agents had to turn to local law to determine the marital status of a widow suspected of living with a man without marriage. Patsey Clark's file illustrates the problems posed by irregular marriage. Clark received a pension in 1885, but only for the few months between her husband's death in early 1864 to December 1865, when she allegedly began marital relations with Farrar Ellis. Their relationship continued until 1872. Clark appealed the short duration of her pension benefits. In her testimony, Clark contended that her relationship with Ellis did not constitute a remarriage, but was illicit. Because the relationship ended before passage of the 1882 law, it had no bearing on her right to a pension. Assistant Secretary Bussey countered Clark's claims with reference to the laws of Mississippi, where Clark and Ellis resided. Unfortunately for Clark, Mississippi was a common-law marriage state. Bussey concluded that Clark and Ellis did contract a legal, valid marriage and that Clark was therefore no longer eligible for a pension.[49]

In a January 4, 1863, letter to Dianna McConnaughey informing her of her husband's death in battle, Captain R. B. Lynch wrote, "In one short moment many widows and orphans are made—families made desolate, and life almost made a burden to us." [50] With those

---

[47] Ibid., 1: 61; and ibid., 2: 119.

[48] See, for instance, ibid., 3: 115, 235; and ibid., 4: 289

[49] Ibid., 4: 134–36.

[50] Letter, January 4, 1863, Dianna McConnaughey Pension File, Widows' Certificate Series, Civil War Pension Files, RG 15.

words, Captain Lynch captured the meaning of the war for countless women who lost their husbands. By applying for a pension, however, McConnaughey ensured that her husband's military-related death would be more than a private tragedy. Her claim and those of tens of thousands of other Civil War widows had a lasting impact on public definitions of marriage.

In the administration of the Civil War pension program, agents of the Bureau of Pensions, commissioners of pensions, and interior secretaries determined what constituted a legal marriage. They did so in a period of dramatic redefinition of familial relations and a reconfiguration of the relationship between the family and the state. Pension officials thus operated on shifting ground. They also contributed to the uncertainty and controversy surrounding marriage in the late nineteenth century. For a short period, the Bureau of Pensions defined, for purposes of awarding pension benefits, what was a legal marriage based on federal, not state, standards. The United States Supreme Court weighed in on the marriage question in the 1870s as well, declaring polygamy unconstitutional in *Reynolds v. United States* in 1874.[51] In 1877, the justices ruled that common-law marriage was valid, unless explicitly prohibited by state law.[52]

This encroachment on state power was short-lived—by 1882, Congress issued a clear statement of state supremacy in this area—but not without significance. Civil War and Reconstruction-era pension policy and Supreme Court decisions challenge the general assumption that marriage is a creature of state, not federal, law. If even briefly, the federal government had a voice in determining what constituted a legal marriage. Moreover, as Nancy Cott argues, for the past one thousand years, authorization and regulation of marriage have been major vehicles of state formation.[53] In the American context, the liberal federal definitions of marriage in the 1860s and 1870s can be seen as part of the expansion of federal power required for

---

[51] Grossberg, *Governing the Hearth*, 123–24; and Carol Weisbrod and Pamela Sheingorn, "Reynolds v. United States: Nineteenth-Century Forms of Marriage and the Status of Women," *Connecticut Law Review* 10 (summer 1978): 828–58.

[52] *Meister v. Moore*, 97 U.S. 76 (1877); and see Grossberg, *Governing the Hearth*, 88; and Koegel, *Commom Law Marriage*, 99.

[53] Nancy F. Cott, "Giving Character to Our Whole Civil Polity: Marriage and the Public Order in the Late Nineteenth Century," in *U. S. History as Women's History*, ed. by Linda K. Kerber, Alice Kessler-Harris, and Kathryn Kish Sklar (Chapel Hill: University of North Carolina Press, 1995), 108–9.

war making and Reconstruction. By the early 1880s, however, the
federal government was ceding power back to the states. Through
postbellum era shifts in pension policy, Congress helped to redraw
what constituted a legal marriage and to restore the balance of power
between the states and the federal government that had been disturbed by the Civil War, and in so doing to remake not only the
family but the nation as well.[54]

---

[54] I am grateful to Peggy Pascoe for thoughts and ideas expressed in this para-
graph.

13

A Different Civil War: African American Veterans in New Bedford, Massachusetts

Earl F. Mulderink III

DURING THE CIVIL WAR, northern African Americans clamored to contribute to the Union cause, believing that they might strike blows against slavery and for their own rights as American citizens. This ongoing and often passionate struggle for citizenship was demonstrated repeatedly in New Bedford, Massachusetts, home to one of the North's most significant African American communities. With a population that comprised the largest percentage of black residents of any New England urban area between 1850 and 1880, New Bedford's black community enjoyed an unusual measure of economic opportunities, political freedoms, and high social standing. In 1860, on the eve of the war, New Bedford's black population stood at 1,518 individuals, or 6.5 percent of the city's total population of 22,300. By comparison, among other northern cities at that time, only Philadelphia counted a larger percentage of African American residents; Boston's black residents comprised less than 1.5 percent of the total population.[1] The relatively large size and favorable position of New Bedford's black community was built by African Americans amid a favorable opportunity structure fostered by a lucrative whaling econ-

---

[1] For background information and elaboration, see Earl F. Mulderink III, " 'We Want a Country': African-American and Irish-American Community Life in New Bedford, Massachusetts, During the Civil War Era" (Ph.D. dissertation, University of Wisconsin-Madison, 1995). Population and census figures are on pages 44–46. See also my " 'The Nearest Approach to Freedom and Equality': Racism, Paternalism, and the Labor Market in New Bedford, Massachusetts," in *Racism and the Labour Market: Historical Studies*, ed. by Marcel van der Linden and Jan Lucassen (Amsterdam, The Netherlands: Peter Lang AG, issued by the International Institute of Social History, 1995), 263–86.

omy and the benevolent local leadership of wealthy Quaker merchants.

Before war erupted in 1861, New Bedford was known not only for its whaling-generated wealth, but also for serving as an antislavery bastion. In 1838, for example, a fugitive slave later named Frederick Douglass arrived in town, pulled by encouraging reports that there he could "make a good living." Douglass found in New Bedford "the nearest approach to freedom and equality that [he] had ever seen."[2] Leading white citizens, many of them wealthy Quaker whaling merchants, founded the city's first antislavery society in 1834, and they worked hand-in-hand with local black leaders, such as Nathan Johnson, through the Civil War.[3] Blacks and whites alike attended numerous integrated antislavery meetings, including dedication of the city's "Liberty Hall" in 1838. Writing in 1858, local Quaker leader Daniel Ricketson opined that African Americans were "among our most respectable and worthy citizens," and he claimed that white residents harbored "little prejudice against color and a general desire that the colored population may enjoy equal rights and privileges with themselves." Ricketson pointed to the city's integrated public schools and the heritage of famed black leader Paul Cuffe as evidence of the community's racial egalitarianism.[4] During the Civil War, Ricketson and other Quakers would forego their pacifist principles to support the claims of African American men to enlist as Union soldiers.

New Bedford's African Americans formed vital connections with

---

[2] Frederick Douglass, *Life and Times of Frederick Douglass: His Early Life as a Slave, His Escape from Bondage, and His Complete History, Written by Himself*, with a new introduction by Rayford W. Logan (New York: Collier Books, 1962), 205, 208. Douglass does note, however, that he endured racist treatment from white tradesmen when he attempted to ply his craft of caulker. See ibid., 208–213. For an overview of abolitionism in antebelleum New Bedford, see Kathryn Grover, *The Fugitive Gibraltar: Escaping Slaves and Abolitionism in New Bedford, Massachusetts* (Amherst: University of Massachusetts Press, 2001).

[3] Nathan Johnson, who gave Douglass his new name, was wrongfully accused of slave kidnapping in 1839, leading to a public investigation that underscored New Bedford's fame as a haven of antislavery activism. Johnson was exonerated fully. See Earl F. Mulderink III, " 'The Whole Town is Ringing With It': Slave Kidnapping Charges Against Nathan Johnson of New Bedford, Massachusetts, 1839," *New England Quarterly* 61 (September 1988): 341–57.

[4] Daniel Ricketson, *The History of New Bedford, Bristol County, Massachusetts: Including a History of the Old Township of Dartmouth and the Present Townships of Westport, Dartmouth, and Fairhaven, From Their Settlement to the Present Time* (New Bedford: published by the author, 1858), 23–24, 252–53, 342–45.

other black communities throughout New England. For example, New Bedford hosted the Convention of the Colored Citizens of Massachusetts, which commenced on August 1, 1858. Black delegates from around the state convened in New Bedford's City Hall to cheer speakers who encouraged activism, attacked slavery, and proclaimed equality for all Americans. Boston's Robert Morris brought the audience to its feet with his pledge to aid fugitive slaves. "If any man comes here to New Bedford and they try to take him away," he promised, "you telegraph us in Boston, and we'll come down 300 strong, and stay with you; and we won't go until he's safe."[5] Similarly, in their religious devotions, New Bedford's black Christians merged local needs with regional and even national efforts. Before 1860, African Americans founded no fewer than five all-black churches in New Bedford, several of which hosted regional conferences and furnished nationally known leaders. The Bethel African Methodist Episcopal Church, for example, was founded in 1842, and hosted the First Annual Conference of the New England AME Conference in 1850. The Bethel congregation then welcomed that group's annual conference five more times before the war.[6] Such participation in antebellum political and religious activities demonstrated the many connections between New Bedford's black citizens and other African Americans within the state and region.

When war erupted in April 1861, northern blacks sought to enlist in the Union cause. Just ten days after Fort Sumter fell to the Confederates, African Americans convened at New Bedford's City Hall to discuss their options. They pledged at least 400 men to "fight for liberty, to be ready at any moment . . . wherever our support may be required." They joined the national chorus led by their one-time neighbor, Frederick Douglass, who called for black military service. In *Douglass' Monthly*, the famed agitator noted presciently that the war "will reach a complexion when a few black regiments will be absolutely necessary."[7] Although nearly two years elapsed before the

---

[5] See Philip S. Foner and George E. Walker, eds., *Proceedings of the Black State Conventions, 1840–1865* (Philadelphia: Temple University Press, 1980), 2: 96–107.

[6] For a detailed treatment of African Americans' religious institutions and activities in New Bedford between 1830 and 1865, see Mulderink, " 'We Want A Country,' " chapter 2, especially pages 68–92.

[7] For an extended treatment of the enlistment of black troops in New Bedford and their military experiences, see chapter 4 of my dissertation. Information about the war meeting is located in *New Bedford Standard*, April 24, 1861, quoted in

federal government authorized the enlistment of black soldiers, New Bedford city authorities worked diligently first to enlist African American men and then to insure their proper and full payment. New Bedford's Committee on Military Relief voted on March 4, 1863, that up to $50 could be granted to "the individuals and families of such of our colored citizens as shall be mustered into the service of the United States." Just five days later, the committee voted a $25 payment "to each colored citizen, resident of New Bedford, who has enlisted, or may enlist, in the 54th Reg. Mass. Vols. and be mustered into the service of the United States." These disbursements recognized the potential hardships and hazards of military service for black men and for their families remaining on the home front, and illustrated New Bedford's strong public support for African American military service.[8]

Black soldiers and veterans from New Bedford proudly described their wartime service and hailed their treatment by white citizens and officials. In describing the recruitment of black men for the 54th Massachusetts Colored Infantry, William Carney recounted that "citizens of New Bedford, both white and colored, were glad of the opportunity, and went earnestly to work in order to aid the governor."[9] During the war, readers of the *New Bedford Mercury* could follow the fortunes of the 54th Massachusetts through the correspondence of a local enlistee, Corporal James Henry Gooding. Gooding's published accounts stand as perhaps the finest extant collection of letters written by a black enlistee in the Union Army, and he undoubtedly claimed a loyal and supportive audience of readers home in New Bedford.[10] Gooding signed up for service with other New Bedford

---

James Henry Gooding, *On the Altar of Freedom, A Black Soldier's Civil War Letters from the Front*, ed. by Virginia Matzke Adams (Amherst: University of Massachusetts Press, 1991), xix; see also *Douglass' Monthly* (May 1861).

[8] Records of the Soldiers' Fund Committee, 1861–1863, Special Collections, New Bedford Free Public Library (NBFPL).

[9] For Carney's account, see Leonard B. Ellis, *History of New Bedford and Its Vicinity, 1620–1892* (Syracuse, N.Y.: D. Mason & Company, 1892), 346–47.

[10] Gooding, *On the Altar of Freedom*. For a compilation of comparable letters, see Edwin S. Redkey, ed., *A Grand Army of Black Men, Letters from African-American Soldiers in the Union Army, 1861–1865* (Cambridge, Eng.: Cambridge University Press, 1992). Also see the excellent collection of letters by black correspondent George E. Stephens, edited by Donald Yacovone, *A Voice of Thunder, A Black Soldier's Civil War* (Urbana: University of Illinois Press, 1997). For recent works on the 54th Massachusetts, see Martin H. Blatt, Thomas J. Brown, and Donald Yacovone,

men in the 54th's Company C, a unit subsequently described by Luis Emilio, the regiment's historian and former officer, as "the representative Massachusetts' company." Although this unit suffered heavy wartime losses, New Bedford's black survivors included men such as William Carney, later awarded the Congressional Medal of Honor for valor at the assault on Fort Wagner in July 1863.

Through the duration of the nineteenth century, African American veterans of New Bedford, including Carney, led the black community in demonstrations of civic pride and appeals to civil religion. Together they created a collective history and memory that commemorated the wartime sacrifices of black soldiers. Like the former city resident Frederick Douglass, New Bedford's lesser-known African Americans used their military participation to push for full equality afterwards. This ongoing quest was played out through various institutions and events, including those sponsored by the impoverished local all-black post of the Grand Army of the Republic. Such segregation permitted the black community to uphold its own patriotic discourse, events, and organizations. Yet these all-black functions demonstrated that the Civil War had not transformed northern society and race relations as African Americans had hoped. In short, for African Americans, the Civil War rendered an ambiguous victory, and the war's meaning and memory would be contested for generations to come.[11]

In their immediate postwar celebrations, white and black citizens

---

eds., *Hope and Glory: Essays on the Legacy of the Fifty-Fourth Massachusetts Regiment* (Amherst: University of Massachusetts Press, in association with the Massachusetts Historical Society, 2001); and Russell Duncan, *Where Death and Glory Meet: Colonel Robert Gould Shaw and the 54th Massachusetts Infantry* (Athens: University of Georgia Press, 1999).

[11] David Blight has offered the most thorough assessment of contested Civil War memories in *Race and Reunion: The Civil War in American Memory* (Cambridge, Mass: Harvard University Press, 2001). In recent years, Americans have acknowledged the role played by African Americans in the Civil War, illustrated by the rededication of the Shaw Monument in Boston, Massachusetts, on May 31, 1997. This centennial celebration included scholarly commentary, historical reenactment, and public commemorations. Historian George M. Fredrickson offered a comparison of the 1897 and 1997 events, suggesting that the latter commemoration focused on black soldiers instead of their white commander. "To me," wrote Fredrickson, "this signified the growth in Civil War historiography, *and to some extent in public memory*, of a realization that blacks were active participants in the process of emancipation rather than passive beneficiaries of white humanitarianism." George M. Fredrickson, "Shaw Monument Rededication Shows Value of OAH and NPS Collaborations," *OAH Newsletter* 25 (August 1997): 9 (italics added).

of New Bedford joined together in demonstrations of civic pride and through depictions of civil religion. At the root of such patriotic rituals lay the myth of egalitarian wartime sacrifices in which all groups— white and black, native- and foreign-born, men and women—played their part in the national drama of the Civil War. Many of these themes centered on the Civil War as an apocalyptic event whose "manifest destiny" was to cleanse and regenerate the nation.[12] Just as African Americans historically have embraced many tenets of American civil religion in their quest for equality, New Bedford's blacks utilized comparable themes to press their claims for full citizenship, sustaining their own versions of civil religion and of their history and memory of the Civil War.[13] To borrow from historian John Bodnar's

[12] For American civil religious themes, see Robert N. Bellah, "Civil Religion," in Robert N. Bellah, *Beyond Belief: Essays on Religion in a Post-Traditional World* (New York: Harper & Row, 1970; reprint ed., Berkeley: University of California Press, 1991), 171–82; Robert N. Bellah, "Civil Religion in the 1970s," in *American Civil Religion*, ed. by Donald G. Jones and Russell E. Richey (New York: Harper & Row, 1974; reprint ed., San Francisco: Mellen Press, 1990); Ernest Tuveson, *Redeemer Nation: The Idea of America's Millennial Role* (Chicago: University of Chicago Press, 1968); James Moorhead, *American Apocalypse: Yankee Protestants and the Civil War, 1860–1869* (New Haven, Conn.: Yale University Press, 1979); and Michael Frisch, "American History and the Structure of Collective Memory," *Journal of American History* 75 (March 1989): 1130–55.

[13] A number of scholars have addressed the unique aspects of African American civil religion, among them David W. Blight, *Frederick Douglass' Civil War: Keeping Faith in Jubilee* (Baton Rouge: Louisiana State University Press, 1989); David W. Blight, " 'For Something Beyond the Battlefield': Frederick Douglass and the Struggle for the Memory of the Civil War," *Journal of American History* 75 (March 1989): 1156–78; David W. Blight, "Frederick Douglass and the American Apocalypse," *Civil War History* 31 (December 1985): 309–28; Wilson Jeremiah Moses, *Black Messiahs and Uncle Toms: Social and Literary Manipulations of a Religious Myth*, rev. ed. (University Park: Pennsylvania State University Press, 1993); David Howard-Pitney, *The Afro-American Jeremiad: Appeals for Justice in America* (Philadelphia: Temple University Press, 1990); Charles V. Long, "Civil Rights—Civil Religion: Visible People and Invisible Religion," in Jones and Richey, eds., *American Civil Religion*, 212–24.

Recent scholarship has focused on memory making among African Americans; see, especially, Genevieve Fabre, ed., *History and Memory in African-American Culture* (New York: Oxford University Press, 1994), which contains essays by David Blight, Genevieve Fabre, Werner Sollors, and others. A very promising recent investigation of antebellum African American communities and the creation of memory is offered by Elizabeth Bethel, *The Roots of African-American Identity: Memory and History in Antebellum Free Communities* (New York: St. Martin's Press, 1997). However, I could find no references to New Bedford or its African American community in Bethel's intriguing account. See also Earl Lewis, "Connecting Memory, Self, and the Power of Place in African American Urban History," *Journal of Urban*

useful conception of memory, African Americans expressed a "vernacular" memory that competed for inclusion within the "official" public memory.[14]

The city's African Americans contributed to larger efforts by Frederick Douglass to use the memory of the war and of African American participation in it to push for full equality.[15] Their social construction of memory was a cultural and political struggle as well, one promoted through at least three overlapping endeavors following the Civil War. First, black Americans underscored their public visibility as veterans and as "militia" members in postbellum parades, a process that can be explored through contemporary newspapers and associational records. Second, black veterans and community members supported an impoverished all-black post of the Grand Army of the Republic, a group whose very segregation and poverty reflected the ambiguous victory of the Civil War. Finally, New Bedford's African Americans created and sustained a heroic icon of the Civil War in a local figure, Sergeant William Carney of the 54th Massachusetts, who became a symbol of black bravery and a rallying point for blacks'

History 21 (March 1995): 347–72; and Kenneth M. Goings and Raymond A. Mohl, eds., *The New African American Urban History* (Thousand Oaks, Calif.: Sage Publications, 1996), which contains relevant articles by Shane White, Elsa Barkley Brown and Gregg D. Kimball, and Earl Lewis.

[14] See especially John Bodnar, *Remaking America: Public Memory, Commemoration, and Patriotism in the Twentieth Century* (Princeton, N. J.: Princeton University Press, 1994). The scholarly literature devoted to "memory" is large and varied. For example, sociologist Barry Schwartz has published a number of works that examine collective memory, often with a sustained focus on Abraham Lincoln; see, for example, Barry Schwartz, "Memory as a Cultural System: Abraham Lincoln in World War II," *American Sociological Review* 61 (October 1996): 908–27. For other discussions of scholarly conceptions of memory, see the recent articles by Susan A. Crane, Alon Confino, and Daniel James in the AHR Forum, "History and Memory," *American Historical Review* 102 (December 1997): 1372–412, along with David Thelen, ed., *Memory in American History* (Bloomington: Indiana University Press, 1991) and the journal *History and Memory*, published since 1989.

[15] According to historian David Blight, Douglass created a "usable past" of enduring myths that would stand as "sacred values, ritualized in memory," utilizing the language and themes of civil religion in preaching for black Americans to join the "high worship" of national inclusion. Douglass sought to "forge memory into action that could somehow save the legacy of the Civil War for blacks," a quest played out by lesser-known African Americans in New Bedford and elsewhere. See Blight, " 'For Something Beyond the Battlefield,' " 1156–78. Also see Blight, "The Meaning or the Fight: Frederick Douglass and the Memory of the Fifty-Fourth Massachusetts," *The Massachusetts Review* 36 (spring 1995): 141–53; and the full-length treatment noted above.

claims for full equality in the postbellum era. African Americans' "memory work" over the course of the late nineteenth century struggled against broader changes in New Bedford and the nation that undercut African American claims for recognition, citizenship, and full equality.[16]

At war's end in 1865, African Americans in New Bedford had every reason to expect favorable and respectful commemoration of their wartime service. They had enjoyed much visibility and support from the white community in the antebellum and Civil War years, and survivors of the 54th Massachusetts and other black units returned home to New Bedford to an enthusiastic public welcome. A typical oration was offered by New Bedford's Mayor John H. Perry in his address before New Bedford's City Council to usher in 1866. Perry offered thanks and congratulations that the Civil War had ended, and he then urged his audience to not forget the dead who had offered their lives "as a sacrifice for their country."[17] Themes of civil religion would surface in other postbellum commemorations that touched upon the Civil War. On the Fourth of July, 1866, Perry officially dedicated the city's Soldiers' and Sailors' Monument, declaring that it had been "consecrated to the memory of our heroic brothers who offered their lives at the altar of our common country."[18]

In the immediate postwar era, integrated public events commemorated black and white veterans through parades and other patriotic rituals, including one of the first efforts to celebrate a "memorial

---

[16] John R. Gillis has written that " 'memory work' is, like any other kind of physical and mental labor, embedded in complex class, gender and power relations that determine what is remembered (or forgotten), by whom, and for what end." See Gillis, "Memory and Identity: The History of a Relationship," in *Commemorations: The Politics of National Identity*, ed. by John R. Gillis (Princeton, N.J.: Princeton University Press, 1994), 3–24; quotation is on p. 3.

[17] Address of John H. Perry, Mayor, Jan. 1, 1866, reel 2, New Bedford City Documents (microfilm) (NBCD), NBFPL.

[18] Fourth of July Address by John H. Perry, Mayor, reprinted with City Documents, January 7, 1867, reel 2, NBCD, NBFPL. By 1910, New Bedford was one of 233 cities or towns in Massachusetts that had built one or more Civil War memorials, according to a survey by Alfred S. Roe, Commander of the Grand Army of the Republic in the Department of Massachusetts. See Alfred S. Roe, *Monuments, Tablets and Other Memorials Erected in Massachusetts to Commemorate the Services of Her Sons in the War of the Rebellion, 1861–1865* (Boston: Wright and Potter Printing Company, 1910), 20–21, 84.

day."[19] Although an official Memorial Day was not mandated by Massachusetts' state law until 1881, New Bedford's citizens began to memorialize the war and its dead as early as May 30, 1866. Significantly, these postbellum rituals were integrated. When citizens and veterans marched publicly to decorate the graves of deceased veterans, participants included sixty-two African American men serving in the "74th Unattached Company," a "militia" led by black veteran Abram Conklin. They claimed public space by marching through the city's principal streets while pausing to hear addresses from the eminent local black attorney, William Henry Johnson, and from white notable James B. Congdon.[20] A local correspondent expressed his hope that New Bedford citizens would not forget "the 74th unattached, so long as a remnant of the 54th regiment shall be found among them."[21] This event reflected the bonds forged between black veterans and the larger community of New Bedford.

Later that summer, the 74th Unattached Company reappeared for the official dedication of the cornerstone for the Soldiers' and Sailors' Monument. A crowd of 5,000 gathered on the City Common to hear songs, prayers, a public reading of the Declaration of Independence, and speeches. Mayor John Perry reminded all present of their mission to maintain the memory of the dead; the Reverend Alonzo Quint

---

[19] Luis F. Emilio, *A Brave Black Regiment: The History of the Fifty-Fourth Regiment of Massachusetts Volunteer Infantry, 1863–1865*, 2nd ed., rev. (Boston: Boston Book Company, 1894; reprint ed., New York: Da Capo Press, 1995), 10, 320–21.

[20] Elsa Barkley Brown and Gregg D. Kimball have offered useful suggestions for merging African American urban history with cultural and social history in "Mapping the Terrain of Black Richmond," *Journal of Urban History* 21 (March 1995): 296–346. Their discussion parallels mine, for they contend that "black militians demanded acceptance in the larger culture through biracial participation in public ceremony." Members of New Bedford's black community faced limited resistance in their initial postwar public assertions of citizenship, and their postwar militias (such as the 74th Unattached or the Schouler Guards) provide "a venue for looking at black rights, citizenship rites, and ritualistic negotiations of manhood and womanhood." See Brown and Kimball, "Mapping the Terrain of Black Richmond," especially pages 304–14; quotations on pages 327 and 305, respectively. For other helpful discussions of parades and public rituals, particularly those that offered "vernacular" memories or "counter-memories," see Susan G. Davis, *Parades and Power: Street Theatre in Nineteenth-Century Philadelphia* (Philadelphia: Temple University Press, 1986); Mary Ryan, "The American Parade: Representations of the Nineteenth-Century Social Order," in *The New Cultural History*, ed. by Lynn Hunt (Berkeley: University of California Press, 1989), 131–53.

[21] *New Bedford Evening Standard*, May 31, 1866.

addressed New Bedford's egalitarian heritage and blacks' military service. Quint explicitly merged civil religion, civil rights, and the Civil War when he declared that "our altar of liberty was the battle-field. . . . [P]eople of New Bedford, you who were the first to pronounce for the freedom of an oppressed race, pledge yourselves and your children forever to maintain liberty."[22] Such powerful expressions of civil religion voiced in a civic ceremony tied together the wartime sacrifices of all veterans, including African Americans, to the larger cause of racial justice and liberty.

Black veterans continued to participate in Memorial Day and Fourth of July celebrations through the 1860s and into the 1870s. Their involvement was duly noted in local newspapers, most notably *The New Bedford Evening Standard*, and by white speakers who memorialized the Civil War. For example, the black militia known as the Schouler Guards stepped out in public commemorations in 1867 and 1868 under the leadership of Wesley Furlong, a veteran of the 54th Massachusetts. On the Fourth of July, 1867, the Schouler Guards presented an independent martial display in which they paraded and performed "military manoeuvres" on Market Street. "The season was one of much festivity and all were highly delighted," wrote one reporter. Black veterans were also feted during Memorial Day celebrations during the nation's centennial of 1876, when sixteen African American veterans in Grand Army of the Republic (GAR) Post 146 marched in the parade under the command of George T. Fisher. Afterwards, the Reverend B. P. Raymond addressed an integrated audience of black and white GAR posts from New Bedford and commemorated the "peculiar sanctity" of a soldier's grave as "holy ground." Another speaker, Robert F. Nichols, past commander of GAR Post 13 in Providence, underscored the significance of the 54th Massachusetts Regiment and the assault on Fort Wagner. A local scribe underscored the impact of Memorial Day events: "The ceremonies of this day had awakened recollections of many memorable events in the minds of members of the Grand Army of the Republic, some of whom were mentioned in well-chosen words by Mr. Nichols."[23]

Yet New Bedford's citizens and city authorities moved toward less

---

[22] Ibid., July 5, 1866.
[23] Ibid., July 5, 1867, May 30, 1876.

solemn celebrations beginning in the late 1860s, with potentially negative repercussions for African Americans' "memory making."[24] For
example, the city allocated $2,500 for Fourth of July festivities in
1869, which included a children's parade and fireworks, leading one
local correspondent to hail a "very pleasant" day that featured "no
long marches or meaningless parade, and as little as possible of hard
work." This trend toward commercialized and less patriotic Fourths
of July became evident in 1871, when the public parade included "a
very amusing display" by the "Bungtown Invincibles." This satirical
group, numbering about 175 men in costumes, lampooned African
Americans through minstrel characters. These included a "darkey on
a horse" and another figure who delivered a talk entitled, "Oh! Ration," in which he insulted public figures in a "black" dialect. In this
same parade, black veterans marched in a division that contained a
satirical group, the Sir John Falstaff Lodge.[25] Judging by the composition of the public parade and limited attention paid to African American veterans in the city's newspaper, New Bedford's black veterans
could no longer claim full and respectful integration into white-dominated activities and commemorations of the war. Indeed, the visible
presence of minstrel figures in the parade posed a direct threat to
blacks' displays of military valor.

To bolster their claims of respectability and citizenship, New Bedford's African American Union veterans could enlist in the Grand
Army of the Republic (GAR). Founded in 1866, the GAR admitted
honorably discharged Union veterans and emerged as the country's
largest fraternal organization in the late nineteenth century. Its members joined comrades in "history making" by telling personal tales of
the war, publishing commemorative stories, printing post histories,

---

[24] In many ways, this turn toward entertainment in New Bedford reflected a later
pattern in Cleveland, as John Bodnar has explained. Immigration and World War I
led to a contested versions of public memory in Cleveland, as patriotic commemorations of the Civil War gave way to the vernacular and distinctive needs of diverse
ethnic groups. See Bodnar, "Public Memory in an American City," in Gillis, ed.,
Commemorations, 74–89. Within New Bedford, similarly, the city was transformed
beginning in the 1870s by an influx of French Canadian immigrants, the increased
public visibility of a large Irish immigrant community, and a significant economic
transition from whaling to textile manufacturing. By 1900, New Bedford had the
nation's third largest proportion of foreign-born residents of any urban area with
more than 100,000 residents, a transition that marginalized the African American
community.

[25] *New Bedford Evening Standard*, July, 5, 1869; July 5, 1871.

and stepping out for public events such as Memorial Day and the Fourth of July.[26] New Bedford was home to the first GAR post organized in Massachusetts. The city hosted the First Encampment of the Department of Massachusetts in 1867, and claimed as a native son the Department's first commander, Major Austin S. Cushman.[27]

Cushman offered a succinct summary of the GAR's purpose in New Bedford and in the nation. Most of the GAR's activities centered on assisting veterans—black and white alike—and in memorializing veterans' participation in the Civil War. Cushman explained several overlapping functions of this important fraternal organization. First, the organization was to preserve "those kind and fraternal feelings which have bound together the soldiers and sailors" during the Civil War. Second, the GAR was to offer material aid to those who needed assistance, and to provide for the "care and education of the orphans of soldiers or sailors, or for the maintenance of the widows of soldiers or sailors." Further, the GAR members would aid disabled veterans, whether hobbled by wounds, disease, old age, or misfortune. In a general sense, Cushman contended, the Grand Army of the Republic would "establish and defend the rights of the soldiers and sailors . . . with a view to secure a proper appreciation and recognition of their services and the acknowledgment of their just claims upon the community." Implicitly, this was a call for a "contractual" claim to pension and other rights. Finally, Cushman emphasized the egalitarian nature of the GAR by noting that its members pledged to maintain "an unswerving allegiance" to the United States and the

---

[26] My discussion of the Grand Army of the Republic (GAR) relies heavily upon Stuart McConnell's excellent history, *Glorious Contentment: The Grand Army of the Republic, 1865–1900* (Chapel Hill: University of North Carolina Press, 1992). An important source for the political context of GAR activities is Mary R. Dearing, *Veterans in Politics: The Story of the G.A.R.* (Baton Rouge: Louisiana State University Press, 1952).

[27] See *Proceedings of the Third National Convention* and *Proceedings of the Fifth National Convention* in *Proceedings of the First to Tenth Meetings 1866–1876 (Inclusive) of the National Encampment, Grand Army of the Republic, with Digest of Decisions, Rules of Order and Index* (Philadelphia: Samuel P. Town, Printer, 1877), 41, 117–18; Address of Department Commander John D. Billings, *Journal of Proceedings of the Nineteenth Annual Encampment, Department of Massachusetts, G.A.R., held at Boston, 1885*, in *Journals of the Encampment Proceedings of the Department of Massachusetts G.A.R. From 1881 to 1887 Inclusive* (Boston: E. B. Stillings & Company, 1902), 249–50 (hereinafter cited as *Encampment Proceedings*); *Early History of the Department of Massachusetts G.A.R. From 1866 to 1880 Inclusive* (Boston: E. B. Stillings, 1895), iii–iv, 5–15.

Constitution and to defend "universal liberty, equal rights, and justice to all men."[28]

Cushman's own post, Number One of New Bedford, served historically and symbolically as the premier GAR post in the Department of Massachusetts. As such, this group played a vital role in structuring war memorialization and myths of postwar life.[29] Significantly, Post Number One was active and racially exclusive, and its whites-only membership reflected national patterns of racial segregation. Although open to all veterans regardless of race or nationality, the GAR permitted de facto discrimination when local posts voted to accept or reject potential members, and in northern areas where the black population was large, black veterans were often able to sustain a separate GAR lodge. In 1887 and again in 1891, national encampments were racked by debates over the racial proscriptions of southern GAR posts, but northern leaders refused to accept a southern-imposed color line. One committee, which included three former national GAR Commanders, reported its opposition to formalized Jim Crow prescriptions. During the Civil War, they noted, black and white soldiers "stood shoulder to shoulder as comrades tried. It is too late to divide now on the color line."[30] Historian Donald Shaffer has argued that white veterans treated black comrades in the GAR as "second-class members," and that whites dominated leadership positions in state and national encampments.[31] Despite the official repudiation of

---

[28] *Early History of the Department of Massachusetts*, 8–9.

[29] Besides planning memorial celebrations, Rodman Post printed promotional pamphlets that included *New Bedford Soldiers' Monument, Ceremonies at the Laying of the Corner Stone of the Soldiers' Monument, July 4, 1866* (1866); *Decoration of the Heroes' Graves by the G.A.R. Post #1, New Bedford, May 30, 1868* (1868); and *The Drummer Boy* (1870). See also Charlene R. Burnett, "Checklist of New Bedford Imprints, 1866–1876" (M.A. thesis, American University, Washington, D.C., 1964). A racially tinged souvenir booklet of "Old War Songs," sold circa 1890, mixed patriotic appeals and commercial endorsements with songs that included references to "darkies." This songbook commingled patriotism, greed, racism, and simplistic sentiments of Civil War memorialization, all underscoring the displacement of African American veterans from Post One activities. See *Old War Songs* (Syracuse, N.Y.,[n.p.] [circa 1890]), located in GAR Records, Special Collections, NBFPL.

[30] McConnell, *Glorious Contentment*, 213–18. Racial policies of the GAR in the South are outlined by Wallace E. Davies, "The Problem of Race Segregation in the Grand Army of the Republic," *Journal of Southern History* 13 (August 1947): 354–72.

[31] Donald R. Shaffer, "An Ambiguous Victory: Black Civil War Veterans from a National Perspective," unpublished paper presented at 1997 Annual Meeting of the American Historical Association, January 2–5, 1997, 14. Shaffer also examines the

racial restrictions, however, segregation was the norm in northern GAR departments, including the GAR posts of New Bedford. In New Bedford prior to 1900, only one black veteran was admitted to Post One's ranks.

Despite such patterns of racially segregated membership among New Bedford's GAR posts, white veterans provided some material assistance to their impoverished black comrades. Although records are sketchy, Post One's relief rolls reflected the interracial bond of postwar veterans and the relative poverty of specific African American veterans or their widows in New Bedford. For example, Ella M. Gooding, the widow of James Gooding who died in a Confederate prison, collected $8 worth of groceries on January 24, 1870. The war hero William Carney claimed food in 1870 and again in 1871. Caroline E. Jackson received aid on several occasions, suggesting problems of serious poverty. On February 7, 1870, Jackson obtained one half ton of coal, $4 for shoes, and $5 for provisions; one year later, she collected $5 for groceries. On April 1, 1875, GAR Post One granted Jackson $5 for food, and again in February 1876 and in January 1877, the post's relief officers supported Caroline Jackson with disbursements for food. Not all applications were accepted, however. Wesley Furlong's plea for aid was "laid on the table" at the Relief Committee meeting of January 24, 1870, and it is not clear if he ever received funding.[32] The postwar penury of black veterans was fortunately met by some assistance by white GAR members.

In line with patterns found in larger northern cities, New Bedford's proud African American veterans created their own GAR post, Number 146, named after Robert Gould Shaw, the martyred white leader of the 54th Massachusetts Regiment. Chartered on December 4, 1871, GAR Post 146 suffered greatly from a lack of members and limited funds, forcing them briefly to surrender their charter in January 1881. At that time, a GAR state official commented that

---

attempts by black veterans and African American historians to keep alive the memory of their wartime sacrifices. He is revising for publication his comprehensive dissertation: "Marching On: African-American Civil War Veterans in Postbellum America, 1865–1951" (Ph.D. dissertation, University of Maryland, College Park, 1996).

[32] Relief Committee Book, vol. 1, GAR Records, Special Collections, NBFPL. The first account book begins on January 10, 1870, and runs through 1899, although there are many chronological gaps in the ledger.

this Post was composed of colored comrades and consequently had a small and limited membership, and against great odds they struggled manfully for an existence, but without avail. It is to be hoped that these comrades will not be lost to the Order and . . . I hope that the mother Post of the Department will take such as are worthy within her membership and thus illustrate the broad foundation stone on which our Order rests.[33]

The "mother Post," Number One of New Bedford, did not admit any black veterans at that time. Instead, African American veterans regrouped under the leadership of Charles Harrison in April 1882 and secured a new charter. By 1883, they claimed eighteen members, barely enough to fill their officers' ranks and perform their rituals.[34]

Through 1900, the Shaw Post's meager relief fund stood as the most glaring indication of black veterans' impoverishment, particularly when compared with the white GAR posts in New Bedford. As reflected in Table 13.1, the high-water mark for Post 146 came in 1891, when it claimed its largest relief fund since 1885—$4.50. Between 1882 and 1900, the Shaw Post disbursed a total of $80 in relief, claiming an average balance of $12.22 in its post fund. Between 1892 and 1900, the post reported no relief funds whatsoever. The plight of this African American GAR post contrasted dramatically with the relative affluence of the leading post, William Logan Rodman Post Number One.[35] Limited funds meant that African American GAR members in New Bedford could not fulfill completely their pledges of fraternity, loyalty, and charity. This small, all-black GAR post sur-

---

[33] At the Sixteenth Annual Department Encampment, held in 1881, the department commander reported that Post 146 of New Bedford (the Shaw Post) surrendered its charter because it lacked the requisite number of members to fulfill basic functions and rituals. *Journal of Proceedings of the Sixteenth Annual Encampment, Department of Massachusetts, G.A.R., Held at Boston, 1882*, in *Encampment Proceedings*, 12, 20.

[34] *Journal of Proceedings of the Seventeenth Annual Encampment, Department of Massachusetts, G.A.R. held at Boston, 1883*, in *Encampment Proceedings*, 99, 101, 112–13, 138.

[35] Another comparison between the all-black Shaw Post and a white one yields similar results. The R. A. Peirce Post 190, founded in New Bedford in 1889, claimed in 1900 a post fund of $2,975.93, and it made charity payments of over $200 per year between 1889 and 1900. Although the new Post 190 claimed property valued at more than $1,200 after its inception, the all-black post never claimed more than $100 in property, and usually reported only $50, as it did between 1895 and 1900. See *Proceedings of the Department of Massachusetts Encampment, Grand Army of the Republic*, 1881 to 1900.

vived through 1902. One local historian, writing in 1918, remembered that the "colored veterans maintained their organization as long as there were enough veterans alive to keep the chapter."[36]

Although military service was confined to men and commemorations of the Civil War featured male veterans and speakers, women often played central roles in public celebrations. Within New Bedford, African American women joined men in promoting postwar commemorations of black men's military service and sacrifices, a contribution that maintained a collective history and memory of the Civil War. Like their male counterparts, however, black women's efforts

TABLE 13.1
POST 1 AND POST 146 MEMBERS AND RELIEF FUNDS, 1881–1900

	Post 1 (White)		Post 146 (Black)	
Year	Members	Relief Fund	Members	Relief Fund
1881	141	$851.98	NA	
1882	155	NA	16	
1883	170	878.99	NA	
1884	214	722.51	NA	
1885	241	800.07	20	$13.15
1886	263	934.00	19	
1887	283	868.75	21	2.55
1888	257	840.00	21	2.90
1889	281	565.76	20	3.90
1890	330	773.10	20	3.60
1891	335	507.82	16	4.50
1892	319	342.24	24	
1893	290	490.53	26	
1894	278	481.91	28	
1895	269	426.87	29	
1896	265	877.02	29	
1897	253	766.44	25	
1898	246	734.10	25	
1899	227	676.58	24	
1900	211	651.12	24	

SOURCE: *Proceedings of the Department of Massachusetts Encampment, Grand Army of the Republic, 1881–1900.*

---

[36] Zephaniah Pease, ed., *History of New Bedford* (New York: The Lewis Historical Publishing Company, 1918), 319–22.

were hampered by similar patterns of postwar poverty. A women's offshoot of the GAR, the Woman's Relief Corps (WRC), was first organized in Massachusetts in 1879, its main work to aid widows and orphans of "suffering comrades." WRC members considered it their "sacred duty" to support Memorial Day celebrations by working closely with GAR members. Within New Bedford, WRC organizations paralleled the racially separated GAR posts. The city's first WRC was founded as an auxiliary to the (white) Rodman Post One in September 1885, and during the next eight years, its members expended over $2,000 in relief and presented their GAR post with gifts of cash, flags, silver, and other items worth $334.34. A second WRC was organized in January 1891 and linked with the recently established R. A. Peirce GAR Post; its members soon donated hundreds of dollars to their GAR fellows.[37] White WRC groups in New Bedford claimed greater success than did their black counterparts.

Black women in New Bedford joined the cause in February 1892, when the Robert Gould Shaw GAR post sponsored a Woman's Relief Corps that initiated thirty-one members and adopted the title of Shaw WRC Corps Number 148. These women tried to "assist as far as possible its Post and their needy comrades," although they lamented that "this Corps has not the facilities for doing the good that many have." Relief payments were paltry compared with those of white WRCs in New Bedford. In May 1893, African American women assisted their male counterparts in "giving an entertainment to raise money to purchase a flag and [they] had the pleasure of seeing the Post carry its beautiful flag on Memorial Day." In 1895, the corps claimed forty members.[38] Like black men within their community, African American women of New Bedford sponsored poorly funded but proudly supported patriotic activities that paralleled those of white groups.

In addition to their public participation in parades and GAR activities, New Bedford's African Americans claimed a full-fledged war hero to highlight and symbolize their community's participation in

---

[37] *History of the Department of Massachusetts Woman's Relief Corps, Auxiliary to the Grand Army of the Republic. From Date of Organization, February 12, 1879, to January 1, 1895. With Appendixes* (Boston: E. B. Stillings & Company, 1895), 37, 205. For fund-raising efforts, see ibid., 235–36. See also *Journal of Proceedings of the Seventeenth Annual Encampment,* in *Encampment Proceedings,* 85–86.

[38] *Massachusetts Woman's Relief Corps,* 271.

the Civil War. Sergeant William H. Carney of the 54th Massachusetts earned fame and the Gilmore Medal during the Civil War for his heroism at Fort Wagner on July 18, 1863. This battle, known as the "Black Bunker Hill" for its symbolic importance, proved to many unbelievers in the North that black soldiers could fight as manfully as white troops.[39] For his defense of the nation's most cherished symbol, the flag, Carney eventually received the country's highest military accolade—the Congressional Medal of Honor—nearly forty years after his act. Carney became an icon to African Americans in New Bedford and other parts of the United States. For example, in January 1898, the *Boston Herald* headlined a story about Carney, calling him the "Bravest Colored Soldier." Describing Carney as a "grizzled hero," the reporter concluded, "The old hero is not as young as when he crawled bleeding into camp, with those immortal words, 'The old flag never touched the ground.' "[40] Although he is largely forgotten today outside of New Bedford, Carney served as an important figure in the perpetuation of African Americans' mythic memories of the Civil War.

After the war, William Carney fulfilled ceremonial roles as both a symbol and object of veneration. In 1870, Carney's black neighbors named him chief marshal of a public commemoration to honor passage of the Fifteenth Amendment, which extended voting rights to black men. Blacks from Boston and southeastern New England journeyed to New Bedford to join the festivities, marching alongside men, women, and children from New Bedford's black churches and

---

[39] The importance of Fort Wagner in overcoming negative stereotypes of black troops is noted by Joseph T. Glatthaar, *Forged in Battle: The Civil War Alliance of Black Soldiers and White Officers* (New York: The Free Press, 1990), 141–42. Luis Emilio also makes this point in his regimental history, based upon his reading of contemporary newspapers and magazines. See Emilio, *A Brave Black Regiment.*

[40] Excerpts and clippings in vol. 4, Addenda, folder 8, Civil War Records of the Fifty-Fourth Regiment, compiled by Luis F. Emilio, Massachusetts Historical Society, Boston (herinafter cited as Fifty-Fourth Records, MHS). The efforts to award Carney the Congressional Medal of Honor nearly forty years after his act appear to have been spearheaded by Christian A. Fleetwood. See "Documents Relating to the Military and Naval Service of Blacks Awarded the Congressional Medal of Honor from the Civil War to the Spanish-American War," Civil War, U.S. Colored Troops, reel 1, National Archives Microfilm Publication M929. Also see the list of "Negro Medal of Honor Men" in ibid., 127, and the melodramatic account of Carney's actions in Irvin H. Lee, *Negro Medal of Honor Men*, 2d ed. (New York: Dodd, Mead, 1967), 24–27.

lodges.[41] The following year, New Bedford's black citizens sponsored a similar event that linked past military service with contemporary concerns for political equality. Featured speaker General William Cogswell connected emancipation, Fort Wagner, and the Fifteenth Amendment, contending that African American soldiers had "defend[ed] a country and a flag which now for the first time had become their country and their flag." Cogswell drew upon William Carney's heroism when he urged his listeners to "see to it, no matter at what cost or sacrifice, that your children are educated and brought up in the faith of a living God; and let the old flag, the emblem of your liberties, never touch the ground."[42] Cogswell's oratory before an appreciative and integrated audience explicitly linked civil religion, the Civil War, and William Carney's bold words and brave deeds.

Carney's wartime exploits were repeatedly used in the aftermath of the Civil War to illustrate the patriotism of African Americans and to support their quest for equal rights. Curiously, Carney became the sole black veteran to be voted into GAR Post One in New Bedford while the all-black Shaw post remained in existence. His case is puzzling. Perhaps Carney's stature as a full-fledged hero allowed white veterans to embrace him as a man who transcended racial boundaries. On a more mundane level, perhaps, Carney may have objected to an abrupt increase in the Shaw Post's membership fee, which jumped from $1.00 to $3.50. Or, possibly, William Carney believed that his admission to the white post was symbolic for all black veterans and that he was striking a blow for equality by crossing the GAR

---

[41] One local correspondent reported that New Bedford's "Schouler Guards made a very good appearance, and are in better drill than ever before." Post-parade events included public addresses in City Hall, an evening oration at Liberty Hall by Dr. E. R. Johnson, and dancing at both City Hall and the Schouler Guards armory. *New Bedford Evening Standard*, April 27, 1870.

[42] Emancipation, according to Cogswell, was "an event greater than the war itself. . . . It was the voice of God . . . and it was the voice of his chosen people, sending back their answer, 'Thy will, O Lord, be done.' It was the beginning of a new era for America." Lincoln had served as the "sainted martyr in the cause of human liberty," whereas Governor Andrew of Massachusetts had been no less "a martyr in the sacred cause." Yet the orator also commended the anonymous men—"those sainted heroes of the battlefield"—who had also joined the "sacred cause." *Address of Gen. William Cogswell, of Salem, at the Grand New England Celebration of the Emancipation Proclamation, The Charge of the Mass. 54th, at Fort Wagner, and the Adoption of the 15th Amendment, Held under the auspices of the colored citizens of New Bedford, July 18, 1871* (Salem, Mass.: Office of the *Salem Gazette*, 1871), located in Special Collections, NBFPL.

color line. According to GAR records, however, no other black veterans left the all-black Shaw Post to join Post One.[43]

Carney's fame stretched beyond New Bedford and into the twentieth century. In August 1887, he acted as chief marshal at a "Grand Reunion of Colored Veterans" at Boston's Tremont Hall. The Grand Reunion, like smaller, more local celebrations, exemplified African Americans' use of civil religious themes to push for full equality with quasi-military rituals and patriotic discourses. Publicity posters featured photographs of and quotes from Carney and Massachusetts' wartime governor, John Andrew. To kick off the event, Carney headed an afternoon parade that contained a special escort for him, along with the officers and enlisted men of the 54th Massachusetts. During the convention, the audience listened to speeches and sang songs such as "We Are Rising as a People," "The Star Spangled Banner," and "Battle Hymn of the Republic." "Rapturously received" at an evening session, William Carney sounded much like Frederick Douglass in his reminders that veterans be "useful citizens" while urging all to "stand firm and see that the results of the war were preserved." Carney eulogized Robert Gould Shaw as a man whom the "colored race will never forget." The evening came to a close with the audience singing "America," followed by "Taps" and "Lights Out," underscoring the use of military symbolism and patriotic appeals by these black veterans.[44]

William Carney's name and fame were used for other purposes, too. For example, the National Christian Congress Association asked for donations to build a "Carney Memorial Hall" in Alexandria, Virginia, to honor "one of the Greatest heroes of the Civil War."[45] Carney attended integrated events in Boston that mixed former officers with rank-and-file veterans, such the annual reunion in 1901 of the Association of Officers of the 54th Regiment. Only two black men were invited to this fete: William Carney and Booker T. Washing-

---

[43] Membership Roll, William L. Rodman Post Number One, 3: 103, in GAR Records, Special Collections, NBFPL.

[44] See *Boston Herald*, August 2, 1887; *Boston Journal*, Aug. 2, 1887; vol. 4, Addenda, folder 8, Fifty-Fourth Records, MHS.

[45] A flyer featured a photograph of Carney clutching his Congressional Medal of Honor with the caption: "Keep the Flag Flying." This building was apparently never built, however. William H. Carney Folder, Black History, Special Collections, NBFPL.

ton.[46] Although known as a modest man, Carney reported that he had met people from as far away as California who were familiar with his famous words. When Carney died in 1908 while working as a messenger in Boston's statehouse, the Massachusetts governor ordered state flags to be lowered briefly, only the second time an African American person had been so honored.[47]

For veterans of the 54th Massachusetts such as Carney, the dedication of the "Shaw Memorial" in Boston on Memorial Day, 1897, was undeniably a proud and patriotic event.[48] One reporter declared it was a "great day for the colored race through the country . . . and the day will remain sacred for all time to the colored race as a day of vindication." He went on to write: "Another Memorial Day has come and gone, but the memory of yesterday will remain peculiarly sacred to all those who witnessed the parade and the unveiling of the Shaw memorial, and to those who heard the intense words of patriotism that were spoken in Music Hall."[49] The "Shaw Memorial" would be the last significant public Civil War monument for a hundred years that featured and feted black soldiers.[50]

---

[46] Vol. 4, Addenda, folders 5 and 6, Fifty-Fourth Records, MHS.

[47] For Carney's own letter to the *New Bedford Sunday Standard* and obituaries, see Carney Folder, Black History, Special Collections, NBFPL.

[48] Kirk Savage offers insightful comments about Civil War memory and memorialization in "The Politics of Memory: Black Emancipation and the Civil War Monument," in Gillis, ed., *Commemorations*, 127–49. Savage points out that black Americans did not create their own Civil War monuments, and he suggests that the Shaw Memorial, "this monument to a local white hero[,] is the closest the country came to erecting a national tribute to the black soldier and the black cause." Savage offers a more complete assessment in *Standing Soldiers, Kneeling Slaves: Race, War, and Monument in Nineteenth-Century America* (Princeton, N.J.: Princeton University Press, 1997). David Blight has explored the Shaw Memorial in several publications, but his *Race and Reunion* provides the best context for understanding the memorial. In particular, Blight argues that dedication of the Shaw Memorial in 1897 provided Americans with a more inclusive memory of the war than that offered by emergent reconciliationist sentiments. See also the essays by Gregory C. Schwarz, Ludwid Lauerhass, and Brigid Sullivan in *The Shaw Memorial: A Celebration of an American Masterpiece* (Conshohocken, Penn.: Pegasus Press, 1997).

[49] *Boston Globe* of June 1, 1897 in vol. 4, Addenda, folder 8, Fifty-Fourth Records, MHS.

[50] See especially Kirk Savage, "The Politics of Memory," 135–37, 139–40. It is noteworthy that the national government has taken a lead role in promoting new memorials to African Americans in the Civil War. For example, the National Park Service helped to organize the rededication of the Shaw Monument in Boston in May 1997, and it has sponsored the African American Civil War Memorial in Washington, D.C. In addition, the National Gallery of Art in Washington, D.C., has now

Dedication of the Shaw Memorial held ambiguous and contested meanings. Black and white citizens from Boston, New Bedford, and New England met on Memorial Day in 1897 to dedicate the handsome sculpture created by Augustus Saint-Gaudens.[51] Newspapers lauded Carney as the "Color Bearer at Fort Wagner," and he explained in an interview that Fort Wagner was not the end to the struggles or heroism of black troops. "[W]hile the government refused to pay us equally," Carney explained, "we continued to fight for the freedom of the enslaved, and for the restoration of our country. We did this, not only at Wagner, but also in the battles on James Island, Honey Hill and Boykins Mill."[52] Carney thus continued to sustain a memory of the Civil War that highlighted African Americans' selfless, principled military service.

The exercises at the Shaw Monument—and the memorial itself—represent a conjunction of history, myth, memory making, and American civil religion.[53] For African Americans, the most memorable oration of the day belonged to Booker T. Washington, then the nation's most prominent black leader. Washington struck a discordant

---

displayed a plaster version of the famed Saint-Gaudens sculpture, a piece that was the sculptor's favorite. The National Park Service is also sponsoring the Civil War Soldiers and Sailors Project, which, beginning with African American veterans, will be a computerized database of individual service records. See Linda M. Rancourt, "Fighting for Freedom: A New Memorial that Honors African Americans Who Fought in the Civil War Is an Important Step toward Broadening Our Understanding of History," *National Parks* 70 (September-October 1996): 24–30; "General Powell Praises Plans for First Memorial Honoring Black Civil War GIs," *Jet* 90 (September 30, 1996): 51–52.

[51] Edward Atkinson, "History of the Shaw Monument," in *Exercises at the Dedication of the Monument to Colonel Robert Gould Shaw and the Fifty-Fourth Regiment of Massachusetts Infantry, May 31, 1897* (Boston: Municipal Printing Office, 1897).

[52] *Boston Globe*, May 30, 1897, in vol. 4, Addenda, folder 8, Fifty-Fourth Records, MHS.

[53] Speaking for the committee of subscribers, Colonel Henry Lee contended that the monument would "commemorate that great event . . . by which the title of colored men as citizen soldiers was fixed beyond recall." Governor Roger Wolcott declared that "on the blood-stained earthworks of Fort Wagner, a race was called into sudden manhood." Boston Mayor Josiah Quincy recalled the regiment's triumphal march through the city's streets in May 1863, declaring that Fort Wagner had proven that the African American soldier "could fight and die for his country, like the white man." William James offered an oration replete with civil religious themes that fit in well with emerging notions of nationalism, manhood, and sectional reconciliation. See *Exercises at the Dedication*, 24–35. David Blight makes an interesting connection between James's speech in 1897 with Robert Lowell's poem, "For the Union Dead," written in 1961. See Blight, "The Meaning or the Fight," 149–50.

note in claiming that the "fruit of Fort Wagner and all that this monument stands for will not be realized" until all black men could have opportunities equal with those of whites. "Until that time comes," Washington intoned, "this monument will stand for effort, not victory complete. What these heroic souls of the 54th Regiment began, we must complete." Washington expressed his wish for interracial cooperation and sectional reconciliation by hoping that under "God's guidance . . . that old flag, that emblem of progress and security which brave Sergeant Carney never permitted to fall upon the ground, will still be borne aloft by Southern soldier and Northern soldier."[54]

The day's events were filled with pageantry and ponderous orations, but the dramatic highlight came during Booker T. Washington's address. He later recalled how, as he spoke, Carney reflexively stood upon the dais, as if still clutching the flag, clad in his military regalia. "In dramatic effect," Washington wrote, "I have never seen nor experienced anything that equaled the impression made on the audience when Sergeant Carney arose. For a good many minutes the audience seemed to entirely lose control of itself, and patriotic feeling was at a high pitch."[55] New Bedford's own living black Civil War hero symbolized the contributions of all blacks in the 54th Massachusetts Regiment and the Union cause, and, in a profound sense, Carney's physical presence brought to life Saint-Gaudens's impressive bronze sculpture.

From 1865 through the early twentieth century, New Bedford's African American veterans strove mightily to sustain the memory of their Civil War sacrifices. They reminded themselves and their fellow citizens of blacks' valor and martyrdom during the Civil War. Although they participated in integrated events, New Bedford's blacks

---

[54] *Exercises at the Dedication*, 57–59. David Blight refers to Washington's speech as a "brief rehash of *Up From Slavery*, combined with artful strokes of Southern sentimentalism and sectional reconciliation." See Blight, "The Meaning or the Fight," 149.

[55] *Exercises at Shaw Memorial*, 57–59. In his autobiography, Booker T. Washington reprints his address and a newspaper account of the moving festivities, then refers to Carney's impact on the audience; see Booker T. Washington, *The Story of My Life and Work: An Autobiography by Booker T. Washington* (Toronto: J. L. Nichols & Company, 1901), 201–12. Interestingly, during the rededication ceremonies of 1997, when a direct descendant of William Carney held up Carney's Congressional Medal of Honor, "the atmosphere was electrifying," according to George M. Fredrickson. Fredrickson, "Shaw Monument," *OAH Newsletter*, 9.

also sponsored unique and segregated activities that perpetuated a proud, patriotic, and African American version of the Civil War. In their GAR encampments, in their public participation during patriotic holiday celebrations, and in their creation of black heroes, African Americans sought inclusion in the social order by pushing their own vernacular memory of the Civil War, one that seemed consistent with the myths and memories of white northern Americans. Sadly, by the turn of the twentieth century, most white Americans chose to ignore—or forget—the service of William Carney and his black comrades in the Union cause.

The unveiling of the Shaw Memorial in Boston in 1897 would endure for nearly a hundred years as the last significant public testament to the bravery and sacrifices of African Americans in the Civil War. Historians such as David Blight have offered perceptive analyses of the racialized memories of the Civil War. For example, Blight contends that the "Great Reunion" of 1913, a commemoration of the fiftieth anniversary of the Battle of Gettysburg, sustained a "deeply laid mythology" of the Civil War that denied the centrality of slavery, race, and competing sectional issues as causes of the war. Black veterans went largely unnoticed at this fete, leading African American newspapers to lambaste the "Peace Jubilee" at a time when racial injustice ruled the nation. W. Calvin Chase, the editor of the *Washington Bee*, declared that the Gettysburg event was "an insane and servile acknowledgment that the most precious results of the war are a prodigious, unmitigated failure." In short, national reconciliation following a tragic civil war was built upon the perpetuation of a racist order that excluded blacks from full equality and denied them a place of honor in the nation's collective memory.[56] Only recently have Americans begun to acknowledge this blind spot in the myth making, memorialization, and historiography of the Civil War.

Despite this century-long national amnesia over the Civil War service of black men, African American families and individuals have passed down through generations stories about the Civil War and

---

[56] David W. Blight, "Quarrel Forgotten or a Revolution Remembered? Reunion and Race in the Memory of the Civil War, 1875–1913," in *Union and Emancipation: Essays on Politics and Race in the Civil War Era* ed. by David W. Blight and Brooks D. Simpson (Kent, Ohio: Kent State University Press, 1997), 151–179. Chase is quoted on p. 176. See Blight's *Race and Reunion* for an extended analysis of national reconciliation over Civil War memories.

artifacts such as letters, documents, and photographs from black veterans.[57] Such was the case for descendants of New Bedford's black Union veterans. Within the larger community, however, the men of the 54th Massachusetts were largely forgotten until the 1980s, when Carl J. Cruz, a local historian and descendant of William Carney, began to publicize Carney's exploits. In July 1988, a local newspaper article trumpeted Carney's bravery, and in the following year, release of the movie *Glory* turned a national spotlight on the history of the 54th Massachusetts Regiment. Building upon this renewed interest, local historians and community members persisted in memorializing and remembering the men of the 54th. In 1998, in the same year that a new "African American Civil War Memorial" was unveiled in the nation's capital, New Bedfordites dedicated the "Fifty-Fourth Massachusetts Memorial Plaza" in the downtown area.[58] This public site, located near where black men first enlisted for army service in 1863, offers a place of repose and remembrance in the midst of the historic "Whaling City" and serves as a tribute to the African American soldiers and sailors who fought for the Union during the Civil War.

---

[57] For a useful study of African American families in Massachusetts that merges genealogy and history, see Franklin A. Dorman, *Twenty Families of Color in Massachusetts, 1742–1998* (Boston: New England Historic Genealogical Society, 1998).

[58] See Michael J. Ryan, "125 Years Ago, Black Soldier Held High His Country's Flag," *New Bedford Sunday Standard-Times*, July 17, 1988; Carl J. Cruz, "Sergeant William H. Carney, Civil War Hero," and "Interview," in *"It Wasn't in Her Lifetime, But It Was Handed Down": Four Black Oral Histories of Massachusetts*, ed. by Eleanor Wachs (Boston: Secretary of State's Office, 1988), 7–16; "Movie Recalls His Kin's 'Glory,'" *USA Today*, January 29, 1990.

14

"I Would Rather Shake Hands with the Blackest Nigger in the Land": Northern Black Civil War Veterans and the Grand Army of the Republic

Donald R. Shaffer

THE "ENCAMPMENT," or national convention, of the Grand Army of the Republic (GAR) was often a contentious affair. Every year during the late nineteenth and early twentieth century, members of the Grand Army, the largest and most important of all Union veterans' organizations, would assemble in some major American city, ostensibly to celebrate the continuing bonds of wartime comradeship and remind the nation of their contribution to Union victory. Yet they also gathered to organize against what they saw as subversion of the war's legacy. Since the earliest days of the organization, GAR men had seen themselves as the guardians of the Civil War, both of the public memory of the conflict and the war's actual consequences. Still, they could not always agree on how best to defend their vision of the war and its outcome, or which aspects were most worth defending.

Emancipation was unquestionably an important legacy of the Civil War, as well as the citizenship and suffrage rights for African Americans that followed during Reconstruction. Yet although virtually all GAR men supported the end of slavery, vast differences of opinion existed within the organization about the proper place of black people in postwar American society. The issue of African Americans was especially relevant because of the presence of black men in the Grand Army of the Republic. In its early years, the GAR adopted membership rules that did not exclude African Americans. Theoretically, any honorably discharged Union veteran was eligible for membership, regardless of his race.[1] Under this policy small numbers of black veterans in the North and Upper South made their way into the organization in the 1860s and 1870s.

By the late 1880s, however, the colorblind membership policy of the GAR clashed with the desire of white Union veterans in Louisiana and Mississippi to keep African American veterans out of their regional organization or "department." Northern GAR men were faced with the dilemma of whether to reaffirm the existing membership rules and risk alienating white members in the Lower South, or accept a color line in the GAR and in effect accommodate their organization's policies to the racial system being put in place in the South by their former Confederate enemies. The rapt attention of the national media to their deliberations did not make the decision any easier.

Many GAR men weighed in with their opinions during the encampment debates. Among them was the department commander in California, Edward S. Salomon. Rising in opposition at the 1887 encampment in St. Louis, Missouri, to what he saw as overly friendly overtures of white Union veterans in the Lower South toward ex-Confederates, he stated, "I would rather shake hands with the blackest nigger in the land if he was a true and honest man, than with a traitor."[2] Salomon's comment was significant on two levels. Taken at face value, he expressed a sincere sentiment of most white members outside the Lower South against any sort of official segregation in the GAR. Yet his statement also reveals the ambivalence of many white Grand Army men toward their black comrades. Salomon's biting language hardly bespoke a full acceptance of African Americans as equals. Only their loyalty to the Union and white southerners' treason reordered racial etiquette—temporarily.

In short, the position of black Civil War veterans in the Grand Army of the Republic in the North was uncertain. Officially, the GAR made no racial distinctions. The organization drew no formal color

---

[1] Robert B. Beath, *The Grand Army Blue-Book: Rules and Regulations of the Grand Army of the Republic and Official Decisions and Opinions Thereon With Additional Notes* (Philadelphia: n.p., 1888), 4.

[2] Grand Army of the Republic, *Journal of the Twenty-First Annual Session of the National Encampment* (Milwaukee: Burdick and Armitage, Printers, 1887), 255.

line. This policy made the Grand Army special among fraternal societies in the post–Civil War period, in which racial segregation or total
exclusion was the norm. Consequently, African Americans joined
predominantly white posts (or local chapters) of the GAR in the
North, with a few even rising to positions of considerable power and
responsibility in them.

Despite such achievements, African Americans in the northern
states still faced discrimination in the Grand Army of the Republic.
If they succeeded in joining the group, black veterans often found
themselves relegated to marginal roles. Racism, differences of memory concerning the war, and the postwar reconciliation of white
Union and Confederate veterans strained relations between black
and white Union veterans. Hence, although the GAR was able to
keep alive the wartime alliance of white and black soldiers, those
bonds became increasingly frayed and tenuous. The result was a dilemma for northern black veterans: whether to remain in the GAR
or to organize separately among themselves. They ended up doing
both, which itself speaks to their conflicted feelings concerning the
Grand Army of the Republic in the North.

The ambiguous position of African Americans in the northern
Grand Army had its origins in the group's early political connections.
With its ties to the Radical faction of the Republican party, it should
not be surprising that the organization tried to forge a race-neutral
policy. Radicals in the GAR, such as its icon, John A. Logan, fought
for the equality of African Americans during Reconstruction and
worked for the equality of black veterans within the Grand Army. To
them, wartime loyalty and service, not race, were the critical criteria
for GAR membership. A group of white veterans well articulated this
position at the 1891 national encampment when they said, "A man
who is good enough to stand between the flag and those who would
destroy it when the fate of the nation was trembling in the balance is
good enough to be a comrade in . . . the Grand Army of the Republic."[3]

Debates about membership criteria in the late 1880s and early
1890s revealed that many white northerners in the GAR not only
accepted African Americans into the Grand Army in the North, but

---

[3] Grand Army of the Republic, *Journal of the Twenty-Fifth National Encampment*
(Rutland, Vt.: The Tuttle Company, Printers, 1891), 250.

they also defended the position of black veterans within the GAR in the Lower South. White Union veterans in the Lower South tried to exclude black veterans because they feared a backlash from native white southerners should they accept African Americans into the organization. They also believed the black veterans, who greatly outnumbered them, would come to dominate the GAR there. But white veterans in the North refused to allow their white comrades in the Lower South to keep black veterans out of the Grand Army. As early as the 1887 national encampment, northern delegates took steps to force open the doors for black posts. When departmental authorities in Louisiana and Mississippi (who, like their counterparts in GAR departments across the nation, normally granted charters for local posts in their region) refused to award charters to black posts, the 1887 encampment passed an extraordinary resolution allowing African Americans denied a charter to apply directly to the national commander of the GAR for authority to establish local posts.[4] Four years later, northern veterans also rejected a proposal from white Union veterans in Louisiana and Mississippi (which made up the Department of the Gulf) to compel black posts to organize into a separate department. The national leadership of the Grand Army subsequently removed the department leaders when they refused to implement the will of the national encampment in favor of an integrated department. Even after a substantial loss of white members in Louisiana and Mississippi following the 1891 controversy, northern white veterans stood firm against an official color line in the GAR.

Still, the relationship between black and white veterans in the North was not as close or cordial as the widespread white support for racial inclusiveness in the Grand Army of the Republic might suggest. Although most white Union veterans in the North accepted blacks as members of the GAR and defended African Americans in the southern departments of the Grand Army, black veterans in the northern states still faced considerable discrimination in the GAR. Gratitude to black soldiers for their Civil War service moderated the racism of many white veterans in the North but did not eliminate it.

Although the GAR formally kept open the doors of the organization to black veterans and insisted on integrated state departments, wherever sufficient numbers existed at the local level, Grand Army

---

[4] *Twenty-First Annual Encampment*, 250–51, 255.

posts often were segregated in the North as well as the South. In the debate within the GAR over the race relations in the Lower South, racially segregated posts were taken for granted. White northerners did not attempt to force whites and blacks into the same posts in the Lower South. Instead, they merely insisted that white and black posts be part of the same department. Under the racial regime for the GAR adopted by the 1891 national encampment, white and black Union veterans would meet at the department encampments, and the departments might have both white and black officers, but the question never arose of requiring former white soldiers anywhere to take African Americans into their posts.

The relatively small numbers of African Americans in the North made their acceptance into the Grand Army in that region in some ways more problematic than in the South. In practice, segregated posts generally proved more agreeable for white GAR men, North as well as South. They relieved white Union veterans from the approbation of mixing socially with black men. In the southern states, the large number of black Union veterans usually made segregation practical. There were enough African American veterans in most southern localities to organize segregated posts. In many places in the North, however, too few black veterans lived to form racially separate posts. Hence, numerous African Americans in the North had no alternative but to apply for membership in a local white post if they wanted to be a member of the Grand Army of the Republic.

African Americans who attempted to join white GAR posts in the North faced an uncertain reception. They discovered that even white veterans who accepted equality in theory could act very differently in practice. Such was the case at the George H. Ward Post No. 10 in Worcester, Massachusetts. By 1870, the Ward post had at least one black member, Amos Webber.[5] In May of that year, a second black veteran, Bassill C. Barker, attempted to join. In a GAR post, an applicant was accepted or rejected by a vote of the existing members. The Ward post voted Barker down at its June 2 meeting. According to Post No. 10's historian, Franklin D. Tappan, quoting from the minutes, "The question being raised, why was he rejected? One comrade vouchsafed the reply that it was because he was a 'nigger.' Upon

---

[5] Nick Salvatore, *We All Got History: The Memory Books of Amos Webber* (New York: Times Books, 1996), 168.

motion a new ballot was ordered, and he was again rejected." The failure to elect Barker despite two attempts proved an acute embarrassment to the post's leaders who had sponsored him. They scheduled a third ballot on Barker's application for the next meeting. Word of the June 2 meeting spread around Worcester, and when the members of Post No. 10 reassembled on June 9, the hall was packed. The post leaders attempted to remind the membership of the GAR's nondiscriminatory policy by sponsoring a resolution that stated "no inquiry as to race, color or nationality of any applicant should, or by right ought to be made, either by any Committee or by this Post." In fact, the resolution, according to Tappan, did pass without "great opposition." Still, when the leadership presented Barker's application a third time, the membership rejected him yet again, prompting three officers to resign from the post in protest.[6]

As Nick Salvatore, the biographer of Amos Webber, points out, it is possible that Barker found himself rejected for membership in the Worcester, Massachusetts, post in 1870 because he was the *second* black veteran to apply for membership. With one black member already, some white veterans in Post No. 10 must have felt they had reached the limit.[7] They accepted another black veteran, Emory G. Phillips, for membership three years after the Barker controversy and brought in about twenty other former black soldiers in the years that followed, but those numbers were negligible in a Grand Army post that at its peak had over a thousand members during the course of its existence.[8]

It is difficult to generalize about which black men in the North successfully joined the Grand Army and which black men were rejected. The reception of African American veterans by northern Grand Army posts was at least in part dependent on the number of black veterans in a given locality. In areas where very few black veterans resided, they had a much better chance of being accepted into a local post. For instance, Robert Anderson, a Kentucky-born veteran, was the only black member of a Grand Army post in Hemingford, Nebraska.

Indeed, Anderson likely found himself welcomed in his post be-

---

[6] Franklin D. Tappan, *The Passing of the Grand Army of the Republic* (Worcester, Mass.: Commonwealth Press, 1939), 23–25.

[7] Salvatore, *We All Got History*, 169.

[8] Tappan, *The Passing of the Grand Army*, 244–64.

cause few Union veterans, white or black, lived in Hemingford, which in the late nineteenth century was a sparsely populated community in the far western frontier section of the state. The special 1890 census of Civil War veterans recorded only twenty-one men with a Hemingford post office address. White GAR men in such small places were probably more ready to overlook skin color in order to maintain a viable post.[9]

The reputation and associations of an African American veteran also made a difference in whether he was accepted for membership in a northern GAR post. Black men who were well known and respected by local white veterans appear to have had a much greater chance of getting into the Grand Army. Amos Webber may have been accepted into the Ward post and Bassill Barker rejected in part because Webber was better known to the white veterans in Worcester. Webber worked at a wire mill, where he became a familiar and well-regarded figure to former white soldiers there, whereas Barker, who worked for a black barber, had less contact with the local veterans' community.[10]

Black men who had the reputation for racially deferential behavior also stood a much better chance of getting into a northern GAR post. White veterans generally expected blacks who joined their Grand Army posts to be seen but not heard. The attitude of white GAR men was that African Americans in their posts should be grateful for their membership and should not attempt to take a very active role in the organization or seek any real power. Consequently, few black veterans served as officers in the predominantly white posts of the North. To be sure, at least two black veterans actually rose to the position of commander, a GAR post's top officer. Robert A. Pinn, a black attorney, residing in Massillion, Ohio, was elected commander of the Hart Post No. 134 in January 1886.[11] Pinn was followed by William H. Dupree, a federal civil servant and prominent black veteran of the

---

[9] Robert Anderson, *From Slavery to Affluence: Memoirs of Robert Anderson, Ex-Slave* (Hemingford, Nebr.: Hemingford Ledger, 1927), 4; 1890 Special Census of Union Veterans and Their Widows, Box Butte County, Nebraska, National Archives Microfilm Publication M123. In fairness, the Hemingford GAR post was no doubt able to draw on men further out in Box Butte County. Robert Anderson himself is not listed as having a Hemingford post office address. Nonetheless, the special census found only 133 Union veterans residing in Box Butte County in 1890.

[10] Salvatore, *We All Got History*, 169.

[11] *Cleveland Gazette*, January 30, 1886.

55th Massachusetts, who became commander of the Benjamin A. Stone Post in Boston in December 1894.[12] More typically, black veterans held no office at all, or like Robert Anderson, who was color bearer in the Hemingford GAR post, the position was purely ceremonial.[13]

The characteristics for an acceptable black veteran in a northern GAR post were well summed up by Andrew S. Graham, a white Union veteran residing in the Lower South, during the 1891 debate over a proposal for a segregated department in Louisiana and Mississippi. With an outsider's observant eye, he told the national encampment: "[In northern posts, you] may have three or four colored men, nice men, respectable men, whom you all know and speak to every day on the street. They come into your post and you treat them well. They are respectful to you. They take no part in the arrangements; they do not elect the officers. You do all the business and everything of the kind."[14]

Given the discrimination and subordination they faced in the Grand Army of the Republic, it is surprising that black veterans in the North rarely organized themselves outside the GAR, and then only temporarily. Significantly, on none of these occasions did the former soldiers explicitly protest their treatment in the Grand Army. Instead, they came together to celebrate the special nature of their wartime experience and to defend what they saw as the legacy of their service: freedom, equal rights, and suffrage.

Nothing was more important to black Civil War veterans than suffrage. Voting became regarded by these men as the most important citizenship right. The significance of suffrage to them began in the arguments against black recruitment early in the Civil War. Opponents of black enlistment argued, among other things, that African Americans could not render military service because according to the Dred Scott decision they were not citizens. They based their position on the notion of the dual nature of citizenship. To nineteenth-century Americans, citizenship meant not only the enjoyment of rights, but also the assumption of responsibilities. Citizens voted and exercised

---

[12] *Boston Journal*, December 30, 1894, in the George T. Garrison Clippings, vol. 4, Garrison Family Papers, Sophia Smith Collection, Smith College Archives, Alumnae Gymnasium, Smith College, Northampton, Mass.

[13] Anderson, *From Slavery to Affluence*, 22.

[14] *Twenty-Fifth Annual Encampment*, 261–62.

other rights, but in return the government expected them to fulfill certain duties, including answering the call to bear arms at the appropriate time. Consequently, the foes of black enlistment feared that if African Americans did join the Union army white supremacy would be undermined, because black men could argue that having performed an important responsibility of a citizen, they were entitled to enjoy a citizen's rights.

Black soldiers in the Civil War clearly understood the significance of the connection between their military service and citizenship rights. During the war, they had aspired to equal treatment with white soldiers, especially as it concerned their pay. When the federal government attempted to pay all black soldiers $10 per month instead of the $13 per month given to white privates, and to deduct a further $3 for clothing, African Americans in the Union army resisted, particularly in the elite 54th and 55th Massachusetts Infantry. The men in these regiments refused to accept any compensation until they received the same rate as their white counterparts. Resisting second-class treatment helped politicize African American soldiers and teach them the skills they would use to defend the position of their race in the postwar period.

As the war concluded, black troops turned their attention to obtaining the citizenship rights to which they believed their military service entitled them, especially suffrage. Although agitation for equal rights occurred in black regiments across the country, it was especially strong in those units recruited in the North. Unlike in the South, where political power after the war quickly fell back into the hands of the old Confederate elite under presidential Reconstruction, in some northern states, African Americans already enjoyed suffrage and in the rest it appeared distinctly possible that grateful legislatures would bestow voting rights on black men as a reward for their military service. This impression was reinforced by the heroes' welcome enjoyed by many northern black regiments as they returned to their home states. But racial prejudice trumped gratitude throughout the North in the immediate aftermath of the war, as state after state rejected attempts to extend suffrage to black men.

Black soldiers responded to the failure of northern legislatures to extend them suffrage with renewed political agitation. As they had with the unequal pay issue during the war, they now protested their lack of suffrage rights. Most vociferous were about 700 of Iowa's black soldiers in the 60th U.S. Colored Infantry, who met in a mass convention at Camp McClellan in Davenport, Iowa, on October 31, 1865. They drew up a petition to be presented to the Iowa legislature. Not surprisingly, their arguments emphasized the connection between military service and suffrage. "He who is worthy to be trusted with the musket can and ought," these Iowa soldiers resolved, "to be trusted with the ballot." They also saw suffrage as the linchpin of all citizenship rights, without which the others were all but meaningless. Bereft of voting rights they contended that "we have no power to defend ourselves from unjust legislation, and no voice in the Government we have endeavored to defend."[15]

The agitation for suffrage rights continued as northern black soldiers mustered out of their regiments and returned to civilian life. African American veterans in the North joined with their southern comrades in 1866 to form the Colored Soldiers and Sailors' League, the first attempt of black Civil War veterans to organize on their own after the war. The league was in no sense a rival to the Grand Army of the Republic, which was itself just getting started. The primary purpose of the Colored Soldiers and Sailors' League was to provide a national group to focus the efforts of African American veterans in favor of black suffrage. By the time the league was organized, black veterans were beginning to develop the idea that they were special advocates for the black community as a whole. They believed that their service gave them a moral authority that would be difficult for white northerners to ignore. Veterans were not alone in this opinion. The *Christian Recorder*, the voice of the African Methodist Episcopal Church, expressed a similar sentiment while promoting the national convention of the League held in Philadelphia in January 1867. "The men, who in open field could bear their bosoms in heroic charge upon the enemy's cannon," the *Recorder* stated, "have certainly force of character, and will know better than any body else can tell them, to charge upon and overthrow the citadel of American prejudice."[16] In short, the Colored Soldiers and Sailors' League was

---

[15] *Muscatine* [Iowa] *Journal*, October 31, 1865; and *Christian Recorder*, November 6, 1865, in *A Grand Army of Black Men: Letters from African-American Soldiers in the Union Army, 1861–1865*, ed. by Edwin S. Redkey (Cambridge, Eng.: Cambridge University Press, 1992), 294–95.

[16] *Christian Recorder*, January 5, 1867, in *Proceedings of the Black National and State Conventions, 1865–1900*, ed. by Philip S. Foner and George E. Walker (Philadelphia: Temple University Press, 1986), 1: 291.

meant to give the moral authority of black veterans organizational force. But the league was apparently short-lived, likely a victim of its own success. After the ratification of the Fifteenth Amendment in 1870 extended voting rights to black men, the Colored Soldiers and Sailors' League disappears completely from the historical record.

Evidently, black veterans were not ready to organize on a more purely social basis, as was the case with white veterans and the GAR. In addition, by the 1870s, there was no doubt a desire on the part of many black veterans to put the war behind them. The GAR itself declined during this decade, only reviving with the rising agitation of Union veterans for more generous pension laws in the 1880s.

Black veterans also did not establish their own national veterans' organization because they wanted to join the Grand Army of the Republic. They associated acceptance into the GAR with equality within the fraternity of Union veterans. They demanded inclusion into the organization they felt represented *all* Union veterans, and promised to gain pensions and benefits for *all* Union veterans regardless of their color. Consequently, former black soldiers initially focused their energy on organizing within the Grand Army after the collapse of the Colored Soldiers and Sailors' League.

Still, disagreement developed among black veterans in the North over the precise meaning of equality as it concerned the Grand Army. Although the focus on equality in the South later centered at the department level, some former black soldiers in the North were more ambitious. They demanded the integration of local posts. In many places in the North, segregated posts were numerically impractical, but this was not the case everywhere, especially in large cities. Some black veterans were willing to accept racially segregated posts in the North, but others believed that all-black GAR posts were objectionable.

The most vocal opponent of racially segregated posts in the North was Robert A. Pinn. He strenuously resisted an attempt to organize an all-black post in Cleveland, Ohio, in the mid 1880s. In December 1886, he wrote to the editor of the *Cleveland Gazette*, the city's black paper, to express his outrage. To establish a separate black post was in Pinn's mind to go against the character of the GAR. "The Grand Army of the Republic is indeed what its name implies," he wrote. "It is a grand institution. It knows no creed, race, color nor politics." Further, he contended a separate black post for Cleveland was unnecessary—and counterproductive. The city had a half a dozen GAR posts already, several of them with black members, "Why set up a 'side show?'" he opined. He feared that by organizing a separate black post, African American veterans would be "drawing a color line for themselves." It was bad enough in Pinn's opinion when whites initiated segregation, but when African Americans took that step, they were encouraging whites to bolster further the ramparts of racial separation. Finally, for Pinn, integrated posts were a matter of honor. Having achieved equality on the battlefield, it would be an insult to accept inequality in the GAR. He wrote:

> We fought side by side with our white comrades; our blood mingled and drenched the Southern soil; our united efforts saved our common country for the abode of freemen, and in this sublime time of peace we should not be the first to say we will have no part with our white comrades in perpetuating and enjoying that which is our common heritage. It is an insult to our comrades, and a slander upon our Grand Army.[17]

Perhaps because of his personal success in the Grand Army of the Republic, Pinn was not prepared to accept that other African Americans were being excluded from the organization on account of their race. Pinn readily acknowledged that some GAR posts had rejected black veterans for membership, but he argued that the grounds were not racial because white men were turned away as well. Acceptance into the GAR, Pinn maintained, was ultimately a matter of individual character, not race. He fervently believed that black men of good character would find acceptance in the Grand Army. "Some men of both races . . . are not fit to belong to the G.A.R.," he stated. "But let a colored man in good standing in society apply and he will not be refused."[18] Pinn was not alone in his opinion. J. F. Burton, a black veteran from Chicago, expressed similar sentiments in the *Gazette* soon after Pinn. "I have been a member of the G.A.R. since 1881," he said, "and have visited Posts in various States, and I have the first time to be refused admittance. The only time that a comrade is refused admittance is when he fails to present himself properly."[19]

---

[17] *Cleveland Gazette*, December 4, 1886.
[18] Ibid.
[19] Ibid., July 16, 1887.

The denials of Pinn and Burton notwithstanding, discrimination did exist within the Grand Army of the Republic in the North. Both men focused their attention on the narrow issue of the initial application of black men to join the GAR. They ignored the subordination of most African Americans once they made it into the organization. They also overlooked the chronic lack of concern in the Grand Army over the special problems faced by black veterans and other African Americans in the postwar period.

The GAR's neglect of black concerns led to renewed independent activity by African American veterans in the North by the mid 1880s. Northern black veterans largely were spared the violence that southern black veterans faced, as former Confederates took revenge against former black soldiers in the South, but their situation was still difficult. Most of these men had been poor before entering military service and returned to poverty after their discharge. This problem was compounded by the fact that many former black soldiers had lost their discharge papers, which made it difficult for them to obtain enlistment bounties and pensions or gain entry into government-sponsored soldiers' homes if they were disabled and had no family to care for them. The widows, orphans, and aged parents of dead black soldiers faced even greater travails in obtaining the government aid to which they were entitled.

Such problems, combined with the inattention of the Grand Army to black concerns, forced black veterans to organize outside of the GAR. In 1884, for instance, a call went out to African American veterans in Ohio to

> meet in a convention for the purpose of considering and laying before Congress our needs and those of the widows and orphans of our deceased comrades in the award of pensions and bounties, and employment in the service of the General Government, and to form a mutual aid society to seek government aid in setting upon the public lands in colonies, for the establishment of a military and industrial school for the heirs of those who served in the Union army during the late rebellion, and for the distribution of half a million of dollars now in the United States Treasury belonging to colored soldiers as unclaimed bounty.[20]

The call to the Ohio veterans was part of a larger effort in the North during the 1880s to organize African American veterans

---

[20] Ibid., July 12, 1884.

toward holding a national reunion of former black soldiers and sailors. State and regional reunion organizations arose in different places throughout the northern and border states. For example, former black soldiers in New England met in Worcester, Massachusetts, in October 1885, to organize the Colored Veterans' Association.[21] Lack of documentation makes it impossible to track all regional manifestations of the black veterans' reunion movement in the 1880s, but its leaders represented regiments originating in Massachusetts, Michigan, Ohio, Iowa, and Kentucky. They met in Dayton, Ohio, in January 1886, to form the Negro Ex-Soldiers' and Sailors' National Reunion Association.[22]

The reunion movement did not emerge as a rival to black activity in the Grand Army of the Republic. Leading members of the movement remained active in the GAR. For instance, Amos Webber was a leader in the Colored Veterans' Association in New England while still participating in the Worcester Grand Army post. African Americans also continued to agitate for their goals within the GAR. The members of the Charles Sumner Post No. 9 in Washington, D.C., for example, at a meeting at Lincoln Memorial Hall in December 1884, advocated the construction of a memorial in the national capital to commemorate the service of black Civil War soldiers and sailors.[23]

Nor did the reunion movement express any hostility toward white Union veterans. Indeed, former white officers were prominent participants in the meetings of the New England reunion organization. Norwood P. Hallowell, former commander of the 55th Massachusetts, was the keynote speaker at the inaugural meeting of the Colored Veterans' Association. Hallowell's involvement is not surprising. Ties were especially close between ex-officers and former soldiers of Massachusetts's black regiments. The state had been an important center of antislavery activity before the war, and abolitionists and their sons volunteered for service as officers in the state's black units. Many of the former officers displayed a continuing interest in the postwar activities of the African Americans who served under them.[24]

---

[21] Salvatore, *We All Got History*, 280–81.

[22] *Cleveland Gazette*, January 30, 1886.

[23] Ibid., December 13, 1884.

[24] For instance, George Thompson Garrison (son of abolitionist William Lloyd Garrison), who had been a 2nd Lieutenant and later Quartermaster in the 55th Massachusetts, painstakingly assembled clippings from Boston newspapers over many years concerning the activities of black veterans of the regiment. See Garrison

The reunion movement also called for tightening bonds between black and white Union veterans. The founders of the Negro Ex-Soldiers' and Sailors' National Reunion Association put closer relations with their former white comrades at the top of their list of goals— even ahead of mutual assistance and defending African American equality. They stated as their top priority that

> the object of this society shall be to strengthen and preserve those kind and fraternal feelings which should bind together the desires and sympathies of all soldiers, sailors and marines who united to suppress the rebellion and the Negro soldiers, sailors and marines especially, who united with the double purpose of crushing the rebellion and to more perfectly establish his own freedom, justice, and equal privileges before the law.[25]

The culmination of the reunion movement was the national two-day meeting of black Civil War veterans held in Boston's Tremont Temple in August 1887. It attracted over 300 veterans and was the largest known assembly of former black soldiers and sailors after the Civil War. Though the meeting was primarily a Massachusetts affair, especially in terms of its leadership, some of the attendees were from regiments raised in the South and other northern states. The president of the reunion was William Monroe Trotter, then serving as the recorder of deeds in the District of Columbia (a lucrative federal patronage post) and a prominent ex-member of the 55th Massachusetts. The men present at the convention listened to speeches by Trotter, William Carney (a veteran of the 54th Massachusetts and a hero of the assault on Fort Wagner), and leading former white officers of the 54th and 55th Massachusetts. They also paraded through the streets of Boston and capped off the meeting with a boat trip to nearby Higham, Massachusetts, to visit the grave of John A. Andrew, the wartime governor of the state and champion of black troops.[26]

Clippings. Burt G. Wilder, the regimental surgeon of the 55th Massachusetts, also conducted a correspondence after the war with Andrew J. Smith, a former soldier in the regiment, who had served as Wilder's orderly for a time before returning to combat duties. Wilder used Smith as a source for his history of the unit, and tried to help Smith get official recognition for saving the regimental colors at the Battle of Honey Hill in November 1864. See Letters and Memorabilia of Color-Sergeant Andrew J. Smith, Co. B, 55th Massachusetts Infantry Regiment, 1842–1932, Civil War Miscellaneous Collection, Archives, United States Army Military Institute, Carlisle, Pa.

[25] *Cleveland Gazette*, January 30, 1886.
[26] *Boston Journal*, August 2, 3, 1887, in the Garrison Clippings.

Like the Colored Soldiers and Sailors' League in the 1860s, the Boston reunion of 1887 was rooted in present realities. While the veterans and their ex-officers commemorated their continuing bonds of comradeship and remembered the special experience of black soldiers in the Civil War, the deteriorating position of African Americans in the wake of Reconstruction dominated the business meeting held on the second day. A resolution passed at the reunion called attention to the fact that, by the late 1880s, the gains black soldiers had made possible by their service were in jeopardy. It complained "that American citizens of African descent . . . are today in a large portion of this great nation denied justice in the courts, deprived of the exercise of the elective franchise, the victims of mob violence, an unprotected and outraged people."[27]

The Boston reunion reemphasized that black Civil War veterans continued to believe they had a special obligation to defend the progress made by African Americans as a result of the Civil War. These men believed they were the liberators of their race. To them, freedom was not a gift of the federal government or white northerners; rather, it had been won with their own blood. In liberating slaves, the veterans added, black troops had done a service for the entire nation. "They washed the blood scars of slavery out of the American flag, and painted freedom there; they snatched the black lies out of every false star upon its folds and set in their stead the diadem of liberty," insisted one black veteran in 1887. "They tore the Dred Scott decision from the statutes and wrote there, 'All men are equal before God.' "[28] Northern black veterans also insisted that their service entitled them to suffrage and equality. Facing death on the battlefield and the threat of execution if captured, they had nonetheless taken the manly course and by their service earned rights to which they believed all free men were entitled.

Black veterans, the heroic liberators of their people during the Civil War, were especially worried about the deteriorating situation of their race, especially in the South, following Reconstruction. The promise of freedom wrought by the war was in eclipse by the late 1880s. The passage of segregation laws and disfranchisement began to extend across the South, the exploitation of black farmers intensi-

---

[27] Ibid., August 3, 1887.
[28] *New York Freeman*, August 20, 1887.

fied, and lynching and other violence directed at African Americans increased and went unpunished. Unless black veterans acted to re-awaken the public conscience, their wartime sacrifice would be in vain.

In that moment of crisis, African American veterans continued to find white Union veterans largely indifferent to their concerns. Northern white veterans might occasionally invite a prominent black Civil War figure, like Frederick Douglass in Baltimore in 1882, to address them, but they paid little attention to the cause he repre-sented.

Persistent racism in part explains white Union veterans' indiffer-ence to growing discrimination against African Americans in the South. But, as Stuart McConnell points out, the GAR's lack of re-sponse to the rise of Jim Crow, disfranchisement, lynching, and the crop lien system also was the product of their outmoded world-view. According to McConnell, it "embraced an antebellum form of liberal capitalism rather than a linguistic-cultural prescription, emphasized republic preservation rather than dynamic change, and treated the Civil War as an unassailable monument rather than an unequivocal triumph. It was peculiar because it described the United States of 1860 better than it described the United States of 1890."[29]

Many white northern veterans continued to hold an idealized ver-sion of the United States as it had been before the Civil War. African Americans fit awkwardly, if at all, into this picture. Black people had been present in the United States prior to the Civil War, but were largely ignored in the significance most white Union veterans in the GAR drew of the conflict. Unlike African Americans, for whom the war had been primarily a war of liberation, for former white soldiers it had remained first and foremost a war to save the Union. Northern white soldiers cheered the end of slavery, which they saw as incom-patible with the free labor system that was an integral part of their liberal-capitalist ideology, but to them the important outcome of the war remained the preservation of the Union. For such white veterans, emancipation did not necessarily translate into support for black suf-frage and citizenship rights.

By the end of the nineteenth century, differing memories of the

---

[29] Stuart McConnell, *Glorious Contentment: The Grand Army of the Republic, 1865–1900* (Chapel Hill: University of North Carolina Press, 1992), 232.

Civil War made a postwar alliance between the white and black Union veterans a dubious proposition. All that mattered about the war for the white veterans was that the Union had been saved (even if in reality industrialization, immigration, and other changes meant that the nation they had saved was fast disappearing). They might suspect ex-Confederates of continued disloyalty and respond when politicians raised its specter by "waving the bloody shirt," if only to insist that the politicians remember to vote pensions for veterans, but few white northern veterans harbored any illusions about a new southern rebellion. For most white veterans, the war was over, northern dominance secured, and nothing more needed to be done but to preserve the status quo.

Another reason why black Civil War veterans found their white comrades in the Grand Army often lukewarm to notions of equal rights for African Americans was the gradual rapprochement between white Union veterans and their Confederate counterparts that gained momentum in the 1890s. Blue-Gray reunions proliferated in that decade as the antipathies of the war subsided, and reconciliation occurred based on a mutual respect for the courage and the authenticity of each side's convictions. Although white northern veterans continued to believe that the Confederates had erred in rebelling against the Union, they accepted their former enemies as men who had made an honorable mistake. The peacemaking between white Union veterans and former Confederate soldiers shunted memories of blacks' wartime service and postwar concerns aside. The growing regard of white Grand Army men for their counterparts in the United Confederate Veterans (UCV) left their black comrades in the GAR in the shadows. The reconciliation of white northern and southern veterans also made it easier for the former to accept the rise of the Jim Crow South. Although not all white Union veterans might have been comfortable with this repressive system, their rapprochement with Confederate veterans was an implicit sign that they did not intend actively to resist it, either.

By the late 1880s, black Civil War veterans also perceived a growing sense of historical amnesia within the Grand Army of the Republic that contributed to white veterans' indifference to black concerns. The black veterans' reunion movement of the 1880s sought to remind white northern veterans (and white northerners in general) of black soldiers' vital contributions to Union victory. In addition to the attempts of African American veterans to keep alive the memory of their participation in war at countless GAR campfires, two of these men fought public forgetfulness by putting out book-length histories of black troops in the Civil War in the wake of the Boston reunion. In 1888, George W. Williams published *A History of Negro Troops in the War of the Rebellion,* a year after Joseph T. Wilson had produced *The Black Phalanx* (1887). Yet such efforts had little apparent effect. Few whites, in or out of the GAR, read the books, and most white northerners had other interests than reliving the war as black men experienced it. This obliviousness led one black veteran, Christian Fleetwood, with a sweeping sense of historical perspective, to lament in 1895, "After each war, of 1776, of 1812, and of 1861, history repeats itself in the absolute effacement of remembrance of the gallant deeds done for the country by its brave black defenders and their relegation to outer darkness."[30]

Unlike Christian Fleetwood, most black veterans in the North did not react to the indifference and forgetfulness of whites in the GAR with outraged frustration. Using different strategies, they attempted to revive the wartime alliance between black and white GAR comrades. For instance, some black veterans in the North consistently, and also gently, reminded white veterans of the assistance they had rendered them during the war. As one African American veteran put it to his white comrades at a national encampment of the GAR in 1891, "Remember that in the dark days when you . . . were struggling to maintain this country, it was the black man that came to your assistance and stood by until the last enemy was gone."[31] Now was the time for white veterans to discharge that debt of honor.

African Americans also tried to revive the wartime alliance by celebrating as heroes those white northerners who had supported their cause during the war. In particular, they singled out Robert Gould Shaw, the commander of the 54th Massachusetts Infantry who had died with his men in the futile assault on Fort Wagner, South Carolina, in July 1863. Shaw became a favorite subject of Decoration Day activities of black veterans. Black Grand Army posts were named for him. George W. Williams, in his history of black troops in the Civil

---

[30] Christian A. Fleetwood, *The Negro as a Soldier* (Washington, D.C.: Howard University Print, 1895), 18.

[31] *Twenty-Fifth Annual Encampment,* 257.

War, proved particularly obsequious in his treatment of the martyred colonel. In making a proposal for a black veterans' memorial in Washington, D.C., Williams suggested naming the park in which the monument would stand for Shaw rather than a heroic black soldier. He thought naming the park for Shaw was "eminently proper." "He came from a noble race of men," Williams wrote. "He was pure as he was just, beautiful as he was good, patriotic as he was brave." Also important, Williams continued, was Shaw's particular service at the head of black troops. "It would quicken the pulse of national patriotism, it would elevate the feelings of the Negro, it would inform the Present, instruct the Future, and bind the friends of freedom to the generous heart of the nation," he wrote.[32] Through Robert Gould Shaw and other heroic white friends to the black race, African American veterans like Williams tried to create connections of memory with white Union veterans. Revered among whites and black veterans in the GAR, Shaw would be the means to link their memories of the Civil War.

Lastly, black Civil War veterans threw themselves on the mercy of their white comrades in the northern GAR. Realizing their powerlessness within the organization, some black veterans were not above self-abasement. One black member of the Grand Army expressed the desperation of African American GAR men quite well in the 1891 debates over separate departments. "If you turn your back upon us," he asked his white comrades, "whom shall we look to, where shall we go?" With a lingering sense of hope, he added, "I see too many honest faces here for that. I see principle here. I see charity here and I see loyalty."[33]

The GAR did not abandon this black veteran in the sense that they stopped white Union veterans in the Lower South from excluding African Americans there from the organization in the late 1880s and early 1890s, and insisting on integration of Grand Army departments. But the GAR deserted him and other African Americans on the issue of equality and suffrage. Likewise, white northern veterans betrayed their black GAR comrades in the process of making peace with their old southern enemies who were denying African Americans their

---

[32] George W. Williams, *A History of the Negro Troops in the War of the Rebellion* (New York: Harper and Brothers, 1888), 330–31.

[33] *Twenty-Fifth Annual Encampment*, 256.

rights. By the early twentieth century, Samuel Salomon no doubt would probably have been more willing to shake hands with a former Confederate foe than with the "blackest nigger in the land." The process of reconciliation between white Union and Confederate veterans continued in the early decades of the twentieth century, and the gulf between black and white Union veterans further widened as the memory of their contribution to federal victory receded further into distant memory. The racism of most white Union veterans, which never had been far beneath the surface, if at all, reasserted its influence. Although black GAR members in the North escaped the establishment of the Jim Crow regime in the South, they proved unable to rally white Union veterans in that region to their vision of the war, with its emphasis on suffrage and equal rights for African Americans. Hence, although northern black soldiers were successful in helping to win freedom for the enslaved and later won a remarkable measure of acceptance in the Grand Army of the Republic—however ambiguous their ultimate status remained—they failed in their biggest battle to guarantee equality for their people in the post-war years.

15

"For Every Man Who Wore the Blue": The Military Order of the Loyal Legion of the United States and the Charges of Elitism after the Civil War

Dana B. Shoaf

THROUGHOUT THE LATE NINETEENTH CENTURY, Civil War veterans formed a variety of fraternal orders to help commemorate their wartime service. The largest of these orders, the Grand Army of the Republic (GAR), which numbered 400,000 members at its peak of popularity, remains the best known of these veterans groups. Unfortunately, the attention it continues to command overshadows other such fraternities, including its nearest rival in numbers and the first such organization established by northern veterans, The Military Order of the Loyal Legion of the United States (MOLLUS).[1]

---

[1] The two most important studies of the GAR are Mary Dearing, *Veterans in Politics: The Story of the GAR* (Baton Rouge: Louisiana State University Press, 1952); and Stuart McConnell, *Glorious Contentment: The Grand Army of the Republic, 1865–1900* (Chapel Hill: University of North Carolina Press, 1992). Numerous journal articles, theses, and nineteenth-century histories further strengthen the historiography of the GAR. MOLLUS has not benefited from such academic treatment. One nine-page pamphlet history titled *History of the Loyal Legion* (no date or publisher) written by current companion Hibbard Gustav Gumpert does exist. There is an oblique mention of MOLLUS in Teresa Thomas's article "For Union, Not For Glory," *Civil War History* 40 (March 1994): 25–47. Wallace Davies, *Patriotism on Parade: The Story of Veterans' and Hereditary Organizations in America, 1783–1900* (Cambridge, Mass.: Harvard University Press, 1957), is the most complete overview of such societies. The epilogue in Gerald Linderman's *Embattled Courage: The Ex-*

During its early years, the Loyal Legion did not merit much attention. It failed to attract significant membership after its founding in
1865 and barely survived past the 1870s. But with new leadership,
the legion began to expand during the 1880s and 1890s, a growth
spurt that brought it renewed attention—not all of it positive. Critical
scrutiny honed in on MOLLUS's membership requirements that
permitted only officers, their direct male descendents, or selected
civilians to join. One reason for the restrictive membership requirements was admirable: founding members believed that MOLLUS
could serve as a reserve officer's pool in the advent of a renewed
uprising. But founders apparently supplemented this patriotic reason
with a more self-serving one: the former officers hoped to use the
organization to maintain the status they had achieved in the military.
With the rebellion quelled, an organization with an officer-only
membership requirement seemed to be one way for the discharged
officers to hold on to their rank when they returned to civilian life.[2]
No matter how naïve or cunning the rationale might have been, the
policy of barring enlisted veterans membership caused the Loyal Legion considerable grief in a nation that prided itself on its democratic
nature.

As the legion expanded in size and reaped the benefits of increased
public awareness, it also harvested hostility over its membership
strictures. The origins of the criticisms are somewhat hazy. Grand
Army of the Republic speeches and pamphlets generally do not reveal any notable criticisms of the Loyal Legion, no doubt because
hundreds of Union veterans enjoyed membership in both organizations. Furthermore, many northern heroes and former officers, including William T. Sherman and Ulysses S. Grant, belonged to
MOLLUS. Their presence on the order's rolls surely helped the order's reputation, causing many potential critics to pause before undertaking a public attack on the legion.

---

perience of Combat in the American Civil War (New York: The Free Press, 1987),
266–97, is a brief but insightful discussion of Civil War veterans and their societies.

[2] Historian George M. Fredrickson discusses at length how America's antebellum
northern elite class rued the democratic impulses of the country, and realized that
the officer class of the military was one of the few hierarchies allowed to exist. A
career in the United States Army was, however, not what many wealthy families
wanted for their sons—until the Civil War broke out and military service was again
seen as desirable. Fredrickson, The Inner Civil War: Northern Intellectuals and the
Crisis of the Union (New York: Harper & Row, 1965), especially 166–80.

Though open criticism of the Loyal Legion is quite evident in the *Army and Navy Journal,* much of the disparagement that apparently drifted back to the fraternal meeting halls was murky in origin. Nevertheless, the criticism was sufficiently real to prompt members to defend their Loyal Legion. The writings and speeches of the legionnaires contain overwhelming evidence of the order's discomfort at wearing an elitist mantle, providing ample evidence of the negative attitudes expressed toward MOLLUS. Furthermore, the legionnaires' defense of their organization made clear that the criticism stung. After all, northerners had fought the Civil War to crush and eradicate an aristocracy based on slavery, and it no doubt bothered the ex-Union officers that their fraternity should be viewed in a similar hierarchical vein. The companions thus undertook numerous efforts to recast their organization's image and present an agreeable public picture of their fraternity to the country.

The shocking catalyst of Lincoln's mortal wounding propelled the legion's foundation. On April 15, 1865, the day after the shooting, former Union officers Samuel B. W. Mitchell, Peter D. Keyser, and Ellwood Zell met in Philadelphia and informally agreed to form a "guard of honor" composed of fellow commanders that would stand watch over Lincoln's body. Five days later, the same three men chaired a meeting to establish the Loyal Legion as a permanent organization dedicated to remembering and honoring the Civil War. Legionnaires always took pride in the fact that theirs was the first Civil War veterans' society to organize.[3] The legion, however, nearly foundered and ceased to exist during its early years. Various reasons account for the shaky beginning, including the fact that most veterans were more anxious to get on with their lives and careers than they were to put energy into an organization that forced them to dwell on the conflict.[4]

Although all veterans' groups had to weather the initial collective disinterest of potential members, the young MOLLUS was suffering

---

[3] J. Harris Aubin, *Register of the Military Order of the Loyal Legion of the United States: Compiled from the Registers and Circulars of the Various Commandaries* (Boston: Commandery of the State of Massachusetts, 1906), 3–9.

[4] Linderman's epilogue in *Embattled Courage* stands as perhaps the best explanation of the veterans' desire to turn away from the bloodshed they had witnessed and return to normal pedestrian routines in the two decades following the end of the conflict. Linderman, *Embattled Courage*, 266–97.

from the additional internal problems of administrative neglect and disorganization. Much of the blame for the legion's dysfunctional nature can be laid at the doorstep of Mitchell, the order's first recorder in chief. The recorder was the most important administrative officer in the legion, responsible for coordinating all of the paperwork that kept MOLLUS functioning. Mitchell was not up to the task.

Co-founder Mitchell was concerned about MOLLUS and wanted it to succeed, but the former Pennsylvania cavalry surgeon seemed overwhelmed by the additional duties the new organization heaped upon his already busy life. A physician, Mitchell spent long hours with his patients, which left him with little time or energy to tend to MOLLUS's needs and to keep its records in order. He failed to send out dues notices in a timely manner, if he sent them out at all, and he did not keep companions abreast of developments within their Loyal Legion. Such disorganization drove away members. Lack of steady leadership also left those members who remained in the order largely uninformed and therefore disinterested, thus contributing to a general malaise among the membership. In short, Mitchell did little to help make the legion a vibrant organization. Years after he had been recorder, companions were still sifting through Mitchell's papers, trying to make sense of them. As one legionnaire politely put it, surgeon Mitchell's records "were very imperfectly kept."[5]

In 1879, Mitchell passed away. His demise most likely saved the order by allowing John Page Nicholson to succeed him as recorder in chief. Nicholson had served in the 28th Pennsylvania Infantry during the war, enlisting as a private and attaining the rank of brevet lieutenant colonel by war's end. It was as a veteran, however, that Nicholson shone, compiling a truly remarkable record of involvement with veterans and military commemorative organizations. In addition to his work with MOLLUS, Nicholson also held posts as the chairman of the Gettysburg National Park Commission and as president of the Valley Forge Park Commission.[6]

---

[5] Charles A. Carleton to John Page Nicholson, January 31, 1893, National Commandery Imperial File, 1893, Military Order of the Loyal Legion of the United States (MOLLUS), Archives, United States Army Military History Institute, Carlisle, Pennsylvania (hereinafter cited as USAMHI).

[6] In Memoriam, John Page Nicholson Memoriam, booklet printed by the Commandary of the State of Pennsylvania and held at the USAMHI. Nicholson also served as a trustee of a veteran's hospital and the War Library and Museum, and enjoyed involvement in a spate of other organizations. His efforts at Gettysburg were

The indefatigable Nicholson reinvigorated MOLLUS during the 1880s, saving it from extinction. He was helped by the fact that the veterans, now moving into middle age, were beginning to look at their service with fondness and pride and were becoming more eager to involve themselves with war-related commemorative activities. Nicholson stepped in to salvage the organization, claimed one of his fellow members, at a time "when the treasury was empty, and the Commandery embarrassed by debt." One admiring companion praised Nicholson for having a "keen realization of the value of order and method" and for his "vigorous administration." Under his stewardship the organization prospered, and in 1885, a National Commandery, also headquartered in Philadelphia, was established to oversee the burgeoning order. Nicholson's success was attributable to having natural administrative ability, but then he also had a distinct advantage in that he devoted himself full-time to veterans' affairs. The volume of surviving papers Nicholson wrote are ample evidence that he spent the bulk of his waking hours dealing with MOLLUS matters.[7]

Nicholson corresponded with members across the nation, cajoled legionnaires into starting new commanderies, made sure the commanderies followed the order's rules, demanded monthly reports from commandery leaders, and quelled internal disputes with aplomb. Fellow Loyal Legion members called Nicholson the "Rarest of Recorders!" and considered him the indispensable "pivot of the order." By 1900, under Nicholson's sage leadership, MOLLUS had grown to include twenty chapters, or commanderies, with a combined membership of approximately eight thousand members or "companions."[8]

---

rewarded with a small marker that notes his involvement with the battlefield. Erected in 1925, the marker can be found along Hancock Avenue. He died on March 8, 1922.

[7] Ibid.

[8] John S. Cunningham to John Page Nicholson, January 29, 1884, National Commandery Letter File, 1882–1884, MOLLUS, USAMHI; Gumpert, *History*, 4. Prior to the National Commandery's existence, the Pennsylvania Commandery functioned as the overseeing chapter for the order. MOLLUS still exists, and today claims a membership of about 950 companions in seventeen commanderies. Though primarily a social society, the legion is still involved in Civil War commemorative and preservation activities. Information about the current state of the Loyal Legion was obtained from a letter written by Recorder-in-Chief William A. Hamann III to the author on July 9, 1995. Sadly, Mr. Hamann is recently deceased.

The organization that Nicholson shepherded to a nationwide distribution was governed by a constitution that stated that the legion's principles centered on a "firm belief and trust in almighty God," and "Allegiance to the United States of America." The fraternal aspects of "cherishing of . . . memories . . . and associations" formed during the conflict, and the advancement of the "best interests" of all Union veterans were claimed as the objects of the Loyal Legion. Such principles and objectives aimed at war commemoration did not vary widely from those of the GAR. MOLLUS did have several features, however, that set it apart from the Grand Army.[9]

MOLLUS's composition, aside from being numerically smaller than the GAR's, was fairly homogeneous, consisting primarily of Anglo-Saxon white males engaged in white-collar professions. Although the most recent study of the GAR determined that society's membership cut across class lines, MOLLUS's membership seems to have been firmly rooted in the middle class. In this sense, the legion conforms more closely to historian Lynn Dumenil's view that late-nineteenth-century fraternal orders were an attempt to recreate communities of like-minded individuals in the rapidly changing social fabric of the Gilded Age.[10]

Table 15.1, comprised of data sampled from the membership applications of the Massachusetts Commandery, reveals the dominance of high-status, white-collar positions held by the Bay State legionnaires.[11]

MOLLUS's most distinctive and controversial feature, its restrictive membership policy, undoubtedly intensified the membership's homogeneity. The policy permitted only a "First Class" of honorably discharged or active-duty U.S. military commissioned officers and a "Second Class" of their first-born or closest direct male descendants

---

[9] USAMHI holds copies of the original MOLLUS constitution and all of its subsequent revisions. For the purposes of this essay, pages 3–12 of Aubin's *Register* were used as the source for this information.

[10] On the multi-class membership of the GAR, see McConnell, *Glorious Contentment*. For Lynn Dumenil's theory concerning the class constructions and cultural meanings of fraternal orders, see *Freemasonry and American Culture, 1880–1930* (Princeton: Princeton University Press, 1984).

[11] The Massachusetts applications are held at USAMHI. This table is modeled on one used in McConnell, *Glorious Contentment*, 59. To obtain a better snapshot of MOLLUS membership, the author is currently compiling data on the Pennsylvania and Michigan chapters.

TABLE 15.1
OCCUPATIONS OF MOLLUS MEMBERS OF THE MASSACHUSETTS' COMMANDERY, 1868–1900.

Occupation	
High-Status White Collar	495 (70.1%)
Proprietors	69 (9.7%)
Low-Status White Collar	50 (7.1%)
Skilled Workers	9 (1.3%)
Semiskilled Workers	4 (0.6%)
Military	48 (6.8%)
Farmers	3 (0.4%)
Unknown or None	27 (3.8%)

to share fraternity as companions of the legion. Although primogeniture helped ensure the "perpetuity of [the] Order," claimed Albert Ordway of the Washington, D.C., commandery, this practice opened the legion to accusations of being "antagonistic [to the] Constitution, Laws and Institutions" of the United States by wanting to perpetuate itself like a European-style military aristocracy. Throughout the last two decades of the nineteenth century, as the legion grew and prospered, it suffered increasingly frequent and intense criticism as an elitist organization.[12]

Detractors pegged the legion's "regulations and purposes [as] dangerous innovation[s]" threatening to the American ideal of equality. Even the *Army and Navy Journal*, normally favorable to the military and its related organizations, on occasion disparaged the legion. One

---

[12] Albert Ordway to John Page Nicholson, May 10, 1882, Commandery-in-Chief Letter File, 1882–1885, MOLLUS, USAMHI. James Smith Rutan to John Page Nicholson, April 18, 1888, MOLLUS Non-Eligible and Rejection Book #1, MOLLUS, USAMHI. Rutan was probably irritated at the legion because it had rejected him for membership because he resigned his officer's commission rather than being honorably discharged. A "Third Class" of members existed that consisted of male civilians that had vigorously supported the North's war effort. This class was always quite small, and no new members were inducted into this category after April 1890. After the turn of the century, out of necessity, the membership and class distinctions were extensively revised. In 1905, primogeniture was abolished, and any male descendent of an officer was eligible to apply. The same year, it was decreed that the most direct descendent of a deceased veteran could become a member of the First Class.

1885 article pointed out that MOLLUS was composed "entirely of officers" and labeled it "one of the most aristocratic organizations of the day." The column continued with the warning that the legionnaires' common backgrounds posed an additional threat as the order could easily become a "powerful body" of political lobbyists.[13] An 1890 *Journal* column concluded that though the First Class members who endured the "crucial tests of war" rightfully belonged to MOLLUS, it also bluntly asserted that the legion's "hereditary distinctions [were] of doubtful utility in this country."[14]

The order's "officer's only" membership requirements sparked further protest and were viewed as being elitist, antagonistic, and "insulting" to the "Private Soldier" that bore the bulk of the fighting during the war. To add to the Loyal Legion's public relations problem, many Americans began to view all fraternal "army societies" as irrelevant and devoid of "any meaning."[15]

Initially, MOLLUS members countered such criticisms by comparing their order to the Society of Cincinnati, an organization formed in 1783 by officers of the Continental Army. The Cincinnati earned the animosity of citizens of the early Republic for restricting membership to officers and their male descendants. Companions at times referred to the legion as "the child of the Cincinnati." They repeatedly pointed out that the members of the Cincinnati had posed no threat to the new country, but instead had peacefully disappeared into society "like snow flakes upon water." No less a companion than Rutherford B. Hayes argued in an 1891 speech that the Cincinnati's and the Loyal Legion's hereditary features represented simple assertions of "ancestry, a natural right of all people."[16]

---

[13] James Smith Rutan to John Page Nicholson, April 18, 1888, National Commandery Letter File, MOLLUS, USAMHI; *The United States Army and Navy Journal and Gazette of the Regular and Volunteer Armed Forces*, February 14, 1885, 525. The article concluded that MOLLUS was "essentially an Aristocracy."

[14] *The United States Army and Navy Journal*, March 29, 1890, 589–90.

[15] James Smith Rutan to John Page Nicholson, November 12, 1887, Non-Eligible and Rejection Book #1, MOLLUS, USAMHI; Carl A. G. Adae, "Our Military Future," speech delivered March 4, 1885, in *Sketches of War History, 1861–1865: Papers Read Before the Ohio Commandery of the Military Order of the Loyal Legion of the United States, 1883–1886*, 2 vols. (Cincinnati: Robert Clarke and Co., 1888), 1: 314–28. Linderman, *Embattled Courage*, 272–73

[16] Davies, *Patriotism on Parade*, 103; Rutherford B. Hayes, "Commander in Chief's Address," delivered on October 7, 1891, in *Personal Recollections of the War of the Rebellion: Addresses Delivered Before the New York Commandery of the Loyal*

Such a contrast might have provided inspiration to MOLLUS's companions, but it formed a weak bulwark against angry broadsides leveled at the legion by critics. The comparison with the Cincinnati hardly explained the roles and purposes of the order to an unknowing public, nor did it explain why the legionnaires deemed a hereditary feature necessary. Members astutely realized that MOLLUS could not rely on the Cincinnati as a crutch. To continue the legion's growth and maintain its existence, members considered it incumbent to develop for MOLLUS an image congenial not only to companions, but one compatible with democratic concepts. Such an identity was considered crucial in order to "give to the world . . . an acceptable reason for [the Loyal Legion's] existence," and to overcome the accusations that MOLLUS only existed to allow the ex-officers to continue "blowin' about" past accomplishments.[17]

The self-defining search for public validity caused MOLLUS to formulate an image as a peculiarly American form of aristocracy. To address the question of relevancy and prove that their organization filled a vital function in American society, legionnaires embarked on an active strategy of public activities designed to cast the order as a "role model" of the martial values of patriotism and sacrifice. The legion also contended that it served as a representative body reflecting the collective patriotism of all Union soldiers, regardless of rank. Hence, the Loyal Legion argued that it only excluded enlisted men in the physical sense, while keeping the memory of their sacrifices alive to the American citizenry. The organization, therefore, was not hostile to those they had at one time commanded.

Legion of the United States, 1883–1891, 2 vols. (New York: Commandery of New York, 1891), 1: 376–77. Hayes belonged to the Ohio Commandery and served as MOLLUS's commander-in-chief from 1889–1892. A brief account of the Society of Cincinnati's origins and the antagonisms faced by this organization can be found in Charles Royster, *A Revolutionary People at War: The Continental Army and the American Character, 1775–1783* (Chapel Hill: The University of North Carolina Press, 1979), 353–58.

[17] James A. Beaver, untitled speech delivered April 15, 1890, contained in the pamphlet, *The Military Order of the Loyal Legion of the United States: Ceremonies at the Twenty-Fifth Anniversary, Held at the American Academy of Music, Philadelphia, April 15, 1890*, (Philadelphia: [n. p.], 1890). Beaver, a former brevet brigadier general, was governor of Pennsylvania in 1890. Orlando Poe, untitled speech delivered June 1, 1887, contained in *War Papers Read Before the Michigan Commandery of the Military Order of the Loyal Legion of the United States, Oct. 6, 1886 to April 6, 1893*, 2 vols. (Detroit: Winn and Hammond, Printers, 1893), 1: 8.

Although forthrightly acknowledging the legion's aristocratic and elitist features, members argued that MOLLUS was not a traditional "aristocracy of blood . . . birth, or wealth . . . [but one] born of gallant and heroic . . . patriotic service," conceived and representative of American values. Ohio companion Ephraim C. Dawes, brother of the Iron Brigade's famous Rufus R. Dawes, struck upon a catch phrase for this mentality when he boasted to Nicholson that their society filled a unique and distinctly American role as an "Aristocracy of Patriotism."[18]

In developing the idea of the "Aristocracy of Patriotism," MOLLUS companions stressed the enlisted origins of many of the men who paid dues to the legion. During ceremonies commemorating the twenty-fifth anniversary of the patriotic order, Massachusetts companion and former Brevet Brigadier General Charles Devens pointed out that "almost a majority" of the Loyal Legion's members at one time "carried the musket and the knapsack" in the rank and file, and advanced in rank due to "their own ability and determination . . . high military qualities, [or the] votes of fellow soldiers." Devens emphasized that "the fame of every General" rested upon the steady service of the common soldier.[19]

Members also stressed the representative ideology expressed in the legion's constitution to help prove that the organization honored Union veterans of all ranks, and that the ex-officers still sought the best interests of their men as they had once done on fields of battle. In other words, MOLLUS was an organization rooted in the traditional American values of republican virtue and democratic action and sympathies, and was not based on the principles of foreign birthright aristocracies.

To avoid the perception that MOLLUS was a meaningless, "self glorify[ing] . . . mutual congratulatory" order, companions considered it vital that they continue to "serve" the American people as role models. This commitment was also reinforced by the legionnaires'

---

[18] Speech of J. P. Morton, Kansas Commandery, *Army and Navy Journal* 25 (June 2, 1888): 904. Ephraim C. Dawes to John Page Nicholson, December 31, 1887, Recorder-in-Chief letter file, 1887, MOLLUS, USAMHI. Ephraim Dawes had most of his lower jaw shot away during the 1864 Atlanta campaign. Though the injury was repaired by crude reconstructive surgery and caused him constant pain, he remained very active in MOLLUS affairs.

[19] Charles Devens, untitled speech in *Ceremonies at the Twenty-Fifth Anniversary*, 12–13.

belief that the "pursuit of gain" symptomatic of America's booming Gilded Age economy was weakening the United States. Ohio Commandery member Carl Adae's 1885 speech illustrates the point. Adae, who served with the 4th Ohio Cavalry, expressed concern that the country's seeming lust for money and material possessions could "overwhelm and drown . . . every vestige" of military elan, and render "war preparations . . . superfluous."[20]

Adae also proclaimed that the Loyal Legion had a "high purpose and import . . . in preserving the martial spirit . . . [and] imbuing that feeling in youths who had grown up without the knowledge of war." Another member ironically used an item of technology representative of the Gilded Age as an analogy when he proposed that "civilians" were to be viewed as "storage batterys" of patriotism and military ardor. Legionnaires were to function as the source of electricity that kept such batteries charged.[21]

The same rationale also justified the hereditary nature of the legion. Second-class companion Negley D. Cochran, the son of a second lieutenant, addressed this issue in an 1897 presentation entitled "What Are We Here For?" Cochran argued that the legion's survival depended on his class of membership, and that longevity was an essential factor in guaranteeing MOLLUS continued to serve as a "school of patriotism" after the First Class companions all answered their final roll call. Such a belief inspired some legionnaires to rhetorical excess, as indicated by Michigan companion Fred Swift's statement that he was "full of hope for the future" because the veterans' sons would continue to serve as "Videttes of the Republic."[22]

Although such oratory and sentiments provided good fare at legion meetings, companions realized that an outward expression of their ideals and engagement in public activities were necessary to prove

---

[20] Carl A. G. Adae speech, "Our Military Future," in *Papers Read Before the Ohio Commandery*, 1: 314–27.

[21] Ibid.; J. P. Powell, untitled speech delivered May 5, 1898, contained in *War Papers Read Before the Michigan Commandery of the Military Order of the Loyal Legion of the United States: Dec. 7, 1893 to May 5, 1898*, 2 vols. (Detroit: James H. Stone and Co., Printers, 1898), 2: 321–22.

[22] Negley D. Cochran, "What Are We Here For?" speech in *The Military Order of the Loyal Legion of the United States: A Stenographic Report of the After-Dinner Speeches at the Fourteenth Annual Dinner of the Commandery of Ohio, May 5, 1897* (Cincinnati: Commandery of Ohio, 1897), 30; Fred Swift, speech delivered May 1, 1890, in *War Papers Read Before the Michigan Commandery*, 1: 23.

the American nature of their order to its skeptics. To this end, the practice of conspicuous patriotism was a vital cog in the culture of the Aristocracy of Patriotism. Throughout the late nineteenth century, MOLLUS members engaged in a variety of projects designed to highlight the patriotic aspect of the organization and its commitment to service.

Beginning in 1884, legionnaires gained direct public attention by venturing into cemeteries and bending their aging bodies to place wreaths bearing the words "Loyal Legion" on the graves of "private soldiers" as well as officers. This was a change from the policies that called for only maintaining the resting places of deceased MOLLUS members. Aside from being a sincere gesture of remembrance, legionnaires hoped that the decorating of enlisted men's graves men would help "take away from public opinion [the] sharp edge [of] criticisms" over the legion's exclusive nature.[23]

As the full name of the order was often too cumbersome to use in full on wreaths and other commemorative banners and signs, "Loyal Legion" became the only accepted shortened version of the society's moniker. This crisp two-word title had a much better ring than MOLLUS, and its punctual yet submissive phrasing helped to create a better public impression. Newspapers were put on notice that the society preferred this abbreviation.[24]

Commemoration of Civil War service formed a large part of the activities of the legion. To help cultivate the study and research of the "War of the Rebellion," each state commandery worked to establish its own "War Library and Museum." These were open to the public, and contained artifacts and books from or about the war, most of which were related to officers, with a few examples of enlisted men's gear. Items ranged from the portraits and uniforms of northern officers to weapons. Esoteric items also found their way to the display shelves of MOLLUS War Libraries. Companion Joseph M. Brown, for example, donated a gavel carved from the "Signal Tree" that had played a key role in the 1864 Battle of Allatoona Pass.[25]

---

[23] Albert Ordway to John Page Nicholson, February 10 and May 10, 1884, National Commandery Letter File, 1882–1884, MOLLUS, USAMHI. Ordway belonged to the District of Columbia Commandery. The term "conspicuous patriotism" is mine, a modification of Thorstein Veblen's phrase "conspicuous consumption."

[24] Ibid.

[25] Joseph M. Brown to John Page Nicholson, April 21, 1887, Recorder-in-Chief Letter File, 1887, MOLLUS, USAMHI. The Massachusetts Commandery was the

Most commanderies also published for popular consumption the speeches and wartime recollections, or "War Papers," of their members in both bound volumes and contemporary periodicals such as the *Republic Magazine*. The essays and transcriptions, designed to reach a wide audience, told of the wartime exploits of the officers now in the legion in order to help "mold . . . future public sentiment" in the appreciation of the North's war effort. In some ways, the effort was very successful, for most modern students of the Civil War know of MOLLUS through these publications, which have become oft-cited sources for battle and campaign narratives.[26]

Another opportunity of a bittersweet nature for companions to gain exposure came as the great heroes of northern victory began to pass away during the last quarter of the nineteenth century. In the sartorial uniformity of topcoats embellished with the legion's rosette-shaped badge, members of MOLLUS exhibited themselves as examples of patriotic service before urban populations as pallbearers in the funeral processions of Ulysses S. Grant, Philip H. Sheridan, and William T. Sherman, among others. At Rutherford B. Hayes's funeral, companions stood solemnly at attention around the casket, a presentation one MOLLUS member found to be "one of the most sublime and effective acts that an organization of officers could tender."[27]

The legion also lobbied Congress in matters patriotic, pressuring

---

first to establish a museum. The Pennsylvania Commandery's War Library and Museum, located at 1805 Pine Street, Philadelphia, Pennsylvania, is the last such facility in existence. As of June 2001, the museum was financially strapped and open on a limited basis. Additionally, a proposal to move the museum's fine collection of Civil War–related documents and material culture out of Philadelphia was being challenged in court.

[26] A. S. Cushman to John Page Nicholson, April 15, 1890, Recorder-in-Chief Letter File, 1890, MOLLUS, USAMHI. Elias R. Monfort, "The Loyal Legion," speech in *After-Dinner Speeches . . . of the Commandery of Ohio*, 1897, 25.

[27] F. Lecke to John Page Nicholson, August 10, 1885, Commandery-in-Chief Letter File, 1882–1885; Albert Ordway to John Page Nicholson, Recorder-in-Chief Letter File, 1888; Arnold A. Rand to John Page Nicholson, Massachusetts Commandery Letter File, 1893; George DeForest Barton to John Page Nicholson, February 16, 1891, Imperial File, 1891–1892, all in MOLLUS, USAMHI. Lecke served as marshal in chief at Grant's funeral. Barton described the dress worn by pall bearers at one funeral consisting of "dark overcoats . . . trousers . . . gloves and black hats." Active-duty officers could wear their uniforms on such occasions. According to several documents in the MOLLUS files, legionnaires also helped to raise funds for statues and memorials dedicated to northern war heroes.

legislators to release more funds to speed up the publications process of the multi-volume *The War of the Rebellion: A Compilation of the Official Records of the Union and Confederate Armies*. The District of Columbia Commandery, in particular, pushed for the undertaking by taking advantage of its access to the seat of national government. In 1888, the D. C. legionnaires drafted a resolution delivered to the congressional sub-committee overseeing the project that called for "increased appropriations . . . so that this work of national importance and interest may be speedily completed." Members were, in part, motivated to try and hasten the process out of the fear that those "who took part in the late war will all die" before the project was finished. Some members even argued for the inclusion of postwar "reports" of engagements, but the publishers of the *Official Records* wisely ignored this idea.[28]

One of the order's most prolonged and ardent lobbying efforts centered around its campaign to see that MOLLUS members still on active duty with the U.S. military be permitted to wear their order's rosette on their uniforms. Companions argued that such an action would uplift the "morale and . . . military spirit" of America's military forces by allowing "younger officers . . . [who had] grown to manhood" without combat experience to recognize the Civil War veterans as patriotic role models. Furthermore, legionnaires believed that such an inspirational service would imbue the order with relevance and help prevent the rosette from being viewed as a "mere badge of hereditary aristocracy." Despite such arguments, the legion's desire met with several rejections and delays, though the order's tenacity on this issue did eventually pay off. The *Army and Navy Journal* reported in its June 16, 1898, issue that the Senate Military Committee had passed a bill allowing the rosette to be worn by active duty military personal on "occasions of ceremony."[29]

---

[28] Rueben D. Mussey to John Page Nicholson, December, 3, 1888, Recorder-in-Chief Letter File, 1888, MOLLUS, USAMHI; Alan C. and Barbara A. Aimone, *A Users Guide to the Official Records of the American Civil War* (Shippensburg, Pa.: White Mane Publishing Co., 1993), vii.

[29] Negley Cochran speech in *After-Dinner Speeches . . . Commandery of Ohio, 1897*, 30; John Page Nicholson to Secretary of War W. C. Endicott, December 20, 1886, Recorder-in-Chief Letter File, MOLLUS, USAMHI; *Journal of the Third Commandery in Chief Meeting, 1887*, 137–38; *Army and Navy Journal* 25 (June 16, 1898): 929. To ensure fairness and parity, this bill also permitted the badges of the Society of Cincinnati, the Aztec Club (a Mexican-American War order), the National

During the late nineteenth century, most patriotic societies—to quote one historian—"worshipped" the American flag, and passed resolutions concerning what they believed to be a proper use of the banner. The Loyal Legion also was heavily involved in attempting to regulate the use of what they viewed as the most "sacred" symbol of their military service. Dismayed by the fact that the banner was being used on advertisements, the legion petitioned Congress to pass a bill that would prohibit vendors from any attempt to "disfigure or prostitute the American Flag" by using it for "private gain."[30]

Although the proposed law was not enacted, the order did not abate its efforts regarding the treatment of the flag. In 1895, the commandery in chief issued a circular that directed members to "rise and uncover" deferentially when the "Star Spangled Banner" was played at athletic events and other public functions, building upon a practice that companion Rossell G. O'Brien, who claimed membership in the Tacoma-based Washington State Commandery, instigated among the members of his chapter in 1893. From Tacoma, the custom spread from one commandery to another until made a uniform policy by the 1895 resolution. MOLLUS still claims that it was the first organization to practice the now ubiquitous tradition of standing for the National Anthem. In this regard, at least, it appears the legion was very successful in casting itself as a role model organization regarding conspicuous patriotic behavior.[31]

To protect the symbol of American unity, an 1887 legion circular directed all commanderies to form "Flag Committees" of twenty members charged with "foster[ing] public sentiment in favor of honoring the flag . . . and preserving it from desecration." To strengthen

---

Association of Veterans of the Mexican War, and the GAR to be worn on ceremonial occasions.

[30] Davies, *Patriotism on Parade*, 218–22 (Davies refers to such flag worship as the "cult of the flag"); *Journal of the Proceedings of the Eleventh Annual Meeting of the Commandery-in-Chief, Held in the City of Washington, D.C. October 16, 1895* (Philadelphia: [n.p.], 1895), 460–61.

[31] Ibid.; an article by C. Herb Williams titled "Star-Spangled Patriot" in *The American Legion Magazine* 95 (January 6, 1976): 12, discusses O'Brien's involvement. The article's credence is bolstered by quotes from the contemporary newspapers the *Tacoma Daily Ledger* and the *Tacoma News* discussing O'Brien's innovation. In 1970, a plaque was placed on the exterior of the former commandery hall commemorating O'Brien's formative role in this custom. Of course, the origins of such a custom are bound to be somewhat obscure. Stuart McConnell, for one, states that the GAR started this custom in 1891 (McConnell, *Glorious Contentment*, 229).

lobbying efforts for laws governing the use of the flag, MOLLUS joined the "American Flag Association" in 1898, an umbrella organization composed of numerous patriotic orders concerned with the desecration of the U.S. banner.[32]

By the 1890s, the Aristocracy of Patriotism identity was well established among the companions of the Loyal Legion. The discourse of the legionnaires reveals that they considered their efforts to bolster the nation's patriotism and to keep alive the memory of the sacrifice of all Union soldiers to have been successful in helping to offset the order's elitist image.

MOLLUS members were proud of developing the Aristocracy of Patriotism concept—and said so. Elias Monfort of the Ohio Commandery exalted in MOLLUS's representative role in 1897, lauding the legion's efforts in representing "good citizenship, morality, charity, fraternity, loyalty and patriotism." The legion constituted a "vast Army" said Monfort, and there existed no "city, town or hamlet where Companions [did] not meet." Furthermore, said the Ohioan, the praiseworthy order had little interest in aristocratic privilege, but stood for the efforts of "every man who wore the Blue" by "preserving and reaffirm[ing] the principles of loyalty and patriotism." Another companion illustrated his confidence in the order's mission by lashing out at those who "sneered at war . . . flout the old soldier [and the] military sentiment" expressed by MOLLUS. Such people, were, he contended, nothing less than "enemies of their country."[33]

Paradoxically, as companions gained satisfaction with the legion's purpose, they became more open in their claims of the order's superiority. In the same speech in which he praised the Loyal Legion's representative and egalitarian nature, Monfort happily proclaimed that the MOLLUS rosette was the "patent of Nobility." Founding companion Peter Keyser told the crowd gathered for the twenty-fifth

---

[32] Commandery-in-Chief Circular Book, 1896–1902, Circular #12, Series of 1897, MOLLUS, USAMHI. The War Department did not adopt a uniform code regarding the handling of the flag until 1923.

[33] Monfort's speech, "The Loyal Legion," contained in *After-Dinner Speeches . . . Commandery of Ohio, 1897*, 22–25; *Army and Navy Journal*, 32 (May 11, 1895): 611. The *Army and Navy Journal* is not clear as to who delivered these remarks, but it is likely that Wisconsin Commandery member Lucius Fairchild, who was serving as MOLLUS's commander-in-chief in 1895, is the quoted source.

anniversary celebration of the legion that MOLLUS "represent[ed] the highest intelligence and best citizenship" of the United States.[34]

Despite such patriotic activities, newspapers and similar contemporary sources do not reveal any amount of pro-MOLLUS editorials occasioned by the order's efforts. One may wonder just how much the public recognized the legion's efforts and its new image. But it is obvious that the Loyal Legion had achieved a level of self-comfort with its Aristocracy of Patriotism identity, and with that increased comfort came a change in how the legionnaires perceived the Society of Cincinnati. Companions who had once proudly claimed the Loyal Legion as the descendent of the Revolutionary-era society increasingly began to cast the Cincinnati in a negative light against the bright glow of the purpose and uniqueness of the legion. This factor was a natural outgrowth of MOLLUS's formation of its own identity, for the legion could hardly claim to be unique if it was preceded by an identical organization.

Companions criticized the Cincinnati for failing to "advance beyond the joys of comradeship and reminiscence" to develop a "purpose" and teach the "lessons of patriotism" as MOLLUS had done. Legionnaires carped at the Cincinnati for its "neutral" stance during the Civil War—a position partially caused by the fact the Cincinnati had chapters in the southern states. Legionnaires argued that if an organization was to be found that was worthy of criticism for elitism, it was the society, whose overdone "pomp and circumstance" would find no acceptance in the democratically oriented legion. Even more important was the fact that the Cincinnati's founders had created the organization "when they were still officers," which belied the very name of the order. MOLLUS's originators, in contrast, started the legion after they had returned to civilian life. Companions now considered their organization the natural answer to the rhetorical question: which order truly typified the lessons of Cincinnatus?[35]

---

[34] Monfort's speech, *After-Dinner Speeches . . . Commandery of Ohio*, 1897, 22–25; Peter Dirck Keyser, untitled speech in *Ceremonies at the Twenty-Fifth Anniversary*, 6.

[35] Charles D. Kerr, "The Loyal Legion," speech read June 10, 1890, in *Glimpses of the Nation's Struggle: A Series of Papers Read Before the Minnesota Military Order of the Loyal Legion of the United States, 1889–1892* (St. Paul, Minn.: D. D. Merrill Company, 1893), 132–34; Irving M. Bean, "The Wisconsin Military Order of the Loyal Legion," speech read May 4, 1899, in *War Papers Read Before the*

MOLLUS members found the greatest vindication of their order, however, neither in peacetime activities nor in comparisons to other organizations, but in America's involvement and success in the Spanish-American War. Celebratory legionnaires considered the United States' quick victory in its first post–Civil War conflict to be a clear proof that MOLLUS served as an inspiration and "influence . . . to all of those brave men who were ready to serve their country in its hour of need." It seemed to members of the legion that no greater illustration could be had of the effect and usefulness of active duty officers wearing the MOLLUS rosette.[36]

Legionnaires additionally saw the conflict as an indication that the American people had not forsaken the martial values preached by MOLLUS. While companions praised the U.S. military for its willingness to give its "best blood to lift up a race," they cheered with equal enthusiasm the American citizenry for patriotically responding with "one voice" to the "wail of the . . . distressed" and so whole-heartedly supporting the idea that "Cuba must be free." Wisconsin companions vigorously applauded Irving Bean's statement that the war's cost of "money and blood" was worth it to prove "valor . . . [had] not passed away."[37]

Only days after Admiral George Dewey's victory at Manila Bay, legionnaire Robert Warnock delivered a stirring address underscoring that the principles that formed the "strength of the Legion" were not just based on "unfurl[ing] . . . flag[s] and beat[ing] drum[s]." Warnock emphasized the service nature of MOLLUS and expressed how the organization viewed its impact on the war with Spain by

---

Commandery of the State of Wisconsin Military Order of the Loyal Legion of the United States, reprint ed., 70 vols. (Wilmington, Del.: Broadfoot Publishing Co., 1993), 3: 336; James H. Howe, "The Loyal Legion," speech (no delivery date) in *Glimpses of the Nation's Struggle*, 281–82. Another reason that the Cincinnati did not more actively decry secession is that by 1861 the organization was almost moribund. It did not rejuvenate until the twentieth century. Davies, *Patriotism on Parade*, has good background information on the Cincinnati.

[36] Bean Speech, "Wisconsin MOLLUS," *War Papers . . . Wisconsin MOLLUS*, 340.

[37] Robert Warnock, untitled inaugural speech in *The Military Order of the Loyal Legion of the United States: A Stenographic Report of After-Dinner Speeches at the Fifteenth Annual Dinner of the Commandery of Ohio, May 2, 1898* (Cincinnati: Commandery of Ohio [1898]), 8; Warnock was being inaugurated as the commander of the Ohio chapter. Bean speech, "Wisconsin MOLLUS," *War Papers . . . Wisconsin MOLLUS*, 341–42.

using an alliterative metaphor that stated the legion's patriotism was based on the "letter D's, to do, to dare, to die . . . [and] Deweying!"[38]

Another indication of the legion's view of their organization was demonstrated by the lithographic rendering on the cover of the Ohio Commandery's booklet containing transcriptions of speeches delivered at the chapter's annual meeting in 1900. The illustration focused on a tropical camp scene, wherein a young officer stood stiffly at attention in the presence of a courtly and gray-haired officer of higher rank engaged in the process of writing orders while seated at a camp desk. The entire tableaux, wreathed in draped American flags, cast an obvious idealized message: MOLLUS, represented by the older officer, was delivering directions and inspiration to the evocation of America's patriotic future, the attentive and respectful young officer. The picture served as the visual essence of the Loyal Legion's crafted image of an Aristocracy of Patriotism.[39]

By the turn of the century, MOLLUS members believed the Loyal Legion's identity stood alone, distanced from the Society of Cincinnati and unsullied by the values acquainted with European-style aristocracies. Legionnaires considered Spain's displacement as a world power vindication and justification of their arguments that the order was a representative and democratic hereditary society, committed to the service of enhancing the patriotism of the American citizenry. The members of MOLLUS, the progenitors of the Aristocracy of Patriotism, were confident they had once more served America as "Videttes of the Republic."

---

[38] *The Military Order of the Loyal Legion of the United States: A Stenographic Report of After-Dinner Speeches at the Seventeenth Annual Dinner of the Commandery of Ohio, Cincinnati, May 2, 1900* (Cincinnati: Commandery of Ohio, 1900).

[39] Warnock's inaugural speech, in *Stenographic Report . . . Commandery of Ohio,* 7–8.

AFTERWORD

Joseph T. Glatthaar

NEVER BEFORE had an American event approached the magnitude of the Civil War. Well over three million men donned the uniform of the Union or the Confederacy, a total that exceeded 10 percent of the entire population in 1860. During the course of four bloody years of fighting, more than 600,000 yielded their lives, a figure that surpassed the number of servicemen in any previous American war. Four million slaves gained their freedom as a consequence of the Civil War, considerably more people than secured their independence from Great Britain as a consequence of the American Revolution.[1]

By comparison with America's past conflicts, the Civil War truly was a massive and complex undertaking. The realities of the war penetrated almost every household, every farm, every factory, and every workshop. In addition to uniformed service, wartime demands, both military and civilian, absorbed the labor of over ten million more people. The United States government alone spent $350 million on clothing and $370 million on subsistence for its soldiers. This did not include anything that family or friends sent to soldiers or that they took for themselves. Nearly all of those goods and foodstuffs came from the hands of northern producers. Limited peacetime capacity transformed into massive wartime output, as opposing sides manufactured an astounding 1.15 billion small arms cartridges and 5 million artillery rounds between them. Despite their comparatively primitive means, the Union and the Confederacy together produced

---

[1] About 30 million people lived in the United States in 1860. Estimates vary dramatically on how many soldiers served in previous wars, but even the most expansive do not approach 620,000, the number of fatalities of the Civil War. See "U. S. Service and Casualties in Major Wars and Conflicts, 1775–1991," in *The Oxford Companion to American Military History*, ed. by John W. Chambers (New York: Oxford University Press, 2000), 849.

enough gunpowder to cause a blast greater in size than the atomic explosions at Hiroshima or Nagasaki. According to the best estimate, the total cost of the Civil War exceeded $20 billion, a figure thirty-one times larger than the federal government's budget in 1860. More than any other single episode, the Civil War defined America as a people, and it changed forever the direction of the re-unified nation.[2]

Because of the war's size, scope, and impact, traditional historians most often fit their studies snugly into distinct components. They focus on the causes of the war and look backward rather than forward, as if those issues were detached from the clash of arms or the results. Others explore the war itself, often concentrating on military events or political and military leadership. But those studies usually end with the campaign or the Confederate surrender at Appomattox, as if the operations and leaders were divorced from the causes or long-term ramifications of the conflict. The last group concentrates on the consequences of the Civil War, usually Reconstruction. Once again, they pay as little attention as possible to causation or to the fighting that preceded the Union victory.

Although the Civil War affected nearly every person in the two sections, those few sweeping studies of the period are either multi-volume works or books that base their entire examination on a narrow theme that tells little about the human condition. These tomes ignore huge segments of the population, focusing instead on political and military leadership. Seldom does the reader get the sense that these were real people who endured the destruction of the Union, the harrows of warfare, and the extended impact and results of the conflict.

The late Bell Irvin Wiley was the rare exception. His three books, *Southern Negroes, 1861–1865*, *The Life of Johnny Reb*, and *The Life of Billy Yank*, are masterpieces in the study of the people who partici-

---

[2] See *Historical Statistics of the United States: Colonial Times to Present*, part 2 (Washington, D. C.: Government Printing office, 1975), 1104; United States War Department, *The War of the Rebellion: A Compilation of the Official Records of the Union and Confederate Armies*, 70 vols. in 128 (Washington, D. C.: Government Printing Office, 1880–1901), series 3, vol. 5, 254, pp. 1042–43; James G. Randall and David H. Donald, *Civil War and Reconstruction* (Lexington, Mass.: D. C. Heath and Company, 1969), 532; Josiah Gorgas, "Essay on the Confederate Ordinance Department," 20, 35, Folder 27, Box 676, Gorgas Family Papers, W. S. Hoole Special Collections Library, University of Alabama, Tuscaloosa; "Nuclear Weapons," *Oxford Companion to American Military History*, 510.

pated in the Civil War.[3] Although Wiley devoted scant attention to causation or consequences, he realized that Civil War scholarship had overlooked the most central component—its participants. His pathbreaking works drew from letters, diaries, and other sources to explain what life was really like for African Americans, Confederates, and Federals.[4]

Despite the breakthrough nature of Wiley's scholarship, no one followed. Wiley's Civil War books were too thorough in research, too comprehensive in their discussions, and too nontraditional to spark an entirely new line of investigation. It was not until decades later that two changes transformed the scene of Civil War scholarship. The first was the expansion of social history and the development of the "new" social history—the application of social science techniques, methodologies, and theories to the study of the past. Historians cast aside notions of history as a discipline written from the top down and began to see individuals as active agents in the shaping of their own world. This belief resulted in renewed interest in various segments of society and provided the previously "voiceless" with a voice.

The second force that reshaped Civil War scholarship was the Viet-

---

[3] Wiley, *Southern Negroes, 1861–1865* (New Haven: Yale University Press, 1938); *The Life of Johnny Reb: The Common Soldier of the Confederacy* (Indianapolis: Bobbs-Merrill, 1943; reprint ed., Garden City, N. Y.: Doubleday and Company, 1971); *The Life of Billy Yank: The Common Soldier of the Union* (Indianapolis: Bobbs-Merrill, 1952; reprint ed., Garden City, N. Y.: Doubleday and Company, 1971). It is a tribute to Wiley's skills as a scholar and a writer that *Johnny Reb* and *Billy Yank* are still in print and now available from Louisiana State University Press.

[4] *Southern Negroes, 1861–1865* is the exception. Wiley admitted in that book that he had great difficulty locating letters and diaries of black civilians and soldiers. More importantly, *Southern Negroes, 1861–1865* eventually helped to spark the extensive study of African Americans during the war, fleshing out many of the topics that Wiley had first introduced. The best of these later works is probably Willie Lee Rose's *Rehearsal for Reconstruction: The Port Royal Experiment* (Indianapolis: Bobbs-Merrill, 1964); but also see Clarence L. Mohr, *On the Threshold of Freedom: Masters and Slaves in Civil War Georgia* (Athens: University of Georgia Press, 1986); and C. Peter Ripley, *Slaves and Freedmen in Civil War Louisiana* (Baton Rouge: Louisiana State University Press, 1976). The Freedmen and Southern Society Project at the University of Maryland, College Park, under the direction first of Ira Berlin and now of Leslie S. Rowland, has published several volumes of source material from the holdings of the National Archives in the series *Freedom: A Documentary History of Emancipation, 1861–1867* (Cambridge, Eng.: Cambridge University Press, 1982–), allowing scholars access to materials that had eluded Wiley.

nam War. Vietnam divided American society like nothing since the
Civil War. Men, women, and children; civilians and military; blacks,
whites, and Hispanics; hawks and doves—all played strong roles in
shaping the national response to the United States's participation in
the civil war in Vietnam. Ultimately, the chorus of opposition significantly contributed to the United States government's abandonment
of its effort in Vietnam, thereby vindicating the arguments of social
historians concerning the importance of that "voiceless" element on
society.

But the lessons of the Vietnam War went well beyond that particular one. The Vietnam experience demonstrated that one could not
truly understand a major event such as the Civil War by looking solely
at the leadership, or even the military personnel. Powerful forces at
home shaped the way the nation fought and the way soldiers perceived the war. More than just anxiety over the enemy, concerns
about family and friends also filled the thoughts of soldiers. Meanwhile, those at home had to cope with life without a husband or a
son, fearful that at any moment the loved one would fall to an enemy
bullet or a fatal disease. The Vietnam War proved that battlefield and
the home front affected each other in ways that previous scholars had
not understood.[5]

The Vietnam experience also awakened scholars to the importance
of viewing that military experience from a broader chronological
framework. The hollow feeling that the American public experienced
eventually sparked investigations into how the United States became
involved in Vietnam in the first place and forced people to come to
grips with the realization that the impact of military service on individual soldiers extended well past their muster-out dates. By applying
the lessons of the Vietnam experience, scholars realized that Civil
War soldiers bore physical burdens for years, sometimes decades,
afterwards, which in turn affected spouses, parents, and children.
Many men died in the service or years later from wartime injuries or
disease, leaving behind widows and children to cope with the resulting hardships. Hundreds of thousands drew pensions, joined veterans' organizations, participated in reunions, and ultimately shaped

---

[5] For an interesting comparison of an aspect of combat across the two war experiences, see Eric T. Dean, Jr., *Shook Over Hell: Post-Traumatic Stress, Vietnam, and
the Civil War* (Cambridge, Mass.: Harvard University Press, 1997).

the way succeeding generations have recollected events and understood the meaning of the war experience. By compartmentalizing the
study of the war into causes, combat, and consequences, scholars had
ignored how the war changed not only a nation but also individuals.

Collectively, the essays in *Union Soldiers and the Northern Home
Front* reflect the influence of social history and the Vietnam experience, what scholars call the "new" military history, particularly in their
breadth of coverage and in their attention to the lives of those people
who endured the Civil War. They demonstrate a more holistic approach to the study of the era, integrating battlefield and home front,
motivations for military service and memory of the war, the thrill of
achieving freedom and its postwar definitions and limitations. Several
essays wrestle with the reasons for entering the service. Rather than
focus exclusively on the soldier, as several recent volumes have done,
they view the call to the colors from the perspective of the home
front, delving into the political, social, and cultural nature of forming
Civil War units. Other essays explore civilian perceptions of combat
and examine military service from the standpoint of disabled soldiers
who continued to aid the cause by joining the Veteran Reserve Corps.
Another addresses what happens to a community when large numbers of locals from a regiment are incarcerated in a prisoner-of-war
camp. Wartime courtship and religion helped to sustain morale and
to preserve links with the world they left behind, so several authors
argue. Three scholars move beyond the role of black soldiers in war,
investigating attitudes toward them and the way a white-dominated
society included them in postwar organizations and events. Although
on the surface the activities of the Grand Army of the Republic and
participation at various Civil War reunions seemed like a typical racial
snub, it had far greater ramifications, largely dictating how future
generations would remember the Civil War. Nor do these essays omit
the postwar consequences, with essays devoted to social acceptance
of amputees and the struggle for widows' pensions.

Over a century ago, Walt Whitman admonished historians to get
the "real war" into the books.[6] The great American poet feared that
historical accounts would record a sterile version of this traumatic

---

[6] See "The Real War Will Never Get in the Books," in *Walt Whitman's Civil War*,
ed. by Walter Lowenfels with the assistance of Nan Braymer (New York: Alfred A.
Knopf, 1960; reprint ed., New York: Da Capo Press, 1989), 283–94.

and bloody four years, devoid of the personal triumphs and tragedies, the glory and the agony so endemic in time of war. In the last few decades, scholars have concluded once again that the human condition and experience were at the heart of the Civil War, as the observant Whitman intuited, but the "real war," the one historians have come belatedly to understand, functioned on different levels, and over a more expansive period of time than from 1861 through 1865.

Perhaps historians should have followed the lead of the person who knew best, the one who directed the Union victory. In his second inaugural address, President Abraham Lincoln counseled his fellow Americans, "Let us strive on to finish the work we are at; to bind up the nation's wounds; to care for him who shall have born the battle, for his widow, and his orphan—to do all which may achieve and cherish a just and lasting peace, among ourselves, and with all nations."[7] In fifty-odd words, Lincoln alerted people in his time and in future generations that the hardships and brutalities of war touched lives well beyond those on the battlefield and affected people long before they resorted to arms and long after the cannons went silent.

---

[7] Roy P. Basler et al., eds., *The Collected Works of Abraham Lincoln*, 9 vols. (New Brunswick, N. J.: Rutgers University Press, 1953), 8: 333.

CONTRIBUTORS

Paul A. Cimbala, professor of history at Fordham University in The Bronx, received his Ph.D. from Emory University. He is the author of *Under the Guardianship of the Nation: The Freedmen's Bureau and the Reconstruction of Georgia, 1865–1870*, winner of the Georgia Historical Society's Malcolm and Muriel Barrow Bell Award. He and Randall M. Miller edited *The Freedmen's Bureau and Reconstruction: Reconsiderations*, *Against the Tide: Women Reformers in American Society*, and *American Reform and Reformers: A Biographical Dictionary*. He also edited (with Robert F. Himmelberg) *Historians and Race: Autobiography and the Writing of History*. He is working on two monographs, one dealing with the Veteran Reserve Corps during the Civil War and Reconstruction and the other dealing with African American musicians and their transition from slavery to freedom in the nineteenth-century South. He is editor of two Fordham University Press book series, *The North's Civil War* and *Reconstructing America*.

Randall M. Miller, professor of history at Saint Joseph's University, received his Ph.D. from Ohio State University. He has published numerous books, including the award-winning *"Dear Master": Letters of a Slave Family*; (with John David Smith), the award-winning *Dictionary of Afro-American Slavery*; and (with Harry S. Stout and Charles Reagan Wilson) *Religion and the American Civil War*. His latest project is a study of immigrants in the American South. He is coeditor of the University Press of Florida book series, *Southern Dissent* and editor of two Greenwood Press series, *Historic Guides to the Twentieth Century* and *Major Issues in American History*.

CONTRIBUTORS

Michael J. Bennett holds a Ph.D. from the University of Saint Louis, where he wrote his dissertation, "Union Jacks: The Common

Yankee Sailor of the American Civil War, 1861–1865." A former Mayer Fellow at the Huntington Library and a King V. Hostick Fellow at the Illinois State Historical Association, he also holds a law degree from Case Western Reserve University.

David A. Cecere is a doctoral candidate in the history department at the University of New Hampshire, where he also taught for a number of years. He is a Program Officer at the New Hampshire Humanities Council in Concord. His dissertation deals with the reformulation of the racial perceptions of Union soldiers.

Frances Clarke is a doctoral candidate in the history department at the Johns Hopkins University. Her dissertation is "The Politics of Sentimentality: Sacrifice and Benevolence in the Civil War North."

Joseph T. Glatthaar, professor of history at the University of Houston, received his Ph.D. from the University of Wisconsin. Among his best-known works are *The March to the Sea and Beyond: Sherman's Troops in the Savannah and Carolina Campaign, Forged in Battle: The Civil War Alliance of Black Soldiers and White Officers*, and *Partners in Command: Relationships between Civil War Leaders*.

Lesley J. Gordon, associate professor of history at the University of Akron, received her Ph.D. from the University of Georgia. She is author of *General George E. Pickett in Life and Legend* and coeditor of *Intimate Strategies of the Civil War: Military Commanders and Their Wives*. She is currently working on a book-length study of the 16th Regiment Connecticut Volunteers.

Earl J. Hess teaches at Lincoln Memorial University, where he is the director of the History Program. He received his doctorate in American Studies from Purdue University. He is the author, co-author, and editor of numerous books about the Civil War, including *Liberty, Virtue, and Progress: Northerners and Their War for the Union, Pea Ridge: Civil War Campaign in the West*, and *The Union Soldier in Battle: Enduring the Ordeal of Combat*. His most recent book is *Pickett's Charge: The Last Attack at Gettysburg*.

Russell L. Johnson is an assistant professor of history at Bilkent University in Ankara, Turkey. He received his Ph.D. from the University of Iowa with a dissertation about the social and cultural impact of the American Civil War. He recently completed writing a book on that subject titled *An Army for Industrialization: The Civil War and the Formation of Urban-Industrial Society in a Northern City.* His present project is an analysis of the Civil War pension system and the construction of social categories such as veteran, disabled, widowed and aged in late nineteenth- and early twentieth-century America.

Megan J. McClintock received her doctorate from Rutgers University. She taught at the University of Washington at Tacoma and at Seattle. She also was the author of several papers and articles, including "Civil War Pensions and the Reconstruction of Union Families," which appeared in the *Journal of American History.*

Earl F. Mulderink III is an associate professor of history at Southern Utah University. He received his doctorate from the University of Wisconsin-Madison. His dissertation, which he is now revising for publication, compares African American and Irish American community life in New Bedford, Massachusetts, in the Civil War era. He has published several articles and reviews and also produces Web-based teaching materials. He was Southern Utah University's Grace A. Tanner Distinguished Faculty Lecturer for 2000.

David A. Raney is an administrator at the University of Illinois at Urbana-Champaign, where he received his doctoral degree. His contribution to this volume was made possible in part by the generous support of a Clarke Chambers Travel Fellowship from the University of Minnesota, as well as a Mellon Research Fellowship from the Virginia Historical Society. He is currently writing a history of the United States Christian Commission.

Carol Reardon received her Ph.D. from the University of Kentucky and is now an associate professor of history at Pennsylvania State University. She is the author of *Soldiers and Scholars: The U. S. Army and the Uses of Military History, 1865–1920;* the award-winning *Pickett's Charge in History and Memory;* and numerous essays and articles on military history and the Civil War. She has held the Harold Keith Johnson Visiting Professorship in Military History at the United States Army Military History Institute and recently was a visiting professor at the United States Military Academy. Her numerous projects include a study of Pennsylvania regiments and their home communities during the Civil War.

Patricia L. Richard received her Ph.D. from Marquette University. She teaches at the University of Wisconsin-Fond Du Lac and is revising for publication her dissertation "Home to the Camp: Images of Family in the Northern War Effort."

Donald R. Shaffer received his Ph.D. from the University of Maryland, College Park. He has taught at the University of Maryland, San Diego State University, SUNY at Plattsburgh, and the University of Wyoming. He is presently a member of the history faculty at the University of Northern Colorado in Greeley, Colorado. He is completing *Ambiguous Victory*, a book about African American veterans of the Civil War.

Dana B. Shoaf is the editor of the magazine *America's Civil War*. He is completing his Ph.D. at Kent State University. The Loyal Legion is the subject of his dissertation.

Mark A. Snell teaches at Shepherd College and is the director of the George Tyler Moore Center for the Study of the Civil War. He received his Ph.D. from the University of Missouri-Kansas City and was an assistant professor at the United States Military Academy. His publications include *Dancing Along the Deadline: The Andersonville Memoir of a Prisoner of the Confederacy* and a biography of Major General William B. Franklin. He is presently editing a collection of Franklin's letters.

INDEX

CPSIA information can be obtained
at www.ICGtesting.com
Printed in the USA
LVHW010013300620
659354LV00019B/2110